Principles of Direct, Database and Digital Marketing

Lecturer Resources

For password-protected online resources tailored to
support the use of this textbook in teaching, please visit
www.pearsoned.co.uk/tapp

ON THE
WEBSITE

PEARSON

At Pearson, we have a simple mission: to help people make
more of their lives through learning

We combine innovative
learning technology with trusted content and
educational expertise to provide engaging and effective
learning experiences that serve people wherever and
whenever they are learning.

From classroom to boardroom, our curriculum materials,
digital learning tools and testing programmes
help to educate millions of
people worldwide – more than any other private enterprise.

Every day our work helps learning flourish,
and wherever learning flourishes, so do people.

To learn more please visit us at www.pearson.com/uk

Fifth edition

Principles of Direct, Database and Digital Marketing

Alan Tapp, Ian Whitten and Matthew Housden

PEARSON

Harlow, England • London • New York • Boston • San Francisco • Toronto • Sydney
Auckland • Singapore • Hong Kong • Tokyo • Seoul • Taipei • New Delhi
Cape Town • São Paulo • Mexico City • Madrid • Amsterdam • Munich • Paris • Milan

PEARSON EDUCATION LIMITED
Edinburgh Gate
Harlow CM20 2JE
United Kingdom
Tel: +44 (0)1279 623623
Web: **www.pearson.com/uk**

First published 1998 (print)
Second edition 2001 (print)
Third edition 2005 (print)
Fourth edition 2008 (print)
Fifth edition published 2014 (print and electronic)

The Financial Times. With a worldwide network of highly respected journalists, *The Financial Times* provides global business news, insightful opinion and expert analysis of business, finance and politics. With over 500 journalists reporting from 50 countries worldwide, our in-depth coverage of international news is objectively reported and analysed from an independent, global perspective. To find out more, visit www.ft.com/pearsonoffer.

ISBN: 978-0-273-75650-7 (print)
      978-0-273-75652-1 (PDF)
      978-0-273-79480-6 (eText)

British Library Cataloguing-in-Publication Data
A catalogue record for the print edition is available from the British Library

Library of Congress Cataloging-in-Publication Data
Tapp, Alan.
  [Principles of direct and database marketing.]
  Principles of direct, database and digital marketing / Alan Tapp, Ian Whitten and Matthew Housden. — Fifth Edition.
    pages cm
  ISBN 978-0-273-75650-7 — ISBN 978-0-273-75652-1 (PDF) — ISBN 978-0-273-79480-6 (eText)
  1. Direct marketing. 2. Database marketing. 3. Internet marketing. I. Whitten, Ian. II. Housden, Matthew. III. Title.
  HF5415.126.T35 2014
  658.8'72—dc23

                                                                              2013029012

ARP impression 98

Print edition typeset in Charter ITC Std Regular 9.5 pt/12.5 pt by 75
Print edition printed and bound by Ashford Colour Press Ltd, Gosport.

NOTE THAT ANY PAGE CROSS REFERENCES REFER TO THE PRINT EDITION

Contents

Part 3 Setting objectives and strategies within direct marketing

Part 4   Direct marketing implementation and control

Preface to the fifth edition

In the five-year period since the fourth edition of this book (then entitled *Principles of Direct and Database Marketing: A Digital Orientation* and written solo by Alan Tapp), the world of direct, data and digital marketing has changed massively.

At that time, Tapp said in his preface that the discipline 'seems to have plateaued out as a mature profession'. He was referring to the way in which commerce used data to drive marketing. But of course since then we have witnessed enormous changes, not just in data management or marketing strategies, but in technological advances:

- The rise and rise of social media (referred to as 'Web 2.0' in the previous edition) as a social, Internet and marketing phenomenon.
- The rise and rise of giants such as Apple, Amazon, Facebook, Google and eBay (each of whom are now worth more than many companies and have surpluses that are the envy of most governments).
- Mobile Internet has risen to prominence.
- Cloud computing promises to make a huge impact.
- 3G is becoming a thing of the past (the 4G auctions were held in 2013).
- Smartphones and other 'mobile' devices will prove the future battle ground for consumer engagement.
- The analogue TV signal in the UK being switched off, meaning all televisions there are digitally enabled.

And yet, other predicted trends have struggled to become reality:

- Companies are still not making as much use of location-based marketing as they could.
- Some 'next big things' have still to fire the public's imagination: Foursquare seemed to come and go with barely a ripple, and Skype has been bought and sold more than once!
- 'Red Button' marketing on TV has not caught on as experts expected, largely due to the advances in technology that mean Web streaming of TV programming changes the way consumers interact with this type of content.

How much of some of these trends are down to the biggest economic downturn since the 1930's is unclear. However, the recession has undoubtedly meant that it is more important than ever for organisations to get the biggest 'bang for their buck' that they possibly can, and here, 'old' strengths of direct marketing – cost effectiveness and measurability – still stand out.

It is tempting to see the future as exclusively digital, but this ignores the recent resurgence of the much maligned origin of the discipline, direct mail. Although slower than e-mail and a darned sight more costly, it is also more difficult to ignore, and a well-designed piece of direct mail can scream 'read me' at its target far more than a subject line on an e-mail. Perhaps rumours of direct mail's demise have been exaggerated.

So what of the future? Will the proposed new EU-wide data protection legislation – with the right to be forgotten – be as bad for the industry as is believed in some quarters, or will it force marketers to think a little harder about how to do things more efficiently and effectively, as the previous round of legislation did? Will 4G take off, or will consumers not be prepared to pay the extra money? Will people finally get fed up of Facebook changing their terms and conditions and resetting our privacy options? Will the promise of cross channel attribution ever be delivered or will digital marketers continue to make many of the mistakes their analogue counterparts made decades ago? Are marketers and marketing able to embrace the full extent of the opportunities that new technology is offering the discipline? Only time will tell.

The development of the Internet and World Wide Web is challenging orthodoxy in politics, society, economics and commerce. In its own way direct, data and digital marketers are in the right place to lead the way for the marketing profession. This book is your first step in being a part of that success story.

New to this edition

The fifth edition sees Alan Tapp joined by Matthew Housden and Ian Whitten. Ian Whitten is an experienced former practitioner and now academic specialising in direct and database marketing. Matthew Housden is an academic and an Institute of Direct and Digital Marketing trainer and consultant. He has worked with many companies looking to implement direct and digital strategies within their overall approach to marketing.

The fifth edition has been extensively updated throughout. Digital and Internet content is now infused throughout the book, reflecting the way in which on-line marketing is now integrated within mainstream marketing.

There are new case studies throughout, some based on author experience and some supplied by some of the best practitioners in the business, including those from Tullo Marshall Warren and Ogilvy.

As you might expect, we have paid attention to the key Internet developments including the impact of Web 2.0, social media in general and Facebook and Twitter in particular.

Finally, there is a new chapter on the Data Protection Act (1998). This piece of legislation plays such an important role in any data activity that it was felt to be a necessary addition to edition five of this book.

We hope you find the book enjoyable and useful, both as a study aid and when you are in practice.

Alan Tapp, Matthew Housden, Ian Whitten
March 2013

Acknowledgements

We are grateful to the following for permission to reproduce copyright material:

Figures

Figures 1.4–1.6, pages 26, 27 from EHS Brann; Figures 3.7–3.15 from SmartFOCUS Ltd; Figure 4.4 adapted from http://acorn.caci.co.uk/infographic, CACI Limited; Figure 6.7 from ONS (2006) UK Time Use Survey, 2005; Figure 6.9, from Sport England – Active People Survey, Oct 2005–2006, Ipsos MORI; Figures 6.10, 6.11 from Sport England; Figures 6.12–6.17 from Sport England – Experian/Taking Part Survey/Active People Survey; Figures 8.5, 8.6, 8.8, 8.9 from Dycem Ltd; Figures 9.2, 9.3 from comScore Media Metrix, Worldwide, October 2011; Figure 9.7 from True Social Metrics, 2013, http://www.truesocialmetrics.com/metric; Figure 10.3 from D. Holder (1992) 'Finders keepers – the basics of customer acquisition and retention', in B. Halsey (ed.) *The Practitioners' Guide to Direct Marketing*; Figure 11.3 from DMA Census, 2003; Figure 11.7 from Sitel and TNS Omnibus 2012 cited in emarketer.com; Figure 11.12 from Harrison Troughton Wunderman – and Xerox; Figure 12.1 from http://www.ft.com/cms/s/0/3f9693bc-113a-11e2-8d5f-00144feabdc0.html#axzz2bSc8quoj; Figure on page 433 from Andy Nairn and Matt Buttrick (2007) Trident (Metropolitan Police) – making a small budget go a long way; Institute of Practitioners in Advertising, Grand Prix & Gold, IPA Effectiveness Awards, 2007; Figure 12.2 from Metropolitan Police 2000/2001–2006/2007; Figure 13.4 from Directors at Large' direct-response press ad; Figure 13.5 from Skeleton in the cupboard, The Story of Red – RSPCA; Figure 13.6 from The UK's Best Buy Time Group ad; Figure 13.7 from Compaq and Bates Worldwide; Figure 13.8 from Still from Sky News – showing scrap metal barge outside the House of Commons; Figure 13.8 from ITN screen grab (still from Channel 4 News) ITN Source; Figure 13.8 from Cover of Financial Times, 7 July 1999, © The Financial Times Limited. All Rights Reserved; Figure 13.8 from Practical Action montage photo – EHS Brann; Figure 13.10 adapted from Foxall, G. and Goldsmith, R. (1994) *Consumer Psychology for Marketing,* Cengage Learning; Figure 13.11 from You always meant to join us; ad – Amnesty International; Figures 14.1–14.3 from 2 Royal and Sun Alliance Group ads; Figure 14.5 after P. Mouncey (2002) 'Using market research for better direct marketing', in B. Halsey (ed.) *The Practitioners' Guide to Direct Marketing*; Figure 14.6 from He'll face 30ft. waves . . . – Royal National Lifeboat Institution ad.

Screenshots

Screenshot 11.1 from Google screenshot – search for 'Adventure holidays'; Screenshot 11.2 from Screenshot from Hastings Hotels web site, http://www.hastingshotels.com/index.cfm/website_key/4/index.html.

Tables

Table 1.3 from WARC, AA 2012; Table 2.1 from Director of Compliance Operations, DMA, 2003.

Text

Exhibit 3.3 from Segmenting according to lifestyle needs: Harley Davidson, *Journal of Targeting, Measurement and Analysis,* 4 (1), pp. 337–62 (Swinyard, W. R. 1996); Exhibit 4.1 from Acxiom UK, 2011; Case Study 4.2 adapted from a slideshow delivered by Tim Harford, Head of Donor Care and Community Fundraising at Depaul UK, on 02 March 2011. Charity case study – iHobo, [Online] Available at: http://resources.mediatrust.org/events/think-mobile/charity-caste-study-ihobo; Exhibit 4.4 from The Direct Marketing Guide, Teddington: IDM (Fairlie, R. 1998); Exhibit 4.6 adapted from http://www.themarketer.co.uk/articles/case-studies/the-national-trust/; Exhibit 4.12 from Acxiom UK (2010); Exhibit 4.13 from Alan Mitchell, www.rightsideup.net.; Exhibit 6.1 from Mass Customization and Open Innovation News, published and edited by Frank Piller; Case Study on page 213 from Alan Tapp and Mihir Warty, Sport England; Exhibit 6.12 adapted from Dig deeper into the database goldmine, *Marketing Magazine,* 11 January, pp. 29–30 (Marsh, H. 2001); Case Study 7.1 from Case Study written by Dr Tim Hughes; Case Study 9.1 adapted from Harding, M., 2012, www.wherethehellismatt.com/about; Case Study 10.2 from Bolger, M., Case Study: Barclaycard Freedom, http://www.themarketer.co.uk/articles/case-studies/case-study-barclaycard-freedom/; Case Study 10.4 from Publicis Dialog; Case Study 11.1 from Harrison Troughton Wunderman and client Xerox; Exhibit 11.7 from Mashable 2012, http://mashable.com/2012/11/27/siri-chevrolet/, Copyrighted 2013. Mashable, Inc. 102589:813PF; Exhibit 11.12 from Hastings Hotesl Group – Battle of Hastings 2005–06: how email marketing overcame heightened competition to generated increased room occupancy and return on advertising investment for Hastings Hotels, Institute of Practitioners in Advertising, IPA Effectiveness Awards, 2007; Exhibit 11.21 from Extracts from Script for the Red Cross Gulf War Appeal, British Red Cross; Exhibit 12.2 from News International Commercial, 2012, News International Case Studies, http://nicommercial.co.uk/times-media/case-studies/california-tourism; Case Study 12.2 from Barda, T., 2009, Case Study: Gillette, http://www.themarketer.co.uk/articles/case-studies/gillette/; Exhibit 12.8 from B. Quinton (2006) 'As seen on the web', www.directmag.com; Exhibit 12.15 from Andy Nairn and Matt Buttrick (2007) Trident (Metropolitan Police) – making a small budget go a long way, Institute of Practitioners in Advertising, Grand Prix & Gold, IPA Effectiveness Awards, 2007.

In some instances we have been unable to trace the owners of copyright material, and we would appreciate any information that would enable us to do so.

PART ONE

Introducing direct and digital marketing

Chapter 1

What is direct and digital marketing?

Objectives

Once you have read this chapter you will:

- have a clear view of what direct and digital marketing is
- understand its importance in contemporary marketing
- understand its role within the wider marketing framework

Introduction

In this chapter direct, database and digital marketing will be introduced. Direct marketing is widely misunderstood and the common areas of confusion are addressed early on. A clear vision of direct marketing as a complete framework for a specialised form of marketing across multiple channels both on and off line will be developed. The reader will probably be familiar with typical general marketing techniques, so these are used throughout as a foil to provide a clear sense of how direct marketing, whether in the physical or on-line worlds, differs from mainstream marketing. The concept of digital marketing is introduced and a case is made for the incorporation of digital techniques within the direct paradigm.

Finally, the reasons for the recent explosive growth in direct and digital marketing practice are analysed.

1.1 What is direct and database marketing?

1.1.1 A distinct marketing system

Direct marketing is simply a way of doing marketing. You may already be familiar with the core philosophy of marketing, summed up by Kotler *et al.* (2009) as:

> 'Marketing is the societal process by which individuals and groups obtain what they need and want through creating, offering and freely exchanging products of value with others.'

This philosophy is exactly the same for direct marketing. So where does direct marketing differ from general marketing?

Direct marketing is a method of marketing based on individual customer records held on a database. These records are the basis for marketing analysis, planning, implementation of programmes, and control of all this activity.

In contrast, general marketing is structured around the creation of brands for each product, and the attainment of market share for that product. The very first marketing department, set up by Colgate Palmolive in 1938, contained that classical department structure: brand and product managers, group product managers, and so on.

In comparing these two approaches, the advantage of the direct marketing framework is that 'the use of the database forces a natural focus on customers rather than products'. Modern direct marketing thinking, for example the Institute of Direct and Digital Marketing (IDM, 2012) holds that it is better to understand one's customers as 'individuals' in more detail than to build up product brands. Direct marketing also encourages us to think in terms of customer relationships with the company – are we talking to 'new prospects' or 'loyal, established customers'? In this respect, there is a natural alignment between direct marketing and 'relationship marketing'.

If the first tangible difference is the database, the second is that direct marketers market to customers with the aim of 'attracting a direct response'. Direct Line Insurance gives you a phone number or website to respond to after seeing its adverts. Direct marketers will often contact customers directly through addressable, one-to-one media. *Marketing Week* magazine will e-mail customers whose subscriptions have run out to ask them to renew, at the same time offering them an incentive to respond quickly. Direct marketers may also distribute direct to customers, missing out the retail link in the chain. Laithwaites, the direct wine company, does exactly this.

What about digital marketing or marketing over the Internet? Much of this is direct in nature, most uses a database, and some is traditional brand building. The mistakes made by digital marketers in the early days of the Internet mirror problems that have always faced marketers. The use of poorly targeted e-mail led to the creation of a new meaning for the word spam and effectively killed a wonderfully cost effective and potentially powerful acquisition medium. This is not so different from brand marketers using broadcast media to target potential customers. Equally, the successes enjoyed by digital marketers are often determined by the use of tried and tested direct marketing principles and techniques that have always looked to target the right individuals with appropriate products, offers and messages at the right time delivered through the right media and channels. Indeed it could be argued that the Internet acts simply as another medium alongside, say, TV, or a channel for service distribution (easyJet tickets), or a marketplace all of its own (eBay). The detailed techniques for managing the medium are new and different but this is not so different from when marketers had to re-engineer their skills to deal with TV or other new media. Of course, for marketers whose skills were formed in the analogue world this new medium has produced challenges and disruption. For consultancies and trainers it produces benefits and opportunities. But it remains the case that many of the principles and some of the techniques used over the net are the same as, or similar to, those used in the physical world.

So far so good. But the problem with the previous descriptions of direct marketing is that, although they are often used to explain the discipline, they do not quite get to the heart of what direct marketing is all about.

In fact, the key to modern direct marketing is the capture of individual customer details at the first sale, so that the marketer can begin a relationship with that customer, 'subsequently treating them differently' over time in order to generate repeat business (see Figure 1.1).

So, if someone texts you an offer to get money off your next cinema ticket, or you join an on-line dating agency, or the charity volunteer leaves an envelope at your home for you to make a donation, or you receive a coupon through the post from Persil to redeem at your supermarket – a lot of this may be described as direct marketing. But it is argued here that direct marketing in its fullest sense happens only when the customer's name, address and details are taken, and the subsequent marketing to them changes as a result.

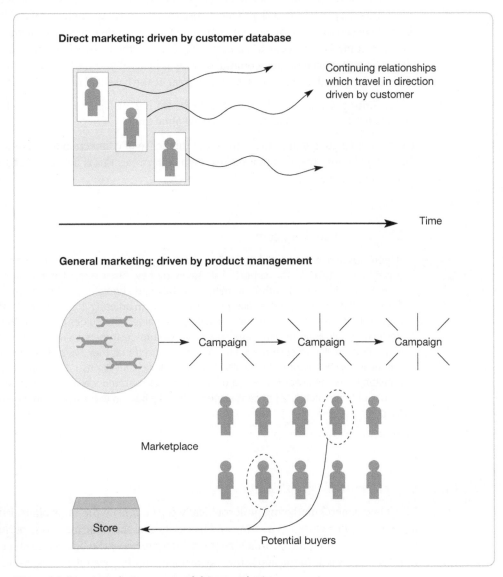

Figure 1.1 Direct marketing: a way of doing marketing

Let us consider the charity volunteer who leaves an envelope at your house for you to make a donation. The volunteer returns three days later and merely picks up your donation without noting your address, or indeed noting your contribution in any way. Although some may describe this as direct marketing, only in the most basic way (direct contact with an individual) can it really be described as such.

At the other end of the scale, it could be argued that the purest form of direct marketing is that practised by business salespeople. What do good computer equipment salespeople do having made the first sale to a company? Forget all about that company until they next have a shortfall on their targets? No, they stay in constant touch, learning more and more about that company's computing needs. Then they will make the company further offers that they know will be relevant to it. Good salespeople will be constantly learning about their customers' individual needs in depth, and will adjust their own product and service offers as far as possible in order to meet customers' needs. An ongoing relationship is established between salesperson and customer, and any changing needs are acknowledged and met. Direct marketing seeks to emulate the sales/customer relationship as far as possible, by gathering personal details, communicating individually, and wherever possible adjusting offers to individual taste. Morris Hite, the great Texas-based ad man said this:

> 'Advertising is salesmanship mass produced. No one would bother to use advertising if he could talk to all his prospects face-to-face. But he can't.'

The goal of all good marketing is to create this sense of connection and intimacy; to create the feeling in our prospects that makes them believe 'yes, this is for me' and to inspire them to act on that belief.

Exhibit 1.1 Ebookers.com

If you buy a flight or holiday on-line these days you get an e-mail confirmation and e-printout to take to the airport. This saves money, but makes it harder for ebookers. com to stay in contact with customers who have just booked. So their agency Stephens Francis Whitson produced a nice piece of creative marketing to stimulate further bookings. It used the customer's name to create personalised city guides based on their booking destination, all done in very high quality to ensure customers valued the guides. These were direct mailed to customers. Ebookers recognised that they have difficulties encouraging loyalty, with customers typically 'Googling' for cheap flights rather than automatically repeating their behaviour. The use of direct mail to customers who had booked was innovative, obtained nearly 2 per cent response directly back in extra sales, and won a Precision Marketing award.

Source: Stephens Francis Whitson.

1.1.2 Direct marketing: a discipline within marketing

Direct and general marketing philosophically start out from the same place. Direct marketing is a discipline within marketing and has as its goal the same aims as general marketing: that is, championing the customer as the primary focus of the business. Direct marketing's rightful place is within the marketing department, adding leverage to the overall marketing effort, and often working alongside other disciplines in an integrated fashion.

1.1.3 The distinctions between direct, database and digital marketing

At this point we can begin to address the differences between 'direct' and 'database' marketing:

- **Database marketing.** This is using a database to hold and analyse customer information, thereby helping create strategies for marketing. There is a big overlap with 'direct marketing'.
- **Direct marketing.** This focuses on using a database to communicate (and sometimes distribute) directly to customers so as to attract a direct response. There is a big overlap with 'database marketing'.
- **Digital marketing.** This broad term encompasses any marketing aimed at consumers using digital channels, from general advertising to closing a sale. Much of this (but not all of it) is direct in nature. The broad principles with off-line direct marketing hold firm, but the techniques change.

In the majority of practices, however, direct, digital and database marketing – whether on- or off-line – are brought together into a direct marketing system:

- **Direct marketing systems.** Database, digital and direct marketing can be brought together to provide a complete, alternative method of marketing analysis, planning, implementation and control. These words have been carefully chosen, and we will see that direct marketing systems have distinct strengths in all four of these marketing activities. This complete direct marketing process is the primary focus of this book.

The use of terms in this book

As we progress through the chapters, the slight distinctions between database, digital and direct marketing will be drawn out. However, given the overlaps, we will avoid clumsy use of language by using the term 'direct marketing' as shorthand for 'direct, digital and database marketing' or 'direct marketing systems'.

Before we move on to full definitions, let us clear up a few misconceptions about direct marketing.

What direct marketing is *not*

The first place that you may have encountered a mention of direct marketing is in a general marketing textbook or in a marketing magazine or blog. Unfortunately, none of these sources captures the entirety of direct marketing systems. Mainstream marketing texts, for example Brassington and Pettitt (2007) (and also marketing communications texts, e.g. Fill, 2009, De Pelsmacker *et al.*, 2010), as well as the syllabus of the Chartered Institute of Marketing (CIM), tend to view direct marketing as confined to the marketing communications mix, while database applications are ignored almost completely.

Meanwhile, the marketing trade press often refers to direct marketing and direct mail interchangeably. Worse, a set of euphemisms, such as 'loyalty marketing' or 'interactive marketing' have emerged (often used by direct marketing practitioners seeking to capitalise on emerging trends) to describe direct marketing. To cap it all, the popular press (and marketers can partly blame themselves for this) sums it all up as 'spam', 'junk mail' or 'cold calling'.

The following section clears up the main misconceptions about direct marketing.

Direct marketing is part of marketing communications.

This is widely believed, but unfortunately it is inaccurate. The discipline of direct marketing began in mail order, which is primarily a method of 'distribution' rather than communication. Indeed it is this functionality of the Internet that is harnessing the skills of direct marketers in acquiring the best prospects and retaining the best customers. Direct marketing systems run through databases, the primary functions of which are capturing, maintaining and, most importantly, analysis, with an additional role as orchestrator of communications. Lastly, direct marketing, via database analysis and the generation of management information and customer insight, has a key role to play in strategy creation, as we will see.

Direct marketing is called something else.

Throughout the marketing world, across different subjects and within the academic and practitioner worlds, words are used sloppily. The word 'marketing' itself is thrown around by various groups to represent totally different things. How many times will you read in a marketing trade journal 'Joe Smith has been moved from advertising to a job in marketing'? But you thought advertising was 'already part of marketing', right? Er, right. But marketing professionals use descriptors any old how. Here Joe Smith, by moving into 'marketing' has presumably moved into what academics would call 'sales promotion', whereas some practitioners might call it 'promotion'. So, promotion = sales promotion then? Er, no, not that simple. Because professional marketers will use the word 'promotion' in many different ways: is 'promotion' not one of the Four Ps (product, price, place and promotion), covering advertising, sales promotion, PR, and so on?

> 'If you would speak with me, you must define your terms . . .'
>
> (Voltaire)

This utter confusion is, unfortunately, just as prevalent in direct marketing. You may have come across direct marketing, database marketing, CRM (customer relationship management), direct-response marketing, relationship marketing, one-to-one marketing, data driven marketing, loyalty marketing and interactive marketing. These are all used by direct marketing practitioners to mean much the same thing.

The only way to cope with this situation is to define each term carefully before using it.

Direct marketing equals direct mail.

Even experienced practitioners often fail to distinguish between the two terms. Direct marketing is a discipline within marketing – a system of marketing. Direct mail is merely one of the media, although an important one, that direct marketers use. But direct marketing is also practised on-line, through the press, the telephone, and a host of other media.

Direct marketing equals junk mail.

Junk mail is direct mail that is poorly targeted, patronising, of low quality, or a mixture of all three. Unfortunately, junk mail is pretty much as widespread as it ever was, and has without question damaged the industry. Financial services, in particular banks, credit card and insurance companies, are the main culprits – and in this age of environmental awareness these people should be called to account. But there are also plenty of well-targeted, relevant and attractive direct mail programmes, which customers describe as 'letters from the company'!

Having (hopefully) dispelled some myths, we can now move towards a more rigorous definition of direct, digital and database marketing.

1.2   Defining direct, digital and database marketing

Direct (and digital and database) marketing is a rather complex collection of principles and practices that together make up an entirely 'self-contained' choice for marketers. We can unravel this complexity by looking briefly at the history of definitions for direct marketing and then moving clearly towards a single definition.

Bird (1989), a practitioner of worldwide authority, originally defined direct marketing as:

'any activity which creates and exploits a direct relationship between you and your customer as an individual.'

This definition is widely quoted, perhaps because of its compelling simplicity and broad, inclusive nature. Bird has widened out direct marketing from being merely part of the communications mix to something that can develop 'relationships' with customers.

The reader should note that other definitions of direct marketing around the world are plentiful. In contrast to the view that direct marketing is a way of doing marketing, commentators in the USA seem to agree on a definition that positions direct marketing as a part of the communications mix rather than as a strategic framework (Baier, 1985; Katzenstein, 1992; Nash, 1995; Roberts, 1989; Stone, 1996).

Some writers have split direct, digital and database marketing, emphasising the use of the database as an information tool for strategies but, in practice, the majority of data driven marketing leads to direct marketing programmes (e.g. Experian, 2008). It is also a fact that most digital marketing is data driven. In this book, then, we will concentrate on a combined view of direct and database marketing.

Newcomers to the discipline might benefit from taking on board the central core of strategic direct marketing:

Direct marketing happens when individual customer details are captured and kept on a database, thus allowing that customer's needs to be better understood over time. This enables subsequent approaches to the customer to be tailored according to that customer's specific needs.

This book is about direct marketing as a complete marketing system through which analysis, planning, programme activities and control are all practised. We can, therefore, more fully define direct marketing in the following way:

Direct marketing is a way of acquiring, keeping and developing customers and, in doing so, meeting the needs both of customers and the organisation serving them. It does this by providing a framework for three activities: analysis of individual customer information, strategy formation and implementation such that customers respond directly.

The first part of this definition springs from Levitt's (1983) famous assertion that

'the purpose of business is to create and keep a customer.'

This neatly captures the notion of direct marketing as a customer management system.

The notion of direct marketing being a framework is also very important. What this means is that all the decisions we make in general marketing – how you segment, brand, position, deliver a service, build relationships with, or deliver a marketing mix to, the customer – are also made within direct marketing, but start from a different place: that is, individual customer information.

So is digital a new way of doing marketing? In his influential text Dave Chaffey defines Internet marketing very simply as:

'Achieving marketing objectives through applying digital technologies'

(Chaffey and Ellis-Chadwick, 2012)

He then goes on to distinguish between e-marketing and digital marketing. E-marketing, he believes, is different from Internet marketing in that it refers to other digital applications, including the use of digital customer data and electronic customer relationship management systems. Digital marketing is defined by Chaffey for the Institute of Direct and Digital Marketing in a more complex fashion.

'Digital Marketing involves:
Applying these technologies, which form on-line channels to market: that is Web, e-mail, databases plus mobile/wireless and digital TV

To achieve these objectives:
Support marketing activities aimed at achieving profitable acquisition and retention of customers within a multi channel buying process and customers' lifecycle.

Through using these marketing tactics:
Recognising the strategic importance of digital technologies and developing a planned approach to reach and migrate customers to on-line services through e-communications and traditional communications. Retention is achieved through improving our customer knowledge (of their profiles, behaviour, value and loyalty drivers), then delivering integrated, targeted communications and on-line services that match their individual needs.'

Chaffey (2012), Thomas and Housden (2011)

The IDM (2012) defines e-marketing as:

'The use of the Internet and related digital information and communications technologies to achieve marketing objectives. Broadly equivalent to digital marketing.'

It goes on to define digital marketing as:

'"Digital marketing" has a similar meaning to "Electronic marketing" – both describe the management and execution of marketing using electronic media such as the web, e-mail, interactive TV, wireless media in conjunction with digital data about customers' characteristics and behaviour.'

(IDM, 2012)

So we see amongst leading commentators on the business a high degree of uncertainty about the scope and extent of digital marketing. In some of the above definitions digital marketing does not always appear to have to be direct in the sense that we are communicating to known individuals. In others digital is simply a new set of techniques within a direct model. This represents a weakness in much of the writing around digital marketing.

The late Professor Derek Holder, founder of the IDM, said that the definition of digital marketing is in many ways the same as the definition of direct marketing except that it is limited to digital media. We can see the simple sense in this statement. It is extremely unusual for any brand to be marketed solely through digital channels. We use a range of channels to reach our customers and customers do not readily see the difference between on- and off-line channels. They simply see a range of communications coming from a company that is relevant to their needs or not. We have also seen that, as brands can be marketed successfully using a mass marketing approach, so brands can be marketed through digital media outside a direct marketing system. We would argue that the most effective use of digital is within the direct marketing paradigm and, indeed, the success of digital techniques rests on the fact that often this is how they are executed.

If digital marketing is carried out with a direct marketing system then it is a direct technique.

If there is a difference between direct and digital, it lies in the organising principle that underpins their use. Once this is determined, the techniques and tactics that are employed are simply ways of delivering mass marketing or direct marketing.

In this book we see 'direct marketing' as fitting within a broader approach to marketing and business, which looks to develop organisations that aim to meet customer needs for mutual benefit, and 'digital' and 'database' as central elements of the direct marketing system.

> **Direct marketing is a way of acquiring, keeping and developing customers and, in doing so, meeting the needs both of customers and the organisation serving them. It does this by providing a framework for three activities: analysis of individual customer information, strategy formation, and implementation such that customers respond directly through a variety of on- and off-line channels and media.**

Finally, with the doubts expressed over the years about the Four Ps framework, and the rise in credibility of relationship marketing techniques, it is important for us to examine the basis of direct marketing from the point of view of both 'Four Ps' and 'relationship' marketing.

1.2.1 Is direct marketing based on relationship marketing or the Four Ps?

We have nearly completed our introduction to direct marketing, but there is one more thing to clear up. Modern marketing now juggles two competing philosophies. The first is the transaction approach epitomised by the 'Four Ps' of marketing: product, price, place and promotion. The second approach is known as relationship marketing, which emphasises building relationships with customers over time and the importance of bringing together customer-led quality, service and marketing within a company.

Which of these philosophies does modern direct marketing follow? If we go back to direct marketing's early development, it concentrated on prompting action from customers to make a 'sale' (for example Bird, 1989). This approach is heavily influenced by the Four Ps approach.

According to Christopher *et al.* (1991), direct marketing has developed as a powerful tool in customer loyalty strategies. Relationship marketing starts with the premise that customer retention is critical to company profitability, which is also the starting point of modern direct marketing, although subsequent relationship marketing thinking has concentrated on service and quality issues as the keys to delivering relationship strategies. By the mid 1990s, however, relationship marketers had started to integrate direct marketing into their thinking (Payne *et al.*, 1995).

In answer to our original question, we can see that direct marketing draws from both philosophies while maintaining its own clear identity as an approach based on a customer database.

But watch out: many writers (and this goes back to the mid 1990s, for example; De Bonis and Nucifora, 1994; Pearson, 1994; Shani and Chalasani, 1992) use the terms 'direct (database) marketing' and 'relationship marketing' interchangeably, and direct marketing is routinely described as relationship marketing in practitioner journals and conferences. Why this is so is not clear, because the term 'relationship marketing', as originally coined by Berry in 1983, clearly did not refer to direct marketing in any way at that time. We will maintain the clear distinctions between the approaches here.

The following section begins our exploration of direct marketing in practice.

1.3 Direct marketing in practice

After comparing direct marketing to general marketing in a little more detail, we will go on to examine the various levels at which direct marketing operates in businesses.

1.3.1 Direct marketing compared to general marketing

Figure 1.2 gives a comparison between a typical direct marketing process and a typical general marketing process. It may be useful to take a look at both processes and spot the different approaches taken by direct marketers.

1.3.2 The similarities and differences between direct and general marketing

Looking at Figure 1.2, we can take a closer look at the ways in which direct marketing differs from the general marketing process.

A TYPICAL GENERAL MARKETING PROCESS

Example: the Sony Walkman

1 A new product or service is developed. Through superb innovation the first personal stereo is invented by Sony.
2 Marketing research is carried out. Sony invites consumers to give their opinions about the Walkman. Opinions are favourable.

A typical general marketing process (*continued*)

3 The Four Ps of marketing (product, price, place and promotion) are looked at strategically. Sony realises that the Walkman will first be bought by innovators, but it will also have wider market appeal, especially to young people. Sony understands that it will be copied quickly by competitors. Therefore the price is set quite high initially, but to drop quickly. Sony maintains a premium position in the marketplace, in keeping with its strong corporate brand. It looks to distribute through typical high-street outlets.

4 Operational details for product, price and place are set. The target audience is assessed in detail. From this, product features are added, e.g. different styles of headphones, graphic equalisers, etc. Typical prices for Sony Walkmans are £30–£60. They are sold through Dixons and other high street outlets.

5 The first customers are sought using promotion techniques. Advertising builds awareness, interest and brand salience. Sony uses corporate brand advertising on television to maintain a high profile. An emphasis on quality and reliability is highlighted.

6 Sales promotions are used to stimulate trial of the product. Limited use is made of these techniques by Sony until the product has been on the market for some time.

7 Customers identify themselves when they buy the product for the first time.

8 Reinforcement advertising is used to build brand loyalty. Existing customers are not identified, nor is any effort made to treat regular customers differently from new customers.

In a typical general marketing process, *brand loyalty* is achieved by:

building a brand that consumers like

building customer satisfaction through excellent service when the customer is in contact with the product, service or company.

A TYPICAL DIRECT MARKETING PROCESS

Example: IBM

1 A new product or service is developed, or a new channel is required.

IBM turns to direct marketing because its traditional markets are saturated and growth is taking place in the consumer and small-business sectors.

2 A database is built and used for analysis.

All IBM's worldwide databases are pulled together into one and this is developed into a marketing database. It is found that IBM is confusing its customers through different brand images in different countries. This is rectified.

3 Strategy is developed. Direct marketers will plan to:

- gather information on each individual customer;
- develop tailored products and communications;
- communicate directly to customers over time;
- consider direct distribution.

A typical direct marketing process (*continued*)

IBM Direct is created, with the remit of creating leads, fulfilling orders, and customer care. An integrated approach with IBM's salesforce is developed.

4 At this point, a clear distinction is made by direct marketers: how much can we sell to our existing customers and, therefore, how many new customers do we need to acquire? What is the split of effort between existing and new customers?

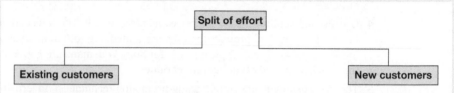

Figure 1.2 A comparison of direct and general marketing

5 Segmentation may be carried out.

IBM Direct looks at segmenting its customers according to product category – its different customer support needs may be calculated according to this segmentation.

6 Communication with existing customers is via personal media (for example, sales force, e-mail, via the website or by telephone).

IBM's database is hooked up to its telemarketing system – 250 operators dealing with inbound and outbound telephone calls to customers. Both sales and customer care are handled in one management operation.

7 The customer responds. A sale is made.

IBM Direct may generate a prospect which the salesforce will take over and look to convert into customers.

8 Sometimes the product or service is delivered direct to the customer.

IBM Direct delivers direct to the customer, bypassing retail channels.

9 This response information is added to the customer's record.

10 Market information and intelligence gathering tends to be centred around the database rather than market research, although research is sometimes used.

Both market research and data analysis are used at IBM Direct.

11 A target audience of possible customers is drawn up by profiling existing customers of other products or services.

12 Direct response media are employed to communicate the product. An incentive or sales promotion may be offered to stimulate this first purchase.

IBM's biggest asset is its brand, and this added value is used to generate responses. Mail and telephone are both used as acquisition media.

13 If a customer responds and a sale is made, as much information as possible is gathered and stored on the database.

The new customer's name is added to the database of 600,000 contacts in 250,000 companies.

> **A typical direct marketing process (*continued*)**
>
> Direct marketers generate loyalty by:
>
> meeting individual needs above and beyond the mass delivery of the product or service;
>
> proactive service to customers using direct, two-way communication.
>
> *Source*: IBM Case Study, based on *Marketing Direct*, November 1995. Reproduced from *Marketing Direct* magazine with the permission of the copyright owner, Haymarket Business Publications Limited.

Similarities

Many of the initial stages that a marketer goes through are the same for general and direct marketing. In particular, at the start of the process, 'new product development' is exactly the same in both camps. Continuing through the process, much of the 'strategic thinking' you need to do, for example matching your strengths with market opportunities, should be the same. 'Research methods' and testing are also used by both marketing camps, although the relative emphasis is very different.

Differences

Although the process of 'strategy' setting is the same, the content of that strategy is likely to be different – direct marketing gives you, the marketer, a choice of different strategies. A focus on customers rather than products; segmenting according to the financial value of customers to you; distributing directly to bypass retail: these are just some of the key areas.

The most obvious operational difference between the two methods is in the area of 'communications'. General marketers tend to use mass media to build brands, and use sales promotions in the retail environment. Direct marketers also sometimes use some mass media when addressing new prospects, in order to get a response. They use personal media – mobile, social media, e-mail, direct mail, telemarketing – when developing a relationship with existing customers.

There are differences in the way classic and direct marketers 'measure' their marketing effort. General marketers will usually use marketing research techniques to understand and predict their customers' likely behaviour. Direct marketers will analyse behaviour using their database in order to predict the best responding people and the best offers to make. They will look to market test new ideas on small samples before rolling out.

Overall, direct marketing is often more expensive, on a per-customer basis, than general marketing. The investment in direct marketing is a way of 'buying' a closer relationship with the customer: first, individual customer information, and then subsequent precision and control in customer contact.

Now that we understand how direct marketing differs from general marketing, we can examine direct marketing practice from a new angle. Let us now look at the different levels that direct marketing operates at within a business.

1.3.3 The three levels of direct marketing

The previous section highlighted how direct marketing can be viewed at a number of different levels, from communications to strategy setting. In fact there are three clear levels at which direct marketing can impact on a business.

Direct marketing drives the business
Example: Direct Line Insurance

Direct Line Insurance has a direct marketing strategy that drives the entire business. Everyone in the company understands that it is the customer who is the focus of their activities. As a result, the product (insurance policies) reflects what the customer wants, i.e. a competitive price, and a no-hassle claims department if the need arises. The 'delivery' of the product to the customer is 100 per cent 'direct': customers are recruited via on-line search engines such as Google, responsive TV and press adverts, and prospects are chased through communications that are timed to coincide with the prospects' renewal period. Once a sale is made, all details are completed using 'direct distribution'. Direct Line has no broker network, nor is any high street outlet used. If you have a query, you ring Direct Line, or access its website and it is sorted out over the phone or on-line. Naturally, Direct Line has a 'database of existing customers' that it uses to organise direct communications aimed at 'keeping customers'.

Since 1984, when it was set up, Direct Line has grown faster than any other insurance company in the UK.

Direct marketing drives part or all of the marketing strategy
Example: British Airways

British Airways (BA), like all the major airlines, is driven by the 80: 20 rule. Twenty per cent of its customers – the frequent flyer business people – contribute 80 per cent of its profits. Not surprisingly, a great deal of BA's marketing effort goes into looking after these precious individuals. Imagine you are a frequent flyer with BA. Do you turn up at the airport two hours before the flight, queue to check in, sit around in the crowded airport lounge and then cram yourself into economy class for the flight? Forget it! You arrive half an hour before take-off at priority check-in. You are whisked through to the Executive Club members' lounge and, in these quiet, relaxing surroundings, you order yourself a free drink at the bar. You unhurriedly make your way to your business class seat where you are pampered for the length of the trip. During the flight, you clock up Avios Miles for your personal use.

All this, of course, is run through direct marketing. A direct marketing strategy is being used here: repeat customers are treated very differently to first-time or occasional customers. This is the core of any strategic direct marketing operation. Direct marketing also directs the tactical implementation: the initial recruitment of a frequent flyer is done via direct-response methods to potential prospects. Once enrolled into the Executive Club (levels Blue, Silver and Gold), your details are placed on a database and continually updated depending on your involvement with BA. Communication with you, to keep you informed of any offers, your latest Avios Miles, totals, etc., is carried out through direct mail.

However, direct marketing is only part of the story for BA. Heavy expenditure is directed towards a strong brand advertising programme, and a lot of emphasis is put on overall service delivery and keeping prices as keen as possible in a highly competitive industry.

Direct marketing, therefore, improves the gearing on other marketing investments: it is one of the disciplines within British Airways' marketing mix.

Direct marketing is used within the communications mix
Example: the university sector

Some universities, when recruiting students, rely on a mix of word-of-mouth recommendations, their prospectus (a detailed brochure distributed to schools and colleges) – and luck (students sticking a pin on the map).

University marketers may not have a database of existing or past students to use for marketing purposes. Use of direct marketing may be confined to one area, such as recruitment of students on to specific postgraduate courses. This could be done through direct-response advertising in key press, such as the *Guardian* or *Times Higher Education Supplement,* or on-line at sites such as **thestudentroom.co.uk**. This sits alongside other elements of the communications mix, of which the major one is PR both on- and off-line. Many universities make heavy use of this, both proactively, with visits, open days, liaison with local events, and the use of Twitter and personalised e-mails once the students have raised their hands and can be identified via a database of prospects; and also reactively via press editorial comment, which has a powerful effect on their public image.

In conclusion, universities do not typically have a developed direct marketing strategy, nor are their marketing operations led in any sense by direct marketing. They use direct-response communications as a part of their overall communications mix.

Now that we have a clearer sense of what direct marketing is, our final task is to understand the historical development of direct marketing, putting it in context as an increasingly important discipline within marketing.

1.4 The historical growth of direct marketing

Direct marketing originated as a form of distribution from mail-order companies, publishers and book clubs (McCorkell, 1992). The mail-order discipline is in fact centuries old, although the industry as we recognise it today emerged in the latter part of the last century. It is often reported in marketing journals that the use of customer data to drive marketing is relatively new. This is not the case, however. *Reader's Digest*, for example, had been using customer databases in various forms well before the invention of computers. 'The Digest' originally used large, specialised filing cabinets to hold its customer records. By turning various handles with rods penetrating the files, lists of customers who fitted different marketing segments could be drawn out!

The expansion of direct marketing from its roots in mail order into mainstream marketing began in the USA in the 1970s. One of the few major companies to grasp direct marketing's potential at that time was American Express. However, in Western Europe very little expansion took place until the 1980s. In the UK, growth was led by financial services companies, which began to make serious use of their account records (Henley Centre, 1995). British Telecom (BT) began experimenting with direct marketing, and by the late 1980s the charity sector had made huge leaps forward in its use of direct marketing, emerging as highly accomplished practitioners by the early 1990s.

The late 1990s and 2000s have seen the coming of age of data driven direct marketing. Thanks in part to cheaper, more flexible technologies, and increasingly well-educated marketing managers, there has been rapid growth in direct marketing. Industries such as airlines, hotels, car manufacturers, utilities, leisure, retail and, latterly, packaged goods have all embraced direct marketing. The mid to late 2000s have seen an enormous leap in on-line direct marketing, making it, at the time of writing, the fastest growing marketing discipline worldwide.

Table 1.1 UK direct marketing spend by channel 2011

Medium	% Spend by channel 2011	£ million
Display advertising	20	2,840.0
Direct mail and door drops	16	2,272.0
E-mail marketing	16	2,272.0
Internet search advertising	15	2,130.0
Telemarketing	5	710.0
Social media	3.4	511.2
Outdoor, transport direct response	3.3	468.6
Experiential marketing	2.6	369.2
Internet banner advertising	2.6	369.2
Freepost and business reply	2.1	298.2
Mobile	1.0	142.0
Interactive TV	1.0	142.0
All other direct channels	12.0	1,704.0
Total	100.0	14,200.0

Source: DMA (2012).

1.4.1 Reasons for growth

A number of sources (DMA, 2012; PWC IAB UK, 2012) have reported on the continued growth of direct marketing. In 2012, the industry in the UK was forecast to grow to £15.2 billion, up from £14.2 billion in 2011.

According to the Internet Advertising Bureau UK (IABUK), despite the backdrop of a depressed UK economy, advertising on the Internet increased by 14.4 per cent to a new high of £4,784 million in 2011, up £687 million year on year. (IABUK, 2012)

The following factors have emerged and are discussed below:

Exhibit 1.2 Direct marketing: new sectors, new ideas

Sometimes we need to remember that entertaining, charming, or even dazzling our prospective customers can pay rich dividends. But why would a client do the following?

Give consumers a scratch card with an 'oily' penguin on it

Mail out a train menu on tin foil

Send out a make-up stick called 'Slap' to young working women

E-mail a movie of a landlord trying to push a pint through the computer screen

Mail out a rain mac to advertise a holiday destination

And the answers are:

Bristol Zoo sent a door drop to potential donors inviting them to scratch the 'oil' off the picture of the penguin using a coin. Once off, the 'oil' revealed the message 'The money you used to clean this bird could clean this bird'.

Virgin Trains used tin foil with a mouth-watering menu printed on it to persuade business travellers to upgrade to first class. The foil was to be handy because 'you won't want to leave any behind'.

The charity Refuge targeted young working women to donate and to raise awareness of the issue of domestic violence with the make-up stick 'Slap' and slogans like 'tested on women by animals'.

Guinness sent a viral e-mail to their birthday list that could be sent on to friends inviting them to the pub to celebrate. The e-mail could be personalised by adding the name of the pub of choice.

Visit Wales had a strategy to change perceptions of rain from negative to positive – impossible if you like lying on a beach, but fine if you are a mountain biker. The mac pack achieved a 19 per cent response rate.

Social/technical reasons for growth

1 **The Internet.** The Internet has established itself as probably the major engine of economic growth and social change worldwide. The dot-com bust of 2000 left Internet entrepreneurs licking their wounds for a while but the underlying business advantages – in particular the low costs of matching buyers with sellers – were, and are, simply too great. As we look back on the first ten years of the 21st century it is clear that this decade will be seen as the decade of the Internet. Much of this activity is of course direct in nature, at least in terms of communications and distribution. A lesser percentage involves the use of customer records to keep in touch. But in this book you will find plenty of material to help you understand Internet marketing.

2 **Fragmentation of society.** Demographic changes to society have continued at an incredible pace. In particular, we can witness changes from the nuclear family as being the hub of society, to a split whereby the traditional married couple with children now accounts for fewer than 20 per cent of households. Just as prevalent is the explosion of individualism. This is known as Popeye syndrome 'I am what I am' and customers want information that is personal, relevant, pertinent and timely to their particular circumstances. There has been a huge growth in lifestyle options, resulting in a more complex society. This gives direct approaches to marketing an advantage as they can differentiate to account for these differences.

3 **Proliferation of media.** Throughout Europe, satellite, cable and digital supply have changed the face of television broadcasting, resulting in rising costs for mass marketers looking to reach a large audience. The same effect can be seen within the UK in radio and magazines. The rise of on-line media has added enormously to the complexity of the media market. Social media sites like Facebook, Twitter, Instagram, Pinterest and LinkedIn have created large and highly targetable markets in a very short space of time. Bloggers are now generating significant audiences and in effect are becoming media owners. Mashable is an extreme example of this with a value recently estimated at around £100 million created since its formation in 2005.

4 **Greater consumer sophistication.** Consumers now demand far better service than companies were allowed to get away with in the past. Part of this is the wish to be treated according to their personal circumstances. How companies communicate to their customers has also emerged as being very important.

5 **Consumers want to be in control.** Customers increasingly want the option of contacting organisations direct through multiple channels and expect their data to be accessible

and up to date across all channels, leading to a big growth in devices such as freephone numbers and care lines.

Business reasons for growth

1 **Ever more competition.** This is a general truism about business – that competition in most markets worldwide has increased over the years. As long ago as 1995 the Henley Centre found that companies were worried about the increasing commoditisation of their markets. Since then companies have seen direct marketing as a way of adding value to their markets and differentiating their offerings.

2 **Criticism of traditional marketing methods.** In a damning report at the time, Coopers and Lybrand (1993) found that marketing departments were considered by senior managers to be inefficient in their spending. As we will see, direct marketing can vastly improve marketing's efficiency through its control and precision, leading to better targeting and campaign measurement. Over the years since 1993, senior executives have slowly inculcated the way in which direct marketing can match spending with revenue – and this is the kind of language that sits well in the boardroom.

3 **Interest in customer retention and loyalty.** This is discussed in detail later **(see Chapter 6)** but, in essence, this took off with a consultancy study by Bain & Co in 1990 that identified existing customers as much cheaper to sell to than new customers. While there is doubt placed on some of their findings, the core idea – that acquiring new customers from scratch is costly – remains a business truism. Over the past 20 years, big firms from IBM to Procter & Gamble have invested millions in customer databases and CRM systems as a result.

4 **Continuing drop in computer processing costs.** Underpinning all of the preceding factors is the biggest driver of all: the relentless advance of the computer. Since the 1960s, the cost of processing has halved about once every four years, on average. Because we are surrounded by this computing power nowadays it is difficult to appreciate sometimes just how much of a phenomenon, how much of a driver of change, this is. Desktop PCs can now handle large customer datafiles and undertake complex calculations, selections by customer type, and so on, *in seconds*. Ten years ago this would have taken two or three weeks. These data can be accessed remotely through the 'cloud' so a sales rep on the road can be kept fully informed about customer details at all time, The use of GPS systems means that we can now access information on the physical location of our customers and prospects, and services such as Foursquare have been set up to exploit this. These changes will be a huge driver of growth for direct marketing at least through the next decade.

1.4.2 Spend and trends in direct marketing

Marketing resources in direct marketing are mostly spent on two things: various media, and database marketing costs. The long-term prognosis remains optimistic for direct marketing as a whole but with some traditional media, particularly direct mail, under threat. The rate of growth of non-Internet based direct marketing has plateaued out or fallen, with growth now being driven by spend in new media arenas. However, we should note that most executives do not describe digital marketing as being 'direct marketing'. They see it as

Table 1.2 Time and cost of one typical data processing operation

	Time (seconds)	Cost (£)
1955	375	9.09
1960	47	1.55
1965	29	0.29
1975	4	0.12
1987	1	0.04
1993	0.1	0.01
2002	0.01	0.001
2008	0.001	0.0005

a separate way of doing marketing. This the authors feel is a significant error. These quibbles aside, compared with the slow shrinkage of advertising budgets this has to be seen as a good performance. The total spend on direct and database marketing in the UK in 2011 was £14.2 billion, nearly treble that of 1995 (see Figure 1.3).

The 2012 UK based Direct Marketing Association (DMA) report 'Putting a Price on Direct Marketing' also suggests that there are reasons for optimism for direct marketers up to 2020 and beyond. One factor is the continued faith that marketing directors show in direct marketing when times are tough – they like the close link between spend and income, and

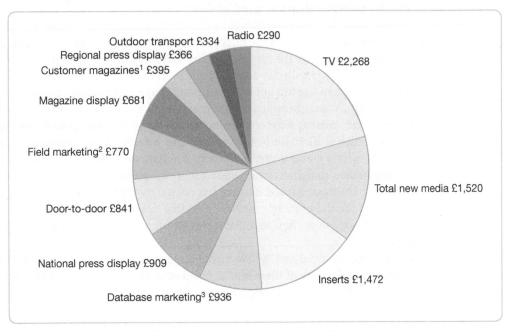

Figure 1.3 Percentage of total budget spent on UK direct media, 2005

Notes
[1] Customer magazines are better known by consumers as loyalty magazines.
[2] Field marketing will include many activities undertaken in public spaces with the aim of identifying prospects
[3] 'Database marketing' is a figure for supplier sales only, and does not include the huge amount of in-house activity that goes on.

Source: Adapted from DMA Census of the Direct Marketing Industry (2005), p. 7. Reproduced by permission of the DMA (UK) Ltd.

Table 1.3 Media spend advertising in the UK, £m

	2011	2011 vs 2010	Share of
	adspend (£m)	(% change)	total spend
*TV	4,159.30	1.9	25.80%
Radio	427	1.6	2.70%
Out of home	886.3	0.6	5.50%
*Press	3,945.10	−8.4	24.50%
Cinema	172.1	−6.6	1.10%
Internet	4,784.10	16.8	29.70%
Direct mail	1,728.60	1	10.70%
Total	16,102.40	2.7	100%

*TV data excludes sponsorship of £224m

*Press includes print only – press websites appear under Internet

Source: WARC, AA (2012) cited in Media Week (2012).

the cost-effectiveness of this approach. Of course, one of the biggest drivers of growth is the proliferation of new media that will grow over the next ten years. The IABUK Internet advertising spend survey for 2011 found that 33.8 per cent of the entire spend on media (£4.8 billion) was in new media, and that this figure is growing by around 10 per cent per year. This explosive growth will not continue at quite this rate, but marketing spend on new media is now greater than the spend on direct mail and TV.

There has been significant change in the direct marketing landscape over the past decade. The traditional media in the direct marketer's armoury, of the phone and direct mail, have been overtaken by the range of on-line opportunities. However, in terms of spend, according to the UK it is display advertising in print that now accounts for the lion's share of budgets. Direct mail has lost out to e-mail, which enjoys significant economies and is effective, especially in customer retention programmes. E-mail is less effective when it comes to acquisition and, indeed, some commentators are suggesting that as an acquisition medium it is not effective at all. In the last couple of years, direct mail volumes have begun to stabilise and, in certain markets, the saturation of e-mail, for example, in business-to-business marketing, means that direct mail's impact is growing again.

The use of outbound telemarketing has passed its heyday. The intrusive nature of the medium and the rise of mobile media means that opt out rates are very high and that lists are not as complete as they were. However, as an inbound retention channel it remains important.

Advertising on social and mobile media remains in its infancy but the ability to target, and the personal nature of these media, means that the authors believe they will show significant growth until they too begin to settle down as part of the media mix.

Summary

In this chapter we found that direct marketing is a way of doing marketing that encompasses both principles and practical tools across a variety of on- and off-line channels. The core of direct marketing is the use of a database to hold customer information on an individual level. This means marketers can treat existing customers in a different way from new prospects in order to create loyalty and profitability.

In the next chapter (Chapter 2) we will take a much closer look at the most important practical tool, the database.

QUESTIONS

1 Since the 1990s direct marketing has enjoyed a period of considerable growth. Some managers believe that its ability to segment customers is direct marketing's strongest asset. Explain the relevance of this benefit, along with other benefits described in the chapter.

2 The managing director of a large, fast-moving consumer goods firm said, 'I have no need for direct marketing. Ours will always be a mass-marketing industry.' Do you think he was right? Explain your reasons.

3 What are the core tangible elements that make up direct, digital and database marketing? Explain how they fit together.

4 What is the difference between relationship marketing and direct marketing? Explain how the two areas of marketing overlap with each other.

5 Retailers have never been so adept at meeting customers' needs as they are now. If this is so, then why is direct marketing growing so fast?

6 Explain how direct marketing can help a company develop sustainable competitive advantage. What are the keys to success?

7 The roots of direct marketing originally lay in the mail-order industry. Modern mail-order businesses will often use direct marketing to drive their business. Explain why direct marketing is still so important to them.

8 You are the manager of a large car dealership. At present, you rely on a large pool of dealers to sell your product, but you have noticed recently that consumer opinion appears to be turning away from car dealers, who are generally mistrusted. One of your marketing team has written a paper advising you to look at setting up a 'direct' operation. What considerations should you take into account before making a decision?

9 Explain the connections between direct and digital marketing. How do the two techniques work together and what are the essential differences between them?

References

Baier, M. (1985) *Elements of Direct Marketing*, McGraw-Hill, New York.

Berry, L.L. (1983) 'Relationship marketing' in Berry, L.L., Shostack, G.L. and Upah, G.D. (eds) *Emerging Perspectives on Services Marketing*, American Marketing Association, Chicago, pp. 25–8.

Bird, D. (1989) *Commonsense Direct Marketing*, Kogan Page, London.

Brassington, F. and Pettitt, S. (2007) *Essentials of Marketing*, FT Prentice Hall, Harlow.

Chaffey. D, 2012 [on-line] **http://www.davechaffey.com/Internet-Marketing/C1-Introduction/ E-marketing-Internet-markeitng-%20definition/** [Accessed August 2012]

Chaffey, D. and Ellis-Chadwick, F. 2012 Digital Marketing Strategy Implementation and Practice 5th Edition, Pearson, Harlow.

Christopher, M., Payne, A. and Ballantyne, D. (1991) *Relationship Marketing*, Butterworth-Heinemann, Oxford.

Coopers and Lybrand (1993) *Report on UK Marketing Departments*, Coopers and Lybrand, London.

De Bonis, N. and Nucifora, A. (1994) 'Progressive databases: the underpinning for relationship micro-marketing', *Journal of Database Marketing*, 2 (2), pp. 134–40.

De Pelsmacker, P. Geuens, M. and Van Den Bergh. J. (2010) *Marketing Communications A European Perspective*, 4th edn, Pearson, Harlow.

Direct Response magazine (1997). For database advert example see p. 50.

DMA (2012) Putting a Price on Direct Marketing, DMA, London.

Experian Ltd (2008) Promotional material.

Fill, C. Marketing Communications Interactivity Communities and Content, 5th edn, Pearson, Harlow.

Henley Centre for Forecasting Ltd (1995) *Dataculture 2000*, Henley Centre, Henley, Oxfordshire.

IABUK (2012), [on-line] **http://www.iabuk.net/video/iabpwc-online-adspend-study-full-year-2011** [Accessed August 2012]]IDM 2012 [on-line] **http://www.theidm.com/resources/ archives/jargon-buster/?glos=E** [Accessed August 2012].

Institute of Direct and Digital Marketing (2012) *Diploma Course Material,* IDM, Teddington,

Katzenstein, H. (1992) *Direct Marketing*, Macmillan, New York.

Kotler, P. Keller, K. Brady, M. Hansen, M. (2009) *Marketing Management*, Pearson Education, Harlow.

Levitt, T. (1983) *The Marketing Imagination*, The Free Press, New York.

McCorkell, G. (1992) 'Direct Marketing – a new industry or a new idea?' in Halsey, B. (ed.) *The Practitioner's Guide to Direct Marketing*, Institute of Direct Marketing, Teddington, Richmond-upon-Thames.

Media week 2012 [on-line] **http://www.mediaweek.co.uk/news/1126667/AA-reports-UK-ad-spend-lifted-27-2011/** [Accessed August 2012]

Nash, E. (1995) *Direct Marketing Strategy: Planning, execution*, 3rd edn, McGraw-Hill, New York.

Payne, A., Christopher, M., Clark, M. and Peck, M. (1995) *Relationship Marketing for Competitive Advantage*, Butterworth-Heinemann, Oxford.

Pearson, S. (1994) 'Relationship management: Generating business in the diverse markets of Europe', *European Business Journal*, 6 (4), pp. 28–38.

Randall L. Schultz, 2013 *"HITE, MORRIS LEE,"* Handbook of Texas Online [on-line] **http://www. tshaonline.org/handbook/online/articles/fhi48** [Accessed August 13, 2012].

Roberts, M.L. (1989) *Direct Marketing Management*, Prentice Hall, Upper Saddle River, New Jersey.

Shani, D. and Chalasani, S. (1992) 'Exploiting niches using relationship marketing', *Journal of Services Marketing*, 6 (4), pp. 43–52.

Smith, P.R. and Taylor, J. (2004) *Marketing Communications: An integrated approach*, Kogan Page, London.

Stone, B. (1996) *Successful Direct Marketing Methods*, 5th edn, NTC Business Books, Chicago.

Thomas, B., and Housden, M (2011) Direct and Digital Marketing In Practice, 2nd edn, A & C Black, London.

CASE STUDY

Volvo: from product to consumer-led response marketing

Thanks to Anita Fox of Volvo, David Williams of EHS Brann, and Tracey Barber of EHS Brann for their help in writing this case study.

The turn of the millennium marked a turning point for Volvo in the UK. The firm decided it could do better and gave itself a bold new target of increasing sales by 50 per cent within a short time. This was against a backdrop of a decline in the overall market sales within the segment Volvo serves. Volvo was also keen to expand its target audience, and asked EHS Brann to consider ways in which it could tap into fresh consumer segments. Up to that point Volvo's approach had been primarily product led.

Back in 2000, Volvo's acquisition strategy was primarily based upon model-specific prospecting. Hence: 'here's a car we think you might be interested in . . .'.

However, in order to support the drive for a significant increase in sales, EHS Brann and Volvo realised there was a need for Volvo to differentiate itself from the competition. The challenge was set to find a new way to attract consumers, involve them in the Volvo brand, and ultimately convert them into a sale.

In 2002, the company moved to 'range based prospecting'. At that point few people understood Volvo's range of cars or their naming convention. So there was a need for an education based campaign to increase awareness of the product range.

These campaigns had early success, with a 276 per cent uplift in average response rate across other programmes. Clearly the company was underselling itself before that point.

But Volvo wanted to keep moving forward. What about segmenting its consumers such that different ranges could be targeted in different ways? This led to its 2003 development of mini ranges 'prestige introduction', 'style and desire', 'diesel' and 'luxury and comfort' (see Figure 1.4) and creative work typical of the time, illustrated below.

With good development of general marketing over the 2000–2004 period, it was time to look more closely at Volvo's direct and Internet marketing. Volvo had always had success in generating lots of 'handraisers' who were aware of Volvo and its cars and may have been interested in them, but Volvo was disappointed with its conversion from direct marketing leads through to test drive and purchase.

But why was there low conversion? In those days Volvo would send out as many as 10 million pieces per annum, but these were not particularly targeted, using little more than broad brush age profiles. So, the idea grew to use the 'science' of direct marketing to get the percentage of conversions up.

Volvo's new approach can be summarised as shown in Figure 1.5.

In the car market, moving with consumers down the AIDA (awareness, interest, desire, action) ladder may take as long as 9–12 months with a car purchase: clearly this is different from more routine purchases.

The year 2004 marked a turning point. With the help of EHS Brann, Volvo decided to develop an even more compelling message by focusing 'mini' range communications around consumers rather than cars.

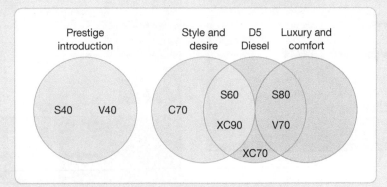

Figure 1.4 Development of mini ranges

Case study (*continued*)

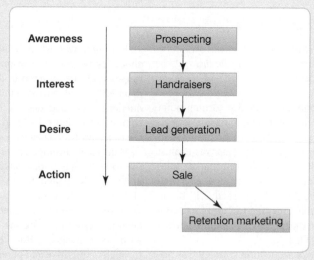

Figure 1.5 Volvo's new approach

It used the concept of lifestage triggers, well-known key points of consideration for vehicle replacement, with the theme turning subtly from 'Volvo for life' into 'Volvo for YOUR life'.

Triggers included:

- expecting first child
- children more active – school age/third child
- retirement

These new programmes continued to be supported by the product-led 'range' 'banker' programmes which had proven successful up to then.

The move to lifestage triggers marked an increasing use in direct marketing. Examples included:

- growing families
- greys
- young families

Growing families

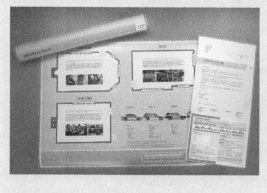

Greys

Young families

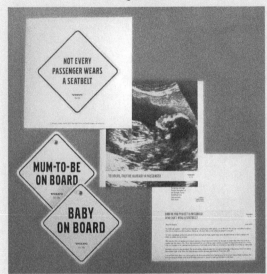

Volvo knew it was going in the right direction: focus group responses were very positive.

2005 saw the extension of the lifestage segmentation into what the team called lifestyle segments with campaigns based around:

- expecting first child
- pre-school campaign (new)
- children more active – school age/third child
- retirement (existing trigger, new campaign)
- lifestyle campaign – high mileage drivers
- cause related marketing campaigns

More sophisticated database work led to pre-collection of trigger and lifestyle data, leading to the kind of complex route map of communications shown in Figure 1.6.

Volvo knew that the average age of its current customer base was quite high at 56. The company was

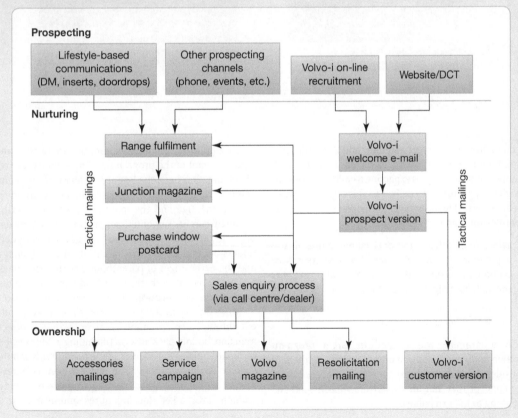

Figure 1.6 **Route map of communications flow**

Case study (*continued*)

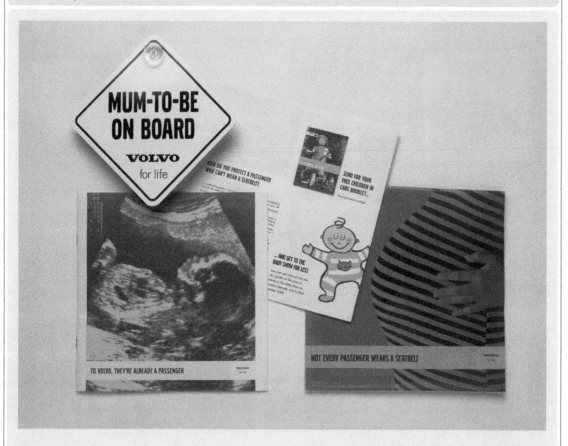

keen to attract a younger audience and the traditional brand emphasis on safety attracted families with young children. Couples expecting a child were seen as an ideal opportunity to deliver to this objective. Volvo created a credible message to this audience by leveraging relevant brand values such as:

- safety (e.g. Volvo is the only manufacturer to use a pregnant 'crash test dummy' and offers advice on how to maximise the safety of child passengers through its 'children in cars brochure');
- environment (e.g. Volvo's cars emit less internal toxins than most other cars).

A programme was created to target pregnant women and young mums in order to persuade them to consider Volvo as their next car – this was based upon the concept that 'not all passengers wear a seatbelt', referring to unborn babies.

To support the communication, the use of accurate data was vital to the programme. The primary source of this data has been the Bounty database of pregnant women. Targeting selections were made according to the income, age and the month of pregnancy/birth. Through careful targeting, segmentation and measurement, EHS Brann and Volvo have developed a good understanding as to what point during pregnancy and the early stages of parenthood are the best times to communicate with these individuals, and subsequently when to encourage them to test drive a Volvo.

Volvo has successfully generated a pool of responders through a programme of award-winning direct mail and 'bounty pack' inserts (including a 'Mum-to-be on board' sticker), which it is nurturing with family specific communications. The interest from this new market segment for Volvo has been impressive – many women have asked for brochures and test drives.

The success of the programme has been recognised throughout Volvo globally, and it is being replicated across other countries. 'Mum-to-be on board' stickers have become so popular that they have been discussed in on-line forums and even traded on eBay!

Nowadays, the direct and Web-driven operations of Volvo are quite large scale. Volvo generates initial awareness in the first instance by a combination of media and marketing activities, from Web and e-mail, to dealer events, SMS and interactive TV.

A new thing for Volvo has been search engine optimisation and search advertising. By 2008, it was realised that 80 per cent of new drivers used the Web at some point in their search process. To attract these Web searchers, banner ads were used on general auto sites. Volvo deploys these in a subtle but clever way to avoid the charge of being intrusive and irritating. Pop-ups are avoided as not appropriate for the 'premium' positioning of Volvo.

Like all its rivals, Volvo has found response rates to traditional direct mail have been slowly dropping as people have read the mailer but have then gone on-line for more information rather than respond directly. This was not necessarily a bad thing, reflecting the way in which consumers wanted to be in control of the information they gathered. Hence, mail assumed the position of being more of an awareness medium – driving traffic to a response medium – the website or e-mail. Coupons were still used within direct mail and coupon fillers were very high quality prospects. Volvo's target market has been carefully profiled as you would expect. Fifty per cent are above 50 years old, with the exception of the C90 buyers who are younger. Volvo drivers come from up-market, older 'mosaic' groups (see Chapter 4 for more details) such as 'symbols of success', 'rural isolation', 'grey perspectives' and 'suburban comfort'. These people enjoy wine, antiques and gardening.

The direct marketing process has to be integrated with other key operations. Volvo has sought to improve the way in which it works with its dealers to maximise their conversions. If a prospect 'handraises' by declaring an interest, they may be passed on to a dealer but if they do not convert to a sale in a few days, then some dealers find it difficult to stay in touch with the prospect.

To try and manage this better Volvo's direct marketers wanted to be more hands-on in making sure the leads were not lost. They asked consumers to help them by asking 'When will you want to change your car?' and 'Would you like a test drive?'. If people say yes to the latter they are referred quickly to a dealer. Getting people to test drive status was the big challenge. Volvo knew that expectations of non-Volvo drivers of the brand sometimes were not that high but that this changed when they got behind the wheel. The driving experience of Volvo is usually perceived very positively. But for those who were some way from a test drive the objective was to make sure these prospects are nurtured and their interest moved to a point closer to purchase. Volvo has the details of over one million people they regard as prospects. Some will subscribe to an e-newsletter: Volvo-i. This features lifestyle, environment, safety and other articles that reflect Volvo's brand attributes. The use of e-mail is important. E-mails cost only about 5–10p compared to about £1 for a high value mailer.

One of the big challenges Volvo faces is integrating its consumer and fleet (business). Why is this a concern? Because costs can be lowered by sharing communication material and also because the business buyer and driver is a consumer as well.

Volvo's fleet market has tended to be among smaller rather than larger firms. The latter have tended to go for the likes of BMW and Mercedes, who offer higher profile 'status' cars. But smaller firms that like 'to be different' tend to go for Volvo. Business buying is probably more complex than consumer buying. Business buyers will be a combination of fleet decision makers and end driver 'user choosers'. For fleet managers, after-sales service and help with fleet management is very important. For the car sector generally, profit on business cars by themselves is not particularly high but the profit on after-sales service is healthier.

As 2010 approached, Volvo felt confident. Direct marketing has been an important tool for the firm in its battle to win customers in the most competitive car market in Europe.

Questions

1. What strategic decisions did Volvo make between 2000 and 2008 that have improved its marketing performance?

2. How has direct marketing helped it grow?

3. Looking ahead, how would you assess the growing importance of on-line marketing?

'Rapid Pizza'

Although most of the case studies in this book are based on real companies, 'Rapid Pizza' is a fictional company. However, the case reflects the pressures acting on commercial take-away operations.

Rapid Pizza is a medium sized chain of pizza takeaway outlets located in the Midlands. The chain is modelled on bigger, well-established names, such as Perfect Pizza. Customers can ring up and order a home-delivered pizza from a menu that is distributed to local homes. Rapid Pizza does the usual choice of popular pizzas, with no particular pretension to cater for any niche group. Its best seller is the 'Rapid Speciale', a spicy chicken based pizza with a range of cheese toppings.

The marketing manager of Rapid Pizza, Colin McVie, has just had a conversation with an old friend, Dan Smith, who happens to be a direct marketing expert. His friend was very enthusiastic about Rapid Pizza's possible use of direct marketing, which surprised Colin, as he had not really given it much thought. He had a website that, to be honest, was a bit under-developed but it did have a map showing people where the restaurant was.

Rapid Pizza uses 'door-to-door' leafleting to distribute its promotional literature through the locality. This includes a menu, a map showing where the outlet is, and a phone number for ordering any time until midnight, seven days a week. Incentives to phone are periodically offered, again through door drops, distributed via the local freesheet. Incentives include an 'order two and get one free' offer, 'free garlic bread with any order over £10', and similar promotions.

The busiest times for the takeaway business are early and late evenings, and in particular Friday and Saturday nights. Most of its customers are in their twenties or thirties, with enough expendable income to afford not to bother cooking occasionally. In order to qualify for the takeaway service, customers have to live within a one mile radius of the outlet. Each outlet caters for about 7,000 households.

The main features of Colin's business are as follows:

- The top priorities for consumers are hot, tasty pizzas, fast delivery and reasonable prices.
- Some consumers are remarkably regular with their orders, wanting exactly the same items each time they phone. Some of Colin's staff have got to know the most regular customers quite well.
- When customers call in to order their pizza they leave their name and address as a natural part of the process. Their transaction details are easily taken and can be kept on a computer based database in each outlet. At present, these transaction details are used only for accounting and stock ordering.
- Menu changes are executed quite regularly. Colin believes that these help to keep customers interested, and are an excuse to launch fresh marketing initiatives.
- Occasional monitoring of the website showed that Web visitors were on the increase, but Colin was not sure whether these visitors went on to buy from him.

When Dan absorbed these details he recommended that Colin should contact a direct marketing agency and invite them to help him.

In a sense, Colin was reluctant to take his friend's advice. He had spent a lot of time and effort setting up the existing business and had an emotional commitment to keeping the status quo. Also he did not feel any particular competitive pressure. 'No one else is using direct marketing, and customers don't seem to be crying out for it. Why should we bother?' he thought to himself.

He decided to give his direct marketing friend another call and discuss it one more time.

Question

Acting as Colin's friend, explain what the benefits of direct marketing would be to his pizza operation. How would it work in practice? How would the website integrate into this operation?

Chapter 2

The database

Objectives

Once you have read this chapter you will:

- know what a database is
- be able to picture what a database consists of
- know what data to hold and where to get it from
- be aware of some of the management issues
- Be aware of the key legal constraints in direct marketing

Introduction

In the introduction to the previous chapter we saw that this book is organised around the direct marketing planning process. Before we start on that journey, however, it is important to give a full description of the most important tool in the direct interactive and digital marketing armoury: the database. The purpose of this chapter is to explain what a database is. We will cover what a database looks like, what data to hold, and how to manage a database. One very important area in direct marketing is to understand the legal constraints, and we have a dedicated section on this subject at the end of the chapter.

As you might expect from the previous chapter, the various uses of database applications are integral to direct marketing itself. Therefore, rather than discuss applications here, they are covered in detail as and when they arise throughout this book.

How this chapter is structured

In this chapter we will begin with a review of database practice. We will then address the question of exactly what a database is. The next section covers what data to hold, and it is followed by a section describing typical sources of data. The intricacies of database management are then analysed and, finally, the important area of legal constraints is examined.

2.1   What is a marketing database?

A marketing database can best be pictured as an electronic version of an office filing cabinet, holding records of customers. Imagine each customer's record held on a card, detailing the customer's personal details, transactions (sales) and communication history with the particular company. The cards are held in various files according to, say, which products the customer has bought. The entire set of records is cross-referenced against the other files so that customers can be selected according to different characteristics (see Figure 2.1).

From Figure 2.1 it follows that:

- a database is a collection of data records in a list that can be manipulated by software
- a data record is the entire set of information that is associated with one customer
- a data field is one item of data within a record: for example, a name, one line of an address, the number of a type of product bought, and so on

This is a useful picture to hold in our minds as we move towards a full definition of marketing databases.

2.1.1 Definitions

There are surprisingly few definitions of marketing databases that have been proposed:

The Data Protection Act (1998) speaks of a database as being 'equipment operating automatically in response to instructions given', which does not really help much!

Armstrong *et al.* (2009, p. 455) say that 'a customer database is an organised collection of comprehensive data about individual customers or prospects, including geographic, demographic, psychographic and behavioural data'.

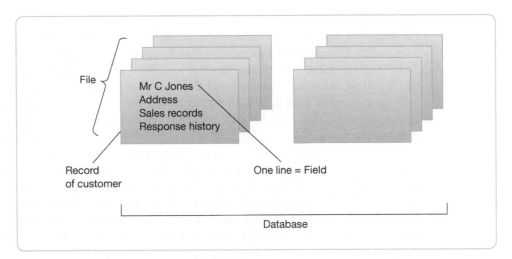

Figure 2.1 Pictorial representation of a database

33

The IDM (2002, pp. 2.2–2) tell us that a marketing database is 'a comprehensive collection of inter-related customer and/or prospect data that allows the timely and accurate retrieval, use or manipulation of data to support the marketing objectives of the enterprise'.

Thomas and Housden (2011, p.109) take things a step further by telling us that the purpose of a marketing database is to 'further relationships with customers'.

An alternative, rather simpler, definition is offered here, which the reader may find helpful in understanding how the database should be viewed in the context of a direct marketing system:

A marketing database is a list of customers' and prospects' records that enables strategic analysis, and individual selections for communication and customer service support. The data is organised around the customer.

2.1.2 The minimum requirements of a marketing database

Data

IDM (2002, pp. 2.2–5) lists four types of data that a marketer is likely to want to store in their database:

- Primary data, such as names and addresses of customers, details of products and/or services your organisation offers, pricing details, campaign details and definitions of various channels of distribution
- Secondary data, which is data used to qualify primary data, such as demographics, lifestyle information, geographical profiles or levels of penetration into markets
- Performance data to record how your customers have responded, what they bought, how much they spent and to which campaigns they responded
- External data, covering everything rented or bought in lists to data from various agencies that can enhance your base data

Database software

For marketing managers, a welcome development in databases is the use of front-end software, which is user friendly, menu driven and removes the need for programming know-how. There are many commercial organisations offering their own proprietary software, which will sit on top of a database and allow the user to interrogate it to create reports, perform analyses or draw up lists for marketing activity. These tools generally only work on Open Database Connectivity (ODBC) compliant databases but, bearing in mind that ODBC is one of Microsoft's babies and the dominance of that organisation in the office computer market, that is a fair percentage of all systems available. The benefit here is that database marketers can take their favoured software with them from one organisation to the next and (usually with a little help from the IT department in setting things up) have a much more portable skill set to offer new employers. Microsoft Access, available as part of the MS Office Suite, has ODBC front-end capabilities (i.e. it can sit on top of more complex databases) and can provide an ideal interface to more complex or unfamiliar databases, as can Excel to some extent.

Basic software functions

Database applications require the following basic software functions, according to one author (Goldwag, 1995):

- **Name and address processing.** This is discussed later under 'management issues'.
- **Being able to make selections.** The database must be able to generate the desired list of customers to be contacted.
- **Having analytical capability.** The most basic requirement here is for simple campaign analysis. Each response is allocated to the promotion that generated it. Percentage response figures for each campaign are then output.
- **Being able to generate reports.** Basic reports would include elements such as counts of customer movements in the database, or campaign reports comparing current ones with previous efforts. Goldwag made the point that business is full of useless reports. Information such as 'we had 1,000 transactions yesterday' struggles for a use, whereas 'we are losing 10,000 of our customers' prompts action.

These basic requirements have not changed since 1995, nor are they likely to.

2.2 The data to hold

2.2.1 Principles of data collection

Information overload is one of the biggest irritations in modern life (*The Economist*, 2011). There are e-mails to answer, virtual friends to pester, YouTube videos to watch and, back in the physical world, meetings to attend, papers to shuffle and spouses to appease. A survey by Reuters once found that two thirds of managers believe that the data deluge has made their jobs less satisfying or hurt their personal relationships. One third thinks that it has damaged their health. Another survey suggests that most managers think most of the information they receive is useless.

Kotler *et al.* (2009) say that marketing managers will sometimes complain about not being about to get hold of critical information while being awash with too much other information that they cannot use. They go on to point out that a marketing information system should be a hybrid of three things:

- What managers think they need
- What managers really need
- What is economically feasible

Kotler *et al.* (2009) go on to suggest the following 'information needs probes':

- What decisions do you regularly make?
- What information do you need to make these decisions?
- What information do you regularly get?
- What special studies do you periodically request?

- What information would you want that you are not getting now?
- What information would you want: daily? weekly? monthly? yearly?
- What magazines and trade reports would you like to see on a regular basis?
- What topics would you like to be kept informed of?
- What data analysis programmes would you want?
- What are the four most helpful improvements that could be made in the present marketing information system?

There is a tendency for marketers to ask themselves 'What data shall I collect?', rather than 'What do I need the database to do?'. The latter question should always be asked first, letting data requirements flow from the answers.

It is suggested (Boddington, 1994) that the following still relevant principles should be taken into account when collecting data:

- Data should be split into 'essential now' and 'possible future use'.
- Data should allow ease of sourcing and updating.
- The cost of raw data, for example external bought-in data, must be offset against benefits

The golden rule for data collection can be summed up as 'only hold data that is required for your strategy. If you don't use it, don't collect it and if you collect it, use it.'

2.2.2 Data to hold

Let us take a look at the data that is typically held in a comprehensive marketing database. If we combine the suggestions from three authors, Goldwag (1995), Stone & Shaw (1988) and McCorkell (2002), and then update for recent technology changes, we arrive at a typical list such as the one shown in Table 2.1. The example on the right hand side of the table illustrates what a full customer record might look like. The example given may resemble a typical record from an environmental charity.

2.2.3 Business data

In addition to many of the above fields, some of the following (or others) may be appropriate:

- Company name, address and main switchboard number
- Inclusion on Corporate Telephone Preference Service (CTPS)[1]
- Web address
- Job title (possibly including a job code and description)

---

[1] The Privacy and Electronic Communications (EC Directive) (Amendment) Regulations 2004, often referred to as 'PECR' (pronounced 'pecker'). These regulations came into force on 25 June 2004. They extended The Privacy and Electronic Communications (EC Directive) Regulations 2003 to allow corporate subscribers to register with a managed telephone register, known as the Corporate TPS, their wish to not to receive unsolicited telephone calls for direct marketing purposes. TPS enables individuals (consumers, sole traders, and (except in Scotland) partnerships) to register their objection to receiving direct marketing calls with a central service. This means that the TPS file contains consumer telephone numbers as well as some business numbers. The CTPS holds data on almost 2.3 million corporate bodies. It also includes schools, government departments and agencies, hospitals and other public bodies (DMA, 2012).

Table 2.1 Typical customer record

Consumer	Example: Charlotte Smythe
Name	Charlotte Smythe
E-mail address	**Charlotte-Smythe@yourinternet.co.uk**
Mobile phone number	07765 111111
House name or number	The Woodlands
Street or road	Princes St
Postal town	Dorking, Kent
Postcode	DS12 3AT
Sex	F
Date of birth	2 /10 / 65
Married	N
Age	32
No. of children, ages of children	N
External data[1]	
Geodemographic indicator	Desirable residential area, young, trendy
Lifestyle indicators	Reads *Guardian*. Interested in current affairs
Credit history and rating	Good
Education	Postgraduate level
MPS/TPS membership[2]	N
Communication history	
Campaign code number	01
Message code	03
Dates of contact	12 /12 / 11
Response	Y
Orders	3 items
Returns	N
Customer complaints	N
Relationship/activity data	
Source of recruitment[3]	07 Mail
Account no.	12223/6789
Product categories purchased	13 24 56
Recency, frequency, value of purchase data	Score: 67 (top third of responders)
Date of purchases	Last two years
Method of payment	Credit card
Date of renewal of subscriptions	1/4/13
Loyalty programme details: points, contact, status in club, and so on	N

Notes:

[1] External data is data purchased from a *commercial supplier* of consumer or business data. This important area of direct marketing is fully discussed in Chapter 4.

[2] The industry association (the Direct Marketing Association or DMA) runs several services on behalf of the public. The Mailing Preference Service (MPS) is a public service set up to hold records of people who do not wish to be sent direct mail. It was set up in the late 1970s and now has about 5 million records. (For more information visit **www.mpsonline.org.uk**.) It is, of course, very much in companies' interests to purge their output lists of these names because they have no chance of getting any response (other than perhaps that from an irate member of the public). The Telephone Preference Service (TPS) was set up in 1994 to hold names of people who do not wish to be telephoned by companies. Currently about 17.5 million people subscribe (for more information visit **www.tpsonline.org.uk**). The initiative was designed to calm fears about the spread of 'cold calling', and is considered very important for the telemarketing industry's credibility. The Fax Preference Service (FPS) was set up in 1999 and makes it unlawful to send an individual an unsolicited sales and marketing fax without prior permission. With the demise of faxes, the FPS is becoming less relevant, though there are still almost 2.2 million numbers on the register. The Idea of Baby MPS is to allow parents to opt out of the many baby-related mailings they receive in the months following the arrival of their little bundle of joy - an option that is especially welcome to all in the sad event of the premature passing of said bundle of joy. As at April 2012, just 24,000 families had taken advantage of this – perhaps because new parents are often sent free samples at a time when money is tight and they are at the start of a new buy learning curve!

[3] 'Source of recruitment' refers to the media/campaign used to acquire the customer. It is often a guide to the subsequent profitability of the customer. For example, charities often find that donors recruited from TV are less profitable than those obtained by mail.

Source: The DMA (2012).

- Department
- Nature of business (Standard Industrial Classification (SIC))[2]
- Number of employees
- Turnover and/or profit

Communications and activity data would be constructed in a similar way to the above example.

2.3 Data sources

2.3.1 Principles

There are two main sources of data: internal and external to the company's records. External data could include commercially available lists, census data, and so on.

Most data is sourced internally. Kotler and Armstrong (2012, p. 125) make the point that internal data will vary in its usefulness to marketing because is often collected for non-marketing purposes, it may be incomplete or in the wrong format and may not be up to date. Quite how much this is the case will depend on factors such as whether you have direct contact with customers as a natural way of doing business.

Direct contact businesses include examples such as retailers and sports clubs – sectors where the consumer and the business have a direct interface and a data-gathering opportunity exists. In these instances, customer purchase data will be held within the company, but it may be held in an awkward form for marketing. Name and address details may not have been collected and it will be necessary to begin tracking customer communications and responses in order to build a true marketing database.

(Bird, 2007) suggests the following sources of data:

Direct contact companies

- Records held by anyone within the company who deals with customers
- Retail outlets, agents, dealers
- Guarantee forms
- Invoices
- Enquirers, past, present and future
- People who visit your stand when you are at any exhibitions or shows
- Competition entrants
- Responders to sales promotions

---

[2] A Standard Industry Classification (SIC) was first introduced into the United Kingdom in 1948 for use in classifying business establishments and other statistical units by the type of economic activity in which they are engaged. SIC codes provide a framework for the collection, tabulation, presentation and analysis of data and its use promotes uniformity. It can also be used for administrative purposes and by non-government bodies as a convenient way of classifying industrial activities. Classifications have been revised five times, most recently in 2007. (*Source*: Office for National Statistics: UK Standard Industrial Classification of Economic Activities 1992.)

Companies with no direct contact

Sectors with no direct contact include packaged goods industries that sell through retail outlets, where no natural and direct consumer data gathering opportunity is present. If a company has no direct contact with customers it could gather data in the following ways:

List purchase

There are literally thousands of lists available in the UK, and many more in Europe. One example of these is 'lifestyle' databases. Lifestyle databases will hold lists of people according to specific products and brands bought in categories such as packaged goods, finance and leisure. For example, a national newspaper could buy a substantial list of its own readers from a lifestyle data company.

For a good idea of what lists are available (and at what sort of costs) visit **www. marketingfile.com** or **www.listbroker.com**. Both sites give an excellent insight into just what sort of data is commercially available, and the former will even allow you to search and buy on-line using your credit card if you so wish. Be warned, the experience is often quite a shock for the uninitiated!

Data building schemes

These might be credit schemes, club membership or promotions. Car manufacturers looking to build up a database of their existing marque owners might run a 'phone in' free prize draw, open to existing owners only.

Other common data building mechanisms include product/warranty registrations, competitions and free prize draws. If you choose to use the latter of these in your business, remember that people enter a free prize draw to win a wheelchair only if they want a wheelchair; so make the incentive relevant to your organisation's offering and not a prize of cash or other item of no relevance. If you do, all you will do is attract people who want cash, not people who want your product.

Introduce new contact channels

New channels that offer direct contact could be opened. Airlines could offer tickets directly over the Internet rather than through travel agents.

Direct contact organisations are increasingly taking advantage of new media channels to allow customers to input their data into the organisation's database themselves. Precious few of us have not filled in an on-line form at some time over the last few years, whether it is for an insurance quote, cinema tickets, to reserve an item in a high street shop or buy from its on-line equivalent.

This has its good and bad points. On the upside, the customer is likely to know how to spell their own name and address much better than you do but, on the downside, they may not be as accurate at typing as a professional data entry clerk and they will almost undoubtedly not stick as rigorously to your entry conventions as you will, if for no other reason than they cannot know what those conventions are. Software such as 'Quick Address' (**www.qas. co.uk**), which fills in a complete address in a standard format from just a postcode, can help overcome such matters, but not all fields can be fixed like that.

Indirect contact companies may also use:

- product registration documents, product warranties
- credit card details

- subscription details
- questionnaire responses
- in-store offer details
- requests for product information
- events/promotions requiring response
- established direct channels

Exhibit 2.1 **The creative use of commercially available lists**

'Pensions transfer' is a process whereby someone who has been saving into a personal pension plan is able to access the money in their pension pot before they retire, as long as they are at least 55 years old. It is usually a bad idea from a financial point of view because it reduces the amount of money available in retirement (sometimes to nil) but, in some situations, it can be the answer to a serious and immediate financial crisis. What is more, the money released never has to be repaid because it is already yours; all you are doing is accessing it earlier than planned.

The one-time market leader in this politically dubious arena used to make full use of direct mail in the early 2000s, and was always on the lookout for fresh names of prospects. One list they found was of people who had entered a free prize draw run by a charity but had not actually made a donation to that charity. Their marketing manager says 'we realised that these people wanted something for nothing, and that was effectively the service we were offering. We tested the list and then went back for all the names we could get. It was one of the most responsive lists I've ever found'.

2.4 Database management issues

Bird (2007) refers to the rapid technological advances of the last 25 years: 'In those days people talked about lists. . . now the simple and inexpensive list has been . . . replaced by the sophisticated (and sometimes very expensive) database'. The rapid change in technology has also been responsible for one of the most frustrating facts facing database marketers today.Most organisations never had a database strategy 25 years ago and, as a result, most do not have a single database so much as many databases scattered throughout different departments, usually in inconsistent formats. It has been identified (Ranchhod & Gurau, 2007) that significant organisational barriers exist to the straightforward use of these databases for marketing purposes, often related to database access protocols or simply because of different rules and structures preventing their implementation at a central level.

This chequered history highlights the need to have a clear view of database management issues. In this section, we take a more detailed look at the tasks that a large database operation demands.

Adapting a list from a previous work (Goldwag, 1995), we arrive at the following four main stages to database management:

1 Manage the data sources.

2 Manage the data entry.

3 Manage the database.

4 Manage the applications.

These steps are summarised in Figure 2.2.

2.4.1   Manage the data sources

Leaving aside on-line trading, in the majority of companies data about customers rarely goes directly from the customer onto a marketing database. It may first arrive at the company via a sale made and be recorded in the sales ledger. Details are passed to accounts, and then perhaps on to billing, who send the bills out. Information goes to stock control, to let them know their stock of the product bought is reduced by one. Even in the case of on-line trading there are often middle databases to allow for the cleaning of poorly entered data.

Into this data 'merry-go-round' comes marketing. Marketing wants the data captured to be organised around the 'customer record'. It wants customer name and address, number of sales, and products bought and owned. It wants this kept on a 'per customer' basis. But sales and stock control wants the data on a 'per product' basis, and in many companies it is

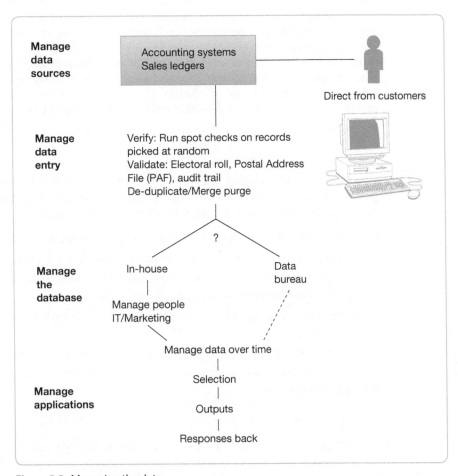

Figure 2.2 Managing the data

the sales department that takes the order. Accounting wants the 'revenue figures': amount charged and amount of cash in. Customers? Who are they?

Your last problem could be much closer to home. Within the marketing department, product managers are interested in customers – but only those who buy their particular product. As a direct marketer you are managing customers, not products, but product managers are targeted on the number of their products they sell, and may not be very co-operative about sharing their data in order to expose 'their' customers to other products the company sells.

Given the preceding competing pressures on the data flowing around the company, it is a very complicated job getting up-to-date, accurate data on to the marketing database in the form you want it.

Exhibit 2.2 The trials and tribulations of marketing databases in the banking industry

Despite spending huge amounts of money, UK banks' CRM programmes are at best still in their infancy. As Emily Cubitt puts it, once you explain what CRM is to many bank customers, they may burst into tears on you.

CRM disciplines were desperately needed for many financial service companies. Most firms had run their operations based on accounts – that is to say products, not customers. Hence, the same customer could be recorded on many different databases, with name and address information often incomplete. Purchase data was incomplete, and no record of any previous communications to the customer held.

A cynic might ask, does it matter, given that UK banks have retention rates for their core products approaching 92 per cent? This loyalty is driven not by satisfaction but by customer inertia: to move requires a lot of effort. At the moment this is the reality in the sector – perhaps until the equivalent of easyJet enters the market and rocks the boat.

Source: Based on Cubitt, E. (2003) 'Bank customers still crying out for service', *Precision Marketing* 15 (29), 5 February, p. 11.

Overcoming these problems is a big job. Marketing needs to isolate the data required from these systems and capture it on a regular basis. It is suggested (*The Absolute Essentials of Direct Marketing* (4), 1992) that the following need to be in place:

- Senior management commitment to ensure co-operation across departments
- Regular audit trails for items of data to ensure it is handled in a quality way
- Training for front-end staff to ensure they understand the importance of capturing the data properly and keeping these standards uniformly
- Introducing systems to ensure customer-inputted data adheres to these standards, even if it is input poorly
- Service-level agreements between departments for delivery of data to the right standard
- The marketing database to update records regularly by downloading from 'live' systems during quiet periods

2.4.2 Manage the data entry

Once the data has been sourced it needs to be added to the marketing database. Wallinger (IDM, 2002, pp. 8.2–2) tells us that data processing may be unglamorous but it is essential to the success of a campaign, which can be undermined by poor selection, mistargeting, incorrect addressing or unwanted duplication. The key is to be structured and disciplined. The data needs to be uniform and in a useful format for the database applications.

The main steps in managing the data entry are:

1 Verification

2 Validation

3 De-duplication

4 Merge purge

Verification

Verifying that the data has been put in accurately should be standard procedure. A common approach is to select records at random for visual inspection and correction, noting the identity of the original data entry clerk to see if there are any patterns identifying a need for further training.

Validation

Validation is checking the accuracy of personal and product data provided by the customer. This could include:

- checking product/source codes for invalid codes against an internal master list. Address checking can be done using the Postal Address File (PAF). This file of all UK addresses is owned and updated 'daily' by the Royal Mail.

- carrying out audits. These involve counts of customers and other data entries, and then comparing these counts to see that they tally.

- carrying out various accuracy checks (as proposed by Woodcock, 1992, and still applicable) such as range validation: What are the valid ranges for each field? Do any of the entries lie outside these ranges?

- doing a sanity check. As mentioned above, pull off 100 records at random and do a visual inspection. Do they look reasonable?

De-duplication

De-duplication is the act of ensuring that the database does not contain duplicate records of the same customer. In many ways de-duplication replicates what humans do in picture puzzles when we are set the problem of 'spotting the ten differences between one picture and another'. A special de-duplication programme has to be run by the computer to ensure duplicate customer records are kept to a minimum.

When adding details of a transaction to your database, it may be obvious that the new data refers to a customer already on the system. However, there are a number of problems in checking the new record against existing records:

- Unless there is an exact match of spelling, conventional record matching will miss the match and two records for the same customer will result. Several matching algorithms exist based on anticipated spelling and typing errors, i.e. a missing character, two letters reversed, or using the wrong vowel.

- Different names within the same household will cause problems. Suppose the husband rang the first time and the wife the second time, about the same query? A duplicate record may be set up.

- When a customer moves house and then makes a further purchase, they will quote their name and order number and new address. The database needs to be able to spot this and update the old record, not create a new one.
- Another big problem area is that of one address divided into apartments. If the database then removed one record, one customer would be lost and that would be regrettable.

In all these cases we would want to ensure that either the new data is allocated to an existing record, or a new record is set up. De-duplication is the art and science of attempting to do this. It is not easy, and much effort is spent by database bureaus in getting this right.

Merge purge

Merge purge is similar to de-duplication, but with merge purge you are merging two files – perhaps two external, or one external and your own internal database – into one. You, therefore, want to make sure you do not have the same customer twice in the final file. This is sometimes difficult to do, but important to avoid mailing the same customer twice. It is also important to make sure that 'existing' customers are not mailed with an offer aimed at 'new prospects'. An offer of 'How about our Gold Card at no annual fee?' would not go down too well with existing full-fee-paying customers, if it were mailed to them by mistake!

Because de-duplication and merge purge are both long processes (each record on one file has to be compared to all the records on the other file), matchkey systems are used to speed up the process. A matchkey shorthand is created: using the key characters, lifted from the name, address and postcode, that define the rest of the customer record. The use of 14 character matchkeys is recommended (Stone and Shaw, 1988). Matchkeys are compared to see whether they are the same or different. Those that are the same may be output by the computer for visual inspection. Given the speed of database development in the quarter of a century since Stone and Shaw suggested this, you could be forgiven for thinking it is ancient wisdom, because it is in computer terms, but it still works and is still widely adopted.

Another approach used is called 'soundex' and is used for data taken down aurally. Do both records sound like each other? If so, one may be erased.

Marketing managers have to make a trade-off between the quality of data on the one hand, and cost on the other. By using bigger matchkeys (more extensive checks) they will eliminate more duplicate files, but this will take longer and cost more. It is up to the individual company to make this trade-off decision.

Suppression files

People become more annoyed about receiving direct marketing materials than they do about anything else that marketers do, simply because direct marketing is personal; it even has their name on it most of the time. Television advertising (for example) is not. People will angrily call the company who had the audacity to send them items, to tell them to 'take my name off your mailing list, NOW', but few will do the same with TV advertisers (though Elvis, the staff at Graceland tell us, shot at televisions for showing things he did not like). But what do you do when someone asks you to take them off your list?

Logic suggests that you take them off, doesn't it? Not really. If you remove Ian Whitten from your database and then buy an external list on which his name appears, you will contact him again, and incur his wrath again for not doing what he asked you to do. And quite right too!

Instead of deleting the record, best practice is that you should create your own equivalent of the various Preference Service lists (see the footnotes to discussions of this above

(Sections 2.2.2 and 2.2.3) and build a suppression file of names who do not want to hear from you. Then, before undertaking any activity on new lists, as part of the merge, purge and de-duplicate routine, you should include your internal suppression file.

2.4.3 Manage the database

Once the data has been sourced and entered, it then has to be stored on the database and managed, ready for use. The company first has to decide whether to hold the data in-house or in a bureau.

In-house or bureau?

The decision on whether to manage the marketing database in-house or make use of an expert outside supplier – a data bureau – will be affected by various factors. An option is to set up the database initially in a bureau. This would allow staff to gain experience while the bureau takes on the job of managing the data. A move back in-house can be contemplated later.

Table 2.2 summarises the advantages and disadvantages of in-house versus bureau management.

If a decision has been made to keep the database in-house, it is probably the IT people who will manage the database on marketing's behalf. In this instance, there are typically some clashes of perspective within the company, which need to be recognised and allowed for. These can be summed up as 'people issues'.

People issues

'IT are cautious. It's their job to be cautious; they know the danger of chaos. Marketing are aggressive. It's their job to be aggressive; they know the danger of delay.'

(NCH Clearing House)

Exhibit 2.3 The balloonist

A man in a hot air balloon realised he was lost. He reduced altitude and spotted a man below. He descended a bit more and shouted 'Excuse me, can you help? I promised a friend I would meet him an hour ago, but I don't know where I am.'

The man below replied 'You're in a hot air balloon, hovering approximately 30 feet above the ground. You're between 40 and 41 degrees north, 59 and 60 degrees west.'

'You must work in IT,' said the balloonist.

'I do,' replied the man, 'How did you know that?' 'Well,' answered the balloonist, 'everything you told me is technically correct, but I've no idea what to make of your information, and the fact is I'm still lost. Frankly, you've not been much help at all. If anything, you've delayed my trip.'

The man below responded, 'You must be a marketing manager.'

'I am,' replied the balloonist, 'but how did you know?'

'Well,' said the man, 'you don't know where you are or where you're going. You have risen to where you are due to a large quantity of hot air. You made a promise which you've no idea how to keep, and you expect people beneath you to solve your problems. The fact is you are in exactly the same position you were in before we met, but now, somehow, it's my fault.'

(With thanks to Mike Bartlett, an IT man).

Table 2.2 Advantages and disadvantages of in-house versus bureau management

Management	Advantages	Disadvantages
In-house	A customised approach is possible	High cost of development
	Day-to-day control	Lack of internal expertise
	Data can be moved easily	Name and address handling is difficult
	Speed of service	Fewer analytical tools available
Bureau	Easier to enforce service-level agreements	Conflicting demands from other clients
	Share costs of hardware experience	On-line access sometimes difficult
		High operating costs

The human chemistry of the interface between the information technology and marketing departments is crucial to the successful integration of database marketing into the company. The differences in perspective can, however, create problems.

The marketing perspective

As a marketer you are rightly obsessed with the customer. You understand that one of the few differentiators we have is customer information. So why does the rest of the company not understand? Why is it so difficult to get them to accept that this is a priority?

Marketers:

- own the objectives of the database: they want it to be up and running quickly to steal a march on their competitors
- do not fix on the cultural 'rules': they are there to be broken
- are often weak on technical details
- know the danger of delay

The IT perspective

IT database managers have a very different view of the world. To them, marketers are only recent arrivals on the scene, coming behind the accounting system, the billing system, the stock-control system and the sales-recording system. What does marketing do anyway? They have never understood it, and no one has bothered to tell them, so what is all the fuss about? An IT manager's job is to make sure the company's internal systems are working properly.

IT people:

- own the technical knowledge of the database and the internal systems to make it happen
- focus on the details
- can feel weighed down by the problems
- need strong guidance on what data to hold and what software applications are required
- know the danger of chaos

The solution to conflict is understanding each other's different points of view, and understanding what each other's roles are in managing the whole picture. It is up to the marketing department to specify what it wants the database to be capable of, and then to work with IT to agree the database solution.

The next issue is the ongoing management of the data 'once it is on the database'.

Data management over time

Here we are concerned with:

- keeping data up to date
- auditing
- archiving

We will look at each of these separately.

Keeping data up to date

The problem with data is that it decays over time, and so money has to be spent keeping it up to date. In the UK, about five per cent of the population moves every year. People die, people change their names, get married or change their circumstances, and they do not even bother to tell you about it!

In a research white paper by Acxiom (DMA, 2011) it is said that 3.2 million UK households move each year (4.5 per cent of all UK addresses) and that consumer data decays at a rate where 22 per cent of mail remains undelivered each year. Other reasons for data decay include registrations with the various preference services (see Section 2.2.3).

The problem of changing data in business-to-business work is even more acute. Because of the rapidity with which managers change jobs, as much as '30 per cent of the data' can be out of date within a year.

Customers whose records become out of date in this way are known as 'goneaways' or 'nixies', and are a cause of great concern to direct marketers. The last thing you would want is to waste money by mailing people who no longer live at that address, to get people's names wrong, or cause distress to relatives by mailing someone who has recently died!

To minimise problems, the following data management procedures are recommended:

1 Verify data against the electoral roll and Postcode Address File before selections of name and address are made. This will:
   - help reduce the number of 'goneaways' mailed
   - reduce data capture errors getting back to the customer (e.g. name misspellings)

   However, the privacy laws contained within the Data Protection Act have been applied directly to the electoral roll since 2002. People are now given the opportunity 'to opt out of usage' of their name in direct marketing. A growing number of people will, therefore, be unavailable for verification. Companies will have to work harder to verify their data. Suppressing records that do not match the electoral roll has become something of a lazy practice, one that will probably have to change.

2 Have your data cleaned regularly by commercial organisations specialising in this. The major players include Acxiom (**www.acxiom.co.uk**) and DLG (**www.dlg.co.uk**), but a Google search for 'data cleaning' will show you a lot more. Such an exercise should be specified to remove all known movers (there are several 'movers files') and deceased persons (again several files exist). Reputable companies will be able to advise on the best order in which to clean the data to keep your costs low. Charging is subject to negotiation and may be made on a 'per name' basis (where you are charged for each name identified for suppression), a 'per thousand processed' basis, or you may even be able to negotiate the cleaning free if you go on to lease a certain number of names for marketing activity use over a given period of time.

3 Use only recent data. What counts as recent varies between industry sectors. For example, a supermarket would count three-month-old data as getting a bit old. A car manufacturer would see three-year-old data as usable, while 20-year-old data may be acceptable for a mortgage company.

4 Run off 1,000 records. Review common mistakes. Analyse sources for data entry: coupon, phone, in-store. Look for patterns and track down the source of the problem, then rectify it.

Exhibit 2.4 What's in a name?

Running off names is useful for idea generation as well as problem spotting. Let us say you were the direct marketing manager for the Royal National Lifeboat Institution (RNLI). Look at the two names and addresses below:

Admiral R D G Harrington	Mr I Brown
The Manor	Flat 2
Abbots Lumley	Cowley Mansions
Staffordshire	Chelsea
WS12 4JG	London
	W3 4HJ

Both the above subscribe to a computer magazine. Which one of them is more likely to donate to the RNLI? An RNLI fundraiser would quickly choose the left-hand name – it sounds older, rural, and with a naval connection – lying squarely in RNLI territory.

Auditing

Audit counts should be carried out regularly for record verification. This should include checking database records against the sources of those records, right back to the original data capture. It may be that mistakes along the way can be spotted and rectified.

Archiving

In order to make decisions about how long to hold records, we need to ask ourselves this question: when does a customer become a former customer? The answer is not as straightforward as we might think. For a magazine subscription, if your customer does not renew, then yes, they are now lapsed customers. But in the case of a credit card company, this

---

Exhibit 2.5 Saving the rainforests

I had a mailer recently from my bank. It eventually reached me after being forwarded by a friend who now lives in a house I vacated over two years ago. The mailer offered me a product which I had already taken up from the bank a while back.

The overall impression was one of inefficiency and a lack of any care being taken. It is likely that proper record verification and de-duplication would have prevented the bank from wasted mailers such as this.

decision is not straightforward. There are many accounts which have not been used for a while. A decision has to be made on the length of time allowed to elapse before the account is considered dormant.

Some data may be completely archived or destroyed. But marketers also need to decide when to archive customer data for active communication. The data is then kept, but used only to aid in the analysis/modelling stage.

2.4.4 Manage the applications

The key area to manage is the accuracy of any data that is going to get back to the customer. There are few things more irritating to customers than seeing their name spelt wrongly, and small details like these are going to reduce the impact of the best thought through strategies and tactics. The major areas to consider are as follows:

Selection

The selection of a customer list from the database is made on the basis of the marketing decisions made in analysis and strategy. A decision can then be made to select customers according to their characteristics on the database. This process of selection needs to be carefully monitored. Some records may need to be suppressed from the final output; for example, it is reputed that vicars are suppressed from many mailing lists because they have a higher propensity to complain than average!

Exhibit 2.6 Happy anniversary! Mistakes with data

A company that sells flowers once mixed up two lists: one was a list of birthdays and the other was funeral anniversaries. Unfortunately, the funeral anniversary people got a letter starting 'Happy anniversary!', while the birthday list letter began 'On this sad day . . . '!

A telecommunications company launched a new product by writing to 1.7 million of its customers. It needed to write only to those customers who were connected to updated equipment. By mistake, however, the list consisted of those customers not able to take up the service. When this had been discovered, the company had to write again to all these people explaining that they had been a bit hasty, and the service was not quite ready. A simple key-stroke error in the database bureau cost the company £700k.

Outputs

Outputs are those fields that are transferred from the database 'to the communication material going to the customer'. For direct mail this would include address, name for the salutation (Dear Mr/s . . .), and also personal data, such as account information for use in the letter.

Outputting data can go spectacularly wrong! Marketers need to be careful of items such as unusual titles, decorations and qualifications. Sensitive customers can be very publicly upset if their title is used incorrectly. If no data is available on the title, then marketers need to decide defaults, for example 'Dear customer . . .', 'Dear Ms . . .', and so on. Another alternative is to simply omit such records which, experience suggests, represent between 2 and 5 per cent of a typical file.

Exhibit 2.7 Who owns our cars now?

A perennial problem for car manufacturers is that, while they know who owns the car just bought from the main dealership, as soon as the owner stops getting that vehicle serviced at one of the manufacturer's dealers, there is simply no way to tell if they have subsequently sold the car or have just defected to a local garage for servicing. This creates all sorts of problems for the marketing department when it comes to creating customer retention programmes.

A well known car manufacturer appointed a new database manager just as a customer survey (costing £500,000, including £25,000 on incentives) was being sent to all known owners over the last ten years. The key objective of the exercise was to tie cars to their present owners and the database manager's very first task at the company was to go through the questionnaire and make any changes he required to allow him to capture the data he wanted for his database. Being young and enthusiastic he set about the task with gusto, and pretty well rewrote the whole questionnaire from scratch. Being of a cautious nature, he had the finished article checked by at least five people from within the company or the advertising agency they used. When everyone was happy, he signed it off, sent it to print and it was duly dispatched via Royal Mail.

On the day it entered the postal system someone from the advertising agency (who had already seen and checked the questionnaire) said 'Hey – what's happened to the question "What is your car's registration number"?' All in the room suddenly experienced that warm wet feeling you get as the blood drains from your legs, with the realisation that the key piece of data required to link cars to their owners had been removed.

Fortunately, the name and address had remained, as had the characters to indicate the year of the car's registration. When the replies came back the team managed to data process their way out of a lot of the mistake, and then spent their contingency budget buying the names and addresses, with registration number, of owners of the manufacturer's cars from commercial sources, much to the amusement of the list brokers involved. By the time the database manager had to confess his mistake to his manager, thanks to the support of his team almost 95 per cent of respondents had been successfully tied to their cars.

Unfortunately I can confirm that this story is true, gentle reader, because I, Ian Whitten, was that database manager. And no, I am not going to tell you which car manufacturer it was!

Managing campaign responses

One of the best things about direct, interactive and digital marketing is that responses can be so easily tracked and, as a result, marketing effectiveness can be measured to the penny. Of course, this is also one of the worst things about the discipline in as much as there is nowhere to hide if you mess it up!

Good old fashioned direct mail can all be sent with a code that responders need to quote, on-line advertising can be simply directed to a specially designed page on a website, unique to that advertising campaign, broadcast media can have a dedicated telephone number for each channel used. E-mail is even more measurable, with the ability to see who opened which mails and work out from that exactly what subject lines pack a punch.

By noting responses against each responder's record, you can then see not only what has worked and who has responded, but you can also use that intelligence to guide your future targeting. The people most likely to buy a product are those most like the ones who already have.

No examination of data management would be complete without considering the legal constraints that impact marketers. The UK Data Protection Act (1998) is covered in another chapter of this book, but at this point it is worth looking at self-regulation.

2.5 Self-regulation in direct marketing

Self-regulation, and the Codes of Practice that come from it, are often referred to as 'voluntary' regulation. Do not be fooled by that. It means that the codes have been drawn up voluntarily: it does NOT mean that organisations can choose to follow them or not!

In the UK, 'the advertising self-regulatory system is based on an agreement between advertisers, agencies and the media owners that each will act in support of the highest standards in advertising, to ensure that all ads are legal, decent, honest and truthful' (Committee of Advertising Practice, 2012).

British advertising is self-regulated by three bodies working together:

- The Broadcast Committee of Advertising Practice (BCAP), responsible for writing and maintaining the broadcast code;
- The Committee of Advertising Practice (CAP), responsible for writing and maintaining the non-broadcast code;
- The Advertising Standards Authority (ASA), the independent body responsible for administration of the codes and for the investigation of complaints.

Together, the codes cover the full gamut of promotions media from print and press adverts to promotions, competitions to cinema advertising, direct mail to e-mail, television, teleshopping, websites and Internet promotions.

2.5.1 The Broadcast Committee of Advertising Practice (BCAP)

The first edition of the BCAP Code came into force on 1 September 2010 and applies to all advertisements (including teleshopping, content on self-promotional television channels, television text and interactive television advertisements) and programme sponsorship credits on radio and television services licensed by Ofcom. It does not cover commercial references made within a programme (these are covered by The Ofcom Broadcast Code).

(Committee of Advertising Practice, 2010)

2.5.2 The Committee of Advertising Practice (CAP)

The 12th edition of The UK Code of Non-broadcast Advertising, Sales Promotion and Direct Marketing (CAP Code) came into force on 1 September 2010. The code applies to advertisements in newspapers, magazines, brochures, leaflets, circulars, mailings, e-mails, text transmissions (including SMS and MMS), fax transmissions, catalogues, follow-up literature and other electronic or printed material, posters and other promotional media in public places, including moving images, cinema, video, DVD and Blu-ray advertisements, advertisements in non-broadcast electronic media (such as on-line advertisements in paid-for space (including banner or pop-up advertisements and on-line video advertisements); paid-for search listings; preferential listings on price comparison sites; viral advertisements;

in-game advertisements; commercial classified advertisements; advergames that feature in display advertisements; advertisements transmitted by Bluetooth; advertisements distributed through Web widgets and on-line sales promotions and prize promotions, marketing databases containing consumers' personal information, sales promotions in non-broadcast media, advertorials.

(Committee for Advertising Practice, 2010)

2.5.3   The Advertising Standards Authority (ASA)

When the ASA feels a complaint is justified, it can take action with the broadcaster concerned. The ASA can require the broadcaster to withdraw the advertisement immediately, amend it or suspend it while investigations are carried out. The ASA Council's interpretation of the Code is final and its adjudications are published weekly on the ASA website, **www. asa.org.uk**. Complainants, advertisers and broadcasters may request a review of Council decisions by the Independent Reviewer of ASA Adjudications. Information about the review process is given in the Broadcast Complaint Handling Procedures document, available on the ASA website (**www.asa.org.uk**).

(Committee of Advertising Practice, 2012)

2.5.4   Other applicable codes of conduct

As well as the three mentioned above, marketing in the UK is subject to many other codes of conduct, including the following:

The Ofcom Broadcast Code

This was mentioned in the BCAP section above. At the time of writing, the current Ofcom Guidance relates to programmes broadcast on or after 28 February 2011 (Ofcom, 2012). The code covers 10 sections (further details available at the Ofcom website, **ofcom.org.uk**):

We are mainly concerned with Sections 9 and 10 of the Ofcom Code because these cover Commercial References in Television and Programming respectively.

The principles behind these codes are designed to:

- ensure that broadcasters maintain editorial independence and control over programming (editorial independence)
- ensure that there is distinction between editorial content and advertising (distinction)
- protect audiences from surreptitious advertising (transparency)
- ensure that audiences are protected from the risk of financial harm (consumer protection)
- ensure that unsuitable sponsorship is prevented (unsuitable sponsorship)

(Ofcom, 2011)

The Code seeks to do this by:

- limiting the extent to which references to products, services and trade marks can feature in programming
- requiring that viewers are made aware when a reference to a product, service or trade mark features in programming as a result of a commercial arrangement between the broadcaster or producer and a third party funder

● helping to ensure that broadcasters do not exceed the limits placed on the amount of advertising they can transmit

(Ofcom, 2011)

The regulations also define the types of programming that can and cannot be sponsored or include product/prop placement. News broadcasts and children's programming cannot, for instance.

The Direct Marketing Code of Practice

Issued by the Direct Marketing Association (DMA), the latest version at time of writing is Version 4 from February 2012 (DMA, 2011b).

The DM Code of Practice sets standards of ethical conduct and best practice. The Code covers all forms of direct marketing, as well as the emerging direct marketing channels, such as Bluetooth, SMS, MMS and other on-line commercial communications, as well as the traditional media such as direct mail, inserts and telemarketing (DMA, 2011b).

In addition to the Code, a number of Best Practice Guidelines set standards that are desirable to achieve. Best Practice Guidelines are supplementary to the Code and are not mandatory except where there is an overlap with the law or with the Direct Marketing Code of Practice.

Your attention is also drawn to the professional codes of conduct issued by the various professional bodies covering the industry (CIM, IDM, etc.), both in the 'home' market and also any overseas markets being targeted.

Summary

In this chapter we found that a database is a collection of customer records that can be analysed and output for communications. The key data to hold is personal data, transaction data and contact histories. Data sources can be internal or external, and great care needs to be taken in establishing the form in which internal data is collected. Managing the database involves managing the entire journey of the data, from its source into the database, and over time on the database, before outputting as lists or on to customer communications.

The most important legal constraints for direct marketers occur in the areas of data usage, sales promotions and customer communications. The Data Protection Act guides the use of data through its eight principles. For international direct marketers, there are extremely complex diverse laws governing the use of sales promotions in each country.

QUESTIONS

1　Explain the role of the database in direct marketing. What are the key applications for an international airline wishing to use its customer records for marketing?

2　According to Boddington (1994), 'a database is a record of our relationships with customers'. Discuss this statement, and discuss how this philosophy guides the type of data that a company may hold on its marketing database.

3 What is the difference between a database and a list? Drayton Bird (1989) said that by understanding what a list was, marketers were some of the way to understanding a database. Do you think he is right? Explain your reasons.

4 A manufacturer of golf products was interested in mailing a list of golfers from a lifestyle database and a list of subscribers to various golf magazines in order to build up a marketing database. What would he need to do with the data before mailing?

5 What is de-duplication and why is it so important?

6 Mr Jones recently received a mailer forwarded to him from the Royal Mail. It was from his building society, and contained an address he had vacated over two years previously. He complained to the company and was told it was a 'computer error'. Explain how the building society could have avoided this problem.

References

Armstrong, G., Kotler, P., Harker, M. and Brennan, R. (2009). *Marketing – An Introduction,* 1st edn (ed.), Prentice Hall, London.

Armstrong, K. (2012). *Principles of Marketing,* 14th edn, Prentice Hall, London.

Bird, 2007. *Commonsense Direct 7 Digital Marketing,* 5th edn, Kogan Page, London.

Boddington, A. (1994). *IDM Diploma Course material,* The Institute of Direct Marketing, Richmond-upon-Thames.

Committee for Advertising Practice (2010). *CAP Code* [on-line] Available at: **http://www.cap.org. uk/The-Codes/CAP-Code/CAP-Code-Item.aspx?q=CAP±Code±new_Scope±of±the+Code** [Accessed 23 April 2012].

Committee of Advertising Practice (2012). *Regulatory system at a glance.* Available at: **http://www. cap.org.uk/About-Us/Regulatory-system-at-a-glance.aspx** [Accessed 23 April 2012].

DMA (2003). *DMA Census,* DMA Records Office, London.

DMA (2011). *Acxiom White Paper – Reaching more consumers with certainty.* Available at: **http:// www.dma.org.uk/toolkit/acxiom-white-paper-reaching-more-consumers-certainty** [Accessed 20 April 2012].

DMA (2011b). *DM Code of Practice.* Available at: **http://www.dma.org.uk/toolkit/dm-code-practice-1**[Accessed 23 April 2012].

DMA (2012). *Exchange of emails.* s.l.:s.n.

Goldwag, W. (1995). s.l.: Smith Bundy and Partners.

IDM (2002). *The Interactive and Direct Marketing Guide,* 3rd edn, The IDM, London.

Kotler, P., Keller, K. L., Brady, M., Goodman, M. and Hansen, T. (2009). *Marketing Management,* Pearson Education, London.

Kotler, P. and Armstrong, G. (2012). *Principles of Marketing,* 14th edn, Pearson Education, London.

McCorkell, G. (2002). *The Interactive and Direct Marketing Guide,* 3rd edn, The Institute of Direct Marketing, Richmond-upon-Thames.

Ofcom (2011). *Ofcom Guidance Notes Section 9: Commercial References in Television Programming.* Available at: **http://stakeholders.ofcom.org.uk/binaries/broadcast/guidance/831193/ section9.pdf** [Accessed 23 April 2012].

Ofcom (2012). *Ofcom Broadcasting Code Guidance.* Available at: **http://stakeholders.ofcom.org.uk/ broadcasting/guidance/programme-guidance/bguidance/** [Accessed 23 April 2012].

Ranchhod, A. and Gurau, C. (2007). *Marketing Strategies – a Contemporary Approach,* 2nd edn, Prentice Hall, London.

Stone, M. and Shaw, R. (1988). *Database Marketing,* Gower, London.

The Absolute Essentials of Direct Marketing (4). (1992). [Film] Directed by N. Woodcock. The Institute of Direct Marketing, United Kingdom.

The Economist (2011). *Too Much Information – How to Cope with Data Overload.* Available at: **http://www.economist.com/node/18895468** [Accessed 14 April 2012].

The Information Commissioner's Office (2007) *Our highlights of 2006/07.* Available at: **http://www.ico.gov.uk/upload/documents/annual_report_2007_summary_html/4_highlights.htm** [Accessed 23 April 2012].

The Information Commissioner's Office (2012). *Home page.* Available at: **www.ico.gov.uk** [Accessed 12 April 2012].

Thomas, B. and Housden, M. (2011). *Direct and Digital Marketing in Practice.* 2nd edn, A & C Black, London.

CASE STUDY

Saco Drive-In

Twenty-one-year-old Ry Russell was looking to start a business when he discovered the local drive-in theatre in Saco, Maine, was for lease. As with many drive-ins, use of the theatre had been declining. The product was dated, but the drive-in had a lot of meaning in the community because it had been there since 1939. It's one of the oldest drive-ins in the United States and, even though the revenue was declining, he thought there was an opportunity to rebrand it and get a younger audience interested.

When he'd leased the theatre, Russell decided to focus only on social media marketing and cut out all other types of advertising.

The theatre had a Facebook page with about 3,200 fans at that point. Analysis of their data showed that the average age of the fans was about 37 years old. There wasn't anything on the page targeting younger people, so Russell set about increasing the fan base and targeting a younger audience by engaging with fans and creating a community on the Facebook page.

It was decided to reposition the theatre as a community event venue, not just a place to go to watch movies. When tickets were sold at the box office, Russell made sure to talk to people and welcome them. He also spent time walking around the theatre talking and engaging with those who were there. Facebook was a way to continue those conversations – visitors were encouraged to like the Facebook page so they could start discussions and provide feedback on their experiences.

Russell was prepared to put the hours into developing the Facebook page – about four hours a day, in fact, interacting with fans and continuing conversations that started at the theatre. The page wasn't used as a sales pitch, but rather as another way to build community, in line with the community event ethos. Postings included community events, and reviews on movies and even suggestions of what movies to play in forthcoming weeks were actively solicited.

One thing that really made Facebook fans feel valued was when Russell recognised them and greeted them by name when they came to the theatre. That helped to build trust with their audience, as did openly posting their prices on Facebook and letting fans know

> **Case study (*continued*)**
>
> that the theatre was there to serve them. The theatre is a business, but Russell also wanted fans to be passionate about the brand and what was happening with it.
>
> The fan base increased from 3,200 to about 9,800 fans throughout the first summer. The attempts to target a younger audience were successful – about 18 per cent of the fans are now in the 18–24 age range.
>
> Aside from just increasing the number of fans, the personal stories from those who visited the theatre were very rewarding. A woman in her late 50s asked for recommendations on novelty ice cream when visiting the concession stand and then went on to recommend the theatre to her friends via Facebook because of the personal interaction she had.
>
> At the end of the summer, a patron came and told Russell that he enjoys the drive-in because it allows him to spend time with his daughter. They would go to the theatre, but sometimes just ended up talking and spending time together instead of watching the movie. He said he really appreciated having a place to connect with his daughter.
>
> The former owner of the theatre would often bring her grandkids to see movies. She remarked that it had a much more communal atmosphere and that there were more people sitting outside and mingling at the concession stand than in prior years. It has helped to recreate the small town atmosphere at the drive-in and redefine what going to the drive-in meant.
>
> **Questions**
>
> 1 Do you think Ry Russell was wise to abandon all advertising except that on social media, or would he have been better to adopt a more balanced portfolio?
>
> 2 What about his approach of trying to attract a younger audience, especially given that older people have more disposable income?
>
> 3 How could the theatre have improved on the data they held on customers more quickly than via the organic method they used?
>
> *Source*: Hunt, L. (2012). Social Media Case Study: Drive-In Theater [on-line] Available at: **http://lindsay-hunt.com/social-media-case-study-drive-in-theater/** [Accessed 23 August 2012].

PART TWO

Using direct marketing to analyse the marketing situation

Chapter 3

The customer database: analysis and applications

Objectives

Once you have read this chapter you will:

- appreciate how a marketing database can help to improve customer understanding
- have an understanding of the techniques used to analyse customer data
- be better able to contribute to the process of database analysis

Introduction

In Chapter 2 we discovered what a database was and what data to hold. In this chapter we can move the focus on to how marketers can manipulate the data in order to understand their customers better. We will review what marketers use the analysis for and explain, in simple terms, some of the intricacies of database analytical tools.

The need for information

When a corner shopkeeper chats to one of his customers as they pop in, as well as being friendly, he is also doing a form of analysis. He is assessing the customer's needs from his shop, and if Mrs Jones makes a regular order of three boxes of eggs a week, he makes sure there are enough ordered to meet demand. Turning the focus inwards, he will understand his own strengths and limitations. He will also quickly find out if a rival opens up a new grocer's just up the road and starts to compete. In short, 'analysis' in this situation is fairly straightforward.

However, as companies have got larger, they have had more and more difficulty staying close to their customers, understanding their own capabilities, or scanning what their competitors are up to. The marketing director of a large company has no 'natural' way of staying in touch. At the same time, the demand for companies to be market focused has become imperative.

Companies try to combat these scale problems by adopting the philosophy that, if they cannot stay close to each of their thousands of customers individually, at least they will try to understand them as groups of people with shared characteristics.

In general, marketing such information is typically obtained through market research, salesforce feedback, competitor monitoring, and so on. However, firms that practise direct marketing have an extra string to their bow, which can help them in understanding their customers in a more precise way. This extra string is the database.

In the previous chapter we talked about databases and the data they hold. It is worth noting at this point that there is a subtle but important difference between data and information. Information has been defined as 'combinations of data that provide decision-relevant knowledge' (Jobber, 2010). Lynch opines that the next IT revolution will happen in the 'I', not the 'T' (Lynch, 2012). A data broker of repute in the industry regularly expresses the view that data (and the information it bestows) will be the drug of this century, in as much as it will bring great wealth to those who control its supply.

Several factors have combined to change the way data is used in marketing over the last decade or so:

- The power of computers has increased massively over this period.
- The cost of computers has drastically reduced over the same period.
- Computers have become mobile, to the extent that over a quarter of adults and almost half of teenagers now own a smartphone (Ofcom, 2011).
- We are all becoming more tech-savvy, marketers and consumers alike.

As a result, the value of data, leading to information in acquiring and maintaining a sustainable competitive advantage, cannot be overstated.

In this chapter we will investigate the ways that marketers can use a customer database to understand their customers better, and we will clarify the particular techniques they use to turn the raw data into useful information.

How this chapter is structured

In the previous chapter we found that companies collect many different types of data on their customers. In this chapter we are concerned with the way in which this data can be turned into management information to help marketers create more effective strategies.

There are two main subjects we need to focus on here. The first looks at the uses that marketers can make of the information that database analysis produces. These are discussed in the following section. The second area is to develop a clear understanding of the analytical 'tools and techniques' themselves, which we will cover later on in this chapter.

3.1 Uses of the database

3.1.1 How data analysis helps marketing managers

Exhibit 3.1 Hard and soft information in direct marketing

Direct marketers have to make decisions in two broad areas. First, we have the quantitative camp: we are faced with decisions on budgets, finance, returns on spend. This is where the database provides a great deal of leverage, helping drive marketing in a precise, numbers driven way.

However, other analysis is more 'qualitative' in nature. These decisions are based on 'words and pictures' rather than numbers. In particular you are looking to answer the 'Why?' question. Your database will tell you who is remaining loyal, and 'what' products they are being loyal to. However, only market research will tell you 'why' they are loyal: is it your brand strength, the appeal of your offers, or your service?

A good direct marketer will not, therefore, seek to use the database to replace market research. Rather, they should be used in tandem, together, to maximise the firm's understanding of customers in a cost-effective way.

The role of marketing research in campaign analysis is fully discussed later (see Chapter 14).

What type of information are we talking about? Table 3.1 summarises the typical approach to marketing analysis in general marketing.

From Table 3.1 we can see that a marketing database can add value to analysis in two main areas. The first area is that of 'measurement' and is covered later (see Chapter 14). The second area, which we are concentrating on here, is that of 'segmentation and targeting'.

It really cannot be overstated how valuable a customer database is to a segmentation strategy. There are two reasons why a customer database is a segmenter's dream. One is the volume and type of data that is available on a good database. Instead of a few hundred sample units of researched, claimed attitude and behaviour, there are potentially hundreds of thousands, or even millions, of data sets that include actual behaviour, plus profile information. The second reason for the database's segmenting value is that, once the segments have been created, each customer can be precisely allocated to each group and then contacted accordingly. The

Table 3.1 The scope of marketing analysis in general marketing

Analysis	Description
Internal information	Understanding the company's strengths and weaknesses
Marketing research	Analysing customer markets and buyer behaviour
Environmental monitoring	Scanning the wider environment for opportunities and threats
Competitor analysis	Assessing competitors in relation to your business
Measuring and forecasting markets	Predicting market demand; measuring company performance against objectives set
Market segmentation	Splitting markets into discrete groups to be treated differently
Market targeting	Selecting the best markets for the company

core requirements of a segment – that it should be discrete, profitable and accessible – are all achieved in an 'integrated' way using the database. In effect (and quite bizarrely) segmentation gives the likes of Tesco and Sainsbury's, the UK's top two supermarkets, similar abilities to those of the corner shopkeeper discussed in the introduction to this chapter.

The single most important application of this data arguably lies in its ability to segment at the 'individual level'. We can look at the data, build up a picture of who the customer is and what he or she wants from us, and create value for them accordingly. This deceptively simple use of the data leads to a one-to-one strategy (Peppers and Rogers, 1993), discussed by many authors (McDaniel *et al.*, 2013, pp. 292–3), (Armstrong and Kotler, 2009, pp. 213–5), (Kotler *et al.*, 2009, pp. 398–9) and which is fully discussed later (see Chapter 5).

Customer segmentation at group level is an aspect of marketing that has been extensively researched and written about by marketing academics, and is very important to marketing 'practice'. Segmentation is based on two main data types: behavioural and profile data. Various segmentation approaches have developed from this data (see Figure 3.1).

A number of authors ((Dibb *et al.*, 2012, pp. 126–30), (Ranchhod and Gurau, 2007, pp. 53–71), (Thomas and Housden, 2011, pp. 110–1) and others) have identified many such segmentation applications. In particular, database marketers have understood how 'purchase (behavioural) data' allows them to segment customers according to their value to the company. Direct marketers can also use purchase data to segment according to product needs.

The second major data type, consumer characteristics data (or 'profile data', as it is often called), is used by direct marketers to build up 'pictures' of those customers who are 'more likely to respond' to a particular campaign. Such profiling is important because, quite apart from anything else, readership and viewership of newspapers, magazines and television

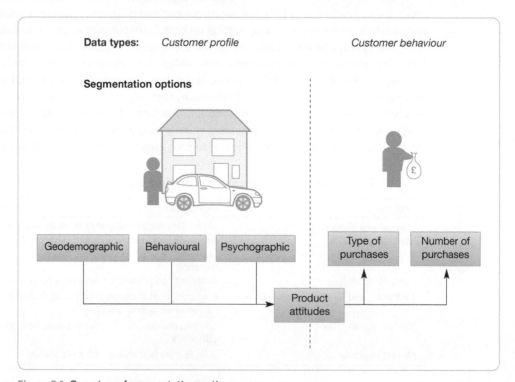

Figure 3.1 Overview of segmentation options

Table 3.2 Summary of segmentation applications

1 Use purchase behaviour to segment by customer value (also, use current purchase behaviour to forecast lifetime values).
2 Use purchase behaviour to segment by product need, and to assess product/market strategy.
3 Use profile data to relate to campaign response (ROI driven marketing).
4 Use profile data to target new customers accurately.

programmes tend to be expressed in that way (Jobber, 2010, p. 269), so such knowledge is a vital tool in the media buyer's toolkit. McCorkell (1997) called this 'Return on Investment (ROI)driven marketing'. Profile data is also used to target new markets more accurately, thereby lowering the costs of acquisition.

A summary of these segmentation options and their uses is given in Table 3.2.

Having introduced segmentation as the key application of database analysis, we can now move on to discuss each of these applications in a little more detail. In order to keep an overview, you may find Figure 3.2 helpful in keeping a visual picture of the database and what it can do.

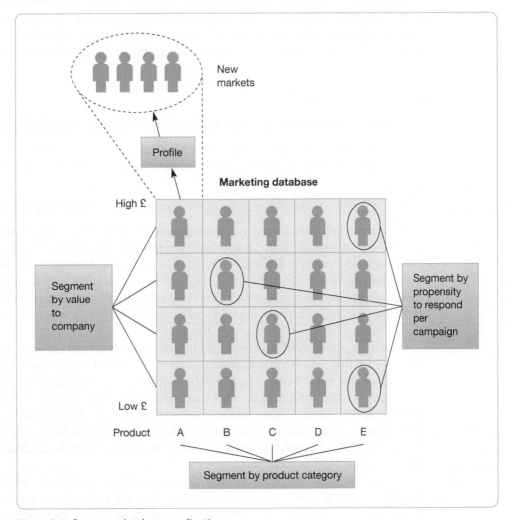

Figure 3.2 Company database applications

3.2 Segmentation applications for database marketers

3.2.1 Using purchase data to segment by value

The importance of this area to the whole of direct marketing thinking, and beyond to relationship marketing, cannot be emphasised too strongly. Not all customers are created equal. Surprisingly, perhaps, some loyal customers can be unprofitable whereas some disloyal customers can be profitable (Kotler *et al.*, 2008, p. 29).

Armstrong *et al.* summed it up when they said:

> 'Today, most marketers realize they don't want relationships with every customer. Instead, companies are now targeting fewer, more profitable customers . . . [using] customer profitability analysis to weed out customers that cost them money and to target ones that are profitable for pampering.'

> (Armstrong *et al.*, 2009)

This phenomenon is explained by applying Pareto's Principle to business. Pareto was an Italian economist who noticed that 20 per cent of the population owned 80 per cent of the land, and that this rule seemed to hold true no matter what area he studied. As a result, he created his principle, often known as the '80:20 rule', which has since been adapted for business.

Pareto's Principle applied to business

> 'Twenty per cent of your customers will provide you with 80 per cent of your profits.'

The actual numbers, 80 and 20, should not be taken as accurate for all businesses. This is not the case. What is crucial is that all businesses exhibit the underlying principle to some extent:

> A small number of your customers provide a disproportionate amount of your profits.

If we once again compare general marketing and direct marketing, we can see the importance of this analysis. In general marketing, this attempt to split off the firm's most valuable customers and treat them differently is not done with the same precision or conviction as it is by direct marketers. The manager of a high street store does not keep records of her customers, and so she does not know who the more valuable ones are. Every customer gets the same marketing effort targeted at them, and no records are kept of who is more valuable to the company.

In contrast, direct marketing spend is often deliberately spread unevenly amongst customers, such that returns are maximised. Hilton Hotels identify their biggest spending customers, who are senior business people who travel frequently. Their database flags up these customers as worthy of special attention, and when they arrive at the hotel they are given priority check-in service. Their every preference, from the size of the bed to the paper they read, is logged and delivered without them needing to ask. What Hilton has done is look to improve loyalty through a strategy of superior service in which the database analysis of customer value plays a crucial part.

In some cases, the definition of 'best customers' may be stretched to breaking point. Patients having laser eye corrections rarely come back for a second treatment, so the definition of a 'best customer' is one who recommends many people for treatment. In 2004, database analysis of a laser eye clinic in London revealed the surprising news that their most prolific referrer was someone who had been found not suitable for treatment himself, but who was so impressed with the initial consultation process which came to that conclusion, that he had referred tens of happy patients over the coming years.

Exhibit 3.2 Segmenting by value: the NSPCC

The National Society for the Prevention of Cruelty to Children (NSPCC) is one of the largest charities in the UK and, as such, has a donor base of about 500,000 supporters. These are segmented according to the level of their support, and NSPCC's fundraising department is organised around these different segments. One department looks after VIP donors (over £2,000 p.a.), another cares for the major donors (over £500 p.a.), while another caters for the group between £100 and £500, and so on.

Segmenting by value has enabled the NSPCC to focus on the differing needs of each group of fundraisers, and maximises their potential to give.

3.2.2 Using purchase data to set budgets

Companies can analyse their customers' purchase data in order to calculate how much each customer is likely to be ultimately worth to the company. This forecast is known as the 'customer's lifetime value'. By predicting how much gross profit we will make from customers, we can then construct a budget, on a per customer basis, which clearly tells us how much we can afford to spend. This calculation is called the 'allowable marketing spend per customer', and is extremely important in direct marketing practice.

Let us say our company is in computer periphery sales. Our customers' average lifetime value is calculated at £100 gross profit per annum. Using this figure to guide us, we can arrive at an allowable marketing spend per customer of, say, £30 per year.

This is a vital application of our existing customer data. Using customer lifetime values, we can take a view of the profitability of different markets. In turn, the allowable marketing spend figure can form the basis of budget setting. Both acquisition and retention budgets can use this figure as the start point. If a target figure of sales is imposed on the marketing department, this can be converted quickly to customer numbers and, hence, to a budget figure, because we have a basis for spend per customer. This budget submission is based on analysis, rooted in current customers' behaviour, not on guesswork or last year's budget. A step-by-step guide to these calculations is provided below (see Section 3.3.2).

These calculations have a number of linkages elsewhere in this book. This includes strategic division of resources between acquisition and retention (see Chapter 5) and the use of the allowable marketing spend per customer to set budgets for tactical programmes (see Chapter 14).

3.2.3 Segmenting according to customer need

Jobber (1995) reported that segmenting by different customer needs is quite common. In general marketing, it is standard to use market research to understand the different benefits obtained by different sets of consumers from the same product.

By studying the behavioural and psychographic data held on each customer, direct marketers can offer an additional tool. As Patron (1994) pointed out, the database can help the marketer to understand the different benefits that the same product may give customers. It may be that market research will be used as an additional way of obtaining insight here, perhaps to confirm a hunch developed from the database analysis. Second, subsequent marketing can be delivered to those customers with precision.

For example, American Express ('Amex') has used advanced modelling techniques to split its customer base according to the products customers have bought with their credit or charge cards. Amex then approaches 'third parties': Shell might be interested in offering tie-in deals with big spenders on petrol, for instance. These deals would then be offered to customers with their statements.

Exhibit 3.3 Segmenting according to lifestyle needs: Harley Davidson

Swinyard (1996) conducted an elegant analysis of Harley Davidson motorbike owners. He analysed their responses to a series of lifestyle opinion statements, and then used cluster analysis to split up and group the riders into six segments, according to how Harley Davidson meets their needs. The following lifestyle segments provide a firm basis on which to split the existing customer database and direct the marketing of Harley accessories accordingly:

1 **Tour Gliders.** Use their motorcycles for long trips. Agree with statements like: 'My bike is made for comfort rather than speed.'

2 **Dream Riders.** Now they have their Harley, but are trying to figure out what to do with it. Agree with statements like: 'Most of the time my motorbike is just parked.' 'I mainly use my bike for short trips around town.'

3 **Hard Core.** Gang bikers who like that sort of society. Agree with statements like: 'Some people would call me and my friends outlaws.' 'I think it's true that real men wear black.'

4 **Hog Heaven.** In love with the Harley mystique. Agree with statements like: 'When I ride, I feel like an old wild west cowboy.'

5 **Zen Riders.** Find spiritual solace in riding bikes. Agree with statements like: 'I like the attention I get when I am on my bike.' 'Most of the time my bike is just parked.'

6 **Live to Ride.** Passionate about motorbiking and do so rain or shine. Agree with statements like: 'I love to ride long distances; to me 500 miles is a short trip.' 'Motorcycles are a total lifestyle to me.'

Swinyard then calculated purchase predictions of new Harleys and accessories for each segment. For example, using historical purchase data, he calculated that Dream Riders and Zen Riders spent much more on accessories than did Hog Heavens.

He concluded that Harley Davidson riders were a much more complex set of people than the old stereotype of 'hard core outlaw gang riders' would seem to imply!

Source: Swinyard, W.R. (1996) 'Segmenting according to lifestyle needs: Harley Davidson', *Journal of Targeting, Measurement and Analysis,* **4** (1), pp. 337–62.

If product information is not available, customer needs may be deduced using psychographic or demographic information. Segmentation may then follow. In the 20 years between 1990 and 2010, the Muslim population of the United Kingdom more than doubled from 1.172 million to 2.869 million and is predicted to almost double again to 5.567 million in the next 20 years (The Pew Forum, 2012). This growing market has its own requirements when it comes to financial services, with Sharia law (as well as state laws) governing the behaviour of organisations in the market, so it is not surprising that Lloyds TSB has developed a range of accounts for this growing segment of the UK population. Lloyds TSB promises that money in these accounts will not be used for any interest based or non-Shariah approved activities (Lloyds TSB Bank PLC, 2011).

Moreover, the Islamic Bank of Britain (the UK's first standalone, Sharia compliant, retail bank in the UK to be authorised by the Financial Conduct Authority) commenced banking operations on 12 October 2004. They provide Sharia compliant retail banking products and services using digital and interactive banking methods. All their products and services are Sharia compliant and approved by a Sharia Supervisory Committee (Islamic Bank of Britain, 2011).

The early identification of this rapidly growing market segment has allowed the Islamic Bank of Britain to differentiate itself from other mainstream bankers who offer Sharia banking only as a part of a non-Sharia portfolio, and thereby gain a lead on any subsequent competitors.

3.2.4 Maximising response on a per campaign basis

Direct marketers use modelling techniques to identify their most 'responsive' customers. This allows us to allocate the marketing budget on a per campaign basis such that return on investment (ROI) is maximised.

Imagine that you are running a small 'direct' operation. You have 100 customer records laid out on paper in front of you. However, you have only enough marketing budget to contact 50 of them. You need to select the 50 customers most likely to respond to your offer. If you have only 100 customers, you can look at each customer and, based on your personal knowledge of them, make a decision about who to contact.

Given the reality of thousands or even millions of customers, we clearly cannot allocate our scarce budget using personal knowledge. The answer is to use predictive statistics, described in the following section, to forecast which individual customers are most likely to respond. A new analysis may be run for each campaign and, depending on the product, the timing, and so on of each campaign, a different set of customers each time will receive the communication.

The advantage of this technique is its firm focus on profitability on a 'campaign by campaign' level, as well as a strategic level: something rarely done in marketing. However, there are pitfalls. If we let the model alone decide which customers receive what communication, it is difficult to envisage a coherent set of messages, over time, going to customers.

Marketers in sectors where coherent communications over time are important, may therefore look to mix these 'profitability driven' methods with 'relationship driven' programmes.

3.2.5 Targeting new prospects based on existing customer descriptions: profiling

The database applications covered so far concentrate on existing customers – those held on the database. But is there any way that this tool can help us find new customers? Here we arrive at a second 'truism' for business in this chapter, which is as important to direct marketers as Pareto's Principle. Provided the new markets are looking for the same benefits from the product as existing markets:

your new customers will have a similar profile to your existing customers.

On giving this a moment's thought, you may not be surprised that similar types of people will like similar products, or will be attracted to similar brand images. Surprising or not, this phenomenon is absolutely crucial to direct marketers. It means that by making the effort to 'profile' our existing customers accurately, we can then 'more precisely target' new customers.

General marketers profile using market research. An aggregate profile based on customer characteristics is built up and related to media habits: TV, press readership and so on. A media buyer is then employed to pick those media that most closely match these profiles. The problem with this approach is the imprecision of the profiling and targeting process. Rather like dropping leaflets from an aeroplane, a lot of people get the message who do not need it!

In contrast, direct marketers take advantage of the sheer volume of their data and use modelling techniques, described later in this chapter, to produce a highly accurate quantitative profile of their customers. Direct marketers can complete the precision of their marketing efforts by matching with external databases or lists, enabling a list of the most likely new market prospects for the company to be generated. This list is then marketed to directly. The use of external databases is fully discussed in the next chapter (Chapter 4).

Now that we know what uses direct marketers make of databases for analysis, the following section describes the techniques that make it all happen.

3.3 Analytical techniques

Table 3.3 links together the 'applications' described previously with the 'techniques' direct marketers use to analyse customer databases.

On the right hand side of Table 3.3 you will notice a number of technical terms. The intention of the remainder of this chapter is to introduce these techniques in a non-technical way in order to make them accessible to readers who may be unfamiliar with statistical

Table 3.3 Summary of applications and techniques in direct marketing analysis

Application	Technique
Setting budgets	Use lifetime value (LTV) analysis to set allowable marketing spend
Understanding customers' value to you	Use frequency, recency, amount, category (FRAC) analysis and LTV analysis
Understanding existing customers as individuals: what they want from you	Database overlays with external data; profiling/modelling techniques; focus on product categories link with customer profiles; combine with market research
Targeting your spend in order to maximise ROI per campaign	Use modelling techniques, FRAC analysis
Profiling existing customers in order to target new customers	Profiling/modelling techniques

methods. Those readers who do not enjoy numbers are urged not to skip this section, as it is the use of these methods that lies at the heart of the superior control and targeting that direct marketing can offer.

3.3.1 Introduction to analytical techniques

The enormous amount of data that a database holds, and huge computing power, has heralded a drive towards heavy use of quantitative techniques that help in deciding where to spend one's marketing pound. One of the greatest concerns marketers have often lies with the future; in particular, who is likely to buy our products and services, and what they are likely to buy. Reflecting this, we are dealing primarily with 'forecasting' techniques, known by statisticians as 'predictive' techniques. However, some focus is also given to 'descriptive' techniques that help us understand what our customers 'look like'.

There are two main methods of predicting a variable (such as customer response): 'time series' and 'explanatory'.

- With time series methods, we make predictions about future levels of customer response by projecting forwards from the trend, cycle and seasonal patterns contained in 'past values' of our data. Time series techniques are the quicker of the two approaches and more accurate in the short term.
- Explanatory methods can predict customer response (the dependent variable) by identifying the factors that drive it (the independent variables), estimating their effects and projecting these forward into the future. Explanatory techniques are generally more useful than time series analyses when looking at the medium to long-term future.

3.3.2 Time series methods

Lifetime value analysis and allowable marketing spend per customer

In lifetime value analysis we are exploring the relationship between, on the one hand, the gross margin that we obtain from customers and, on the other hand, the amount we can spend marketing to them. This spend is used to attract customers in the first place, and then to ensure they maintain or increase their value to us. The allowable marketing spend is calculated *not* as one departmental total but, more usefully, for individual customers.

First, let us understand what lifetime value is, because if we understand this concept and know a customer's lifetime value, we can use this intelligence to determine how much we can spend to recruit the customer; and it may be more than they spend with us in their first transaction.

Explanation of lifetime values

Lifetime values are the sum of all future net incomes expected from a customer, translated into present-day terms.

In plain English, it is the total amount of money we expect to get from a customer during their lifetime as one of our customers. In some cases this may run to hundreds of thousands of pounds. Lexus has been said to estimate that a single satisfied customer is worth US$600,000 to them in their lifetime as a customer (Kotler and Armstrong, 2012, p. 44), (Armstrong *et al.*, 2009, p. 22).

There are two things to note particularly about this definition.

- The first is net income: this is income after direct costs have been taken into account. A direct cost is one that can be completely attributed to the production of specific goods or services. So, if my company makes cakes, the costs of flour, sugar, eggs and water are direct costs; the cost of heating and lighting the bakery are not, nor are my accountant's fees.

- The second is the reference to the present day. This is an adjustment made to future incomes, based on the principle that £10 next year is not the same as £10 today. In fact it is worth less – maybe only about £9 – depending on the 'discount rate' you set. The principle here is that money in the future is always worth less than the same amount today.

To turn this economic logic on its head, another way of thinking about it is this: if you had £10 today, you could invest it and it would be worth more than £10 next year. Therefore, it is better to have £10 now than £10 next year. This adjustment figure is known as the 'net present value'.

Lifetime value assessments vary according to the product sector. For some sectors, where revenues are stable and predictable, the calculation is simple (Dupin, 1992). This is true of much of financial services. For example, a mortgage document will anticipate all the revenue received by the company over the entire lifetime of the relationship. However, other product sectors, in particular classical direct sectors such as book clubs or china collectibles, have what has been called 'front-end' and 'back-end' revenues to consider (Stone, 1996):

- The front end refers to the revenue obtained from the initial sale, which may well be lower than subsequent sales because an acquisition offer was used as an enticement.

- The back end refers to all revenue obtained from subsequent sales, which can make the difference between loss and profit for each customer.

Calculating lifetime value

To calculate customer lifetime values accurately, we need three key pieces of data. These are:

- the number of years a customer buys from a company
- the percentage of customers remaining loyal to the company
- the amount spent per annum

It is possible to predict lifetime values by using previously observed trends and projecting them to the future. This is a useful approach in the absence of historical data (perhaps for a new startup company, for instance) and is appropriate if you want to play 'what if . . .' with some theoretical figures. However, a more accurate method involves taking an historical approach to calculating lifetime values. The success of this approach will, of course, be reliant on having built up a store of historical data on the above variables (Stone, 1996).

Assuming that our database contains such data, we can now press on with understanding the method used to calculate lifetime value and allowable marketing spend.

There are four steps to calculating LTVs:

- Identify a 'cell'. A cell is a group of customers, all of whom were recruited through the same medium, and who first bought from us in the same time period (the same day, week, month, quarter, year, etc. – whatever is relevant to your business. For the sake of example we will assume it is a year).

- Record the sales revenue for this group each year.

- Calculate costs (and thus profits) for each period.

- Discount each profit figure to arrive at the net present value (NPV) for each period.

This is perhaps best illustrated by example and Table 3.4.

That's great! . . . But what does it mean?! Let us go through it slowly and you will see that it is actually nowhere near as scary as it may first appear.

- In Year 1 we recruited 1,000 customers (row A) via (let us say) our website.
- On average, each of those customers spent £100.00 (row B) with us in year one.
- That gave us total year one sales from this cohort of customers of $100 \times £100 = £100,000$ (row C).
- Our net profit (in this example) is 20 per cent, so the cohort generated £100 000 $\times$ 20% = £20,000 net profit in year one (row D).
- For the sake of this example, we have assumed a constant discount rate of 6 per cent (row E) on the previous year's figures. This is to account for the fact that £10 next year is not the same as £10 today, as previously discussed. (This is used in row F, below). In reality, this rate may or may not be constant, depending on predicted economic factors.
- We calculate the NPV contribution (row F) by multiplying net profit (row D) by the discount rate (row E). In year one this is £20 000 $\times$ 100% (£10 this year IS worth £10 this year, so there is no discounting as there is in following years; in Year 2 the NPV is £15 147 $\times$ the discounted 94% = £14, 238).
- Cumulative NPV contribution (row G) is calculated by adding all the net present values (row F) up to and including that for this year. For Year 1 there is only one value, for Year 2 row G is the sum of year one's NPV plus year 2's NPV and so on in subsequent years.
- Lifetime value at net present value (row H) is simply the cumulative NPV contribution (row G) divided by **the original 1,000 customers,** not by the number of customers remaining.
- Retention (row I) shows us how many customers stay with us to the next year. So in Year 1 we had 1,000 customers, 72.1% of whom were retained, giving us a starting point in Year 2 of 1,000 $\times$ 72.1% = 721 of the original cohort remaining.

By following this process for the period we determine to be reasonable for our organisation, we can work out the 'lifetime value' of our cohort of customers. In the above example, the lifetime value of our cohort after five years is £58.70 each. This will continue to increase over time as the (probably ever-declining number of) remaining customers continue to buy from us.

For those of you who love mathematics, the formula for estimating customer lifetime value is:

$$\text{CLV} = \Sigma \frac{T^* (P_t - {}^c_t)}{T = 0 (1 - i)^t} - \text{AC}$$

Where

P_t = Price paid by a customer at time t

${}^c_t$ = Direct cost of servicing the customer at time t

i = Discount rate

$$t = \text{Expected lifetime of a customer}$$

$$AC = \text{Acquisition cost}$$

(Kotler *et al.*, 2009, p. 835)

However, the rest of us may wish to ignore that in favour of the above method!

Of course, there are often massive difficulties involved in calculating the lifetime value of a customer. It has been suggested (Ranchhod and Gurau, 2007) that these fall into the following broad categories:

- **Defining a customer.** Is a customer an individual, account, household or business address, for instance? See also the laser eye clinic example above. (Section 3.2.1)
- **Evaluating costs.** Not all costs in an organisation can (or should) be attributed down to customer level.
- **Evaluating the length of the customer relationship.** Markets and customers are both prone to change and change $\times$ change = a difficult calculation!

These aside, by preparing different LTV tables for cohorts of customers recruited via different media, we can compare how well each medium is performing compared to the others. This will allow us to determine where to best spend our advertising budget, as well as how much we can afford to spend on a) recruiting them as customers and b) keeping them as customers, which brings us neatly on to allowable marketing spend per customer.

Calculating allowable marketing spend per customer

Two separate allowable marketing spend figures need to be decided upon:

- The first is the amount we can spend to attract a customer for the first time. This figure may well have to be greater than the revenue from the first sale.
- The second is the amount we can spend on existing customers in order to keep them with us.

In the example in Table 3.4, a lifetime value of £58.70 for each customer over a five-year period sets the boundary for our 'target' allowable spend. It is vital to set the allowable spend at a realistic value, but it must allow for the realities of the company's profitability expectations.

Let us set an allowable spend for recruitment at £20 per customer, and an allowable spend for retention at £3 per customer, per year. The much higher recruitment figure

Table 3.4 **Example lifetime value calculation (£)**

		Year 1	Year 2	Year 3	Year 4	Year 5
A	Customers	1,000	721	536	410	323
B	Average sales p.a.	£100	£105	£110	£115	£121
C	Total sales	£100,000	£75,737	£59,081	£47,471	£39,287
D	Net profit (20%)	£20,000	£15,147	£11,816	£9,494	£7,857
E	Discount rate (6.0%)	100.0%	94.0%	88.4%	83.1%	78.1%
F	NPV contribution	£20,000	£14,238	£10,441	£7,886	£6,135
G	Cumulative NPV	£20,000	£34,238	£44,679	£52,565	£58,700
H	**LTV at NPV**	**£20.00**	**£34.24**	**£44.68**	**£52.56**	**£58.70**
I	Retention		72.1%	74.3%	76.5%	78.8%	81.2%

reflects the high costs of acquisition, something we will be discussing in greater detail later (Chapter 5).

Having set this target figure, we can now set the marketing budget required to achieve the exercise – acquiring and retaining 1,000 customers. First, we need to look at acquisition:

Acquisition marketing budget
= allowable recruitment spend per customer × target number of customers
= £20 × 1000
= £20,000

(The allowable marketing spend for acquisition also allows us to calculate quickly a target response rate for a campaign. Let us say we use direct mail to attract customers from a list of prospects. An amount of £20,000 would allow us to send about 40,000 mailers (see costs of media) (Chapter 10). We need 1,000 customers, which is a response rate of 2.5 per cent from the mailer. (This is our target response rate.)

Second, we assess retention:

Retention marketing budget for years 2 to 5
= number of customers × allowable marketing spend for retention

A total is then calculated depending on the number of customers each year.

For a customer who stays with us for all five years, we will spend the initial £20 plus £3 p.a. for four years, making a total of £32. This is the total allowable marketing spend over a customer's 'lifetime'.

Calculation of expected return on investment

This is best done by looking at returns on investment per customer, over the expected lifetime. Subtracting the marketing spend per customer (Step 2) from the lifetime value income per customer (Step 1), we arrive at:

Expected return on investment per customer = £58.70 − £32.00 = £26.70

We can express the surplus in terms of return on investment per annum. As the expected 'lifetime' of each customer is five years, the total figure of £26.70 is divided by 5.

$$\text{Expected ROI per annum} = \frac{£26.70}{5} = £5.34$$

The next technique we shall consider is FRAC scoring.

Frequency, recency, amount and category (FRAC) scoring on the database
Explanation of FRAC

FRAC is a breakdown of behavioural data on customers into its constituent parts. Frequency refers to the time elapsed between purchases. Recency is the date of the most recent purchase. Amount is the average value of that customer's purchases. Category refers to that segment which the product bought comes under.

What is FRAC scoring?

FRAC scoring is a way of assessing each customer on the database, based on their purchase behaviour. The outcome of the scoring procedure is that each customer has a number, a score, attached to them. Using these scores, a prediction can be made of each customer's likelihood of responding to your next campaign. However, in addition to this tactical emphasis, FRAC can also be used as a strategic tool, to help understand the bigger picture. It is the basis on which customer segmentation by value is carried out, enabling segmentation marketing to be practised, as described earlier.

The principle behind FRAC scoring

In explaining FRAC, it is possibly easier to start with the 'C' element – Category. (Maybe the model should be called 'CFRA', but that does not have the same ease of pronunciation!)

FRAC scoring is one of the most valuable analyses to carry out on your database (Stone and Shaw, 1988). In a nutshell, they say that this is because 'past transactions are one of the most important indicators of future transactions'.

The way in which past transactions guide future transactions depends on the market sector – the Category. In some sectors there are well-established gaps between purchases, for example the private purchase of cars. Here, a customer who has just bought a car from us is unlikely to buy another straight away: the score may indicate a customer maximum propensity to repurchase when, say, five years have passed (five years is a typical average gap between new car purchases).

In other markets, direct marketers have found some more surprising patterns. In mail order, and other classic direct sectors, the following 'principle' seems to hold:

Your next customer is likely to be one who has just bought from you.

Whereas in financial services, a bank may find that:

A customer with many accounts is more likely to purchase further products from you than one with few or no accounts.

In general, collective direct marketing practice has revealed the following important truism:

The more your customers have spent with you, the more they are likely to spend with you in the future.

Does this sound obvious? Let us turn it on its head for a second. It can be argued that, if I have bought one item from your catalogue, then surely I am less likely to buy a future item than someone who has not bought anything? In fact this is rarely the case, and this underlies the principle that a company's existing customers are its most valuable asset, something we will discuss more later (Chapters 5 and 7).

Example calculation of FRAC scoring

In a typical simple FRAC scoring method (Stone, 1996) a points system is used, with purchases broken down by quarter years. A typical formula might be as follows:

Recency points:

24 points	purchase in current quarter
12 points	purchase in last 6 months
06 points	purchase in last 9 months
03 points	purchase in last 12 months

Frequency points:

$$\text{No. of points} = \text{No. of purchases} \times 4$$

Table 3.5 Gains table description

Segment	Score	Decile	Responses	Typical marketing decision
1	60+	0–10	600	Five outbound telephone contacts
2	54–59	11–20	400	Four outbound telephone contacts with mailer to follow
3	48–53	21–30	300	Three outbound telephone contacts with two mailers to follow
4	42–47	31–40	280	Two outbound telephone contacts with two mailers to follow
5	36–41	41–50	120	One outbound telephone contact with two mailers to follow
6	30–35	51–60	100	One outbound telephone contact with one mailer to follow
7	24–29	61–70	80	Three mailers
8	18–23	71–80	60	Two mailers
9	12–17	81–90	30	One mailer
10	6–11	91–100	10	No activity

Monetary points:

No. of points = 10 per cent of purchase value, with a ceiling of 9 points.

Each customer's score is then calculated and held on the database. The marketer then makes targeting selections according to these scores.

Ranking your customers

After each customer has been scored according to their FRAC data, we then organise them according to that score. Customers are divided up into cells (or 'segments') according to their predicted response levels. Typically ten cells, known as deciles, are used with segment one (or decile 0–10) being the most responsive and segment 10 (or decile 91–100) being the least responsive. A 'gains table', such as that shown in Table 3.5, is then produced.

The typical marketing decision shows the sort of activities that may be directed to each different segment, with the most responsive receiving the most contacts (at the greater cost to the company, in a reflection of the LTV of each segment's typical customer) and the least responsive segment receiving perhaps no activity at all; that is not to say we do not want their custom, it is just that we recognise that, if we spend any money trying to get that customer, there is a good chance it will be wasted.

It is said that 'a picture paints a thousand words', and so it is with statistical analysis, where graphs are often easier to understand than tables of numbers. First, we need to do some very small manipulation of the data in the chart above – nothing complicated, don't worry!

First, we can see that each of the segments above represents 10 per cent of the total customers, so let us re-label that column and change the data to show the 'cumulative' percentage of customers mailed, assuming we start with the best segment and work our way down, as we have in Table 3.6 below.

If all customers were created equal, we would expect to get 10 per cent of all responses from each segment. So, if we mail 10 per cent of the list, we would expect to have 10 per cent of the responses, if we mail 30 per cent we would expect to get 30 per cent of the total responses and so on. Let us put that expectation in the second column of Table 3.6 and call it our 'baseline', and then put the cumulative figure (assuming we start with the best segment) in column three.

Table 3.6 Gains table

Segment	Baseline	Cumulative baseline	%age of responses received	Cumulative responses
10%	10%	10%	30%	30%
20%	10%	20%	20%	50%
30%	10%	30%	15%	65%
40%	10%	40%	14%	79%
50%	10%	50%	6%	85%
60%	10%	60%	5%	90%
70%	10%	70%	4%	94%
80%	10%	80%	3%	97%
90%	10%	90%	2%	99%
100%	10%	100%	1%	100%

The data in the 'responses' column of the original Table 3.5 tells us how many responses we got from each segment. Let us convert that to percentages of the overall response and put that in the fourth column of Table 3.6.

Finally, we add up the cumulative response percentages and put that in column five of Table 3.6.

This allows us to produce some interesting graphs. The first one (Figure 3.3) is a 'cumulative gains chart'. It shows the cumulative effect (in terms of response) of adding each new cell to the marketing activity.

The second graphic we can produce shows how well each segment performs compared to the expected 10 per cent per segment (see Figure 3.4).

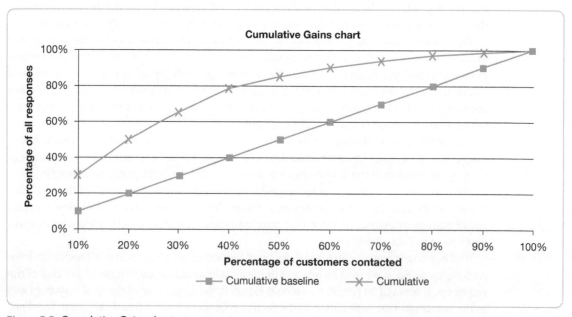

Figure 3.3 Cumulative Gains chart

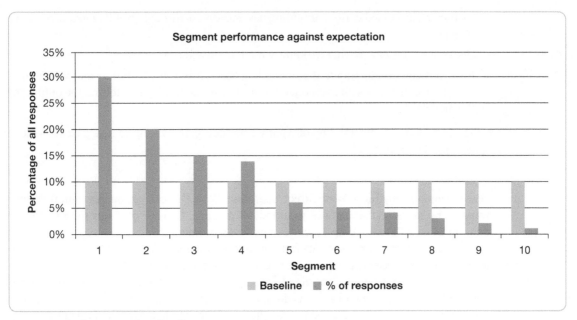

Figure 3.4 Performance of each cell versus expectation

3.3.3 Explanatory analytical techniques

In this section we will first introduce modelling techniques, before exploring some of the more common techniques used in database analysis. We will look at cluster analysis, neural networks, regression analysis and CHAID analysis.

Modelling techniques introduced

This is a vast and complex area, and detailed coverage of all the techniques useful to direct marketers is well beyond the scope of this book. However, it is perhaps not good enough for marketers to throw up their hands and say, 'I don't understand this area. Let's leave it to the statisticians.' The best results from modelling techniques spring out of a debate between marketers and modellers, with the marketers specifying what they want out of the model, and the modellers trying to interpret these instructions. There are many objectives that a marketer can set, and there are many techniques to choose from, as we will see.

Modelling is as much an art as a science. The factors that drive, say, response to a mailer are a mix of 'orderly' and 'random' factors. It is to some extent possible to model the orderly influences on response to a mailer. However, random factors, by their very nature, are unpredictable and their effects cannot be included in a model. The marketer's intuitive understanding of the market is required to recognise when the influence of random factors, or perhaps the correlation between two or more orderly factors, is affecting the model. Very often in modelling, variables such as age and income are quite likely to be related 'to each other' as well as response to a mailer – the factor we are trying to model. Marketers need to be aware of these common problems in modelling. These can be understood and overcome by building up familiarity with both the data to be used in modelling and the limitations of modelling techniques.

The responsibilities for marketers, therefore, are to:

● Specify what we want the model to do: what are the marketing objectives? These have already been established as either maximising response from our existing customers, discussed earlier, or finding new customers through profiling, discussed later (Chapter 4).

- Understand our data so that we know what it is we want to model.
- Have sufficient understanding of modelling 'jargon' and techniques so that we can discuss these objectives with the modelling specialists and be able to interpret the outputs of the models.

To improve our understanding of what we are doing, it is useful to take a closer look at some typical customer data.

The nature of customer data

Let us examine a mythical 'Wine Direct' operation. Wine Direct is expanding, and therefore wants to target new customers as accurately as possible. Can the company use its existing data (in Table 3.7) to build up a picture of its best customers?

If we take a closer look at the data from the five customers outlined in Table 3.7, we may be able to spot how those people who have bought the most wine (high responders) are different from those who have bought less wine (low responders). The data implies that older people seem to be responding a bit better, as do those with more income and those who live in the south. However, car ownership seems unrelated, as does their liking for classical music.

As a result of this analysis, we decide to contact 'new prospects' based on age, income and where customers live. The logic we used is this:

Provided there are associations between variables, then knowledge of one variable (say, age) will help us increase the accuracy with which we predict the values of another variable (say, likelihood to respond).

In the example we have used, we have just built a mental 'model' of our data. Statistical modelling techniques do just the same, except that they establish the patterns in the data mathematically, using thousands of data sets rather than our five. The model establishes 'associations', or linkages, between response and other variables, that will help us predict our best future customers.

Identifying these associations lies at the heart of quantitative techniques. However, there is a difference between an 'association' between variable A and variable B, and any hint that variable A may have 'caused' variable B to change. This is an important distinction to make. As marketers, we are very interested in any 'causal' relationship between variables because this can help us understand our customers just that little bit better. For example, if we are selling exploration holidays it is very useful to know that our customers are mostly, say, people who are searching for some personal meaning from their holiday experience; it enables us to talk to them in their language. This psychographic variable is a probable 'causal' factor in the purchase of the holiday. On the other hand, our customers may also be

Table 3.7 Wine Direct customer data

Customer	Cases of wine bought	Age	Income	Own a car	Classical music fan	Live in south
1	20	45	35,000	Y	N	Y
2	5	28	20,000	Y	Y	N
3	10	35	30,000	Y	Y	N
4	15	52	15,000	N	Y	Y
5	25	60	28,000	Y	Y	Y

higher-than-average purchasers of sports cars. This variable is merely 'associated' with the holiday purchase, but is unlikely to be a causal factor in its purchase.

Having made the effort to examine data in more detail, we are now ready to look at the more common explanatory techniques.

Cluster analysis

The process of clustering can be visualised by imagining a piece of paper with iron filings spread randomly all over the sheet. Each filing represents a customer, as yet not assigned to any group. Then picture what happens as a set of magnets is slowly drawn closer to the underside of the paper. The magnets represent the clustering process. As they get closer, so the filings start to separate out into groups that are pulled towards each magnet, depending on the filing's position on the paper. At the end, the original spread of filings (customers) has been replaced by clusters, or groups, depending on the position (customer characteristics).

Cluster analysis is one of the techniques used by direct marketers to produce quantitative profiles of customers. Geodemographic profilers also use cluster analysis to manipulate the census and other data in order to profile postcode areas, discussed later (see Chapter 4). In a nutshell, cluster analysis provides a picture of how the data clusters together.

The clustering process for geodemographics can be 'visualised by imagining each of thousands of postcodes as a centroid of about 25 rays, the length of each describing the value of an independent variable (income, size of house, etc.). Cluster analysis involves the simultaneous comparison of the length of these 25 rays, pair-wise, among all the postcodes and it brings together, as the clustering proceeds, those postcodes that are most alike on all dimensions' (Stone, 1996).

Exhibit 3.4 Quantitative jargon explained

Variable A variable is simply a concept that varies; for example, age, income, response.

Dependent variable This is the variable you want to predict. In direct marketing this is often 'response', 'sales' or 'profit'.

Independent variable Independent variables are other variables on the database that may be related to, and so help predict, the dependent variable. Independent variables may be 'age', 'income', 'attitudes', 'prior product purchase'.

Regression This takes two variables – one dependent and the other independent – and uses statistical formulae to describe how strongly the two are linked.

Correlation The closeness of the relationship between variables that are related to each other.

Measure of association (correlation coefficient) The correlation coefficient is a single number that expresses the strength and direction of a relationship between two variables, say age and response. It measures the extent to which the variation in an independent variable, say income, explains the variation in a dependent variable, say response to an offer of a credit card. If all responders to the offer have a high income, and all the non-responders have a low income, then income is a strong 'explainer' of the variance of response to the offer. It is also said to be highly 'correlated' or associated with response.

Coefficient of determination (R^2) This statistic lies between 0 and 1. It identifies what percentage of the variation in the dependent variable is explained by the overall model we have constructed. A model with an R^2 close to 1 will produce more accurate predictions than those from a model with an R^2 closer to 0.

Cluster analysis literally tries to aggregate customers into groups. The data is analysed and customers are placed in groups that have two characteristics: both the 'inter-group differences' and the 'intra-group similarities' are maximised. Each group or segment then contains customers that are as alike as possible to one another and, at the same time, are as different as possible from customers in other groups.

Cluster analysis is often used as an 'initial' exploratory technique by a database modeller. At this early stage, the important explanatory variables (those that best explain the variation in response) are not yet identified. This first stage will help the marketer understand how the mass audience splits into various segments. This is an important input into the marketing strategy: it can help us understand that we have different groups of customers who have used our business for different needs. Product development, targeting and marketing-mix decisions may all stem from this kind of analysis.

Cluster analysis does not predict how a dependent variable, say response, will vary between customers. This prediction analysis is the work of techniques such as regression and CHAID modelling, both of which are covered later in this chapter.

Neural networks

The practical application of neural networks has been described in the industry as being a bit like teenagers and sex – everybody is talking about it, but hardly anyone is actually doing it! In the previous edition of this book it was stated that results (Courteux, 28–29 June 1995), (Patron, 1994) seem to indicate no particular advantage in using any one modelling technique and that, indeed, when considering direct marketing models, a minor advantage, if one exists, seemed to lie slightly with regression techniques. Things have moved on in the time since then. Some researchers (Cui et al., 2008) have found that neural networks outperform many other statistical techniques but their results suggest that the other techniques vary in performance across different criteria and validation methods. Others (Raza et al., 2010) found that neural networks proved to be better than other techniques in classifying and predicting results. In other words, the jury is still out! It should be borne in mind, however, that increases in both available computer power and the technical expertise of people entering the marketing profession mean that neural networks may well be set to become a very important asset to direct marketers. On paper, they are reckoned to be potentially the most powerful of all the techniques and, as such, it is worth having a basic understanding of what they are and what they do.

It has been explained (Patron, 1994) that neural networks are not a statistical technique but a relatively recent development from a branch of computer science known as artificial intelligence. The technique actually simulates the way the human brain learns, memorises and reasons, although in a greatly simplified way. The internal structure of a neural network consists of cells and connections between them known as neurons. This simulates our own biological neurons/cells set-up.

Neural networks work in the following way. Imagine a baby first learning to recognise a set of keys. At first, she will not be able to understand the difference between the shape of a set of keys and, say, a pen. With correction by parents, and constant exposure to the two distinctive shapes, she gradually gets closer and closer to the perfect identification of the two shapes – a process that is characterised by certain electrical emissions through her neurons. By a process of trial and error, the end result is achieved. Neural networks replicate this pattern-recognition approach, using a computer.

To use neural networks to predict response, you have first to train the computer using 'training data'. Initially the computer will make good predictions only by chance but, as you feed into it the results, it learns more and more. When this process stops, the computer has 'learned' the way in which the variables relate to one another. The real data is now exposed to the model and the output, in the form of scored predictions for each record, is produced.

Regression analysis

As stated in Exhibit 3.4, regression analysis takes two variables – one dependent and the other independent – and uses statistical formulae to describe how strongly the two are linked.

There are numerous statistical techniques but a simpler technique involves drawing a type of scatter graph and being able to find the average of a few numbers to plot a line on that scatter graph so we can visually determine how far away from the line the scattered points lie.

All advertisers want to know if there is a link between their advertising spend and the revenue that advertising generates, so let us take that as a starting point for an example.

We have two sets of variables:

- An independent variable (advertising)
- A dependent variable (sales, which we <u>hope</u> will depend on the amount of advertising we do)

For the last five months, we have been varying the amount we spend on advertising on-line. Our spend and resultant income looks like this:

Table 3.8 Spend and resultant income

Month	Ad spend	Sales
January	£20,000	£600,000
February	£50,000	£1,000,000
March	£40,000	£700,000
April	£60,000	£900,000
May	£30,000	£800,000

When we plot this to a scatter graph (with the independent (ad spend) variable on the X (horizontal) axis and the dependent variable (sales) on the Y (vertical) axis), it looks like Figure 3.5 (concentrate on the X's, ignore the O's and the line for the moment, we will be back to them soon):

The basic purpose is to see if there is a pattern among the points: the more distinct the pattern, the more closely related are the sets of variables. The crosses show the data points from the table above; the value of the scatter graph can be increased by including on it a 'line of best fit', which will allow us to see rough estimates of income for a given spend. The most accurate method of calculating this is by using regression analysis formulae, but a far simpler, quicker and generally serviceable method is known as the Three Point Method. Here is how it works – (see Table 3.9 below for the practical application of this):

- Keeping the advertising and income data in their pairs, rank them according to the independent variable.
- Find the average of the lowest two values of independent variables (advertising spends) and their associated dependent (sales) variables.

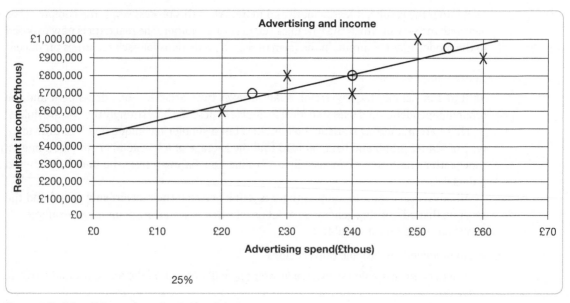

Figure 3.5 Advertising and resultant sales data

● Find the average of the highest two values of independent variables (advertising spends) and their associated dependent (sales) variables.

● Find the average of the whole dataset of values for both the independent variables (advertising spends) and their associated dependent (sales) variables.

● Plot those three average figures on the graph and draw a line through them so that it passes through the overall average coordinates and is as close as possible to the high and low averages.

The line is plotted on Figure 3.5 with the 'O's' representing the data points. From this, we can see that the spend and income figures *do* follow the line quite closely, so we can say that there is a quite a strong link between the dependent and independent variables.

Table 3.9 Advertising and resultant sales data

	Advertising (Independent X)	Sales (Dependent Y)	
'X1 Average' £20,000	£20,000	£600,000	'Y1 average' £700,000
	£30,000	£800,000	
	£40,000	£700,000	
'X2 Average' £55 000	£50,000	£1,000,000	'Y2 Average' £950 000
	£60 000	£900 000	
Totals	£200,000	£4,000,000	
Overall average of X =	£40,000	£800 000	= Overall average of Y

We can also look at the line and say that we can reasonably expect to get something like £550,000 in sales for a spend of £10,000. Of course, these figures are probably wildly inaccurate for the sale of anything that is legal, but it makes the point.

There is a lot more to applying regression models than this, but the reader is reminded that this is a marketing text and is directed to statistics texts for greater, more in-depth coverage, if required.

CHAID analysis

CHAID stands for Chi-squared Automatic Interaction Detector. This technique was developed in 1978 by Gordon Kass (Kass, 1980). It is simpler to picture than multiple regression and so remains a popular technique, particularly when it is necessary to explain your results to senior managers.

It is a useful exploratory technique, often used prior to regression modelling or neural network development (Patron, 1994). Table 3.10 compares regression analysis and CHAID.

In CHAID analysis, each record is put into a discrete cell, generated by the analysis, rather than producing a score (Polock, 1992). The essence of the technique is that the marketer first chooses the likely discriminating variables, i.e. those that best explain who responds. CHAID uses chi-squared statistics to confirm which of these variables best explains the variance in response.

Steps in CHAID analysis

Take a look at Figure 3.6. Using the example of 'Wine Direct' and assuming the company has carried out an offer, CHAID output is constructed by using the following six-step process:

Step 1

Compare the records of 'responders' with those of 'non-responders'.

Step 2

Computer model asks, 'Which variable best explains the difference between responders and non-responders?' This is done in a systematic rather than an intuitive way.

Step 3

Split the responders' file into two cells according to the biggest difference in response between the cells.

Step 4

The model then looks at each of the segments separately to see if they can be broken down any further. Different variables may now be appropriate to segment the cells further.

Table 3.10 Regression analysis versus CHAID

	Regression	CHAID
Complexity	Complex	Simpler
Minimum sample size	300	1,000
Software	Extra needed	No extra needed
Data type	Better with continuous	Better with categorical
Output type	Equation which allows score model	Tree segmentation
Interaction of variables	Ignores it	Detects it

Source: Portlock (1992).

83

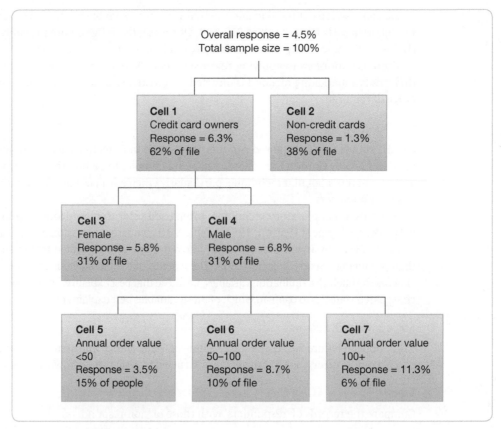

Figure 3.6 Tree segmentation for CHAID

Step 5

Continue process until cell sizes are too small for it to be of value to split them further.

Step 6

Output as a tree segmentation, as illustrated.

The appeal of CHAID modelling is that the output, a tree segmentation, automatically produces the desired end for the direct marketer, which is a set of customers split into segments according to their marketing potential.

Summary

One final word on modelling. Many authors have urged caution when using modelling techniques. There is a kind of aura that surrounds these techniques, because they are quite complex, but they are easily used with computers. A rather appealing 'answer' pops out at the end of the modelling process, which can be very attractive to pin your money on. However, such models are only as good as, first, the data and, second, the hard thinking that has gone into them. Care is needed.

QUESTIONS

1 Compare and contrast the analytical needs of a direct marketer in charge of a business-to-business car rental firm and a brand manager of a soft drink.

2 'A relationship marketer would never choose which customers to communicate with based on statistical methods.' Examine this statement, debating the extent to which marketing communications, driven by forecast responsiveness and value, may damage customer relationships.

3 A charity marketing manager is looking to understand which of her donors are the most valuable to the charity. Explain which techniques she should use to achieve this. What would she do with the information?

4 'The only certainty with forecasts is that they will be wrong.' How does this statement apply to lifetime value analysis? Recommend a way of calculating a customer's lifetime value.

5 A database owner wants to obtain a broad description of his customers to establish whether any obvious segments can be identified. Recommend to him which major technique(s) he should employ to analyse his data.

References

Armstrong, G. and Kotler, P. (2009). *Marketing – An Introduction,* 9th edn, Pearson Prentice Hall, Upper Saddle River.

Armstrong, G., Kotler, P., Harker, M. and Brennan, R. (2009). *Marketing – an Introduction,* 8th edn, FT Prentice Hall, London.

Courteux, R. 28–29 June (1995). *Workshop Masterclass,* IDM Conference, Surrey, UK.

Cui, G., Wong, M. L., Zhang, G. and Li, L. (2008). Model selection for direct marketing: performance, *Marketing Intelligence & Planning,* 26(3), pp. 275–292.

Dibb, S., Simkin, L., Pride, W. and Ferrell, O. C. (2012). *Marketing Concepts and Strategies,* 6th edn, Cengage Learning, Andover.

Dupin, D. (1992). Lifetime Marketing: Assessing Return on Marketing Spend, using a magazine subscription as an example. *Journal of targeting, Measurement and Analysis,* 1(1), p. 29–33.

Islamic Bank of Britain (2011). *Investor Relations,* [on-line] Available at: **http://www.islamic-bank.com/investor-relations/** [Accessed 09 May 2012].

Jobber, D. (2010). *Principles and Practice of Marketing,* 6th edn, McGraw Hill, London.

Kass, G. V. (1980). An exploratory Technique for investigating large quantities of categorical data. *Journal of Applied Statistics,* 29(2), pp. 119–27.

Kotler, G. *et al* (2009). *Marketing Management,* 1st edn, s.l.:Pearson Prentice Hall.

Kotler, P. and Armstrong, G. (2012). *Principles of Marketing.* 14th ed. s.l.:Pearson Education.

Kotler, P., Armstrong, G., Wong, V. and Saunders, J. (2008). *Principles of Marketing,* 5th European edn, FT Prentice Hall, London.

Lloyds TSB Bank PLC (2011). *Current Accounts – Welcome to your Islamic Account* [on-line] Available at: **http://www.lloydstsb.com/media/lloydstsb2004/pdfs/islamic_account_welcome_pack.pdf** [Accessed 09 May 2012].

Lynch, D. M. (2012). *Data wars: Unlocking the information goldmine.* [on-line] Available at: **http://www.bbc.co.uk/news/business-17682304** [Accessed 04 May 2012].

McCorkell, G. (1997) *Direct and Database Marketing,* Kogan Page, London.

McCorkell, G. (2002). *The Interactive and Direct Marketing Guide,* 3rd edn, The Institute of Direct Marketing, Richmond-upon-Thames.

McDaniel, C., Lamb, C. and Hair, J. (2013). *Introduction to Marketing,* 12th International edn, s.l.:-South-Western, Cengage Learning.

Ofcom (2011). *The Communications Market Report: United Kingdom – A nation addicted to Smartphones* [on-line] Available at: **http://stakeholders.ofcom.org.uk/market-data-research/market-data/communications-market-reports/cmr11/uk/** [Accessed 04 May 2012].

Patron, M. (1994). A Comparison of Four Profiling Techniques. *Journal of Targeting, Measurement and Analysis,* 2(3), pp. 223-32.

Peppers, D. and Rogers, M. (1993). *The One-to-One Future,* Piatkus, London.

Polock, W. (1992). An examination of regression and CHAID and their application for direct marketing. *Journal of Targeting, Measurement and Analysis,* 1(1).

Ranchhod, A. and Gurau, C. (2007). *Marketing Strategies – a Contemporary Approach,* 2nd edn, FT Prentice Hall, Harlow.

Raza, J., Liyanage, J. P., Al Atat, H. and Lee J. (2010). A comparative study of maintenance data classification based on neural networks, logistic regression and support vector machines. *Journal of Quality in Maintenance Engineering,* 16(3), pp. 303–318.

Stone, B. (1996). *Successful Direct Marketing Methods,* 5th edn, NTC Business Books, Chicago.

Stone, M. and Shaw, R. (1988). *Successful Direct Marketing Methods,* Gower, London.

The Pew Forum (2012). *The Future of the Golbal Muslim Population* [on-line] Available at: **http://features.pewforum.org/muslim-population/** [Accessed 09 May 2012].

Thomas, B. and Housden, M. (2011). *Direct and Digital Marketing in Practice,* 2nd edn, A & C Black, London.

CASE STUDY

Segmentation in action

In the past few years software innovations have moved on to reach a key stage for direct marketers. Using software from firms such as SmartFOCUS we now have the ability to conduct relatively advanced analyses of our customer database simply and quickly. Turning such analyses into customer selections, and outputs of names and addresses ready to go, is then a simple matter of a couple of clicks of the mouse.

It is easy to become blasé about these software improvements, but it is important to realise that the effect of this speed and convenience has yet to be fully felt in marketing management. As you follow the example below, picture the scene for direct marketers only 10–15 years ago: they would decide on the need to analyse customer data, contact the IT department, wait two weeks for first results, after poring over these, ask for more analyses, wait another two weeks, decide to select and output customer data anyway as time was short, wait two weeks for selections, and finally move to the campaign itself. . .!

The description below illustrates how times have changed.

Example: A brand manager for a wine merchant wishes to increase sales of champagne to existing customers

Before planning the campaign, she will need to:

● segment the customer base into those who have bought champagne and those who have not

● identify the appropriate target audience for the campaign

Her experience tells her that customers who buy sparkling wine and more expensive wine, such as claret, are likely to also purchase champagne.

Therefore, it is reasonable to assume that those people who buy sparkling wine and claret but have not bought champagne would make a good target group for a campaign.

We can create a Venn diagram of these different customers, and their overlaps, by simply clicking on the customer-product list headings (see Figure 3.7).

We can see from this diagram that 7,269 customers have bought sparkling wine and claret *but not* champagne. This group could be the target audience for the campaign and could be exported as a mailing segment.

This is a simple cross-sell approach, but makes no attempt to profile champagne buyers from scratch. If we wanted to do this we could examine some simple demographic data that should shed light on champagne buyers. Let us choose age, gender, home ownership and income (see Figures 3.8, 3.9, 3.10 and 3.11).

We have now established that, historically, most of our champagne buyers are:

- male
- 36 to 45

- home owners
- earning between £15,000 and £22,500

What we can now do is apply these same criteria to people who have not bought champagne to give us a better target segment for the marketing campaign.

To do this, we will create a Venn diagram of customers matching the above criteria (see Figure 3.12).

The final stage of this operation is to apply these criteria to customers who have *not* purchased champagne. Hence we drop the query *non-champagne buyers* onto the Venn diagram (see Figure 3.13).

We can now see that we have, in the centre segment, 4,254 existing customers who match the criteria of champagne purchasers but have not bought any. By mailing this new group we can expect a higher return than the previous group of claret/sparkling wine buyers, because our target group has been profiled as very similar to champagne buyers.

So far, the brand manager has:

- used assumptions and experience to select a potential target audience for a cross-sell campaign

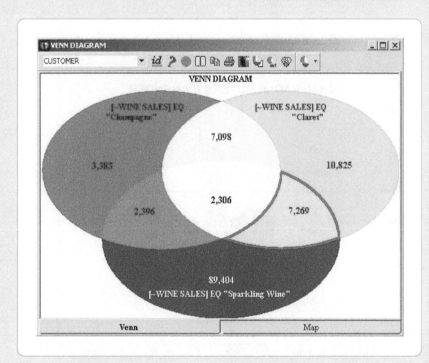

Figure 3.7 **Target audience**

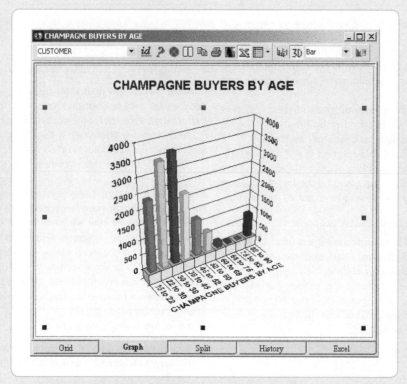

Figure 3.8 Champagne buyers by age

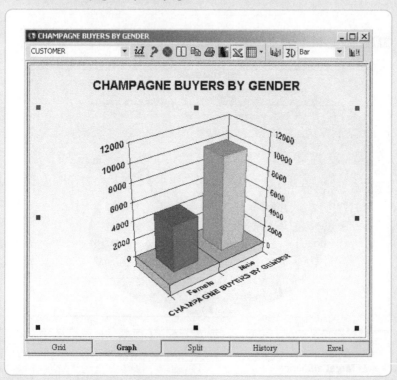

Figure 3.9 Champagne buyers by gender

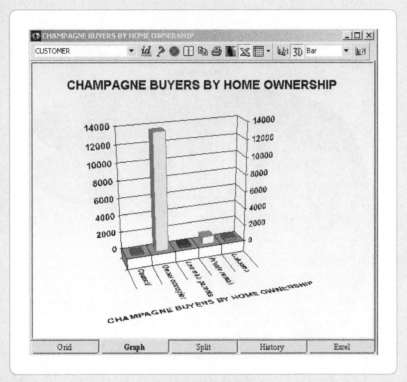

Figure 3.10 Champagne buyers by home ownership

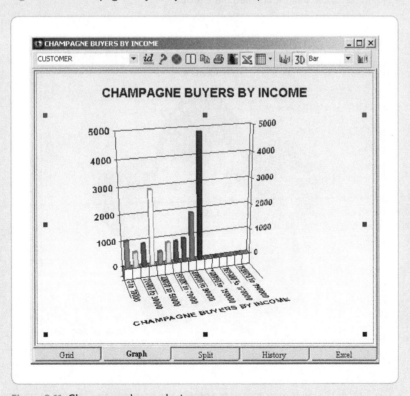

Figure 3.11 Champagne buyers by income

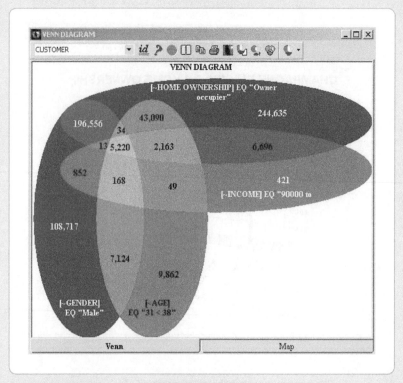

Figure 3.12 5,220 customers match the profile

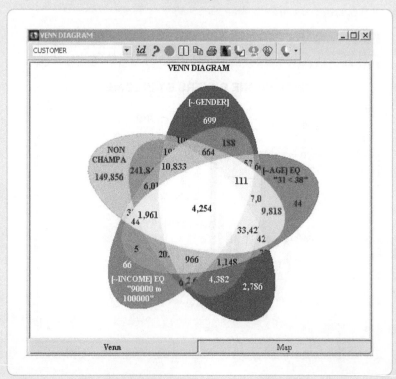

Figure 3.13 4,254 customers match the profile and have not purchased champagne

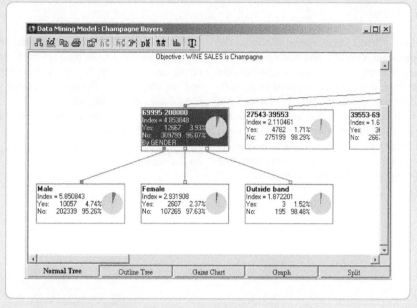

Figure 3.14 CHAID identifies high responding segments

• identified a more targeted audience for the campaign by analysing existing champagne customers against a series of criteria and then matching these criteria to non-champagne customers

At this point the brand manager might export this segment for the marketing campaign, sending the output to the mailing house. However, an alternative may be to refine the target audience further by using a data mining technique such as CHAID to create 'a propensity (or likelihood) to buy' model.

Once more this is now a simple matter with software such as this. An example output (below) is quickly created. Here, CHAID is run on non-champagne buyers.

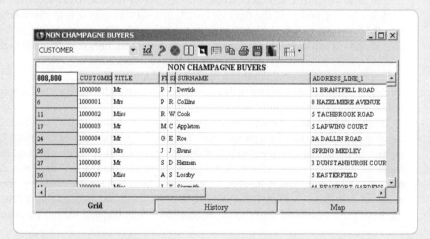

Figure 3.15 Non-champagne buyers

In Figure 3.14, CHAID has identified gender as the next most important variable, and has split the file into males and females. It anticipates a 4.74 per cent response rate from a campaign to males only, compared with 3.93 per cent for both sexes. Should you choose the both sexes option the final stage would involve very simply calling for the names and addresses of those customers who form that very high propensity segment identified by the CHAID model, removing those who had already purchased champagne.

To summarise: with just a few clicks of the mouse, starting from scratch, we have selected a specific list of actual customers who fit our profile of high response, and we are ready to communicate with them. All in five minutes (see Figure 3.15).

For more information about SmartFOCUS see **www.smartfocus.com**.

Source: Adapted from a case study developed by SmartFOCUS Ltd. Reproduced with permission.

CASE STUDY

Tesco Clubcard

Even if only 10 per cent of the hype is true, UK supermarket giant Tesco has still had huge success with its loyalty card Clubcard. Not many humble cards have books written about them: Tesco's direct marketing agency Evans Hunt Scott has teamed up with Clive Humby of analyst DunnHumby (now owned by Tesco) to write the story of Clubcard – such is the interest. Clubcard's fame is now such that it is probably the best known example of direct marketing in British commercial history.

Tesco Clubcard was launched in 1995 under conditions of some secrecy. After a few trials the national launch was carried out in a wave of publicity. Now, every quarter Tesco sends out a statement to its 10 million regular Clubcard users, but only one in every hundred of the recipients will receive the same communication. It now mails 100 000 variants of its quarterly statement – arguably, therefore, getting closer all the time to the idea of 'perfect' 1–1 marketing.

The investment in Tesco Clubcard was driven not by the idea of loyalty from a discount card, but by the power of the data gathered. Not surprisingly, it is in the marketing area that the biggest benefits of the information are being felt. The principle is that Tesco is now able to understand its customers' needs in more detail and, hence, improve the relevance of products, sales promotions and communications to individuals.

Tesco collects data down to single product/item level and can, therefore, link individual products to individual customers. It also collects personal details such as lifestage, household details, occupation and so on, on the joining form.

Tesco quickly realised it was faced with a mountain of data and, in order to cope, it has developed a hierarchy of segmentations. The top level broad segments relate household details, in particular lifestage, to broad shopping habits such as breadth and intensity of shop. So, we have 'single adults', 'urban professionals', 'pensioners' and so on. Shoppers have also been categorised into 'price sensitives', 'foodies', 'heavy category users' or 'loyalists' of particular brands (Mitchell, 2002). For each segment, using FRAC analysis, marketers can assess average spend, frequency of visit, lifetime value, retention rate and similar variables, and then monitor the impact of marketing initiatives on these variables over time.

Further sub-segments could also be identified, based on shopping behaviour. These segments may be described in terms of customers' use of competitor supermarkets as well as Tesco. The lifestage data can lead to detailed tracking of, for example, families, the key target for Tesco. The focus of the analysis covers product groups as well as customer groups. In theory, therefore, Tesco could take any particular product, say milk, and assess penetration, spend and purchase frequency of any of the customer segments against this. For example, a family who fell in the 'high behaviour' category may spend, let us say, over £6 on milk in about four visits each month. Tesco could compare this data with 'external market research' as well as internal profiles that would indicate potential take-up of the product. The outcome may be a list of customers whom the analysis has identified as seeming to be under-purchasing milk compared with a (researched) expected volume. Interestingly, Tesco has learned that it is far easier to move a top shopper to higher levels of spending than it is to get a non-shopper into the store.

The analysts have also carried out detailed cluster analyses that map out relationships between the different product groups. Therefore, a cluster of a particular profile of customers who tend to purchase milk, bread and staples regularly, but only occasionally buy, say, ready meals, could be identified. This series of customer clusters, or segments, may cut across the broad scale top line segments described earlier, to provide a new focus for marketing activity.

The Clubcard is used to communicate more effectively with customers. Promotions are targeted more precisely – for example dog food is targeted at dog owners – using coupons given out at the checkout and with Clubcard statements. These are delivered at the same time to all Clubcard users, four times each year. Executives joke that it is like Christmas four times each year, such is the uplift in traffic.

Stock control, product take-up and comparative store performance are just some of the areas where the data is helping the business. Different stores are arranged differently according to the customer data. Hence, Tesco effectively lets customers decide what each store should stock, fundamentally changing its supply chain from 'push' to 'pull'.

More recently, Tesco now offers specific details of segments of customers, minus names and addresses, plus analyses of direct marketing tests, to its suppliers – provided customers give permission of course. Manufacturers such as Kraft and Procter & Gamble are keen to take advantage of such offers. This, plus Tesco's sales of advertising space in its Clubcard magazine, makes the retailer a source of marketing research and a media owner, as well as a retailer. It also points to possibly increased links with suppliers in the future.

In March 2002, Tesco signed a deal with Air Miles, allowing points from Clubcard to be redeemed for air travel. It saw a 400 per cent uplift in traffic to its website and a surge in Clubcard members, illustrating the continuing power of Air Miles in attracting customers.

Questions

1 Why is the term 'loyalty card' a misnomer?

2 What are the keys to Clubcard's success?

3 How has Clubcard changed Tesco's non-marketing processes?

4 Identify the different segmentation approaches adopted by Tesco. How would you describe its segmentation strategy?

CASE STUDY

Training and Enterprise Councils

Imagine you have set up a small business, let us say importing and distributing software to retailers. What are the characteristics that an outsider would notice about your business? They might find that:

- you lack time – everything is done in a rush
- you focus on selling not buying, therefore you need your suppliers to deliver to you on a plate with no lapses
- you rely on word of mouth a lot, and relish the chance to talk to other small businesspeople
- you do not consult within the company before taking decisions, everything is quick

Small businesses, therefore, like direct marketing. If it can save them time, in particular from possibly unwanted sales visits, it can be an invaluable aid to their business. But they are relying on their suppliers to use direct marketing intelligently. Amongst their suppliers are the Training and Enterprise Councils or TECs.

Although primarily government funded, TECs have a surprising amount of freedom to act. They tend to be limited companies by guarantee. Their aims are to help local businesses (and hence local people) improve their competitiveness by raising the standards of business. This is done through training, education and development initiatives offered to SMEs (small and medium enterprises).

More specifically, the TECs offer:

- help in attaining the Investors in People industry award
- National Vocational Qualifications
- Business Link – access to experienced consultants who may be able to offer advice and help
- access to training of all types – open learning, practical courses
- work experience for job seekers
- in partnership with Chambers of Commerce, membership and networking opportunities

And so on. Asked what they do, Norfolk and Waveney TEC said they 'bring experts and potential together'. In other words, TECs are enabling organisations.

Each of the country's 81 TECs has packaged up various 'products', which they offer to small businesses at prices that are affordable. For example, a course called 'getting your Investors in People award' may be offered at £250. Of course, the TECs compete with private enterprises that are also operating in the training and consultancy markets.

In the past, the TECs have tended to be 'product' driven. Most TECs have a team of salespeople who have concentrated on one of their services. Each product group has tended to be competitive with other groups within the TEC, perhaps not an ideal way of ensuring maximum success for the partnership between TECs and businesses.

More recently, TECs have started to show an interest in database and direct marketing as a way of interacting with businesses. Initially, it was thought that direct communications could just be an effective way of selling their services, and indeed this has proved to be the case. However, most TECs have had the foresight to take this to the next step and begin to record their sales on a customer database. The expertise with which these are deployed varies quite considerably around the country, but it would be fair to say that many TECs still need more help in making full use of their databases.

At a recent national conference of TECs, the following ideas were raised by a consultant for TECs to consider:

- *Membership schemes*. Typical business associations (for example the Chartered Institute of Marketing) offer membership facilities, such as regular information about their sector, chances to go to talks, networking and conferences, and training and consultancy.
- *Profiling and segmentation*. One experienced manager in a chamber of commerce had developed a typology of small businesses according to their attitudes and behaviour to TECs and chambers. He came up with the following segments:

'sole traders' – new businesses that were just starting up

'entrepreneurs' – successful business people who were looking to expand their businesses

'philanthropists' – people who wanted to give something back to the business community

'smash and grab' – businesses that spotted one course they wanted, joined for one year only and then would leave

Other ideas included the potential for loyalty schemes. Recently, TECs had developed fairly extensive websites that the database people knew they should be integrating into their activities.

What was needed was a proper plan, a full database driven programme that would help the TECs' customers meet their needs.

Questions

Develop a strategically driven plan for how each TEC should use its marketing database to best advantage. What other segmentation possibilities are open to them? Remember that you are operating in a business-to-business market.

Using external databases in direct marketing

Introduction

The previous chapter concentrated on how we analyse 'internal' data, on the company's own database, to understand our customers better. In this chapter we will explore the use that direct marketers make of 'external' data, held on large, commercially owned databases. In Chapter 3 we outlined four distinct marketing analyses important to direct marketers. It is the last two of these, 'segmentation by customer profile or customer need', and 'targeting new prospects based on existing customer profiles', that external databases can particularly help with. However, external databases have a key additional benefit that lies outside their analytical capabilities. They are a valuable 'source of lists' of prospects for new market development.

In this chapter we will investigate what external databases are and why they are so useful to direct marketers. The chapter is organised into three main sections as follows:

1 A short introduction describing the industry.
2 The uses that direct marketers make of external databases are analysed. A discussion of the advantages and pitfalls of using these products.
3 The products – external databases – are described in detail.

4.1   Introduction to external databases

The company's own database is an enormously powerful tool, as we saw in the previous chapter. There are, however, occasions when direct marketers could use some help from outside. We may want to add to the data on our existing customers in order to understand their personal characteristics better. If we are expanding into new markets we will want accurate profiles of our intended targets; and best of all, we would like to have a list of 'interested' individuals whom we can contact with an invitation to be a customer of ours.

It is these needs which external databases are in business to meet. External databases consist of records of individuals, available for sale to interested companies. They are split into two main areas: geodemographic products and lifestyle databases.

4.1.1   Geodemographic products

Every ten years in the UK a government-run census is carried out, through which enormous amounts of (geographically based) demographic information are gathered. These data are used by the government for a number of purposes, but are also available for purchase by interested companies. The data are only available in aggregated form, not at individual level, and so are not useful to direct marketers in their raw form.

This is where geodemographic profilers add value. Using techniques such as cluster analysis, they first place households into groups according to their common demographic characteristics: age, social class, size of house and so on. They then take each postcode in the country, and allocate a description to that postcode according to its typical household profile. This is useful information to direct marketing clients, who will buy this data from the profiling company.

4.1.2   Lifestyle databases

If you have ever completed a product registration form after buying some music equipment, or filled out a questionnaire sent to your home in return for some vouchers, you are probably recorded on a lifestyle database. These operators collect their data using these methods, and together hold millions of records of individuals and their contact details.

The data held vary from attitudinal and opinion data to lifestyle data, but the most important category is product purchase data, details of individuals' current product and brand preferences across a range of sectors of interest to direct marketers. As well as providing lists of individuals for contact, the data are also of great use as a research and segmentation tool.

A complete description of all these products is given later in this chapter, but first we will take a closer look at how direct marketers make use of this data.

4.1.3   The Electoral Register

Anyone who wants to vote in any elections held in the UK must be on the Electoral Register (The Electoral Commission, 2012a). The details you are required to provide for inclusion on the Register include your name, address, nationality and age (The Information Commissioner's Office, 2012). It used to be possible to buy the entire Electoral Register for the United Kingdom; in other words the name and address of every adult registered to vote was available to marketers. Then in November 2001 the 'Case of Brian Beetson Robertson v City of Wakefield MDC and Secretary of State for the Home Department' changed that.

Mr Robertson argued that his right to vote should not result in any commercial organisation having the right to contact him for marketing purposes. The courts agreed and, as a result, two versions of the Electoral Register were created: the full version and the edited version. Everybody's details appear on the full version, but it is possible to opt out of the edited version when registering. The full register is used for elections, preventing and detecting crime, and checking applications for credit (The Electoral Commission, 2012b). A copy of this version is available in public libraries (The Information Commissioner's Office, 2012). The edited register is available for general sale and can be used for commercial activities such as marketing (The Electoral Commission, 2012b).

With the level of sophistication of other external databases commercially available, the data on the Electoral Register may not be gold dust to marketers, but it is certainly silver dust. However, let us consider what uses this gold and silver may be put to, and look at the more useful and lucrative alternatives.

4.2 What are external databases used for?

Direct marketers use external databases for two major applications: first, adding data to existing internal records in order to understand their existing customers better; second, using lists selected from the external database to contact new prospects directly. (External data is also used for retail site location analysis, but this lies outside the scope of this book.)

A well-established process is used by the database operators with their direct marketing clients to help them achieve this. We call this process 'profiling'.

4.2.1 Profiling using external databases

The following process, which is based on still relevant research (Stone, 1996), outlines how geodemographic/lifestyle operators merge their data with clients' records and what is done with this new information.

Step 1

A 'matching process' is undertaken between the client's internal database and the external geodemographic or lifestyle database. 'Matching' means letting the computer identify the common names/postcodes held on both the internal database and the external database.

If a geodemographic system is used, then postcodes are matched; however, if a lifestyle system is used, then individual names and addresses are matched.

Step 2

The effectiveness of matching external lifestyle databases with a given customer file will vary massively depending on factors such as whose lifestyle database you use, how well your database has been structured and maintained, how niche your product is and so on.

As an example, Acxiom UK claim that their Infobase Lifestyle Universe can deliver lifestyle, demographic and behavioural data across 90 per cent of UK households. However, some of this data has been imputed (or derived, based on assumptions drawn from other data variables) and the coverage of known data ranges between 5 and 61 per cent, depending on the variable used (Acxiom Corporation, 2012a).

Infobase has 330 data variables you can ask to have appended to your database, ranging from the basics (what TV region you are in, how many children are in the house and their ages, type and age of building) to the more social aspects (what papers are taken, what hobbies are enjoyed, what type of holiday is the norm) and others in between (Acxiom Corporation, 2012b). Other lifestyle databases are available.

For geodemographic systems, a complete overlay is achieved, based on 'postcode'. So, a 100 per cent match should be achieved at this level of data.

For those postcodes or individuals that are matched, 'the existing customer record is then expanded to include the outside data'. So, you provide the external database owner with a list of names and addresses, they return your list with details of (for instance) the number of cars in the household, when the owners plan to replace them and when their insurance is due.

There are then two main uses for these data (see Figure 4.1).

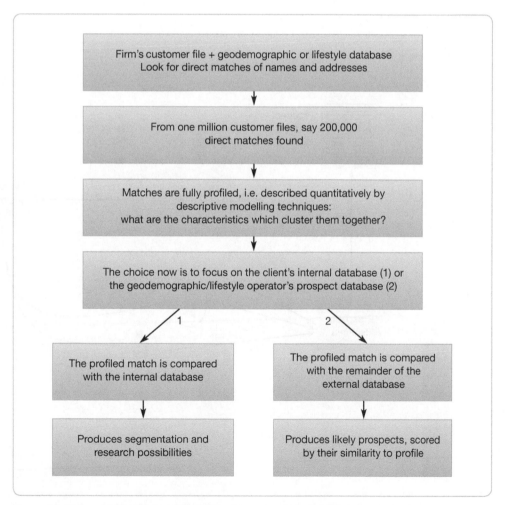

Figure 4.1 Using profiling to identify prospects on an external database

Step 3

If the data is to be used for 'researching/segmenting existing customers', then the external data supplier's outputs are clustered descriptions of the client's customers according to their geodemographic or lifestyle attributes. In other words, data will be appended (based on known or imputed external data) to allow you to identify common attributes and patterns in the data that can be used to identify customer segments, or the differences between customers and non-customers.

The external database company will offer a bespoke service to clients; that is, they will go back to their 'raw data', not aggregated clusters they use to sell to new entrants, and use this raw data to build up clusters that are relevant to the client's products.

Step 4

If the output is 'new market targeting' of prospects, the output is different. The variables that occur most frequently among the customers who are profiled will be used to select 'lookalikes' from the remainder of the lifestyle database, and a prospect list will be generated, ranked in order of greatest similarity to existing customers (Sleight, 1993) (see Figure 4.2).

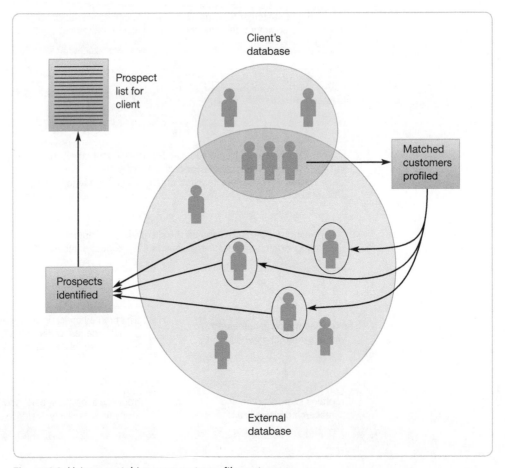

Figure 4.2 **Using a matching process to profile customers**

4.2.2 Using external data for market research/segmentation

A typical situation that many firms face with customer data is that, although they have the basic transaction data 'what customers have bought', they may not know very much at all about the customers themselves. In particular, they may not know 'why' their customers buy from them and what customers use their products for. General marketers would use market research to overcome this.

However, direct marketing provides an alternative in the shape of the external database. By adding geodemographic and/or lifestyle data to our customers' records, we can understand how these attributes drive our customers' purchase behaviour. Once we have added geodemographic and lifestyle data to our internal databases, we have enhanced customer profile data, which can be quantitatively analysed. We can begin to understand what might be driving our customers' behaviour.

Lifestyle data or market research?

The pros and cons of these two approaches to gaining additional intelligence on customers and prospects are neatly summed up by Table 4.1:

Table 4.1 Conventional research vs research based on lifestyle surveys

Conventional research	Research based on lifestyle surveys
High cost. Even at the minimum level required for statistical significance, conventional research is expensive; extended to any substantial scale it becomes extremely expensive, with costs closely related to number of persons surveyed.	**Low cost.** The methodology is cheap: the design, printing and distribution of questionnaires, the data capture of response, and the analysis of results, should give a cost measured in pence per respondent.
Use restricted to research applicants. The statistical tabulations produced from this kind of research are its sole output: the rules of the Market Research Society positively forbid the attribution of names to research data.	**Respondents can be mailed.** The chief by-product of the whole process is a potentially valuable list of self-submitted names and addresses, with a wide range of information about each.
Inflexible. The methodology requires 20:20 vision at the time of designing the questionnaire: it really is not practicable to look at the response and discover some interesting further question one would like to explore with certain respondents.	**Ease of follow-up.** Because this list of names is available, any kind of follow-up suggested by the results of the original questionnaire is simple.

Source: Webber, 2002, pp. 3.5–18.

Webber goes on to identify a major weakness in using this approach: it is rare that lifestyle databases will generate a representative sample of anything definable because people who do not complete lifestyle surveys are not included (Webber, 2002, pp. 3.5-19)!

Exhibit 4.1 Lifestyle data as research: super-concentrated Persil

When replacing its dilute liquid detergent with a new super-concentrated formula, it was business critical for Persil to communicate the benefits of this greener and more convenient alternative to its core customer base. Using Acxiom's Personicx data profiling solution to identify target groups for tailored communications allowed OgilvyOne to extend its campaign reach to a wider audience, while only targeting recipients to whom the campaign was relevant.

Personicx data was used to profile responders to previous marketing campaigns. Based on this Personicx profiling, OgilvyOne was then able to identify new data that had similar characteristics to the existing respondent list. Twenty four different segments were identified, and these were then sent a communication tailored to that segment.

As well as extending the reach of the campaign by 10 per cent, Personicx helped identify which types of household were most responsive, which provided an important insight to help with future marketing activities.

Source: Acxiom UK (2011).

Advantages of market research

Market research does have its advantages over the lifestyle database route:

- Accuracy of data
- Representativeness

Accuracy of data

Market researchers argue that the anonymity which they guarantee allows them to elicit more accurate, in-depth data that gives a truer understanding of respondents' motives and deeply held beliefs. They, therefore, claim that their data are more accurate than lifestyle data.

Exhibit 4.2 Watch out for the Suggers and Fruggers

Sugging is 'Selling Under the Guise of Research', Frugging is 'Fundraising Under the Guise of Research'. Some unscrupulous companies will approach prospects and pretend to be market research companies. They will then gather the individuals' names, addresses and details about them, which are relevant to the company's products. At the end of the questionnaire, they may ask, 'Are you interested in a sales call from/making a donation to. . .?'

This activity is frowned upon by the Market Research Society, because it feels it is giving legitimate market research a bad name. It feels there is now increasing suspicion from the public when approached by genuine researchers that they are about to be 'sold to', and this is leading to higher refusal rates.

Clearly there is some danger that lifestyle questionnaires could be seen as 'sugging'. The lifestyle database operators completely refute this, and say that they make their purpose perfectly clear. Indeed, lifestyle database questionnaires do not state their purpose as market research, and make it quite clear that respondents may be followed up according to the data they submit.

However, there has been long running tension at times between market researchers and lifestyle database operators. This goes back decades. In 1994, a caricature comparison between market researchers and lifestyle database operators showed the former being regarded as 'unworldly, corduroy wearing types', whereas the latter were 'sharp suited salesmen'!

(Sleight, 1994).

Representativeness

Lifestyle databases consist of individuals who have selected themselves by their interest in filling in the survey – arguably because they are attracted by the rewards of coupons, prize draws and so on. Market researchers assert that this means the database is only representative of people who are interested in such rewards, and does not reflect the population as a whole.

However, both Webber and Sleight make the point that market research and lifestyle databases can be collaborative rather than competitive and, as we shall see later, combination products are becoming more the norm.

In explaining how the two disciplines can collaborate, Webber notes that one of the hardest problems in market research is knowing in advance what questions to ask. External data can provide a vital 'initial' perspective that can subsequently inform what questions to ask in research. By adding lifestyle data to our internal data, trends in lifestyle and demographics can be picked up, and theories developed as to how these characteristics impact on customer behaviour. This can save on expensive market research profiling exercises and give a sharper focus to supplementary research.

Using external data as a basis for segmentation

The use of internal database information to segment customers according to their value to us, and their product needs from us, has already been discussed **(Chapter 3)**. External databases can potentially add a lot of value to the second of these, the 'analysis of customers' product needs'.

This is because product needs are often 'related to', or even 'caused by', lifestyle or demographic factors. For example, age is a key factor in driving the take-up of financial products such as mortgages, loans and pensions. Therefore, it is possible to use lifestyle and geodemographic variables, such as age, to act as 'surrogates' when segmenting according to product needs.

However, internal data is still more valuable than external data. Logic surely dictates that it is more valuable to know how often a customer buys from you, when they last bought, what they paid and what it was for (see FRAC analysis) (Chapter 3) than it is to know what sort of house they live in, or if they have a dog or a cat. There is general agreement on this key principle by direct marketers:

> **It is usually the case that a company's internal data is more valuable than external data in determining customer behaviour.**

In summary, external data may sometimes be used when firms find it difficult to extract their internal data; when they want to append more data on to their own customers; and when they want to obtain a wider picture of how consumers are using competitor products as well as their own.

Exhibit 4.3 Lifestyle data to drive segmentation: *Bike Magazine*

The publisher of *Bike Magazine,* EMAP, needed to increase subscriptions and news-stand circulation of the title. *Bike Magazine* was the UK's second best selling monthly motorcycle magazine. To help its analysis, lifestyle data was added to EMAP's existing database. To the publisher's surprise, two distinct magazine readers became apparent. The first was the typical young biker, but the second was an older, more affluent 'born again' biker who perhaps lived a conventional life with a steady job and family, but rode motorbikes as an exciting hobby to stand out from the crowd.

Subsequently, the product itself was adjusted to take this new segment into account. Targeting new customers was based on profiles of both segments, using lifestyle databases as lists (see the following section).

4.2.3 External databases as lists of new market prospects

Taking the hard work out of prospecting

As long ago as 1987, *Maximarketing* (Rapp and Collins, 1987) succinctly described what is still a key benefit of external databases:

> 'A public database has done most of the hard work for you. It has identified by name and address the people most worth bothering with, that use your product or service category, but do not use your brand; or those who have exactly the lifestyle that your product calls for.'

So far in this chapter we have considered external databases as something we can use to help us profile our own database, and/or can be used for segmentation and/or research purposes. However, there is a much simpler use for external data too, and that's simply to buy lists of people who sound like our customers for prospecting purposes. The sheer volume of list brokers in the UK becomes evident by just Googling 'Commercial Database' (in quotes), and this, in turn, is indicative of the fact that this application of external databases is far more prevalent than that we have so far discussed. If we compare the use of commercially available lists by direct marketers with the methods employed by general marketers to acquire new customers, we find direct marketers have major efficiency advantages, as shown in Table 4.2.

Making the decision to use profiled external lists

The economics of the purchase of data to use as prospect lists are clear: it is worth doing so provided the gain in response from better targeting outweighs the costs of purchasing the external data. Here the devil is in the detail, so let us have a look at the example calculation in Exhibit 4.4.

The costs in Exhibit 4.4 have been simplified for the purpose of illustration, and relate to the use of traditional direct mail. In such a case, if the economics of the exercise do not add up, the miracle that is e-mail may well change that situation by reducing your costs considerably: but that is covered in another chapter!

Now that we understand the economics of prospect lists, we can analyse the extent to which our external list options can help with new market development.

Table 4.2 Comparison of general marketing and direct marketing operations for the attraction of new markets

General	Direct
Segmentation and targeting aided by market research	Segmentation established by understanding of existing customers, overlaying external data. Profiles based on large volumes of data
↓	↓
Targeting operationalised by media/retail choice	Targeting achieved by exact match of accurate profiles to well-understood new market profiles
↓	↓
Brand building and communication to a mass audience: awareness and interest built up	Communication goes precisely to profiled prospects. Can be segmented according to type of prospect, e.g. competitor buying could be acknowledged
↓	↓
Sales promotion in store or in pack: mostly wasted on existing customers	Sales promotions directed to definite prospects only

	Existing products	**New products**
Existing markets	Market Penetration	Product Development
New markets	Market Development	Diversification

Figure 4.3 Ansoff's Matrix

Prospect lists: strategic options

Ansoff's Matrix (Ansoff, 1957) of strategic options shows a number of different ways in which lifestyle and geodemographic data can be used for market penetration, new market targeting, or new product development. See Figure 4.3.

Lists of competitor customers based on purchase behaviour: market penetration

This category consists of prospects identified as known users of a direct competitor's products. Prime prospects for brand switching offers, these prospects can be contacted by you without your competitors knowing what you are doing; the ultimate in stealth marketing!

For example, 50 local Mazda dealers used lifestyle data to write to drivers of rival BMWs, Audis and Mercedes. They also wrote to prospects who were not claimed drivers of such cars, but whose profiles suggested they could be.

Lists of prospects from profiles of existing customers: market penetration

This is the core business of external database operators. The majority of their revenue is obtained from clients who use the matching, profiling and targeting process described earlier. These profiles are used to identify people, or postcodes, on the external database whose descriptions match the profiles generated, the output being a list of names and addresses of prospects.

Exhibit 4.4 Example calculation: the costs versus benefits of a demographic system

Let us look at a credit card company trying to target owners of 'gold' credit cards, as they have been identified as the best prospects for a new card the company is launching.

The market size for gold cards was found to be 700,000. On matching a sample of these people to a typical geodemographic system, the company found that one group called 'ageing professionals' gave an 'index' of 300 compared with the national average of 100. In other words, the penetration of gold card holders was three times greater in these clusters.

The company decided to mail the affinity card offer to all households in the postcodes that fitted the 'ageing professionals' cluster description. This represented 250,000 households (hidden within which are 15,000 gold card holders: the company's primary target). Accordingly it purchased a list from a geodemographic operator and mailed its offer.

The results were as follows:

Response from gold card holders is 5%:

5% of 15,000 = 750 responses

Non-gold card response is 0.5%:

0.5% of 235,000 = 1175 responses

Total response = 1925

Costs:

250,000 mailers @ £400 per thousand = £100,000

Geodemographic list @ £150 per thousand = £37,500

Total costs = £137,500

Therefore, it cost the company £71 to obtain one new customer.

What would happen if the company decided not to bother with the geodemographic profiling and just mailed randomly?

Assume it mails 250,000 again, but this time randomly chosen from the electoral roll. There are 5,000 gold card holders among this random group.

This time the results were:

Response from gold card holders is 5%:

5% of 5,000 = 250 responses

Non-gold card response is 0.5%:

0.5% of 245,000 = 1,225 responses

Total response = 1,475

Costs:

250,000 mailers @ £400 per thousand = £100,000

Electoral roll @ £75 per thousand names = £18,750

Total costs = £118,750

Therefore, it cost the company £80 to obtain one new customer by mailing randomly.

Source: Adapted from Fairlie, R. (1998) *The Direct Marketing Guide*, IDM, Teddington.

This is an example of the calculation that needs to be made by a marketer wishing to use geodemographic profiling for new customer acquisition.

The same calculation process can be used to estimate the return from investing in a lifestyle data list. Here, the costs per thousand names may be higher. If, say, actual gold card carriers were requested, this list could be over £200 per thousand to buy. Responses would, however, most likely be higher than those of a profiled list, which only gives a higher probability of targeting the right prospects.

Pura Foods was looking for new customers to purchase its Light Touch sunflower oil product. The company profiled its existing customers, and used this profile to target new customers from a lifestyle database. With a mix of offers, including money-off coupons, it generated an impressive 19 per cent response from a direct mail campaign.

Banks and building societies use lifestyle profiling to help target campaigns to recruit prospects for their branch network salespeople to follow up. If a typical customer is found to be (say) aged 35 to 64, married, and with a known interest in financial products, then that becomes the base profile for searching for lists of just such people. Regional targeting of such prospects can be carried out using, among other sources, external lists from a lifestyle database and, by doing so on a monthly basis, it becomes possible to generate a drip-feed of leads for the salesforce.

External data used for marketing new products: product development

When launching a new product, lists of the appropriate target market may be obtained as supplements to the internal database. In Ansoff's Matrix this is the existing market, so we have the benefit of knowing their profile reasonably well. For example, most of the major car manufacturers are developing alternative fuelled vehicles; and the market for these will almost certainly reveal itself to be a subset of their existing customer base. Should it be a subset that is too small to be able to offer sufficient development potential, the first port of call will be external lists, with the required profile description ready to go!

Exhibit 4.5 Launching a new product: the Co-operative Bank Visa gold card

This new product was the UK's first gold card that was guaranteed free of annual charges for life. The target audience was well defined: an income above £25,000 p.a., homeowners, aged 25+ who had an existing credit card.

Four different sources were tried for a direct mail approach. The top performing list gave a 7 per cent response. This mailer was rolled out to 300,000 prospects, achieving 21,000 responses.

A new type of customer: market development

Although the majority of business for external databases consists of lists based on existing customer profiles, some business has also been generated from clients pursuing a new market development strategy. Here, a new profile may be built up, perhaps from market research initially, or by adapting the existing customer profile obtained from internal and external data.

One such example of this approach was an old campaign by Croft Original (see Exhibit 4.6) with a lifestyle database firm NDL, now renamed and part of Acxiom.

We now have a complete understanding of how direct marketers use external databases. Our final task is to complete the description of the products themselves: who are the main players in the business, and what are their products?

Exhibit 4.6 New market targeting: The National Trust

Marketers at the National Trust, which manages 300 historic properties throughout Great Britain, were acutely aware of their organisation's stuffy image and limited appeal, mainly to the over fifties. They decided to do something about it by positioning the Trust as the gateway to a wide variety of experiences for all ages, including children.

Three target groups were identified: 'Explorer Families' (ABC1 families seeking a quality day out together), 'Out and About' (those looking for outdoor relaxation, adventures and social opportunities) and 'Curious Minds' (people who like exploring and discovering history).

Media was selected by looking at what previously worked for the trust in general terms, then finding more specific sub-media based around what would be seen by the target audience.

The number of people visiting National Trust properties increased by 16 per cent and memberships grew by almost 18 per cent. In an opinion survey, 70 per cent said their view of the Trust had improved. Encouraged by the results, the National Trust now has an aim of increasing memberships by a further 25 per cent to five million by 2020.

Source: Adapted by the author. This case study first appeared in the Chartered Institute of Marketing magazine, *The Marketer* 2012.

4.3 External databases explained

Both geodemographic and lifestyle databases are now described under the following headings: 'product overview' and 'how the products are created'.

4.3.1 Geodemographic databases

Product overview

There is a British saying that sums up geodemographic products: 'birds of a feather flock together'. The premise is that similar people have a tendency to live near one another. It is not difficult to picture this: consider two people, one very rich, and the other poor. The rich person is far more likely to settle down near other people who are in a similar financial position, and the poor person likewise. What drives this is our desire to associate with people similar to ourselves. Humans have a strong basic need to form into groups, and we feel most comfortable in groups of like-minded, socially similar people. What this means is that where we live is a predictor of what we buy. As one senior practitioner of CACI puts it: 'Without ever having met or heard of somebody, we aim to predict likely spending, ownership of goods, readership, and reactions to offers – and get it right!'

Geodemographic profiling suggests there are a number of factors that will be common to neighbourhoods. One would expect that our income, the size of our families, our stage of life and so on, could be predicted by where we live. But the profilers have found that it is also our interests, lifestyle and psychographic variables, such as our social image – how we want others to see us – that are predicted by where we live. These findings are useful to direct marketers: geodemographic, attitudinal and lifestyle traits often 'explain' what we buy.

We cannot take this 'birds of a feather' premise too far. You only have to ask yourself, 'Hang on, to what extent am I like my neighbour in personality? Do we really feel the same way about things, do the same things at weekends and have the same amount of expendable income?' Probably not to the extent one might imagine on first reading the above paragraph. It is important to remember that the basis of these products is in descriptions of 'groups of people', not individuals.

Therefore, there is no guarantee that a postcode profile will be accurate for a particular household within that postcode. If we were to market to a postcode assigned 'affluent blue collar', we would still be approaching individuals within that area who are, say, college students or unemployed older people.

Geodemographic products provide a 'statistical probability' that people living in a described area are more likely than average to fit that description. In other words, in the absence of perfect information, you are better off using these products to target prospects than relying on random chance. Geodemographic operators will give you scores that reflect the extent to which the chosen postcodes fit the descriptions.

Interestingly, it has been commented that all of the geodemographic systems are better at locating areas of poverty than affluence (Fairlie, 1992). Fairlie asserted that they are also better at broad descriptions of geographical areas (of a kind invaluable to retailers or marketers to whom geography is important) than they are at picking out individuals for new market acquisition in direct marketing. This conclusion may be disputed by the operators themselves, who will claim that many direct marketers have had great success in new prospect targeting using geodemographics.

Exhibit 4.7 **Sparrows of a feather . . .**

Poorer people 'flock together' more than well-off people do. In other words, there is clearer discrimination against the average when identifying areas with low incomes than there is in high-income areas.

Geodemographic industry structure

The major players in the UK are CACI and Experian. In recent times Experian has launched its Mosaic product across the world. The first geodemographic product released in this country was CACI's ACORN (A Classification Of Residential Neighbourhoods). To show how the industry has developed, Exhibit 4.8 gives a summary of the early history of UK geodemographics.

How the products are created
Sources of data in geodemographic systems

The core data source of all these systems is the census. Each operator then adds value to these data using sources such as the electoral roll, credit referencing data, market research, mail-order trading data and County Court Judgments.

The census is carried out every ten years, in years ending with '1'. Traditionally, it consists of a paper based questionnaire sent to the entire population, though the 2011 version could also be completed on-line for the first time ever. Each time the census runs it is slightly different, reflecting the changes in society as a whole and what the government (who run it) wants to know about us. Returning the form is a legal requirement but, typically, only about 94–96 per cent of households actually do return the census, despite the risk of a £1,000 fine for failing to do so. This return rate is in line with international standards for such censuses.

In 2011, the census consisted of 14 household level questions (a total of 365 possible answers because most questions had more than one potential response); 43 individual level questions for up to six people per house (6×146 possible responses) and four questions about each of three visitors per household. . . in other words, it contained a lot of questions!

Contrary to popular belief, the census does not 'provide' data at the individual level, although it does, as explained, 'collect' data at an individual level. Data is reported in units of geography called Output Areas; there are 175,434 such Areas, 80 per cent of which contain between 110 and 139 households (Office for National Statistics, 2012a). Only after 100 years will data be made available with names attached.

Table 4.2 illustrates how UK postcodes are built up from the basic postcode unit, and where output areas fit into this arrangement.

Given that the census data is published at output area (OA) level, but the most useful output for marketers of this sort of data is the postcode level, one of the tasks for geodemographic operators is to represent the source data at postcode level. Fortunately, output areas are built largely from postcodes (Office for National Statistics, 2012a). This has some significant implications for the creation of neighbourhood segmentation.

Perhaps the most significant downsides to the census data are that the census only takes place every ten years and analysis of the data prior to release is a mammoth undertaking.

Experian's Mosaic, a typical geodemographic product, sources 38 per cent of its data from the census. In the decade between censuses, they produce current-year estimates by utilising its other data sources to track change in key census variables (Experian Limited, 2010).

Since at least the run up to the 1991 census, the inclusion of a question has been debated and left out as being too sensitive to ask. And yet we are asked to give that data when we apply for even the smallest of loans or a credit card, and happily do so! As a result, 'income' is inferred for an OA, using other variables as surrogates: house size, occupation types, education.

Seven new questions are included: two about the household (number of bedrooms and type of central heating), and five about the residents (passports held, national identity, year of entry to the UK and intended length of stay for recent arrivals, main language and whether or not they have a second residence) (ESRC Census Programme, 2012). Go to **www.statistics.gov.uk** for more details and lots of free information on the census.

Creating the geodemographic product

There are two major analytical processes that need to be applied to the raw census data. First, the initial 1,200 or so possible variables need to be 'reduced' to the key independent variables that are seen as driving consumer behaviour. Second, the areas need to be 'combined' into segments that the variables tell us will contain similar people.

Many of the analytical techniques that were used to build the 2001 Mosaic date back to a study that was commissioned by the Heath government in 1975, to examine ways of combating inner city deprivation in Lambeth, Birmingham and Liverpool (Webber, 2003).

Table 4.3 How postcodes are built up

Postal type	Example	No. in UK	No. of households in unit
Total delivery points		27.5 million	
Postal areas	B (Birmingham)	124	220,000
Postal district	B31	3000	9,000
Postal sector	B31 4	9000	3,000
Postcode	B31 4AN	1.8 million	15

The problem with a lot of the census data is that it exhibits co-linearity; in other words, some variables are associated with each other. One can imagine that, for example, 'family size' and 'number of cars' are associated with each other. There is a need to ensure that independent variables are associated 'with each other' as little as possible. Factor-analysis techniques achieve this. The data is then reduced to between 40 and 100 variables.

To combine the records into segments that reflect the differences between areas, an exploratory, descriptive technique is needed. Cluster analysis has been found to be ideal for this job. A good segmentation is one which maximises the differences between segments, while minimising the differences between individuals within the same segment. This is exactly what cluster analysis does in a logical, quantitative way. See above for more on cluster analysis (Chapter 3).

Geodemographic products

Each of the operators uses slightly different data, analysed using some different techniques and, hence, the outputs – the products – are slightly different. However, all products consist of major clusters and sub-groupings described to give an indication of the type of people within them. To give you a flavour of these products, CACI's Acorn is described in Figure 4.4. Acorn consists of 162 Acorn types, aggregated into 18 groups and six categories (five of which are shown in Figure 4.4, the sixth being "Not private households" (Source: Acorn CACI, 2013). You may wonder whether Acorn categories are over segmenting the market – why not just have 'rich' and 'poor'? The geodemographic data sellers argue that in some product areas it is the 'clever capitalists' who represent the best market, in others it is the 'chattering classes', while the 'prosperous pensioners' and 'rising materialists' can also head the league in a number of product areas (Webber, 2003).

One of the most fascinating underpinning realities of geodemographics is that geography itself is important. It has been pointed out (Webber, 2003) that, if we take two families of matching income and age, education, employment structure and ethnicity, these two families will display very different spending patterns according to the type of neighbourhood in which they live. Put differently, a typical postman in Bradford is different from a typical postman in Bristol. This was looked at in detail by Elliston Allen as long ago as 1968: as examples he pointed out that (not surprisingly) not much Lancashire cheese is eaten in Yorkshire; that Midlanders prefer sourer beer while Londoners are more fashion conscious. Another famous example, showing that neighbourhoods could be seen to be a significant discriminator, was the comparison of the *Sunday Telegraph* and the *Observer* readership profiles, the latter being far more heavily skewed towards high status, inner city neighbourhoods.

Geodemographic products are important internationally: Experian's Mosaic was first built not for the UK but for the Netherlands in 1985. This was because Experian's then parent company, Great Universal Stores (GUS), wanted a marketing tool to set up an equivalent to Experian within its Dutch mail-order business, Wehkamp. (Experian was demerged from GUS in 2006 (Experian Limited, 2012a) and has since gone on to be a constituent of the FTSE 100 companies in its own right (The London Stock Exchange, 2012)). Since the 1986 launch of UK Mosaic, Experian has built and updated classifications for a further nine European markets, and eight more countries outside Europe including the US Mosaic, Brazil and China.

There are other dimensions to geodemographic products. CACI have developed a system (MONICA) for calculating the age of individuals within each postcode. The systems are based on the idea that age is linked to first names. There are a lot of Chloes and Jacks who were born since the 1990s; but not many parents call their children Violet or Herbert any more, although there are often cyclic trends, so it is important not to be too dogmatic here! Even then, CACI has been a bit clever in its approach: if a household has Jack living with Doris and Ian, there is a good chance that Jack and Doris are married and Ian is their middle-aged son (those being the current approximate ages of people born when such names were popular). If Herbert lives with Ian and Amanda, the same logic improves the chances that he is the father of either Ian or Amanda. CACI has identified 13,000 first names, which it obtains from the electoral roll, and uses its system, MONICA, to predict age. It is not something they actively push as a stand-alone product (it is a bit hit and miss on its own) but, in conjunction with other data sets, it gives a little extra insight.

Building up an individual profile

Figure 4.4 shows how geodemographics can build a complete picture for any name and address. This example comes from Experian.

Figure 4.4 Infographic

4.3.2 Lifestyle databases

Product overview

Lifestyle databases are probably one of the most remarkable developments in marketing over the last 20 years. In the UK, anyone can now go and buy the data that reveals the products purchased, the attitudes, opinions and beliefs and the personal geodemographic data of over 15 million individuals in the country.

It has been reported (Sleight, 1994) that the market research industry has every reason to be concerned with these developments, especially when a company wants to understand simple descriptive data about its customers. Also Experian, then one of the lifestyle data operators, are reported to have correctly predicted the result of the 1992 general election as a narrow Conservative victory. This contrasted with all the major research companies whose polls predicted a clear Labour victory only the day before the election.

We are told (Fairlie, 1992), that lifestyle databases were originally developed by consumer goods manufacturers who were finding conventional advertising and market research methods either inadequate or poor value for money. Indeed, Experian (owners of the Mosaic system discussed in this chapter, and now one of the world's leading marketing information services) was originally set up as a part of Great Universal Stores, the catalogue shopping company who owned Kay and Company and who, since the demerger of Experian in 2006, has gone on to be known as Home Retail Group and encompasses the likes of Argos and Homebase.

Lifestyle databases were introduced into the UK in 1983. Claritas opened its London office in 1985, followed quickly by Customer Marketing Technologies (CMT), with Experian entering the market in 1988. However, it was not until the very late 1980s that Claritas and CMT's databases were sufficiently large to be of use to marketers as lists to rent (Sleight, 1994). Following a period of mergers, takeovers and other acquisitions during the first ten years of this century, the UK market became dominated by Acxiom, Data Locator Group (DLG) and Experian, with Equifax specialising in consumer credit information. More recently Call Credit has also successfully entered this market.

Exhibit 4.8 The changing face of Britain and Europe

The census is only run every ten years and it takes a further 18 months for data to be released. In the time between, data decays and statistical profiles become out of date, which is bad news if, like Experian, you depend on accurate data as your stock-in-trade. So what can you do to overcome such a potentially massive problem?

Experian is able to produce current-year estimates by utilising its other data sources to track change in key census variables (Experian Limited, 2010) and it is by using this great wealth of data all together that they are able to keep an up to date picture of the country and its residents.

Mosaic is Experian's market leading people classification model and its most recent version (2009) draws on over 440 separate variables and 21 billion individual data items to create a rich and detailed picture of modern British society. The classification now includes 15 lifestyle groups, 67 lifestyle types and 141 person types and will be updated every six months to provide a completely contemporary view of UK consumers at person, household and postcode level.

Some of the more significant social trends identified in the new version of Mosaic are likely to be confirmed once 2011 Census data starts to become available, such as the following:

- **Ageing society** There will be an estimated three million people over 55 by 2019 but it must be remembered that there is a distinction between the active and less active phases of retirement.

- **Migration** Britain has an increasingly multicultural and contemporary nature. There are communities where we have seen the growth of mono-cultural enclaves and, by contrast, neighbourhoods which have embraced multiculture through assimilation and integration.

- **Change in household composition** The last ten years has seen a massive rise in single person households. This has created a mismatch between housing supply (typically three bedroom houses built for families) and actual housing needs. A significant trend has been the growth in concentrated student populations, which has fuelled an increase in multi-occupancy households dominated by single people.

- **Marginalisation of rural Britain** A strong rural segment of society has been identified, which has separated itself from creeping urbanisation and materialism. This has emerged as a result of the increasing gentrification of rural communities within commuting distances of large towns and cities, driving country people further into rural Britain.

- **The network society** The UK has grown from 10 per cent to almost 70 per cent broadband coverage since 2003. This massive transformation has brought a range of new social behaviours as people develop on-line social networks to keep in touch with family and friends, recommend products, services and experiences and transact business.

- **Impact of recession** Not everyone has been equally affected by the recession. Those most affected include those who have seen their savings and investments seriously eroded, those who have to support grown-up children financially, and those who (having bought properties in the last few years) now find themselves in often serious negative equity.

Source: Adapted by the author from an Experian press release (Experian Limited, 2009).

How the products are created

The whole basis of lifestyle database data is different from that of geodemographic databases. Lifestyle databases use data collected at the 'individual' level, obtained from commercially operated surveys, or product registration forms filled in by individuals who choose to take part.

Four broad categories of data are collected by lifestyle companies (Reynolds, 1993):

- Name and address information
- Data relating to the purchase of products and services, known as 'lead-to-purchase' data
- Demographic and socio-economic information
- Values and lifestyle (VALS) information

Clients can also add sponsored blocks of questions to the surveys, and the data obtained from these questions is then passed to the sponsoring client, usually with a period of exclusivity built in. For example, cinema goers can be identified by the appropriate questions, and a list of cinema goers, with all their lifestyle information, can be built up.

> ### Exhibit 4.9 Lifestyle databases: what data do they collect?
>
> Which toothpaste do you use? What books do you buy? Have you got a DVD player? Do you eat out a lot? Do you smoke? Which brands of cigarette? Do you have a pet? What about your financial products: credit cards, PEPs, life insurance?
>
> As an example, a 2003 Consodata survey contained 129 questions in 14 separate sections, ranging from where you do your weekly shop to which charities you support (or may consider supporting) and what car you drive and your purchases of financial services.
>
> Some surveys are branded, like the one above that was presented as a *Sun* Reader Survey and may offer an incentive to complete the questionnaire. These range from a free prize draw to win £10,000 to a free box of chocolates for everybody who leaves a completed survey on their doorstep two days after it was delivered!

VALS data

When the original concept of lifestyle databases was being devised by its founder (Mitchell, 1978) the question that the VALS project was trying to answer was well summed up (Rapp & Collins, 1987): 'Is there not some psychic predilection, based on a prospect's value system, that once uncovered can tell us why people choose one brand over another?' In the intervening quarter of a century, it is possible that nobody has put it better.

VALS looked for a link between product/service consumption and the attitudes held towards benefits sought from the service; activities, interests and opinions; and value systems subscribed to by consumers. Simply put, one might envisage that someone who responds that they regularly go on foreign holidays would be interested in sun cream products.

It is this correlation of psychographic data with product and service behaviour data that provides the bases for some of the lifestyle database analyses.

As we move well into the 21st century, the marketplace is still working to make psychographic segmentation work. There is still interest, but a real breakthrough in profitable data has yet to be made. One initiative involved a consortium of agencies, academics and clients working on examining the decision-making processes for those people on 'the margins of response'. These are the consumers who would respond if they could 'get their bums out of their chairs' as one commentator put it. Such initiatives have yet to reach commercial fruition.

Modern lifestyle databases: 'lead-to-purchase' data

Lifestyle operators have found that so-called 'lead-to-purchase' data is a better predictor of prospect behaviour than psychographic attributes. Lead-to-purchase data is data on consumers' 'actual purchases', past, present and future. Responders are asked questions such as 'Which of the following magazines do you subscribe to?', 'What make of car do you currently own?', and so on. In some categories, consumers are asked when they are next considering a purchase: 'When do you plan to replace your car?'

There is an increasing trend towards collecting this type of data. Says Richard Jackson of R J Data Solutions Ltd: 'there is a move away from providing thousands of names of people who look like they 'should' make a purchase and towards providing a very few names of people who have positively indicated that they are ready to do so in the immediate short term. A list of names of people who said they will consider replacing their car in three or six months may sell for 50p per name; a much smaller list of people who said they are actively looking for a new car now will probably sell for upwards of £5.00 per name. There's less waste (and so less costs) for the marketer, so the increase in price is effectively negated' (Jackson, 2012).

Further than this, the concept of mass collected lifestyle data is taking an interesting turn. Certain comparison websites are collecting data from people who apply for a car insurance quote (to carry the example on) for their ten year old Honda Civic and then passing that data to their partners – say Ford, for example – who will then send the prospect a brochure on their equivalent of the Honda Civic. Any responses (requests for further information or test drives, perhaps) are then passed by Ford to their local dealership network at a price to reflect the immediacy of the lead (Jackson, 2012).

As a summary, we can construct a table that illustrates the hierarchy of prediction power of different data categories. Table 4.4 compares the value of data for a bank looking to maximise response from a credit card offer.

The end product

Over the last 15 years, there has been a flurry of lifestyle product launches in the UK. Claritas (now part of Acxiom) launched the Lifestyle Universe (a list of individuals) in 1997, PSYCL£ (classifies people according to their financial behaviour) in 1998, PRIZM (a post-code based segmentation system) in 2000 and, more recently, Personicx (a suite of segmentation tools analysing the lifestyle and purchasing behaviours of the individuals who live in a given postcode).

As well as Mosaic, Experian launched Pixel (a model to predict behaviour in the business-to-business market) in early 1999, and has gone on to bring in Consumer View (a database of over 40 million contacts offering a view of consumers based on aspects such as hobbies and interests, lifestyle choices and attitudinal data); Delphi for Marketing (comprehensive consumer credit data, covering the credit information of all UK consumers); True Touch (Classifying consumers by their channel preference and promotional orientation); Financial Strategy Segments (insight around the impact of the recent recession on the way consumers utilise financial products and services); and Fashion Segments (a person-level system that describes attitudes towards fashion and brands, and consumer

Table 4.4 Typical predictive power of data categories in lifestyle databases

Data type	Description	Typical score against random mailer response (random mailer = 100)
Entire list	No targeting	100
Demographic only	Profiled against Bank X's own customers	About 180
Attitudinal and lifestyle	Profiled against Bank X's own customers	About 250
Mail order	Upmarket mail order, e.g. 'wine direct operation'; pay by credit card	About 320
Lead-to-purchase data	Responders have credit card	About 400

Notes:
1. The 'scores' are illustrative only and should not be used as precise 'rules'.
2. A 'super responsive' list may be created by merging, say, lead-to-purchase data and attitudinal and lifestyle data, providing profiled credit card holders. This may have a response index of 1000+ against an indiscriminate mailer, but the total list volume is likely to be small.

behaviour related to types of clothes, stores visited and the frequency, value and purpose of shopping trips).

In addition, CACI, Equifax, DLG, Call Credit and any number of other smaller players have all introduced their own proprietary systems. The point to take with you from this is that it is not a lack of data, analysis or insight that is the problem, it is more a case of 'paralysis by analysis': where do you start with all that lot (and more) available to you?!

Each system has used different methods of data collection, and each has collected different data from the others. We need to remember that personal data is dynamic – constantly changing – and, therefore, lifestyle database operators need to spend significant amounts of money to 'stand still', that is to keep their existing data fresh. As mentioned earlier (Chapter 2), it is said that 3.2 million UK households move each year – 4.5 per cent of all UK addresses – and that consumer data decays at a rate where 22 per cent of mail remains undelivered each year (DMA, 2011). Then there is the need to contend with births, deaths, changes of name through marriage/divorce/other reasons, and so on.

A summary of some of the major systems is given in Table 4.5.

Many of the systems discussed in this chapter are based on merged data, known as data fusion products. These interesting products are particularly appropriate for a company wishing to improve its understanding of its marketplace for strategic marketing planning, and they merit a closer look.

Data fusion

Data fusion is the combination of information on individuals or groups using data from different sources to present a more complete picture. This has only really been commercially possible in a truly successful way since the turn of the century. It is an extremely exciting development for the direct marketing industry because it increases its ability to compete with other marketing approaches. The two key areas of data fusion are combining geodemographic and lifestyle data, and combining market research databases with lifestyle data.

Table 4.5 Some major lifestyle databases (in alphabetical order only)

Supplier	Product	Data	Source
Acxiom	Home Lifestyle List Selector	15.8 million people	Completers of Lifestyle Surveys
CACI	Ocean	40 million people	Edited electoral register, surveys, share registrations, mail order data and others
Call Credit	UK Consumer Universe	37.4 million people	Edited electoral register, in-filled with names from lifestyle surveys, transactional data and on-line data collection methods.
Data Locator Group (DLG)	Data Assets	29.3 million people	Survey
Experian	Consumer View	49 million people	Edited electoral register plus Experian's proprietary data assets and other data sources
Scientia Data	Active homes and lifestyles	16.2 million people	On- or off-line product registrations

Note:
Much of the above lifestyle data is inferred using profiling techniques from source data that actually relate to individuals and come from dedicated surveys deployed for that purpose.
Sources: Websites of the various suppliers listed.

Exhibit 4.10 Ensuring the baby boom never ends for mamas and papas

Nursery brand, Mamas & Papas uses data driven marketing techniques to create more fruitful relationships with its customers and generate more value from its customer lifecycle.

Through its website and UK stores, Mamas & Papas offers innovative and high quality prams, pushchairs, nursery furniture, clothes and toys. With a purchasing journey that typically extends from early pregnancy to a child's toddler years, the brand has a time-limited opportunity for customer engagement.

Mamas & Papas has been able to analyse its customer data and map the ideal purchasing journey through pregnancy and beyond by identifying key customer touch points.

With help from Experian, the retailer has been able to build an accurate picture of every customer, understand their purchasing behaviours and segment effectively. This insight then drives the deployment of targeted marketing communications to allow the brand to engage on a consistent basis with parents and grandparents, delivering e-mail marketing campaigns based on different trimesters and targeting special offers at specific groups.

The result has been a significant increase in the value derived from its customer database. Customers opted into marketing communications are worth 50 per cent more than those who are not opted in, and when the due date of the child is known (allowing for even more relevant and accurate communications) Mamas & Papas has found that these customers are worth 130 per cent more in terms of spend than non opted in customers and transact twice as many times. Repeat customers on-line have also increased by 27 per cent year on year.

Rob Jennings, E-Commerce Director at Mamas & Papas commented: 'Through in-depth customer analysis, Mamas & Papas has mapped what the ideal customer purchasing journey is for the expectant and new parent. We can now tailor communications to that journey, enhancing the customer experience by pre-empting their needs and deploying reactive communications whenever a customer deviates from that path to extend and enhance the value of each customer. This is a win for both Mamas & Papas and our customers, in that by providing targeted, relevant communications we are offering improved customer service, whilst also driving the lifetime value of each customer.'

Mamas & Papas and Experian Marketing Services are now extending their relationship to draw on more cross channel data derived from in-store and mobile activity to build a consistent view of individual customers, create more effective customer segmentation and deliver ever more relevant communications.

Source: Adapted by the author from an Experian case study (Experian Limited, 2012c).

Combining geodemographic and lifestyle data

As has been seen above, most lifestyle data providers are now creating their databases by combining a variety of data sources: the Electoral Register, lifestyle surveys, product registrations, census data and shared databases to name but a few.

It is the product of these combined databases that is used to create 'virtual customers', and Figure 4.6 shows how this happens.

Exhibit 4.11 How geo-lifestyle products helped re-elect the world's most powerful man

In the mid 1990s, American political consultants acting for President Bill Clinton were looking for ways to improve his popularity as the US elections loomed. While looking for breakthrough ideas, they began to get increasingly interested in geo-lifestyle products. (American lifestyle categories include 'pools and patios', which describes middle-income, white suburbanite, married people with kids; and 'caps and gowns', which refers to urban intellectuals living near universities. Each of these lifestyles has been identified within the American equivalent of enumeration districts known as 'census tracts'. Each is about as big as a city block.)

Clinton's advisers knew that the key to the election was swing voters, those people in the middle who tended to vote either way at different elections. What were swing voters' characteristics, and how could they be targeted? To answer this, the consultants carried out a large survey of about 10,000 people, asking questions about their lifestyle habits and enabling them to be placed into one of the lifestyle categories. Then the respondents were asked whether they preferred Clinton, Dole or were 'swingers'. From this data, those lifestyle segments corresponding to swing voters could be identified.

It turned out that a significant proportion of swing voters were campers and hikers. As a result, the President was urged to go camping and hiking for his next vacation, in spite of the fact that he allegedly disliked outdoor holidays. In the end, Clinton did venture out on a hiking trip.

Bill Clinton was re-elected in November 1996.

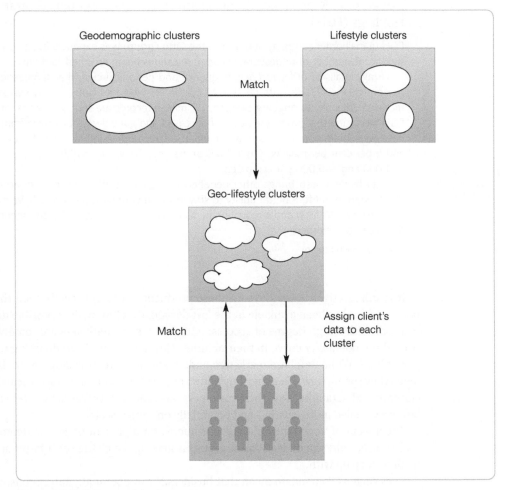

Figure 4.5 Building up virtual consumers

Combining lifestyle and market research information

The attempt to bring together the worlds of marketing research with its depth of data, and database marketing with its breadth of data, has been going on for some time now. Indeed, as far back as 1994 Sleight pointed out that various parties were looking for areas of synergy between market research and lifestyle information (Sleight, 1994). The idea is to develop 'T-cubes' of data that would greatly add to the power of the data to predict our behaviour (see Figure 4.6).

The term T-cube was claimed to have been coined by Greg Ward at Taylor Nelson Sofres (TNS), a market-research firm in the WPP group of companies. Research and database data is either joined (literally looking for duplicates of the same person on both datasets), or fused (linking together data profiles to create 'virtual' profiles that are claimed to predict what is actually happening - see preceding sections of this chapter). However, we need to be clear about what the database will then hold. Some of the data will be the actual, real information gathered from individuals, but other data will be inferred (often referred to as "imputed data") from the models built up by the market research. The latter represents probabilities of the individuals possessing that attribute.

Exhibit 4.12 Reaching customers with certainty – Freemans Grattan Holdings (FGH)

FGH (a mail order company and part of the Otto Group) was experiencing an ongoing and significant number of undeliverable communications being returned to them.

Using details of order recency, frequency and periodical customer suppression figures, Acxiom cleaned FGH's data relating to customers who had bought between six and 48 months earlier. As an ongoing exercise, 1.7 million records are sent to Acxiom for cleaning. FGH has found that prompt removal of deceased and gone away customers from the database saves them 18p per record, which equates to a suppression rate of between 2 per cent and 5 per cent per mailing. On 1.7 million names, this works out as a saving of between £34,000 and £85,000 per campaign.

Data hygiene also brings other benefits, such as a reduction in the instances of fraud due to identity theft, a better ability to stay in touch with customers who have moved (via Acxiom's movers lists) and a reduction in distress caused to relatives by erroneously writing to deceased customers.

Source: Acxiom UK (2010).

It is still relatively early days for these products. It has only really been the computer power, which has been available in the last decade, that has made it possible to apply such methods with a high degree of success; and, as a result, marketers are somewhat lagging behind the possibility curve in their abilities. However, there is no doubting the potential power here. While database marketers understand what their customers are buying, how much they spend, how often they buy and so on, the fusion of marketing research gets them closer to understanding why their customers buy. The factors leading up to the decision to buy are revealed more clearly – and potentially on a mass scale.

The advent of 'social media' (which is almost omnipresent in certain demographics of society, especially the under 30s age group) is making the change ever faster and more difficult to keep up with.

Sites such as Foursquare mean that businesses can potentially target consumers in real time based on proximity. The ability to 'like' a product, service or company on Facebook can

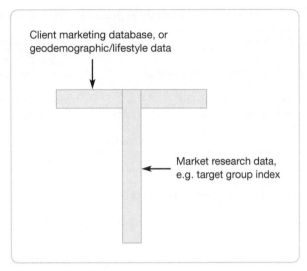

Figure 4.6 T-cube data

increase that offering's profile exponentially overnight, whereas the possibility of opening up a website telling the world how much you hate a product can be devastating in the same timescale. Blogs empower would-be writers and journalists to publish their own thoughts and views from the comfort of their own bedroom, removing the need for prohibitively expensive printing presses and distribution methods in getting their voice heard.

These are truly exciting and volatile times!

That concludes our sketch of the lifestyle data industry. We are now ready for an overview of geodemographic and lifestyle data products, and how these are changing.

Issues and trends in external data
Lifestyle versus geodemographics: which is best?

Lifestyle database suppliers have historically been at (very public) loggerheads with geodemographic suppliers over whose product is the 'better' offering. Although the bringing together of these databases in more recent commercial offerings has largely negated that argument, the sum is still made of its parts and it is worthwhile understanding the various main points of the arguments for both sides. These are presented in Table 4.5.

Probably the key strength of lifestyle data is that it is based on individuals, not aggregates. The key weakness lies in the data itself. First, the data will be biased towards people who like filling in surveys, have got time to do so, or are attracted by the incentives to fill in. A marketing manager once noted that people seem to get into 'box ticking mode' in completing surveys and had worked out that, if they had ticked more than six answers to one particular question, then it was a good sign that the data would not perform well when used for prospecting. It also brings into question the validity of profiling clients' own customers based on a sample of lifestyle survey returners that may be flawed.

Finally, there is the question of honesty. The entire lifestyle data industry depends on the accuracy of data filled in by the individuals themselves. However, market researchers have long known that people may distort personal data in order to present themselves in a better light. Said one high ranking industry insider (who has asked to remain anonymous!): 'if you were to believe lifestyle surveys, nobody watches TV, especially not *East Enders* or *Coronation Street*, everybody reads books instead. Nobody goes to pubs either, except for a

Table 4.6 Strengths and weaknesses of geodemographic versus lifestyle products

Lifestyle strengths	Geodemographic weaknesses
Individual data	Only at OA/postcode level
Behavioural/attitudinal data as well as geodemographic data	Only geodemographic data
Income is actual not modelled	Modelled income only
Claimed update at tens of thousands of records per day	Census records decay by 12 years at end of life
Major lifestyle strength: more precision	
Lifestyle weaknesses	**Geodemographic strengths**
Partial coverage only	Census is 100% sample
Records biased to people who like incentivised surveys	No bias
Claimed behaviour anecdotes suggest quality is variable	'Official' survey more accurate?
Not based on geography	Whole basis is geographical, and therefore ideal for direct targeting
Consumers worried about data protection	
Major geodemographic strength: wider coverage and balance	

meal with family or friends, certainly not to drink! Geodemographic operators claim that the official nature of the census improves the validity of the data. However, there is little absolute evidence for any of these claims or counter claims.

Issues in client usage of external data

Use of external data gets easier as desktop computing becomes more powerful. Marketers can now do their own analysis on their desks with user-friendly software. This is a major step forward from having to ask a supplier to run a particular analysis for you. Good analysis is all about trying things, seeing what results are, and re-inputting more analyses. This can now be quite easily done.

Recent trends, future developments

In the first decade of this century interactive digital marketing was seen as the future, leaving traditional media in its wake. More recently, however, there are questions being asked about whether this trend is about to reverse.

The Head of Consulting with Experian's Marketing Services Division points out that on-line acquisition costs are starting to creep up, citing the fact that it is pretty well impossible to target key words at only new customers, and any existing customers clicking through on keywords will naturally result in increased acquisition costs and often dissatisfied customers, if they think the acquisition offer was not available for them. He goes on to point out that it is far easier to de-duplicate a traditional mailing list than it is to do so with any new medium, except perhaps e-mail addresses (Gosling, 2012).

Another trend that may be about to go back on itself is the boom in the number of organisations requesting e-mail data for marketing purposes. The reason for this initial trend is simple and easy to understand.Compare the price of the stamp alone to the cost of sending an e-mail. Then take into account the various design costs associated with each, the comparative time delays involved and so on. It is a no-brainer. At least, it is, at first.

Recently, however, organisations are beginning to realise that they are losing out on a lot of the profiling and segmentation ability discussed in this chapter simply because you cannot tell from an e-mail address where someone lives, and a postcode is a mighty powerful piece of data, as I am sure you will appreciate by now. Another factor influencing the reversal of this trend is that e-mail addresses are often out of date or that people will use their 'give it to anyone' e-mail address – the one that they rarely check because they use it for avoiding spam.

It has been pointed out that e-mail marketing simply is not the panacea everyone thought it would be. It is too easy to ignore and often comes down to the simple question of 'is the subject line interesting enough?' (Jackson, 2012) in much the same way that traditional direct mail is so reliant on the envelope used. But an e-mail is even easier to get rid of than poorly targeted direct mail.

Even in traditional marketing routes the dynamic is changing. One industry stalwart says that telemarketing has been massively hampered by an unforeseen side effect of the Telephone Preference Service (TPS) described earlier (see Chapter 2) and the fact that it has phone numbers at its heart (Jackson, 2012). If James Monday registers his phone number with the TPS and then sells his house to Arnold Shanks, the phone number stays registered unless Mr Shanks goes to the hassle of un-registering it, assuming he knows it is even registered in the first place. Furthermore, the chances are good that James Monday will register his new phone number too, and so two numbers are struck off for one person's preference. Given the statistic quoted elsewhere, that almost 5 per cent of housing stock is sold each year, the impact of almost 20 years of TPS on telemarketing becomes clearer.

But let us finish on a warning note. We must be careful to differentiate clearly between data that customers have willingly given us to help themselves assess their options, and that which we use to infer their buying intentions. The latter is much less predictive. Alan Mitchell explains this in more detail in Exhibit 4.13.

Exhibit 4.13 An alternative view: button pressing baloney by *Alan Mitchell*

Right now a new service is being touted to UK marketers, combining 20 different databases and promises to provide over 100 million data records on 40 million named UK individuals.

The service offers marketers access to names, addresses, telephone numbers, e-mail addresses and so on, plus a comprehensive analysis of their geodemographic status (income, etc.), their spending habits, newspaper reading habits, what they buy on the internet, and current spending plans (for example, whether they intend to change mobile phone service provider in the next few months).

It is being sold as the holy grail of direct marketing. In fact, services like this are part of the problem, not part of the solution. They underline the fact that the direct marketing industry has a big problem. A very big problem that lies deep in the unstated assumptions by which the industry currently operates.

Here are three of these assumptions:

First, that good marketing is about effective messaging: if only we can find the right message – the right stimulus – we can be assured of the right response. Thus, when firms talk about pressing the right consumer buttons they are treating 'the consumer' – a living, breathing human being with his or her own purposes, priorities and intentions –

as if 'it' was a non-sentient automaton which, if you can press the right buttons, you can get to do what you want it to do.

The second assumption follows from the first: to discover the right buttons and how to press them you need more and better data. So increased marketing effectiveness depends on gathering ever more data and mining and analysing it in ever more sophisticated ways. The more you know about 'the consumer' the more effective your button-pressing, that is the greater your influence and control.

A third assumption is that this consumer data is a natural resource, like fish in the sea, there to be harvested and used by anyone who has the investment and technology to do so (subject to the laws of the land). Since the only entities capable of making these investments are companies, direct marketing naturally revolves around helping companies harvest as much data as possible from consumers, and then to use it as efficiently and effectively as possible to 'press their buttons' and get them to do what companies want them to do.

So what's wrong with these assumptions?

Well, first, as sentient beings with their own purposes and priorities, individuals do not always respond well to having their buttons pushed by others – especially by hundreds of different button-pushers all at the same time. The real secret of marketing effectiveness does not lie in bigger, better button-pushing. It lies in offering consumers better value. (That is hardly news, but it is amazing how often marketers think that better messaging, rather than better value, is the real secret of success.)

Second, rather than seeing consumer data as a commons – a resource which is there to be harvested and used by anybody with the means to do so – we should see it as a private, personal asset. In which case, the main benefits of this asset should accrue to the asset's creator and generator: the individual.

That is how most individuals see it already. Thus, Information Commissioner research that shows protecting people's personal information is now the third highest priority issue for UK citizens, with 83 per cent of individuals nominating it as a cause of concern (behind improving standards in education and preventing crime). That is what lies behind recent changes to electoral roll regulation, which means that today one third of the electoral roll database is no longer available to direct marketers.

Third, if the first two alternative views are right, then the future for direct marketing and CRM lies not in harvesting, selling and using consumer data behind individuals' backs and mostly without their knowledge, influence or control. Instead, it lies in encouraging and facilitating individuals to volunteer information about what they are planning to do and when.

There are two points to note about this alternative. Firstly while predictive patterns of possible future behaviour can be derived from historical data about attitudes, attributes, transactions and behaviours, there is only one entity that actually knows the answer to the question: 'what is this individual going to do next?' It is the individual himself. Even the best predictive models are exercises in guesswork, and most of the effort that currently goes into predictive modelling is invested in attempts to reduce the levels of error and waste it inevitably creates. Secondly, individuals will only bother volunteering significant amounts of information in a sustained fashion, if they have a good reason for doing so (if they profit from it and can trust it) and if it is easy for them to do so. And that points to a completely different type of service: one that acts for, and on behalf of, the individual, helping that individual make the most of their personal information.

Today, every technology, public opinion and legislative trend is pointing towards this alternative. A new personal information management or 'personal information logistics' industry is emerging – an industry that adds value for individuals by helping them access the right information about the right things at the right time and to acquire, collect, store, secure and protect, analyse and pass on the information they want and need to manage their lives better.

As this industry matures (driven mainly by technology providers, not marketers) the centre of data gravity is beginning to shift: from many different and separate organisations, holding small, isolated bits of information about many individuals (and desperately struggling to fill the resulting holes by clever bits of modelling and data fusion), to individuals holding ever larger amounts of data about themselves, and letting chosen organisations access and use discrete elements of this data on a permission-only basis, for clearly defined purposes and clear benefit to the individual.

If you are in marketing, as you look towards the future, where should you be investing? In harvesting ever more data from consumers and using it to 'press buttons'. Or in a new model of value creation that wins the consumer as its biggest, most active ally?

Source: Alan Mitchell, www.rightsideup.net, accessed November 2007.

Summary

This chapter described lifestyle and geodemographic databases and outlined how they can help direct marketers. Although quite different products in content, in the way the data are collected and how they are output, both product types can add to existing, internal data. Through a process of matching, then profiling using modelling techniques, external data can be a valuable research, segmentation and targeting (through subsequent list generation) tool.

Companies such as Sky, and even the President of the United States, have used lifestyle and geodemographic data effectively to segment and target existing and new customers more effectively.

QUESTIONS

1 The manager of a publishing firm is looking to raise subscription numbers for her portfolio of 'house and home' and gardening magazines. What use could she make of external databases? Would the costs be worthwhile? Debate the likely returns on her investment.

2 'Lifestyle databases are much more useful than geodemographic products because the data is held at individual level.' Make an alternative case in favour of geodemographic products.

3 Pick any one of the case studies contained in the chapter and outline why external data was used. Were there any alternative strategies and if so what advantages do external databases offer?

4 There are instances when a marketer may decide to use broad scale media to attract new prospects rather than a list from an external database. Name these instances.

References

Acxiom Corporation (2012a.) *Infobook.* Available at: **http://www.acxiom.co.uk/site-assets/reports/acxiom-infobook-optimise-customer-engagement-at-every-intersection/** [Accessed 30 May 2012].

Acxiom Corporation (2012b). *Infobase Enhancement Variables.* Available at: **http://www.acxiom.co.uk/site-assets/factsheet/infobase-enhancement-variable-list/** [Accessed 31 May 2012].

Acxiom UK (2010). *Reaching Customers with Certainty - Freemans.pdf.* [on-line] Available at: **http://www.acxiom.co.uk/site-assets/case-study/reaching-customers-with-certainty---freemans/** [Accessed 05 August 2013].

Acxiom UK (2011). *Precision Targeting Keeps Persil at No1_Persil.pdf.* [on-line] Available at: **http://www.acxiom.co.uk/site-assets/case-study/precision-targeting-keeps-persil-at-no1---persil/** [Accessed 05 August 2013].

Ansoff, I. (1957). Strategies for Diversification, *Harvard Business Review,* 35(5, Sep–Oct), pp. 113–124.

DMA (2011). *Acxiom White Paper – Reaching more consumers with certainty.* Available at: **http://www.dma.org.uk/toolkit/acxiom-white-paper-reaching-more-consumers-certainty** [Accessed 20 April 2012].

ESRC Census Programme (2012). *What questions were asked in the 2011 Census?* Available at: **http://census.ac.uk/News/2011Questions.aspx** [Accessed 01 June 2012].

Experian (2008a). *Case Study: JD Williams.* Available at: **http://www.experian.co.uk/assets/decision-analytics/case-studies/case-studies-global/ExperianDA_CS_JDWilliams.pdf** [Accessed 31 May 2012].

Experian Limited (2008b). *Case Study: Coventry Building Society.* Available at: **http://www.experian.co.uk/assets/consumer-information/brochures/Coventry_V4.pdf** [Accessed 11 June 2012].

Experian Limited (2009). *Experian reveals the changing face of UK society.* Available at: **http://press.experian.com/United-Kingdom/Press-Release/mosaic-uk-2009--experian-reveals-the-changing-face-of-uk-society.aspx?&p=1** [Accessed 11 June 2012].

Experian Limited (2010). *Optimise the value of your customers and locations, now and in the future.* Available at: **http://www.experian.co.uk/assets/business-strategies/brochures/mosaic-uk-2009-brochure-jun10.pdf** [Accessed 31 May 2012].

Experian Limited (2012a). *History.* Available at: **http://www.experianplc.com/about-experian/history.aspx** [Accessed 01 June 2012].

Experian Limited (2012b). *Mosaic UK Interactive Guide.* Available at: **http://guides.business-strategies.co.uk/mosaicuk2009/html/visualisation.htm?011121** [Accessed 01 June 2012].

Experian Limited (2012c). *Mamas & Papas' customer relationships bloom with Experian's data driven marketing.* Available at: **http://www.experian.co.uk/marketing-information-services/mamas-and-papas-press-release.html** [Accessed 11 June 2012].

Fairlie, R. (1992). Making the Most of Geodemographic and Psychographic profiles, In *The New IDM Practitioner's Guide,* The IDM, Teddington.

Gosling, C. (2012). *Articles and Blogs – Showdown! Online Marketing vs Direct Marketing.* Available at: **http://www.experian.co.uk/integrated-marketing/articles-and-blogs-digital-marketing.html#anchor12** [Accessed 11 June 2012].

http://census.ac.uk/News/2011Questions.aspx, 2012. *What questions were asked in the 2011 Census?* Available at: **http://census.ac.uk/News/2011Questions.aspx** [Accessed 01 June 2012].

Jackson, R. (2012). *Telephone conversation* (Interview 01 June 2012).

Mitchell, A. (1978). *Consumer Values: a Typology,* SRI International, Menlo Park, California.

Office for National Statistics (2012a). *Output Areas.* Available at: **http://www.ons.gov.uk/ons/guide-method/census/census-2001/data-and-products/output-geography/output-areas/index.html** [Accessed 01 June 2012].

Office for National Statistics (2012b). *Release Plans for 2011 Census statistics.* Available at: **http://www.ons.gov.uk/ons/guide-method/census/2011/census-data/2011-census-prospectus/release-plans-for-2011-census-statistics/index.html** [Accessed 01 June 2012].

Rapp, S. and Collins, T. (1987). *Maximarketing,* McGraw-Hill, New York.

Reynolds, J. (1993). Lifestyle Databases, Strategic Marketing Tools? *Journal of Targeting, Measurement and Analysis,* 2(1).

Sleight, P. (1994). Can Lifestyle Databases and Market Research Learn to Live Together? *Journal of Database Marketing,* 1(4).

Sons of Maxwell (2009). *United Breaks Guitars.* Available at: **http://www.youtube.com/watch?v=5YGc4zOqozo** [Accessed 11 June 2012].

Stone, B. (1996). *Successful Direct Marketing Methods.* 5th edn, NTC Business Books, Chicago.

The Electoral Commission (2012a). *Voter Registration.* Available at: **http://www.electoralcommission.org.uk/voter-registration** [Accessed 30 May 2012].

The Electoral Commission (2012b). *What is the Electoral Register?* Available at: **http://www.electoralcommission.org.uk/faq/voting-and-registration/what-is-the-electoral-register?** [Accessed 30 May 2012].

The Information Commissioner's Office (2012). *Electoral Register.* Available at: **http://www.ico.gov.uk/for_the_public/topic_specific_guides/electoral_register.aspx** [Accessed 30 May 2012].

The London Stock Exchange (2012). *FTSE100 Constituents.* Available at: **http://www.londonstockexchange.com/exchange/prices-and-markets/stocks/indices/summary/summary-indices-constituents.html?index=UKX&page=2** [Accessed 01 June 2012].

The Marketer (2012). *Case Study: The National Trust.* Available at: **http://www.themarketer.co.uk/articles/case-studies/the-national-trust/** [Accessed 31 May 2012].

Webber, R. (2002). Using Geodemographic and Lifestyle *Segmentation* Systems, in R. Fairlie, ed. *The New IDM Practitioner's Guide,* The IDM, Teddington, pp. 3.5–18.

Webber, R. (2003). *Experian Publicity Material.* s.l.:s.n.

CASE STUDY

The Salvation Army

Background

The Salvation Army is a worldwide Christian church and registered charity. Working in 124 countries, The Salvation Army demonstrates Christian principles through practical support; offering unconditional friendship and help to people of all ages, backgrounds and needs. Today, The Salvation Army extends a helping hand to people who are homeless, friendless and in need.

Campaign objectives

In 2010, The Salvation Army planned to door drop their banker pack prior to Christmas as this is the most responsive time of year for people to give and to recruit new supporters. However, because of heavy snow during the delivery period, some of the packs were delivered later than planned (post Christmas).

The banker pack did not work as well as expected, so The Salvation Army wanted to door drop the pack again in 2011 to ascertain whether the snow and late delivery had impacted the results. The Salvation Army believed they could also improve on the 2010 results

Case study (*continued*)

through better targeting, so they asked TNT Post to produce a door drop plan as part of their donor acquisition media mix to generate donations and raise awareness for their Christmas 2011 Appeal.

Solution

TNT Post used The Salvation Army's donor database to analyse the responder files from the previous year and look at historic performance, donations and potential. This information was then profiled and scored throughout the UK, to understand the best sectors to deliver to for the 2011 appeal, for the best return on investment.

TNT Post looked at specific Mosaic characteristics of a typical donor and fed them into the model for the door drop campaign but also to understand the impact of door drop media and its place within the media mix for acquisition appeals.

The door drop was part of a larger media campaign, including DRTV, radio, inserts, press and cold mail. The charity wanted to have as many touch points as possible to engage and recruit new supporters. Door drop was key to this marketing mix, as traditionally the response was good.

Creative

The envelope had 'Urgent Delivery' on the front of the pack to grab consumers' attention. There were pictures and case studies of The Salvation Army's work with homeless and older people and families living in poverty to engage consumers and ask them to donate a Christmas gift. The pack also contained a Christmas card and encouraged consumers to sign the card and send it back, so The Salvation Army could give it to a homeless or lonely person to show them that someone cares.

Results

The number of donations increased from the previous year by 42 per cent. The campaign generated a total ROI of £2.12; this was an improvement on the previous year's ROI by an additional £0.58

Comment from The Salvation Army

'We were really pleased with the results from the 2011 Christmas door drop appeal and we hope to build on the success of the profiling model with a larger campaign in 2012. (Alex Kelly, The Salvation Army)

Source: DMA (The Direct Marketing Association), 2012. Case Study: Salvation Army. Available on-line at: **http://www.dma.org.uk/toolkit/case-study-salvation-army** [Accessed 23 August 2012].

CASE STUDY

Depaul UK – 'iHobo' app

Depaul UK is a charity that helps young homeless, vulnerable or disadvantaged people. With an ageing donor database (the average is over 65), limited success through traditional campaigns and a low brand awareness, Depaul recognised that they were facing a media and creative struggle to meet their aims of raising awareness of both their cause and themselves. Working with Publicis, the charity set about devising a campaign to target young, affluent, socially conscious, 30-somethings.

A problem faced by homeless charities is that we have largely become hardened to their plight. Such people are sadly all too common a sight on the streets of most of the UK's cities and we just mentally tune them out as we pass by. Also, as a fundraising prospect, the homeless are not as appealing as (say) a cute looking polar bear cub. As a result, it was decided that, whatever solution was devised, it would have to be something innovative.

Recognising that it is just as difficult not to ignore the beep on your mobile phone, as it is to ignore a homeless person on the streets, was the first step in creating that innovative solution. As a result, the world's first charity app, iHobo, was created.

Described as 'Tamagotchi with a conscience', a virtual homeless person has to be cared for by the user. If he was treated well during the three days of the app's life, the 'hobo' would thrive: if he was left uncared for, his inevitable decline was played out. The app used live action, not animation, to make things as realistic as possible and users got to witness first hand (albeit virtually) how tough life on the street can be, which built a sense of empathy for the hobo. Depaul got round Apple's no donation rule with a 'one click text to donate' .

Even the name iHobo was chosen carefully. Attention grabbing and self-explanatory, the name alone prompts conversations about youth homelessness and the labels we put on the homeless, and would have been far more provocative than 'Depaul UK fundraising App', or similar. The app was sent to influential technology bloggers and journalists to maximise word of mouth publicity.

Within five days of the official launch, it was the number one app (both free and paid for) in the UK. There were half a million downloads in just a few weeks. The value of equivalent media coverage on conventional and other channels was estimated at £1.2 million, with mentions in such diverse publications as the *Los Angeles Times*, the *Guardian* (in the UK) and the British charity sector's trade publication, 'Third Sector'.

A sum of £10,000 was received in donations from 4,000 new donors, including five new direct debits being set up. Overall, that is 74 times the number of new additions from typical previous Depaul campaigns. In addition, 1,200 new e-mail addresses were gathered and Depaul's website traffic was up by 59 per cent as a result of the campaign.

At the outset, Depaul were worried about the controversial nature of the app they were planning and did not realise it would take so long to come to fruition (the process took about 18 months to put into action). On the other hand, they were not prepared for the approach to be quite as successful as it was. Depaul's server crashed in the first week due to unexpected demand. Now plans are in place for the release of iHobo 1.2, with integrated facts on homelessness, connection to social media sites, point scoring for positive actions and an ability to utilise elements of the app to expand Depaul's database for ongoing activity.

Questions

1 How could the approach taken by Depaul have backfired on them?

2 What are the ethical considerations associated with using apps, and finding ways around Apple's no donations rule, for fundraising?

Source: Adapted by the author from a slideshow delivered by Tim Harford, Head of Donor Care and Community Fundraising at Depaul UK, on 2 March 2011.
Depaul UK (2012). Charity case study – iHobo. Available on-line at: **http://resources.mediatrust.org/events/think-mobile/charity-caste-study-ihobo** [Accessed 23 August 2012]

PART THREE

Setting objectives and strategies within direct marketing

Chapter 5

Direct marketing objectives and strategies

Objectives

Once you have read this chapter you will:

- be able to set direct marketing objectives for any business that requires them
- understand the elements of direct marketing strategies
- be able to create direct marketing strategies when required

Introduction

In this chapter we begin by discussing what direct marketing objectives are and how they are set. This acts as our platform for the most complex and important step in the planning process: designing the direct marketing strategy.

The remainder of the chapter will be devoted to outlining a broad framework, which you will be able to use to develop direct marketing strategies. The close links that direct marketing strategy has with the overall marketing strategy will be explored. Later (Chapter 6) we will take a more in-depth look at the wider considerations influencing direct marketing strategy: relationship marketing, loyalty marketing and the company's marketing mix.

How this chapter is structured

This chapter takes the planning process onwards (from Chapter 4), moving from analysis to objective and strategy setting. Once the analysis has been completed, and the 'Where are we now?' question has been asked, you are ready to move to objective setting, or 'Where do we want to get to?'

Beginning with a discussion of 'general' marketing objectives, we move on to 'direct marketing' objectives, showing how they differ. The use of lifetime value analysis as the basis for setting 'allowable marketing spend per customer' objectives is included.

The second part of the chapter introduces direct marketing strategy, which direct marketers need to develop as their guide for subsequent tactical activities.

The key influences on direct marketing strategic philosophies are outlined before laying out a framework that direct marketers can follow to set a strategy. The final part of the chapter explores this framework in more detail.

5.1 Setting direct marketing objectives

5.1.1 Marketing objectives

The next stage in a company's planning process, after the analysis of the current situation is complete, is to set the objectives (McDonald and Wilson, 2011). As a result of the analysis, we now have a clear view of the likely opportunities and threats. This enables us to set objectives that realistically represent what the company can achieve over the next planning period.

If analysis sorts out 'where we are now', objectives are a statement of 'where we want to be' by, say, this time next year.

Marketing objectives are best approached by understanding the broader context within which they are set. Objectives should be set in a hierarchical fashion; that is, the objectives of marketing, finance, and operations should all fit together so that, on meeting all of them, the corporate objectives are met. Similarly, all the different marketing function objectives should come together to achieve the prime marketing objective.

The hierarchical links described are illustrated in Figure 5.1. Here, we can see that at the corporate level 'increasing sales' is viewed as a strategy. However, coming down to the level of the marketing function, 'increasing sales' may be delegated as an objective. Marketing objectives are, therefore, derived from corporate strategies.

Exhibit 5.1 Setting corporate objectives based on retention

Most corporate objectives are concerned with profitability. An alternative view of corporate level objectives was taken by Reichheld (1996) in his work *The Loyalty Effect*. In his view, backed up by extensive work with companies across many sectors, corporate objectives should not be set around profit, but around retaining customers. He found that companies that set customer retention as their reason for existence, with profit following as a consequence of this, were extremely successful, for a number of reasons we shall explore later in this chapter.

Following Reichheld's reasoning, a typical corporate objective might, therefore, be 'to retain 98 per cent of our current customer base this year in order to generate £3 million revenue'.

When we come to set our marketing objectives, we have to be aware of the potential for confusion. It is tempting, when looking at the immediate marketing problems facing the company, to set marketing objectives that are too tactical. For instance, at first sight a legitimate objective might be 'to establish a database of 10,000 prospects by the end of the year', or 'to obtain 30 per cent awareness of our new product among our target market within six months'. However, it is important at this point to recall the need for the 'prime' marketing objective to reflect a corporate strategy. In this instance, 'marketing objectives are

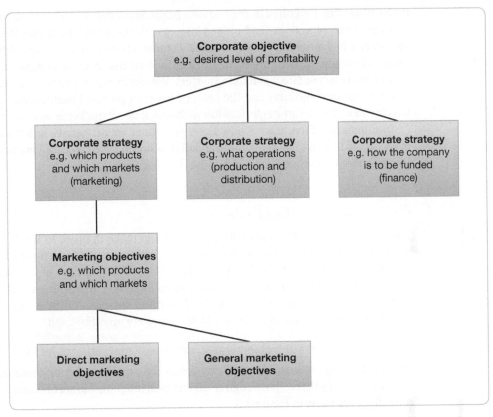

Figure 5.1 How objectives fit together

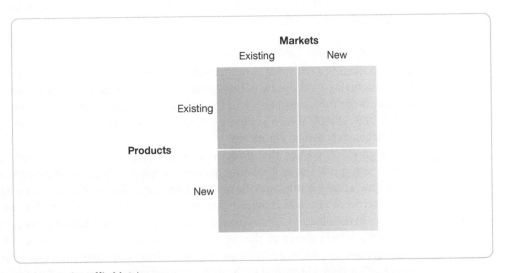

Figure 5.2 Ansoff's Matrix

concerned only with markets and products'. In other words, objectives may be set in terms of numbers of customers, numbers of products sold, revenue, or market share.

A useful tool to guide the setting of marketing objectives is Ansoff's (1968) Matrix (see Figure 5.2). Ansoff's Matrix is one of the few marketing models to have withstood the test of time – it was first published in the Harvard Business review in 1957. Ansoff suggests simply that marketing objectives (and indeed strategy) decisions can be simplified into only the decisions, which product to which market? For markets we can substitute a direct marketing variation because markets are made up of individual customers or companies. Ansoff links very nicely to a core direct marketing system. We can interpret Ansoff in terms of new business and retained business and the balance between acquired business and retained business is essentially the strategic decision with which direct marketers are concerned.

To summarise, then, if we follow these guidelines we may arrive at a typical marketing objective such as this: 'To sell X thousand of new product Y to acquired market Z at a cost of V to generate W revenue by the end of the financial year.'

5.1.2 Direct marketing objectives

There are a number of considerations we need to make in order to set direct marketing objectives. We first need to link our direct marketing objectives to the overall marketing objective. We can then gain clarity of purpose by converting sales objectives to customer based objectives. Further guidance can be given by setting allowable marketing spend and retention rate objectives. Finally, we should remind ourselves of the need to abide by the SMART approach to objective setting. These issues are now discussed.

Linking direct marketing objectives to the overall marketing objective

Direct marketing objectives lie at a level below the overall marketing objective. Consider a clothing company that sells through retail and mail order. Its full set of objectives might look something like those in Figure 5.3.

As Figure 5.3 illustrates, direct marketing needs to be positioned alongside other marketing disciplines, with the total sales, or revenues, from each discipline adding up to equal the overall marketing objective.

The emphasis on customers

Direct marketing's emphasis is on markets (customers) rather than products. As a result, direct marketing objectives are usually set in terms of numbers of customers, the revenue available from these customers and the costs of achieving these sales rather than products sold. In the example shown in Figure 5.3, we need to take the direct marketing objective a step further, as shown in Figure 5.4.

In Figure 5.4, we see that direct marketers have established that they need to find 10,000 customers. The next obvious question to ask is: where are these customers coming from? This is really getting into the realms of strategy, which is discussed at length in the following section and a later chapter (Chapter 6). But we have one more job to do yet with our customer based objective. Let us examine Figure 5.5; Ansoff's Matrix gives us our options.

Ansoff's Matrix shows us that we can obtain our required customers either from our 'existing customer base', or by 'acquiring them' from our competitors or from totally new markets. Our final adjustment to the direct marketing objective set in Figure 5.4 is shown in Figure 5.6.

Setting direct marketing objectives in this way, splitting up existing and new customers, gives clarity to the process. It guides the next step, the setting of strategy, and ensures that everyone knows the worth of existing customers, rather than concentrating too much on searching for new people.

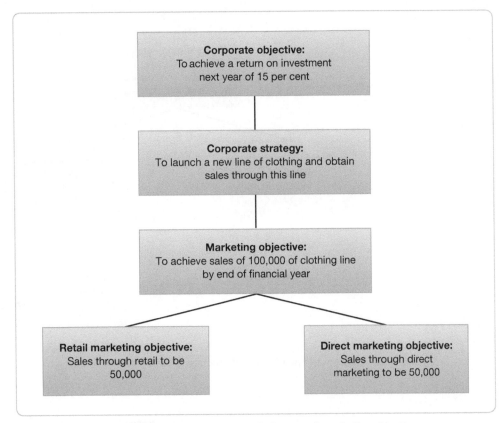

Figure 5.3 Linking direct marketing objectives with the overall marketing objective

The allowable marketing spend per customer

Direct marketing objectives can be set for more than just revenue. We have already found (Chapter 3) that our marketing database can help us to allocate costs precisely to each sale and to each customer. Hence, we can closely control the profitability of what we are doing. In simple terms, we can make sure that 'what we spend on marketing does not exceed the worth of the customer to us'. If a customer has spent £100 with us over the last year, with a gross margin of £60, then we know that we can spend, say, £30 in retaining that customer and encouraging the same spend next year. This can and should be included in the direct marketing objectives set. Allowable spend should be set based on projected lifetime values, the calculation of which was previously outlined (see Chapter 3).

Allowable spend objectives can be set for both existing and new customers. For example:

- to recruit 5,000 new customers by the year end, at an allowable marketing spend of £30 per customer;
- to retain 90 per cent of our existing customers by the year end, at an allowable marketing spend of £10 per customer.

These objectives give clear guidance to strategy: if your acquisition strategies are costing more than an average of £30 per customer, and your retention more than £10, your marketing is too expensive.

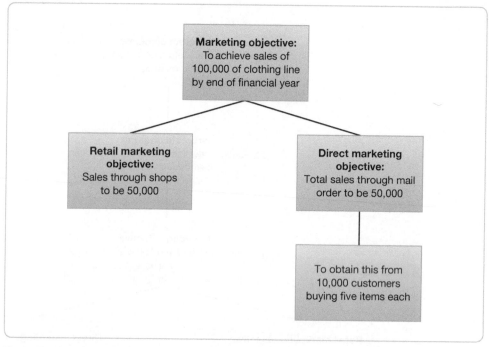

Figure 5.4 Direct marketing objectives emphasise customers

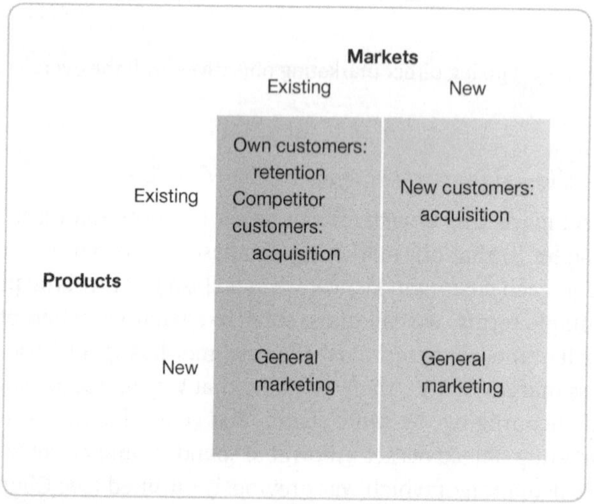

Figure 5.5 Using Ansoff's Matrix to link objectives
and strategy

It may be that you have been allocated a budget (say £100,000) and given a target of recruiting, say, 2,000 customers, and told to get on with it. In this instance, your calculation is simple:

recruit 2,000 customers with £100,000;

allowable spend per customer $=100,000 \div 2,000 = £350$.

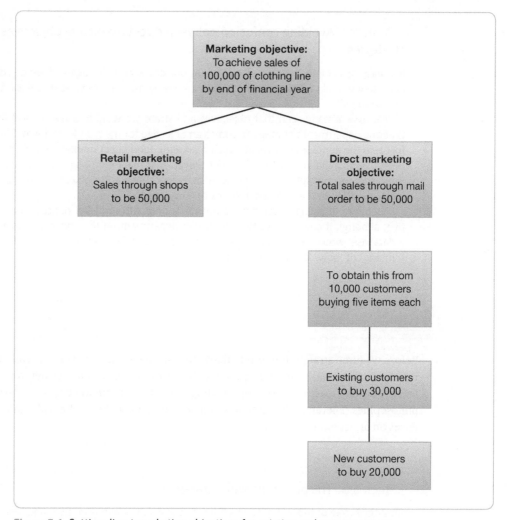

Figure 5.6 **Setting direct marketing objectives for existing and new customers**

Setting SMART objectives

Finally, we should remind ourselves of the need to ensure all objectives are set in a disciplined manner. The SMART formula is well established although there is some debate about the precise meaning of each part of the formula:

Specific/Simple Objectives must be set focusing on specific products and markets and associated revenues and costs.

Measurable/Manageable A key advantage of direct marketing is its facility to measure precisely the actual performance against a numbers based objective. This links to the idea of managing output against objectives.

Aspirational/Achievable The objective should motivate but also be achievable in the context of market conditions.

Realistic Unrealistic objectives are demotivating.

Time based A time limit should be set to enable measurement criteria to be established.

Exhibit 5.2 Avoiding confusion between direct marketing objectives and strategies

It is easy to fall into the trap of mixing up objectives and strategies. If we decided it was necessary to build a database of 100,000 names by the end of the year, is this an objective or a strategy?

We have already seen that objectives and strategies work in a hierarchical fashion, so that one department's strategy becomes an objective for the next level down. The key is to fix on to the appropriate level at which marketing (and direct marketing) objectives should be set. McDonald and Wilson (2011) believed that marketing objectives should be about 'products and markets'; we have seen that direct marketing objectives, set at the same level, are often best expressed in terms of 'customers'.

Therefore, building a database is not an appropriate top level direct marketing objective, although it could be set for a particular department. In the above example, 'building a database' would be part of the direct marketing 'strategy', an expression (albeit a rather thin one) of 'how' the objectives are to be achieved.

5.2 Creating direct marketing strategies

Before we jump straight into direct marketing strategies, it is worth our while understanding the background to modern practice in our field. Modern direct marketers see direct marketing 'as a part of marketing', adding value to other marketing tools, strategies and philosophies. Therefore, it is essential that we take a look now at the wider marketing influences on direct marketing strategy.

Exhibit 5.3 The problems with strategy

Strategy is one of those words which has become rather overused by marketers.

You have probably seen statements described as communication strategies, media strategies, research strategies, campaign strategies, and so on and on until the original meaning of the word has got lost. In this book, the word strategy is used to mean one thing: important decisions that 'guide the direction the company is taking' over the planning period.

5.2.1 The major influences on direct marketing strategy

Classical direct marketing

Direct marketing has expanded considerably from its original roots in mail order, but many of the core principles of direct marketing strategy were established and fine-tuned by the original, highly disciplined industry. In particular, the following principles were established:

- Measurement of lifetime values and the setting of allowable marketing costs per customer to drive marketing activity
- The use of testing to minimise risk and to gain understanding of the relative leverage of different direct marketing elements

- Database segmentation based on customers' responses to previous offers and the use of statistical techniques to predict responses
- The use of existing customer profiles to target new customers

In summary, classical direct marketers established the principles of testing, control, targeting and continuity.

The importance of customer loyalty

In his book *The Loyalty Effect,* Reichheld (1996) outlined a study by Bain and Co. that has profound implications for businesses because it underlines the strategic importance of customer retention. Bain and Co. found that increasing customer retention by, say, 5 per cent could improve company profitability by as much as 125 per cent. We will take a close look at this work in the next chapter (Chapter 6), which gives important guidance to direct marketing strategies aimed at keeping customers. It will also show us why so many of today's 'loyalty schemes' are, in fact, badly flawed concepts.

Relationship marketing and customer relationship management (CRM)

Relationship marketing is an approach to marketing that emphasises a 'relationship' rather than a 'transaction' approach to business. First coined by Berry in 1983, relationship marketing concentrates on customer service, quality as the concern of all, and partnership marketing between all the business stakeholders. Given its emphasis on relationships, relationship marketing not surprisingly focuses on customer retention over time, and in this respect there is an area of convergence between relationship marketing and direct marketing. Direct and, in particular, database marketing approaches are also useful support for good service, something seen as key for productive relationships. CRM, meanwhile, is a more recent addition to the marketers' lexicon, and has been largely driven by powerful IT firms selling database technology. However, we need to be careful not to confuse CRM, relationship and direct marketing – something that happens a lot with the marketing press. You can find a full discussion later (Chapter 7).

The marketing mix

As direct marketing has been increasingly utilised by major players in many different sectors, so its integration with general marketing, espoused by the Four Ps mix, has become a key part of direct marketing strategy.

(General) marketing strategy has been defined by Kotler *et al.* (2009) as follows:

> 'Marketing strategy is the marketing logic by which the business unit expects to achieve its marketing objectives. Marketing strategy consists of making decisions on the marketing mix, marketing expenditures and marketing allocations in relation to expected environmental and competitive conditions.'

As well as the Four Ps of marketing, Kotler *et al.* emphasise the importance of segmentation, positioning and branding as strategic decisions. This marketing mix approach (although being challenged by relationship marketers) remains an important element of the discussion on direct marketing strategy. Just to take pricing as an example, it is clear that direct marketers must pay attention to price as a strategic tool; indeed the ability of direct marketing to offer different prices to different segments, and vary pricing over time to maximise lifetime values, can be a vital corporate asset.

The product/market decision and competitive advantage

Again within general marketing, a second school of thought takes the line that marketing strategy and corporate/business strategy are closely linked. This view is summed up by Aaker (Fifield, 1998):

'The marketing strategy concept can be encapsulated into two core elements: the product market investment decision, and the development of a sustainable competitive advantage to compete in those markets.'

This second definition is an important feed into direct marketing strategy. The product/market investment decision, which Ansoff's Matrix describes, divides markets into existing and new customers, which is the major 'scene setter' for direct marketing strategy. Porter's (1985) well-known concept of 'sustainable competitive advantage' is also important to direct marketers. Fletcher *et al.* (1995) believed that privately held customer information, and its use, can provide sustainable competitive advantage.

The Internet

When it first became available as a business tool, direct marketers said to themselves 'Here's a nice medium for our direct approaches'. And they were right, but of course the Internet has proven to have a much wider influence on business life than being just another medium. The unique characteristics of the Internet make it an entirely different and very exciting place to conduct business. The Internet has had a huge influence on all aspects of direct and database marketing. However, the basic principles of objective setting and strategy development remain as relevant to the on-line environment as they do to the off-line environment. The basic business decision of what markets (customers) to serve with which products remains key to business success. When the authors hear of companies 'losing control' of their brands in social media, for example, we are really just seeing bad marketing practice.

Now that we have an understanding of what can influence direct marketing strategy, we are ready to tackle the subject head on.

Exhibit 5.4 Strategy tip

Examiners often complain about the lack of thought that has gone into strategy formulation. One common fault is to mistake a marketing technique for a marketing strategy. For example, sometimes students will employ a 'strategy' of 'using direct marketing in getting new customers'. Although this may be part of a strategic approach, by itself this is not much use as a guideline for a company. Marketing strategies must clearly explain in a persuasive manner how the firm will achieve its objectives, fully acknowledging the circumstances at the time.

5.2.2   The essence of direct marketing strategy

Traditional marketing strategy emphasises a Four or Seven Ps approach, in which the focus is on developing something within the company that offers superior value to customers, compared with that offered by its competitors. The whole approach begins with the company's offering. Direct marketing takes a different approach, because it starts with customers, not products.

The essence of direct marketing's role in a company's strategy is the way in which 'customer information', held on the database, can be used to guide the company's actions. Because the information is held around customers, not products, it has been said that a business can 'manage' groups of, or even individual, customers over time. But let us be very careful not to blindly follow marketing rhetoric: to what extent is 'customer management' a reality? This concept needs refinement: often customers like to be in control themselves, not handing it over to companies.

Ponder this for a moment. What do consumers want from marketing? Think about yourself. The Internet has probably changed the way you live your life. It has put you much more in charge of how you buy things. Take holidays: years ago you would go and get help from travel agents. You might still do, but you might also want to search for yourself on-line and seek reviews of other holiday makers via sites like TripAdvisor. In doing this, you are the one leading the approach to market; you are in charge of the 'process' of making a deal. It is being done by you, at your convenience, and on your terms – at least in the sense that you search for as much information as you want before making a decision, or putting it off until tomorrow. Does this mean there is no place for promotional marketing led by marketers? Of course not. Sometimes we still want to lie back and be sold to. We still like attractive brands, we still like a bit of glitz with our marketing. So, back to the question, what do consumers want from marketing? They – we – sometimes want to be in control, and sometimes they want to sit back and be marketed to. Direct marketers can help deliver this, using information that, at its best, can be deployed in a real time manner, in a way that consumers welcome. This has yet to be truly made a reality, but a combination of Internet and customer database might make it so in the near future.

In the authors' view then, the essence of direct and database marketing does **not** lie with the idea of customer management. Rather, a **'direct' firm's competitive advantage stems from information held on its customers and the use of this information to offer existing customers consistent, superior value.**

Other key factors impact on direct marketing strategy. As far back as 1996, Reichheld asserted that ultimately the key to profitability was the effort to retain the firm's existing, stable, profitable customers. In view of this, perhaps the most important strategic role of direct marketing is its ability to identify and contact a firm's most valuable customers. Given the hue and cry about loyalty over the last decade, let us be clear – the prevailing evidence is that absolute loyalty cannot be regarded as the norm in most markets. Hence, we are talking here about share of wallet – improving the amount that customers will spend with us. Direct marketing can help: customer information helps to drive development of products and services, which are then directed to individual customers according to their needs from the company and their value to the company. It must be said that most 'loyalty marketing' remains immature and over-emphasises price; but, for some companies, the marketing database allows them to be quite specific. They identify those 'profitable, but vulnerable' customers, then make quite specific efforts to keep them. The dilemma for marketers remains the same: are we wasting money with promotional efforts that are not needed – would they have stayed anyway? Direct marketers get closer than anyone else to solving this targeting conundrum.

The relationship approach to marketing proposes the development of relationships with various groups, including customers, as key to business success in high involvement markets. There are sometimes close links between direct marketing and 'relationship marketing', as direct marketing ways of thinking and techniques often emphasise the building of relationships (Spiller and Baier, 2010). While relationship marketing literature develops a conceptual business strategy, it is less clear how relationship marketing is actually developed in reality. This is where direct marketing maybe enters the debate: it is a proven method of delivery for customer dialogue, and can also help deliver breakthrough levels of 'service', a key facet of relationship marketing's philosophy. We should not over claim here though – unless the firm uses a database in an advanced manner to create a permission based dialogue with the customer, it is stretching a point to suggest relationships are created through direct marketing.

There is more than one way of building a relationship with, and maximising the profitability of, customers. General marketers may concentrate on building brands as a way of differentiating from competitors. Direct marketers, however, would often focus on 'segmentation'. In particular, 'behavioural (value and product category) segmentations' are well supported by a customer database as already discussed (see Chapters 3 and 4). Direct marketers are extremely efficient at driving the initial segmentations, guiding the marketing mix development, and then delivering the segmented offerings precisely to those who are most likely to buy. At the extreme, direct marketing can take segmentation down to the 'individual' level. Mass customisation and one-to-one communications allow products and communications to be tailored according to each individual's wants (Peppers et al., 1995). In his seminars, Bird (2007) describes direct marketing as potentially a 'perfect system of marketing'. If so, it is perhaps Peppers' '1–1 marketing' that is the ultimate manifestation of a truly customer-led direct marketing strategy, although the development of 1–1 remains slow. To make a big difference, 1–1 marketing requires consumers to invest time, sharing detailed information with business on a regular basis. Given its ease and low cost for sharing information, in practical terms this means developing on-line vehicles to adopt such a role: one could imagine, say, **www.moneysupermarket.com**, Ask, or Google itself considering this model. But, as we move towards 2014, no one has really come up with a model that delivers enough value to both consumers and businesses to make 1–1 marketing work in the all encompassing way Peppers originally predicted.

This focus on customer information (and sometimes relationships) does not mean that direct marketers should discard the traditional marketing mix driven approach. Getting an appropriate marketing mix right, so that customers feel attracted to the product and it is competitive, is still very important. For example, the root of direct marketing, mail order, is an example of a direct distribution method. Here, the 'place' element of the Four Ps approach is the remote delivery of products, providing a different shopping experience to customers. However, the marketing mix as a strategic approach to customer management does begin to feel dated and not fully capable of describing the complexity of direct consumer/company relationships in the digital era.

The final perspective is the view of direct marketing from within the business. Here, the very cornerstone of direct marketing is the extra 'control' it offers the marketer. Thanks to the precision of the database and the demand of a direct response from the customer, any returns on investment can be precisely measured. The use of individual media allows precise testing, minimising financial risks.

Let us summarise by going back to the big picture: in terms of corporate strategy, where should we locate direct and database marketing? Look at Figure 5.7.

Figure 5.7 first divides up strategy into two key questions: where and how we should compete; secondly, it suggests the creation of differential advantage as the central requirement of strategy; and finally it suggests links between this and the start point of marketing strategy – positioning. Volvo has a differential advantage in safety technology. Its positioning – the safest car in the market – naturally follows from this. The strengths of direct marketing

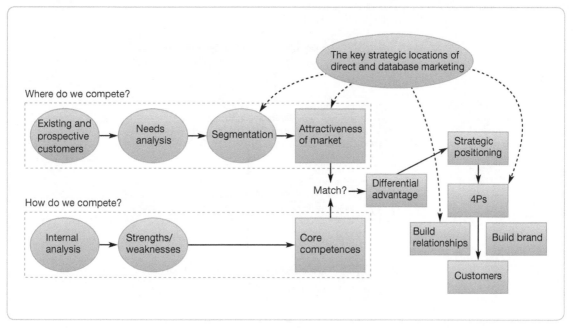

Figure 5.7 The key strategic locations of direct and database marketing

lend themselves to it being strongly linked to market analysis and its key output – segmentation and identifying attractive markets. Then, moving to marketing delivery, direct marketing may help in building relationships, and also in delivering a Four Ps marketing mix.

There is, of course, much more to any discussion of direct marketing strategy than this summary. The next section shows how to develop a complete direct marketing strategy.

5.2.3 A framework for creating direct marketing strategies

Now that we understand the essence of direct marketing strategy, we are ready to tackle the detailed work of creating a complete strategy. Although the final strategy statement may be only a paragraph in length, for it to be powerful it must be rooted in hard work and the consideration of all strategic issues.

To help us, what we need is a clear, simple framework that we can use as a 'map' to guide us through the decision making. Such a 'map', a framework, is shown in Figure 5.8.

Examining the direct marketing strategic model in Figure 5.8, we can see that we have four primary decisions to make.

We first have to decide what will be the role of direct marketing in achieving our marketing objectives. Second, how much emphasis do we put on existing versus new customers and markets? Third, how are we going to keep our existing customers with us and maximise their profitability? Lastly, how are we going to attract new customers? In the remainder of this chapter we will take a closer look at these questions.

We will also introduce the marketing considerations – loyalty, relationship marketing, branding, and so on – which will shape our discussion of strategy. However, with these we are entering a vast and potentially complex area, so to keep things clear a fuller discussion of these considerations will be given later (see Chapter 6).

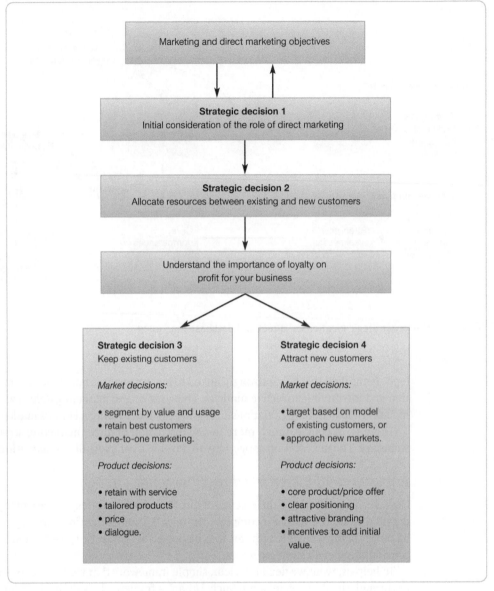

Figure 5.8 **The direct marketing strategic model**

5.2.4 Using the direct marketing strategy framework

'Acquire with Product. Retain with Service.'

(Professor Tom O. Jones, IDM Conference, 1996)

Decision no. 1: the role of direct marketing

The first strategic decision to take is to consider what the role of direct marketing is in achieving our marketing objectives. (Indeed, as part of this we should decide whether or not to use direct marketing at all.) In reality, we are considering the role of direct marketing 'throughout' this strategic process. However, at this early stage, the most important thing is to take a look at 'macro issues', such as industry structure, how our business is set up, and so on, and decide to what extent the 'natural strengths' of direct marketing make it a viable system to use. If it is going to be well nigh impossible to build a database, for example, then there is little point giving detailed consideration to direct marketing.

First, then, we need to understand in what conditions it is favourable for direct marketing to be part of the solution for the marketing strategist. Like most strategic decisions, there are no such things as foolproof 'rules' that guarantee success in this matter. The following should, therefore, be seen more as an initial focus for thinking than rigid guidelines.

A marketing strategist could consider direct marketing within the strategy if one or more of the following apply:

- The profitability of the company is heavily dependent on the loyalty of existing customers (which will only be ascertained through detailed analysis).
- The Pareto Principle applies strongly to the relationship between customers and profit as discussed earlier (see Chapter 3).
- Internet activity is likely to be high perhaps with website based sales, customer searches for information, and on-line only businesses competing. These events make a Web basis essential, perhaps backed up with a consumer database.
- There is scope to differentiate the product offering to different audiences;
- The gross margin of products sold, or customers' lifetime value, is high enough to justify the costs of direct marketing (media, database, management).
- The target audience is relatively small and/or tightly defined.
- There is scope to gather individual customers' details and hold them on a database.

The following **may** also be important:

- Products in the sector are primarily sold on 'logic' rather than 'emotion'.
- Control over the customer relationship is important.
- There is an opportunity to distribute direct.

It is worth re-emphasising that the above should **not** be taken as 'rules'. There will be business situations where few or none of the above apply but direct marketing is still used successfully. Few would have thought that Procter & Gamble would be one of the largest spenders on direct marketing worldwide. Equally, sometimes many of the previous points may apply, but the marketing people may still opt for a more general approach to marketing strategy. Many of the conditions apply to the business-to-business 'fleet' car market, but direct marketing is used sparingly by most car manufacturers in this area.

Having made an early exploration into the possible use of direct marketing, but keeping our options open, we move to the next level of decision making.

Exhibit 5.5 The role of testing and control in company politics: evidence defeats doubt

Testing and control are internal management issues that have a bearing on strategic decision making. If your company is risk averse, then it would want to test any initiative carefully before committing significant resources to it. If your company wants to allocate resources carefully to resulting income, the control offered by direct marketing will be attractive. Because it is driven by a database, direct marketing is often centrally run within an organisation, increasing headquarters' control over what the firm does.

These advantages of direct marketing over general marketing often underpin any strategic decision to use direct marketing.

Decision no. 2: allocating resources between existing customers and new customers

The second strategy decision for direct marketers is equally important: what should be the allocation of company resources between keeping existing customers and acquiring new customers? More particularly, how should we prioritise the following?

- Defending market share by keeping our existing customers
- Improving existing customer profitability by increasing existing customers' spend
- Improving existing market share by acquiring customers from direct competitors
- Growing the market by acquiring customers from new market development

Answering these questions requires analysis of the current situation. A number of factors specific to your company and its customers may be important. If you are just starting up a business, you obviously do not have any existing customers. Clearly then, in the first year of operation the vast majority of your budget is allocated to new customer acquisition. Or perhaps you have a large database of existing customers but you have depressingly high levels of defection. Here, your priority is customer retention: stemming the flow.

Exhibit 5.6 Getting the acquisition/retention balance right: the credit card sector

Companies that sell credit, such as American Express, know they have to strike a balance between encouraging loyal behaviour from existing customers and allocating resources to attracting prospects from competitors or new markets. To achieve these aims they may use commercial partners to attract new custom (affinity marketing). They may create a reward scheme, which rewards card spend by giving some value back to loyal customers. Inevitably, some existing customers are lost through bad debt, defection to competitors, or just no longer needing credit. In order to keep its customer base at the same level, Amex will have to allocate resources to replace these people.

It is all a question of balance.

As we saw earlier (Chapters 3 and 4), we can use analysis techniques to look at our database of existing customers. We need to focus on valuable, loyal customers, and look at their current and potential lifetime values and defection rates. To what extent can the marketing objectives be met by obtaining a bigger share of customers? Or by stemming the rate of defection through a commitment to loyalty? Other considerations lie outside the database analysis: if there is heavy competitor activity we may need to counteract it; any new opportunities or threats need to be dealt with.

A strategic guide emerged in the early 1990s to assist us in making this first key resource decision. Work by Boston-based Bain & Co. found that, assuming that you are dealing with a mature business in a mature market, 'your primary focus should be on keeping existing customers rather than obtaining new customers' (Reichheld, 1996). Their research suggests that loyal behaviour can be directly linked to company profitability across a very wide array of sectors. In the late 1990s, a lot was made of Reichheld's work because it provided a bedrock for direct marketers' emphasis on loyalty. Since that time other schools of thought have rained on the loyalty parade somewhat, notably Reinartz and Kumar (2002) who challenged the idea that loyal customers were always more profitable than fly-by-night customers. You will find much more on loyalty later (Chapter 6), but a reasonable summary is that direct marketers should note that:

- acquiring new customers is usually an expensive business, but that . . .
- not all loyal customers are automatically profitable, so . . .
- careful analysis of different customer groups, using research and database analysis, will help us make sensible decisions about where to prioritise our marketing efforts.

Acquisition versus retention guidance also comes from McCorkell (1997), Thomas and Housden (2011) and the IDM (2012), who point out the classic direct marketer's 'numbers driven' route. Tests can establish the lowest cost of acquiring a new customer and, similarly, how much needs to be spent to obtain a similar sale from existing customers. McCorkell proposes that the point at which funds are transferred from existing customers to new customers is when it is cheaper on a like-by-like basis to obtain sales from new customers. The strength of this approach is its foundation in financial logic. Its weakness is that it is tactical in that no account is taken of investment in existing customers, which may not pay immediate dividends but are ultimately profitable.

Decision no. 3: decide how to keep customers

Once the strategic decision between existing and new markets has been made, we are ready to move to the next level of the model – deciding how to keep our current customers with us.

Returning to Figure 5.7 we can see that for both retention and acquisition the strategy decisions come under two basic headings: 'product' and 'market'. The elements under each will now be briefly introduced, with a fuller discussion given later (Chapter 6).

'Market' (customer) decisions

The obvious question to ask here is: which customers do we want to keep? Here is where the database marketers' ability to 'segment by customer value' becomes so important. By understanding the differing value of different customers, we can separate out those who are so important to the company that it is vital they are looked after (see Figure 5.9).

Exhibit 5.7 Angels and Demons: isolating genuine high value customers

Neff tells the story of Mike Seidenman, a salesman who had earned some top-level rewards from US airline Delta by flying very frequently with them each year. Yet he was sacked from their top value loyalty scheme. Why? Seidenman had reached Platinum Medallion status and earned over 100,000 loyalty miles. But he had done so using the lowest fares available, by-passing the premium priced flights that the scheme was aimed at. Delta changed the rules for its SkyMiles scheme and Mike was sent packing.

Delta is just one of many firms trying to identify brand-loyal but penny-pinching consumers. Banks have introduced steep fees on less profitable accounts; insurers have refused to renew policies of homeowners who make as few as one or two claims, and retailers have started refusing refunds to frequent returners, tracking their car registrations to ensure these people are identified. These initiatives reflect the backlash against 'blind loyalty' – where once long standing consumers are automatically assumed to be profitable, this is no longer the case.

Source: Based on information in Neff, J. (2005) 'Why some marketers turn away customers', *Advertising Age*, **76** (2), pp. 1–10.

As we saw previously (Chapter 3), direct marketers also have the ability to segment by loyalty to the company (Reichheld, 1996), by customer needs (Armstrong and Kotler, 2009), by lifestyle, or by profiled likelihood of responding to the next offer (Thomas and Housden, 2011). All these can improve the accuracy and profitability of our marketing.

As we saw earlier in this chapter, the ultimate segmentation is to separate down to segments of one. Using this idea, a new way of thinking about keeping customers has emerged, dubbed one-to-one marketing by Peppers *et al*. (1995), pioneers in this area. Using a database, the firm learns over time, together with the customer, how to meet customer needs more and more efficiently until the firm is regarded as being such good value for money that the idea of going somewhere else is not considered.

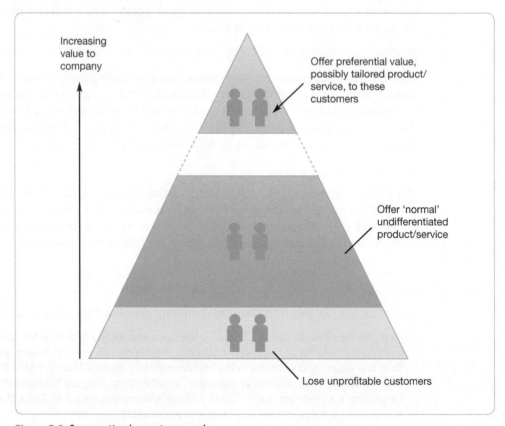

Figure 5.9 **Segmenting by customer value**

'Product' decisions

What can the company offer customers in order to keep as much of their spend with the firm as possible?

To achieve greater retention, direct marketers have been increasingly influenced by relationship marketing philosophies at the expense of traditional Four Ps transactional thinking. The emphasis, therefore, switches from product to service. In particular, the importance of delivering 'superior service' has become apparent in many markets, including the hotel industry (see Exhibit 5.8).

Exhibit 5.8 Tailored service from business hotels

Business people who travel a lot are worth an enormous amount to hotels over their lifetime. By assiduously recording these people's service needs, and making the details available to staff in live situations, these hotels can deliver a 'proactive' tailored service in every aspect of hotel service delivery, from the check-in desk to the bar. Fast check-in and payment, courtesy drinks from the bar, and so on, will add to the convenience of the customers' stay and imbue them with a sense of privilege.

Source: See for example Gale D., (2005) 'From data to dollars', *Hotels*, **39** (10), pp. 61–4.

Another facet of relationship marketing is the opening of meaningful dialogue with customers. The dialogue can help the firm to understand individual needs better, but also can create value by delivering communications.

Exhibit 5.9 Zoom in: keeping customers with high value communications by Mazda

Godsell (2006) reported on car company Mazda planning to launch a new customer magazine to support its CRM programme. Published in ten languages, the first edition was launched in autumn 2007 and the UK version featured lifestyle articles from exotic Lake District cookery to climbing, as well as one or two in-depth features on the latest Mazda range. The magazine was supported by on- line delivery, **www.mazda.co.uk/MazdaLife/**.

An in-depth study of customer magazines is provided later (see Chapter 10).

The other side of the value equation is price, and direct marketing systems that allow differential pricing based on spend have become very popular. These 'loyalty schemes' will be examined in more detail later (Chapters 6 and 10).

Decision no. 4: how to attract new customers

The biggest strategic decisions in attracting new markets often involve the creation of attractive brands, distinctive products or innovative distribution systems. The role of direct marketing in a strategic sense is sometimes, therefore, quite minimal, although its role as a targeting and communications vehicle is often very important. This contrasts with the key strategic role of the database in keeping customers, as we saw in the preceding section.

Nevertheless, there are some important elements of strategy for us to consider in direct marketing acquisition, especially if we picture direct marketing as a part of the overall marketing effort. Once again, we can split our focus between market and product.

'Market' decisions

For any marketer, the core strength of direct marketing for acquiring new customers is 'targeting'. Direct marketers are dealing with individuals, and they have the analysis and media tools to pinpoint prospects more precisely than general marketers. Strategically, there are a number of targeting approaches that depend on the company's strengths (does it have a database; does it have a clear idea of precisely who its new customers are likely to be?) and the marketing environment (the need to go for new types of customers, competitive activity, whether its markets are niche or mass, and so on).

Within this strategic framework, the targeting options for direct marketers are:

- asking new customers to identify themselves
- targeting based on the principle that new customers will be similar to existing customers
- targeting based on predicted loyalty to the company, again based on existing customer profiles
- targeting a commercial partner's customers, known as affinity marketing (covered later (see Chapter 6))

'Product' decisions

In the acquisition of new customers, marketing practice is arguably still more influenced by the Four Ps transaction approach than by relationship marketing theory. Certainly, a look at direct marketing practice suggests that it is the 'formal product' that is more important in attracting prospects than add-on service. This, however, is mentioned here more as a thought provoker than a firm principle.

A customer seeking to buy from a supplier for the first time will seek lots of things, but some benefits may be more important on first purchase. These may include 'trust', 'reassurance' about the quality of their purchase, being able to buy 'conveniently', or having an extra 'incentive' as a temptation to purchase.

Both direct and general marketers will need to pay attention to these issues, and perhaps place them at the core of their product strategy. There are occasions where strategic advantage can be obtained by delivering these benefits more effectively through direct marketing systems.

General marketers look to imbue feelings of trust and reassurance through 'building brands' that prospects will be familiar with and like, even though they have yet to purchase from that firm. Direct marketers can either 'support' brands built through general marketing or take a 'lead role' in building different types of brand values themselves. The links between branding and direct marketing are becoming more important, and this subject is given further attention later (Chapter 6).

The use of 'direct distribution' – whether mail order, on-line e-tickets for a flight, or direct services like telephone banking – is a powerful weapon in the direct marketers' armoury when it comes to attracting new customers. The benefit they are offering is convenience. The growth of electronic media heralds the possibility of new modes of shopping by consumers who value convenience over the tangible shopping experience itself. This will offer firms the strategic advantage of bypassing retail channels and is, therefore, an attractive option for FMCG (Fast-moving Consumer Good) sector manufacturers, among others.

Finally, a decision must be made whether or not to use 'incentives' to stimulate purchase. This decision may rest on branding, pricing, competitive usage or targeting decisions, and it is with the latter that incentives used through direct marketing may well provide a huge advantage (Thomas and Housden, 2011). The idea is that, instead of most of your incentives to attract new users being taken advantage of by existing customers, as happens in retail situations, incentives can be directed to the intended audience – prospects. Of course, this runs counter to the philosophy of rewarding loyalty: are you doing the right thing by incentivising switchers over loyalists?

Summary

In this chapter we found that direct marketing objectives should be linked to the main marketing objectives, which in turn encompass separate acquisition and retention objectives.

A model of strategic decision making for direct marketers was developed.

The most important strategic roles of direct marketing were identified as a focus on customer understanding and the ability to deliver improved customer retention through powerful segmentation and targeting strategies. The service and dialogue links with relationship marketing were seen as vital in many markets. Finally, the strategic roles of direct marketing in acquiring new customers were pinpointed as efficient targeting, direct distribution, and brand building and support.

QUESTIONS

1 What are the core strengths of direct marketing over general marketing? If you were marketing director of a children's toy manufacturer, what would be your arguments for using a direct marketing system in that sector?

2 Give three reasons why a clothing company should consider distributing direct rather than through retail.

3 What are the overlaps between relationship and direct marketing? In what ways do the two approaches to marketing differ?

4 Give two differences and two similarities between direct marketing objectives and general marketing objectives.

5 Why are packaged (supermarket) goods companies less likely than business-to-business suppliers to use direct marketing?

6 'Direct marketing's strength is its focus on customers.' Explain how this market focus influences the development of direct marketing strategy.

References

Ansoff, H.I. (1968) *Corporate Strategy,* Penguin, Harmondsworth.

Armstrong, G. and Kotler, P. (2009) *Marketing – an Introduction,* Pearson, New Jersey.

Berry, L.L. (1983) 'Relationship marketing' in Berry, L.L., Shostack, G.L. and Upah, G.D. (eds) Emerging Perspectives on Services Marketing, American Marketing Association, Chicago.

Bird, D. (2007) *Commonsense Direct and Digital Marketing,* Kogan Page, London.

Fifield, P. (1998) *Marketing Strategy*, 3rd edn, Butterworth-Heinemann, Oxford.

Fletcher, K., Wheeler, C. and Wright, J. (1995) 'The role and status of UK database marketing' in Payne, A., Christopher, M., Clark, M. and Peck, H. (eds) *Relationship Marketing for Competitive Advantage,* Butterworth-Heinemann, Oxford.

Gale, D. (2005), 'From data to dollars', *Hotels*, 39 (10), pp. 61–4.

Godsell, M., (2006), 'Mazda backs CRM drive with customer magazine', *Marketing*, 11 August.

IDM (2012) *Course Material Diploma in Direct and Digital Marketing,* Teddington.

Kotler, P. Keller, K., Brady, M. and Hansen, M. (2009) *Marketing Management*, Pearson Education, Harlow.

McCorkell, G. (1997) *Direct and Database Marketing*, Kogan Page, London.

McDonald, M. and Wilson, H. (2011) *Marketing Plans: how to prepare and how to use them*, 7th edn, Butterworth-Heinemann, Oxford.

Neff, J. (2005) 'Why some marketers turn away customers', *Advertising Age*, 76 (7), pp. 1–10.

Peppers, D., Rogers, M. and Pine, J. (1995) 'Do you want to keep your customers forever?', *Harvard Business Review*, March–April, pp. 103–14. (See also Peppers, D. and Rogers, M. (1993) *The One-to-One Future*, Piatkus, London.)

Porter, M. (1985) *Competitive Advantage: creating and sustaining superior performance*, The Free Press, New York.

Reichheld, F.F. (1996) *The Loyalty Effect*, Harvard Business School Publishing, Boston, Mass.

Reinartz, W. and Kumar, V. (2002) 'The mismanagement of customer loyalty', *Harvard Business Review*, 80 (7) pp. 86–94.

Spiller L, and Baier, M. (2010) *Contemporary Direct And Interactive Marketing*, Pearson, New Jersey.

Thomas, B. and Housden, M. (2011) *Direct and Digital Marketing in Practice*, A and C Black, London.

CASE STUDY

Nissan GB Qashqai Launch 2011 TMW and Indicia

This case study is based on the actual events surrounding the launch of the Nissan Qashqai in the UK in 2011. Work was carried out for Nissan UK by their Direct ad Digital agency Tullo Marshall Warren (TMW) and Indicia. Indicia provided strategy and data planning input. TMW worked on creative, production strategy and data planning. Reproduced with kind permission of TMW.

Setting the scene

The task was to raise awareness of the QQ's new technologies, including the 'Around View Monitor' (AVM) and the now more fuel efficient and environmentally friendly 1.6L diesel engine.

QQ launched in 2007 as the first crossover of its kind, creating a new car category. True to its revolutionary origins, it has continued to offer ground-breaking innovations since. The latest of these is the AVM: a cutting-edge four-camera system that makes parking easier by sending real-time images to the central console, forming a bird's eye view of the car. QQ is the first affordable family car to offer this technology.

Campaign strategy

We used a unique approach to drive the strategy and targeting. Using the characteristics and attributes of QQ households such as demographics, attitudes and behavioural variables, we could understand what would be interesting and compelling for them when choosing a car. From this understanding, we created two distinct segments, 'Practical Couples' and 'Trendy Families', dialling up the key benefits of Nissan and QQ appropriate to each.

To drive urgency and desire to buy, we sent a combination of mail packs and/or e-mails. First, a tease e-mail to excite prospective buyers just before the new registration period and to take them out of the market. Second, a pre-launch to build anticipation and drive pre-orders. Finally, cut-through launch communications when the car was available to buy and drive.

Creativity and strategy

Armed with powerful data insights, the tack was to tell the story in stages, particularly as we knew people would be in the market for a new car well before they could order or test drive QQ.

Cue the tease e-mail, which boldly announced 'Change is coming'. Alluding to the eureka moment the new QQ was conceived, TWW created an animated gif that showed lights flickering on in a secret building where it seemed the final touches were being made to the QQ.

From then on, activity was tailored to each segment. For 'Practical Couples' after the latest gadgetry and style, TWW led with the AVM. For 'Trendy Families' wanting a reliable, high quality, reasonably priced car from a trusted brand, the agency dialled up the fuel efficiency and Nissan credentials.

The pre-launch direct-mail and e-mail brought to life the 360° view enabled by the AVM, by inviting the audience to 'see the city from a new perspective' and pre-order the QQ.

The launch direct-mail then led with 'Inside, a little peek at what it's like to drive the ultimate urban car'. The box contained a pair of mirrored 'eyes in the back of your head' glasses, a preview of the benefit offered by the Around View Monitor. The pack also contained a highly personalised letter (with over 90 variants) and brochure, inviting recipients to book a test drive with their local dealer.

Each piece also featured graffitied characters who follow the car on its urban travels, integrating fully with the look and feel of the TV campaign.

How results confirmed creative stratgey

The success of the launch stemmed from an innovative new strategic approach that recognised that speaking to the right household about pertinent product details would ultimately trigger sales.

The data insight enabled a highly targeted and impactful creative approach, driving interest in the innovative AVM technology, and sales, despite a lack of major product changes. The look and feel also aligned with the TV Campaign, capitalising on awareness that had already been generated.

The agency also understood that we would need a simple yet dramatic way to announce and explain the car's new technology.

In the absence of any other new product news, the execution succeeded in making the QQ feel fresh and exciting to a largely conquest audience always on the look out for the next new thing.

Case study (*continued*)

As a result, TMW increased loyalty to the brand, achieving stand-out in a crowded market, recruiting a legion of Nissan devotees with a higher lifetime value and reaffirming QQ as a highly innovative category leader.

Results

The campaign generated a total of 1516 sales.

Return on investment was 5:1 from those that were in market.

E-mail engagement levels were 60 per cent higher than expected, with the tease e-mail having generated 40 per cent open rates, exceeding the target of 25 per cent.

CASE STUDY

Managing acquisition and retention – BK Bank

This case is based on a real bank operating in the UK. The bank is not one of the 'big four' retailers. The name of the bank and the names of key personnel have been changed to preserve confidentiality, but the core material reflects the bank's commercial situation.

Introduction

David DeLorean sat staring out of his office window from its vantage point high up in the headquarters' building of BK Bank in Macclesfield. The view was as pretty as ever, looking out over the rolling hills as far as the Peak District in the distance, but David was not really taking any of it in. His thoughts were far away as he pondered the problems that had been handed to him by his superiors. As a businessman, he had grown used to pressure, but this was going to take some beating . . .

David DeLorean is the Direct Marketing Manager at BK Bank. The directors of BK had just had a meeting at which they had decided to reverse a key decision of three or four years ago. The meeting had concluded that BK needed to increase its revolving credit (credit card) account base urgently. Naturally, the task had fallen to him to resolve. But how . . .?

The credit card business

Credit cards were introduced in the UK in 1966 when Barclaycard launched its service, although credit cards have been used in the USA for a good deal longer. Indeed, the first known credit card was introduced in stores in the USA in the early part of the twentieth century.

The early UK market was dominated by Barclaycard (card issuer), which was backed up by 'network organiser', Visa. Companies like Visa and Access spent a great deal of capital laying down the infrastructure of the credit card business. They arranged deals with retailers and built up the card processing facilities. The next chain in the business was the card issuers, such as Barclays Bank and BK Bank, which began the process of building up credit card awareness and recruiting customers.

In the early 1980s, more players, such as TSB and the building societies, entered the market.

The market soon broke into different sectors, defined by the plethora of different cards that were available. At one end, corporate clients who had high spending power were attracted by the status of 'gold' and 'platinum' cards. These charged a high fee, were exclusively marketed and were highly profitable to the issuers. Another emerging sector was that of the high street charge cards, which gave credit to regular customers of particular stores. One of the early problems encountered by these cards, however, was their impulse nature. This led to a large volume of bad debt being built up, especially among people from lower social profiles. That said, the high debt utilisation (i.e. a low number of dormant cards) made these cards a great success with card issuers.

The mid 1980s saw a new development with the arrival of 'affinity' cards into the UK. These products were the result of partnerships between two businesses: the issuer (for example BK Bank) works with a well-known organisation to provide a credit card branded by that organisation. The card is then aimed at the existing customers of the partner.

There has been a steady growth in the number of these cards and now organisations as diverse as Cambridge University, charities, the Automobile Association and many others, have affinity cards.

However, this has not been the end of the product development. The end of the 1980s saw the fall off in growth in credit card usage as consumers' ability to raise debt dropped off. In 1993 an attempt was made to restart market growth with the launch of 'product based', value-added credit cards. Barclaycard launched a new type of card in partnership with Ford with which customers could get up to £2,500 off a new Ford by accumulating points according to credit card spend. A similar deal was struck between General Motors and HFC Bank, backed by Visa, giving money off new Vauxhalls.

The market-place

The credit card market is highly diverse, with many sectors of the population using credit cards for many reasons. However, there are two sectors in particular that contribute a major part of industry profits:

- Generally well-off sectors of the population. These people tend to be of AB social class, highly educated and they spend money reasonably freely. They will not be too upset at paying either interest or other charges.
- Less well-off people, who may be working class in background and may be tempted to run up quite large credit card bills. A subset of these consumers has been dubbed 'Essex Man' in popular culture.

The market-place is now reaching its mature stage, with the early growth slowing down. In particular, the most wealthy sectors have been exposed to a very high amount of marketing and are largely saturated. In the affinity card sector, charities have been extensively targeted and new openings are hard to find.

BK Bank

BK Bank Limited is a wholly owned but independent UK subsidiary of Chase Chicago, an American conglomerate that wanted to get a toehold in the UK banking sector. BK Bank is a large financial organisation with assets of over £9 billion. These assets are based on lending to companies and individuals on a range of different products, from mortgages to lease, HP, personal loans and credit cards.

Origins

BK's traditional form of business was to provide finance through credit cards and loans. However, through the years, BK has moved into a number of new market sectors to provide finance. These include professional groups, industrial concerns, membership groups and retailers. BK spotted these partnership opportunities very early on and was the most profitable group in its sector.

The BK business

The name BK, however, is not well known to the public, even though hundreds of thousands of them make use of its services every day through its various credit cards. The reason for this lack of awareness by British consumers is that BK does not brand its product and services itself. Rather, its products are marketed by business partners. For example, if BK and Thistle Hotels, say, were to launch a credit card, then BK would provide the card processing facilities and the marketing know-how, but the card would be branded by Thistle Hotels with no mention of BK Bank at all. As David DeLorean described it:

> 'We are like a chameleon in a way. We take on the identity of whoever we happen to be in partnership with. It's a symbiotic relationship and it works very well.'

BK describes itself as a wholesaler of funds, preferring to work behind other companies' own brands. It is BK, however, that does the marketing on behalf of the business partner: BK sets out the product specification, for example the APR rate, loan facilities, etc., and BK does the marketing of the cards, often acting under the name of its partner. If a customer rings in with a service issue, the BK staff who take the call take on the identity of the affinity partner. They will, therefore, answer the phone 'Hello, Red Cross', and so on.

Main business areas

BK Bank's main business is in loans, whether by big-ticket finance to corporate customers, or fixed and revolving accounts to consumers. A fixed-term loan is one that was traditionally offered to consumers by high street banks. Consumers would be expected to pay back a fixed loan in instalments, to which interest was added. These loans were typically 'one-off' affairs. However, the problem with fixed-term loans was that, on average, customer turnover would be 100 per cent in six years, with less than half the customers renewing their loans or taking up another product at the end of each payment period.

The introduction of credit cards marked the start of revolving accounts. These had the advantage of allowing the customer to build up and pay off debt again and again.

Over ten years ago, BK was responsible for the launch of several large retailer credit cards now known in the market. Through this programme it has managed to recruit many tens of thousands of customers, which it has retained on its database. In tandem with this, BK is an issuer of Visa cards in the UK and, additionally, has several large operations that are over-branded with other organisations' names: affinity cards.

Of the customers who use credit cards, about 30 per cent will build up debt and not pay it all off within a month. These are amongst the most profitable customers for BK because they pay interest on longer term debt. The bank also earns revenue through the additional charge it makes of a fixed annual fee of £12 to consumers, other customer charges (for example, late payment fees) and merchant fees (charges levied on retailers for the use of BK's credit cards).

Recent situation

In 2009, BK Bank decided to have a major review of its involvement in consumer revolving accounts. This product was making some money, but was rather slow moving compared with other parts of BK business. Costs at the time were high; marketing costs, the capital and ongoing costs of processing and customer service were all biting deep. In return, the revenue payback was quite long in coming. The conclusion of the review, after looking at the situation, was that BK should not continue to market proactively the cards to consumers.

When looked at from the point of view of the prevailing culture at BK Bank, this was not a surprising decision. BK had always gone for a strategy of steady, short-term growth across a broad range of products with no particular commitment to long-term strategy in any one area.

BK's strengths

The company has considerable resources at its disposal. Its marketing budget is fixed on a cost-justification basis and by comparison with the rest of its sector is quite large. It has its own large marketing department, which is able to handle the large volumes involved. BK also has enjoyed good relations with many of the UK's top direct marketing agencies, leading to some award winning campaigns in the past.

BK's advanced systems allow processing costs to be kept to a minimum. It has an advanced relational database that allows any required customer profiling analyses to be done very quickly but, up till recently, BK had not actually used statistical techniques to help with its marketing.

BK had the following data on most of its customers:

- Name
- Address
- Transaction data including date of product purchased, which products: loans, credit cards, insurance, value of transaction
- Marketing history: what promotions had been aimed at the customer, response history
- Age, personal geodemographic details
- What loans were used for, for example car purchase

David had recently been on a direct marketing course and had picked up some basic tips on the use of modelling techniques. He knew that predictive techniques could lower the cost per response for his acquisition and retention activities. However, he needed to get a clearer picture of what could be done.

Used in tandem with the database was a sophisticated inbound and outbound telemarketing system which allowed a screen of customer information to be on every telemarketer's desk. There were over 100 personnel potentially available for a telemarketing campaign. BK Bank had established an impressive system of inbound and outbound customer contact, which it used with customers who had loans (see Figure 5.10).

Staff were well paid and well trained, backed up with good systems. This ensured the quality of customer contact was kept very high. The same outbound operatives were always used with a particular customer to ensure a genuine relationship was built up over time. Customers came to trust the advice they were given. The customer record contained details

Case study (*continued*)

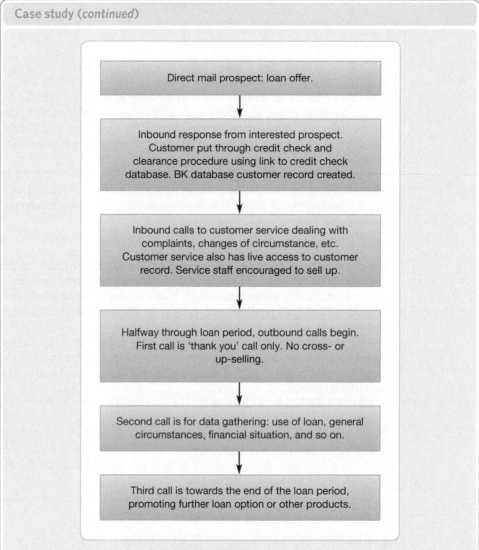

Figure 5.10 **Inbound and outbound customer contact**

of the last three conversations they had had with BK Bank, so that service and outbound staff always knew what was going on.

BK Bank had carefully tested this relationship building system against controls in which no contact was made, and it knew that the system paid for itself for loan products. A typical loan of £3,000, paid back over five years at 18 per cent APR (Annual Percentage Rate), made a gross profit of £280 per annum. Set against this was the initial costs of acquisition. A typical mailer costing £500 per thousand would generate an average response of 0.2 per cent, although this varied dramatically depending on the affinity partner. Then there were the costs of service and outbound calling, estimated at about £120 p.a. per customer. However, David had found that, under the service and telemarketing system, retention rates increased for loans (i.e. a customer with a loan renews with a new loan or takes up another product on expiry of the original loan) from under 40 per cent to nearer 60 per cent.

David's problem now was to decide whether such a system would be profitable with credit cards. The acquisition costs of credit cards were less than for loans; mailers to affinity partners' databases averaged about a 1 per cent response. However, profitability per annum was lower, at about £30 per customer.

The problem

As the fiscal year drew to a close, the marketing department at BK Bank was considering its marketing plan for the following year. David and his colleagues had for some time been increasingly concerned about the consequences of the decisions made four years earlier to slow down activity in the credit card sector. In the meantime, BK's competitors had been far from idle. Using incentives, sales promotions, awarding larger credit limits, removing the annual fees and promoting new uses of credit cards were just some of the tactics successfully employed to renew the momentum of the sector.

Over the last four years or so, BK Bank's recruitment of credit card (revolving) accounts had dropped sharply compared with the early 2000s. BK was, therefore, beginning to miss out on a highly profitable sector. The directors had met and hurriedly decided to restart marketing activity in the revolving-account sector. This decision was hardly surprising to David and his department; after all, the marketing department had been keeping a close eye on the credit card market-place for some 18 months now and could see which way the wind was blowing.

A budget of £600k had been set for marketing activity for 2012–13.

David looked back into the office to see the team looking at him anxiously. He knew they depended on a strong strategy and plan to provide the right start to the new financial year. Fortunately, they had some plans on the table already.

BK Bank's traditional strength had always been to pick up particular niches that were too small and undeveloped for the likes of Visa and Access to bother with but could, nevertheless, be highly profitable. Some ideas (which do not have to be adopted) were:

1 The previous year a staff suggestion scheme had suggested what a good idea it would be to have a credit card aimed exclusively at women. A lot of research had been done on this idea and, while not all the findings had been positive by any means, there were some possibilities to be explored.

2 David had just finished very fruitful negotiations with Toyan, a major Japanese car manufacturer with a strong UK presence, with the objective of launching a new 'product' based credit card branded as Toyan.

The brief

Your group has been commissioned as a direct marketing agency invited to pitch for the BK Bank account in 2012–13. In your pitch include the following:

- The key issues
- Carefully planned, detailed marketing and direct marketing objectives
- An explanation of the role of direct marketing
- Strategies for retention and revenue from existing customers and strategies for generating new prospects

How will BK achieve competitive advantage?

Coventry City Football Club

Introduction

The ticketing manager, Jim Whelan, and the commercial manager, Ron Chippo, got their heads together and decided to approach the chairman with a plan to implement direct marketing to supporters in a more strategic manner than had been attempted to date.

It would be fair to say that, up to now, the use of direct marketing had been patchy.

Club structure

With some exceptions, football clubs have traditionally treated ordinary supporters as somewhat of a 'cash cow'. Senior managers in football have tended to focus their attention on sponsorship and business-to-business marketing – conference and corporate entertainment revenues – while the major supporter focus has been the short-term gains afforded from merchandising. Football clubs have never had classical marketing departments as such. They have tended to organise around ticketing – hence, Coventry City had a Ticket Office Manager – and 'commercial activities', needing a 'commercial' or 'marketing' manager. Commercial activities typically include the main sponsorship deal, perimeter advertising, corporate hospitality boxes on match days, and off-field sales of the ground's facilities, conference hire, wedding hire and so on. Consequently, there is a less developed marketing approach towards ordinary supporters, and it is this that has limited the growth of database marketing. At Coventry, the commercial manager Ron was well aware that there was a cross-over between the ordinary supporter and his corporate guests, and that a database of fans would be of great use to him.

The other major business unit in football clubs is merchandising. At clubs like Manchester United, merchandising is a worldwide operation taking advantage of a global brand. In 2004, income from this source alone for Manchester United is likely to have exceeded £50 million. The rest of the football world is playing catch-up in comparison, but even for a local club such as Coventry City, retail and merchandise is important. The retail manager at Coventry City was keen to get in on the database marketing initiatives being discussed at the club. At the moment the club has two retail outlets, one at the ground and one in the city centre. The retail manager knew that capturing purchase data and linking it to supporters' personal details could help his operations. If only he had time to do something about it!

The second major barrier to database marketing investment was the low priority given to long-term projects. However, while it is sometimes easy to criticise, let us reflect for a moment on the frantic scramble for cash that clubs need to buy and pay players and, hence, stay in their division. The lower divisions are littered with once highly placed clubs who have dropped into a vicious circle of lower gates meaning less money available to buy or keep the players they need to climb the table. It is this unforgiving and volatile nature of football that sometimes militates against the business side of the operation feeling that it can take a long-term approach. As a result, any new ideas had to be very thoroughly sold to the board to stand a chance, and that included direct marketing.

Current use of database marketing

The situation that Jim and Ron had inherited is represented in Figure 5.11.

A few years ago, the only 'direct marketing' from the club would have been the season ticket renewals in June and July. More recently, some affinity marketing had been started, but all on a small scale (see later (Chapter 6) for a section on affinity marketing). A small

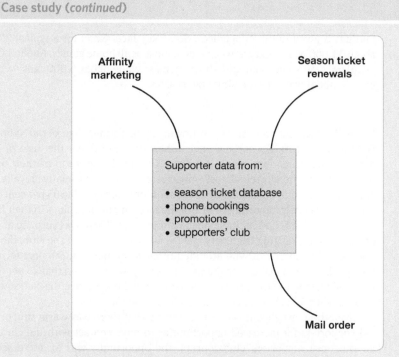

Figure 5.11 Limited direct marketing at Coventry City

mail-order operation had been started by the retail manager, who used the database as a route to his customers, but with no attempt to record sales or to look at targeting.

New initiatives

At the time the future looked bright for Coventry City. The club planned to move to a state of the art stadium at the edge of the city. Holding 45,000 spectators and with a retractable pitch, the new facilities would rival any in Europe. At the moment, at Highfield Road (capacity 24,000), the club averaged just over 20,000 for a home fixture. It sold out for the arrival of big draws, such as Arsenal or Liverpool, but the home support shrank a little to a core of about 16,000 for, say, Southampton on a wet Tuesday night.

The club management knew that they needed to set in place initiatives that would draw new support to fill the new stadium. The mood was favourable for expenditure on items like integrated database systems. Accordingly the club had invested in a new system called Arena, which had the capability to integrate with the important functions of the club: ticketing, retail, corporate hospitality, finance and so on. The database held records of all transactions, sorted by supporter name and personal details. Of course, at busy times in the shop or in the ticket office on match days, it was difficult or often impossible to record details of a supporter purchasing tickets with cash. But, otherwise, the club was encouraged by the amount of data it had been able to collect. A total database size approaching 50,000 people had been accumulated.

Coventry City supporters

In conjunction with the local university (Coventry Business School), an extensive amount of market research data had been gathered about its supporters. A summary of the main findings is given in the Appendices. Some key facts were: for a typical 20,000 audience, about 11,000 were 'fanatics' who went to most or all home games. About 3,000–4,000 were 'regulars' who went to about half the games; while about 6,000 fans were 'casuals' who went to about five or fewer games per season.

'Fanatics'

Football is more than a business. As Rogan Taylor, former chair of the National Supporters' Federation, put it: 'No one has their ashes scattered down the aisle of Tesco's'. At the extreme end, some fans placed Coventry City at the very top of their priorities in life; indeed the researchers felt almost embarrassed to test their relative loyalty to the club versus their own family! A fan survey backed this up: an incredible 65 per cent of fans said that their club was very important or one of the most important things in their life.

Committed fans had multiple links with football. There was surprise at the multiplicity of associations, ranging from personal friends who worked at the club, those having some link with the players, or who attended other local matches. Support for this 'football as lifestyle' behaviour came from the Carling survey, which found that 25 per cent of Coventry fans had been to see the reserves, 14 per cent had been to see the Nationwide league that season, while 13 per cent had seen non-league action.

Given these insights, it was not surprising that there was warm support from committed supporters for increased opportunities to have contact with the club. Based around an enhanced supporters' club concept, the opportunity was for increased dialogue and improved interaction within the community. Practically everyone was eager for more information and more news than they were currently getting, and some supporters looked for increased contact with other supporters, maybe through 'supporter evenings' and so on. At present, only about 10 per cent of Coventry supporters belonged to one of the supporter club options, which indicated both the supporter club product and promotion may need addressing in order to meet the needs of these committed fans.

The special nature of loyalty

Among supporters, there were complex and sometimes contradictory sets of feelings towards loyalty and value. Some diehard fans actively defined their entire experience with Coventry City through loyalty. Unlike most business relationships, loyalty was explicit and extremely important to these fans. The link with behaviour was important for credibility among their peers: they were 'required' to turn up to less exciting home games, and maybe away fixtures as well.

Other fans also 'described themselves' as loyal, but, over the years, their attendance was more varied. They may have 'drifted away from watching Coventry City live' and then come back. Interestingly this was behaviour they felt they needed to justify, because of the peer pressure to be seen as loyal.

Casual supporters

At the other end of the scale were 'casual' supporters: those who went to an average of five or fewer games per season. For these, loyalty was not an issue they had considered. They viewed Coventry City as an entertainment option, not a lifestyle, and were, therefore, not subject to any pressure to attend from peers. Compared with committed fans, they tended to be more critical of the value for money they were getting. Casual supporters explained that they typically made decisions on the match day or maybe only decided to attend the game a day or two before, perhaps after driving past the ground accidentally during the week. Appendix 5 gives some more details on 'casual' fans' attitudes.

Other segments

Coventry Business School had conducted research amongst the fans, and key segments were identified as:

- Women. 50 years ago it was rare to see any women attending football games. The national average is now over 10 per cent, and Coventry was no exception.
- 'Professional wanderers'. These were casual fans, with professional occupations, who had moved around the country and formed relatively weak associations with more than one club.
- 'Repertoire fans'. 27 per cent of fans said they attended matches not involving Coventry City. This pattern was typical around many other clubs. These repertoire fans were more likely to fall into the 'casual' bracket above.
- Collectors. Many dedicated supporters we spoke to had varying degrees of 'collecting behaviour'. One even wrote down transcripts of all the radio interviews involving Coventry City! The commercial opportunities were definitely there.

Match day behaviours were often different among different groups. For examples see Appendix 7.

Possible marketing initiatives
The idea of club membership

At various points, Ron had been approached by third parties who wished to discuss initiatives with him. These people were keen to act as middlemen beween Coventry City and suppliers of goods and services. What these agents knew was that the relationship between a football club and its fans was a powerful one. In short, the club had immensely powerful brands that, at present, were probably being under exploited.

One way to exploit them was to develop affinity goods.

The growing role of the Internet

Coventry City's website was up and running by early 1999. It would be fair to say that the club had operated a 'follower' rather than leader strategy with its use of the Internet. Some managers at the club had seen the net as merely another possible channel from which to make money. However, others had seen the potential for more strategic uses. For example, they had noted the following:

- Fans were heavy users of unofficial sites.
- One club executive had heard that on one Sunday a small Premier League club with a supporter gate averaging 25,000 had received over 250,000 'hits' to its website!
- International fans were heavy users of the Internet. One group of 20 Coventry City Fans who lived in Canada had organised a trip to the UK to see a game via the Coventry City website.
- Other clubs were looking at selling tickets over the Web. But how could they manage this facility, given that for some matches the sale of tickets needed tight control?
- Merchandise was sold over the Internet.

Case study (*continued*)

- Most of all, fans used the Internet to talk to each other. The Internet provided the ideal place for communities to establish themselves, and relationships to be built. The potential for fans to build themselves up as one voice was also greatly increased – fan power had a forum!

Other issues, such as future media rights and the interest of agents in acting as middlemen between consumers and suppliers, had to be considered.

The brief

The scene was set for a push to invest more in direct and database marketing. In the future, filling the new stadium was top priority and, as a result, the club needed to think about acquisition and retention. This being football, loyalty was clearly important, but the club perhaps needed to be more proactive. The management at the club were very concerned to get things right. Was a points scheme a good idea? What about the Internet? The first thing to do was to take a closer look at all the research the business school had produced for them. Ron and Jim opened the first of the reports.

Your task

Produce a direct marketing plan for Coventry City for the next three years, including recommendations on the club's use of the Internet.

Appendix 1
Extracts from research carried out with season ticket and ex-season ticket holders, November 1999

Reason ex-season ticket holders are not loyal (tick any that apply)	Frequency
The letter from CCFC came at a time when I was short of money for just that time.	20
The team performance last year put me off.	18
I expected a poor team performance this year.	5
I did not get round to it when CCFC sent me the renewal letter.	2
I feel less loyal than I used to.	5
I am watching other teams more.	6
I am doing other things on a Saturday.	19
I have to work on match days.	16
My family commitments have increased.	17
My job has changed from last year to this.	16
I have less money to spend on things like this compared with last year.	35
The people/person that I went to matches with do/does not go any more.	15
I found myself not enjoying going last year.	11
I would rather pay to get in match by match because my life is more complicated this year.	37
Season ticket price rise.	38
I would rather watch football on TV.	1
None of the above.	3
Other.	25

APPENDIX 2
Extracts from research carried out at an open day, June 1999

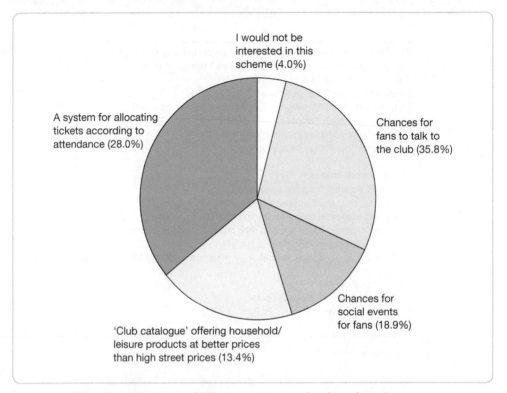

I would not be interested in this scheme (4.0%)

A system for allocating tickets according to attendance (28.0%)

Chances for fans to talk to the club (35.8%)

Chances for social events for fans (18.9%)

'Club catalogue' offering household/ leisure products at better prices than high street prices (13.4%)

Figure 5.12 What the supporters would like to see in 'a membership scheme'

APPENDIX 3
The typical fan – research findings

Your typical fan does not exist! The findings show:

- a range of ages, incomes, occupations
- the fans are more likely to be men (80 per cent) than women
- 50 per cent have incomes between £10k and £30k but 10% have incomes >£50k
- about 40 per cent have children under 16
- about 10 per cent have children under 5
- own a three-bedroom house
- a mix of occupations with a slight C1/C2 bias but also many with AB jobs
- an equal split between living in the city and living outside
- the fans are more likely to be aged 19–34, but with plenty of fans across all age groups

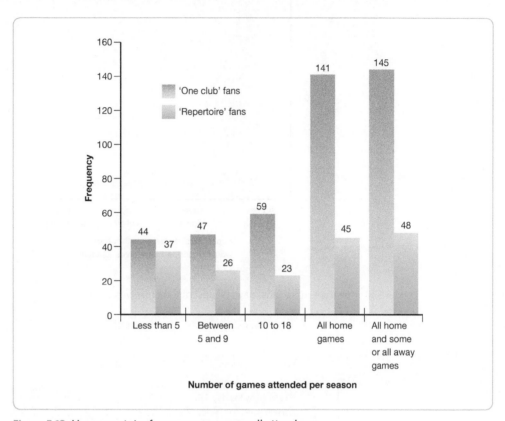

Figure 5.13 How repertoire fans vary versus overall attendance

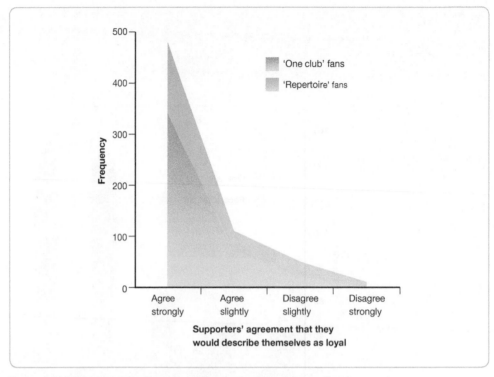

Figure 5.14 How repertoire fans may still describe themselves as loyal

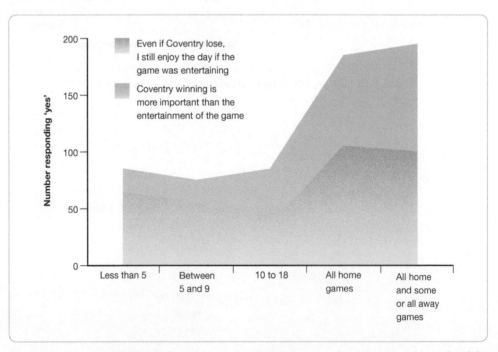

Figure 5.15 How attitudes towards winning and entertainment vary by supporter value to the club

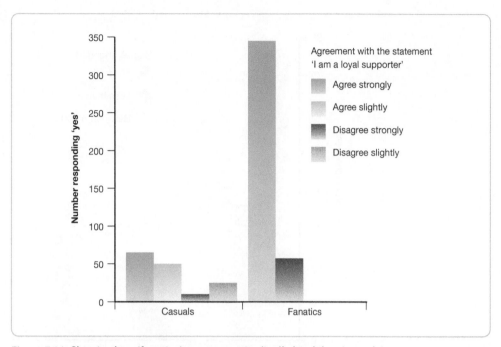

Figure 5.16 Showing how 'fanatics' are more attitudinally loyal than 'casuals'

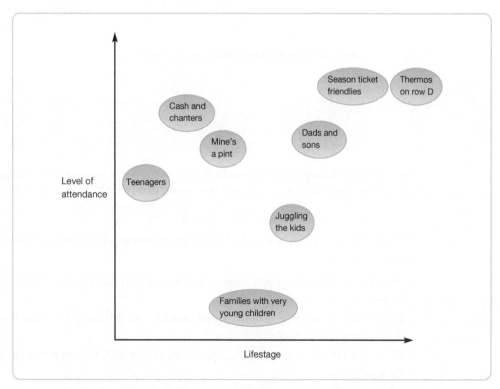

Figure 5.17 Behaviour based segments mapped against level of attendance and lifestage

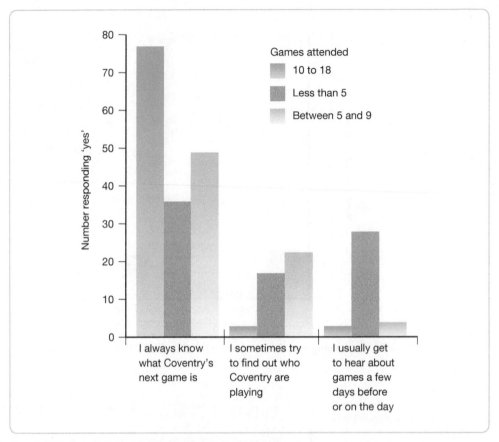

Figure 5.18 Reactions to marketing: casual and loyal fans

APPENDIX 5
Casual fans: two types of casuals

On examining the research findings in detail, 'two types of casuals have emerged'. We have called these the 'carefree casuals' and the 'committed casuals'. These are defined as follows:

Carefree casuals (57 per cent of casuals)

Defined as those casuals who only slightly agree, or disagree, with the notion that they are loyal supporters:

● 88 per cent of carefree casuals prefer to see an entertaining game, even if Coventry City loses.

● 50 per cent of carefree casuals attend matches not involving Coventry City, compared with 27 per cent of all fans.

● 88 per cent describe watching Coventry City as just one of a number of choices for them on a Saturday.

● 63 per cent do not know when Coventry City's next home game is.

In summary, carefree casuals may be football lovers but see Coventry as an entertainment option, and being Coventry City supporters is NOT part of their self-image.

Committed casuals (43 per cent of casuals)

Defined as those casuals who strongly agree that they are loyal to Coventry City:

- Only 26 per cent go to non-Coventry City games.
- 38 per cent claim Coventry City winning is more important than an entertaining game (close to the percentage of fanatics who think the same).
- 78 per cent of committed casuals know when Coventry City's next game is.
- However, 75 per cent still see Coventry City as one of a range of things they will consider.

In summary, committed casuals are genuine fans of Coventry City, but for them some non-football activities are of equal or greater priority (family? playing sports/activities?). They, therefore, value variety and choice, and perhaps have their football support in perspective with the rest of their lives.

APPENDIX 6
The loyalty issue

When we took a closer look at how fans expressed their loyalty, we started to notice some strange contradictions. This is what we found:

27 per cent of fans (even regular/fanatics (24 per cent), but especially casuals (46 per cent)) 'go to competitor games'.

'Of these, 68 per cent would strongly agree that they are loyal supporters'. Thus, the stereotype of the typical football fan as being a one-team person, perhaps having nothing but contempt for other teams, does not seem to be borne out by their behaviour.

In other words, when people describe themselves as loyal to one team, we should NOT take this as read. More than one in four of them will attend other matches.

APPENDIX 7
Groups distinguished by match-day behaviour

Mine's a pint: people who like a drink or two either side of the game. These fans will arrive early, 'to park', will often meet casual acquaintances at the bar or maybe read the programme.

Juggling the kids: families trying to fit in two or three events in the day. They may arrive at the ground at the last minute, but be high half-time spenders on snacks and so on. Families are also high spenders on merchandise.

'**Thermos on row D':** creatures of habit who get into the ground quite late, they are not interested in talking to anyone and may not spend much money at the ground on programmes or food.

Season ticket friendlies: enjoy the social event of meeting fellow supporters by virtue of always having the same seat.

Loyal cash and chanters: buy tickets with cash when they get paid and have a good shout at the game. May be 'regular' fans.

Dads and sons: quiet supporters, and not part of a group. They are loyal, 'club' rather than 'football' orientated, and critical of 'disloyal' boys being Manchester United fans.

Chapter 6

The strategic influences on direct and digital marketing

Introduction

We have introduced direct marketing strategy and provided a model for strategic decision making in direct marketing (Chapter 5). Within the model, we encountered a number of very important strategic elements that deserve more consideration than was possible during the introduction to the model. In this chapter we will take the opportunity to examine these elements, and their links with direct marketing, more fully.

In this and subsequent chapters we will pick up from the previous discussion of strategy and also develop some new themes. But we start the chapter with perhaps the most important discussion: where is direct marketing headed in the future? The optimism of the late 1990s reached its zenith with the arrival of Don Peppers and his one-to-one ideas. New technology promised almost cost free systems for customer contact, with response rates exponentially rising. The gloss has faded a little, at least for the present. What has happened? We take a look in our first section.

We then move on to developments that have had a major influence on modern direct marketing. We will look at the twin influences of customer loyalty strategies and the Internet and the rise of digital marketing; and also the potential importance of database marketing as a knowledge management tool beyond the marketing function and into the wider business environment.

The influence of relationship marketing has become intricately tied up with direct marketing, and not always in a clear and appropriate manner. In order to deal with this important subject properly, and to discuss fully its offshoot, customer relationship management (CRM), a separate chapter (Chapter 7) is dedicated to these discussions.

The Internet and digital is of course a massive consideration for direct marketers and is a fast changing environment.

The second part of this chapter deals with the specific techniques of direct marketing strategy, introduced previously (Chapter 5), in more detail. These include segmentation and targeting, service delivery, creating a dialogue, pricing schemes, and finally techniques for adding value to the product: positioning, branding and incentives, and the integration of on-and off-line media and channels (see Figure 6.1).

6.1 Influences on direct marketing strategy

Let us start by painting the picture of why, in the past ten years or so, direct marketing has been 'talked up' as potentially supplanting other forms of marketing. We begin with the story of one-to-one marketing.

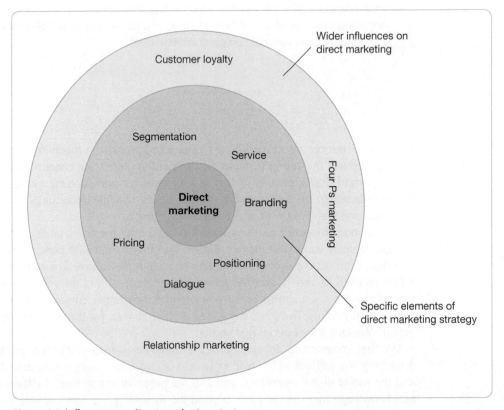

Figure 6.1 Influences on direct marketing strategy

6.1.1 Techno-driven 'perfect marketing': the one-to-one future?

It has been quite a while since Peppers and Rogers (1993) first wrote *One-to-One Marketing*, outlining a new paradigm for marketing, and predicting irresistible changes to the way marketing is practised worldwide. Peppers and Rogers predicted a marketing revolution based on the twin technological breakthroughs of, first, mass customisation and, second, the plethora of electronic media that offer the opportunity for one-to-one interaction with customers. Let us have a look at the theoretical idea first, then get to what has happened since those original ideas were floated.

Mitchell (1997) made the point that the financial logic of traditional mass advertising has always depended on the economies of scale generated by mass production. – the two have had a symbiotic relationship. However, mass production economies of scale are now breaking down: car companies can make an assembly line pay with very few cars of one specification rolling off. Companies such as Dell can 'make individually specified orders within hours'. Microsoft's recent advertising campaign for its smartphone promises a product made for each individual with its strapline 'reinvented around you'. According to Peppers and Rogers, this means that mass advertisers will ultimately be outflanked by those companies that can make their products tailored to the individual, driven by instant, one-to-one media contact with the customer. However, their one-to-one marketing idea takes these concepts a step further, in two main ways:

Learning with customers

In *One-to-One Marketing*, Peppers and Rogers gave a new spin to the notion of 'relationships' with customers. They proposed a partnership with customers whereby customers are given incentives to share their needs, as they understand them at the time, with you. Electronic media are used to make it as easy as possible for customers to share their needs in a recordable way. With their use of the firm's products over time, more chances abound to learn more about their particular needs.

Peppers and Rogers discussed the idea of a birthday card company that uses electronic kiosks to allow customers to design their own cards, which are then printed off instantly. A record is kept of customer designs, linked to that customer's details. Further designs are then 'proactively offered' in the future when the next anniversary arrives. Customers value the convenience and are impressed with the card company's effort in getting to know them, so they buy more from that company at full price. However, the firm must make it easy for the customer to share information – hence the electronic kiosks.

Companies such as Moon Pig and Funky Pigeon have brought this vision to life using ubiquitous and cheap Web based technology to create value for, from and crucially with customers.

Overall, Peppers and Rogers describe the interaction as a partnership, not the 'stand-off' approach of much conventional marketing.

What you have read so far represents the ideas that were first endorsed in the mid 1990s. Today, with the advent of social media, collaborative creativity and crowd sourcing Peppers and Rogers' vision is beginning to reach fruition. In 2012, the US crowd funding business **KickStarter.com** arrived in the UK. This simple business concept uses micro funding from individuals to help support the development of new product ideas. The focus was initially in the arts but now runs across many different sectors. The concept of monetising on-line social networks and the exploiting of 'wisdom of the crowd' (Surowiecki, 2005) to create value is something that Peppers and Rogers did not fully predict and in certain areas their ideas are now being overtaken.

However, for the majority of businesses most would agree that this open, collaborative and highly targeted approach is rather different from the reality of most direct marketing that we still see. In most instances, direct marketers do not address customers with one-to-one communications. At best they analyse and communicate with customers in groups.

Clearly, the one-to-one approach is potentially powerful; but how realistic is it for a company – a large bank say, with millions of customers – to treat 'all' of its customers as individuals? At present, it is clear that most banks are a long way from genuine one-to-one marketing! Peppers and Rogers' solution here is straightforward. 'Ring fence' your most valuable customers, 'one customer at a time', with a one-to-one approach. As this process continues down to less valuable customers, a point is reached where it does not make economic sense to attempt one-to-one marketing. At this point customers must be approached as aggregated segments (see Figure 6.2).

Linking mass customisation with rapid one-to-one communications to create individualised products for customers

The twin logic of mass customisation and one-to-one communications, using fast response media, means that customers have the ability to contact companies and say, 'I'll take that product, uniquely made the way I want it.' In their Harvard *Business Review* article of 1995, Pine, Peppers and Rogers (Pine *et al.*, 1995) described how Motorola made pagers to any of over 11 million different specifications. But as we have seen technology has moved on.

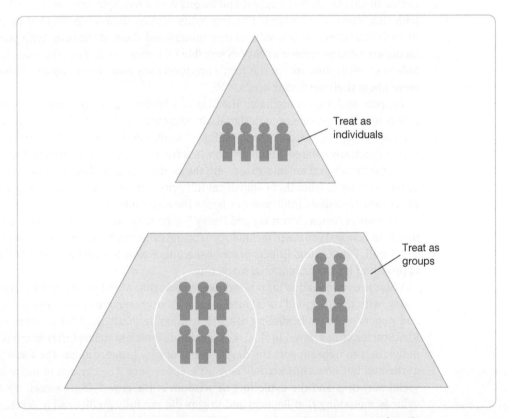

Figure 6.2 One-to-one approach to valuable customers and a mass approach to the rest

---

Exhibit 6.1 'Men need more help: smart mirrors and smart shelves'

Radio Frequency Identification or RFID technology, is leading another mass customisation push forward. A German department store, the Galeria Kaufhof in Essen, uses RFID to help men buying clothes in their store. For example, when they go to a dressing room to try a suit, a 'smart mirror' will tell them what kind of shirt or tie they need to buy with it. The RFID reader on the 'smart mirror' checks which clothing has been brought into the room from a tag attached, then displays other clothing choices. The system is used alongside 'smart shelves' so that customers can be shown choices in sizes that are available, and in various styles and colours. Bill Colleran, chief executive of Seattle based Impinj, said the exciting thing about the Kaufhof deployment is that it demonstrates that RFID can be used as a sales driver: 'People joke that this is the ideal place to start because men need more help in making choices,' he says.

Source: mass-customization.blogs.com (2007). *Mass Customization and Open Innovation News* published and sourced by Frank Piller, RWUT/MIT.

Mass customisation is most important in those markets that have changing customer needs, technological advances and diminishing product life cycles. So, mass customisation is emerging (in 2013) as making a difference across many sectors such as personalised authoring of books, clothing, birthday cards, personally designed vacations, etc. Where markets are stable and predictable, with convergent customer needs (fuel for cars?), there is less scope for this strategy. For interesting and up to date examples emerging in Germany, see **www.mass-customization.de**

Mass customisation can be:

- **Collaborative.** The dialogue takes place with and between customers before product design – the full one-to-one marketing concept. This is particularly useful for businesses whose customers cannot easily articulate what they want, and hence need the dialogue.

- **Adaptive.** One standard product, but customisable by the users themselves, e.g. games that are programmable by customers to suit them.

- **Cosmetic.** The same product is presented differently with a minor amount of actual product change, such as the customer's name on the product.

- **Transparent.** Observation of regular customers' needs creates a customisation of service or product that is done automatically without the customer asking.

All four modes of customisation require different direct marketing approaches. What Peppers and Rogers (1993) and Pine *et al.* (1995) provided was a clear call to action to direct marketers to expand their thinking outwards from 'communication' and embrace interaction that feeds back into product strategy, via mass customisation, an area hitherto given little attention.

However, in general, companies have found it difficult to implement one-to-one strategies. There are obvious places where entire industries have been transformed into mass customisation by the Web, the most prominent being the music industry. Apart from this the most conspicuous success has probably been Dell Computers, which remains a world player in the computer hardware market. It is no coincidence that Dell is a major user of the Internet as a part of its business, and there is little doubt that the major future for one-to-one marketing lies with Web based applications: more fully discussed later (Chapter 8).

Exhibit 6.2 One-to-one marketing: a DIY company

Let us say you run a chain of DIY 'out of town' warehouse stores. You have two ways of running the company. Traditional thinking would push you to competing on market share terms with your rivals, trying to get as many customers in as possible to buy your products. You may advertise in local press or radio. To boost sales you run incentives and broadcast these, hoping to pinch some of your competitors' customers.

Your alternative is one-to-one marketing. A customer comes in and buys some tomato seeds. He mentions that he is starting up a greenhouse in his garden. You note this on to a database with that customer's name and address, which you asked him for at the till. When a new book, *A Guide to Greenhouse Gardening,* comes out, you e-mail him, telling him about the book and offering it to him with a couple of packets of seeds thrown in. If he wants it, you suggest, he need only reply and you will send it to him. Next time he pops in you learn more about what he is doing with his garden and again you note it. He shares this e-mail with the members of his local horticultural society and they also are able to take advantage of the offer you are making, and you are able to capture more information for your database.

What you are doing is learning with the customer what they want from you and who they network with and influence. We will read more about this amplification effect later (Chapter 9). You are offering them value by giving them relevant, timely information. You are making it easy for them to do business with you and share the offers with their friends and social network. You have tailored your product and your communication to that individual in an attempt to increase your business from that one customer.

6.1.2 The future of direct marketing: glass half full or half empty?

The direction of travel of direct marketing over the past 20 years tells us quite a lot. During that time there is no doubt that direct and database marketing has grown in scale, expanding out of its home territory of financial services, non-profit, mail-order and other niches into the bigger time of retail, leisure, business-to-business, travel and telecoms, to name but a few. The engine of the Internet and other digital media fuel further growth and on-line direct spend new accounts for around 30 per cent of total marketing spend in the UK. What underpins this scale growth is the underlying success of direct marketing in delivering demonstrable sales: our discipline has been described as 'salesmanship in print' (Cruikshanks and Schultz, 2010), and although this goes against the grain of thinking of a customer database as the central core, it does recognise that selling is one of direct marketing's core competences.

So much for the scale growth of direct and database marketing; what about its growth of scope? By this we mean the list of strategic opportunities that have been attributed to direct marketing: its ability to help create relationships with customers over time, perhaps as part of a CRM system; its scope as a knowledge management tool within the business; and, as we have just seen, its potential as a deliverer of one-to-one marketing. Looking back (see Chapter 3), we see the most conspicuous success has come with the Tesco Clubcard and the system that enables customer segmentations to be linked to a powerful way of lowering marketing costs by directing marketing spend to segments where it is most needed. This is an example of segmentation working, and of the database creating a bank of knowledge that is spread about the business. We shall talk about this later in this chapter.

But in most other respects the progress of increased scope has been disappointing, and one-to-one returns are, as yet, modest. CRM systems have been reined back within most industry sectors to more modest dimensions, and we await decent returns. The principles of relationship marketing are still largely confined to face-to-face dealings in business-to-business markets. One piece of good news is that direct marketers have slightly shifted their spend from hunting for prospects towards contact with existing customers – in 2011, according to a survey by Forbes coremetrics cited by **www.marketingcharts.com** (Marketingcharts, 2011) 39 per cent said that customer retention took the largest proportion of their marketing budgets. Customer acquisition was allocated the largest proportion of budget for 36 per cent of companies. 52 per cent of respondents said that customer retention was their highest priority. It appears that little has changed from 2007 when about 55 per cent of UK spend was on marketing to existing customers and we do not see strong signs that this spend is moving from tactical selling.

None of this would matter quite as much if direct marketing's ability to shift goods was as strong as ever. But this is not the case. Response rates across all media have yet to really step up from the 2 per cent or less mark, and in many cases, for example with cold e-mail and pay per click advertising, these are slipping significantly. At the heart of database marketing is the principle that future sales can be predicted from past behaviour. This depends on high quality data, best of all being a firm intention by the consumer to buy. These kinds of data are in short supply because the industry has largely lost the trust of prospects so they feel that it is not worth their while sharing their data with sellers. Hence, direct and database marketers rely on basic transaction data that is often hit-and-miss for predicting. The advent of 'big data' or the pooling of data from the vast range of data sources available to businesses, and its mining for insight, has not yet fully and widely realised revenue opportunities other than for the consultancies selling 'big data solutions'. In fact, we need to be absolutely clear about this. The lesson of the past 20 years is that it is a mistake to believe that a mish-mash of data about people will enable us to do more than slightly improve our prediction odds to much better than random. Work by the Gartner Group (2003) suggests that attempts at seller driven 'customer management' – for instance predictive direct mail with cross-sell offers – are typically seen as intrusive, and yields are typically 2–3 per cent response at best. If, however, the marketing contact is related to a customer event, for instance moving home, customers regard such contact as much more convenient for them. Response rates may rise to values like 20 per cent. Best of all is to cross-sell when the customer contacts the company on the 'customer's' initiative – you may get 40 per cent response to these approaches. These figures tell us a lot about how customers wish to be approached. They are quite happy to be approached about goods and services – but the timing has to reflect their position – do they want to buy and do they want to buy from you?

The future of direct and database marketing is probably at a crossroads. Digital and Internet technology give us an opportunity to create data driven systems for going to market that uses up-to-date real time data hitherto undreamt of. Run on behalf of consumers, these new ways of doing marketing will work, if they demonstrate to consumers a type of marketing that puts their interests first, rather than tricking them into sharing data in a grudging manner as happens so often now.

Facebook's success has been phenomenal but perhaps the gloss is beginning to wear off. As Facebook seeks increasingly to monetise the data that are captured from our 'personal' profiles, Google trends reveal that searches using the term 'delete Facebook permanently' have increased significantly since 2009.

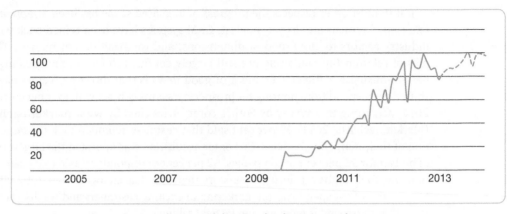

Figure 6.3 Search trends using the term 'delete Facebook permanently'
Source: Googletrends.com.

One-to-one marketing would be a manifestation of such an approach, as would the idea of relationships, and response rates would shift from 2 per cent to 30 or 40 per cent. You will find much more about this paradigm shift idea later (Chapter 8). Without these developments it is hard to see one-to-one marketing becoming a large scale reality.

Perhaps the best thing is for us to stay in touch with these arguments as they develop. Meanwhile, let us get on with the substance of direct marketing, and get back to its core business – acquisition and retention marketing.

6.1.3 The importance of customer loyalty

'Corporate leaders today can't understand why the troops won't rally behind a mission statement that places maximising shareholder value as the highest corporate goal.'

(Reichheld, 1996)

There have been a number of major corporate management trends over the last two decades that have been hailed as breakthroughs in how to do business, but have not quite lived up to their early promise. These include Total Quality Management (TQM), Business Process Re-engineering (BPR), virtual teamworking, and so on. Throughout the 1990s, customer loyalty was another 'craze' and, as we move towards 2014, it remains a talking point, arousing the concerns of senior managers, who, unfortunately, often do not act on these concerns. A recent study found that while about 80 per cent of marketing directors claimed customer loyalty was a high priority for them, only about 50 per cent said they measured loyalty, and even worse, only 30 per cent did 'anything at all' about improving loyalty.

In spite of this, we argue here that, handled correctly, managing customer loyalty is very important to companies and should not be seen as another 'fad'. Loyal behaviour has been directly linked to company profitability across a convincingly wide array of sectors. Indeed prioritising customer loyalty as the primary generator of profit is not new. Traditional direct marketers, such as mail-order companies, have understood the superior profitability of existing customers, compared with new customers, for many decades.

Linking loyalty with direct marketing

An emphasis on loyalty is of great interest to direct marketers. This is because there is a 'natural alignment' of direct marketing – philosophy, measures and systems – with the notion of retaining customers. In particular, direct marketing can do the following:

1 Direct marketing can orchestrate the targeting of the most valuable customers and those who are intrinsically loyal.

2 Direct marketing can help 'create' customer loyalty. It is often claimed that direct marketers can create loyalty – direct marketing initiatives, tied to price, the product or service, can improve the value the customer gets from the company. Potentially more powerful, the customer database can orchestrate the development of one-to-one relationships, which, if they come to pass, will surely have an impact on loyalty. However, the reader is cautioned: as yet there remains a paucity of evidence to back this up; it is still early days for the one-to-one concept.

3 We are on much more solid ground in asserting that direct marketing can 'take advantage' of customer loyalty to maximise revenue. We can take advantage of the loyalty by understanding how to market to existing customers so that both they and the company get maximum value from the association.

4 Finally, direct marketing systems can measure customer retention. Both Reichheld (1996) and the relationship marketing academics (Payne, 1995) have pinpointed this as an absolutely crucial area. It is a truism in business that little gets done unless it can be measured. Customer retention is very difficult to measure, and unquestionably the most efficient tool for the job is the database. Where other systems measure customer satisfaction, and use this as a surrogate for retention, a database can track customer spend over time – the only way to measure customer retention.

In order to decide the allocation of resources to customer loyalty, we need to understand how loyalty and profit are linked.

The economics of customer loyalty

The primary figure in clarifying the connection between loyalty and profit has been Reichheld, whose original book *The Loyalty Effect* (1996) and other work (for example *Loyalty Rules!*, 2001, and a *Harvard Business Review* article in 2003 'The one number you need to grow') set out clearly why loyalty is so important.

The following example illustrates the point.

Example

In this example we examine the relative profitability for a company that achieves 90 per cent versus 95 per cent retention rates over seven years. The retention rate is the percentage of customers with the company at the start of the year, who remain with it at the end of the year.

The figures in Tables 6.1 and 6.2 compare the situation of 100 customers over a seven-year period. Each customer costs an average of £30 to recruit. Each customer that leaves has to be replaced, at a cost to the company. Each customer is worth £10 per annum in gross margin.

If we ignore net present value calculations for the sake of simplicity, what are the comparable profit figures after seven years?

Example
(cont'd)

Table 6.1 90 per cent retention rate

	Year						
	1	2	3	4	5	6	7
100 customers' recruitment cost	3,000	0	0	0	0	0	0
Replacement costs if ten leave each year		300	300	300	300	300	300
Margin @ £10 per customer per year	1,000	1,000	1,000	1,000	1,000	1,000	1,000
Margin (cumulative)	−2,000	−1,300	−600	+100	+800	1,500	2,200

The final cumulative profit of 100 customers at 90 per cent retention is **£2200**.

Table 6.2 95 per cent retention rate

	Year						
	1	2	3	4	5	6	7
100 customers' recruitment cost	3,000	0	0	0	0	0	0
Replacement costs if five leave each year		150	150	150	150	150	150
Margin@ £10 per customer per year	1,000	1,000	1,000	1,000	1,000	1,000	1,000
Margin (cumulative)	−2,000	−1,150	−300	+650	1,500	2,350	3,200

The final cumulative profit of 100 customers at 95 per cent retention is **£3,200**.

In other words, in this example, 'a 5 per cent increase in customer retention has led to a 45 per cent increase in cumulative profit' over the seven-year period.

Bain and Co. (Reichheld, 1996) conducted research into this effect and found that a small increase in retention rate had a hugely disproportionate effect on profit 'in every sector examined'. Most spectacular of all was the credit card industry, where a 5 per cent increase in customer retention led to a profit improvement of 125 per cent! In general, given that a typical company loses 10–30 per cent of its customers in a year, the potential for improving profitability by focusing on loyalty is dramatic.

This example highlights the potential leverage that loyalty has on profitability, but it does not clearly explain 'why' retaining customers is so profitable. There are a number of reasons that are important for direct marketers.

Reasons for retention leading to higher profits
No acquisition costs

The importance of acquisition costs on profitability is highlighted in the previous example. Whether you use direct marketing or not, acquisition costs in most businesses are high. One major financial services company found the average acquisition cost per customer for loans was £280. Acquisition costs in credit card companies are typically £50 or more; in insurance they are often over £100. Charities now expect to lose money on fundraising activity aimed at acquiring new donors. As we saw in the example, the more we can keep customers, the less costly acquisition we need to do.

One way to visualise the importance of retention is to think of a company as a bucket with a hole in the bottom. Customers are acquired through the top of the bucket, while at the same time the company is leaking customers who defect (see Figure 6.4). Let us imagine two companies, both of which acquire customers at a rate of 10 per cent per year. One loses 5 per cent of its customers per year and the other loses 10 per cent. The company with the lower rate of loss doubles in size every 14 years. The other company has zero growth.

Price premium

Reichheld's (1996) research found that 'old' customers pay higher prices than new ones. This is partly because of the mechanics of trial discounts aimed only at new customers (discussed at length later (see Chapter 10)). However, more fundamentally, Reichheld

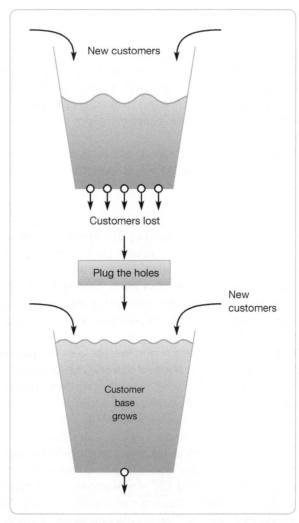

Figure 6.4 Preventing the 'leaking' of customers increases company growth

suggested it is because loyal customers are happy with the value they are getting from the company. Loyal customers ignore vouchers and coupons, and are less price sensitive on individual items than new customers. However, as a blanket rule, we should be wary of concluding that loyal customers are always less price sensitive: this was disputed by Reinartz and Kumar in 2002 – something we will discuss more fully in a moment.

There is an interesting irony here. Many companies have 'loyalty schemes' that offer lower prices via points systems in return for loyal custom; but companies whose customers only stay with them because of a loyalty scheme do not have genuinely loyal customers. Reichheld (1996) asserted again and again in his book that companies cannot 'buy' loyalty. They can only earn it through consistently creating superior value for their customers.

Direct marketing can help to take advantage of the price-premium effect. Database driven marketing allows us to know who our most loyal customers are. We can market to these customers accordingly, ensuring they receive excellent service and avoiding offering them unnecessary discounts.

Referrals

Mature, satisfied customers tend to give more referrals; that is, they recommend the company to their friends. Referred prospects in turn convert at a higher rate than prospects recruited 'cold'. Referred new customers end up staying longer, because they were originally similar types of people to existing customers anyway, and so are more likely to stay. In other words, retained customers help to lower the average acquisition cost of new customers.

Direct marketing is excellently placed to maximise this effect by using a tactic called Member Get Member (MGM), which gives a company's own customers incentives to recommend it to others.

Revenue growth

In most businesses, customers buy more from you when they get to know you better. In retailing, for example, as customers get to know more of your product lines, they buy more; as their trust in you increases, they buy more. Direct marketers can proactively learn with customers, anticipate their future needs and develop more products to meet them. Customers of a car dealer may start with a basic car service, but loyal customers may move to valeting, warranties, hire cars and so on, as they get to know more of the dealer's business and learn to trust them more.

However, as mentioned above, Reichheld's work has been questioned by Reinartz and Kumar in a high profile *Harvard Business Review* article (2002). They found little or no evidence to suggest that customers who purchase steadily from a company over time are necessarily cheaper to serve, less price sensitive or particularly effective at bringing in new business. Their conclusions were based on a four-year study of four different businesses in the USA and Europe, and found only a moderate link between loyalty and profitability. Sometimes short-term customers were very profitable, but not worth chasing because they would not come back. Sometimes long-term customers were basically unprofitable.

It may be that Reinartz and Kumar's analysis is a more accurate reflection of business reality than Reichheld's. This is not necessarily bad news for direct marketers. Reinartz and Kumar conclude that the use of data mining on customer data is a sound approach that helps identify who is profitable and who is not. Let us take a closer look.

Table 6.3 Database marketing strategies for Reinartz and Kumar's model

Name of segment	Description	Strategy
'Strangers'	Customers who have no loyalty and bring in no profits	Identify early and do not invest anything
'Butterflies'	Customers who are profitable but disloyal	Milk them for as much as the short time they are buying from you
'True friends'	Profitable customers who are likely to be loyal	Adopt a softly-softly approach
'Barnacles'	Highly loyal but not very profitable customers	Find out whether they have the potential to spend more than they currently do

The trouble with loyalty

To what extent are customers naturally loyal, and to what extent can their behaviour be changed? As long ago as 1972, work by Ehrenberg found that customers exhibited little brand loyalty across all the sectors studied, including many packaged goods categories, airlines, clothing, retail and others. An analysis of car insurance (Cram, 1994) found that 60 per cent of customers had switched companies in the preceding five years, many more than once. Of the remaining 40 per cent, many will only be 'loyal' through a lack of interest in shopping around. Hardly a ringing endorsement.

Exhibit 6.3 Understanding loyalty

Customers can be loyal to many different things. They can be loyal to people – perhaps to a friend they make who is their contact in a business supplier, or to a friendly cashier at the bank, or to their local village shopkeeper.

They may be loyal to a brand, which in some way symbolises a group of people. Bikers who ride sports motorbikes nod to other sports bikers, although strangers, when they pass them on the road. Mini car drivers may be members of a club where they meet and socialise around their common passion.

Reichheld (1996) reports that Josiah Royce, Professor of Philosophy at Harvard University, wrote a book, *The Philosophy of Loyalty*, in 1908 in which he asserted that the highest form of loyalty is to values and principles. Reichheld holds that this is relevant to businesses too; but most companies do not earn loyalty through too much commitment to self-interest. In the charity sector, there is a great deal of interest currently in developing fundraising strategies around shared values.

Reichheld believes philosophically that business loyalty is all about 'finding that elusive balance between self-interest and team interest'.

In retail the story is similar. Pressey and Matthews (2000) emphasise that, despite the recent use of loyalty cards and database marketing techniques by UK retailers, most transactions are 'discrete, short-term, one-off acts'.

Customers exhibit more complex patterns of behaviour than just 'loyalty' or 'switching'. In fact, customers see the whole issue of loyalty in a different way to marketers. As McCorkell (1997) noted: 'The notion of customer loyalty is important to marketing people, but not, on the whole, to customers. Customers don't see why they should not accept a good offer from a new supplier just because they are satisfied with their present one.'

A lot of frequent purchase behaviour (e.g. supermarket goods) is based on 'repertoire' purchasing, in that customers retain a basket of brands, which they jump between in a 'polygamous' fashion. A number of reasons may account for repertoire purchasing:

- **Different brands satisfying different needs.** We may buy one brand of coffee for everyday use and quite another for a dinner party.
- **Deal switching.** Some people prioritise getting a discount for their brand choice.
- **Time/convenience factors.** Customers of airlines usually make their choice of carrier based on route and time. Brand loyalty is, therefore, low. Similarly, petrol purchases depend largely on convenience.

The clear conclusion from these different pieces of work is that exclusive brand loyalty cannot be regarded as the norm in most markets.

What are direct marketers to do with this finding? First, it is important to recognise reality, especially in the face of so much emphasis on loyalty in texts and trade press, much of which do not recognise the inherent complexities of 'loyal' customer behaviour. Second, we should recognise that striving for exclusive loyalty in some markets, for example wine purchase, is not a realistic goal; it is better to aim to be a part of customers' repertoire. Third, companies need to identify active loyals (those who have assessed other options and made an active decision to stay) and seek to keep them happy.

Most important, we can recognise that Reichheld's, Reinartz and Kumar's, and Ehrenberg's findings can sit alongside each other: loyalty may not be the norm, but any improvement in retention of the right – that is, profitable – customers will be extremely beneficial. Attaining loyalty is, however, hard work.

Exhibit 6.4 Loyalty: why don't companies practise what they preach?

Loyalty was probably *the* management 'buzzword' of the 1990s. However, very few companies have really believed in its principles and convincingly gone about building loyalty. In truth, most people seem to smile and agree that loyalty is important, but do they really believe, deep down, that customers can be loyal? Perhaps not. In many companies, employees do not trust their customers: the managers talk about service but the day-to-day attitudes betray a belief that their customers are out to rip them off. These cultural attitudes are in direct conflict with a commitment to loyalty, and form a vicious circle: less loyalty means more acquisition, more acquisition means more of the 'wrong' type of customers and less trust in the system.

Investigating business priorities, the recent research by Circle Group (Circle Group, 2012) found that business people put generating more leads and cross- and up-selling at first and second place in a list of priorities. Reducing customer churn came in at eleventh place. So although business people may say they want more customer satisfaction, their actions often suggest otherwise. And it is argued throughout this book that it is customer retention, not customer acquisition, that is the real strength of direct marketing. Undue emphasis on the merry-go-round of customer acquisition creates problems, as customers become loyal to bribes rather than brands.

How can direct marketing help firms achieve customer loyalty?

In their sales pitches to clients, direct and digital marketing agencies may claim that database driven marketing can create loyalty. A strategy for a car manufacturer who wants to increase loyalty from consumers may be to maintain contact with the customer in between purchases. This could be done using, say, a quarterly magazine and well-timed mailings inviting the driver for a test drive of the latest range. But will this really enhance loyalty? Customer magazines have worked very well for many companies, and the trigger to come along and enjoy a test drive is an important part of the selling process; but it is hard to believe that these measures 'in isolation' will cure a car company's churn rate.

Reichheld (1996) pointed out right at the beginning of his book that the creation of loyalty is a corporate rather than a marketing strategy. It, therefore, cannot be just delegated to the marketing department as a bolt-on extra, a 'campaign'. Imagine a situation where an airline with limited routes, a poor safety record, sullen service delivery, ordinary meals in-flight, and so on, had a 'loyalty' pricing scheme based on Air Miles. As common sense would indicate, this is not a successful recipe for customer retention. There is now substantial evidence going back many years (Hartley, 1997; Nunez and Dreze, 2006, Pressey and Matthews, 2000) that loyalty schemes used without a strong underpinning have little or no effect on loyalty.

According to Reichheld, and underpinned by many influential marketing strategists such as Piercy (1997) and Doyle (2002), the key to retention is 'creating superior value for customers'. Loyalty is a consequence of creating value for customers, and profit is a consequence of loyalty. Reichheld found that those companies that enjoyed superior levels of loyalty had focused on people – employees and customers – not systems. In some industries where service is not a prime consideration, it may be pricing that has irresistible power over consumers' decisions.

Direct marketing's true role in creating loyalty is moulded by these wider considerations. If we accept Reichheld's logic, then direct marketers should recognise that they are part of a 'corporate' effort to concentrate on creating value for customers. We will take a close look at how direct marketing can contribute to improved customer loyalty later in this chapter.

In summary, in spite of the doubts and difficulties surrounding it, improving customer loyalty remains important for businesses and it is an important strategic influence on direct marketing. Let us now turn to an area that, more recently, is increasingly recognised as also very important: the use of database knowledge throughout the company.

6.2 The use of marketing databases in the wider company environment

In this section we take a look at how direct and database marketing can influence events in non-marketing areas of the company – outside of the marketing department. This can be illustrated in Figure 6.5.

The marketing database can help companies whose service would otherwise be disabled by their sheer size. DeTienne and Thompson (1996) pointed out that larger companies tend to lose track of minute market information. Often this information lost includes key elements of what the customer values in his or her personal relationships with the company. However, recording personal information can help customer service people deliver the best service to customers (Bessen, 1993; Gronroos, 1996; Stone and Woodcock, 1997). This is now common business practice for service companies that make heavy use of inbound channels, and

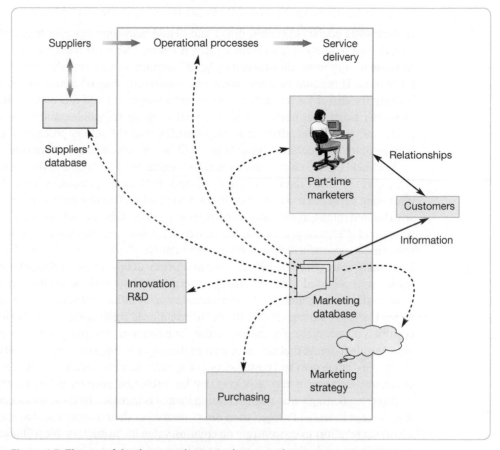

Figure 6.5 The use of database marketing in the internal company environment

in sectors such as hotels that deliver priority service to high-value customers. In all these examples, however, the marketing database is not enabling the marketing department to provide better service; rather, it is helping part time marketers (Gummesson, 1991) in the customer facing functions give at least an impression of familiarity with the customer.

Another important measure of the quality of the marketing database is the ease with which its data and information can be accessed by the organisation as a whole (Bessen, 1993). For example, Fletcher and Wright (1997) argued that database marketing (DBM) information could help to strengthen the supplier/buyer position by using market information to cut out inefficiency, share stockholding with suppliers, optimise sales channels and measure supplier performance. More recently the so-called 'efficient consumer response' (Piercy, 1997) approach that describes manufacturing firms' relationships with retailers also makes use of networked databases.

This new role for database marketers, 'as facilitators', reflects the work of writers such as Gronroos (1996), Gummesson (1991) and Christopher (1996), who argue that a marketer's role is to motivate the company to adopt a greater market focus. These are just some examples of the potential of marketing databases in company wide situations.

In summary, as DeTienne and Thompson (1996) point out, if the organisation is good at learning, the database transcends the status of a record keeping device and becomes an implement of ever increasing organisational knowledge. This knowledge is transferable to any part of the company, thanks to the increasing simplicity of user interfaces provided by modern technology. If an operator in the research and development arm of the company wants to see what types of customers are using what products, he or she can do so.

These are, in fact, all examples of important developments in sharing knowledge throughout the business. This quite separate area of study is known as knowledge management, and is discussed next.

Exhibit 6.5 Using data for company wide knowledge management – Tesco Clubcard

UK retailer Tesco had stolen a march on its main rival, Sainsbury's, through the launch of its loyalty scheme, Clubcard, in 1995. By 1997, however, Sainsbury's had responded with its own Reward card scheme. Tesco knew it had to work hard to maintain its lead. Its next challenge lay not with marketing communications – the card had been accepted by customers – but instead 'within' the company. How could Tesco best use the data throughout the business? It identified a number of areas.

First, price. Tesco was keen to avoid a damaging price war, with Asda in particular. Yet it needed to remain competitive. It used shopping basket analysis to identify price sensitive customers through the clever device of homing in on Tesco value margarine buyers. Tesco knew these buyers would be price sensitive right across the range. Special efforts were made to look after these customers.

The second area was purchasing. Purchasing from suppliers is one of the most important and powerful functions in retailing. The aim was to ensure that all the 60,000 lines on sale in an average superstore accurately reflected what customers wanted. This will of course vary geographically, and according to the social make up of the clientele.

Third, new product development. Areas such as gourmet eating, organics, food allergy sufferers, dieters or healthy eaters provided rich pickings for the developers who, week by week, would look to innovate. Clubcard data was invaluable, not in directly answering these questions, but in setting the scene. It helped them understand better who tried what, and allowed them to build mental pictures of the lives of their customers.

Finally, competitive strategy. So far the Clubcard had primarily been used for loyalty – defence. Tesco's analysts now turned their attention to improving their market share. Clubcard allowed them to know more than either of their main rivals: the challenge now was offensive marketing.

Source: Humby, C., Hunt, T. and Phillips, T. (2003) *Scoring Points, How Tesco is Winning Customer Loyalty,* Kogan Page, London.

6.3 Knowledge management

6.3.1 What is knowledge management?

Perhaps triggered by the widespread adoption of business process re-engineering, which has involved shedding large numbers of middle managers, many of whom left the company taking vital knowledge with them, interest in knowledge management has exploded since the mid 1990s. Knowledge management (KM) has been widely adopted by practitioners who have led academics in developing the area. A lot of the interest in KM has been generated by the large management consultancies such as McKinsey, Ernst and Young and so on, who have used KM extensively in their own internal organisations. Bassi (1997) defined knowledge management as the process of creating, capturing and using knowledge to enhance business performance. The dominant discourse of KM is how better to exploit the knowledge of employees through tools and methods.

The possible use of database marketing in knowledge management was first put forward by DeTienne and Thompson (1996), who pointed out that a customer database is an opportunity for organisations to mechanise the process of learning about customers. As they state: 'The usefulness of DBM for organisational learning is partly in its iterative nature.' In a later chapter (Chapter 14), the subject of testing in direct marketing explores this iterative learning in more detail. The point here is that iterative learning could be expanded beyond tactical promotions to a wider environment within the firm. What we will do now is to explore in more detail what knowledge management actually is, and create a picture of how database marketing could help companies improve their knowledge.

6.3.2 The nature of knowledge

Much of KM theory is based on positivism, the idea being that 'knowledge is truth', and a matter of 'linking facts' to assemble ever more knowledge. In this sense a marketing database is a positivist tool, with knowledge presented in a logical manner, and the emphasis on testing and quantitative analysis. One example of this is data mining, the use of powerful analysis tools to extricate patterns from large volumes of complex data, which has become the subject of great interest by database marketers (Finerty, 1997).

An alternative view of knowledge management is that presented from a social constructivist paradigm. Here, knowledge is an everyday experience, embedded in the unwritten systems and cultures of the organisation. One illustration of this is database marketers' 'ways of thinking' about business, and their 'market sensing', i.e. a focus on managers, understanding of the market rather than on market information (Piercy, 1997). Database marketers build up their market 'understanding' through examination of customer data, and through their experiences of how customers react to direct marketing initiatives.

Many writers seem to agree that knowledge is much more subtle than, say, the output of a data mining analysis. It is more difficult to define than that: it could be the outcome of everyday experience. Some insights were that knowledge is 'messy'; it travels via language; it slips away the more it is pinned down; it does not respond to rules and systems; and the more loosely it is managed the better. It seems that attempts to 'manage' knowledge too closely will lead to problems. The big success story of database driven knowledge management is Tesco. It seems to understand when to manage closely the analysis and when to let it go its own way; when to go with a hunch based on experience and when to question conventional wisdom.

Writers have split knowledge into two types.

6.3.3 Tacit and explicit knowledge

Hansen *et al.* (1999) distinguished between 'tacit' and 'explicit' knowledge. Explicit knowledge is important when existing knowledge needs to be re-used to tackle problems with known solutions. Tacit knowledge is 'deep' knowledge needed for complex problems not encountered before. McAdam and McCreedy (1999) identify the distinctive characteristics of tacit and explicit knowledge. They quote Polanyi (cited in McAdam and McCreedy (1999)) defining tacit knowledge as non-verbalised, intuitive and unarticulated. Explicit knowledge is specified as being in writing, drawings or computer records. Clearly, knowledge held on marketing databases is explicit, while much of the knowledge held by database marketers will be tacit.

Bearing all this in mind, we can now take a look at a model of how database marketing can help with the management of knowledge.

6.3.4 How database marketing can help with knowledge management

Knowledge management is about the capture or creation, codification, distribution, sharing, combination, use and finally retention of knowledge within a company. However, the emphasis in the model (see Figure 6.6) is on using DBM knowledge in non-marketing environments, probably by 'combining' it with local knowledge. This is illustrated in the central box of the model.

The role of database marketing – transforming knowledge

Marketing databases have a role to transform (and record) explicit knowledge. Moreover database marketers themselves may have a vital role in helping combine explicit and tacit, or tacit and tacit knowledge in order to solve complex problems, for example in a business undergoing change. Database marketers can also help by using the powerful analysis tools available (see Chapter 3) to transform explicit knowledge into higher forms, which (when combined in another department such as finance) may transform to 'tacit' knowledge through an internalisation process.

The final element to the model is the use of the (transformed) knowledge. The temptation for database marketers has been to use the database to 'record' (explicit) knowledge, yet the

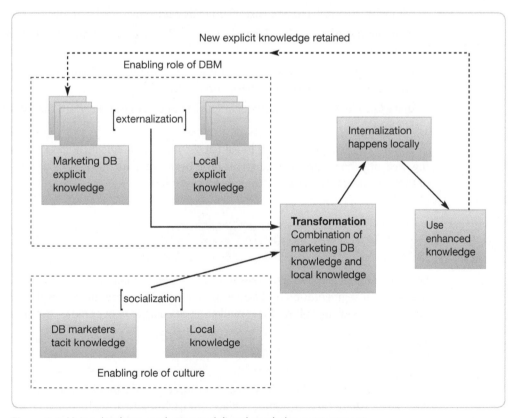

Figure 6.6 Using database marketing to deliver knowledge management

emphasis of the model in Figure 6.6 reflects recent literature by emphasising the 'creation' and 'use' of knowledge rather than its recording. As Scarborough *et al.* (1999) put it: 'Technology should be viewed more as a means of communication and less as a means of storing knowledge.'

It is undoubtedly 'usage' (i.e. acting knowledgeably) which appears to be the Achilles heel of knowledge management theory and practice. McAdam and McCreedy (1999) and Scarborough *et al.* (1999) see employee motivation, reward and benefits as the key elements in solving this dilemma. Meanwhile Harris (1996) sees measures of success as key to motivating managers to be market focused. Taking our cue primarily from these authors, the following initiatives may encourage the use of marketing databases across the business:

● Introducing customer related measures of management performance

● Using database marketing knowledge as shared currency between different departments, thereby encouraging 'shared language' and, hence, helping to break down barriers

● Encouraging the use of DBM information as a powerful way of making market focus a reality

If the steps shown in Figure 6.6 can be implemented, then better market orientation should result. According to Kohli and Jaworski (1990) market orientated firms will: place a priority on the collection and understanding of customer information; encourage the sharing of this information throughout the company; and place a company wide priority to respond to these needs. Using this definition, it is proposed that database marketing can improve market orientation by:

● facilitating the collection of customer needs data across the business

● overcoming organisational barriers by enabling easier dissemination of customer knowledge

● using simple user interfaces to facilitate easy analysis and combination of customer knowledge with other knowledge centres in the firm

● using knowledge management techniques to encourage and reward the subsequent market focus

So far in this chapter we have looked at the major strategic influences on direct marketing. Recently, however, some concerns have been raised about the lack of practice of some of these elements. The next section takes a closer look.

6.4 Delivering direct marketing strategies

Our earlier direct marketing strategy model (Chapter 5) highlighted the importance to direct marketers of segmentation and targeting. We will, therefore, now consider these in more detail, before looking at how direct marketing can help to deliver more customer value.

6.4.1 Delivering segmentation and targeting

Segmentation

Direct marketing has the ability to deliver 'precisely defined' segmentations of existing customers, where each customer is placed in each segment with complete accuracy based on historical data. This contrasts with segmentations in classical marketing, where it is educated guesswork that a customer lies in a particular segment. Because of the inevitable wastage, this raises the costs and reduces the accuracy with which classical marketing works.

The first step in our retention strategy is, therefore, to decide whether we should segment at all. Segmenting in order to communicate with different groups of customers in different ways, or to offer each a different product, costs money and takes a lot of effort. We have to decide whether it is worth it: will our customers value a more individual approach and be more profitable as a result? Harley Davidson found that for its motorbike business segmenting by product usage was worthwhile and has strategically gone down this route. Most retail banks in the UK, however, undertake little segmentation for much of their business; they have many managerial hurdles to overcome in order to segment with much sophistication, and in many instances they opt for a 'mass direct marketing' approach.

Probably the most powerful methods of segmentation, executed very effectively by direct marketing, are splitting by value – what customers are worth to us; splitting by need – what customers want from us; and segmenting by predicted response. All these have been extensively covered (see Chapter 3), so we just need to remind ourselves here of their strategic importance. The other key segmentation approach to add is segmenting by loyalty.

Segmenting by loyalty

Reichheld (1996) recommended isolating valuable customers in a slightly different way. He proposed that top priority be given to targeting those customers who are predictably loyal and stable. He found many businesses that boasted customers who were 'inherently' more loyal than others. MBNA, a US credit card provider, found that professions were the important loyalty segmenter. Teachers, accountants, nurses and engineers all showed more 'innate' loyalty than the average. So did older, married people living in rural areas. These people were more attracted to familiarity and, hence, less deal conscious than average. MBNA, at considerable expense, targeted only affinity groups showing this innate loyalty. It has paid off: MBNA's profit levels are among the highest in the world in its sector.

Another key group may be those whose current spend with the company is modest, but whose potential is much greater. Frequent business flyers typically belong to a number of airline 'clubs' at the same time. For each airline, they may not register as a heavy spender, but their potential, if they were to focus on one carrier, is great. Using a mixture of behavioural and profiled data, it is possible to segment and then market to these customers accordingly. For example, the high potential frequent flyers may be offered more value in the form of better service or a one-off offer of free Air Miles.

Exhibit 6.6 Segmenting by loyalty: business-to-business markets

Research has found the following segments that exhibit different loyalties:

- **Programmed buyers**: small customers, less price sensitive, purchase is a routine
- **Relationship buyers**: small, more knowledgeable, seek partnership
- **Transaction buyers**: large customers, very knowledgeable, balance price and service
- **Bargain hunters**: large customers, switch readily, price/service sensitive

---

Faced with these segmentation options, the direct marketer needs guidance. Certainly, Reichheld's loyalty based segmentation is worth serious consideration, given his evidence of the link between loyalty and profit. However, at present, relatively few companies appear to segment in this way, possibly because loyalty is relatively difficult to measure. What we need to do is keep an overview of all the above options and decide which is best for our situation.

Targeting

When targeting 'existing' customers in order to keep them and maximise their profitability, priority segments include:

- the most valuable customers
- the most loyal customers
- customers with great potential for revenue growth: these may be low spenders with us, but big spenders with our competitors
- loss making customers: we can look for ways to make our company unattractive to these customers, edging them out of the business
- 'segments' identified through statistics as most likely to respond to the next offer, based on their buying history or other data

Targeting 'new' customers is more problematical. Our options depend on two things: first, the market choice – are we trying to attract our competitors' customers, or are we looking for entirely new markets? Second, the extent to which we know who our prospects are – do we have a tightly defined profile? If we have a well-defined profile and are looking for prospects in our existing market, we can be much more precise in our targeting than if we were looking for poorly defined prospects in unfamiliar markets.

The top priority categories for targeting are:

- **recently lapsed customers**
- **former customers:** used the company in the past but are now with a competitor
- **enquirers:** have contacted the company but are not yet customers
- **referrals:** recommended by existing customers
- **profiled prospects:** statistical profiles based on existing (loyal) customers
- **'handraisers':** prospects who select themselves via the use of responsive advertising

The lowest priority are suspects contacted through market research profiles, new markets and the use of responsive advertising.

Figure 6.7 shows us that our options are as follows:

- Targeting prospects based on previous contact of some sort with the company
- Targeting based on the principle that new customers will be similar to existing customers
- Targeting based on 'predicted loyalty' to the company, again based on existing customer profiles
- Targeting a commercial partner's customers, known as affinity marketing
- Asking new customers to identify themselves

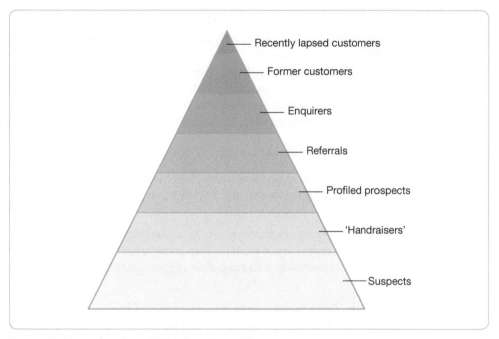

Figure 6.7 Hierarchy of acquisition targeting options

Targeting based on previous contact

Our top priority lies with enquirers, former customers and recent lapsers, who should all be held on the customer database. They have already shown an interest in the company and its products. Indeed, former customers and recent lapsers may not, in their minds, have lapsed at all. People drift in and out of relationships with companies without seeing this as active switching. They may have a repertoire of brands to provide variety; they may have forgotten to renew their subscription; or a dozen other factors may have affected their status with you. The only instance in which lapsers are not your best prospect is when they have experienced dissatisfaction with your company and this has not been resolved. (In this case, they may still be top priority for contact, to try to recover the situation. Relationship marketers (Payne, 1995) have pointed out the dangers of ignoring dissatisfied former customers who have a tendency to tell many others of their horror stories!) Referrals, motivated by word of mouth recommendations, are the next highest priority.

Exhibit 6.7 Timing: the unsung hero of direct marketing

Much of marketing these days consists of getting the right offer to the right audience but at the wrong time. Direct marketing acquisition can be accurately timed so that the offer reaches prospects when they are actively in the market.

This can be done using data collected on external databases; for example, the likely date of next car purchase can be collected. Timing to enquirers or lapsers can be even more accurate. If you ask Direct Line Insurance for a quote on car insurance and then decline to take up the offer, you are held on file as an enquirer. Exactly one year later, the company can be pretty sure you are in the market for car insurance once more, and it can time its offers very precisely.

Targeting based on profiles of existing customers

Targeting based on profiling was fully described earlier (Chapter 4); here we can see where the technique fits strategically.

If you have a database of existing customers, the opportunity exists to build up detailed 'profiles' and match these statistically with 'prospect lists'. A golf supplier may find his existing customers have a high propensity to live in 'leafy suburb' geodemographic areas. The supplier can then rent a list of such prospects from a geodemographic system agency.

Targeting the most loyal customers

> It's hard to concentrate on acquisition quality when quantity is so much easier. . . Winning more and more new customers could slowly put you out of business.
>
> (Reichheld, 1996)

Reichheld (1996) argues that the best new customers are those that are similar to your own most loyal customers. We can get help in targeting based on loyalty from Cram (1994), who, taking a relationship marketing view, suggests the following prospects as being the top priorities:

1 **Referrals.** Cram found that people who respond because of the recommendation of a friend or colleague are more likely to stay than those who respond to an advertisement.

2 **People who buy at the standard price.** These are more loyal than sales promotion respondents – 'deal conscious' consumers who are loyal to the discount, not the brand. According to Reichheld, getting these 'wrong' customers can quickly erode the efficiency and strength of the company.

3 **Risk averse consumers.** These are more loyal than experimenters. Cautious customers are more likely to stick with you.

4 **Customers looking for high levels of service.** Cram asserted that customers who value service, and are willing to pay for it, are in turn more loyal than those who do not.

5 **Customers seeking a high level of personalisation.** Tailored service inspires loyalty. A book club that tailors its offers depending on individual tastes will attract consumers interested in that service.

Exhibit 6.8 IBM and analytics

IBM needed senior business decision makers to associate IBM with analytics by leveraging Wimbledon via a 'seeing is believing' approach. Their agency Ogilvy One used five years' tennis player history to create win/lose predictions.

A $7.2m projected revenue represents an ROI of £27 for every £1 spent.

One of IBM's biggest challenges was to be seen to offer software and analytics solutions, rather than just infrastructure, particularly among senior business decision makers (BDMs) outside the IT community. We know that communicating what software does can be difficult in conventional media, so Ogilvy One London chose an animated visual approach, in a channel that reached BDMs effectively. The new Executive Channel media met all criteria, with digital screens in 80 large offices around London and an average dwell time of 40 seconds. They also took advantage of the strong public interest in Wimbledon when it was most likely to be top of mind. Wimbledon was used to make analytics interesting, along with a channel that could deliver a 'seeing is believing' demonstration of software in action and a can't-miss BDM channel that only needed 40 seconds of their time.

Analytics were at the heart of the idea, predicting the likelihood of players winning or losing. A staggering 75 per cent accuracy was achieved – powerful proof of IBM's strength in analytics. IBM analysed the last five years of top tennis players' match data to generate three unique keys to victory for every player. By continually monitoring this data during the two weeks of Wimbledon, predictions were presented in real time. The execution took full advantage of the media to present visually just enough top line tennis data to intrigue the audience, without oversimplifying the technology. Match predictions were also tailored to the media using workplace humour, e.g. 'It looks like Federer won't be coming in tomorrow', increasing relevance.

Results. Product purchase cycles were generally between 6 and 18 months, therefore sales were projected based on historical conversion rates. A £7.2m projected revenue figure represents an ROI of £27 for every £1 spent.

This projection comprises a total campaign cost of £159 591 and an average deal value of £180,000 or approximately 40 product sales. Brand recall was 27 per cent higher than the next nearest brand advertised in the medium. The call to action 'Search: IBM tennis' contributed to a 9.7 per cent search cost per click-through (CTR), 67 per cent higher than the previous year, with a third of the spend.

Source: Ogilvy One, DMA Awards.

We now turn to a special case of targeting for acquisition, known as affinity marketing.

Affinity marketing

An entirely new method of acquisition has been developed, primarily by direct marketers, known as affinity marketing. Affinity marketing is the use of a commercial partner's brand and customer base to provide a ready market for your product. Thus, a typical set-up may be a bank promoting a credit card to a charity's audience. The credit card is co-branded with the charity logo and the bank marque. In return for access to the charity list and use of the logo, the bank pays a sum to the charity each time a transaction is made, typically 0.25 per cent of the transaction.

The point of affinity marketing to acquire customers is the extra leverage that the strong branding bond your partner has with its customers can offer you. People often have a strong affinity for organisations such as their favourite charity, their university, or the football team they support. They are, therefore, more likely to take up offers that come from such organisations.

Strategically, affinity marketing is an important area because it raises the crucial concept of 'partnership's between 'non-competing organisations' for mutual gain. Partnership marketing can be a way of overcoming the often stifling similarity of many companies to their competitors. Direct marketers can take advantage of such strategic alliances in many different ways to acquire customers. Mutual reinforcement is obtained by merging the different customer service capabilities to add to each company's offer.

Exhibit 6.9 To affinity and beyond: Beneficial Bank

The name Beneficial Bank is not widely known, not even to its own customers! This is because it offers third-party affinity cards to people, and the branding on the cards is that of the affinity partner. Beneficial has teamed up with organisations such as Tottenham Hotspur, the Law Society, the Police Federation and Cambridge University.

The benefits of these tie ups go to all parties involved. The card holder receives a Visa card with no annual fee and a highly competitive APR. For the affinity partner, Beneficial pays a one-off fee of about £5 for every member who takes up the card, plus 25p for every £100 spent on the card. These amounts soon add up for the partner: Open University has benefited to the tune of hundreds of thousands of pounds.

A 2004 Mintel report found that over three-quarters of adults felt they belonged to an affinity group of some sort – whether a charity, sports or arts club, or common interest. The benefit to banks like Beneficial is that they do not have to go out and find customers – a significant saving. Beneficial saves on brand creation, incentives, prospect database costs and so on.

The real growth of affinity cards took place in the mid 1990s. Since then the market has flattened and is probably saturated. The 2004 Mintel study found that affinity members tended to be up-market and better educated. Further affinity growth may well come from on-line Web based sales, with websites providing a natural basis for membership schemes, and for the sales of financial products.

Sources: Adapted from Denny, N. (1996) 'Affinity way to do business', *Marketing Direct*, June, pp. 42–4. Reproduced from *Marketing Direct* magazine with the permission of the copyright owner, Haymarket Business Publications Ltd; and adapted from Precision Marketing (2003) 'RSPCA tests DRTV for affinity card promotion', Precision Marketing (2003), 17 January, 15 (14) p. 6. Mintel Report, Affinity Marketing – UK, November 2004.

In the USA, one credit card in four is an affinity card, compared with one in 20 in the UK. Growth in Europe is a strong possibility over the next few years.

Finally, a warning about cards and their use in direct marketing. Be careful not to confuse affinity cards with co-branded loyalty cards, for example the HFC Bank/General Motors credit card. The latter also involve partnerships, but not primarily to attract new customers; rather, they are a deal for the loyal customer who benefits from points accrued through loyal spending – a General Motors customer gets points towards money off a new car, for example. Co-branded cards are fully discussed later (Chapter 10).

Targeting suspects

In instances where there is little chance of using any of the previous methods of targeting, direct marketers may mimic general marketing, relying on market research to build up rough profiles of suspects. These could be:

- competitors' customers within existing markets
- prospects in new markets
- new entrants into the market

It is important to distinguish between these market 'pools' of prospects, because the approach – the message or the product offer – may change in each instance.

Using the targeting hierarchy to guide strategy

The targeting hierarchy gives a strong guide to our resource allocation: we should spend our targeting money from the 'top down' (see Figure 6.7). For example, if we have only enough budget to contact one group, then we should aim for recently lapsed customers. There would be less return in allocating spend to prospects or suspects. Once each level of potential is exhausted, any further acquisition budget is used on the next level down, until the money runs out.

Of course, this targeting 'rule' is there to aid our strategies, but it is not set in stone. We may, for other reasons, wish to expand into new markets, or learn something about the attractiveness of our products to a totally new set of customers. In this instance, we would allocate resources to targeting suspects, even though better prospects were available to us.

Targeting decisions may also depend on whether our firm is 'customer' led or 'product' led. Let us take the example of the small-car market. The customer led marketing philosophy tells us to find out people's needs first and then meet them. In this instance, we may use a list of people who have expressed the desire for a small economic car. We approach these people and obtain details of their preferences for the car, design and launch it, and precisely target our list with details of the car.

The product led company would follow research and development, relying on good ideas internally to design a competitive car. Here, only a broad, rough idea of possible customers has been considered. It may then be best to use primarily awareness advertising and local dealers to sell the product. Here, the firm relies on customers 'identifying themselves' when they show an interest.

The example used highlights two different marketing strategies, which then direct two targeting routes. The higher the commitment by the firm to being customer led, the more likely it is to target precisely; and the more precisely it targets, the more effective direct marketing is compared with general marketing.

Which is the better route? Clearly, the customer led route more precisely follows the marketing philosophy; but it is interesting to observe that a lot of successful firms routinely use 'handraising' to identify their customers.

Let us move on from segmentation and targeting issues. What about the proposition, or offer, made to the customer? Direct marketing undoubtedly has a strategic role to play in delivering elements of this offer, and in the next section we focus on direct delivery of 'service, dialogue with customers, pricing and product value'.

6.5 The total product/service

The 'total product' is the sum of everything a company offers to customers. For a supermarket chain this might include fast checkout facilities, bigger trolleys, cheaper price, notifying the customer of exciting new products, on-line ordering and home delivery and indeed everything else that would make a difference to the customer's experience.

6.5.1 Delivering service

Relationship marketing focuses on employee satisfaction as a major factor in service delivery. Direct marketing can link with employees in delivering 'help, convenience and reassurance'. It can also be a major method of delivery of 'after-sales service'.

Help, convenience and reassurance

When people are in the middle of buying a house they are often in a state of high anxiety. Juggling suppliers, dealing with lawyers, the mortgage, the seller and the sale of their existing house is stressful. What they need above all is 'help', if possible proactively delivered by the supplier. A database can go some way to delivering this by recording progress and anticipating pressure points, thus helping the customer manage their way through.

After-sales service

Direct marketing can sometimes offer a crucial advantage here over general marketing. The following example shows how.

A customer buys, say, a second-hand car from a dealer for a few thousand pounds. A few days later the customer gets a call to ask if everything is all right with the car. At the same time, the dealer suggests the customer books in for her six-monthly service and free steam clean. In this way, the customer is well on the way to being retained for her next car purchase. Why? Because she has started a genuine relationship with the dealer, which she would actively have to break in order to buy from somewhere else. It is much easier for the customer to say yes to the deal she is offered by the dealer than actively to look elsewhere. Moreover, this strategy provides sustainable competitive advantage. Only the dealer knows when the customer will need the service and what the particular needs of that customer are.

Tailored service delivery

In sectors where tailored service is important to customers, direct marketing can be absolutely fundamental to high quality delivery. We have already looked at the way executive hotels manage their frequent customers. Such frequent visitors are highly profitable and are treated lavishly with a highly personalised service. The database orchestrates a lot of the face-to-face contact that occurs. It is the 'proactive delivery of convenience' to customers that is the key to this strategy. As an aside, the customers also enjoy a feeling of exclusivity, of specialness, because they know that they are getting special treatment.

Another plank of relationship marketing that can be delivered through direct marketing is 'dialogue'.

6.5.2 Loyalty through regular communications

Relationship marketers advocate communication that emphasises listening to and learning from the customer, rather than the 'we speak, you listen' school of marketing. Direct marketing is one way of making this happen in practice. Questionnaires can be sent out to customers asking them what they want and when they want it. Suggestions can be made on how the products can help make that particular customer's life easier, with easy access provided for further dialogue via the telephone, e-mail or social media.

There are many business sectors where there is little opportunity for regular contact with existing customers. Take the mortgage lenders. Once the mortgage is agreed, the house is bought and regular payments are established, there is no 'natural' occasion for any further contact between company and customer. Indeed, the better the customer, the less they will contact the company! Similarly, car manufacturers, financial services companies, utilities and car breakdown companies all have little contact with their biggest assets – their existing customers.

To overcome this, a strategy of regular communication direct to existing customers can be adopted. These companies can use direct marketing to maintain contact with customers using vehicles such as membership clubs, customer magazines, or e-newsletters. These vehicles need to be of high quality – they need to be of value in their own right – in order to work. It is no use bombarding customers with newsletters that are little more than glorified sales brochures. The Walt Disney Children's Club is an example of a communications vehicle that creates value for customers. You will find much more about customer magazines, clubs and so on later (Chapter 10).

Communications to enhance loyalty has now become a mature industry. While cynics may argue that much of this activity is companies 'running to stand still' against each other, provided the campaigns are well executed the evidence suggests they are still valued (Bolton *et al.*, 2000).

Exhibit 6.10 Intense competition drives investment in improving loyalty using direct marketing

The Marriott rewards scheme is one of the industry's most successful schemes. In 2003, worldwide hotel chain Marriott stepped up its drive to retain its customer base with a refreshed loyalty scheme. The campaign included 2 million inserts and direct mail shots featuring a mini brochure. Frequent travellers can also earn 'elite level' benefits after staying 15 nights or more in a year, including hotel and gift shop discounts, room type priority, reservation guarantee, bonus point earnings, free room upgrades. Marriott commented that it was looking for an approach that included 'brand planning combined with hard nosed number oriented direct marketing'.

By 2010, Marriott Rewards had a membership of over 20 million worldwide. Marriott wanted to emphasise the benefits of joining, which include room upgrades and discounts, Avios and other airline miles, discounts and offers on eleven leading partner brands and, as the programme has developed, there are now over 250 ways in which members can redeem points. Members are able to use their points to help victims of natural disasters, for example Hurricane Sandy, as well as to help support wounded servicemen. The scheme has also been extended to include certain Ritz Carlton hotels.

Source: Based on: **http://www.marriottreards.com**, accessed 2012. *Precision Marketing* (2003) 'Marriott Hotels embarks on loyalty offensive', 27 June, **15** (37), p. 2.

6.5.3 Creating loyalty through pricing strategies

'You can't buy loyalty. You can only buy the next purchase.'

(Simon Roncorroni, MD, The L&R Group)

'Whoever invented the term "loyalty card" has a lot to answer for.'

(Mitchell, 1998)

Direct marketers can tie a price based loyalty scheme to individual spend. Rewards can be in the form of a straight price discount or can be 'points based systems'. These are widely known as 'loyalty schemes'. Loyalty schemes are an established, important weapon in the direct marketer's armoury, and we will take a detailed look at them later (Chapter 10). However, the decision as to whether to adopt a loyalty scheme, or to look for alternative actions, is a strategic move, and as such merits some discussion here.

Loyalty schemes have for some time been criticised by a number of commentators (Nunez and Dreze, 2006; Dowling, 2002; O'Brien and Jones, 1995; Peppers and Rogers, 1993; Uncles, 1994). Peppers and Rogers suggested that when used as part of an overall strategy of creating value for existing customers they make sense, but otherwise they are essentially just another costly marketing promotion. When the airlines created frequency rewards in the form of free Air Miles, they also created a structure of preferential service in which frequent flyers benefited from upgrades, priority check-in, and so on. Car rental companies, in contrast, rewarded customers with free rental, followed by gifts in exchange for points, but with no service extras. What they quickly found, however, was how easily this approach was copied by competitors, and how quick customers were to switch, depending on who offered the best reward.

Uncles (1994, 1996) found that, as schemes are copied, customers realise there is no particular advantage and their behaviour is unchanged. Worse, customers become bored with all the deals, and basically filter out all loyalty scheme messages from all the players.

Taking these perspectives on board, Lynch and Mitchell (1997) examined the use of loyalty cards in supermarkets. They questioned the effectiveness of loyalty cards in actually generating loyalty or 'relationships' towards supermarkets. By 2008 each of us, on average, participates in three schemes. So loyalty needs careful definition. Loyalty schemes should be used as follows:

● When we have little choice. In some markets, such as credit cards, service issues are not as important to customers. Product/price benefits must, therefore, be concentrated on ways to differentiate.

● When we have the chance to reinforce brand associations (Uncles, 1996). If the loyalty scheme can reinforce the brand 'relationship' with the company, then it may be considered. American Express's Membership Miles scheme achieves this.

Exhibit 6.11 Keeping customers in commodity markets

Are there any alternatives to price-led loyalty?

The problem with price-led loyalty is that, when the price is not right, customers are being trained by the deals to walk. This is very unprofitable for all concerned. The answer? This is not easy. One idea may be to use the database to identify the right customers; then look for innovative ways to share value with them. If we take car insurance, service is not a big issue in this market. So to turn away from price means creating value for customers in other ways. What about donations made direct to customers' favourite charities, based on loyal customers' no-claims records?

Exhibit 6.12 The strategic use of loyalty card data

The key player in the UK and one of the most important schemes in commercial history has been that of Tesco (see also the case study ending Chapter 3). It has revolutionised the way a multi-billion pound industry is run. Individual-level data has been systematically gathered on most of Tesco's 12 million customers, allowing the company to understand each customer's value to the company and how it may be able to increase that value, or prevent losses.

One key area has been in fighting off competition from US Giant Wal-Mart which took over Asda in 2000. While Asda's 'EveryDay Low Pricing' strategy guides its mass discounting across a range of products, Tesco's individual data enables it to understand which price drop is valued by which customers. It therefore focuses on those customers who may be price driven rather than, say, convenience driven. The scheme is also used to analyse behaviour and segment customers, and test different promotional efforts. More strategically, it is about rearranging stores, and redirecting supply chains.

Some loyalty schemes enable a value based segmentation to be built up, meaning firms can save money by not contacting low responsive or low value customers: instead of mailing 100 per cent of a database, just mail maybe 50 per cent.

Others enable segmentation by product need. Music retailers can send thousands of e-mails to customers, but offerings will depend on that customer's particular buying pattern.

Recent linkages between data and supply chains has been made, moving database information out of the realms of marketing departments and into the genuinely strategic domain in companies. Clothing retailer Marks & Spencer analysed its customer profiles in different stores and adjusted its merchandise accordingly. It noticed huge increases in men's and women's fashion sales.

Some sectors are better than others. Credit card firms have been noticeably less successful in using their data from loyalty schemes: special offers tend to be untargeted and rather bland, customer segmentation is undeveloped.

Sources: Marsh, H. (2001) 'Dig deeper into the database goldmine' in *Marketing Magazine,* 11 January, pp. 29–30. Mitchell, A. (2002) 'Consumer power is on the cards in Tesco plan', *Marketing Week,* 2 May p. 30.

- We have the opportunity to meet most or all of the rules outlined by O'Brien and Jones (1995) for effective schemes. O'Brien and Jones propose five attributes that a successful scheme should have: cash value, offer convenience, relevance, aspirational value, and offer choice.

- Extra value can be created outside the core programme. This could be service benefits, for example British Airways' Executive Club.

- We want to gather transaction data and this is the best way of doing it. Retailers use loyalty schemes to gather transaction data, which would not otherwise be available. This data is then used to create 'tailored' added value for customers, perhaps with coupon offers related directly to individuals' spend. This is often the key advantage for companies' schemes.

Verhoef (2003) finds that loyalty schemes remain popular in spite of the problems. Customers are now more expert at filtering the good deals from the mundane.

Apart from service and pricing issues, direct marketing can help deliver a differentiated 'augmented product strategy'.

6.5.4 The product

Direct marketing systems do little for core product strategies; these depend on innovative research and development, good market research, portfolio analysis and so on. However, direct marketing is an important consideration when we focus on the extended product. Strategically, we may use direct marketing to offer 'convenience through direct distribution, positioning and brand-related benefits', and 'incentives to trigger purchase' in getting new customers.

Convenience through direct distribution

Direct distribution, the original form of direct marketing (via mail-order), is still an important tool. Direct distribution, when viewed from the customer's perspective, is a 'service' issue. Customers who respond to direct offers may be attracted by the convenience of purchasing goods and services from the comfort of their own home.

Mail-order was originally seen as catering for relatively downmarket sectors but, in the 1990s, new entrants such as Racing Green, Lands End and Next Directory, and the move to on-line, changed the profile of the industry. Moving towards 2013, industry standards for direct delivery have been transformed. Companies typically set 48- or even 24-hour delivery promises, reflecting customer dissatisfaction with traditional mail-order performances. As a result, home shopping is increasing, and even conservative companies like Marks & Spencer have launched on-line operations to complement their retail activities.

Of course, there are many sectors in which most customers prefer the shopping experience of the high street. Some people want the instant satisfaction of ownership. You, therefore, need to make a strategic decision on whether to distribute through retail, directly or a mixture of both. The pressure on the high street retailers at the moment is intense and the recent closure of major names in retail business has highlighted a sector that is in crisis.

Technological developments may provide another swing towards direct distribution. Supermarket chains have set up on-line operations that offer direct delivery of groceries. Consumers can be given the trigger of their previous week's shopping list and asked if they want any changes made. The Internet of things means that your kitchen cupboards and fridge can send automated rebuy signals to a shopping list held on your tablet computer or directly to a supplier. Recently Tesco has experimented with mobile shopping at Gatwick Airport, using mobile phones and quick response (QR) readers. Tesco billed this as the UK's first interactive virtual grocery store. Located in the departure lounge at Gatwick Airport the 'shop' consisted of four interactive touchscreens that the shopper could slide by hand to show fixtures with around 80 essential items. To buy them the shopper simply scanned the barcode with a mobile phone. So travellers could use the downtime waiting for planes to order a basket of groceries for their return. This test followed a similar trial on the South Korean metro system.

It can be speculated that, at some point in the near future, consumers will divide into two groups: those who like the shopping experience but do not want to pay fees for delivery; and those who want convenience and can pay for it. To compete, companies will have to choose between retail and direct distribution operations or a combination of both.

Positioning

Positioning is two things:

- The dimensions chosen by the company to describe the product
- Where the product fits in the consumer's mind in relation to its competitors

To take a simple example, BMW is positioned as a car of '*engineering excellence*', and also as a '*high status*' car.

Positioning is as important to direct marketing as any other type of marketing. The company and product must be positioned clearly, using direct marketing communications, if you are to succeed in attracting people to you. Direct marketing has an extra string to its bow here; it can segment your positioning dimensions to appeal to different groups. For example, a mobile phone supplier could position its products simultaneously to young adults as status symbols, and to women with young families as security aids. The precision of direct marketing allows this to be done very efficiently.

Branding

General marketers often look to differentiate their products (especially in markets where the core products are closely matched, such as most supermarket goods) through 'building a brand' that prospects will be familiar with and like, even though they have yet to purchase from that firm (Aaker, 1991).

Brands are 'intangible values' added to the core product or service. The values are deliberately created and nurtured by the marketer, and exist as images held in the consumer's mind.

Direct marketers, in contrast, have not traditionally used branding techniques to the same extent, relying more on rational appeals based on products' unique selling propositions. In short, brand building came a poor second to the unique selling point (USP) school of thought exemplified by Rosser Reeves: what is the USP – why should I buy from you? These cultures stemmed from the world of mail -order, where product benefits were always more important than brand symbolism. More recently, however, the idea of marrying the worlds of DM and branding has become more important as DM has become more important in sectors where branding is strong – the automotive sector, for example. Pearson (1996) argued that brands can and should be built up through direct marketing. Pearson's argument is more concerned with service sectors. He asserted that modern consumers want things like help, convenience and a relationship with their supplier, and that branding these attributes as belonging to your company will build a sustainable competitive advantage.

Pearson's assertions were lent credibility by the upsurge in companies whose brands have been built by, or are related to, direct marketing. Examples include Direct Line and First Direct, to add to traditional big players worldwide such as American Express. Indeed, the word 'direct' itself has taken on positive brand values of its own, being associated with values like lower price, efficiency and convenience.

Because of these developments, brand strategy options need to be understood by the direct marketer. De Chernatony *et al.* (2010) and Cowley (1991) outlined the branding strategic options, of which those most relevant to direct marketing are as follows:

Branding as a device for recognition or shorthand

Visual brand entities can act as a shorthand for reasons to buy: quality, trust, price, value. The most important visual entities are the name and logo. Direct marketing communications usually reinforce this added value by prominent display of the brand name and logo.

Branding for reassurance

Imparting trust and reassurance is an essential part of marketing. People want to minimise the risk of making a purchase they will come to regret. Brands such as McDonald's reassure customers that they will receive a consistent product and service on each visit.

When recruiting customers through direct 'distribution', reassurance is particularly important. This is because consumers are buying remotely: they cannot assess the product at first hand before purchase, and they do not meet the seller face to face. The classic direct marketers, distributing direct, made an art form out of trust and reassurance by using various devices. The mail -order clothing company, Boden, offers a 'no quibble' product guarantee for on- or off-line sales, encouraging new customers to see their purchase as very low risk; and this is replicated across almost all companies operating in the sector.

Branding that communicates functional values

Functional values are the product or service benefits that are on offer. Functional branding is an important area for direct marketers, who have traditionally operated primarily on functional benefits and logical reasons to buy. Lakeland, a mail-order operation, sells products by emphasising unique selling points.

Branding that communicates symbolic values

Here the focus is on brand values that help the buyer express their personality. The consumer associates the brand's glamour, sexiness, high performance, youth and so on, with themselves. Direct marketing has not traditionally been used in order to build symbolic values; this technique has been more suited to large TV advertising budgets. However, one customer value where direct marketers do make a difference is status. Companies such as American Express, BMW and Ritz Carlton Hotels use direct marketing as a way of building and maintaining a feeling of exclusivity and privilege to both recruit and keep customers.

Exhibit 6.13 Developing a brand with direct marketing – Kern

This experiment used a travelling gnome to prove a little known theory about Earth's gravity. Beyond business results – a 21 per cent sales uplift – the story reached more than 350 million people in 150 countries, propelling Kern to the top of Google rankings. The experiment became a TED talk and was even added to several national curricula.

Kern makes some of the planet's most precise scales. It wanted to build its reputation and revenue in the global laboratory and education sector, but there are millions of these institutions and no credible data on who buys science equipment. Plus, Kern's marketing budget was small. The strategy was a global experiment, with the aim of creating a globally newsworthy campaign without the usual costs. This would help boost Kern's search rankings, which are critical to success; around 20 per cent of Kern's sales result from on-line search. The media plan included the direct mail 'gnome kit', an e-mail invitation, the gnome's Twitter account, the gnome's Tumblr account and seeding the story with key influencers.

This was the world's first mass participation gravity experiment, one that reveals an amazing, little known phenomenon. Earth's gravity actually varies, with fluctuations that would not register on typical scales – but do so on Kern scales. Carefully selected Kern customers and scientists around the world were invited to play a starring role. They received a kit with scales and a special test weight: a chip proof garden gnome. Participants weighed the gnome, recorded the results on the website, toook photographic evidence, then sent him on. Each world famous institution the gnome visited was a highly credible endorsement for Kern, from the South Pole to CERN. He is even set to experience weightlessness in NASA's 'Vomit Comet'. As he travels, he drives traffic to the site and explains the science through his very own Tumblr and Twitter accounts.

Results. Within two days of his reaching the South Pole, the story was Twitter top news, reaching more than 355 million people in 152 countries, having been shared by blogs such as *New Scientist*, NASA, *Huffington Post*, *Reader's Digest*, *National Geographic* and the BBC, as well as appearing on TV. After two weeks, 16,386 websites had linked to **GnomeExperiment. com,** resulting in an 11 per cent sales uplift and 1,042.00 per cent ROI. After a month there was a 21 per cent sales uplift across the entire Kern range. All of this was achieved on a production budget of £24,000 and without spending a penny on traditional media space.

Sources: Ogilvy One, DMA Awards (2012).

This is not the end of direct marketing's influence on symbolic branding, however. If we probe a little deeper, we can distinguish between using advertising to create a 'communications based brand', and using the customer experience of the product to create an 'experience based brand'.

In instances where communications driven brand values are very important, direct marketing usually plays a support role; its communications maintain and enhance advertising driven values. The launch of the Audi A1 car in the UK illustrates this. All the Audi marketing communication, including social media, direct-response press and direct mail, contained the basic brand building creative elements, including consistent imagery and the strapline 'A1 Big Idea Condensed' as well as the ubiquitous 'Vorsprung Durch Technik' endline.

With experience based brands, direct marketers can often take more of a lead role. A prime exponent of an experience based brand is First Direct. First Direct offers a 24-hour telephone banking operation, delivering high quality service to its customers. The ease with which everyday transactions are conducted contrasts hugely with many retail banking operations and, as a result, First Direct's own customers are its biggest asset in spreading the news. 94 per cent of First Direct's new business comes through word of mouth; over 10,000 new customers per month are joining it as a result.

Using incentives

Unlike branding, the use of incentives to trigger purchase is not new to direct marketers. Incentives have been used by direct marketers in the traditional direct sectors, such as mail-order and publishing, for a long time. The accumulated knowledge of extensive testing has provided considerable evidence of the improved cost per sale often achieved using sales promotions (discussed in more detail later (Chapter 10)).

However, the long time 'love affair' that direct marketers have had with sales promotion techniques has been challenged by some practitioners (Rapp and Collins, 1987). Reichheld (1996) proposed that people recruited through powerful incentives were more likely to switch again to another competitor. Such customers were loyal to deals rather than to companies. The cellular phone industry in the US has defection rates as high as 40 per cent p.a., thanks to overuse of incentives to stimulate new custom. O'Brien and Jones (1995) raised the whole philosophy of rewarding people to switch rather than to stay loyal.

In acquisition, there are two decisions that direct marketers have to make about incentives at the strategic level:

1 For the situation at hand, should we use incentives to stimulate first time purchase?

2 If we decide to use incentives, what strategic guidelines should govern the choice of incentive?

An examination of the advantages and disadvantages of using incentives will help to answer these questions for whatever specific situation arises.

Advantages and disadvantages of using incentives

Rapp and Collins (1987) suggested that incentives used in public media or retail environments led to high wastage because they could be used by existing customers who would have purchased anyway. In contrast, direct marketing is used to target incentives precisely, so avoiding this wastage.

Incentives are often used as tie-breakers in parity brand markets. It may be that the incentive is the only point of differentiation between suppliers. This is often the case in financial services markets, such as insurance, where brands are weak and service has not been developed such that consumers will regard it highly.

If the company has a clear cost focus strategy, incentives can be used to draw attention to reduced prices. Similarly, if the company operates a differentiation strategy, appropriate incentives may add value. Direct marketing systems can administer complicated mechanics that tie in first time customers to deals, locking them into future purchases (Stone, 1996). This ensures that payback on acquisition spend is reached through retained customers. An example of this might be a book club offering any three books for £1, on the condition that the customer buys six more books at full price within a year.

One problem with using incentives as a point of difference is 'me-too-ism'. Your competitors quickly copy any successful promotion that you offer. The result is a zero-sum game, creating additional costs of doing business. Another downside is the possible damage to the brand of inappropriate incentives; many financial services' 'brands' sometimes seem to consist of free watches or alarm clocks rather than attractive brand values.

Summary

In this chapter we found that loyalty has had a major influence on direct marketing, in directing resources to retention and in understanding how to achieve better retention levels. The increased awareness of the importance of marketers using their influence company-wide was also assessed – indicating the importance of a database as a strategic tool. The impact of a number of marketing tools in helping to deliver direct marketing strategies was assessed. Perhaps the greatest strength of direct marketing is its ability to deliver powerful segmentation and targeting strategies. It can also support service delivery, differentiate prices to different customers, and help in an augmented product strategy. The links between brand creation and direct marketing are a possible development area for the future.

QUESTIONS

1 Give an example of a sales related objective for a retailer and an acquisition objective for a direct marketer, and explain the distinction clearly.

2 Give an example of an acquisition objective and a retention objective for an airline. How might the two objectives be clearly related to one another?

3 Both relationship marketing and the Four Ps approach to marketing have influenced direct marketing strategic approaches. Outline the key areas of direct marketing thinking affected by both paradigms, and give examples of firms following either approach in their direct marketing.

4 The Institute of Direct and Digital Marketing argues that accountability and control are two cornerstones of direct marketing. These are internal management benefits. Others argue that it is direct marketing's focus on the customer that is its best feature. Argue the merits of the various benefits direct marketing offers, focusing on the differences between direct and general marketing.

5 Why is it that it is usually more cost effective to market to an existing customer than to acquire a new customer? Can you think of any business situations where this may not be true?

6 Tour operators selling package holidays often do very little in persuading previous customers to return for another trip. As a consultant, offer advice on customer retention and revenue maximisation strategies for a tour operator. What role would direct marketing play in such strategies?

7 A leading, up-market credit card brand is considering the use of incentives within a direct marketing strategy in order to acquire more new customers. Debate the pros and cons of this move.

References

Aaker, D. (1991) *Managing Brand Equity,* The Free Press, New York.

Bassi, L.J. (1997) 'Harnessing the power of intellectual capital', *Training and Development,* 51 (12), pp. 25–30.

Bessen, J. (1993) 'Riding the information wave', *Harvard Business Review,* September–October, pp. 150–60.

Bolton, R., Kannan, P. and Bramlett, M. (2000) 'Implications of loyalty program membership and service experiences for customer retention and value', *Journal of the Academy of Marketing Science,* 28 (Winter), pp. 95–108.

Christopher, M. (1996) 'From brand values to customer value', *Journal of Marketing Practice: Applied Marketing Science,* 2 (1), pp. 55–66.

Circle-research.com/wp-content/uploads/2012-06/B2B-Barometer-Q2-20121.pdf [Accessed Dec. 2012].

Cowley, D. (ed.) (1991) *Understanding Brands, by 10 People Who Do,* Kogan Page, London.

Cram, T. (1994) *The Power of Relationship Marketing,* Pitman Publishing, London.

Cruikshanks, J. and Schultz, A. (2010) *The Man Who Sold America: The Amazing (but True!) Story of Albert D. Lasker and the Creation of the Advertising Century*, Harvard Business Review Press, Boston, Mass.

De Chernatony, L. McDonald, M. Wallace, E. (2010) *Creating Powerful Brands,* 4th Ed Taylor and Francis.

DeTienne, K. and Thompson, J.A. (1996) 'Database marketing and organisational learning theory: toward a research agenda', *Journal of Consumer Marketing,* 13 (5), pp. 12–34.

DMA Census (2003) Direct Marketing Association.

DMA Awards (2012) Available at: **http://www.dmaawards.org.uk/2012-winners** [Accessed February 2013].

Dowling, G. W. (2002) 'Customer relationship management: in B2C markets, often less is more', *California Management Review,* 44 (Spring), pp. 87–104.

Doyle, P. (2002) *Marketing Management and Strategy,* FT Prentice Hall, Harlow.

Ehrenberg, A.S.C. (1972) *Repeat Buying: Theory and applications,* North Holland, London.

Finerty, L. (1997) 'Information retrieval for intranets: the case for knowledge management', *Document World,* 2 (5), pp. 32–4.

Fletcher, K. and Wright, G. (1997) 'The challenge of database marketing', *Journal of Database Marketing,* 5 (1), pp. 42–52.

Gartner Group (2003) Presentation to Relationship Marketing Colloquium, England, September.

Gronroos, C. (1996) 'Relationship marketing: strategic and tactical implications', *Management Decision,* 34 (3), p. 13.

Gummesson, E. (1991) 'Marketing orientation revisited: the crucial role of the part-time marketer', *European Journal of Marketing,* 25 (2), pp. 60–75.

Hansen, M.T., Nohria, N. and Tierney, T. (1999) 'What's your strategy for managing knowledge?' *Harvard Business Review,* March–April, 77 (12), p. 106.

Harris, L. (1996) 'Cultural obstacles to market orientation', *Journal of Marketing Practice: Applied Marketing Science,* 2 (4), p. 14.

Hartley, M. (1997) *It wouldn't stop me going somewhere else: supermarkets and their loyalty cards,* 31st Annual Conference, Academy of Marketing, 8–10 July, Manchester.

Humby, C., Hunt, T. and Phillips, T. (2003) *Scoring Points, How Tesco is Winning Customer Loyalty,* Kogan Page, London.

Kohli, A.K. and Jaworski, B.J. (1990) 'Market orientation: the construct, research propositions and managerial implications', *Journal of Marketing,* 54, April, pp. 1–18.

Lynch, J.E. and Mitchell, P. (1997) *Supermarket loyalty cards: low involvement relationship marketing,* 31st Annual Conference, Academy of Marketing, 8–10 July, Manchester.

Marketingcharts.com/direct/customer-retention-top-marketing-priority-17975/forbes-spending-june-2011jpg/ [Accessed, December 2012].

McAdam, R. and McCreedy, S. (1999) 'A critical review of knowledge management models', *The Learning Organization,* 6 (3), pp. 91–101.

McCorkell, G. (1997) *Direct and Database Marketing,* Kogan Page, London.

Mitchell, A. (1997) *Marketing Week,* 14 March, p. 28.

Mitchell, A. (1998) 'The one–one gap', *Management Today,* July, pp. 90–1.

Nunez, J. and Dreze, X., (2006) Your loyalty program is betraying you', *Harvard Business Review,* November–December, pp. 124–31.

O'Brien, L. and Jones, C. (1995) 'Do rewards really create loyalty?', *Harvard Business Review,* May–June, pp. 75–82.

Payne, A. (1995) *Advances in Relationship Marketing,* Butterworth-Heinemann, Oxford.

Pearson, S. (1996) *Building Brands Directly,* Macmillan, Basingstoke, Hants.

Peppers, D. and Rogers, M. (1993) *The One-to-One Future,* Piatkus, London.

Piercy, N. (1997) *Market-led Strategic Change,* Butterworth-Heinemann, Oxford.

Pine II B J, Peppers D and Rogers M, (1995) 'do you want to keep your customers forever?', *Harvard Business Review*, March–April, pp. 103–14.

Pressey, A. and Matthews, B. (2000) 'Barriers to relationship marketing in consumer retailing', *Journal of Services Marketing,* 14 (3), pp. 272–86.

Rapp, S. and Collins, T. (1987) *Maximarketing,* McGraw-Hill, New York.

Rapp, S. and Collins, T. (1994) *Beyond Maximarketing,* McGraw-Hill, New York.

Reichheld, F.F. (1996) *The Loyalty Effect,* Harvard Business School Publishing, Boston, Mass.

Reichheld, F.F. (2001) *Loyalty Rules!* Harvard Business School Publishing, Boston, Mass.

Reichheld, F. (Dec. 2003) 'One Number You Need To Grow', *Harvard Business Review* [on-line] **http://hbr.org/product/one-number-you-need-to grow/an/R0312C-PDF-ENG** [Accessed May 2013].

Reichheld, W. and Kumar, V. (2002) 'The mismanagement of customer loyalty', *Harvard Business Review,* 80 (7), pp. 86–94.

Reinartz, W. and Kumar, V. (2002) 'The mismanagement of customer loyalty', *Harvard Business Review,* 80 (7), pp. 86–94.

Scarborough, H., Swan, J. and Preston, J. (1999) *Knowledge Management and the Learning Organisation,* Institute of Personnel and Development, London.

Stone, B. (1996) *Successful Direct Marketing Methods,* 5th edn, NTC Business Books, Chicago.

Stone, M. and Woodcock, N. (1997) 'Database marketing and customer recruitment, retention and development: what is "state of the art"? Part 1 – Strategy', *Journal of Database Marketing,* 4 (3), pp. 236–47.

Surowiecki, J. (2005) *The Wisdom of Crowds: Why the Many Are Smarter Than the Few,* Anchor Books, New York.

Uncles, M. (1994) 'Do you or your customers need a loyalty scheme?', *Journal of Targeting, Measurement and Analysis,* 2 (4), pp. 335–50.

Uncles, M. (1996) 'Loyalty, behaviour – the direct marketing issues', Presentation to IDM Educators' Day, 30 March, Wembley, London.

Verhoef, P. (2003) 'Understanding the effect of customer relationship management efforts on customer retention and customer share development', *Journal of Marketing,* 67 (4), pp. 30–45.

CASE STUDY

Social marketing in action: how direct marketing could be used for social good (Sport England)

How segmentation can help us from becoming a nation of couch potatoes

Many thanks to Mihir Warty, Director of Policy and Performance, for his help and permission in compiling this case study

Sport England is the brand name for the English Sports Council and is a non-departmental public body under the UK Government's Department for Culture, Media and Sport. Its role is to provide the strategic lead for sport through advising, investing in and promoting community sport in England. Its ambition is to get a 1 per cent year-on-year increase in participation, or 2 million people more active in sport by 2012.

Sport England distributes over £230 million a year to grassroots sport projects. It has recently been told to refocus on community sports and away from generic physical activity. In June 2008, Sport England published its new strategy for 2008–2011(**http://www.sportengland.org/index/get_resources/resource_downloads/sport_england_strategy.htm**). What is not in doubt is the need for sport and exercise in westernised societies.

Mihir Warty, Sport England's Director of Policy and Performance, makes a number of critical points. As he explains, the core challenge is that over half the population do not participate in sport on a regular basis. This is bad news: sport and exercise contribute to lower levels of obesity, better general health and well-being, lower cancer levels, and a fitter and happier population. Interest in sport *per se* is not the problem. It would not be unfair to say that England is a nation obsessed by sport – at least, in watching sport. What it seems is not so clear is the nation's appetite for participation.

This is important, not just for children in school but also for adults. England's levels of obesity are rising alarmingly, with nearly 25 per cent clinically obese. Obesity is linked to type II diabetes and this costs the nation billions of pounds each year in healthcare costs.

So, the stakes are high.

Sport England know that the challenge for sport participation is competing for people's attention and time.

The time use study illustrated in Figure 6.8 hints at the complexity of the challenge facing Sport England. Modern life offers a bewildering set of choices for people's travel, home life, work life and, crucially, leisure time. Home based entertainment has skyrocketed over the past 30 years. Similar trends have taken place with consumerism, cinema and so on. Outdoor based activities expanded into huge choices that compete with sport.

Sport England conducted a survey of activity across England, the Active People Survey (**http://www.sportengland.org/index/get_resources/research/active_people.htm**). They looked at regions, as shown in Figure 6.9, and age and social class, as shown in Figure 6.10.

Some of these items identified predictable links between age and sport, for instance how basketball is linked to younger people, while skiing is an up-market, middle class pursuit, and bowls is for the more mature player.

These early findings convinced Sport England that it would benefit from segmenting the population according to different ways in which different groups engage with sport. Sport England sought to understand behaviours, or lack of them, triggers to be active, and barriers to activity. For example, in research people often say that they are 'too busy' to exercise, but good researchers will try and get under the skin of this remark to find deeper seated reasons for lack of activity.

Case study (*continued*)

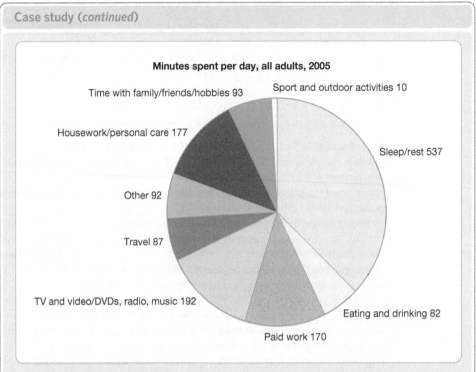

Figure 6.8 **Activity by region**
Source: ONS (2006) *UK Time Use Survey 2005.*

With the help of Experian, Sport England developed 19 segments falling within four 'super-groups'. The segments were based on the Active People Survey and the Taking Part Survey in which Sport England asked people about their behaviour with regard to sport participation (**http://www.sportengland.org/index/get_resources/reseach/se_ marketingsegmentation.htm**). This research was data fused with Experian's geodemographic Mosaic database which is based on the UK Census.

The segments are driven by demographics – particularly sex, age and social group. The segmentation is rich in consumer behaviour information. Motivations for participating vary from health and keeping fit through to the more sociable and fun aspects.

Triggers and barriers were investigated in some depth. There are a variety of factors that could encourage greater participation but it was noted that few of these motivated the older segments.

The power of these segments is made clearer when we look at specific segments.

The full list of names and descriptions is interesting.

Looking to the future, Sport England knew the next step was to examine 'social marketing mix' solutions: activities that people will find attractive enough to tempt them from their sedentary lifestyles.

Let us take a look at an example. Two of the segments are known as 'Leanne' and 'Chloe'. Leanne is from C2DE social group and aged 18–25. Chloe is the same age range, but ABC1 social group. Figure 6.15 shows how these two segments might play out in London.

Mapping the two segments in London according to the penetration levels of the segments shows how geography can be important (Figures 6.16 and 6.17).

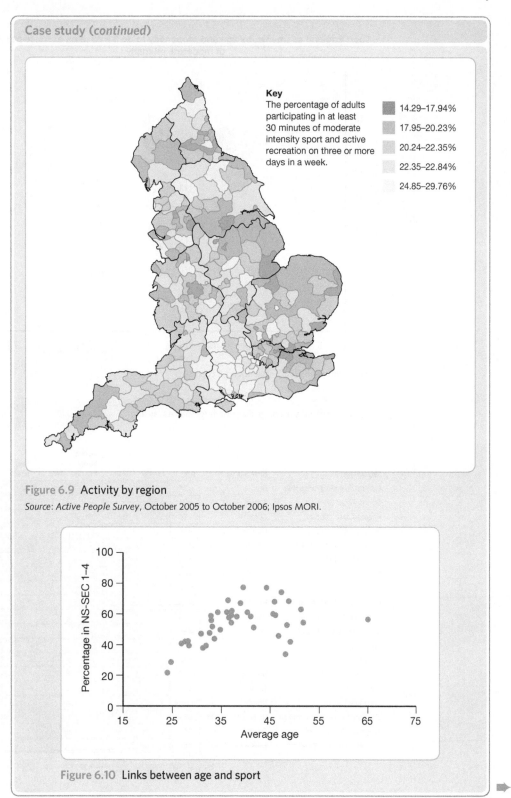

Key
The percentage of adults participating in at least 30 minutes of moderate intensity sport and active recreation on three or more days in a week.

14.29–17.94%
17.95–20.23%
20.24–22.35%
22.35–22.84%
24.85–29.76%

Figure 6.9 Activity by region
Source: *Active People Survey*, October 2005 to October 2006; Ipsos MORI.

Figure 6.10 Links between age and sport

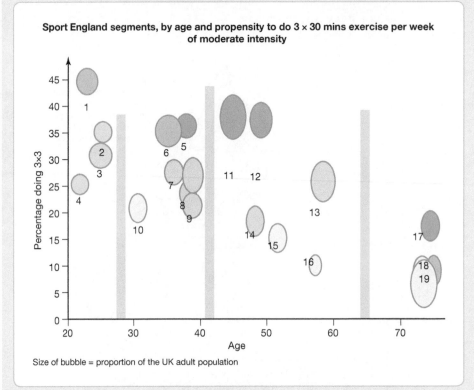

Sport England segments, by age and propensity to do 3 × 30 mins exercise per week of moderate intensity

Size of bubble = proportion of the UK adult population

Figure 6.11 **Segments arranged according to lifestage**

Segment name	Forename (s)	Age	Female	C2 DE	Income below £13,500	BME	Poor health	Obesity
Competitive Male Urbanites	Ben	<24						
Sports Team Drinkers	Jamie	<24						
Fitness Class Friends	Chloe	<24						
Supportive Singles	Leanne	<24						
Career Focused Females	Helena	26–45						
Setting Down Males	Tim	26–45						
Stay at Home Mums	Alison	26–45						
Middle England Mums	Jackie	26–45						
Pub League Team Mates	Kev	26–45						
Stretched Single Mums	Paula	26–45						
Comfortable Mid-Life Males	Philip	46–64						
Empty Nest Career Ladies	Elaine	46–64						
Early Retirement Couples	Roger and Joy	46–64						
Older Working Women	Brenda	46–64						
Local 'Old Boys'	Terry	46–64						
Later Life Ladies	Norma	46–64						
Comfortable Retired Couples	Ralph and Phyllis	65+						
Twighlight Years Gents	Frank	65+						
Retirement Home Singles	Elsie and Arnold	65+						

Key: ▨ High incidence ▧ Average incidence ▨ Low incidence

Figure 6.12 **Segment profiles**

Source: Experian/*Taking Part Survey*/*Active People Survey*.

Case study (*continued*)

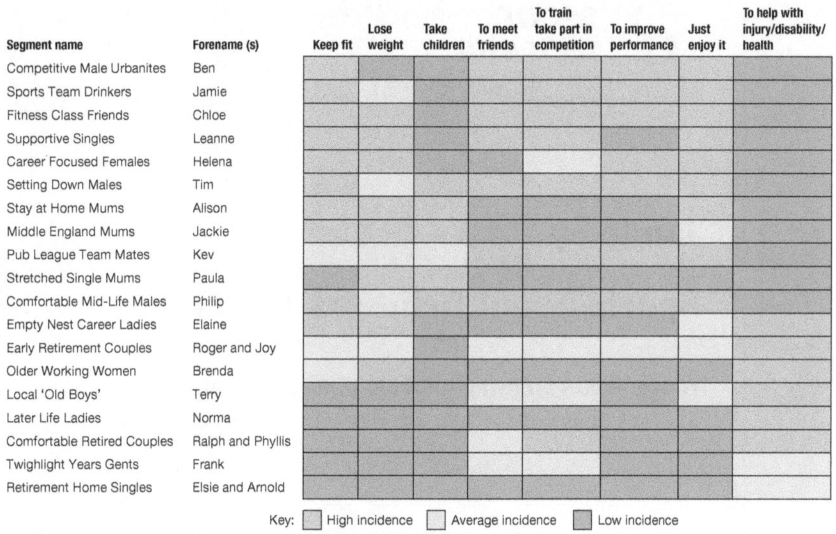

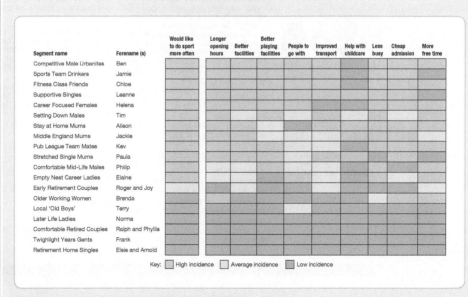

Figure 6.13 Segments, by reasons for taking part

Source: Experian/*Taking Part Survey*/*Active People Survey*.

Figure 6.14 Segments, by reasons to do more

Source: Experian/*Taking Part Survey*/*Active People Survey*.

Case study (*continued*)

SPORT ENGLAND

Jamie

Sports Team Drinkers (A02)

Jamie
Age 18-25
Single
Vocational
Student

Young blokes enjoying football, pints and pool
5.4% of adults, 11.1% of adult males, 22.9% of Group A

Jamie

Jamie is 20 and has just finished studying for an HND at his local college. Since finishing the course he's been unable to find a related job, he works at the local supermarket full time, but hopes to find something better soon. He lives with his parents in the family home, still very much hangs around with his school-mates.

Jamie plays football in the local youth league, and often plays computer games with mates from the team. Tight finances mean that Jamie puts a lot on his credit card. His spare cash goes on nights in the sports bar with the boys, drinking and playing late night pool. On Sundays after matches, its back to the bar to get in a few pints before the working week starts again.

Jamie isn't fussed about his health or diet. He smokes and enjoys fast food, curries and plenty of lager.

What Jamie likes to do

● Second highest participation rate of all the types; enjoy watching and playing team sports, especially football. Fitness classes and swimming are not appealing to them, but combative sports, social activities or weight training would be.

● Least likely of the Group to be member of health/fitness club, but is sports club member.

● Motivations for participation include improving performance and being with mates.

● Better sporting facilities locally would encourage this type; people to do exercise with and finding time may be barriers.

Sports that appeal to Jamie

Football	Karate
Martial Arts	Weightlifting
Boxing	Rugby

Social Activities

Jamie is least likely to participate in the arts compared to his peers, being not particularly interested or finances being a barrier.

If Jamie volunteers, he might help to coach or give tuition in a sport. He also enjoys watching live events.

Media and Communications

Jamie is a prolific mobile user, particularly using sms text alerts and checking out the football scores on his mobile using wap. He has a pay-as-you-go phone, rather than being tied into a monthly contract.

Jamie is a medium to heavy TV viewer, enjoying C5, interactive TV and sports packages. He also particularly enjoys internet gaming and online social messaging. Jamie reads tabloid newspapers and 'lads' magazines.

Towns such as

Hounslow
Croydon
Slough
Coventry
Leeds

Similar to live near
B08 Jackie
A02 Jamie

SPORT ENGLAND

Jamie

Sports Team Drinkers (A02)

Number of days participating (for at least 30 minutes) in the last week

Activity Participation Rates

Utility Cycling
Recreational Cycling
Utility Walking
Recreational Walking
Golf
Football
Bowls
Winter
Water
Team
Sailing
Racquet
Projectile
Motorised
KeepFit/Gymnastic
Equine
Cue/Darts
Combat
Athletics/Running
Aquatic
Adventurous
Any recreational physical activity

0 25 50 75 100 125 150 175 200
very unlikely   not likely   average   likely   very likely

Segment Groups & Types

The 19 Types sit within 4 Groups (A to D) which are designed to broadly reflect age bands. For example, Types A01 to A04 comprise Group A, which is generally 18-25 year olds; Types D17, D18 and D19 constitute those of retirement age. Within each of the 4 Groups and 19 Types there are obvious differences in terms of lifestyle, affluence and participation rates - it is therefore equally as important to compare an individual Type with other Types within its peer Group as it is to compare across all 19 Types or to compare the 4 Groups.

Index Values

The index value compares the percentage of the target and base populations, to identify over or under representation for a variable. An index of 100 shows average representation, above 100 shows over-representation, below 100 shows under-representation. For example, if Group A are more likely than average to cycle, then the index would be greater than 100 - similarly, if Type A01 is less likely than their peers (Group A) to enjoy equine sports, then the index is less than 100.

Case study (*continued*)

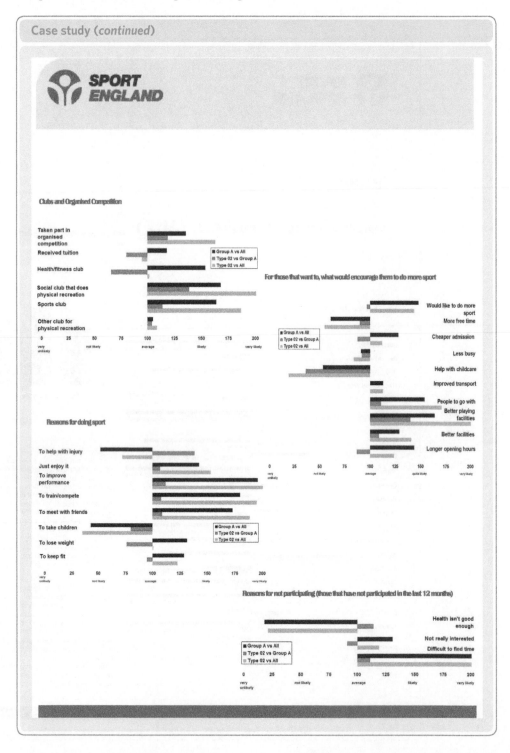

Jamie

Sports Team Drinkers (A02)

How to reach Jamie

Jamie
Age 18-25
Single
Vocational
Student

Channel Preferences

TV/RADIO

Jamie is a medium to heavy TV viewer, enjoying live sport, music channels, reality TV and using interactive services. He notices sponsorship and advertising and is likely to be influenced by this. Jamie is unlikely to listen to the radio often, preferring to use personal music players instead.

INTERNET

Jamie uses the internet for entertainment rather than practical purposes. He enjoys internet gambling sites, social messaging and online gaming. He is also likely to download music and ring tones. The internet feeds his thirst for entertainment and informs his decision making, complementing his experiential and inquiring style. He is less likely to directly respond to a targeted email, unless it's value-driven.

POSTERS/DIRECT MAIL/NEWSPAPER

Jamie reads 'lads' magazines and tabloid newspapers. He is influenced by branding in these but would not respond to offers in them.

TELEPHONE

A prolific mobile user, he likes to text rather than talk. He uses sms text information services and WAP for sports results.

Newspapers and Magazines, such as...

Front	Maxpower
Match	Maxim
Playstation Magazine	Ride
The News of the World	The Daily Star
What Car?	The Sun

Tone and message...

Young	Funky
Off-the-wall	Cutting-edge
Experiential	Transitory
Relaxed	Urban
Edgy	Informal

Brands such as...

Adidas	Burberry
Carling	Topman
Strongbow	MacDonald's
Lynx	Nintendo
Umbro	Xeox

Case study (*continued*)

SPORT ENGLAND

This document can be provided in alternative languages, or alternative formats such as large print, Braille, tape and on disk upon request. Call the Sport England switchboard on 08458 508 508 for more details.

Further information
To find out more about Sport England and to get the latest news and information about our various initiatives and programmes, please go to: www.sportengland.org

Sport England
3rd Floor
Victoria House
Bloomsbury Square
London, WC1B 4SE
T 08458 508 508

Stock code number SE-1106-006
Date of publication November 2006
Designed by Company name
Photography by Name Surname
Printed by Company name

This document is printed on a woodfree matt coated paper, whose primary fibre is made from sustainable forestry and exceeds the applicable environmental requirements.

The 19 Types

The Sport England classification is built primarily from the 'Taking Part' and 'Active People' surveys, and helps explain individual's motivations, attitudes, behaviour and barriers towards sport and active recreation. It is underpinned by key socio-demographic variables to ensure the segments can be geographically quantified and appended to customer records.

The clustering process has created a two-tier solution driven by key lifestage and lifestyle identifiers such as age, affluence, marital status and parental obligations. Within these, the levels of participation and the activities undertaken vary enormously. Each typology has been described within the context of sporting activities and levels of participation. Also, through providing underlying variables pertaining for example towards attitudes, socio-demographics, health statistics and marketing communication preferences, a fully-rounded picture of each segment has been developed.

	Segment Name	Forename (s)	% Pop	% M	% F
A01	Competitive Male Urbanites	Ben	6.4	13.3	0.0
A02	Sports Team Drinkers	Jamie	5.4	11.1	0.0
A03	Fitness Class Friends	Chloe	6.9	0.0	13.4
A04	Supportive Singles	Leanne	4.7	0.0	9.1
B05	Career Focused Females	Helena	5.0	0.0	9.7
B06	Settling Down Males	Tim	9.4	19.3	0.0
B07	Stay at Home Mums	Alison	4.6	0.0	8.9
B08	Middle England Mums	Jackie	4.0	0.0	7.7
B09	Pub League Team Mates	Kev	5.8	12.0	0.0
B10	Stretched Single Mums	Paula	3.8	0.0	7.4
C11	Comfortable Mid-Life Males	Philip	7.8	16.0	0.0
C12	Empty Nest Career Ladies	Elaine	5.3	0.0	10.2
C13	Early Retirement Couples	Roger & Joy	6.2	6.2	6.3
C14	Older Working Women	Brenda	4.0	0.0	7.6
C15	Local 'Old Boys'	Terry	3.4	7.0	0.0
C16	Later Life Ladies	Norma	2.0	0.0	3.6
D17	Comfortable Retired Couples	Ralph & Phyllis	3.7	5.0	2.4
D18	Twilight Year Gents	Frank	3.5	7.1	0.0
D19	Retirement Home Singles	Elsie & Arnold	8.3	2.5	13.8

SPORT ENGLAND — Sports Segments — *Creating an active nation through sport* — South West Region

(Shaded segments are where there are a greater proportion of these people in the SW than England)

Segment name and description	Segment characteristics	Age	Socio econ	3x30 / 0x30	% Eng Pop	% SW Pop	Prominent locations (LAs)	Sports	Media and Communications	Key brands	Activity characteristics
 **A01 Ben** Competitive Male Urbanites	Male recent graduates, with a work-hard, play-hard, drink-hard attitude	18–25	ABC1	40% / 19%	6.4	7	Bath+NES, E Dorset, N Somerset, S Glos, Kennet	Football, Golf, Cricket, Rugby Un+Lge, Skateboard, American Ftball	Ben is a heavy internet user and has a high speed broadband connection at home. He uses this for sports news, personal emails, buying films and games and in recent months playing online poker.	Gap, Diesel, Virgin, Sony Ericsson, FHM	Ben is well educated and well informed, and is the most likely of his peers to appreciate live music, photography and graphical design, especially if combined with his thirst for the latest gadgets.
 **A02 Jamie** Sports Team Drinkers	Young blokes enjoying football, pints and pool. Single, Vocational Student	18–25	C2DE	32% / 30%	5.4	4.4	Exeter, Plymouth, Bristol, Bournemouth, Cheltenham	Football, Weight Lifting, Pool	Jamie is a prolific mobile user, particularly using sms text alerts and checking out the football scores on his mobile using wap. He has a pay-as-you-go phone, rather than being tied into a monthly contract.	Adidas, Carling, Topman, Burberry, Lynx	Jamie is least likely to participate in the arts compared to his peers, being not particularly interested or finances being a barrier.
A03 Chloe Fitness Class Friends	Young image-conscious females keeping fit and keeping trim. Single graduate professional.	18–25	ABC1	28% / 34%	8.9	7.5	Cotswolds, Kennet, Bath+NES, E Dorset, N Somerset	Aerobics, Horse Riding, Yoga, Netball, Trampoline	Chloe is a heavy mobile phone user, keeping in contact with all her friends almost daily, and probably uses it more than a landline. She uses the internet a lot, for social messaging, booking music tickets, or movie information.	Nokia, iPod, Maybelline, Starbucks, Wagamama	Chloe is very likely to participate in the arts, having been encouraged from an early age. She particularly enjoys crafts, photography and dance classes, including those not just for fitness. It is a good way to meet new people and learn new skills.
A04 Leanne Supportive Singles	Young busy mums and their supportive college mates. Likely to have children. Student, Pt vocational.	18–25	C2DE	23% / 44%	4.7	4.1	Exeter, Plymouth, Bristol, Torbay, Gloucester	Aerobics, Dance Exercise, Netball, Body Combat, Ice Skating, Rounders, Gymnastics	Leanne is a heavy mobile user, for personal rather than business use. She regularly texts and calls her friends, and is likely to use pay-as-you-go rather than be tied to a monthly contract.	Spar, Superdrug, Reebok, Primark, H&M, Aldi	Leanne enjoys participating in some arts activities, to meet people and also to take her children. She is the most likely of her peers to participate in dance classes both for fitness and general enjoyment, and may also enjoy textile crafts.
 **B05 Helena** Career Focused Female	Single professional ladies, enjoying life in the fast lane. Single, Full time professional.	26–35	ABC1	33% / 33%	5.0	5.8	Bournemouth, Cheltenham, Cotswold, South Hams, Carrick	Aerobics, Yoga, Home Riding, Pilates, Netball, Hockey, Body Pump	Helena always has her mobile on hand so that she is contactable for work and social calls. As a heavy internet user it is her primary source of information on events, holidays and restaurants.	Habitat, Harvey Nicols, Clinique, Selfridges, Abu	Helena is the most likely of her peers to participate in arts, having been encouraged from an early age. She enjoys going to museums, art galleries and the theatre and also listening to live music.
 **B06 Tim** Settling Down Males	Sporty male professionals, buying a house and settling down with partner. Single/Married, may have children, professional	26–35	ABC1	32% / 27%	9.4	10.1	Bournemouth, Cheltenham, Cotswold, South Hams, Carrick	Football, Golf, Squash, Cricket, Rugby U, Shooting, American Ftball	Tim loves to embrace the latest technology –the internet is his primary source of information, and he is a heavy mobile user for both personal and business purposes	Pampers, Fcuk, Gap, Waterstones, Volvo, Debenhams	Tim enjoys participating in the arts. He is the most likely of his peers to play a musical instrument, enjoying developing and learning new skills. He may also enjoy photography or use his computer for graphical design, especially if these activities can be combined with his thirst for top of the range gadgets.
 **B07 Alison** Stay at Home Mums	Mums with a comfortable, but busy, lifestyle. Married, Housewife, Children	36–45	ABC1	25% / 33%	4.6	5.2	S Glos, N Wiltshire, Kennet, N Somerset, W Wiltshire	Aerobics, Yoga, Home Riding, Pilates, Netball, Skiing, Trampoline, Body Pump, Rounders	Alison is a medium TV viewer, watching mainly children's programmes but also cookery shows and dramas. She enjoys reading higher-end women's magazines, the Telegraph or Times.	Next, John Lewis, Brabantia, Sainsbury's	Alison enjoys participating in the arts including dance, music, textile crafts and drawing. She finds it relaxing, likes to take the children and also likes meeting new people at events and classes. Alison takes the children to the library regularly, and picks up a book for herself also.
 **B08 Jackie** Middle England Mums	Mum juggling work, family and finance. Married, Part-time skilled worker, Housewife, Children	36–45	C1C2D	21% / 47%	4.0	4.0	Kerrier, Kennet, Restormel, Gloucester, S Somerset	Aerobics, Trampoline, Ice Skating, Rounders, Step Machine, Rollerskating	Jackie is a medium TV viewer, enjoying soaps, chat shows and dramas. She is a cautious internet user, but is being encouraged by her children's prolific usage and is becoming more confident herself.	Iceland, Focus, Tesco, IKEA, Matalan	Jackie enjoys participating in the arts, including textile crafts, dance, painting and drawing, having been encouraged from an early age. She finds these activities relaxing, and also takes the children to them.
B09 Kev Pub League Teamates	Blokes who enjoy pub league games and watching live sport. Married/Single; may have children; Vocational	36–45	DE	19% / 51%	5.8	3.4	Plymouth, Bristol, Gloucester, Swindon, Exeter	Football, Fishing, Weight Training, Snooker, Pool, Darts, Sea Fishing, Weight Lifting	Kev is a heavy TV viewer, particularly favouring ITV and C5. He is also likely to have a digital/cable package for live sports coverage. Kev's mobile phone is important for his plumbing business and getting the footy lads organised, his landline is seldom used.	JJB, Matalan, Pukka Pies, Wickes, Woolworths, Benson & Hedges	Kev is generally uninterested in arts participation, or unable to for heath reasons. He was also not particularly encouraged to participate at an early age and is unlikely to encourage his children to get involved.
B10 Paula Stretched Single Mums	Single mums with financial pressures, childcare issues and little time for pleasure. Single, Job seeker or part time low skilled	26–35	DE	16% / 61%	3.8	2.3	Plymouth, Bristol, Swindon, Exeter, Penwith	Aerobics, Keep Fit, Trampoline, Ice Skating, Step machine, Rounders, Rollerskating, Skipping	Paula is a heavy TV viewer, enjoying quiz and chat shows, reality TV and soaps. She is likely to have a digital or cable package and enjoys the extra choice this provides, particularly the shopping channels.	TK-Max, Butlins, Toys R Us, Peacocks, Argos	Paula is likely to participate in a few arts activities, perhaps textile crafts or craft and design with the kids – these may have been encouraged from an early age or through her kids' primary school.
C11 Philip Comfortable Mid-Life Males	Mid-life professional, sporty males with older children and more time for themselves	46–55	ABC1	20% / 39%	7.8	8.8	S Hams, S Glos, Cotswold, N Dorset, Caradon	Golf, Football, Squash, Cricket	Philip is a medium TV viewer, enjoying business and current affairs programmes and live sports coverage. He is likely to have digital TV and also use interactive TV services for sports and business news.	Financial Times, John Lewis, Homebase, Canon, Sky	Having been encouraged from an early age, Philip enjoys participating in the arts – he may play a musical instrument, enjoy photography, visit theatres and be an active all rounder.
 **C12 Elaine** Empty Nest Career Ladies	Mid-life professionals who have more time for themselves since their children left home	46–55	ABC1	25% / 44%	5.3	6	W Devon, S Harris, Torridge, Bournemouth, E Dorset	Yoga, Aerobics, Dance Exercise, Step Machine, Rollerskat, Horse riding, Keep-fit, Fitness	Elaine is a light TV viewer, choosing programmes that reflect her interests in art or cookery. She uses the internet at home, for news and emails but does not have a high speed connection.	Waitrose, Lakeland, Monsoon, BBC, Fairtrade	Well educated and well informed. Elaine enjoys participating in the arts, including dance, painting, drawing, textile crafts and reading for pleasure.
 **C13 Roger & Joy** Early Retirement Couples	Free-time couples nearing the end of their careers. Married, retired or part-time.	56–65	ABC1	19% / 54%	6.2	8.1	Purbeck, N Somerset, E Dorset, W Dorset, Christchurch	Golf, Yoga, Keep Fit, Pilates, Bowls, Aqua Fit, Tai Chi, Ceiling Skirfen	Roger and Joy are medium TV viewers and heavy radio listeners. They read newspapers regularly, usually the Times or Daily Telegraph, and also subscribe to some personal interest magazines.	Hobbs, Pier, Laura Ashley, Sainsbury's	With more time available to them, Roger and Joy like to participate in arts such as painting, drawing, sewing and reading – they also use the local 'university of the 3rd age'.
 **C14 Brenda** Older Working Women	Middle aged ladies, working full time to make ends meet. Single/Married. May have children. Low skilled worker	46–55	C2DE	14% / 64%	4.0	2.7	Plymouth, Bristol, Gloucester, Forest of Dean, Swindon	Keep Fit, Aerobics, Dance Exercise, Step Machine, Health + Fit, Skipping	Brenda is a medium TV viewer who likes to keep up with the soap storylines and the latest reality TV show on cable. She also enjoys reading soap magazines and newspapers such as the Mirror or Sun.	Heinz, Hobbycraft, Bella, Weight Watchers, Haven	Although lack of time is a barrier, Brenda is still likely to participate in some arts. She may enjoy dance classes and also textile crafts.
 **C15 Terry** Local Old Boys	Generally inactive older men, low income, little provision for retirement. Single/Married. Low skilled worker, Job Seeker	56–65	DE	12% / 68%	3.4	2.4	Plymouth, Bristol, Gloucester, Penwith, Weymouth + Portland	Fishing, Weight Training, Snooker/Darts, Pool, Sea Fishing, Weight Lifting, Shooting, American Ftball	Terry is a high TV viewer, both at home and in the pub, particularly enjoying live sports coverage. He is a heavy reader of the Mirror, the Sun or the Daily Star. Terry doesn't have internet access at home, though it isn't something he feels he misses	JSP, Racing Post	Terry was not encouraged to participate in the arts at an early age. He has a general lack of interest, which is reflected by his low participation.
 **C16 Norma** Late Life Ladies	Older ladies, recently retired. Single/Married. Low skilled worker. Retired	56–65	DE	9% / 78%	2.0	1.3	Plymouth, Bristol, Penwith, Weymouth + P, Gloucester	Keep Fit, Aqua Fit, Dance Exercise, Tai Chi, Step Machine, Skipping	Norma is a high TV viewer, enjoying quiz shows, chat shows, soaps and religious programmes. Most new technology has passed her by, having no internet access or mobile phone.	Matalan, Iceland, Wilkinson, Freemans, Lambert & Butler	Norma enjoys participating in the arts, particularly enjoying reading, textile crafts such as knitting, sewing and embroidery, and some painting or drawing. She will also regularly visit her local library
 **D17 Ralph & Phyllis** Comfortable Retired Couples	Retired couples, enjoying active and comfortable lifestyle. Married, Retired	66+	ABC1	14% / 70%	3.7	5.2	E Dorset, S Hams, W Dorset, W Devon, E Devon	Golf, Bowls, Keep Fit, Tennis, Shooting	Ralph and Phyllis are medium to light TV viewers, preferring to be out and about instead. They like to read the Daily Telegraph or Independent do not have access to the internet, but they have a mobile phone.	Gardener's World, Volvo, Saga, Waitrose	Ralph and Phyllis enjoy participating in the arts – they paint, read for pleasure and may play a musical instrument. They regularly enjoy visiting museums and heritage sites and taking foreign holidays.
 **D18 Frank** Twilight Years Gent	Retired men with some pension provision and limited exercise opportunities	66+	C1C2D	9% / 78%	3.5	3.7	Christchurch, N Somerset, Torbay, E Devon, Bournemouth	Golf, Bowls, Snooker, Fishing, Pool	Frank is a heavy TV viewer enjoying live sports coverage. He doesn't have access to the internet, or a mobile phone. He enjoys reading the Daily Mail or Express.	Greggs, Benson & Hodges, Sunblest, Post Office	Frank has limited participation in arts activities, having not been particularly encouraged in his early years. However, he does enjoy visiting heritage sites and museums when given the opportunity.
 **D19 Elsie & Arnold** Retirement Home Singles	Retired singles or widowers, predominantly female, living in sheltered accommodation. Widowed, Retired	66+	DE	5% / 85%	8.3	8.0	Christchurch, N Somerset, Penwith, Torbay, E Devon	Bowls, Yoga, Keep Fit, Aerobics, Aqua Fit, Tai Chi, Dance Exercise	Elsie is a heavy TV viewer enjoying old films, and BBC2. Elsie does not have an internet connection or mobile phone. She will use her landline to call family	Bonril, Londis, Tetley, Woman's Weekly, Post Office	Elsie is keen to participate in the arts, particularly enjoying the dance afternoon in the community lounge. She loves listening to old music and having a waltz with other residents.

Case study (*continued*)

WHERE ARE THESE SEGMENTS IN THE SOUTH WEST?

The maps below provide a visual on geographical location for some of the segments where there is a greater proportion in the South West. Dark colour represents more of the particular.

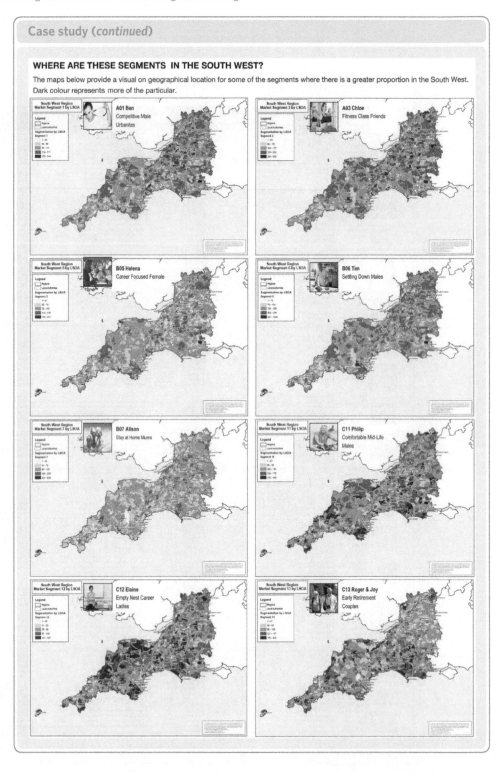

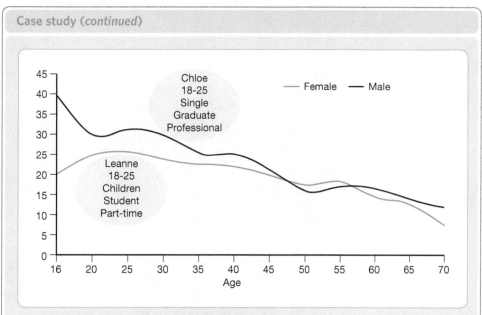

Figure 6.15 Sports participation in London, 2005–06
Source: Experian/Sport England/*Active Life Survey*.

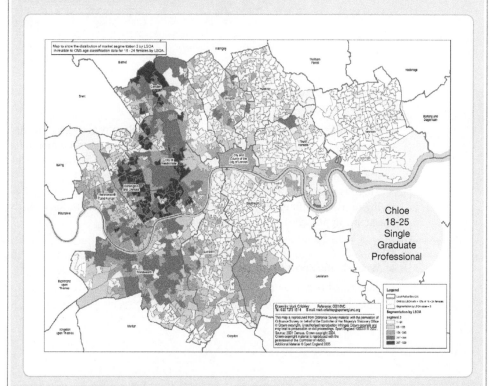

Figure 6.16 Sports participation, Chloe
Source: Experian/Sport England/*Active Life Survey*.

Case study (*continued*)

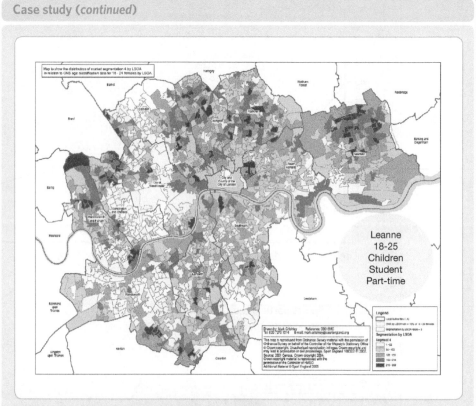

Figure 6.17 **Sports participation, Leanne**
Source: Experian/Sport England/*Active Life Survey*.

Certain offers can be developed that are aimed specifically at these segments. For instance, women-only classes in gyms, expanding dance as an option, or three-month free trials.

These offers can be tailored and channelled appropriately for our target audiences using media highlighted by the research (Figure 6.17).

There is a lot of work to do yet, but Sport England feel they are on the right lines by trying to use consumer attitude and behaviour driven segmentations to drive their social marketing approaches to encouraging sport.

Task

● What should Sport England do next?

● How can direct and on-line techniques help them?

CASE STUDY

Sony Professional

Sony Professional 'extra.ordinary' campaign

Challenge

The brief was to increase the number of registrants to Sony's videographer eCRM programme across Europe. TMW were briefed to create a campaign that would inspire videographers and showcase Sony's role in their world as unique and irreplaceable, helping them achieve their vision on a daily basis and giving them an edge over their competitors.

Strategy

'extra.ordinary' is a digital campaign featuring inspirational films, behind-the-scenes tutorials, interviews and tip sheets on how to get more from the equipment.

To bring the concept to life, we teamed up with well-known film maker and director Philip Bloom to produce content that helps videographers take an ordinary situation and turn it into something magical and visually stunning.

Solution

The films were executed on a tight budget and within a limited timeframe to mirror the constraints faced by professionals every day. Each film is accompanied by a behind the scenes video explaining how to get the best possible results from the product.

The campaign was included on the on-line Videographer Hub on the Sony Professional website and the content was also accessible through social media Sites, including You Tube and Vimeo. The campaign was supported by banner advertising, paid search, e-mail communications and webinars.

Results

- 10,948 registrants in the first three months of the campaign.
- E-mails achieved 44 per cent open rate and 49.5 per cent click-through rate.

Reproduced with kind permission of TMW.

Chapter 7

Relationship marketing and CRM

Objectives

By the end of this chapter you will:

- be aware of the growth and importance of CRM
- be familiar with the concepts of relationship marketing and CRM
- understand how these two things differ
- understand the overlaps and also the differences between these and direct marketing
- be aware of the practical implementation problems

'If your company is good at managing customers you should shout about it, because company valuation experts in the City are starting to take CRM seriously.'

(Woodcock and Starkey, 2005)

Introduction

In this chapter we continue with the theme of understanding the strategic influences on modern day direct and database marketing. Academics, commentators and writers often discuss relationship marketing as part of their assessment of what is happening in marketing practice. An even hotter topic recently has been the billions spent by firms on customer relationship management systems.

This chapter devotes itself to clarifying the extent to which relationship marketing (RM), customer relationship management (CRM) and direct marketing are intertwined. This necessitates an introduction, definition and discussion of the theory of RM and CRM. Just as important, however, will be a recognition of how practitioners have used these concepts and turned them into philosophies, strategies and activities. In fact, theory and practice often diverge with relationship marketing and this will be one of the main talking points of this chapter.

7.1 Relationship marketing

7.1.1 Introduction

Those of you who have embarked on a marketing career will have had plenty of contact with the use of the phrase 'relationship marketing'. One only has to read the popular marketing press to find innumerable instances of direct marketing managers describing the 'relationship building' programmes they have put into place. Usually these are replete with claims that customers have struck up relationships with the company, or the other way round. A 'dialogue' will have been built, 'two-way communications' established, and maybe even 'commitment' made.

This is the language of relationship marketing. So what is the concern? The problem here is the use of language but without very much of the substance. At a guess, a conversation with some customers of that manager might be rather revealing. 'A relationship? With my bank? Sorry. I haven't a clue what you're on about.' And so on. There are a number of issues here. One is the wanton use of language by professional marketers (and academics) that mitigates against us all being able to communicate properly with each other. Another is the attempt to dress up really quite trivial tactical campaigns under the guise of a strategy, perhaps in the hope that our efforts really will change customers' behaviour, this time. The final problem, linked to these two, is a fundamental lack of understanding of what the concept actually means.

This then is our first job here – to understand what relationship marketing is, and to clearly distinguish it from direct and database marketing.

7.1.2 Understanding and defining relationship marketing

Relationship marketing is one of those areas of marketing theory that owes its development largely to academics working in competing schools of thought centred in both Europe and the USA. A rather unseemly scramble to claim first coinage of the term has ensued, but the publicity prize must go to Berry, whose publication in 1983 is widely quoted when reviewing the subject. One of the most prominent Europeans has been Gummesson who as early as 1987 called for the Four Ps of marketing to be replaced as the dominant paradigm, arguing it is poor in theory, exaggerating some aspects such as advertising and competition, and limiting others such as inter-relationships and co-operation. He still expounds his proposal that the Four Ps model should be replaced with the 30 relationships approach but it has yet to gain serious traction in mainstream marketing practice. The latter had been made prominent by the excellent work done by the IMP group years previously when examining business-to-business partnerships. According to exponents of relationship marketing, the use of 'hard sell' selling tactics is seen as misguided, and the customer now defines the nature of the business exchange. With increased competition, and companies realising the value of their existing customers, market leadership can no longer be maintained simply with short-term, sales orientated transactions. Customers are demanding more quality in their relationship with their sellers.

Another advocate of RM, Francis Buttle, described the transactional model as 'hit and run' marketing: get in, make the sale, and leave (1996). This traditional transactional marketing model is now seen as outdated, with relationship selling taking its place. Gummesson (1994) described transactional marketing as manipulative and exploitative of the customer's ignorance. The balance of power lies with the seller, with few mutual benefits apparently existing.

In comparison to relationship selling, there is little or no after-sales service, and there is a limited commitment to meeting customers' expectations (Payne *et al.*, 1995). (Cynics of the relationship concept would probably hit back by pointing out that consumers are often quite happy to buy into so-called exploitative marketing; that most 'relationship marketers' would usually take the opportunity to exploit ignorance and make a quick buck; and that unless the product or service is of high quality, customers would not buy it in the first place. These cynics are perhaps being a bit too harsh, but it may be prudent to take with a pinch of salt these claims that, after years of contempt for customers once they have sold to them, companies have completely repented and are now bending over backwards to solve our problems!)

Payne *et al.* (1995) argue that the key elements of relationship marketing are as follows:

- A shift in emphasis from transactions to relationships between suppliers and customers.
- A focus on maximising the lifetime value of desirable customers and segments.
- An emphasis on customer service as a key element in retaining customers. Providing high contact with customers and easy access back to the company are priorities.
- Quality is the concern of all rather than merely the concern of production. Quality is measured by what the customer perceives as good quality, rather than by internal measures of quality.
- Relationships are maintained with a wide set of groups, with the ultimate objective of feeding into the customer relationship. These groups could include distributors, suppliers, stakeholders and so on.

Relationship marketing is best understood by following a story of what might happen when two businesses start to interact with each other. Imagine an IT executive meeting up with, say, a hotel manager for the first time. The hotel needs a new accounts system put in place and the manager is happy to chat it through. The dialogue begins. They have a series of meetings, phone calls and exchange e-mails. After a while they find they have some personal things in common, both enjoying football, and this becomes infused into their business conversations. An agreement is reached about the new system, but the IT firm is let down by its suppliers, so the initial promises have to be amended. Throughout this difficult time, the IT executive keeps the hotel manager fully informed and is truthful about the delays. Both agree it is better to be 'honest in business, even if it means losing the sale'. They find they have values in common. The experience builds up trust for both parties and the hotel manager is committed to stay with the IT firm. Their interpersonal relationship improves further at Christmas, when the IT firm puts on a party for its customers and the two men get together over a few drinks.

The point of this story is to illustrate the key elements of relationship marketing. According to O'Malley and Mitussis (2002) the full extent of RM is to engage in dialogue, develop trust and demonstrate respect for customers. Another hugely important element is the actual relationship built up between two people. If a personal relationship is promised but all customers get is impersonal delivery, then 'customers will have a hard time feeling human presence in the relationship' (O'Malley and Mitussis, 2002). Unlike mass consumer markets, business-to-business and service markets involve exchanges where the individuals are known to each other rather than anonymous. This face-to-face element is vital for giving credence to the relationship idea.

In adding to dialogue, trust and mutual respect, Gronroos (1996), a key figure in the development of the theory of RM, would supplement 'shared ideals', 'mutual benefit', and a 'commitment to continue the relationship'. For Gronroos, relationship marketing is more than a set of activities, more even than a 'strategy' for the company. For him it is the very essence of business: a philosophy, that is deeply held by all in the company, that places a commitment to its customers higher than making a quick buck. Gronroos observed that relationship marketing is often done in a very superficial way – and implementation is often unsuccessful because the firm sees RM as a strategic option to be tested, rather than as a set of beliefs.

The fields of key account management and channel management are often the areas where relationship marketing lives and breathes most strongly. Interaction intensity, mutual disclosure of information and co-operative intention are all mentioned by Crosby *et al.* (1990). Meanwhile Selnes (1993) talks about the trust that is gained from safety, security and credibility in dealings with suppliers. Interestingly, there has been some suggestion that women are superior to men in relationship building in account management situations (Corner and Jolson, 1991). They are more likely to empathise with the customer, and more likely to disclose personal information.

Thus far we have not mentioned where satisfaction, as a crucial output of a business exchange, fits into this model. Some research suggests trust and commitment, rather than satisfaction, are the key components of commercial relationships. Little and Marandi (2003) saw satisfaction as a key initial element of a customer's feelings towards their relationship partner.

Exhibit 7.1 Key concepts that are part of commercial relationships

Satisfaction could be defined as 'the feelings we get when our expectations are met or exceeded'. It seems common sense that satisfaction must be a precursor of an ongoing relationship. Dissatisfied people do stay with suppliers, but only in the absence of reasonable alternatives. However, satisfaction in itself is not enough to secure retention.

Trust is a 'decision to rely on a partner in whom one has confidence'.

Commitment is a 'decision to stay with a supplier in the future'.

To summarise so far, we may describe RM thus:

$$\text{Dialogue} + \text{mutual values} + \text{mutual interests} \rightarrow \text{trust} \rightarrow \text{commitment} \rightarrow \text{retention} \quad (1)$$

This may be contrasted with a typical transaction model:

$$\text{Communication of benefits transaction} \rightarrow \text{satisfaction} \rightarrow \text{trust} \rightarrow \text{retention} \quad (2)$$

Given the scepticism about relationship marketing in some quarters you may want to run with Equation 2 as having more widespread application to commercial situations, especially with consumer markets. As a consumer, you might be satisfied with a wine supplier. You may trust them, feel committed to buying from them in the future. But you may still scoff at the idea that you have a relationship with them.

A business-to-business situation may be different. An acquaintance of the author who works for a large food manufacturer is trying to solve problems in the supply chain with a retailer. She feels very much part of a partnership with the retailer's employees as they battle together to get this problem solved. She has a relationship with them. This story is typical of how the relationship marketing concept is frequently exhibited in channel partnerships. Relationship marketing is the 'thread that stitches all channel members together' (Bruhn, 2003).

Customers become active partners with producers, wholesalers or retailers. This more involved role for the customer means that they are more proactive, and tend to feel more in control of their marketing channels. Berman (1996) goes as far as calling relationship marketing 'partnering', thus reflecting the strong mutual basis of these relationships.

One of the authors of this book, employed by a business school, has some of his time bought out by a direct marketing agency to work on projects of mutual interest. Here individual relationships are very much at the heart of the partnership between the agency and the business school: the concept is very apt in describing what is happening with this arrangement.

7.1.3 The boundary between relationship marketing and direct marketing

As we have seen, the heart of relationship marketing is dialogue, human interaction, identifying mutual benefits, having shared ideals and keeping promises. The outcomes are trust, mutual respect and a commitment to continue the relationship. Relationship marketing, hence, has a clear focus on existing customers and is concerned with retention and loyalty.

As we discussed previously (Chapter 5), the essence of direct marketing (as it is currently 'practised') is predictive transaction marketing based on advanced segmentation approaches. However, like RM, direct marketing (DM) also has a clear focus on existing customers – to sell to them. Like RM, DM can be used to prolong and improve customer loyalty, but DM tends to rely on transaction marketing approaches – product/price packaging, pricing offers, or maybe charming customers through brand symbolism. Some direct marketers have drifted into the habit of interchangeably using the terms 'direct marketing' and 'relationship marketing' as if they were the same thing. This is misleading: there is a distinct difference between, say, loyalty schemes, or lock-in cross-selling, and any genuine attempt to build partnerships or learning relationships.

Most direct marketing replicates relationship ideals only in a remote, second-hand kind of way. It is true that the act of buying and selling goods or services always involves the 'keeping of a promise' in the sense that the seller promises something to the buyer in return for cash. It can be argued that Four Ps based transaction marketing involves keeping promises just as much as relationship marketing. But until one reaches the theoretical end-point of one-to-one marketing (creating a learning 'relationship') there is no sense in which this mass, branded, standardised delivery of service reaches a state in which it could be called a 'relationship'.

There is, however, important overlap between relationship marketing and direct marketers in one sense. Both direct and relationship marketing have at their core the idea that customer lifetime value should be valued over and above the individual transactions that take place. Both approaches emphasise the importance of this, and keeping existing customers is seen as more important than acquiring new ones.

However, can we be more specific about where the overlaps between relationship and direct marketing exist? Direct marketing systems exist primarily to transact efficiently with customers. However, there are some aspects of DM communications that can contribute in a relationship sense. These may be split into 'service' and 'dialogue'.

Service

There has been much work devoted to establishing the link between service and retention. Cram (1994) reported research by Rapp and Collins that illustrates the value of service in retaining customers.

Table 7.1 Reasons why customers were lost

Reasons	Percentage
Moved away/died	4
Relationships with other companies	5
Competitive activity	10
Product dissatisfaction	14
No contact, indifference, attitude of sales force	65

Relationship marketing advocates the provision of excellent service to customers as a critical part of improving their satisfaction with the company. Service and quality are inter-mixed so that quality is defined as customers' service expectation. Thus, quality is defined by the customer – if they get what they expect, that is quality (Gronroos, 1984).

Direct marketing may take a lead or support role in helping ensure customers get what they expect. The strategic advantage of using a database to drive service is that this is a proactive stance. Instead of waiting for customers to ask, and then reacting, McCorkell (1994) pointed out instances where direct marketing's predictive capabilities are invaluable in anticipating needs.

Delivering service through direct marketing systems has been fully described previously (Chapter 6).

Dialogue

Relationship marketers argue that dialogue is central to the idea of fruitful relationship development. A two-way exchange of information needs to be constantly maintained if the relationship is to be genuine. But how can this be done with large volumes of customers? Clearly, database marketing has a potential position of strength here. One way to deliver a genuine relationship through direct marketing systems may be through customer clubs or communities.

Customer clubs

Clubs are discussed in detail later (Chapter 10) but here we consider the idea that a customer club is a surrogate for a relationship between company and customer. Clubs are a good idea when the customer takes a sense of status from belonging, when they want to interact with other consumers, and when they have high involvement and interest with the product or service. In the latter two situations it may be appropriate to instigate elements of the club that could be described as relationship marketing (Pryce, 2003). For example: a baby club set up by, say, Kimberley Clark or Procter & Gamble may move beyond information about baby products and into advice about raising children, and maybe act as a mechanism for mums to get together. This may be delivered through discussion forums on-line as well as through e-newsletters and direct mail. A product like, say, Jaguar Cars could successfully run a club that would physically bring together customers to events and functions celebrating classic cars of the past. Such customers would quickly form relationships with each other, but would they form relationships with Jaguar? The answer is probably at least partly yes: perhaps directly with Jaguar people running the events; perhaps via e-mail with customer service representatives; and (less clearly a relationship) they may form intense affinities with the 'brand' that go beyond weak associations. The authors of this book would argue that 'brand liking' or even 'brand love' is more accurate than 'brand relationship' to describe these feelings. Trust, commitment, respect may well be there from customer to brand, but not in a dynamic two-way fashion – the brand does not 'know' the customer! Still, this is complex: the customer will not separate out the above effects – to them, the brand includes the people of the company whom they have met or corresponded with.

7.1.4 How RM and DM fit into marketing planning

Throughout this book we have referred to the marketing planning process in an effort to provide a framework into which different elements of direct marketing can be positioned. Earlier (Chapter 1), we decided that direct and database marketing provided a process, or system, of marketing. This is worth reminding ourselves of now as we contrast direct with relationship marketing. Little and Marandi (2003) point out that relationship marketing is a strategy, i.e. a guide for the company in how to conduct itself. They point out that RM, as a strategic guide, necessarily 'depends on the customer' one is having a relationship with for its direction. Therefore, there is no attempt to exert an independent 'predict and control' approach that the 1950s' business managers would have wanted. With RM, the future depends on mutually agreed outcomes between the firm and customers. The predictive component of RM strategy, such as it exists at all, comes from the initial choice of customer and the strategic emphasis placed on each customer. However, Little and Marandi (2003) report Gronroos' insight that the 'essence of RM implementation lies in processes rather than in planning'. Here is the insight into where direct marketing and relationship marketing meet. Both relationship and transaction marketing could be described as 'strategies', and, if chosen, there are a variety of processes businesses could deploy to help 'implement' either strategy. Direct marketing is one of these 'processes of implementation'.

Different sectors, different situations

For the most part, relationship and direct approaches to marketing address different sectors, though there are overlaps. What does seem to emerge is that relationship marketing as an approach arguably has more relevance within the business-to-business and service industries, in particular with 'high involvement' products, for example a business purchasing a computer system. What is less clear is the extent to which these ideas apply in 'low involvement' products, such as, say, filling up the car with petrol. Focusing on the latter, it may well be the case that direct marketing techniques become relatively much more important as a way of delivering relationship marketing in 'low involvement' markets (see Figure 7.1).

Figure 7.2 shows us the differing roles played by relationship and direct marketing depending on the sector.

Exhibit 7.2 Paradigm shift or hot air?

By no means everyone is persuaded by the messages of relationship marketing. A leading light among the heretics is Stephen Brown, who, in *Postmodern Marketing Two* (1998), started by pointing out that RM, if it exists, is a testimony to the complete failure of the original marketing concept. After all, if the original concept had delivered on its promises there would be no dissatisfied, possibly defecting, customers for us to attend to. He also points out other commentators for whom RM is problematic: Baker (1994) finds RM nothing more than an attempt to teach old dogs new tricks; yet others consider the talk of trust, commitment and partnership between typically large companies and small suppliers, or even smaller consumers, little more than a smoke screen for the continued coercion, exploitation and manipulation of the weak by the strong (e.g. Chen *et al.*, 1992).

In the same vein, Brown asks us to 'ponder what customer in their right mind would want to establish a relationship with a marketing organisation? Do marketers really believe that today's consumers, after having been shafted for years, have concluded that marketers have turned over a new leaf and really, really care about their customers' welfare?' Brown: 'Something tells me that consumers have probably concluded that our sobbing on their shoulders and promises to be a better boy in future are little more than pathetic attempts to elicit sympathy prior to picking their pockets . . . Marketers would be far better off being open about their commercial intent: we don't love you, we just want your money – and lots of it!'

Sources: Baker, M.J. (1994) 'Research myopia: recency, relevance, reinvention and renaissance (the 4Rs of marketing?)', Department of Marketing working paper series 94/2 Glasgow, University of Strathclyde. Brown, S. (1998) *Postmodern Marketing Two: Telling tales,* International Thomson Business Press, London. Chen, I.J., Calantone, R.J. and Chung, C. (1992) 'The marketing–manufacturing interface and manufacturing flexibility', *Omega,* **20** (4), pp. 431–43.

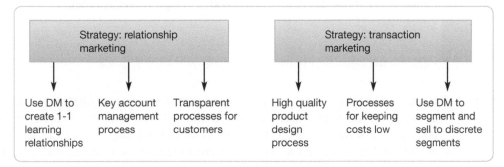

Figure 7.1 The strategic planning linkages between RM and DM

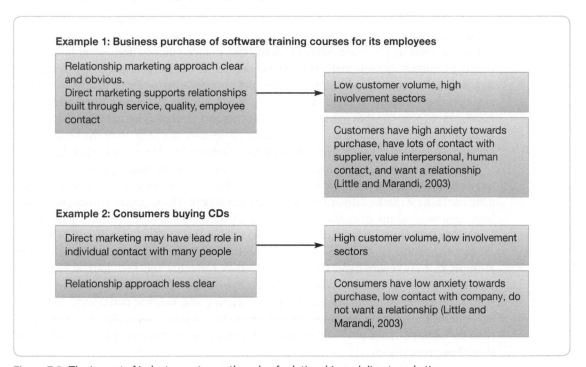

Figure 7.2 The impact of industry sector on the role of relationship and direct marketing

7.1.5 Conclusion

Relationship marketing has strong roots. The extent to which RM happens in practice may be something we in the West are sceptical about but in Asian, South American and some European markets the building of personal relationships is a prerequisite of business-to-business marketing. So maybe our scepticism is unjustified. But just before we buy wholesale into the rhetoric of relationship marketing we must always keep one crucial question in mind: would your business relationship partner forgo some short-term profit in order to maintain or strengthen the relationship they have with you? If they would, then that is at least one definition of a 'true' business relationship. If they abandon the relationship the moment it no longer suits them in the short term, then one must question whether words are matched by deeds.

Transactional selling is far from ineffective. Transactional and relationship selling can co-exist, suggesting that relationship marketing should not be viewed as a replacement for transactional selling strategies, but as another perspective in marketing.

7.2 Customer relationship management (CRM)

If you read an article about customer relationship management (CRM) in the popular marketing press, you might finish it a little mystified about the difference between direct and database marketing. In fact, CRM is one of those marketing phrases that takes on a life of its own depending on the vested interests of the person writing about it. Consultants will promote it as philosophy, strategy and systems that will solve their client's headaches. Academics have had relatively little to say on the subject, but will most likely focus on its relationship building aspects. Commentators in the direct marketing world often use it interchangeably with direct marketing.

CRM is important because rarely in history has so much money been spent by so many clients on improving their marketing. The sheer size of the budgets has concentrated the minds and the attention of CEOs and directors on marketing as never before. What this means is that – and this is highly significant – the size of the investment has forced senior managers to focus on what marketing departments and marketers actually do. This is both an opportunity and a threat for the marketing profession: are they up to the challenge of being in the spotlight in their lead role in ensuring returns on these huge IT spends?

CRM is also important because it provides us with an understanding of 'the problem large organisations have in focusing on their customers'. Unless you have worked inside a big company it can be difficult to appreciate the way in which customers become somehow remote from the everyday life of many of the firm's staff. Even in functions like marketing departments, customers can be somehow lost in the 'fire fighting' of the latest product problems, or dealing with the politics of the research agency, or whatever. Multiply this into every department in a complex company and then look at that complexity from the boardroom. Who keeps their eye on the ball in making sure the organisation stays focused on its original purpose – getting and keeping customers? The CRM movement, flawed as it has undoubtedly been, has at least raised the visibility of the need to 'manage customers' – or at least to remind people internally of the priority that should be given to them.

Exhibit 7.3 How IT is changing marketers' lives

The author was centrally involved in a recent study commissioned by the UK Chartered Institute of Marketing that investigated the impact of e-business on marketing practice. The initial flurry of excitement around the dot-com 'revolution' has been replaced by the more stolid reality of using the Internet and its associated technologies to improve the value chain of the company. The study found that marketers were reasonably innovative in taking new technology and applying it in 'tactical' ways to their marketing communications campaigns: using SMS advertising was one example. However, less impressive was the marketer's strategic grasp of company-wide IT initiatives that, in theory, marketers should be heavily involved with, but in practice had largely abandoned to IT, operations, HR or finance people. Examples of such initiatives included knowledge management systems discussed earlier (see Chapter 6), supply chain exchanges on the Internet, and even CRM – in theory a central domain of marketing – often now run by IT specialists. Sadly, senior managers' opinions of marketers, as professionals deserving serious power within the company, had not improved since the days of the 'mid-life crisis' ten years ago. One quote from someone very senior in the industry aptly summarised marketers' preference for glamour rather than leadership:

> Marketers need to develop mini-entrepreneur skills – strategising, devising a business plan, making resource allocation decisions, understanding risk. In short, commercial acumen. What marketers lack are MBA graduate skills. At the moment these are in very short supply.

> Marketers should develop IT/new technology skills. We cannot influence the development and usage of IT within companies unless we know something about it.

> [Marketers should] stop wasting time hiring and firing agencies. Marketing departments are fiddling with deckchairs on the Titanic. We are playing marbles at the wrong end of the playground, while the grown ups are doing business at the other end.

Source: Chartered Institute of Marketing (2001) 'The impact of e-business on marketing and marketers', October. Website for CIM direct purchase: www.connectedinmarketing.co.uk, tel. 44 (0) 1628 427427.

A major supplier of CRM auditing and measurement worldwide is SAP. Their website **http://www.sap.com/solutions/bp/customer-relationship-management/index.epx** is a useful resource for you, with a large database of publications available.

7.2.1 What is CRM?

One of the most important writers and commentators on CRM is Merlin Stone. He, Woodcock and Gamble (1999) defined CRM:

> 'CRM is an enterprise-wide commitment to identify your named individual customers and create a relationship between your company and these customers so long as this relationship is mutually beneficial.'

A glance at academic papers or at practitioner literature will illustrate the impossibility of obtaining definitive agreement about what CRM is, but what we can do is identify its centre of gravity in terms of what it substantively consists of in the commercial world. If CRM in its totality was adopted by a firm, that firm would have in place:

● people who regard serving the customer well as the top priority of their job and – crucially – are motivated to deliver this day after day

● processes that cut across traditional departmental boundaries and create ways of serving the customer better

● customers identified by their value to the company and prioritised accordingly (also a key part of traditional direct marketing discussed earlier (see Chapter 3)

● a customer database that is independent of individual channels and is an integral part of live service delivery to inbound contact

● the database at the centre of planning and execution of direct marketing programmes for outbound contact (what much of the rest of this book is about)

So, compared with direct marketing, in its execution CRM:

● is associated with large companies that have multiple channels, and possibly multiple sources, of customer data

● is centred around the idea of data driven 'service'

● focuses on 'inbound' customer contact at least as much as outbound

According to Hansotia (2002), CRM works best in sectors where

● there are frequent customer interactions

● a high level of expertise is needed to guide purchase decisions

● multiple products and services are purchased by customers

Thus, a bank with multiple products is going to get more out of CRM than an insurance company selling only life insurance.

Customer relationship management as a marketing idea has large overlaps with both direct marketing and relationship marketing, and we will pin down these overlaps in a moment. But what is crucial here is to recognise that CRM in practice has been driven by the supply of complex IT applications created by firms like SAP and Oracle, and by the demand for these systems by large firms. In practice, the billions of dollars spent on CRM has been driven by two things. One is the opportunity to nudge customers into ways of contacting the business that are cheaper for the firm: in some instances this may mean 'Let us close down some branches and open up telephone or Web channels'. Second, and linked to this, has been the desire of (usually big) firms to sort out the chaos that their basic customer contact has slipped into. A few years ago, if you rang up a bank to order a new service, then walked into their retail branch the next day, there was little hope that your order record would be known about or that staff would be able to help you. Companies that have successfully installed CRM systems will allow 'live' processing of customer enquiries irrespective of the channel chosen by us – retail, telephone, on-line, sales force, or whatever (see Figure 7.3). Given how low service standards often are in practice, this 'channel free customer management' may be a source of competitive advantage rather than a hygiene factor.

There have been many claims, usually by management accounting/consultancy firms, that CRM is a way of delivering the philosophy of market orientation (MO). MO asserts that better profits result from the whole company sensing and responding to customer needs in a dynamic way: the customer is top priority for everyone in the firm. However, in reality

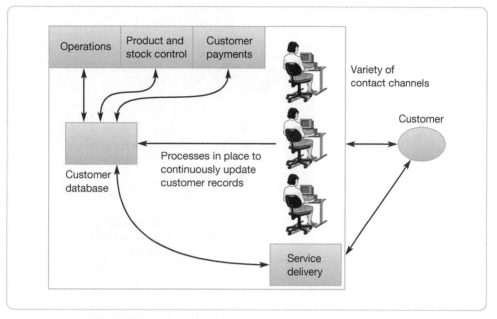

Figure 7.3 CRM in large firms

the growth of CRM has not been driven by MO. In practice, as mentioned above but worth repeating, 'CRM has largely grown from a more tactical imperative – to cope with all the channels of contact that customers have been offered and now expect'. The language of vision and values that puts the customer first may have been taken up by managers, but the reality is often that internal politics still dominates and, in the worst cases, the customer is attended to 'in spite of', rather than because of, management philosophies.

Firms such as SAP try and make some sense of what CRM should be about – and they try to provide some clarity and perspective to senior non-marketing managers. So, they will very sensibly position CRM as being led by a process that includes a firm 'understanding of its target market; its proposition to this market; how this proposition should be delivered in order to acquire and then manage selected groups of customers through sales, marketing and service on a day to day basis; what they should measure to show they are doing this effectively and efficiently; and what infrastructure (people, processes, data and IT) is needed'.

Sound familiar? It should, because this process is pretty well accepted as covering the major elements of modern strategic marketing. However, CEOs of big service companies, such as banks, often do not understand this – because their firms have, up to now, never been 'marketing led'. This lack of understanding is what leads to the problem of the whole CRM process being led by IT sellers. If you examine the paragraph above once more, you will see that 'IT' comes last rather than first, summing up quite neatly the troubles that so many firms got into in the early 2000s, when they spent so much money on large IT infrastructure without understanding the strategic context of that spend.

7.2.2 What is the difference between CRM, RM and DM?

In the light of the possible confusion between these concepts, an explanation seems in order. In short, relationship marketing (RM) is a business-wide strategy. Direct marketing (DM) is a system that allows us to implement marketing plans driven by customer data. And

Figure 7.4 CRM, RM and DM – a memory aid

CRM is a system and process driven attempt to improve contact between large firms and the customer.

The first thing to say about Figure 7.4 is not to take it at face value – it is over-simplistic. But it may be useful as a partial explanation of the key differences between the concepts.

An ideal linkage between the three concepts would be as follows. Relationship marketing is a management ethos that pervades everything the company does, and is 'top-down' from the CEO and board. In this RM driven firm, both CRM and DM are 'tools and processes' that support this ethos (and this means, for instance, not exploiting customer ignorance, but rather informing the customer when it is to their advantage to do something). CRM systems allow convenient two-way dialogue to build, and allow tailored service at the point of delivery. DM systems may be centred around the marketing department, but are part and parcel of CRM, and support the relationship ethos through predicting customer needs and placing good service above sales.

So far so good. But we have to add one more sauce to the mix of RM, CRM and DM. We have forgotten transaction marketing.

7.2.3 Transaction or relationship marketing – the tension in CRM

At the heart of the confusions endemic in CRM implementation lies the transaction – relationship marketing dialectic. In other words, are we primarily interested in using CRM tools for better targeting, creating propositions, selling directly and avoiding wasting marketing budget? Or do we want to generate a two-way dialogue, give up market power to customers, make and keep long-term commitments, and nurture that most precious of commodities, trust? In many ways this debate, yet to be resolved by academics or commentators of practice, lies at the heart of this entire book. One may summarise the present position, perhaps rather cynically, as one of 'talking the talk' of relationships, but 'walking the walk' of transaction marketing. And who is to say these practitioners are wrong? For all the academic work on relationship marketing, there has been little study as yet that links a genuine relationship approach with enhanced profitability.

A recent study that the author was involved with found that practitioners were by and large struggling to get past the first stages of CRM. Just aligning the channels properly, so that a common view of the customer could be obtained between them, was difficult work. Spotting and co-ordinating tactical 'selling' initiatives was probably the next stage. As so often, 'cross-sell' dominated the business case for investment. The customer who has just rung in fits the profile for a credit card, but does not have one. So offer them a credit card. Nothing wrong with this, but it is as yet a long way from learning and growing together, building trust, nurturing relationships.

As things stand you may be justified in asking: where is the 'R' in CRM? Most companies are probably committing 'relationship fraud' at the moment, or operating a CSUGBR strategy: Cross-Selling Under the Guise of Building Relationships. Not much seems to have changed since Gronroos said: 'relationship marketing is done in a very superficial way – and implementation is unsuccessful because the firm hasn't bought into the relationship marketing philosophy of shared ideals, mutual benefit, trust, commitment and dialogue' (Gronroos, 1996).

Such a lack of authenticity can make a mockery of attempts to operate in a one-to-one marketing mode (O'Malley and Mitussis, 2002). At that time (2002), O'Malley and Mitussis offered the opinion that CRM IT expenditure for solving the 'tricky problem of developing and enhancing consumer relationships without interpersonal interaction is highly problematic and must be questioned'. It is interesting to note, therefore, how some CRM auditors have amended CRM to plain 'Customer Management', which they define as:

> How a company aligns its resources and deploys any set of business techniques (not just marketing and sales) to:
>
> ● attract existing customers
> ● maintain or change how existing customers relate to the company as a buyer of its products or services

They then note that 'this definition does not presume that customers are managed in a relationship. There are many different models of customer management'. This is very interesting. What is being pointed out here is that the notion of 'managing customers' more often than not does NOT involve relationships – whether it is called CRM or not. You can see that account management, for example, which usually involves face-to-face communication between an account handler and a business buyer, can more often than not be accurately described as a relationship. At the very least the buyer and seller have to interact as human beings. Usually in business-to-business (B2B) account management things progress to a situation where the two individuals get on together, may become friendly, may go to corporate entertainment functions and so on. But CRM is put into place in larger scale B2B or consumer situations where a firm deals with thousands of customers and does so in an automated way. It is hard to justify calling this 'relationship' marketing. Customer management is better – and this phrase also highlights how organisations will segment their base with a view to losing unattractive customers, buttering up valuable customers and so on.

Exhibit 7.4 Why don't direct marketers strategise?

Why is it that professional marketers often seem so poor at strategising? It is not as if the principles of business strategy are a great secret: there are over 50 textbooks produced in Europe alone with the words 'corporate strategy' in the title. Anyone who has an MBA will be more than familiar with Porter and Hamel. Yet this material still seems to come as a shock or as a startling revelation to marketers – year after year. The strategic process is 'unveiled', slightly altered, with new buzzwords, as a brand new panacea by management consultants, or by slick business school 'academics' selling under the guise of academia.

The other issue that astonishes many is just how bad many senior managers are at strategising. One presumes that the reason they rose to these senior positions can only be down to their undoubted skills at people management – lobbying, influencing, maybe making things happen by driving change. But strategy? A foreign language, it seems.

CRM – the state of play

CRM is big business. Some IT business brands, notably Oracle, SAP and IBM, have made global names off the back of CRM purchases by large companies. CRM has been a serious driver of hardware and software sales for big players like IBM and Oracle. Across the USA and Europe, nearly 50 per cent of the companies in sectors such as high technology, aerospace, retailing and utilities have invested in CRM systems. Two-thirds of all US telecom operators and half or more of all US financial services, pharmaceutical and transportation companies are either implementing or already operating them. In 2006, companies around the world spent $3.5 billion a year on CRM software, and that was only a fraction of the total; implementation, training, and integration outlays can be many times higher. All in all, a highly complex CRM installation can cost more than $100 million and take three years to complete (Giga, 2002). Agnes Nairn (2002) reported a global survey by the Data Warehousing Institute of 1670 global CRM users, which found that 'most are now adopting CRM as a mission-critical business strategy'. Even allowing for our suspicions about any group that uses the phrase 'mission critical', there is little doubt that CRM has created a lot of fuss.

However Nairn, quite rightly, suggests that the case for allocating budget on CRM initiatives has yet to be proven. There is at present some concern about the wisdom of these investments: Patron (2002) reports that over 80 per cent of CRM projects fail in Europe. In many instances CRM has failed to yield the improvements expected in cost savings, customer service improvements, satisfaction scores or, ultimately, profitability. When managers were asked to assess three key functions of CRM – marketing campaign management, call centre management and marketing analytics – no more than 35 per cent of the respondents said that their expectations had been met in any function (International Data Corporation, 2001).

Making CRM work – the strategy gap

Discussions with consultancy QCi in 2008 revealed that most large companies still find it difficult to align themselves with customers. After the CRM difficulties of the early–mid 2000s some firms have attempted to solve this by appointing a senior manager in charge of customer management. QCi's experience is that this has been a mistake (Woodcock and Starkey, 2005; discussions with, for example, CRM expert Merlin Stone and others, 2008). They will advocate embedding CRM within the major business functions rather than attempting to manage it separately. They advise firms to move from a focus on customer satisfaction towards focusing on customer commitment: why should customers be committed to staying with a particular supplier? If this can be answered correctly, the organisation might have an insight into the kind of experience that customers want to have when they consume that firm's service – and this might in turn link to enhanced loyalty and robust profitability.

Customer service experience will have a physical component (right service, at the right time, delivering the right products, at the right price, conveniently) but in the developed world these components of service are increasingly replicated by competitors. This is why the other factor – an emotional component – is so vital. As QCi points out, if your customers say 'I enjoyed that', 'That was fun', 'I believe in those values as well', 'I was so impressed with that' and so on, they have strong, positive feelings about your service. These emotional dimensions are becoming more important but are still frequently ignored.

Direct and database marketing can undoubtedly help deliver good service, enabling firms to use customer data to serve customers better. But we should not be blind to the vital role that well-motivated and trained employees play in delivering good customer experiences. This is harder to achieve in some sectors than others. Imagine you work in a large bank in a service role. The intrinsic nature of account handling here is important to consumers, but not particularly interesting on a day by day basis for yourself as an employee. Now contrast this with employment in a leisure interest sector such as, say, cycling. Bike shops are often staffed by enthusiastic bikers who enjoy working with bikes and can talk about them all day. Staying enthusiastic and committed to customers is much easier in these scenarios. The challenge then for big business service delivery is keeping employees motivated for consistently high levels, day after day.

QCi points out that these customer management and employee issues have important implications for infrastructure, and by this we include customer data management, channel management including on-line channels and so on. At present the infrastructure is rarely aligned to customer management processes across different departments. Instead, IT and other support structures are usually situated within departments that operate quite a lot in isolation. Solving this requires strong senior management to force people in different disciplines to get together and see themselves as part of a bigger process. This does not happen spontaneously – because as human beings we rather like working in small teams of like-minded people. Overcoming this is the next big challenge for businesses.

The literature explaining how to implement CRM successfully is increasingly substantial. Its origins lay with authors such as Gamble and Stone (1999), and Foss and Stone (2002), and moved to more recent work by Woodcock and Starkey (2005). Fletcher (2002) found that the effective use of CRM is achieved by marrying *organisational* capabilities and market contexts, rather than by uncritical adoption and development. Organisational and strategic barriers are more important than technical barriers but this is still not generally recognised. In other words, too many companies have bought the technology but avoided the more difficult organisational and cultural changes needed to make the most of it. According to Foss and Stone (2002), 'people' and 'organisational' issues are the greatest contributors – and in many cases the greatest obstacles – to successful adoption of CRM practices. Often big firms fragment into departments that exist as separate silos that communicate poorly with one another. Patron (2002) reports that CRM requires an organisational change inside the company, away from products/silos and towards customer service delivery. Organisational changes mean people having to change who they work for and where they work. This in turn means the inevitable political jockeying for position that always happens at senior levels of the firm. Cultural changes are often even more difficult.

If you have worked in a large firm you will know how difficult it is to ask someone to change the way they work, the things they do on an everyday basis. O'Malley and Mitussis (2002) suggest that without a shared, culturally bound vision, the implementation of CRM systems might fail because of political infighting over the ownership of systems and data. This type of infighting has been well documented in the information systems literature. Woodcock and Starkey (2005) noted the link between a powerful brand and successful customer management.

The underlying problem behind much of the above discussion is that senior managers often do not focus on the underpinning strategy behind the CRM decision or its implementation. If we list culture, strategy, organisation and technology, then the 'least important' of these is technology, but this is often the element receiving most attention.

Foss and Stone (2002) cite the drivers of success as:

- making CRM a strategic priority, driven by the CEO (Slow progress is made due to lack of commitment across the organisation)
- an inherent customer service culture in the organisation (When ringing a firm as their customer, do you sometimes find they sound as if they do not want to hear from you, or that they are doing you a favour?)
- keeping staff happy so that they keep customers happy
- collaboration across departments

The flipside – obstacles to success – were listed as:

- approaching CRM on a piecemeal basis rather than as an holistic investment
- continued emphasis on acquisition at the expense of retention (Acquisition has often – thoughtlessly – got priority because its budgets are controlled by one department – marketing. Acquisition spend is mainly media. Retention spend on the other hand requires cross-departmental resource in people and processes and is more long term. The latter are more difficult for companies to deal with.)
- perhaps most difficult, culture change (Changing the mindset of the organisation from being, say, product, production or sales led to being customer (service) led is a long, hard road that must be driven from the CEO downwards. To return to our earlier debate about transactions versus relationship cultures, it is often this culture change that most starkly divides: has the firm introduced CRM systems to cut channel costs, increase cross-selling or create relationships? The CEO would probably say all three. But if a firm is not truly committed to the precursors of relationship marketing – treating customers with respect, as equal partners and sharing information – then relationship building is less likely.)

Once the strategic context has been established, Fletcher also points out that good CRM requires an operational level of marketing expertise in gathering and using customer data. Here, the use of customer data to understand different segments and to manage them profitably over time comes to the fore – if this sounds familiar it is because these skill sets are core to good direct and database marketing.

7.2.4 Putting CRM into operation

This chapter has emphasised the need not to under-estimate the complexity of introducing CRM systems into large firms. There are three major stages.

The first consideration is that the channels – Web, call centre, e-mail, mail, text – all have managers that guard their channels very carefully, often for good reason – security of access, etc. But these all need to be amalgamated into one customer file for CRM to stand any chance of being effective. More importantly than internal politics, the customer viewpoint has been terribly neglected when managing channels. The Future Foundation has done work on the self-service customer, the idea being that we actually want two things from company channels. First, the ability to navigate around the 'skin' of the company, hopefully getting what we want quickly and easily, without having to queue. Then, if this does not work, the chance to speak to someone and get help, again hopefully quite quickly and easily.

The second consideration is that, in order to work well, CRM systems require access to accounts data to give marketers the opportunity to share decision making on high-value customer account enquiries. Linked to this are database marketing systems, inventory systems to ensure stock is controlled, and call centre management systems in order to ensure that customers' queries about products, support calls and the like are factored into decision making. Finally, enterprise resource planning software must also be integrated into the mix to ensure these systems talk to each other.

The third dimension of complexity is the different product lines – these need to be similarly amalgamated so that cross-sell opportunities can be identified. However, in many companies each product has its own manager who often competes with other products for access to the customer. All very well in the old days of 'product push' and 'market share is king', but from a customer perspective this may mean receiving competing communications – anyone for a loan and a savings plan mailer on the same day?

Figure 7.5 summarises the evolution of CRM from a channel integrator to a fully fledged supporter of relationship marketing. This illustrates many of the debates we have had in this chapter.

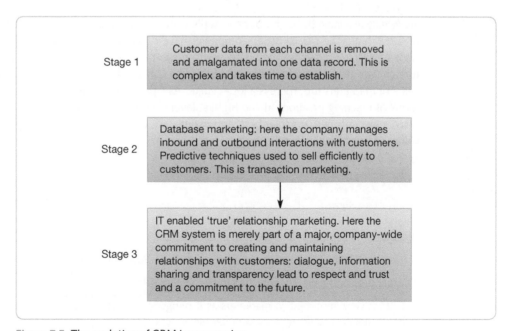

Figure 7.5 The evolution of CRM in companies

Finally – the bottom line

CRM auditors and consultants QCi have plenty of examples of CRM success and failure (Woodcock and Starkey, 2005). They regressed their CRM scores for companies against the profitability of those firms to assess the relationship between the two, and found a significant link. They have also used a series of case studies to further illustrate the link between customer management and profitability. This latter approach is wise because attempts to associate 'CRM' with profitability statistics, even in the sophisticated way QCi measures CRM, are probably over simplistic. A case by case basis can be more illuminating. On the positive side, cases they highlight include a European finance firm that adopted a model similar to the ideas discussed earlier (Chapter 3), dividing its customers into deciles according to loyalty rates, and then looking to redirect resources to profitable deciles and away from loss-making customers. This firm doubled its profitability within three years using this method. That is fine, and shows us how carefully deployed C(R)M can work. Equally, there are plenty of case studies we could raise to highlight failure. The point is that context, local conditions for the firm, the type of customers it deals with, the sector it is in, all contribute to immense complexity that must be tackled on a case by case basis. In this chapter we have laid out in some detail the warnings about what can go wrong if good practice is not followed.

Summary

To understand the state of play with CRM in business you are referred to Tim Ambler of London Business School's comment that 'most companies exist in a state of chaos and shambles' (Ambler, 1996). In the author's experience, he was not exaggerating. Many commentators report that global service levels have remained static, or even declined, in the last 20 years. The theoretical principles behind managing customers and building relationships are widely available (though not necessarily widely understood) but it is the implementation of CRM that is the crucial issue. Companies have collectively spent billions of dollars worldwide on CRM IT systems. They have yet to make the leap to process and, in particular, culture change that will make the most of this investment: it remains to be seen whether they will. For marketers too, there is a lot at stake. As a profession, they have under performed in terms of reaching positions at the highest level in companies. The company-wide focus on CRM represents perhaps their best, and maybe last, opportunity to make a mark on genuine value-adding organisational change.

QUESTIONS

1 How are relationships and direct marketing related?

2 Think about 'relationships' you have as a consumer. How would you describe your associations?

3 What problems have big firms had implementing CRM?

4 CRM is very important to marketers as it brings marketing to the board's attention. Explain how marketers could act more strategically in future.

References

Ambler, T. (1996) *The Financial Times Guide to Marketing: from advertising to zen,* Financial Times Prentice Hall, London.

Berman, B. (1996) *Marketing Channels,* John Wiley & Sons Inc., New York.

Berry, L.L. (1983) 'Relationship marketing' in Berry, L.L., Shostack, G.L. and Upah, G.D. (eds) *Emerging Perspectives on Services Marketing,* American Marketing Association, Chicago, pp. 25–28.

Brown, S. (1998) *Postmodern Marketing Two: telling tales,* International Thomson Business Press, London.

Bruhn, M. (2003) *Relationship Marketing: Management of customer relationships,* Financial Times Prentice Hall, Harlow.

Buttle, F.B. (1996) *Relationship Marketing Theory and Practice,* Paul Chapman, London.

Corner, L. and Jolson, M.A. (1991) 'Perceptions of gender stereotypic behaviour: an exploratory study of women in selling', *Journal of Personal Selling and Sales Management,* XI (Winter), pp. 43–59.

Cram, T. (1994) *The Power of Relationship Marketing,* Pitman, London.

Crosby, L.A., Evans, R.K. and Cowles, D. (1990) 'Relationship quality in services selling: An interpersonal influence perspective', *Journal of Marketing,* 54, pp. 68–81.

Fletcher, K. (2002) 'The role of CRM in changing and facilitating competitive advantage', *Journal of Database Marketing,* 9 (3), p. 203.

Foss, B. and Stone, M. (2002) *CRM in Financial Services,* Kogan Page, London.

Gamble, P. and Stone, M. (1999) *Up Close and Personal? Customer relationship marketing @ work,* Kogan Page, London.

Giga Information Group (2002) Market Overview: E-business/enterprise software applications in 2001 to 2005: Giga planning assumption, 5 March.

Gronroos, C. (1996) 'Relationship marketing: strategic and tactical implications', *Management Decision,* 34 (3), p. 13.

Gummesson, E. (1987) 'The new marketing: developing long-term interactive relationships', *Long Range Planning,* 20 (4), pp. 10–20.

Gummesson, E. (1994) 'Making relationship marketing operations', *International Journal of Service Industry Management,* 5, pp. 5–20.

Hansotia, B. (2002) 'Gearing up for CRM: antecedents to successful implementation', *Journal of Database Marketing,* 10 (2), p. 121.

International Data Corporation (2001) Demand-side survey: a reality check on CRM software, a 2001 study of 300 companies. AMR Research.

Little, E. and Marandi, E. (2003) *Relationship Marketing Management,* Thomson, London.

McCorkell, G. (1994) *The Best of Graeme McCorkell,* Institute of Direct Marketing, Teddington.

Nairn, A. (2002) 'CRM: helpful or full of hype?', *Journal of Database Marketing,* 9 (4), p. 376.

O'Malley, L. and Mitussis, D. (2002) 'Relationships and technology: Strategic implications', *Journal of Strategic Marketing,* 10 (3), p. 225.

Patron, M. (2002) 'If database marketing was so good, why is CRM so bad?', *Journal of Database Marketing,* 10 (2), p. 102.

Payne, A., Christopher, M. and Peck, H. (1995) *Relationship Marketing for Competitive Advantage: Winning and keeping customers,* Butterworth-Heinemann, Oxford.

Pryce, K. (2003) 'Consumer clubs and relationships in fmcg markets', Dissertation for Bristol Business School, UK.

Rapp, S. and Collins, T., (1994) *Beyond Maxi Marketing*, McGraw Hill, New York.

Selnes, F. (1993) 'An examination of the effect of product performance on brand reputation, satisfaction and loyalty', *European Journal of Marketing*, 27 (9), pp. 19–35.

Woodcock, N. and Starkey, M. (2005) 'State of the Nation IV: 2005, a five year study of how organizations manage their customers', publ. by QCi Ltd.

CASE STUDY

Insureco – from direct sales to direct CRM

Insureco is a long established insurance company selling both life and general insurance products. It has a direct marketing unit with a large database of policyholders. However, the company recognised a few years ago that its direct marketing was not as effective as it could be. There was a requirement to increase average product holdings per customer. At the same time, there was also a need to improve customer retention as levels of customers cancelling policies were above industry averages. The challenge for Insureco was that it had traditionally been a sales and operations based culture, driven by income rather than long-term profit. The efforts of the direct marketing unit had primarily been focused on direct mailings to recruit new customers.

The appointment of a customer relationship manager was an important step in changing this approach. In particular, the customer relationship manager recognised that improving cross-selling and customer retention required a far greater degree of integration between marketing and the operational units dealing directly with customers. For example, customer retention needs to start at the point of service: 'We don't make customers aware of the pitfalls of surrendering policies and the options open to them. We need to contact lapsers within three days of defaulting, but currently we don't, and all the customers receive the same letters. We need to change the internal culture in the service centre' (Customer Relationship Manager).

This is a common problem in organisations where customer service is based around operational centres that are driven by efficiency of processing rather than by a relationship perspective.

Following a review by the customer relationship manager, a number of steps have been taken at Insureco to implement a more proactive approach to dealing with customers. A segmented marketing plan has been developed based on an understanding of the profitability of different customer segments, rather than a plan based simply on existing products that are available. Telemarketing has been integrated with direct mail activities (for instance following up direct mail with a telephone call for the best prospects). Research has been conducted into why customers cancel policies. As a result of this, new customer retention initiatives in the form of proactive new customer communications (policy pack, welcome pack, newsletters) and ongoing communications (anniversary communication) have been put in place. New products have been developed specifically for achieving better retention of customers holding maturing products. A new recovery unit has been formed to contact customers surrendering policies or lapsing on payments. Finally, operational units have been encouraged to focus on quality of service as well as turnaround times. The results so far have been impressive, with a significant uplift in sales to existing customers and a major improvement in customer retention. The customer relationship manager concludes that 'CRM is not rocket science, it's common sense'. However, he stresses that if marketing is separate from operations there is a danger that the operational emphasis will purely be about efficiency rather than long-term effectiveness in dealing with customers. Achieving an integrated approach is not easy.

Question

Compare and contrast the challenges and issues facing a customer relationship manager with those facing a direct marketing manager.

Written by: Dr Tim Hughes, who is an expert in CRM at Bristol Business School. The authors would like to thank Dr Hughes for this case study.

Chapter 8

Digital marketing and the Internet

Objectives

Once you have read this chapter you will:

- have an appreciation of the Internet and digital marketing as a business tool
- understand the important implications of the Internet for business strategy
- gain a clear idea of the way in which direct and digital marketing link together

Introduction

There are two ways in which the Internet is important for marketers. The most visible is the use of the Internet as a medium for marketing promotion and advertising: search ads, banner ads, Web design, e-mail marketing. We cover this topic in detail later (Chapter 11). The second way is the more strategic role of the Internet in changing the way businesses go to market. This latter topic is the subject of this chapter.

A lot has happened in the world of Internet marketing in the last few years. After the crazy boom and bust years of the 'dot-com, dot-gone' era of post-2000, Internet marketing has regrouped and slowly but surely gone from strength to strength. Buying and selling over the net has reached maturity and is accepted as everyday business by the sellers, and a behavioural norm – seen as nothing out of the ordinary – by consumers. This is true throughout the developed world, with business-to-business Internet usage very high, and consumer Internet access at home at typically over 60 per cent. The latter half of the decade since 2000 has seen the rise of 'Web 2.0' – so-called user generated content or, in plain English, people creating their own material and taking advantage of Facebook, YouTube and other social media to communicate with each other in new ways. These new developments deserve detailed treatment, so we will look at those in the next chapter, as well as embedding principles of integration of on-and off-line channels and media throughout the book.

But, in the meantime, what of 'mainstream' digital marketing? In this chapter we deal with its development and growth, and move to the special features of the on-line world that lend special flavour to marketing strategies on-line. Digital (direct) marketing shares some key principles with mainstream marketing, but is inherently different in its use of a medium in which power has profoundly shifted to everyday people. Direct and database marketing is deployed in a different way – and this requires some explanation, which we offer to complete the chapter. You may like to note also that later (Chapter 11) we focus on the more tactical, everyday use of the Internet as a medium and, using the AIMRITE model developed there, produce a comparative analysis of the Internet as a medium in competition with other direct media such as direct-response TV, direct mail, and so on.

8.1   What is the Internet?

The Internet is a collection of inter-related networks of computers that span the globe. Anyone with an appropriate Internet connected device and appropriate software and hardware can hook up via an Internet service provider (ISP).

The Internet can be thought of as a giant spider's web of connections that link together a large proportion of the world's computers. Much larger computers called Web servers are responsible for holding and sending the content, websites, onto the Internet in response to a request to see the site by ourselves. The Internet itself is laid out in a manner similar to the international road network – motorways (backbone trunk lines) serving major long distance routes, main roads serving cities and minor roads (local lines) leading to small villages (Figure 8.1).

We connect to the Internet using the World Wide Web, the interface designed by Tim Berners Lee. The Web is accessed using domestic or business based computers, or through a variety of mobile devices ranging from tablets to smartphones to game consoles. Finding the most useful websites has been revolutionised through extremely powerful search engines, of which Google is the most well known.

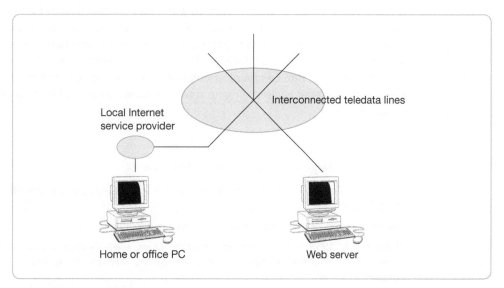

Figure 8.1 **The Internet**

8.1.1 Websites

Historians in 100 years' time will probably look back at late 2000s websites as slow, clunky and primitive, and there is little doubt that there is room for improvement. However, there has been a great deal of innovation by newcomers to the business, some leading edge players such as Facebook, eBay, Amazon and Dell, and most impressively by private individuals seeking to make their mark in all manner of ways. Traditional firms are catching up from a very slow start, often outdone by specialist on-line operators who may offer more interesting, social and entertaining places for us to gather information.

Websites are typically multiple electronic 'pages' of text, artwork, pictures, video and sound put together using specially created Internet languages, such as HTML or Java. Hypertext links allow us to click from one page to another, hence affording relatively easy navigation around the site. Security buffers are now well established, affording the chance to offer pay-per-view sites, or to encourage consumers to enter their details, including payment by card, and receive goods in return. These may be delivered to the customer electronically if the goods are, say, software, or delivered by traditional post.

Websites are of great potential interest to companies operating a genuine database driven marketing strategy, because they can 'capture the details of visitors to the site'. Therefore, an action initiated by a visitor can trigger return e-mails, in which the communication can be made more relevant according to which parts of the site they visited.

8.1.2 Electronic mail

The use of e-mail as a direct marketing medium is given full attention later (Chapter 11) where it is considered alongside the other key media of direct marketing. It is worth noting here the extraordinary impact e-mail has made globally on both working and now domestic life. What did we do before e-mail? The low cost and convenience of the technology allows mass communication cheaply and easily. In theory e-mail dovetails extremely well with websites, encouraging faster two-way communication between the firm and its customers. However, business use of e-mail to contact consumers is now threatened by spammers and fraudsters who impersonate legitimate businesses to steal data or fraudulently receive money. This is to the extent that the value of e-mail as an acquisition medium has fallen significantly, although it remains very important as a way of keeping in touch with customers.

E-mail is being used most effectively by on-line marketers as an inbound channel but is still used for outbound communications. Most websites encourage users to e-mail them with enquiries. E-mail is also being used as an outbound channel by direct marketers to build databases.

Exhibit 8.1 Jargon – what you need to know

For those who are not up on Web jargon, here is your essential guide to terms relating to direct marketing:

Ad impression: a single viewing by a customer of a Web page advert.

Browsers: in 1993 a 23-year-old programmer called Marc Andreessen invented the first browser. This is software that we use to access the Internet, for example, Netscape or Internet Explorer.

Clickstream: the route a customer takes through a website. This software allows Web owners to track the navigation paths used by customers, hence assessing the most popular pages and how the site is being used.

Cookies: websites often compile and share information on the browsing practices of net users by means of a small electronic name-tag (a 'cookie'). Each time you visit the site, the cookie identifies you, tracks what pages you visit and the data you enter, and records where you were before and where you are heading next. Such information can be aggregated into huge direct marketing databases, creating a composite profile of an individual Web surfer's habits; often without their knowledge. Direct marketers can then use this data to place targeted ads in front of us as we browse. Data items that can be gathered on-line very easily include: how many visitors; from which countries; when visitors accessed the site: time and date; where on the site they have been; and how many have requested information.

Disintermediation: a posh word for going direct. The removal of intermediaries. Most commonly seen by financial services companies that replace brokers and salesmen with a website. Now common in many sectors.

E-business: Web and other electronic technologies acting as an enabler for the way a company operates – supply chain, internal operations and customer links. Wider than e-commerce.

E-commerce: selling over the Internet.

Extranet: the linking of two or more intranets between partner organisations. Again private rather than public.

HTML and Java: HTML is Hyper Text Mark Up Language. HTML and Java are the software languages used to build websites. Java is the more advanced.

HTTP: Hypertext transfer protocol. The way in which websites are requested by a user using the domain name – the Web address.

The Internet: a collection of inter-related networks of computers that span the globe. Anyone with a PC, a modem and a telephone line can hook up via an Internet service provider (ISP).

Intranet: a closed mini Internet that connects PCs within a company or organisation and allows private interaction secure from the public Internet.

Opt-in email: the customer opts to receive e-mail by explicitly asking for it. Opt-out customers instruct the company not to contact them.

Paradigm shift: an entirely new technology that comes along infrequently and disrupts the norms of an industry, allowing new business models to be set up. A recent example could be 4G mobile technology.

Portals: 'portal' sites are those that are used as gateways to the Internet and include the major directories or search engines, such as Google or Yahoo! as well as the sites run by Internet and on-line service providers, such as AOL. 'Destination' sites are those that Internet users go to for their content, including news, personal finance, sport, travel, community and entertainment sites. One of the biggest destination sites in Europe is the media company, the BBC, at **www.bbc.co.uk.**

Search engines: a place to go if you wish to find websites dealing with a particular subject. They use Web-crawler technology called spiders that gather sites relating to key words and provide indices that users can click through to get to the site quickly. Content providers can register with a search engine and also advertise, both for a fee.

World Wide Web: invented in the early 1990s, a newer multimedia version of the Internet. When most people talk of the Internet, they probably mean the WWW.

8.2   The growth of the Internet

The Internet has already had a massive impact on many of our lives. Radio took 38 years to acquire 50 million listeners worldwide while TV took 13 years. The Internet achieved the same figure in just four years.

It was during the week of 10 March 2000 that the UK went dot-com mad. First there was the news that a number of traditional companies had been ousted from the FTSE 100 list in favour of a few Internet based firms. Then came the launch of **Lastminute.com** as a public company. Within a matter of minutes frantic share buying had taken this tiny company, with its sales of £409,000 and losses of £6 million, to a paper value of £760 million, an astonishing figure. This soon gave way to a prolonged cold shower as the realisation dawned that the Internet was not a quick route to business riches. The dot-com bust probably cost the world three or four years of arrested development while innovators went back to the drawing board and tried to unravel ways of making money from on-line activity. Could the Internet be a business tool as well as a vehicle for entertainment? Recent growth suggests it can.

In fact, growth in the USA and Europe has followed a classical 'S shape': a slow start, a rapid increase as the early and late majority mainstream came on-line (beginning about 2000) and a flattening-off of growth as new demand slows. This plateauing began about 2005 and, in 2013, consumer penetration rates in the USA and most of Europe (on-line access at home) were around 50–80 per cent. Non-take-up is primarily among people with low incomes, with a skew to older age groups also less likely to be on-line at home.

There is an increasingly established knowledge base investigating the way in which business and marketing are conducted on the Internet. Hoffman and Novak's (1997) original assertion that the Internet would create a paradigm shift in business, and fundamentally change the relationships that exist between businesses and their customers, is coming to pass, driven not by the dot-com boom of the early 2000s, but instead by the power shift to consumers that Google, in particular, provides. Search engines such as Google are a major consideration for direct marketers of course, and we will deal with these in detail later in the chapter. But it is no exaggeration to say that Google has changed the world.

Exhibit 8.2 The story of Google

Google has changed the world. Most of us use it every day, sometimes many times a day. Google is a major part of an enormous change for marketers – especially direct marketers. To understand this we need to go back a step. Ask yourself this: how much of marketing – adverts, promotions, mailers, and so on – is actually welcomed by consumers? The answer is: not a lot. Most of it, most of the time, is seen as an irritant, possibly dishonest, manipulative, annoying or irrelevant. All this changed with Google. Google placed the consumer in charge, enabling them to search on their terms, in their time, for information in ways that they control. Whenever consumers are asked what they want from their contact with companies, they respond that they want to be in control of the contact so it is on their terms, but also that they want to be quickly and conveniently able to understand what the firm can offer them, and how this offer measures up against other offers out there. Once we understand this, we then understand the limitations of one company, on its own, sending marketing material out to an individual semi-blindly, hoping that this material will somehow be just what that consumer wants. In contrast, Google is about convenient, quick access to comparative information available on demand: just what the consumer wants!

So how did it all happen? Here's the story of Google . . .

Google began when Sergey Brin and Larry Page met as PhD students at Stanford University in California in the 1990s. Page described his viewpoint as 'having a healthy disregard for the impossible', and took an optimistic view of what he could achieve. Sergey Brin too had an interesting background: his parents had fled Russia during a period of strong anti-semitism and settled as immigrants in the USA. But Brin's father was a maths professor, instilling in Sergey the need to study hard and how this could open up new worlds.

Google is located at the slightly crankily named 'GooglePlex', located close to San Francisco, California. Googleplex looks a lot like a university campus, and indeed Google runs its headquarters in this way. Most Google employees are located in small project teams, and 20 per cent of their time is completely free and controlled by themselves to work on projects of their own choosing – something adopted from the academic model of how academic staff have some free time to develop personal research interests. The word Google is actually a misspelling: the word means 1 to the power of 100 – a very big number. Brin and Page overlooked its proper spelling: Googol.

It is only relatively recently that it has become clear how Google makes money. For quite a long time after its inception in 1999 Google struggled to make money, delivering search results for its increasing army of users for free. At that time the big search engine players were AltaVista and Excite, with Yahoo! waiting in the wings as the apparent inheritor of the search crown. But Brin and Page knew they had the best search engine and formed relationships with influential people who could spread word of mouth about Google. Indeed, in its early years Google never had to advertise. In those days what Google needed was a way of making money without compromising its trusted position of being unbiased and on the side of the searcher – whereas existing ad funded search engines were inherently biased towards the advertisers. The good news was that Google was recognised as the best search engine. There were other names in search around the dot-com boom–bust of 1999–2001 but none of them foresaw how search would become pre-eminent in the Web mix. Yahoo! and America Online had both betted on e-mail as their key revenue generators, with their e-mail lists creating opportunities for advertisers, and latterly Microsoft's MSN had done the same. Microsoft, for so long having made the correct moves in the IT business chess game, took a wrong turning by not investing in search engine technology in the early 2000s.

By 2001, although it had yet to make money, Google was highly regarded for reasons important to direct marketers. First, Brin and Page disliked flashy banner ads that popped up unannounced and irritated Web users who found them annoying and irrelevant – mimicking the problems of off-line advertising. Second, some rival search engines, short of money, had accepted payments from sellers in return for placing these sites high up in searches – known as paid placement. This was more likely to lead to a breakdown of trust between the search engine and the consumer. Google made a crucial decision: they would continue to provide free, unbiased search, and sell adverts as an added extra. These ads would be marked up as adverts by displaying them in a different colour. All this would, they hoped, keep consumers onside. Users would only see adverts related to the search they did: so people searching for car insurance did not see ads for dog food, or rock music – they saw ads for car insurance. Hence, these ads tended to be read quite carefully by users. Another interesting marketing decision was to keep their homepage clear of adverts – something else that continues to mark Google out to this day as a company that does things its own way. Google's risks paid off, thanks to the quality of its search results, which spread to new users rapidly by word of mouth and kept people coming back. Even by early 2001, Google was running a staggering 100 million searches per day.

It has not all been plain sailing. For example, Google got itself into potential trouble by allowing firms to advertise themselves based on searches to competitor names – so, in theory, Marriot Hotels could buy advertised links for a search on, say, Hilton. This reached court in late 2004 when an insurance company, Gieco, took Google to court, as they believed consumers were being deliberately confused by typing in Geico, then having a competitor advert displayed. Google won the day in court on this issue, but a much bigger challenge was soon to emerge: click fraud. Google makes money by charging advertisers a small amount whenever a searcher clicks on an advert link. Click fraud happens when a firm deliberately clicks on a competitor's advert, obviously with no intention of buying, but knowing that each time they clicked on an advert, their competitor was being charged. This could have been a real show stopper for Google and they had to act fast. They had a dilemma: they could employ enormous teams to track abnormal clicking and, through this, they would be able to find offenders and reimburse their victims. But such teams would cost enormous amounts of money. Yahoo! and its search engine have faced similar problems. Since then, and to date, click fraud continues to be a problem – but one that has reached a slightly uneasy compromise between search providers and advertisers. At the moment between 5 and 10 per cent of clicks are estimated to be fraudulent; and where it is spotted the advertiser will be reimbursed. But both sides lack a cyber-police to hunt down fraudsters.

As we motor towards the mid point of the second decade of the 21st century, Google goes from strength to strength. By some measures it is now the world's most valuable brand. It has so far seen off any challenge from Microsoft in the search sector, although the launch of Facebook search represents another attempt to challenge this dominance, and in 2012 it made more than $50 billion in revenue. To power its search service, Google runs custom designed programmes on over 200,000 PCs linked and stacked together, an awesome combination of computing power. Google has influenced all our lives more than any other firm since a young upstart called Microsoft challenged IBM. But watch this space. The bigger they are the harder they fall. Who will be the young upstart to challenge the complacent giant of Google in the future?

Sources: Mills, E. (2007) 'Google rises at Yahoo's expense', CNet **news.com**, 23 April. Richards, J. (2007) 'Search is history! says Yahoo', *Times Online*, 4 June. Vise, D. (2005) *The Google story*, Bantam Dell, New York. BBC.co.u, 2013k.

The geographical remoteness and community enhancing effects of the medium support the case of a shift in paradigms. Belk *et al.* (1988) add to this by noting that many businesses are already making the transition from entities operating in the physical marketplace to those operating in the virtual marketplace.

Exhibit 8.3 The net: facts and figures

- The worldwide Internet population is estimated at over 2.4 billion in 2012. In 2000 there were 400 million users and, in 1995, 20 million users.
- In most countries it is increasingly a myth that the Internet is dominated by young people. This was true in the early years of the Internet. But, for example, by 2013 in the UK as many 55+ people were on-line as 18–24 year olds.

- On-line reach in most of 'Western' Europe now stands at over 60 per cent. In the UK it is about 80 per cent.
- According to the US department of commerce, the number one activity on the Internet is consumers gathering purchase information, but not necessarily then buying on-line.
- Native English speakers represent 43.5 per cent of the on-line population, although they are less than 10 per cent of the world population. Native Chinese speakers represent the second largest group: 37 per cent of the on-line population.
- A gender gap exists in access and usage of information and communication technologies. Women represent 25 per cent of Internet users worldwide. In the developed world this gender imbalance is evening out.
- Over £50 billion was spent on-line in the UK in 2012, up from £30 billion in 2007. This indicates the kind of growth e-commerce is experiencing at present.
- The most popular uses of the net were accessing social media, e-mailing, checking bank accounts, study/research, instant messaging, and using on-line auctions.
- The most popular purchases remain travel, accommodation or holidays, music, tickets for events and books. But general household goods, and even clothing, is increasingly bought on-line.
- Four seconds is the maximum length of time an average on-line shopper will wait for a Web page to load before potentially abandoning a retail site.
- On-line buying behaviour continues to be driven largely by price across all customer segments. Free shipping remains a very popular on-line promotion.

Sources: **www.Jupiterdirect.com**, Comscore media matrix, Yahoo!

The next section explains in more detail the different ways in which companies use the Internet as a business tool.

Table 8.1 Worldwide Internet population 2012

	Population	Internet population
Africa	1,073m	4,167.3m (mostly dial-up)
Middle East	223m	90m
North America	348m	274m
Asia	3.9bn	1,076m
Europe	820m	519m
Latin America	594m	255m
Oceania/Australia	36m	24m
UK	60m	48m

Source: Based on **www.internetworldstats.com**.

8.3   How companies use the Internet

In this section we will scope out the commercial use of the Internet, focusing in particular on the new models of e-business that have emerged.

Given the learning curve that needs to be travelled in order to use e-commerce effectively, we would have expected that the first movers in e-commerce would have been those firms that had experience of computer based systems, were used to dealing with customers at a distance and had ready made purchasing and customer supply systems. These firms should, therefore, be direct marketers. However, when we examine the major e-commerce companies, there seems little doubt that traditional direct marketers are not the companies exploiting the full functionality of the Internet. A look at the e-commerce press reveals the entrepreneurs as those who have sprung directly from specialised e-commerce.

At one extreme, organisations may see the Internet as merely another channel or medium through which they can raise a profile. Here, usage of a website would be little more than as a 'corporate brochure'. At the other extreme, some businesses are created entirely out of the opportunities afforded by the Internet, and all their operations are conducted on-line. The extent to which the Internet should be used as an awareness raiser, or information site, rather than as a medium for selling, is important. In turn, how far firms should go in seeking to attract informal or *ad hoc* Internet users to become regular interactors and then, if the medium is to be used for selling, how to encourage transactions should also be examined. These considerations give us the following typology of Web based businesses:

- A corporate brochure/brand building site. Here no attempt at selling on-line is made. Customer contact may be encouraged and the site will usually make provision for enquiries (see for example **www.kraft.com**).

- A mail-order style direct distribution site, which uses the website for taking sales enquiries. Purchases may be confirmed on-line (see for example **www.wru.co.uk**).

- A full database marketing driven on-line operation, in which data from on-line sales are fed directly to a marketing database, which is then used for proactive marketing possibly including e-mail (see **www.amazon.com**).

- Services orientated relationship building websites. Not surprisingly these are dominated by business-to-business supplier sites. Chaffey and Ellis Chadwick (2012) use the examples of professional management accountant/consultancy sites that will offer users papers and technical information that may help in their workplace (examples include **www.accenture.com**).

- Dedicated e-commerce business models. Here the Internet provides the entire environment for the business, which is often an intermediary of some kind. Portals act as key points for information delivery (see for example **www.yahoo.com** or **www.lastminute.com**).

Exhibit 8.4 *Profile of* **lastminute.com.** *A dotcom fairy story*

Lastminute.com was unique. Its success was based on a simple premise: offering late details on anything from flights to concert tickets at knockdown prices. It used a model of business that is impossible to emulate in the normal business environment. In short, its central idea was to use the 'searchability' and scope of the Web in order to access suppliers and get the best deal for consumers. It was, therefore, one of a new breed of intermediaries that have set up on the Internet.

The company was launched in November 1998, based on an idea of Brent Hoberman, the co-founder and managing director of **lastminute.com**. He and his co-founder, Martha Lane Fox, formed the company with a relatively modest $600,000 of funding. However, the company is now well funded, having fetched about £400 million when launched on the stock market in March 2000. **Lastminute.com** acts as a virtual marketplace by bringing together the best offers and placing them in front of customers. The key to its future success was the speed and convenience afforded to customers, as with so many of the successful Internet companies. It took advantage of the perishability of services by providing a 'shop window' for deals that are counting down to the time of the service itself. The value added by **www.lastminute.com** was that it does the searching around the Web, which takes time and effort, and may also force suppliers to improve their offers, because of the transparency of the 'shop window' allowing customers to make quick comparisons.

Interestingly, the company had to spend a considerable sum promoting itself using off-line media such as press, posters and Underground advertising. It also used partner companies such as Freeserve, **www.timeout.com** and Tesco.

Lastminute moved into operating profit by the third quarter of 2002. Its rosier financial position was achieved by the nitty-gritty task of running the business efficiently. UK marketing director, Carl Lyons, claimed it cut the costs of acquiring a customer in the UK from £24 a year to £6.24. It also increased the value of existing customers in partnership with Dunnhumby, the database marketing company used and majority owned by Tesco.

In 2006, Hoberman stood down as chief executive following the sales of the business to Sabre Holdings/ Travelocity in order to help rationalise the complexity of its business model. Martha Lane Fox had left the business in 2003. In 2007 it was taken over by a private equity company.

Lastminute.com has rationalised the business model; taken control of its cost base and structural complexity and removed the pressures that came from PLC status. The great ambitions of the dot-com boom years have been tempered and the business now competes alongside a number of other players that have had the opportunity to learn and benefit from the mistakes made in the early years of operation The business also exists as, in today's economic climate, there is still a great deal of unsold inventory available.

Lastminute was a leader of its type and very successful, but it faced the challenge of fighting off new entrants looking for a piece of the on-line booking market. At the same time **www.lastminute.com** is itself looking to diversify by shaking off its image as a late booking holiday service as it looks to broaden the brand's appeal.

For example, in 2007 the company launched a campaign to encourage customers to book their summer holidays early. It targeted the grey market and affluent families as well as its traditional audience of 20- to 30-year-olds.

However it insists its core strategy has not changed: it wants to be a consumer champion, acting as a 'social assistant' in pulling together holidays on demand.

A spokesman has said the brand stood out for its emotional, romantic connections that other, functional, on-line brands lacked. Sometimes, however, this is not enough.

Sources: Chandiramani, Ravi (2002) 'Winning the net survival battle', *Marketing (UK)*, 15 August. City Comment (2003) *Daily Telegraph*, 6 August. Jardine, A. (2000) 'Lastminute wonders', *Marketing*, London, 16 March. Kilby, N. (2006), 'Dot-com survivor', *Marketing Week*, 21 December, 29 (50), pp. 22–3. *Marketing* (2007) '**Lastminute.com** aims to widen appeal', 12 May, p. 3. Murphy, D. (2000) 'The last minute waltz', *Marketing Business*, February, pp. 22–3. Uhrenbacher, S. and Therezien, L. (2000) 'Lastminute recruits two for Euro growth', *Marketing*, 13 January, p. 9. *Venture Capital Journal* (2000) 'Profile of **Lastminute.com**', Wellesley Hills, 1 May.

When the Internet first started growing, Berryman reported on a variety of different models of business used by e-commerce specialists (Berryman *et al.*, 1998). His categorisation of seller controlled sites, buyer controlled sites and neutral sites is still useful. Mitchell (2000) described examples of agents of each market type in a traditional setting as:

- the 'sellers' marketplace' – car dealers acting on behalf of the seller

- 'the neutral marketplace – a typical supermarket retailer provides a setting which favours neither the consumer nor the supplier

- the 'buyers' marketplace – the local doctor is an agent who acts on behalf of the patient rather than the suppliers

This last model is rare in commerce, but the Internet has the potential to introduce such a model into commercial sectors on a major scale.

On-line, these three models translate as follows:

8.3.1 Seller-controlled sites: example – Web based retailers

Convenience for the consumer and cost savings for the business have been an unstoppable combination. Entertainment, finance, books and travel were the pioneering growth sectors, but high street products such as clothes and household goods, while slower to pick up on-line have grown too. Recent players learnt from the mistakes of pioneers of the dot-com boom and bust, and no one crashed harder than **Boo.com**.

Exhibit 8.5 It's boo hoo for Boo

Writing in *Management Today* in November 1999, Matthew Gwyther got it spot on: 'There are anxieties, however, about Boo's ability to deliver. And when you hype to the extent that Boo has, you must deliver. Sceptics anticipate the first big-time British net flame-out. Boo's is an incredibly ambitious strategy because it is hoping for a seven-country launch, which has been postponed twice. The intricacies of selling and delivering clothes over the net are a little short of nightmarish. We wish it well.'

Gwyther's instincts were right. 'Yah Boo Sucks', 'From Boo to Bust' and 'Bang goes Boo' were just a few of the headlines in the financial pages of the weekend press in late May 2000. **Boo.com** had crashed.

Originally launched as a pure dot-com company selling sports clothes and trainers over the Internet, **Boo.com** had achieved an incredible profile in a short time. After months of hype and delay, **Boo.com** launched in November 1999 with £90 million of backing from investors. Launched by three photogenic young Swedish millionaires, one of them an ex-model, and with an address in Carnaby Street, it always had news value. It launched a TV ad push, although this was criticised as gimmicky, not explaining what Boo was and what it sold.

What Boo lacked, however, was a decent business proposal. It was argued that these are the kind of products young consumers not only want to be seen to wear, 'but be seen to purchase too'. Perhaps buying on the Web was too invisible for this appearance obsessed market. Yet, even if the basic business model stood up to inspection, its delivery on the Web did not. The site's launch was delayed by five months. When it did go live, its programming was incompatible with many Web browsers, to the point of being a no-go zone for iMac users, a consumer group that Boo needed to target. The site itself used flashy graphics and featured a personal shopping assistant called Miss Boo. But consumers complained it was confusing and required a high speed connection.

What can businesses learn from this? First, spend less on advertising the brand and more on making each customer contact pleasurable and memorable, and ensuring goods are available and delivered to promise. Second, do not launch too early. Boo did the 'equivalent of Tesco opening a flagship store when the automatic doors don't work and there's a cement mixer in the vegetable aisle', as Rosier (2000) put it. Third, and most importantly, make sure business proposals are sound. What is the company's core competence? Can this be turned into an advantage that customers value? Has this been checked with the chosen market target? These strategic questions do not go away just because a company is a groovy dot-com outfit.

Sources: Dignam, C. (2000) 'Boo's failure does not mar the whole **dot.com** economy', *Marketing*, London, 25 May. Gwyther, M. (1999) 'Jewels in the Web', *Management Today*, London, November. Rosier, B. (2000) 'What went so horribly wrong with **Boo.com**?', *Marketing*, London, 25 May.

> **Exhibit 8.6 How not to retail on-line**
>
> Visit **www.webpagesthatsuck.com** for examples of what not to do. Created by Vincent Flanders, this site provides a light hearted look at typical cock-ups made by firms' websites. Flanders highlights some examples: the *Silly Flash*: 'Flash is a tool and like any tool can be used for good or evil or stupid.' *Random Mystery Meat Navigation*: 'We should all know by now that *Mystery Meat Navigation* is not for use on "real" sites. I wondered how I could make MMN even worse. Well, how about making the links random?' *The Silly Art Fart*: 'You should be able to look at any home page and know what the site is about within 10 seconds. Without the explanatory text, you wouldn't have a clue.' The *Making it Bad*: over-use of Java design including sound files, mouse-over text, pop-up windows, flash, and everything else that irritates the user.

In summary: when designing a website, do not try too hard.

The formula for success of on-line retailers includes features such as a simple Web home page, which directs new and existing customers alike quickly around the site, a 'basket' with which the customer buys goods as they browse around the virtual store, and security in transactions to protect customers' credit card details. The retailer could run features, such as an interactive on-line magazine for customers who have a particular interest in fashion, and various other opportunities for browsers to interact with the site.

As the World Wide Web gets more and more crowded in each category, marketing costs for retail operators will rise significantly, and have already started doing so. It is important to keep a clear view of how net based business costs are different to high street costs. The back-up processes that in the high street are owned by the retailer – stocking, warehousing and so on – with e-commerce are typically partnership arrangements. The Web based company providing the 'front end' (what the customer sees) typically concentrates purely on marketing. Therefore, operating costs for Web businesses are significantly lower (typically about 4 per cent, compared to 15–20 per cent for high-street retailers). Despite distribution costs being high this still leaves on-line retailers at an advantage. However, marketing costs may well be higher as the Web business has to work hard in attracting customers to its site. The importance of branding for Web based retailers is, therefore, very high. Basic awareness, particularly at this early stage in the new world of the Web, is vital. Some research suggests that some consumer segments will spend a couple of months getting to know their 10–12 favourite sites and not bother with much more surfing. But other segments will surf for enjoyment and to maximise their knowledge of what is available. Therefore, it is likely that even e-commerce specialists will have to attract some people using traditional methods; while retaining existing customers. They could do this with a mix of on-line and traditional methods of marketing – the so-called 'clicks and bricks' approach. For example, football clubs have created leads into their websites through search engine optimisation or via stadium advertising.

8.3.2 Neutral sites not controlled by buyer or seller: example – the auction house

One of the first auction houses to be established – and certainly the biggest – is eBay, a US firm.

Exhibit 8.7 eBay: the world's biggest car boot sale

Desperate for an 'original' Barbie Doll? Keen to get hold of a used baby carrier at low prices? If neither of these particularly appeals, don't worry, eBay has millions more items for sale, to be captured by the highest bidder. eBay has over 233 million registered users, and has recently finished a huge TV ad campaign in the USA and Europe that lasted two years, telling consumers that you can buy 'It' at eBay. The idea was to change people's perception of the site from 'This is a place you go to buy quirky stuff' to 'This is a place where you go to buy all of your stuff' according to the senior director of brand marketing for eBay.

Launched at the inception of the Internet in 1995, eBay is by far the world's biggest on-line auction house, and one of the secrets to its success is that however much you may feel that what you are selling is junk, it is always exactly what someone somewhere is looking for. The key once again lies in the unrivalled ability of the Internet to match supply with demand. Another insight comes from a quote from the brand director: 'Nobody walks out of Wal-Mart and gives each other a high five and says, "Let's go do that again!" We have to make sure that it is fun to get a rockin' deal – not just value, but a rockin' deal. At the heart of all that is connecting people.'

This is the philosophy of eBay: the understanding that people love – just love – hunting down a bargain, and getting a great deal. The Internet is about using search to bring together buyers and sellers – no one does this better than eBay. Indeed, many small business people now do most of their trade on eBay.

eBay charges sellers a small fee and this is its main source of income. Unlike many other Internet start-up companies it is now generally very profitable, although it recorded a third quarter loss in late 2007 with the poor performance of its acquisition of Skype. But in 2006–07, eBay looked on course to record over $6 billion in revenue and healthy net margins.

eBay today has a presence in 37 markets and in 2011, the total value of goods sold on eBay was $68.6 billion – more than $2,100 every second and, through all its activities, eBay enabled transactions totalling over $175 billion.

Sources: Diaz, A. (2007) 'eBay', *Creativity*, 15 (11), p. 80. Wolfe, D. (2007) 'eBay profit up as PayPal volume grows', *American Banker*, 20 July, 172 (139), p. 9.

8.3.3 Buyer controlled sites: example – the reverse auction house

Auction houses, such as eBay, are the traditional auction model of consumers bidding against each other for a product or service.

In a reverse auction the consumer names the price they want for a particular product and sticks to it. The reverse auction house then surfs the Web and looks for the product at that price. If they find it, the consumer is contracted to buy. Perhaps the best known supplier of these services is **priceline.com** – a US based organisation, best known for its 'name-your-own-price' model for flights, rental cars and hotels, plus its quirky William Shatner anchored commercials. However, the model may not be transferable to every sector. Consumers are not well equipped to name their own price for a house mortgage, nor would they wish to want to name a price for a big-ticket item like a car and then be committed to buying it.

Exhibit 8.8 Alternative views of e-commerce – the bubble about to burst?

Everyone has their views on the future of e-commerce.

According to this opinion piece, e-commerce is a 'retrogressive step dressed up as modernism'. 'If in the dark ages they'd invented the idea of shopping by staring into a glass icon and looking at foggy images of things you'd like to buy, picking them, and then waiting for a messenger to bring them to you, today we'd be excitedly welcoming the dawn of walk-in shops, where you can see the goods, feel and touch them and walk out with them.'

Morris (2000) describes e-commerce as 'no more than glorified catalogue shopping' (mail order), and extols the joys of spontaneous supermarket shopping in which the customers make any number of on-the-spot decisions about purchases based on what they pass in the aisles. Morris believes that the computer will become a place where only the basics are bought on-line, while we go shopping for the 'interesting stuff'.

The conclusion is that neither e-commerce nor high-street shopping will dominate. The likely end-game is a sensible, genuinely progressive amalgam of on-line and real shops, or 'clicks and mortar'. Then at last, as one US e-commerce expert put it, the letter 'e' can return to its rightful place as the fifth letter of the alphabet.

Source: Based on Morris, G. (2000) 'Hall of infamy (no. 40 – e-commerce)', *Guardian*, 11 February.

Another model of business that was tried during the dot-com bubble was 'community' or 'aggregate' buying. Here, groups of consumers got together in order to increase their buying power by offering companies economies of scale. For example, Internet start-up company Adabra offered a product for sale (let us say a video player) for a set period, say a week. The price Adabra paid the supplier depended on the number of buyers. Adabra's website exhibited the common high street price for the goods, say £300. The site also displayed a number of other prices, all lower than £300. Buyers logged on and chose the price they would ideally like to pay. The 'gamble' they took was that if they chose too low a price, there might not be enough buyers at that low price. If enough buyers chose, say, £250, the price was forced down to this level because enough sales at this price will still be profitable to the seller, and to Adabra, which pocketed the difference between the buyer's price and a price it negotiated with the supplier.

Adabra did not survive the dot-com crash, however, and other community buying sites such as **LetsBuyIt.com** have been forced to re-examine their business model. The case for aggregate buying is uncertain: whether this is down to flaws in the business model or mistakes made by operators is uncertain.

So far in this chapter we have examined the growth of the Internet and begun to look at how companies use it. One of the strategic issues raised has been the way in which the Internet encourages different types of marketplace – buyer, seller or neutral. We are now ready to look in more detail at the distinctive features and benefits of the Internet, before turning to the impact of the Internet on direct marketing. In these sections you may like to note the emergence of the other major strategic planks of e-business: the Internet as a channel, possibly with new types of intermediaries growing in the future, and the Internet as a network that brings groups of people together.

| 8.4 | Distinctive features and benefits of the Internet |

'The most radical difference (of the net) is the shift in power from the merchant to consumer.'

(The Economist, 10 May 1997)

8.4.1 The Internet has the power to change the rules

When it first arrived, Bill Gates called the Web 'friction-free capitalism'. What did he mean by this? In traditional, non-Internet markets, there is what might be termed high 'transaction isolation'. In other words, we as consumers buy without full knowledge of alternatives. Consumers often have a high inertia barrier (we are too lazy to change suppliers), so businesses can take advantage of our laziness and charge high prices knowing that we will not look around too much. In many cases big companies will exploit their power of greater distribution.

On the Internet the leverage of big companies using their 'distribution' power does not exist, although they have resources to leverage marketing power by spending more search advertising, for example. On-line customers are much more likely to undertake an information search for different alternatives (or use an agent to search for them: see later for a description of 'infomediaries'), because of the ease of searching on the Web. In addition, companies themselves can benefit from the slickness of the Web to lower their own costs with suppliers, delivering a highly efficient value chain to the consumer. These efficiencies and ease of comparison mean that the Internet, therefore, comes close to providing a 'pure' marketplace – i.e. one in which any business that provides similar content to competitors, but at a higher price, will go bust. In its early days, sampler and business guru Gary Hamel (1998) described the Internet as a 'noose for mediocrity'.

The Internet is also 'quick'. This has enabled a new breed of dedicated e-commerce businesses to emerge. Companies like **www.lastminute.com** and **www.priceline.com** rely on speed and flexibility for their operations. They use the speed of the Web to quickly establish customers' needs in, say, airline flights, and then search quickly to pull together the best last minute deals for them. Here, the supplier uses the net to match supply with demand in a way that is convenient for the customer, and links easy buying with the special feature of the Internet as a giant marketplace that is dynamic. Internet businesses are easily dissolved and re-formed – therefore the Internet favours companies that can think and change quickly. 'Nimble businesses' have been more successful than those slow to change.

As a 'many to many' medium, the Internet enables 'consumers to co-operate with each other' to get the best deals, something that has had an uncertain start but may grow in the future. As we saw earlier with eBay and **www.priceline.com**, live auctions are much more likely, again utilising the ability of the net to bring lots of suppliers and buyers together easily and quickly.

Having been introduced to the radical nature of the Internet, we are now ready to examine its individual features in more detail.

8.4.2 Features

Customer control

If we view the Internet as a medium or channel to market, and therefore compare it to other media, the Internet has one unique characteristic: customers control when, or indeed if, they are exposed to the advertising/selling message. Customers also know that they can leave the site at any time and return at their own convenience, without having to make or break any social relationships with salespeople along the way. Contrast this with traditional advertising followed by a visit to, say, a high street clothes store. In this scenario, a significant amount of control lies with the company rather than the customer.

Information flows upwards and sideways from customers as well as downwards to customers

In traditional markets, information is passed 'down' to customers from companies taking advantage of their control of the act of going to market. However, the Internet's low cost of access allows customers (or agents acting on their behalf) to take control of going to market. In addition, the Internet caters for easy 'sideways' information flows, allowing customers to talk to each other, forming communities of interest extremely quickly (Mitchell, 2000). Instead of one type of marketplace, where companies tell customers what they have to sell and customers react or choose as a result, we now have three types of marketplace on-line, as we saw earlier.

The Internet is like a flea market

If you have ever browsed amongst the antiques in a street market on a Sunday morning, you are in a flea market. One of its characteristics is that a flea market will attract casual passers-by who see the idea of wandering through the market as a pleasurable activity. Belk *et al.* (1988) suggested that the Internet is analogous to such an entity. For Zwass (1998), the challenge for business is how to engage users by promoting the transition from casual browser to active buyer.

Disintermediation and reintermediation

One of the most significant impacts of the Web has been the emergence of its disintermediating and reintermediating effect. The roles of established intermediaries (such as supermarkets) are reduced or eliminated, to be replaced by new intermediaries between a business and its customers. For the firm, this has the effect of increasing the speed of products and services to the marketplace. This is something we will examine more closely later in this chapter in the section examining the links between direct marketing and the Internet.

The Internet offers freedom from economies of scale for smaller businesses

Website and e-mail facilities help to reduce the costs of establishing physical distribution channels for businesses (O'Connor and Galvin, 1997). For small businesses the net offers true equality in the sense that it allows open access. As a result, the Internet site of one business cannot drown out that of another; each has a unique position and can be accessed by all net users.

Ubiquity and omnipresence, or 'it's always there and it's all there'

The Internet is a medium and marketplace in one – it allows buyers and suppliers to come together and transact. It can be accessed at any time by the customer, so that customers know that, if they want to buy an airline ticket at 10 o'clock on a Saturday night, they can do so.

Transparency

The Internet acts like a shopping centre in that customers can make price/value 'comparisons' very quickly. Indeed, the Internet is probably superior to a shopping centre in terms of speed and convenience of making these comparisons. Everything is just a 'mouse click' away. Increasingly, in markets such as tourism customers are able to treat the Internet as a one-stop shop, in which they can gather information, make comparisons, then make a purchase all in one session. It is this ease of comparison which means that an 'average' offer will, therefore, not survive – as Hamel and Sampler (1998) predicted, the Internet is a noose for mediocrity.

Convenience

We need to make the basic but important point that a large proportion of the population now spend some or a lot of their day in front of or near a computer. Therefore, customers using the Internet have proximity to it as a buying channel for much of their day. This suits the (often random) way in which people suddenly think 'Heck, I need to check my bank account', or 'Damn, I forgot to order that wine for the weekend'. For people who are 'time poor' (well-off people with busy jobs) or are less organised, and whose buyer behaviour is convenience driven, the Internet is unrivalled as a convenient channel.

Interactive capability

Early Internet academic writers Hoffman and Novak (1997) pointed out that the Internet allows a change from a one-to-many model of communication (e.g. TV advertising) to a one-to-one or even many-to-many model (e.g. interactive 'chatlines' on the net). This allows for significant interaction between customer and firm. For example, banks may offer customers the chance to record or plan their finances, while bookstores such as **www.Amazon.com** allow customers the chance to search for titles quickly, and to post their own reviews on the site. Dell Computers uses the Internet as a way of displaying help manuals.

Speed

Weiber and Kollman (1998) distinguished between traditional businesses and cyberspace business in terms of the grounds on which they compete for competitive advantage. While traditional businesses compete on cost and quality grounds, Web based businesses can compete according to the speed with which they gather and use information, and the quality of the information they gather.

Improved service for repeat customers using the Internet linked to a marketing database

If you access the Tesco (a UK supermarket) website to take advantage of its direct delivery service, you will find that it takes a few hours to key in all your shopping when you do it for the first time. However, the next time you may find it only takes a few minutes. The database has saved your previous shopping list and now you just need to adjust your needs to suit. The service for existing customers has, therefore, improved markedly. In 2007, **www.Tesco.com** announced increased margins of over 25 per cent – **www.Tesco.com** is now one of the most successful supermarket on-line operations in the world. The Internet provides an easy link between the customer and the company database, so enabling a personalised service to be provided.

Companies can further improve their on-line service to existing customers using e-mail. In this way firms can correspond outbound with existing customers in the same way as with direct mail or the telephone. An in-depth comparison of e-mail and websites with other media is provided later (Chapter 11).

Other examples of this kind of one-to-one service come from some banks, which may provide interactive on-line services similar to a First Direct style operation. However, in general note that, as yet, tailored delivery of services or products is still a rarity.

The Internet can lower the cost base of the business

Fraser *et al.* (2000) pointed out the importance of the Web to internal workings as well as customer interfaces. They felt that intranets and extranets, as well as the Internet, will facilitate lower costs in purchasing departments.

Fraser *et al.* addressed the fundamental question of costs and benefits of e-commerce solutions for businesses. They listed the following sources of competitive advantage for e-commerce:

1 A reduction in intermediation costs associated with wholesale and retail activities

2 Lowering of supply and logistics costs by curbing time and effort in these operations

3 Improved information gathering and processing that allow improved management of the supply chain

4 Lowering of the costs of gathering customer information, allowing greater chance for effective marketing

However, there may be a disadvantage in being the first mover in the use of e-commerce because of the high costs of establishing capital and human resources. In other words, Internet technologies have high 'learning' costs. The dot-com crash illustrated this: many first movers do not succeed.

In summary, e-commerce is a new paradigm or a way of doing business that generates its own rules. Direct distribution is part of this, but the real heart of it is that the Internet acts as a highly efficient marketplace, which dynamically brings buyers and all suppliers together. Therefore, buyers and suppliers can all react to each other and the deal or offer changes depending on demand and supply. This replicates a town centre market, but on a global scale. The system has even more power from the convenience and control that it gives to the customer.

We can now turn to a more in-depth analysis of how database marketing techniques 'overlap' with e-commerce.

8.5   The impact of the Internet on direct and database marketing

This section discusses the impact of the Internet in changing the very heart of direct marketing concepts. As this is potentially complex, we will divide up the discussion under two headings: 'What has changed?' and 'What stays the same?'

8.5.1   What has changed? Power is shifting to consumers

In a far reaching article written at the turn of the century, Mitchell (2000) went a long way towards explaining the impact of the Internet on direct and database marketing. He pointed out the implications of the Internet's ability to transfer power from sellers to buyers. As we have seen, direct marketing strategy is predicated around the idea of customer management. Here, companies use their transaction histories with customers to understand customers' present needs and predict their future needs – what they want, when they want it, how much they would be worth to the company and, therefore, how much discount the company could offer so that both sides win. Mitchell said that with the new world order the Internet is enabling customers who will no longer put up with being 'managed'. In this old world, the power in the relationship lay squarely with suppliers, who would decide who to target, what offer to make and when to pull out of the deal if it did not suit them and so on. In the Internet driven marketplace, customers (via agents such as infomediaries) will have the upper hand. The infomediary is potentially the most powerful of all the new Internet models of doing business, and is discussed later.

There are a number of skills of database marketing that do not transfer well to e-commerce. These include modelling, segmentation, targeting and so on. This is because the dominant paradigm so far has been the use of websites to attract inbound customers, rather than the use of e-mail to target customers proactively. In other words, as we said earlier, 'it is the customer not the company who controls the contact'. Ironically, the importance of traditional advertising may increase as the company will have to rely on keeping its name in the customer's mind. The firm will also have to make sure its offer is competitive.

Although it is still relatively early days, perhaps we can tentatively make some predictions about likely segmentation approaches on the Internet. For e-mail driven proactive marketing, there is every reason to believe that transaction segmentations based on the customers' value to the company, and needs from it, should be possible. It will depend, firstly, on the company's ability to link sales data from the Web traffic to a customer based database and, secondly, on customers' willingness to be targeted by e-mail.

For inbound traffic on the website, customers 'will segment themselves' based on their needs and wants – all the company can do is position correctly, offer value competitively and make itself as attractive as possible.

How does this power shift affect acquisition and retention on-line?

e-acquisition and e-retention

The ability to find different options quickly, and easily choose between them, has shifted market power to consumers. Take the idea of customer acquisition. It now makes more sense to talk of prospect customers acquiring companies rather than the other way round. At the heart of the acquisition 'problem' is search – prospective buyers and sellers finding each other so that a transaction can potentially be done. This process – the process of going to market – has traditionally been led by the marketer, but on-line search engines are turning this on its head, allowing the prospective consumer to control the searching. This awesome searching power, dominated by Google, has changed the business landscape. Consumers have learnt a new language of key words that they deploy with increasing efficiency as they grow more used to search engines.

So, is traditional acquisition marketing dead? No. It is true that consumers will have no need of acquisition marketing, if they broadly know what they are searching for. But we are still open to hearing about deals – provided they are relevant. So, let us say we are a supplier in the market to find new customers for adventure holidays, mountaineering, extreme sports and so on. We need to understand the journey that is made by our prospects and ourselves in getting together. Who leads the search? As we have noted already, prospects are increasingly searching for us: so, prospects will type 'adventure holidays' into a search engine such as Google and see what is found. This is fine – maybe we can place an ad with Google search, and optimise our website to improve our chances of the generic search placing us near the top. We can place links on affiliate sites so that searchers find us via them. Or pay influential portals in the vacation sector to place us. But, more strategically, we should also try to drive traffic proactively on to our website. Maybe we promote a special offer, using off-line media to encourage 'handraisers' to visit our site (see Figure 8.2).

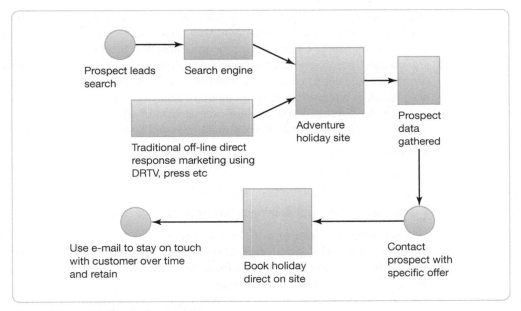

Figure 8.2 e-aquisition and e-retention

e-retention relies on the same principles as any other kind of retention – extensively discussed earlier (Chapter 6). Customers will prefer to stay with one supplier if that supplier offers superior value. On-line, this may mean making offers to the customer to make their life easier; using e-mail to make timely offers, offering click- through links to make navigation easier, reducing the hassle of search. Internet based businesses may have some cost and price advantages, though this is by no means a 'given'. A popular perception has built up that Internet goods are cheaper, but this may not be the case in all markets. What has happened is that some high profile 'low cost' brands have based themselves on the Internet: easyJet or Direct Line spring to mind. These have helped build a perception of low cost/price, which of course will help retain customers. Price comparison sites have been another force placing power in the hands of consumers. Those who want to 'shop around' will use these sites. So, the convenience of the Internet is a two-edged sword for retention: sellers can easily stay in touch with existing customers; but existing customers can easily be tempted away.

8.5.2 Infomediaries

We have just argued that convenience is a double-edged sword. The same is true for choice and control. In spite of the power of search engines, consumers still sometimes do not have the time, patience or perhaps ability to work out the best offer to suit them. What many of them will want is to take advantage of the better value the Internet can offer them, but seek help in doing this. This opens up the field to a new type of player called infomediaries. In fact, these were first proposed by Hagel and Singer (1999) and Mitchell (2000) but have yet to reach their potential. But they are very important to us in direct marketing and so we will describe them in detail here.

Traditional intermediaries, such as brokers, act on behalf of the sellers rather than consumers. In contrast, infomediaries will act on behalf of consumers. They take on consumers as clients and gather data about their needs across a wide variety of categories. They would also record data about purchases made through themselves and, hence, increase their knowledge over time about consumers, in the same way as a traditional database. Infomediaries are in a much more powerful position than traditional database marketers, however, as they can record data across competitors and across sectors, getting a holistic picture of consumers' purchases and preferences. Infomediaries may also issue smart cards and credit cards for use in the physical world, enabling more information to be gathered.

It could be predicted then that infomediaries will offer the following services:

- Lowering customers' search 'costs' – probably time
- Finding the best value for customers
- Shielding customers from unwanted marketing messages
- Leveraging customers' combined buying power in a reverse auction model

What infomediaries can also do is to get back towards Peppers and Rogers' (1993) one-to-one concept, discussed earlier (see Chapter 6), but this time 'act on behalf of the customer'. They can gather information from customers about their preferences and how much they have to spend. They can then react at that time to scour the Web for the best deal to meet that need, as above. But they can also then do the 'database marketing' bit, which is to forecast the future needs of the customer and proactively scour the Web for deals for the customer. This all-sector model has yet to emerge but, within a single sector, one example of this is **Amazon.com**, which uses the customers' travels through its website to gather information on that individual in relation to book sales. The next time the customer accesses the site, they get information on the company's best deals for that customer. In a sector such as where new products are rife and there is a vast array of choice, this kind of marketing makes sense.

The impact of infomediaries on suppliers

If the efficiency of the process proves to be high (depending on consumer participation and the ability of infomediaries to deal with large amounts of data in an individual manner) then the costs of going to market for partner firms should also be lowered. As a channel to market, infomediaries may be attractive if they can lower the cost per sale, because response will be higher than the firms would get using traditional methods. However, it may also be that firms' existing customers may be encouraged by infomediaries to shop around for deals and, therefore, while acquisition costs may be lowered, retention costs may be higher, depending on the competitiveness of the supplier.

The infomediary market at present

At the time of writing, infomediation is starting to happen, but as yet is undeveloped. The most exciting initiative to date is probably that of **moneysupermarket.com**, which is worth a visit. This is a cross-sector price comparison site that also offers a community element. This promotes 'money supermarket' as a consumer champion acting on behalf of customers rather than business vested interests. So, they have site features such as 'ask the expert', 'jargon buster', 'discussion forums', 'hot topics', and weekly polls asking questions like 'Do you feel that energy prices are acceptable?' (This could be argued as a bit of a cheap shot – the answer most people will give is of course 'no', but this 'voting' on-line requires e-mail sign-up, and so is a device to build a database). All of this positions **moneysupermarket.com** as a very useful site for prospects. Click-through links are provided to buyer sites on the basis of reviews or searches for 'the best deals' provided by **moneysupermarket.com**.

A small fee is paid to **moneysupermarket.com** for each click-through. The consumer has saved time and effort on the search, and may trust **moneysupermarket.com** to conduct a more effective search than the consumer would do on their own. Thus, the basis of the infomediary is born, although there is more to the concept than this – see Exhibit 8.9.

Possible problems for the infomediary concept

Mitchell's vision of personal information management looks compelling. He may be ahead of his time: there has been little sign to date of big players willing to set up a business model as he describes. If one were established, the key to success would be whether consumers saw enough value in volunteering their information. As Mitchell points out, the key is trust: at present, consumer trust levels in businesses holding information about them are low. Time will tell if this changes.

The next major change to consider is the Internet's impact on loyalty.

Exhibit 8.9 (Direct) marketing needs a paradigm shift: the rise of personal information management

This exhibit is based heavily on the work of Alan Mitchell; see Alan's website **www.rightsideup.net** *for more details of the arguments presented here.*

In the land of marketing, the sun still revolves around the earth

In order to understand what is wrong with so much of today's commercial marketing, we need to go back a step. Successful marketing happens when richer win–wins are achieved at lower cost. A win–win is when both the consumer and the marketer are happy with the value they both get from the purchase, the price paid, and from the experience of the transaction. Unfortunately most marketing, as practised, replaces this with the assumption that the purpose of marketing is to improve the performance of the company. It sees all outcomes as emanating from its own actions: marketing is what marketers 'do to' consumers, who simply react and respond to marketers' initiatives. 'Better marketing' means getting more of the responses we want. This sets marketing on the road of seeking to be more 'effective' at changing customer behaviours and attitudes (to deliver greater wins to itself). Sometimes, by happy coincidence, this works: the times when marketing is successful are when what marketers do aligns very well with what customers want. But because marketers see success in terms of what they do to customers, rather than in terms of alignment, they cannot distinguish between actions of theirs that align and actions of theirs that do not align. So they are continually mystified as to why some things 'work' and others do not.

Figure 8.3 sums up the thesis. The pale blue circle represents the sphere of corporate activity (including marketing). This is where marketers are focused on improving their own 'performance'. The darker blue circle represents the sphere of consumer activity and potential consumer wins.

Because the corporate sphere is only focused on its own 'wins' it is oblivious to the parts of the darker blue circle that do not overlap with its interests. And because it does not see the darker blue circle, it cannot therefore distinguish between the darkest blue (win–win) area, and the pale blue (no-benefit-for-the-consumer) area. From its point of view it is all pale blue. It is all just 'marketing activity': doing stuff to and at customers. And it is an unending puzzle why some marketing activities seem to work so well and some do not.

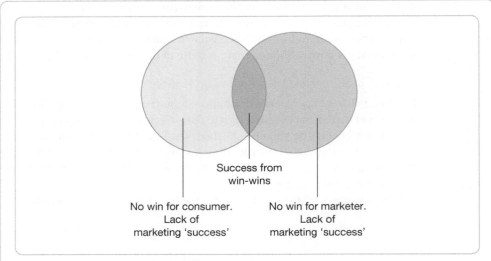

Figure 8.3 Lack of win–win overlap for markets and consumers

How can we avoid this seller-centric inefficiency? Mitchell suggests a new way of doing marketing that he calls Personal Information Management.

The future of direct marketing? 'Personal information management'

Let us think about this. What if individuals were incentivised to . . .?

- volunteer information about themselves
- collect and store information about their lives, attitudes and transactions
- keep this information up-to-date and accurate
- make this information available to organisations

How many benefits could be unleashed, for both individuals and organisations, if this happened? How many misunderstanding and conflicts could be avoided or resolved?

Alan Mitchell's idea is to deploy a new service that he calls Personal Information Management Services – PIMS for short – to help individuals collect, store, protect, analyse, use, trade and exchange, and maximise the value of personal information for and on behalf of the source of that data: the individual (see Figure 8.4).

Personal data management

The first pivotal departure point for PIMS is the simple and obvious notion of individuals as builders and managers of their own personal data.

There is nothing new here. We all collect, store and access personal data, such as telephone numbers, addresses, diary appointments, and transaction records, such as insurances – and we fume and fret if we lose this data. But increasingly that data is going digital. And we are collecting more and more of it, and using it for more and more purposes.

This is the foundation for PIMS: the simple need to manage personal data and to access and use the knowledge it contains. But we also want to do more with our data, and to exercise more control over how this data is used and who uses it for what purposes.

And that leads us to some more building blocks.

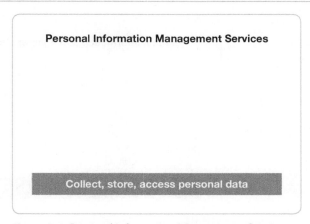

Figure 8.4 Personal Information Management Services

Security and identity verification

See Figure 8.5. This is an absolute prerequisite of everything that follows. Individuals have to know their data is secure, and organisations using this data have to know that the data relates to the person it says it does.

Filtering and blocking services

See Figure 8.6. The next pillar is blocking, filtering and editing services.

On the marketing front, many individuals are sick and tired of being bombarded by intrusive, irrelevant marketing messages, which they have to pay for in the products and services they buy.

In the USA, 69 per cent of consumers now say they would like a service that helps them 'block, skip or opt out of' receiving marketing messages.

By protecting users' anonymity and by using configurable firewalls and so on, PIMS will help individuals ensure they only receive the incoming information and messages that 'they' value – that add value for the receiver rather than the sender.

But even more important is that PIMS will also block unauthorised third party access to individuals' personal data, to ensure privacy and confidentiality – and therefore trust.

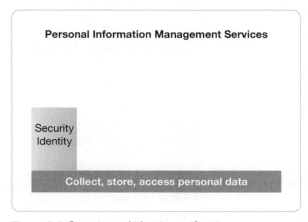

Figure 8.5 Security and identity verification

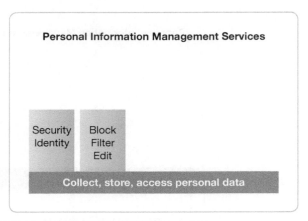

Figure 8.6 Filtering and blocking services

By doing so, they will help individuals assert more control over what information they do wish to divulge to whom, for what purposes. Which leads to the next key building block.

Search

At the same time PIMs will help individuals enrich their knowledge and information by helping them search for and retrieve the information that is useful to them.

Search helps to underline an important point – that PIMs are personal services that earn their keep by helping individuals achieve what they want to achieve (see Figure 8.7).

Search underlines this point because search processes are driven by the purposes of the individual, not the organisations the individual deals with. And the process of search is under the individual's control: the individual, not an outside organisation, decides on the content of the search and its timing.

But search is not only an information gathering exercise. It is also an information 'generating' exercise. While transaction histories tell you what you have done, search histories tell you what you like to do. One other thing about search: it is driven by volunteered, personal data, and the commercial value of this data is huge. Search reveals – instantly and cheaply – what no corporate database, data-mining tool or CRM algorithm can ever reveal. What individuals'

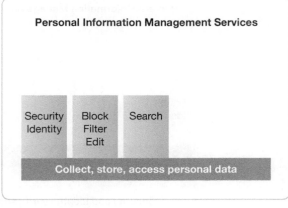

Figure 8.7 Search

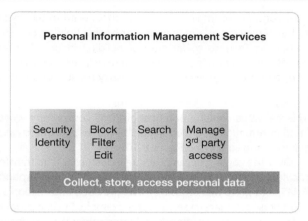

Figure 8.8 Manage third-party access

'intentions' are in real time. Not what I 'might' do tomorrow, or what I 'might' be interested in but what I want to do, now.

Which is why it is single handedly turning the world of marketing upside down. And why, on the back of it, Google is now the biggest media company in the world in terms of market capitalisation.

Manage third-party access
The other side of blocking is 'filtering', allowing chosen parties access to those parts of my personal data that I am willing to divulge on the clear and specific understanding that these data are to be used in a way that I understand – and that brings a clearly identifiable benefit to me (see Figure 8.8).

Business model-wise, this means that PIMS will not only help individuals maximise and trade the value of their 'intentions', they will trade 'permissions' – permissions to organisations to access and use specified fields of personal data, and to communicate on the basis of this data.

Personal publishing
See Figure 8.9. PIMS will also help individuals publish data, when and if they want to. This is not just billions of blogs. But potentially valuable information about wants, needs and

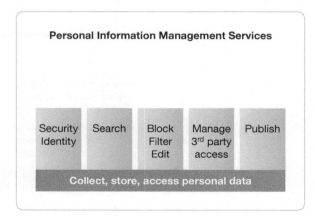

Figure 8.9 Personal publishing

intentions. For example, information that I want to sell my car or my house; or that I intend to buy a new car or a new house, or book a holiday, and so on.

But the features so far are just building blocks. The real interest, and value, is what comes next – which is using this data to help individuals maximise the value of this information, both for themselves and third-party product and service providers.

Maximising the value of personal data

The real value creating potential of PIMS comes from what we can do with this accumulated information to enrich people's lives, to spur the creation of ever better products and services, and so on (see Figure 8.10).

Over the coming decades, entire industries will be transformed by PIMS as, increasingly, providers configure the services they have to offer around the information contained in PIMS, and go to market using PIMS provided information and channels.

In personal financial services, for example, PIMS will not only provide information about individuals' plans and intentions – information that no financial service provider's corporate database can ever access – they will also provide a genuine 'single customer view'. Not the view that sellers have of their – and only their – transactions with that individual, but all the individual's transactions with many different providers. Again this is information that no individual provider can ever gain access to.

The data provided by the PIM service provider then, will not only be much more up-to-date and accurate. By adding in the volunteered information of the individual's personal plans, preferences and priorities it will offer service providers the information they really need to construct a service around that individual's particular needs.

The same goes for health services. And for education. And for public services. And for media and entertainment. And for manufacturing – think of customised products and services made to order. And for retailing, driven increasingly by 'if you like this you might like that' and 'if you already have this, you might need that' recommendations.

A catalyst of change

See Figure 8.11.

A paradigm shift

Stepping back a bit, the big picture is this. For the past 100 years, in information and knowledge management terms wealth has been created by producers applying accumulated

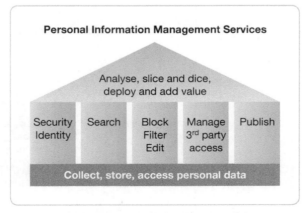

Figure 8.10 Maximising the value of personal data

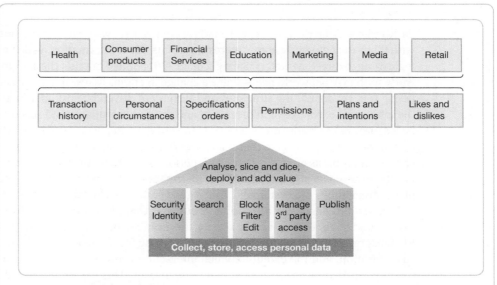

Figure 8.11 A catalyst of change

knowledge about raw materials, technologies and processes to make things. They then distributed information about what they had made to potential customers to organise and stimulate demand (what we now call marketing).

Wealth creation was driven by corporate information and knowledge.

With the emergence of Personal Information Management services, the centre of value creating gravity is shifting. Increasingly, effective value creation will start by gathering knowledge and information about the specific shape, nature and extent of demand from individuals and organising and configuring the provision of products and services on the basis of this information.

Personal information will become the 'fuel' that drives efficient, effective wealth creation; and PIMS will become the fuel's extractors and refiners, using and 'selling' this fuel on behalf of its owners: individuals.

Source: Alan Mitchell, see **www.rightsideup.net**.

8.5.3 The reduced importance of loyalty programmes

In an early article on the subject, Evans and Wurster (1997) contended that as it becomes easier for customers to switch from one supplier to another – something that is now commonplace on the net – the competitive value of traditional approaches, such as one-stop shopping and established relationships, will drop. They predicted that cross-selling would become more difficult. In fact, with a crack of doom appearing behind them and lightning flashing, they intoned that, if this scenario became reality, the entire concept of customer loyalty to one company may need re-examining.

An alternative view is that, as the trend of customers buying from remote sources increases, the importance of branding may grow, as trust in intangible suppliers becomes more important. Further light was shed by Yang and Peterson (2004) who found that on-line companies that strive for customer loyalty should focus primarily on 'satisfaction and perceived value'. No surprises there then. Of course the Internet makes switching easier – so loyalty levels to one supplier are likely to drop as consumers switch about. But, if you provide great value, consumers will stick with you.

8.5.4 The new role of customer information

Early writers about the Internet did not have our perspective of a decade or more of experience with it but they did make some interesting points about information, which are of great strategic value to direct marketers. Sahay *et al.* (1998) pointed out that the shift from the physical world to the virtual world necessitates a change in emphasis towards information based marketing (i.e. the marketing strategies and tactics are driven by customer interactions) where the interactive exchange of information, and the content, quality and speed of responses can be a source of competitive advantage. Meanwhile, Walters and Lancaster (1999) contended that 'information is the glue that holds together the structure of all businesses. A company's value chain consists of all the activities it performs to design, produce and market its product. But the value chain also includes all the information that flows within a company and its suppliers, distributors and customers'. This is good stuff for us in database marketing to ponder.

Walters and Lancaster also pointed out that there is a trade-off between information 'reach' and 'richness'. Reach is simply the number of people exchanging information. Richness refers to the amount of information going from sender to receiver, the extent of its customisation, and the extent to which interaction is possible. The richer the information, the more difficult it is to manage in a mass market. This has underpinned the difficulties that companies have had in implementing one-to-one marketing.

As we enter the world of 'big data' this still has not happened, but eventually new technology or a breakthrough company may force increased richness at decreased cost, allowing for more reach. This has huge implications for the company's supply chain, as shown in Figure 8.12. As we pointed out in our discussions about buyer control and infomediaries, the Internet allows customers to initiate the value chain process, and to infuse it with information about their needs. In theory this supports mass customisation: in practice this has been at a superficial level.

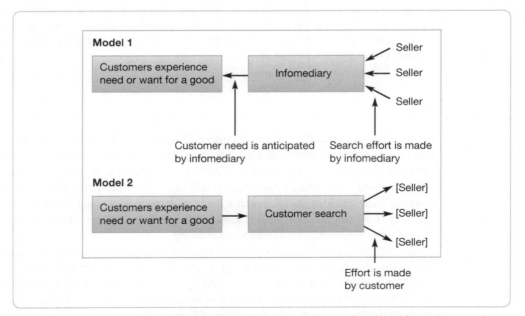

Figure 8.12 In the first model infomediaries add value by removing the effort of searching. In the second model customers do it themselves. In the first model the value chain is extended towards customers so they do less

8.5.5 Reactive versus database marketing

Mitchell (2007) discussed marketing as something that is mostly 'done' to customers in traditional markets. The Internet presents us with a new world in which customers are the 'marketers' who target companies – here companies react to customers' approaches. This debate raises a number of profound questions. On the Internet companies may still use transaction information to do data driven proactive marketing. The weakness of the customer management model in traditional database marketing has always been that it was a set of guesses, by the company, about customer needs (timing, product) and preferences for that supplier (driven by one company when maybe the customer uses others as well). Therefore, there is a lower chance of success in efficiently going to market – it is just the company 'giving itself a chance' rather than acting on firm instructions from the customer.

The power of the Internet may lie in its ability to mix up reactive and proactive marketing. Take **Amazon.com,** which lets the customer tell it when they are ready to enter the market for books (reactive marketing). It then proactively offers customers choices of books based on previous customer transactions (database driven proactive marketing). Customers then take back control and complete the transaction as it suits them, without pressure. This is a powerful way of doing business.

With infomediaries, another slight variation is possible. Customers may initiate the action by contacting the infomediary, which then takes over and manages the transaction on behalf of the customer. In this sense infomediaries are practising 'customer management', but with the customers' consent and knowledge. The customer has asked to be 'managed' because they see this management as a service to them: infomediaries are carrying out a search on their behalf.

8.5.6 Interactive marketing

Interactive marketing can be described as the firm and customers having multiple two-way dialogue in which information is shared. Note that this is essentially the same as one-to-one marketing! The speed, convenience and low cost of dialogue on the Internet led some early commentators (Hoffman and Novak, 1997; Hagel, 1999; Peters, 1998; and Spalter, 1995) to describe interactive marketing as the new marketing paradigm, superseding traditional transaction marketing or even relationship marketing. The extent to which this has come about is discussed later (Chapter 9) because it is through Web 2.0 – Facebook, Twitter, etc. – that interactive marketing has its greatest dynamism. Well before their time, Hoffman and Novak correctly predicted Web 2.0 developments when in 1996 they described the Internet as a many-to-many mediated environment, 'allowing a lot of people to talk to each other at the same time'. Compared to other media, this feature is unique and replicates a group of people meeting in a traditional community. Businesses try to capitalise on these many-to-many relationships. Sports websites are an example of this. Supporters have high involvement with their club and supporter 'chatlines' are extremely popular. A typical English Premier League site may get hundreds of thousands of 'hits' on the day after a game. Another example is the bookseller **Amazon.com,** which has a facility for consumers to post their own book reviews on site.

However, not all examples of interactive marketing are paradigm changes. We need to be careful not to lump in all aspects of business through the Internet as being wildly innovative, when much of it is merely replicating existing business practice. Examples include sellers letting customers fill their own baskets with goods. This may well be a good, efficient use of the Internet but, as a customer/supplier way of interacting, it is exactly the same as mail-order shopping. Another rather prosaic example of 'interactivity' might be an insurance company asking consumers for information and offering quotes for car and house insurance. While this is more interactive than using, say, direct mail (as you may get instant feedback from the supplier telling you that your order has been accepted), it is less interactive than the telephone.

Recording interactions for database marketing

Here we need to ask to what extent firms should attempt to record interactions, learn from them and then change the marketing to that individual as a result. Sceptics would argue that this is never going to be realistic as the management of such a process will be too expensive and customers do not require such minute segmentation. On the other hand, we have already seen from the work of Peppers (see earlier (Chapter 6) for a discussion of one-to-one marketing) that such ideas may have possibilities. Perhaps in between recording all interactions and studying them, and recording none at all may lie a reasonable compromise, so that there is some sort of two-way link between general customer interactions on the net and any database marketing activity driven by it. In this instance, there will be a need to distinguish transactions and non-transaction interactions, and to decide the worth of managing such data.

Now that we have examined what has changed or will change in direct marketing thinking as a result of the Internet, we can ask ourselves what will stay the same.

8.5.7 What will stay the same? The Internet as a 'direct channel'

Some product based companies are using the Internet as the front end of a direct distribution operation. Here the Internet replicates a mail-order style of business, and the skills of traditional direct marketing agencies will be vital (see Exhibit 8.10). Businesses whose service can be delivered electronically can go one step further and can distribute the product on-line as well. In some instances, we need to examine the motives of the companies: it may be that the customer is getting a better on-line service, but it is often the case that costs may be lowered, particularly for banks. When launched, it was reported that financial services company Egg was only taking on-line business because costs for on-line banking were four times lower than telephone transactions and ten times lower than high street branches.

Exhibit 8.10 Life at the sharp end – fulfilling an order efficiently is not easy

As e-commerce matures, performance levels for efficient delivery of products to customers slowly improves. In the early days of an on-line operation, getting the idea up and running and the website designed is just the start of the battle. Early Web based businesses found delivering on customer service promises just as difficult, if not more so, than their traditional counterparts. Companies found it very difficult to maintain consistency of service between different channels; for example, customers were accessing information on the website and then receiving a letter telling them something quite different.

One of the problems is the technology itself. The speed and convenience alluded to many times in this chapter tend to raise expectations for subsequent service. But, for those firms that get it right – Dell, Amazon, ASOS and so on, it is not the technology that makes the relationship work, but the people in the company wanting to respond to customers' needs. As all traditional direct marketers know, in a 'direct company' it is the back end of operations, fulfilment, that is the hardest part of customer service to get right; it is also the most important.

8.5.8 Capturing customer interactions and using this for knowledge management

The Internet has changed many things, but what is unlikely to change is the strategy of capturing customer interactions and learning from them. This may not help greatly in the company's targeting – since it is primarily the customer who targets – but it can help in areas such as supply chain management and purchasing operations, all of which feed into a more competitive value proposition.

Mitsubishi is one example of a company using the Internet to improve its supply chain management. Mitsubishi uses a dealer extranet to give dealers access to product updates and technical bulletins and also to allow on-line ordering and order tracking, handing the dealer full control of the ordering process.

Exhibit 8.11 Merging Web-based business and database marketing: ticket management systems for stadiums

Companies like Talent Sport specialise in sophisticated ticketing systems. Their systems are used by big-time sports clubs, particularly in the world of professional football. Talent Sport numbers Liverpool FC, Newcastle United FC, Panathinaikos FC, amongst its clients. They offer much more than just ticket sales and printing. On-line, telephone and face-to-face bookings are all managed as one; a customer database enables proactive targeting to be carried out, and features such as on-line virtual viewing of the stadiums enable supporters to choose their favourite view and then purchase tickets accordingly.

8.5.9 Testing

Another aspect of Internet business that replicates physical marketplaces is testing. This may be relatively trivial, for instance trying new creative approaches in website design. The testing process will lack the control obtained by testing using private media – direct mail and the telephone – because different websites will have to be tried one after the other. However, the speed and low costs of the Internet will bring other rewards: bookseller Waterstones has used its website to explore otherwise risky new ventures in new markets at low cost. It has tested books that in a bookshop environment may be considered too risky.

Summary

In this chapter we took a close look at what is likely to be a crucial development for direct marketers in years to come. The Internet has the power to alter the entire economic structures of many businesses, to change the way businesses are created and to change consumer behaviour, permanently.

Direct marketers should understand that the Internet revolution will not be based around customer data. Instead it will be based around customers taking more control of the buying process. The new home of direct and database marketing in the future may lie with agents such as Mitchells' Personal Information Management ideas helping customers, provided that such help is driven by customer data, in other words is proactive.

The context of data usage will also change. Transaction data will still be important but it may be that 'customer needs' will be expressed directly by the customer, removing the need for future purchases to be inferred from past purchases. Also, transaction data will encompass many companies rather than just one.

Strategically, developments such as the growth of infomediaries may have profound implications for database marketing. The next decade promises to be an interesting one!

QUESTIONS

1 As the marketing manager for an airline, how would you sum up the strengths and weaknesses of the following channels: travel agent, direct via a call centre and classified adverts; and the Internet?

2 Examine the following websites:

www.easyjet.com	www.dell.com	www.tesco.com
www.amazon.co.uk	www.priceline.com	www.ford.co.uk

Compare and contrast the features of each, and comment on how each company has used the functionality of the Internet to give themselves an advantage.

3 Click onto **Amazon.com**. Look at the associates and member page features. Take a close look and then ask yourself why they may be doing this from a data-gathering point of view. Does this make **Amazon.com** an infomediary? Discuss the implications for new business models.

4 Think of a business, leisure or pastime activity in which you may be involved at the moment. Using the tips you have picked up in this chapter, construct a Web based business idea for that sector, and then outline the features of the net that will help your business idea. Think about services as well as products. For example, a friend has moved from London to the Yorkshire Dales. He is considering setting up a website based, short break business for busy London executives, providing them with a no-hassle, two-day, mountain biking weekend in the Yorkshire Dales.

5 Take a look at the list of Internet features and benefits listed in the chapter. Which do you think will have the most profound effect in changing the way businesses operate? Explain why.

6 Imagine that you have decided to run a direct business on-line. What features would you want to include in your website to attract as many customers as possible, and maximise your revenue? Before you answer this, surf a number of Web addresses to look for ideas. Question 2 above contains a number of such sites.

References

Belk, R.W., Sherry, J.F. and Wallendorf, M.A. (1988) 'Naturalistic inquiry into buyer and seller behaviour at a swap meet', *Journal of Consumer Research,* 14 (4), pp. 449–70.

Berryman, K., Harrington, L., Layton-Rodin, D. and Rrerolle, V. (1998) 'Electronic commerce – three emerging strategies', *McKinsey Quarterly,* no 1, pp. 152–9.

Chaffey, D., Ellis-Chadwick, F., Mayer, R., and Johnston, K. (2006) *Internet Marketing, Strategy, Implementation, and Practice,* FT Prentice Hall, Harlow.

Chaffey, D., Ellis-Chadwick, F. (2012) *Digital Marketing*, FT Prentice Hall, Harlow.

Evans, P.B. and Wurster, T.S. (1997) 'Strategy and the new economics of information', *Harvard Business Review,* September/October, pp. 70–82.

Fraser, J., Fraser, N. and McDonald, F. (2000) 'The strategic challenge of electronic commerce', *Supply Chain Management,* 5 (1), p. 10.

Gwyther, M. (1999) 'Jewels in the Web', *Management Today,* London, November.

Hagel, J. (1999) 'Net gain: expanding markets through virtual communities', *Journal of Interactive Marketing,* 13 (1), pp. 55–65.

Hagel J. and Singer, M. (1999) *Net Worth,* Harvard Business School Press, Boston.

Hamel, G. and Sampler, G. (1998) 'The e-corporation: more than just Web-based, it's building a new industrial order', *Fortune,* 7 December.

Hoffman, D. and Novak, T. (1997) 'A new marketing paradigm for electronic commerce', *The Information Society,* 13 (1), pp. 43–54.

Jardine, A. (2000) 'Lastminute wonders', *Marketing,* London, 16 March.

Marketing Week (2000) 'The rapid impact of the Internet', 20 January, p. 40.

Mitchell, A. (2000) 'In one to one marketing, which one comes first?', *Interactive Marketing,* pp. 354–68.

Mitchell, A. (2007), 'Is it time for direct marketing to follow the trend and opt out?', *Marketing Week,* 26 July, 30 (30), pp. 18–19.

Morris, G. (2000) 'Hall of infamy (no. 40 – e-commerce)', *Guardian,* 11 February.

Murphy, D. (2000) 'The last minute waltz', *Marketing Business,* February, pp. 22–3.

O'Connor, J. and Galvin, E. (1997) *Marketing and Information Technology,* Financial Times Pitman Publishing, London.

Peppers, D. and Rogers, M. (1993) *The One-to-One Future,* Doubleday, New York.

Peters, L. (1998) 'The new interactive media: one-one but to whom?', *Marketing Intelligence and Planning,* 16 (1), pp. 22–30.

Rosier, B. (2000) 'What went so horribly wrong with **Boo.com**?', *Marketing,* London, 25 May.

Sahay, A., Gould, J. and Barwise, P. (1998) 'New interactive media: experts' perceptions of opportunities and threats for existing businesses', *European Journal of Marketing,* 32 (7–8), pp. 616–28.

Spalter, M. (1995) 'Maintaining a customer focus in an interactive age', in Forrest, E. and Mizerski, R. (eds) *Interactive Marketing, the future present,* AMA Publications, Chicago, ch. 12, pp. 163–87.

Uhrenbacher, S. and Therezien, L. (2000) 'Lastminute recruits two for Euro growth', *Marketing,* 13 January, p. 9.

Walters, D. and Lancaster, G. (1999) 'Using the Internet as a channel for commerce', *Management Decision,* 37 (10), p. 20.

Weiber, R. and Kollman, T. (1998) 'Competitive advantages in virtual markets – perspectives of information-based marketing in cyberspace', *European Journal of Marketing,* 32 (7–8), pp. 603–15.

Yang, Z. and Peterson, R. (2004) 'Customer perceived value, satisfaction, and loyalty: the role of switching costs', *Psychology & Marketing,* 21 (10), pp. 799–822.

Zwass, V. (1998) 'Structure and macro-level impacts of electronic commerce: from technological infrastructure to electronic marketplaces', **http://www.mhhe.com/business/mis/zwass/ecpaper. html** [Accessed 9 April 1999].

CASE STUDY

Dycem Ltd

The MD of Dycem, Mark Dalziel, had just jumped on the Tokyo–Heathrow plane. Seated comfortably, waiting for the plane to taxi, he had time to ponder what had just happened. His time in Japan had opened his eyes to just how hard it was going to be to expand his business. He suspected that the problem was that Dycem was very product led and had not considered in enough detail how its customers went about their buying process.

It was early 2007. With a presence in the UK, USA and most of Europe, in 2007 Dycem sought to further expand sales and distribution networks internationally. The question for Mark was: how could he take that next step to becoming a truly marketing-led firm?

Dycem Ltd is a classic small manufacturing firm based in Bristol in south-west England. The company is proud of being one of the few true manufacturing concerns still totally run within the UK – most having outsourced production overseas.

Dycem manufactures and sells specialist flooring products, designed to control contaminants such as dust and dirt. Dycem's customer base is composed of both large global blue-chips and SMEs, from a wide range of industries including pharmaceutical, medical device, healthcare, optical and automotive industries. Dycem's products are used predominantly but not exclusively in 'cleanrooms' and 'controlled environments'.

As manufacturers of specialist industrial flooring the company serves a diverse range of industries, which complicates its direct and on-line strategy.

The product range

Dycem's products are very good. Their top end product is called CleanZone. CleanZone Premier is a high performance contamination control zone designed to attract, collect and retain contamination, preventing particles and microbes from getting into a critical area.

Dycem offer ProtectaMat in the mid range. The ProtectaMat is a High Performance Contamination Control Zone designed to attract airborne particles to its surface and decontaminate soles of personnel shoes and booties. This contamination is held on the surface until cleaning takes place.

All Dycem's products are considered to be of higher specification than the generic 'tacky mat' low-price alternative offered by the corporate giants such as 3M and Johnson & Johnson. These competitors tend to offer loose-laid versions only. Dycem offer both

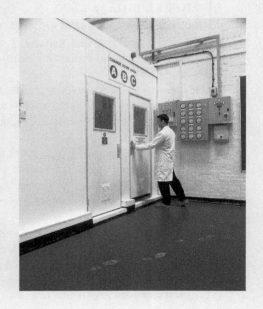

loose-laid mats and permanent fixed flooring systems. Dycem's products effectively offer peace of mind to firms for whom controlling the spread of dirt, virus or contamination is vital.

Strategic issues in 2007

As a smaller company, Dycem typically has limited resources, making it impossible to compete with corporate giants, who can open up overseas subsidiaries overnight and take on the appearances of a domestic company. The Five Forces analysis shown in Figure 8.13 illustrates Dycem's strengths and weaknesses in the market.

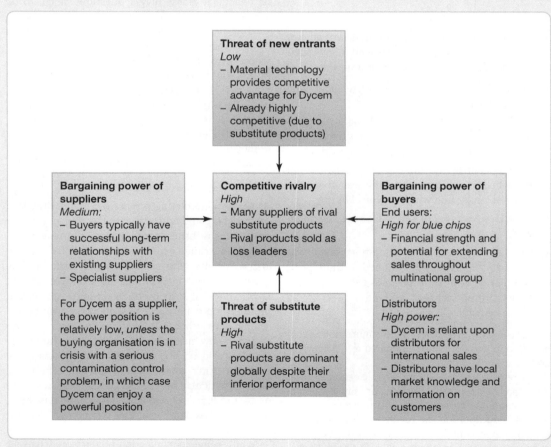

Figure 8.13 Five Forces Analysis of Dycem

Looking back to its roots, Dycem would regard itself as typical of most small companies. They typically start with just one route to market, often a direct or salesforce channel. Dycem's salesforce was an example of this. Since then, Dycem has established a reputation amongst its regular customers of selling superior product alternatives, and it has achieved a good level of success in many market sectors. However, it has been unable to make the transition to being the dominant product in any of its geographic markets or market sectors. The salesforce were very loyal to the top-of-range CleanZone and WorkZone products. These were sold using instant product demonstrations that were very effective with the visual, tacky feel of the product that gives a strong instant impression. But it was felt that there was more headroom for ProtectaMat sales.

Marketing was under used

Mark's initial meetings with his new marketing advisor from Bristol Business School confirmed a few things in his mind. These boiled down to the following:

- Dycem did not really know much about who their customers were.
- It was not clear why customers bought the products – what their motives were, or why they bought from Dycem rather than a cheaper competitor.
- There was little information about who bought and who did not buy, and even less about the decision maker unit within a typical buyer.
- The website was out of date, a bit tired and under used.
- The use of marketing communications was very light, being largely confined to trade press adverts that had cost thousands each year, were not monitored very well, and did not seem to be very successful.

The company had relatively little information about how Dycem was positioned compared to the competition in customers' minds.

There were implications for the role of communications and Dycem's media channel. For example, potential customers who were new to the category often required education on the fundamental principles of contamination control, and may not even be aware of how contamination affected their business. In contrast, more experienced customers, looking to modify their current products with a replacement, needed less education and already had a fairly clear idea of their needs.

How Dycem addressed the issues

Mark knew his local university – University of the West of England – offered 'Knowledge Transfer Partnerships' schemes, funded by the government's Technology Strategy Board, to help small businesses who may be able to make use of academic expertise. A KTP was set up with the Marketing Department of Bristol Business School with the initial intention of growing distributors for international sales, but the academic partner suggested that a more strategic approach – including managing customer contact across the business – could be beneficial. Some bigger questions began to be asked. Was the product line optimised? Was Dycem starting its marketing from a good understanding of its suspects (the broad market), their prospects (those who have signalled an interest but nothing more), and its customers (already bought and may buy more)? Was Dycem missing a lot of opportunities by confining itself to a well-trodden path of salesforce visits?

A rough plan was made in which the company re-thought their contact strategies and re-worked these around prospect and customer groups (Figure 8.14).

Integrating the website

As the new marketing project got underway Mark realised he could add power to the project by integrating his website operations into the new initiatives. He recruited a talented team of Web designers and assistants who started to ask some serious questions about integration. For example, should Dycem offer all of its products on-line? Are certain products more amenable to Web based promotion/selling than others? Do on-line channels provide access to new customers? And, crucially, how does Dycem avoid on-line channels taking sales away from the firm's conventional channels? The latter was of particular interest to Dycem because some of its products require installation and, as such, there is a considerable service component to these products.

Whilst some contamination products may be sold on-line, this was not ideal for Dycem because Dycem

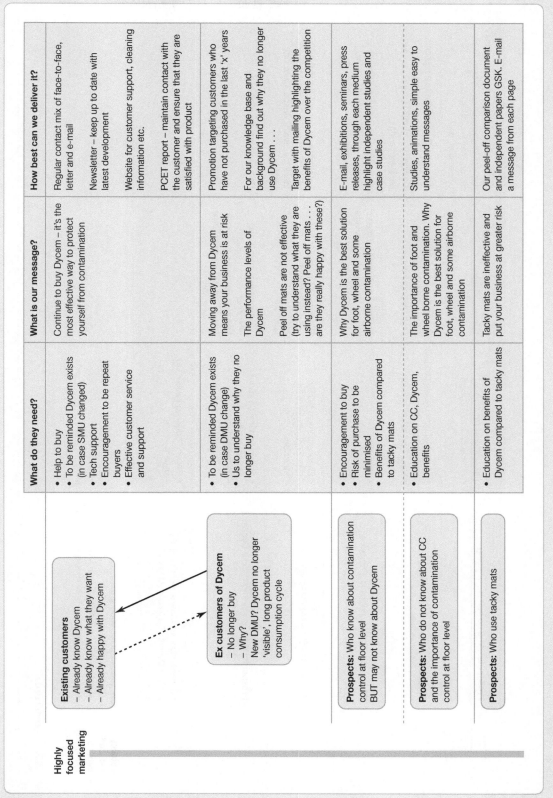

Highly focused marketing

	What do they need?	What is our message?	How best can we deliver it?
Existing customers – Already know Dycem – Already know what they want – Already happy with Dycem	• Help to buy • To be reminded Dycem exists (in case SMU changed) • Tech support • Encouragement to be repeat buyers • Effective customer service and support	Continue to buy Dycem – it's the most effective way to protect yourself from contamination	Regular contact mix of face-to-face, letter and e-mail Newsletter – keep up to date with latest development Website for customer support, cleaning information etc. PCET report – maintain contact with the customer and ensure that they are satisfied with product
Ex customers of Dycem – No longer buy – Why? New DMU? Dycem no longer 'visible', long product consumption cycle	• To be reminded Dycem exists (in case DMU change) • Us to understand why they no longer buy	Moving away from Dycem means your business is at risk The performance levels of Dycem Peel off mats are not effective (try to understand what they are using instead? Peel off mats . . . are they really happy with these?)	Promotion targeting customers who have not purchased in the last 'x' years For our knowledge base and background find out why they no longer use Dycem . . . Target with mailing highlighting the benefits of Dycem over the competition
Prospects: Who know about contamination control at floor level BUT may not know about Dycem	• Encouragement to buy • Risk of purchase to be minimised • Benefits of Dycem compared to tacky mats	Why Dycem is the best solution for foot, wheel and some airborne contamination	E-mail, exhibitions, seminars, press releases, through each medium highlight independent studies and case studies
Prospects: Who do not know about CC and the importance of contamination control at floor level	• Education on CC, Dycem, benefits	The importance of foot and wheel borne contamination. Why Dycem is the best solution for foot, wheel and some airborne contamination	Studies, animations, simple easy to understand messages
Prospects: Who use tacky mats	• Education on benefits of Dycem compared to tacky mats	Tacky mats are ineffective and put your business at greater risk	Our peel-off comparison document and independent papers GSK. E-mail a message from each page

Figure 8.14 Dycem marketing strategy

Prospects: Who do not use anything	• Education about importance of floor-based CC • Education about Dycem	Not using anything puts your business at risk	Case studies contamination problems that can be resolved by Dycem. Fear factor – can you afford to put your business at risk?
Prospects: Who have a problem	• To be told how Dycem can help address their problem • Help + advice to solve it	Dycem can help contribute towards bringing your contam problem under control	Advice on Dycem website a reason to visit apart from overt selling. Fear factor – subtle scare copy how to pass your audit
Prospects: Who do not have a problem	• Nothing	You need to protect yourself against the risk of contamination	Scare copy – this happened to x company could happen to you etc. E-mail campaign
Prospects: Who know about Dycem	• Encouragement to buy • Risk of purchase to be minimised	Reinforce the message that we are the best solution	Emphasize via e-mail/Web that we are cost-effective low risk purchase, can trial if they wish? Assure them with test etc.
Prospects: Who do not know about Dycem	• Generic education about Dycem Limited • Samples/demos	The importance of foot and wheel borne contamination. Why Dycem is the best solution for foot, wheel and some airborne contamination	Help them find us. How? ???
Suspects: Do not know about CC, tacky mats or Dycem. Could benefit from CC products	• Generic education about CC, Dycem	???	????

Loosely focused/ generic marketing

Key questions for each group:
1. Can we find them?
2. What do they want from Dycem – what can we offer them?
3. How do they behave? How should we interact with them?

Figure 8.14 (*continued*)

flooring was a high value 'non-consumable' and was often considered capital expenditure. Its high value inevitably meant that the decision making unit (DMU) was more complex and, as such, any purchase often required financial approval. The high value of the product implied some risk for the buyer, especially if they perceived their organisational culture held them accountable for a poor or incorrect purchase.

The functionality of the products sold by Dycem was not easily conveyed or explained without demonstration. Face-to-face selling was considered vital for the success of most of Dycem's products in both existing and new markets.

Consequently the Internet has taken on a different role of supporting the distribution channels. The Web was a useful tool to demonstrate product functionality. Video imaging and animation was incorporated on the Dycem website, to provide a cheap and effective method to demonstrate the more complicated products and services. Video could also enhance understanding of products by supporting literature and other existing media channels.

At an early stage in its development the website was not easy to navigate and was very product led.

Early work concentrated on updating the website. The second version was felt to be an improvement but had yet to make the leap from product to customer focus. Further development work was needed.

The third version was the result of a lot of work in updating all of the site to cater for the increased emphasis the firm wanted to place on Web based lead generation. The team now grappled with the issue of making the site more customer led. This meant placing themselves in the position of three audiences: their regular customers, interested prospects or even new entrants into the market.

By early 2008, the site looked like the fourth version. This reflected a more attractive up-to-date design with easy-to-navigate features, focusing on to core areas of interest to most visitors. However, the academic advisor suggested the site could be further refined to channel visitors to different pages according to their level of knowledge – effectively asking where the prospect is with their own education and, hence, leading them step by step through the buying process. This makes their navigation much simpler. So, by clicking on the blue button of the fourth version we get through to a clear screen that offered options depending on where the customer was.

Customers were segmented into three broad categories of buy phase. Consideration was given to the needs of the customer at specific stages in the buying process. Information was then categorised into corresponding groups or 'funnels' and organised according to the customers' knowledge and buy phase. The intention was to 'walk' the prospect through the website,

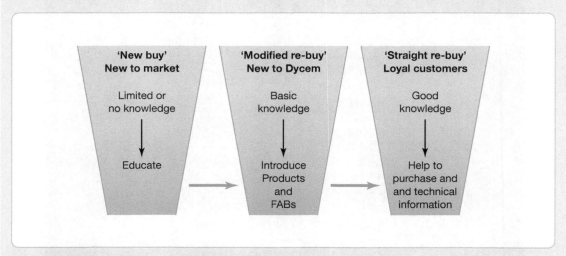

Figure 8.15 Using 'funnels' in the Web 'walk through'

Case study (*continued*)

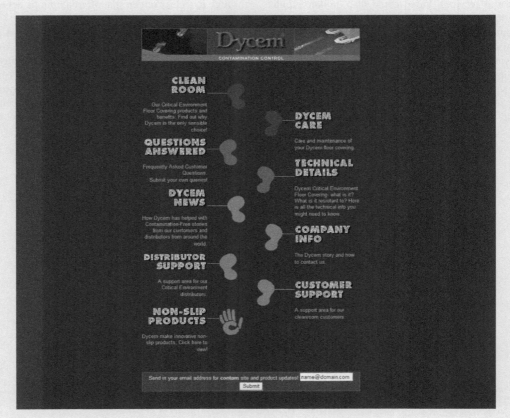

Early Dycem Web page prior to the project

providing the prospect with information appropriate to their own circumstances (see Figure 8.15).

Dycem recognised that new buyers were likely to have very little knowledge of contamination control. The aim was to educate them by providing general information about contamination and contamination control, without any 'hard product sell'. The prospect was guided through the website eventually reaching the section designed for modified re-buyers. Modified re-buyers typically have some knowledge of rival products, but will probably not know a great deal about Dycem. Therefore, at this point the prospects are introduced to Dycem products, but only at a generic level, which allows comparison with rival or alternative products. Features and benefits of the products are also emphasised.

Straight re-buyers are customers who have purchased products from Dycem before and so could be expected to have considerable knowledge of contamination control. Therefore, these customers were provided with full product information and services (technical, FAQs, after-sales service information, etc.). This section also sought to achieve conversion and, as such, used various calls to action.

Push and pull: the website as support for lead generation

Part of the Dycem marketing strategy was to support the distribution network by driving a transition from 'push' marketing to 'pull' marketing. Providing stimulating market communication messages could encourage awareness, interest, desire and ultimately action. A variety of mechanisms were trialled, including the use of e-zines, search engine optimisation

Second version of website

Case study (*continued*)

Third version of website

(SEO) and Web content built around appropriate end user 'buzz words'. Use of pay-per-click (PPC) advertising within search engines also proved a useful mechanism for attracting new customers. The results in the table below suggested PPC was a cost effective method to generate prospect leads.

Advertising on different search terms allowed Dycem to focus on the needs of particular industries or

Some early results for Dycem Google ads

5 Nov–9 Dec (6 weeks)	Before PPC ads	After PPC ads	Percentage increase (%)
Absolute unique visitors	Index 100	Index 204	102
Total visits	Index 100	Index 159	59
Total page views	Index 100	Index 111	11
% of new visits	61%	76%	15
Length of visit: pages viewed/ duration or visit (min/sec)	5.68/ 6.22	4.0/3.05	–

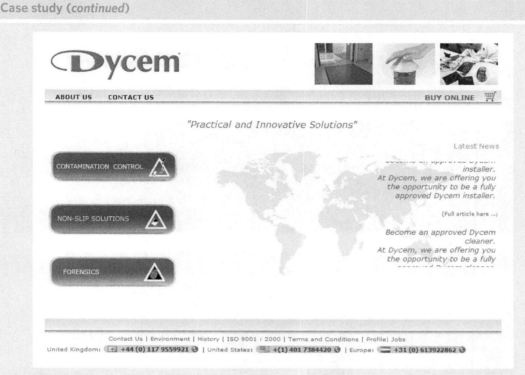

Fourth version of website

even focus in on a specific problem within an industry, for example MRSA in hospital markets or food hygiene in food industries. So, if someone typed 'MRSA control' into Google, then a Dycem ad appeared on the side of the Google search results page.

Overseas markets

Dycem had a relatively light presence in Asian markets. With no local reputation, it was vital to make the most of successes achieved elsewhere. Dycem wanted to capitalise on a phenomenon known as mimetic isomorphism – a tendency for organisations to imitate other successful organisations. Organisations facing a level of uncertainty, or doubt about a given technology and product functionality, will follow a successful role model. Could Glaxo in Tokyo be influenced by Glaxo buying Dycem in the UK? The team were keen to find out, with various activities deployed accordingly. For instance, a newsletter was sent to intermediaries containing information about recent successful sales to blue-chip companies. The newsletter was used when approaching other sites affiliated with the blue-chip.

Retention strategies

Some Dycem products have a long consumption cycle of three to five years. After-sales service is particularly important, not least as a chance to engage in long-term dialogues for repeat sales. Dycem needed to guard against the natural churn of employees at the customers' facilities, such that those people who were part of the decision making unit may have left the company or moved internally. This often meant that important knowledge on how to maintain and care for Dycem disappeared, and when this happened there was increased likelihood of customer dissatisfaction. The second problem with employee churn was that regular contact with customers was not maintained. When the new salesperson returns at the end of the product's life they are faced with a 'new task sale' rather than a straight re-buy.

Case study (*continued*)

Fifth version of website

These challenges were that much greater with distributors. To encourage high standards of care and sales, distributors were encouraged to 'mirror' Dycem's website, including branding in their own native language, use of the Dycem name, and provision of shirts and uniforms to enhance their sense of being part of Dycem. All this helped create the impression with new customers that they were working with the manufacturer.

The future at Dycem

It was 2008. Mark, the MD, took stock. Dycem were a successful small company. They had consolidated with a loyal customer base and competed against much bigger rivals. The KTP with the university had helped galvanise the marketing strategy across direct and Web marketing, both in supporting sales and distributors and, more strategically, moving to being genuinely marketing led.

The challenge now was to make that final leap: using Web and direct operations to help create a complete market led culture throughout Dycem.

Many thanks to Mark Dalziel and Nick Cook of Dycem Ltd for their help in writing this case study. The study leans heavily on a paper created by Nick Cook for a conference in early 2008.

Chapter **9**

Social media

Objectives

Once you have read this chapter you will:

- understand the impact of social media on consumer behaviour
- understand the opportunities and challenges they represent for brand owners
- understand the value of social media marketing as an integral element of marketing strategy

Introduction

At the time of the last version of this book (2008), the new kid on the block was being referred to as 'Web 2.0' and referred to the move from web content created by the site owners to content being created by users. In the intervening years, that move has accelerated and is now referred to by the familiar term 'Social Media'.

Social media have been defined as '[incorporating] the on-line technology and methods through which people can share content, personal opinions, swap different perspectives and insights, using text, images, audio and visual (Dibb *et al.*, 2012).

The advent and popularity of such websites has meant many things for marketers (McDaniel *et al.*, 2013):

- Marketers often no longer control content relating to their brands.
- The ability to share experiences takes word of mouth to a whole new level.
- Social media allow us to listen to (or ignore!) customer complaints more easily.
- Social media are mobile so we can communicate while customers are on the move.
- Social media facilitate a more direct and meaningful dialogue with customers than has previously been possible.

Social networking has developed very quickly and is still in a period of rapid change. Marketers are unsure as to how to make the most of such sites for their corporate benefit, and many organisations are supplementing their marketing departments with social media experts.

Social media experts must have more to offer than an addiction to Facebook. They need to be able to think strategically, integrate social media with other on-line advertising and the marketing strategy in general, work with people who do not have a clue what a tweet is and persuade them that their ideas are sound business sense. They need to understand the market, the company's offering and what competitors are doing, as well as recognise the difference between the requirements of various stakeholders. In other words, they have to be fully fledged marketers.

Social media are a phenomenon that is not going to go away, though the popularity of different sites grows and declines over time. In 2008, Bebo was THE social networking site with an estimated 11 million users in the UK alone (compared to 1.5 million UK members on Facebook). Popularity is almost a self-fulfilling prophecy: the more members a site has, the more content it gains and, as a result, the more members it gains . . . and so on until the next new idea comes along and re-writes the popularity tables.

Social networks and blogs now account for almost 23 per cent of the total time spent on-line. This is twice the amount of time spent playing games on-line (9.8 per cent) – the number 2 category. Next up was e-mailing (7.6 per cent) (Mogg, 2011).

There are many ways of defining and measuring the popularity of websites:

- **Alexa.com** is an **Amazon.com** owned site that collects data from users of the Alexa toolbar (said to number in their millions) to compile popularity statistics (**www.alexa.com,** 2012).

- **Compete.com**'s panel comprises a statistically representative cross-section of US consumers who have given permission to have their internet clickstream behaviours and opt-in survey responses analysed anonymously as a new source of marketing research (**www. compete.com,** 2012).

- **www.quantcast.com** uses cookie distribution data to determine the number of views enjoyed by Web pages (**www.quantcast.com,** 2012).

Other analytics tools and methods are available. For instance, **www.ebizmba.com** uses an algorithm that combines data from all three of the above sources to provide a constantly updated average of each website's traffic. According to that algorithm, the top ten most popular social networks globally are shown in Table 9.1.

It is somewhat surprising to see some maybe unfamiliar names in the second half of the list; at least in the UK they are unfamiliar. Also notable by its absence is Bebo, which was (as previously mentioned) at the top of the list in the UK at the time of publishing the previous version of this book. The numbers above are vast. To put them into a context, if the sites

Table 9.1 Top ten most popular social networking sites (worldwide)

Website	Est unique monthly visits
1. Facebook – Peer to peer social networking	750,000,000
2. Twitter – Microblogging via instant messaging	250,000,000
3. LinkedIn – Business based networking	110,000,000
4. MySpace – Audio, video, games and general entertainment	70,500,000
5. Google+ – General social networking	65,000,000
6. DeviantArt – Social network for artists	25,500,000
7. LiveJournal – Blogging, community involvement and a gift shop!	20,500,000
8. Tagged – Social network for meeting new people	19,500,000
9. Orkut – Common interest based on-line community	17,500,000
10. CafeMom – Meeting place for mothers	12,500,000

Source: eBizMBA.com (2012).

were countries and the number of users their populations, Facebook would be bigger than all countries except China and India, and Twitter would be just a little smaller than the USA.

Social media may be broken down into many different categories, as well as some that do not fall into any category at all. Some of the most common categories are shown below in Table 9.2. See also Figure 9.1.

9.1 Social media objectives

As with all marketing, social media needs to have clear objectives set so that its success can be measured and evaluated. Some of the following are suggested (McDaniel *et al.*, 2013) when drawing up such media objectives:

- **Sell**. Social media are increasingly generating sales.
- **Listen and learn.** Monitor what is being said about the brand and its competitors and glean insights about audiences. Use on-line tools and do research to implement the best social media practices.

Table 9.2 Social media technical enablers

Technology application	Description	Example
Blogs (or web logs) and micro blogs	An on-line diary where writers can express opinions, often combined with Podcasts (digital audio or video that can be watched or downloaded). It is estimated that 40,000 new blogs launch daily (Callan, 2012) Estimated 15 per cent UK population run a blog (Johnson, 2007).	**www.blogspot.com, www.wordpress.com** **www.twitter.com** (micro blogging)
Social networks	Websites that enable users to build a personal Web page, and allow their 'friends' within the network to view their page, sharing personal content and communications.	**www.facebook.com** **plus.Google.com** (Google+) **www.myspace.com www.clubpenguin.com** (targeted at young readers)
Communities	Websites that enable users to organise and share particular types of content amongst their user base.	**www.youtube.com** (video sharing) **www.instagram.com** (photo sharing) **www.pinterest.com** (content and image sharing) **www.tumblr.com** (blog hosting platform with social plug ins) **www.flickr.com** (photo sharing) **www.wikipedia.org** (on-line encyclopedia) **www.spotify.com** (music streaming) **www.slideshare.net** (for sharing presentations) **www.linkedin.com** (business–business community) **www.skillshive.com** (virtual teambuilding and networking site)
Forums/bulletin boards	Websites that enable users to share information and exchange ideas. Tend to be formed around a specific interest.	**www.eopinions.com www.cafemom.com**
Content aggregators	Applications that enable users to fully customise which types of Web content they access.	**www.netvibes.com**

Source: Based on Constantinides & SJ (2008).

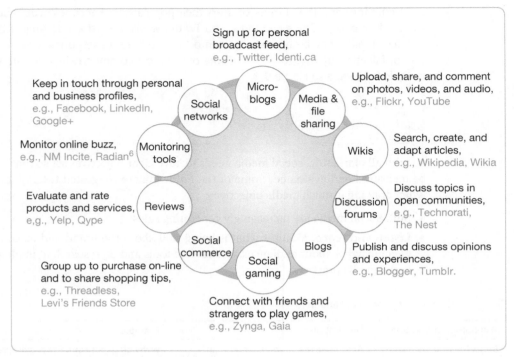

Figure 9.1 Social media utility and applications

Source: McKinsey, 2013.

- **Develop new channels to market.** Social media provide unique and credible new routes to market. They allow for interaction and dialogue to and between customers and the companies that serve them.

- **Build relationships and awareness.** Open dialogues with stakeholders by giving them compelling content across a variety of media. Engage in conversations and answer questions candidly. This will both increase Web traffic and boost your search engine ranking.

- **Promote products and services.** The clearest path to increasing the bottom line using social media is to get customers talking about products and services, which ultimately translates to sales. Creating a buzz about your products and services and using the ability of social media to share content can allow messages to 'go viral' with both positive and potentially negative consequences.

- **Manage your reputation.** Develop and improve the brand's reputation by responding to comments and criticisms that appear on blogs and forums. Position yourself as helpful and benevolent by participating in other forums and discussions. Social media make it much easier to establish and communicate expertise. Look at how companies engage with review sites. Trip Advisor has some influence in the travel market. Jury's Inn has an excellent approach to the monitoring of, and engagement in, this channel, quickly dealing with negative postings and thanking customers for their positive comments.

- **Improve customer service.** Customer comments about products and services will not always be positive. Use social media to find displeased customers and engage them directly to solve their service issues.

- **Create through collaboration.** Many companies are using the power of social media to develop their business. **www.kickstarter.com** and **www.getitmade.com** are examples of companies linking into the power of social networks right at the heart of their business strategies. Ben and Jerry's ice cream use Facebook fans to help develop new products and help with marketing research.

- **Develop relationships with key influencers.** Companies can identify key opinion formers and influencers in their market and use this influence to develop the brand. 'Handmade' in London is targeting fashion bloggers on behalf of their designer clients (**www.handmade.uk.com**). The passion of brand advocates can be harnessed and used to drive positive messages about products and services.

9.2   How consumers use social media

Social media were initially seen as a young person's waste of time but increasingly, as with other aspects of the Web, the social media space is becoming gender, age, and class neutral (see Figures 9.2 and 9.3).

In the UK the figures are similar although again the figures are dominated but for younger males the gap is closing (see Figure 9.4).

A joint project from comScore and search marketing specialist Group M Search claimed that half of consumers use a combination of search and social media to help their purchasing decisions (Rubin, 2011). The survey went on to say that more than a quarter of those surveyed (28 per cent) said sites such as YouTube, Facebook, and Twitter help them learn about new brands and products. Thirty per cent said they used social media to eliminate brands from contention.

Another survey by NM Incite shows that the number one reason consumers use social media sites when related to commerce is not to receive discounts but to read what others are saying about products or brands in which they are interested (Olenski, 2011).

Disgruntled consumers can also use social media to be creative in their complaints, reaching audiences of millions, as can be seen in the following exhibit.

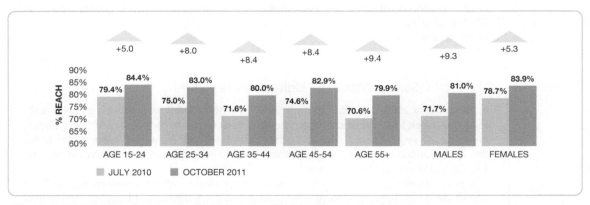

Figure 9.2 Social networking penetration among worldwide demographic groups

Source: comScore Media Metrix, Worldwide, October 2011.

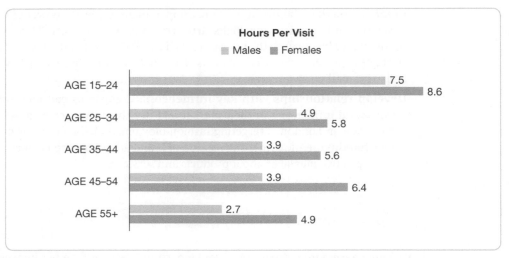

Figure 9.3 Social Networking Engagement Among Worldwide Demographic Groups
Source: comScore Media Metrix, Worldwide, October 2011.

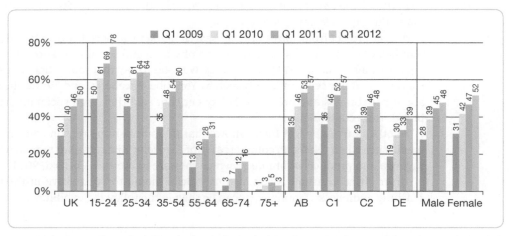

Figure 9.4 Proportion of adults who live in households where social networking sites are accessed:
Q1 2009 to Q1 2012
Source: Ofcom (2012).

Exhibit 9.1 Sons of Maxwell – United breaks guitars

In the spring of 2008, American country band 'Sons of Maxwell' were travelling to Nebraska for a one-week tour. While sitting on the aeroplane (or perhaps that should be 'airplane', in this case!) singer Dave Carrol and other passengers saw his prized Taylor guitar being thrown by United Airlines baggage handlers in Chicago and Dave later discovered that the $3,500 guitar was severely damaged.

United did not deny this had happened, but for nine months the various people Dave communicated with seemed more concerned with putting the responsibility for dealing with the damage on everyone else than they were with resolving the situation; and they finally said they would do nothing to compensate Dave for his loss. Sons of Maxwell decided to take direct action, country style.

They penned three songs relating this experience and posted them on YouTube for the world to see. The first of these songs has, at the time of writing, gained almost 60,000 likes (and nearly 1,200 dislikes) as well as, crucially, over 12 million hits – that is 12 million people who would not have heard about this 20 years ago.

Whether or not it was as a result of this, United Airlines decided to offer Sons of Maxwell compensation within four days of the original posting on YouTube.

Dave Carroll now makes his living on the corporate speaking circuit and as an author. His subject – service recovery!

Source: Adapted by the Author from the YouTube posting notes (Sons of Maxwell, 2009).

9.3 How businesses use social media

The value of social media sits right across the value chain. A recent study by management consultants McKinsey showed the use to which business are putting social media (see Table 9.3).

The same study showed the uses to which companies are putting social media. See Figure 9.5.

The use of social media is generating several benefits, as shown in Table 9.4.

The McKinsey report shows that certain benefits are increasing in importance (see Figure 9.6).

9.4 Other commercial users of social media

The FT reported that athletes leaving the London Olympics were hoping to extend their peak period for commercial endorsements through increasing their popularity on social media. Ricky Simms, Director at Pace Sports Management, who looked after Usain Bolt's interests, said 'Brands always ask how many followers an athlete has. For many companies, this is the way they want to reach their target customers' (Steel, 2012).

The Olympics helped generate a massive increase in the number of social media followers that many athletes have: Usain Bolt's Twitter following increased from 620,000 before

Table 9.3 Social media across the value chain

Value chain step	Case example	Impact
Product development	Procter & Gamble	R and D costs − 6% p.a.
Marketing	Old Spice	Sales +16%
		Campaign costs − 80%
Sales	**Ricardo.ch, Sellaround.net**	Transactions +18,000 per month
Service	Example from telecommunications industry	Resolved customer queries +30%
External communication	McDonald's	Stock price +5%
Human resources	Allianz, Bertelsmann, Henkel, McKinsey and Comany	Reach +20%
		Cost −27%
		Quality +36%
Internal applications	Mountain Equipment Co-op	Efficiency gains ≥90%

Source: Press research, corporate websites, McKinsey.

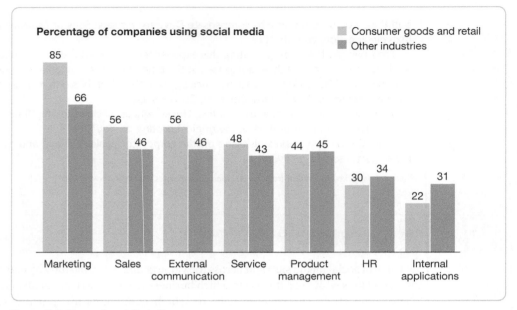

Figure 9.5 Uses of social media

Source: McKinsey 2013 Social Media Excellence Survey.

the games to 1.6 million after the event. US gold winning gymnast, Gabby Douglas, saw her Twitter following increase from 29,000 to 654,000; the winners were organisations that sponsored her before the Olympics, getting in when her following was low (Steel, 2012).

Kevin Adler, founder of Engage Marketing (who specialise in sports and entertainment marketing) suggested that athletes should be aware of this and build future success into new contracts: 'There is no arguing that Gabby's value as an endorser is exponentially more valuable now than it was when they signed her. If I am a creative and smart athlete agent, I would include bonus clauses that trigger financial incentives if social media audiences grow' (Steel, 2012).

Charities are beginning to wake up to the idea of using social media as a method of promoting their cause. See the 'iHobo' case study at the end of a previous chapter (Chapter 4).

Like athletes, stars of popular music and culture are also using social media to stay in front of their fans. The video for Lady Gaga's 'Bad Romance' is said to hold the title of the most viewed video ever on YouTube (McDaniel *et al.*, 2013). It has currently had 483,746,617 viewings (Interscope Records, 2009), over twice the population of the USA. In

Table 9.4 Companies' use of social media, $n = 3,000$ companies

Utility	% companies benefiting
Improving marketing effectiveness	63
Increasing customer satisfaction	50
Reducing marketing costs	45
Lowering customer care and support costs	35
Reducing travel expenditure	29
Faster time to market for NPD	26
Increasing innovations	24
Improving revenues	23

Source: McKinsey, 2012.

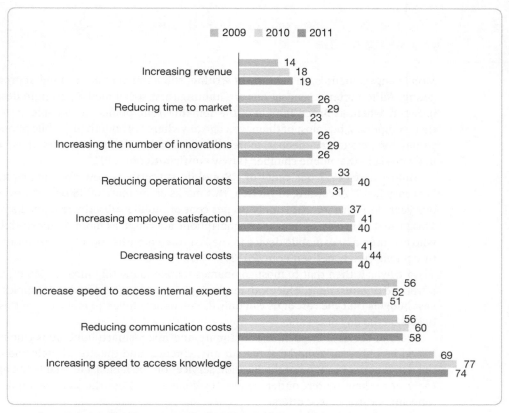

Figure 9.6 Gains from implementation of Web 2.0 applications, % companies benefiting 2009–2011

Source: McKinsey (2012).

the time between writing this book and proofing it, events have taken over and the music video for Psy's 'Gangnam Style' has had a massive 1.733 billion views – approximately a quarter of the population of the planet! (YouTube, 2013).

Exhibit 9.2 A social drink

The 'Captain's island' promotion for Captain Morgan rum was launched on Facebook. Fans of the brand could enter a contest to win a trip to a tropical island. Contestants completed challenges such as posting pictures of themselves dressed as the captain or collecting keys found in bars, supermarkets and on websites that integrate the camping with the product.

The unique keys allow Diageo to track the connection between on-line engagement and sales by mining the data associated with each key to understand where they bought the drink and which websites influenced them. The contests generated so much interest that the keys became valuable and a market was created on eBay.

Source: Marcus Dyer and Mark Wheeler (2011) cited in McKinsey (2012).

9.5 Geo-location based offers – how businesses COULD use social media

Mobile engagement is, at the time of writing, still a much under utilised approach to marketing. All too often organisations are limiting their social media design to desktop based browsers when, as Bruce Temkin of the Temkin Group points out, 'people aren't always at their computers, but most of them won't go anywhere without their mobile phones. As companies compete to gain deeper, more relevant insights about customers, they will increasingly invest in the mobile channel' (**www.confirmit.com,** 2012).

Almost half (49.7 per cent) of US mobile subscribers now own smartphones, as of February 2012. According to Nielsen, this marks an increase of 38 per cent over the previous year; in February 2011, only 36 per cent of mobile subscribers owned smartphones. This growth is driven by increasing smartphone adoption, as more than two-thirds of those who acquired a new mobile device in the last three months chose a smartphone over a feature phone (**www.neilsen.com,** 2012).

So why is it then that to most companies mobile marketing means SMS or, to the more advanced organisations, Bluetooth marketing? Even the 2012 London Olympics (with their vast budgets that the rest of us can only dream about) failed to make use of this for selling tickets on the day of events.

Users of social sites such as Foursquare and many smartphone apps (including those issued by pubs, supermarkets, restaurants, cinemas and theatres, hotels and others) ask the user's permission to use the location services on the handset to enable the app to direct the user to their nearest outlet, so few (by comparison) use the same technology to make time and location based offers.

Research conducted by mobileSQUARED in April 2011 revealed that approximately 70–80 per cent of brands that are active in mobile are now enquiring about how they can capitalise on the location element that mobile delivers. This research is in stark contrast to the views expressed 12 months previously, when the majority of media agencies claimed their clients were expressing little or no interest in location as part of a mobile campaign (Lane, 2012).

9.6 Measurement and control of social media

One of the great characteristics of social media is that it is highly measureable. There are many services available to marketers to help with measurement, some of which are free of charge. The major issue that many companies are facing today is the ability to integrate social media channel metrics with other on-line media and with off-line media metrics to produce a true '360 degree' view of the customer. There remains a silo based approach to measurement and Don Schultz, one of the doyens of integrated marketing communications, has reflected that digital marketers are repeating the mistakes of their analogue counterparts.

'Marketing communication planning and results have historically been measured on a function or a medium-by-medium basis – one measure for advertising, another for public relations, yet another for sales promotion and so on. The new electronic communication systems have fallen into the same trap, one measure for web, another for word-of-mouth, another for mobile. Yet, consumers seem to use all these communication systems concurrently, simultaneously and, one would assume, synergistically. If this is true, what are the challenges in measuring the impact and effect of these integrated systems?'

(Schultz, D., and Patti, C., 2009)

The industry is begnning to respond to these issues but the holy grail of a truly integrated approach to customer metrics appears, at time of writing, to be some way off. The core metrics in social media remain the same as any channel.

● How much does it cost to acquire a customer in this channel?

● What is their cross-sell up-sell rate?

● What retention rate can we achieve?

● What is their lifetime value?

In addition, the key area for most businesses to measure is monetisation or, in other words, what is the value of a Twitter follower or a Facebook follower to the topline.

Kauschik in his excellent blog Occam's Razor (Kauschik, 2013) suggests some additional social measures:

● **Amplification.** How do Social media work to enhance the impact of other channels through sharing, retweeting, etc? For example, if my Twitter followers are 10,000 but they are being followed by three million unique followers then my reach is clearly larger than my following.

● **Conversation rate.** This is the number of comments or replies to a posting. Kauschik here reinforces Schultz and Patti's point above 'Individually (by channel) this is not that hard to measure. But across channels there does not seem to be an option' (Kauschik, 2013).

● **Applause rate.** The number of likes, favourite clicks, etc. Again, easy to measure by channel, harder to achieve across channels.

● **Economic value.** This relates to the revenues available from social media and the cost of achieving revenue directly from social commerce or linked to other channels.

True Social Metrics was a system set up in response to Kaushik's blog post on Social Media Measurement (see Figure 9.7).

There is clearly a range of other measures that may be relevant. Dave Chaffey talks about the need to benchmark effectively across the competition looking at:

● conversation volume or brand mentions across media

● conversation share volume compared to competitors for targeted phrase and words

● conversation sentiment or polarity; automated and/or human assessment of brand mentions that are positive or negative

(Chaffey, Cited in Kauschik 2013).

There is a range of measurement tools available in the social media space.

In its report on social media monitoring, Ideya Consulting identified 250 different social media monitoring tools. These contained a variety of features including:

● data management features such as data coverage, data latency, alerts, data export, Application Programming Interface (API) integration, data archiving;

● data analysis and visualisation features, including sentiment analysis, influencer profiling and analysis, viral content tracking and analysis, trend analysis, topic and theme

	Connect Twitter	Connect Faebook	Connect Google+	Connect Blog	Connect YouTube	Connect Pinterest	Connect LinkedIn	Connect Tumblr	Connect Instagram
You can connect any social media account even your competitors' if you know the url of needed social media page.									x
#Posts	0	0	0	0	0	0	0	0	0
#Comments	0	0	0	0	0	0	0	0	0
#Reshares	0	0	0	0	0	0	0	0	0
#Favorites	0	0	0	0	0	0	0	0	0
1. Conversation rate Comments per post	0.00	0.00	0.00	0.00	0.00	0.00	0.00	0.00	0.00
2. Amplification rate Re-shares per post	0.00	0.00	0.00	0.00	0.00	0.00	0.00	0.00	0.00
3. Applause rate Favorites per post	0.00	0.00	0.00	0.00	0.00	0.00	0.00	0.00	0.00
4. Economic value Value per visitor				Connect Google Analytics					

Figure 9.7 True social metrics analytics screen
Source: True Social Metrics (2013).

analysis, word/tag cloud, competitive monitoring and analysis, campaign management and measurements;

● process management and user interface, including dashboard, workflow management, client relationship management (CRM);

● analysis of factors influencing purchasing decisions, including pricing, key clients and the year when the tool or service was made publicly available.

(Source: Ideya, 2012)

Of these tools, 191 were offered on a paid for basis and 48 were offered free of charge. The rest were in testing or were hybrid offers.

Chaffey (2013) does something similar on the Smartinsights blog and categorises the tools available in the following seven groups:

● **Category 1** Wide scope analytical and reporting tools for all aspects of monitoring customer opinions and campaign effectiveness

● **Category 2** Blog based influence assessment tools, designed to gain access to influential customers/commentators

● **Category 3** PR and media management tools for reputation management and assessing opinion forming influence

● **Category 4** Social media tracking and intervention including free tools

● **Category 5** Fraud protection, security and threat detection

- **Category 6** News media tracking
- **Category 7** Social media within sales management, for identifying B2B prospects

(Source: Chaffey, 2013)

Listed below are some of the social media monitoring tools available and their Web addresses:

Free or services with some free content

Hootsuite: www.hootsuite.com – Allows the user to manage unlimited social networks and profiles under one interface, schedule Facebook posts and Twitter messages, track key words and trending topics. Measure engagement and campaign success and has a colaborative element.

Klout: www.Klout.com – Measures influence across several social networks and shows users how they impact the people connected to them.

Facebook insights: www.developers.facebook.com/docs/insights/ – Gives Facebook developers and page owners metrics about their content. It covers trends within user growth and demographics, consumption and creation of content.

Social Mention: www.socialmention.com/about/ – A social media search and analysis platform that aggregates user generated content from across the universe into a single stream of information. It allows the user to track and measure social media content from over 100 social media sites, including Twitter, Facebook, Google+ and YouTube.

Tweetreach: www.tweetreach.com/products – A social analytics tool that provides metrics on the impact of Twitter conversations. It measures how many accounts received tweets, how far a message has travelled, and who is influencing conversation about brands or products.

Paid for tools

Salesforce Marketing Cloud/Radian 6: www.radian6.com – Helps organisations to understand and gain insights about social media through metrics, measurement, sentiment and analytics reporting. The system covers listening, tracking, monitoring and engagement.

Adobe Social/Omniture: www.adobe.com/uk/products/social.html – Includes the ability to publish content across social networks, amplify that content with social ads, listen to the conversation and respond. It also links social to purchases and brand value.

Brandwatch: www.brandwatch.com – A monitoring tool to help identify what people say about brands, products, competitors, industry or any related topics. It claims to cover 50 million sources including blogs, forums, news sites and major social networks across the world. It covers 25 languages.

Trackur: www.trackur.com/social-media-monitoring – A comprehensive social media monitoring tool covering basic metrics, buzz and sentiment analysis.

Whatever system used, think about the link back to KPIs (key performance indicators) and business objectives. Not all systems will deliver all the analytics and data that you want and many will deliver more than you can use.

Among the features you may expect to be offered are the following:

- Core metrics, including volume of mentions, media trends, share of voice, day parting, buzz metrics, sentiment analysis, etc.
- Real time monitoring and data analysis

- The ability to create graphs and charts as well as dashboard presentation
- Trend analysis over time
- Campaign tracking tools
- Influencer and sentiment analysis
- Topic trends
- Competitor benchmarking
- Data exporting function
- Multi user and workflow management systems
- Database integration

9.7 Some social media sites (not mentioned elsewhere so far) offering great potential for marketers

Foursquare

There are currently 20 million Foursquare users and 1 million partner businesses world-wide (**www.foursquare.com**, 2012).

Foursquare uses the location services facility on smartphones. Once the site knows the device's location, it directs users to local businesses that may be of interest. Users are encouraged to 'like' and 'check in' to a location/business. When they have done so more than once, Foursquare considers them to be loyal customers and will automatically share partner business's updates with them when they are nearby.

Exhibit 9.3 McDonald's Foursquare day

McDonald's randomly selected 100 people who had 'checked in' to one of their stores on Foursquare to receive $5 and $10 giftcards. They publicised the giveaway in advance, and saw an increase before, during and after the promotion:

- Check ins during the promotion day were 33 per cent up on the previous day.
- The rest of the week saw check ins 40 per cent up on normal.
- The campaign resulted in 50 articles and blog posts, 600,000 new fans and followers with 99 per cent positive feedback.

Overall, it was a successful and easily measured campaign.

Source: **www.foursquare.com** (2012).

Pinterest.com

Pinterest is a virtual pinboard that allows you to collect pictures and other items of interest and 'pin' them all in one place. It is the third most popular social network in the USA with over 20 million members at the end of January 2012 (Boxall, 2012).

Users start by installing a 'Pin It' button in the favourites bar of their browser, and from there they can grab an image from any website and pin it to a Pinterest board. As part of the pinning process, Pinterest automatically grabs the source link so that the original creator can be credited (**www.pinterest.com,** 2012a). Images can also be uploaded from the user's PC if required. There are Pinterest apps available for both Android and iPhone.

Just like Twitter and Facebook, people can follow someone's Pinterest board. This makes it ideal for such things as creating wedding or other present wish lists. Links to the Pinterest board can be placed on other websites and blogs.

People use pinboards to plan their weddings, decorate their homes, and organise their favourite recipes (**www.pinterest.com,** 2012b). On a simpler level, it appeals to a special interest group by bringing scrapbooking into the 21st century!

For commercial organisations, Pinterest offers the chance to be included not only in gift lists, but to gain the attention of special interest groups through followers seeing the original source of the Pin and driving traffic to that website. At the time of writing, some Pinterest users have over 10,000 followers (**www.pinterest.com,** 2012c) and the ability to be brought to the attention of such numbers of specifically targeted niche groups is not to be sniffed at. Just as websites include a Facebook 'Like' button, they can include a 'Pin it' button, thus making it even easier to access Pinterest.

Tumblr.com

Tumblr is a microblogging site that allows users to post multimedia content to their 'tumblelog'. Research company, Nielsen, says that Tumblr is a social network to watch, having almost tripled its audience in the twelve months to September 2011 (Mogg, 2011). At time of writing, Tumblr claims to have 70.7 million blogs incorporating 30.5 billion posts (**www.tumblr.com,** 2012a).

From a commercial perspective, Tumblr makes getting feedback, opinions and answers simple: by ending a post with a question mark you are given the option to allow the post to be answerable by the Tumblr community. You will see a new option in the right-column of the website's screen for 'Let people answer this' (**www.tumblr.com,** 2012b).

Eopinions.com

This site has been selected as typical of the many consumer review sites available. It offers consumer reviews on items as diverse as cameras and clothes, sports equipment and cars, books and baby care. Other review sites specialise in one particular area, such as **www. tripadvisor.com,** which focuses on travel reviews, and **www.moneysavingexpert.com,** which focuses on financial matters. Then there are category comparisons: **www.compare themarket.com** and **www.uswitch.com** being examples here.

www.eopinions.com carries reviews posted by people who have bought a product and who want to act in a community led way; to help others, who are also considering buying the product, know how it works in the real world.

Businesses need to realise how important these sites are to consumers. A survey carried out in the UK, US and Canada found that approximately 72 per cent of consumers surveyed said that they trust on-line reviews as much as personal recommendations, while 52 per cent said that positive on-line reviews make them more likely to use a local business (Anderson, 2012).

LinkedIn

LinkedIn has grown quickly over the last ten years and is an increasingly important way of building reputation, credibility, profile and, ultimately, leads. Businesses should realise that their employees' LinkedIn profile may have an important bearing on corporate reputation and profile and a LinkedIn strategy is advised for all staff.

Companies should ensure that employees' descriptions of professional titles are appropriately connected to corporate goals and rich in key words. Key words should also be included in summaries and other areas of the LinkedIn profile. This means a LinkedIn profile will be more searchable around key terms and your profile will have a greater chance of being found.

You should avoid putting negative material on a LinkedIn profile and it is not the place to include information on your capacity to handle all-night parties.

Group strategy is also important. Individuals are limited to 50 groups and should join groups where their customers are found. LinkedIn groups should be actively followed and it is important to contribute to discussion groups in a credible and engaging manner.

A LinkedIn strategy can also achieve increased traffic for the corporate website through links to your website. LinkedIn can also improve page ranking and SEO results.

Ultimately LinkedIn can be used for lead generation. For example, key players in a market may be invited to link in and this can be the start of a conversation that leads to a sale. Better still, look at your first line contacts and see if any are linked to the targets you want to connect with and ask for an introduction. Like all social media LinkedIn works best on a personal level. Always use your own message rather than the standard LinkedIn templates. Your own LinkedIn groups can be used to establish your authority on certain key areas. People trust experts in their field and expertise can be established on LinkedIn through participation and sharing of appropriate resources, including white papers and presentations. LinkedIn ads can also be used to target professionals working in your area.

LinkedIn can also be integrated with other social media to amplify activity and there is a range of widgets that can help with this. LinkedIn profiles should be included on all marketing collateral to extend the reach of the medium. LinkedIn should always be kept vibrant and up to date with examples of recent work and quick responses to LinkedIn messages. You can track LinkedIn activity using your own analytics tools to track the clicks on your announcements and to look at the source of traffic into the website.

References

Alexa.com (2012). *About Alexa Internet.* Available at: **http://www.alexa.com/company** [Accessed 29 August 2012].

Anderson, M. (2012). *Study: 72% Of Consumers Trust Online Reviews As Much As Personal Recommendations.* [on-line] Available at: **http://searchengineland.com/study-72-of-consumers-trust-online-reviews-as-much-as-personal-recommendations-114152** [Accessed 30 August 2012].

Boxall, A. (2012). *Pinterest now third most popular social network in the US, beats Google+ [Updated].* [Online] Available at: **http://www.digitaltrends.com/social-media/pinterest-now-third-most-popular-social-network-in-the-us-beats-google-plus/** [Accessed 30 August 2012].

Callan, D. (2012). *How to launch a successful hight traffic blog.* [on-line] Available at: **http://www.akamarketing.com/launching-a-blog.php** [Accessed 29 August 2012].

Chaffey. D. (2009). *Online brand reputation or social media monitoring tool comparison review* Available at **http://www.smartinsights.com/online-pr/reputation-management-online-pr/online-reputation-management-software/** Accessed February, 2013.

Comscore (2013). Available at **http://www.slideshare.net/Briancrotty/comscore-top-10-needtoknows-about-social-networkingandwhereitisheaded** Accessed February 2013

Compete.com (2012). *Where does Compete's data come from?.* [on-line] Available at: **http://www.compete.com/us/about/our-data/** [Accessed 29 August 2012].

confirmit.com (2012). *Key Considerations for Implementing a Mobile Engagement Strategy.* Available at: **http://knowledgebank.marketingweek.co.uk/documents/2012_05_30_Mobile_ Engagement_White_Paper_FINAL.pdf** [Accessed 29 August 2012].

Constantinides, E. & SJ, F. (2008). Web 2.0: Conceptual Foundations and Marketing Issues. *Journal of Direct, Data and Digital Marketing Practice,* 9(Special Issue Paper), pp. 231–244.

Dibb, S., Simpkin, L., Pride, W. and Ferrel, O. (2012). *Marketing Concepts and Strategies.* 6th edn, (ed.) Cengage Learning EMEA, Andover.

eBizMBA.com (2012). *Top 15 most popular social networking sites – August 2012.* Available at: **http:// www.ebizmba.com/articles/social-networking-websites** [Accessed 29 August 2012].

foursquare.com (2012). *foursquare for Business.* Available at: **https://foursquare.com/business/** **[Accessed 29 August 2012].**

foursquare.com (2012). *Merchant case studies – McDonalds.* Available at: **https://foursquare.com/ business/merchants/casestudies/mcdonalds** [Accessed 29 August 2012].

Harding, M. (2012). *About.* Available at: **www.wherethehellismatt.com/about** [Accessed 29 August 2012].

Ideya (2013). *Social Media Monitoring Tools and Services Report 2012* Available at: **http://ideya.eu. com/images/SMMTools%20ReportExcerpts%2009072012Final.pdf** [Accessed February 2013].

Interscope Records (2009). *Lady Gaga – Bad Romance.* Available at: **http://www.youtube.com/ watch?v=qrO4YZeyl0I** [Accessed 30 August 2012].

Kauschik, A. (2013). Available at: **www.kaushik.net/avinash/best-social-media-metrics- conversation-amplification-applause-economic-value/** [Accessed February 2013].

Lane, N. (2012). *Mobile Geo-location Advertising Will be a Big Number in 2015.* Available at: **http:// adfonic.com/wp-content/uploads/2012 ÷ 03/geo-location-white-paper.pdf** [Accessed 29 August 2012].

McDaniel, C., Lamb, C. and Hair, J. (2013). *Introduction to Marketing* international edn, (ed.) s.l.:Cengage South Western.

McKinsey (2012). *The Social Economy: Unlocking Value and Productivity through Social Technologies* Available at: **http://www.mckinsey.com/insights/mgi/research/technology_and_innovation/ the_social_economy** [Accessed February 2013].

McKinsey (2013). *Turning Buzz Into Gold* Available At: **http://www.mckinsey.com/client_service/ business_technology/latest_thinking/turning_buzz_into_gold** [Accessed February 2013].

Mogg, T. (2011). *Report: Americans can't get enough of social networking sites.* Available at: **http://www. digitaltrends.com/social-media/report-americans-cant-get-enough-of-social-networking- sites/** [Accessed 30 August 2012].

neilsen.com (2012). *Smartphones Account for Half of all Mobile Phones, Dominate New Phone Purchases in the US.* Available at: **http://blog.nielsen.com/nielsenwire/online_mobile/smartphones- account-for-half-of-all-mobile-phones-dominate-new-phone-purchases-in-the-us/** [Accessed 29 August 2012].

Ofcom (2012). Availble at: **http://stakeholders.ofcom.org.uk/binaries/research/cmr/cmr12/ CMR_UK_2012.pdf** [Accessed February 2013].

Olenski, S. (2011). *When It Comes To Brands, Consumers Use Social Media For This More Than Anything Else.* Available at: **http://socialmediatoday.com/steve-olenski/370277/when-it-comes-brands- consumers-use-social-media-more-anything-else** [Accessed 30 August 2012].

pinterest.com (2012a). *Goodies.* Available at: **http://pinterest.com/about/goodies/** [Accessed 30 August 2012].

pinterest.com (2012b). *About.* Available at: **www.pinterest.com/about** [Accessed 30 August 2012].

pinterst.com (2012c). *Most Followed Pinterest Users.* Available at: **http://pinterest.com/ pinterestpower/most-followed-pinterest-users/** [Accessed 30 August 2012].

Psy, 'Gangnam Style'. Available at: **http://www.youtube.com/watch?gl=GB&v=9bZkp7q19 fO&hl=en-GB** [Accessed 12 August 2013].

Quantcast.com (2012). *Quantcast Methodology FAQs.* Available at: **http://www.quantcast.com/how-we-do-it/methodology** [Accessed 29 August 2012].

Rubin, C. (2011). *Shoppers Combine Search, Social Media to Fuel Decisions.* Available at: **http://www.inc.com/news/articles/201102/half-of-consumers-combine-search-and-social-media-for-help-buying.html** [Accessed 30 August 2012].

Schultz. D, and Patti. C (2009), *The evolution of IMC: IMC in a customer-driven marketplace.* Journal of Marketing Communications Vol. 15, Nos. 2–3, April–July 2009, 75–84.

Sons of Maxwell (2009). *United Breaks Guitars.* Available at: **http://www.youtube.com/watch?v=5YGc4zOqozo** [Accessed 29 August 2012].

Steel, E. (2012). *Social Media could turn athlete earnings gold.* Available at: **http://www.ft.com/cms/s/0 ÷ 19d16d1a-e55b-11e1-8ac0-00144feab49a.html#axzz251hQOeXa** [Accessed 30 August 2012].

True Social Metrics (2013) Available at: **http://www.truesocialmetrics.com/metric** Accessed February 2013

tumblr.com (2012a). *About.* Available at: **http://www.tumblr.com/about** [Accessed 30 August 2012].

tumblr.com (2012b). *Tips!.* Available at: **http://www.tumblr.com/tips** [Accessed 30 August 2012].

CASE STUDY

Where the hell is Matt?

Matt Harding is a computer games designer who, at the age of 23, moved from America to Australia, and then decided to travel the world before settling down. Being a programmer, he set up a website to let his family know where he was and what he was up to.

A few months into his trip, he and his friend were taking pictures on the streets of Hanoi when the friend suggested Matt should do a stupid dance to be filmed for the website. Matt did so. They agreed it looked funny and should become Matt's signature for filming everywhere he went.

A few years later, in 2005, Matt found his video on YouTube, where someone else (pretending to be Matt) had uploaded it. Matt says that 'something like a million people had watched it' and whoever had posted it was collecting donations!

Around this time, Matt got an e-mail from a chewing gum company called Stride. They asked if he would be interested in making another dancing video for them. He said he would, if they would pay for it and he could go wherever he wanted. To his amazement they agreed, so he set off, with camera in hand and his girlfriend, Melissa, beside him to film it.

On that trip, Matt mostly just danced in front of iconic landmarks. When he was in Rwanda he could not find any world famous landmarks, so instead he just went to a small village and danced with some of the village's children, who joined him immediately and without hesitation.

This gave Matt an idea, and he went back to Stride to pitch it to them. He told them his films would be much better – and would gain more on-line followers – if they included Matt dancing with other people, rather than just in front of landmarks, and suggested he should make another trip with that approach. Stride agreed, again.

Case study (*continued*)

In 2008, Matt put out another video that showed thousands of people from all around the world laughing, smiling, and dancing with him. The site's Internet following exploded and Matt was hired by Visa to do his dance in a series of TV ads that air across Asia and the Middle East.

Since then, Matt has bought a house in Washington, settled down and had a child with Melissa. He says he 'doesn't have to worry about money so much anymore'.

Source: Harding (2012).

Questions

Go to **www.wherethehellismatt.com/videos** and watch the films mentioned in the case study.

1 Matt's trips were sponsored by Stride Gum. Who actually gained the most from this, Matt or Stride?

2 Do you think this sponsorship was a good investment for Stride Gum or not? If not, what could they have done to increase their exposure and/or their return on investment?

3 How could Matt have used social media to amplify this activity?

4 How could the impact of this have been measured?

PART FOUR

Direct marketing implementation and control

Chapter 10

Offers and incentives in direct marketing

Objectives

Once you have read this chapter you will:

- be able to define 'offers' and 'incentives'
- understand the difference between offers and incentives
- appreciate the roles that different offers and incentives play in acquiring and keeping customers
- be able to make appropriate tactical decisions in this area

Introduction

Previous chapters (Chapters 5 and 6) gave us the tools we need to make the major direct marketing decisions. The next step is to decide tactics. The individual steps we need to take in delivering direct marketing programmes are outlined in the nine-step process shown in Table 10.1.

From Table 10.1 we see that Steps 1 to 3 have already been covered, subsumed within the analysis and strategy sections of previous chapters. There are two steps (4 and 5) still to take before moving into the communication phase. We need to use our strategic guidance to design our proposition, or offer, to customers. This will include the core product/price offering and also augmented product add-ons, including incentives.

Table 10.1 Nine-step process for delivering direct marketing programmes

Step	Programme process	Chapter
1	**Set objectives**	5
	The market	
2	Segment (based on existing customers if possible)	3
3	Decide on final target markets	5
	The offer	
4	Decide product/price proposition	10
5	Decide incentive approach	10
	Communication	
6	Decide media and contact over time	11& 12
7	Decide timing issues	11& 12
8	Develop creative platforms	13
9	Design a detailed test programme	14

Exhibit 10.1 The difference between strategy and tactics

The key elements distinguishing strategies from tactics are difficult to pin down. There is widespread disagreement among academics and confusion among practitioners about what constitutes a marketing strategy.

A pragmatic approach is offered here, as something to clarify the way in which the phrase 'marketing strategy' is used in this book.

Marketing strategies are decisions that are made on what products should be developed for what markets (existing and new), competitive positioning and the marketing mix, which 'provide the direction' for individual campaigns or programmes. Strategies typically have timeframes of many months and often years. Whatever the time period, it is always longer than one single marketing action.

For example, if we take American Express, we can see that its strategy is to differentiate itself as the charge card of exclusivity and status. It seeks to differentiate itself through its brand. A tactic may be a single mailshot to a group of prospects, which emphasises the exclusivity of the card.

Having read this chapter, you will be able to make specific tactical choices applied to your particular business problem. Direct marketing is concerned with both developing relationships and obtaining a definite response from consumers to purchase. To achieve either goal, you could decide to develop a club, to launch a 'loyalty card', or to use an 'opt-out' acquisition device. But have you made the right move? The answers to these problems are tackled in this chapter.

How this chapter is structured

In this chapter we will start by defining offers and incentives in direct marketing. Then, leaving aside offers for a moment, we will examine the case for using incentives in some detail.

The third section brings together offers and incentives in a discussion of contact programmes to existing customers. The final section looks at the same for attracting new customers.

10.1 Defining offers and incentives

10.1.1 The product model

This well-known model is used in most general marketing texts (Dibb *et al.*, 2012) to describe what a product consists of, and is illustrated in Figure 10.1. Take a look at the augmented product elements. It is these that direct marketers use to make offers to customers.

10.1.2 The offer

The need to define 'the offer' becomes apparent when you hear two direct marketing practitioners talking to each other. 'Offer' is a very common jargon word used in the world of direct marketing, and like so many other words in marketing, often seems to have more than one meaning when used by practitioners.

Offer and proposition are not the same thing. The difference between the two is neatly summed up by the following example (Boothby, 2002a):

learn French in 30 days (the proposition);

. . . and receive a free DVD (the offer).

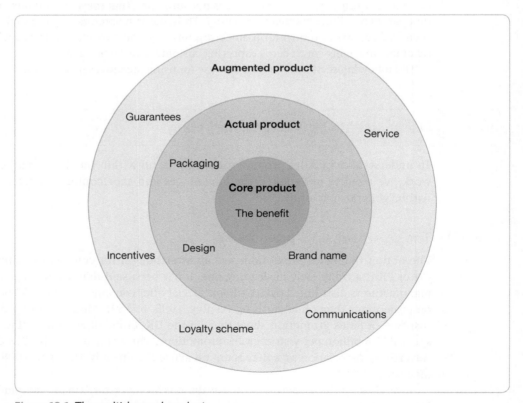

Figure 10.1 The multi-layered product

10.1.3 Incentives (sales promotions)

It is often the case in commodity markets, or those where differentiation is difficult to achieve, that a new way of standing out, or of triggering a response, is needed. In these instances, incentives (or sales promotions) can have a key role and are an important subject for us in direct marketing.

Sales promotions are defined in many marketing textbooks:

'Marketing activities – other than personal selling, advertising and public relations – that stimulate consumer buying and dealer effectiveness'

(McDaniel *et al.*, 2013, p. 651)

'Short term incentives to encourage the purchase or sale of a product or service'

(Kotler & Armstrong, 2012)

'An activity or material that acts as a direct inducement by offering added value to or incentive for the product to resellers, sales people or consumers'

(Dibb *et al.*, 2012)

'Classical' direct marketers Rapp and Collins (1987) coined a more colourful expression to describe sales promotions:

'Sales promotion is the art and science of making something happen.'

Recalling that part of the direct marketing process is the need to 'stimulate', 'encourage' or 'induce' a response (i.e. 'action'), it is not surprising that sales promotions are an important part of the direct marketer's armoury. Thus, direct marketers may use simple incentives such as free gifts in return for a quick response, or complex mechanisms such as 'loyalty schemes', involving smart cards capturing customer transaction data.

The following section examines the case for using incentives in direct marketing.

10.2 Using incentives in direct marketing

To understand why sales promotions are so useful within the direct marketing framework, we need to understand the advantages and shortcomings of sales promotions within 'general' marketing.

10.2.1 The growth of sales promotions

The notion that sales promotions are an afterthought for companies behind advertising or PR is a completely misleading one. It has been said that, as long ago as 1981, US manufacturers distributed over a trillion special offer coupons and spent 60 per cent more on promotions than on advertising (Ogilvy, 1985, p. 169). More recent figures from the Institute of Sales Promotion show that, in the UK, branded good manufacturers alone spent £25.6 billion per year on sales promotions. This compares to the £18.6 billion the Advertising Association says they spent on above the line advertising in 2008 (Marketing Magazine, 2009).

Several factors have been identified as reasons for this growth in promotional popularity. First, product managers are faced with increased pressure to increase current sales, and promotions help them achieve this. Second, increased competition has led to a greater need to differentiate products from those of competitors, and promotions help do this (in the short term, at least). Third, advertising efficiency has declined through rising costs and increased legislation. Finally, we as consumers have become more advertising savvy and deal-driven, so we like sales promotions! (Kotler and Armstrong, 2012).

Exhibit 10.2 Incentives encourage loyalty

Almost half of all shoppers (48 per cent) fail to remain loyal to a favourite brand if a competitor is running a promotion, according to a survey by research group TNS.

A further 24 per cent were unsure whether they would purchase a preferred brand when presented with rival offers, suggesting they may consider swapping if the offer was enticing enough. Only 28 per cent said they would remain loyal to a brand in the face of a promotion.

The social grouping with the most disposable income, ABC1, is the most likely to shop around (53 per cent) for a bargain.

Source: Institute of Sales Promotions (2008), **www.isp.org.uk**.

10.2.2 The objectives of sales promotions

Both direct and general marketers tend to use sales promotions for the same objectives as this list (Dahlen *et al.*, 2012, p. 429) demonstrates:

1 Educating customers and affecting target audience awareness of the brand
2 Helping the conversion of prospects
3 Encouraging early trial and eventual adoption of new products
4 Attracting competitor customers
5 Encouraging increased usage of the brand
6 Cross-selling and up-selling a product

However, a number of commentators have expressed disquiet about the effectiveness of sales promotions. Sales promotions should be tactical offers, designed to gain a short-term advantage or increase in sales. There is a danger that relying too heavily on promotions can result in price erosion, as the over used promotional price lowers the average selling price of your product or service, which in turn can lead to an erosion of company image in the mind of a public who associate quality with price. It can also be the case that, depending on the longevity of your product, customers merely buy up stock at the low price and store it through the non-promotional periods, thus all your promotion ends up doing is bringing high priced sales forward into the low priced timeframe, effectively cannibalising your own sales and profits. This is not a new phenomenon as the following examples show. It has been noticed for at least the last quarter of a century.

10.2.3 The problems with sales promotions in general marketing

Next time you go to the supermarket, take a close look at the promotions on offer. When Heineken offers two cans of lager free when you buy four, what is its objective? It is unlikely to be a reward for loyal buyers. Heineken is probably trying to attract trial from purchasers of other lagers. However, numerous early studies (Rapp and Collins, 1987)

(Smith, 1993) showed that most of this promotion is wasted: in fact most of the purchases are made by:

- customers who would have bought anyway
- deal conscious, compulsive brand switchers

Therefore, relatively few takers of the promotion are genuine 'triallists'.

Kotler and Armstrong noted extensive evidence of an apparent 'lack of any lasting change' in consumer behaviour after the promotion has finished (Kotler and Armstrong, 2007), although it was also found, when reviewing criticisms of sales promotions, that most evidence so far has centred on price promotions rather than added-value promotions (Peattie and Peattie, 1993).

Coming from a direct marketing perspective, the following list of problems have been identified (Rapp and Collins, 1987) (Cram, 1994) associated with sales promotions used in general marketing (especially retail) situations:

- Profitability studies have found that companies using higher sales promotions/advertising ratios have lower profitability.
- A lot of sales promotion is used for the 'wrong' reasons, for example because product managers want short-term gains in market share, or that retailers expect it. Or worst of all, because 'everyone else is doing it'.
- Consumers may be educated/trained to look for the deals and to cry out when they do not get any. Anecdotally, a colleague in the business described these as 'greedy grabby' people who are out to save every penny!
- The trade needs to be given an incentive to carry the manufacturer's brand, and tends to be hostile to many manufacturer-based promotions because they have to be administered through the trade, adding costs without improving total throughput for the retailer.
- Consumers' price expectation will be lowered by continual price promotion. In these instances, the brand franchise is lowered because consumers frequently use price as a surrogate for quality.
- Consumers deliberately misredeem coupons for products other than the intended item.
- In retail stores in the USA, 60 per cent of coupons aimed at new trial customers are in fact redeemed by existing customers, 30 per cent by 'cheaters' who redeem one company's coupons against another's product, and 10 per cent by 'brand hoppers' (loyal to incentives, not brands) and interested triers.

New technology has found a way around some of these problems. For example, the last two in the list above are not so much of an issue now that the vast majority of shops have barcode scanners that will link purchases to coupons and only allow the offer if the correct item has been purchased.

Others of the identified issues arise because of the highly fluid retail environment, with the resulting complete lack of ability to discriminate between existing customers and prospects. The following section explains how direct marketers overcome this.

10.2.4 Using sales promotions in direct marketing

Direct marketers can take a different approach to sales promotions. The direct marketing system 'allows different customer categories to be identified, split and treated separately' (Rapp and Collins, 1987). Separate treatment is the key to success.

Direct marketers can start by using external lists to identify prospects of, say, competitors' products. The sales promotion can then be exclusively targeted at the right audience, rather than wasting such promotions on existing customers. We can subsequently use our own data to highlight loyal customers who can be exclusively rewarded with price or addedvalue incentives to stay.

It can be seen that direct marketing brings superior targeting and control to marketing.

The following process can be used to construct a programme of incentives through direct marketing.

Process for delivering an incentive programme using direct marketing

When planning to use sales promotions in direct marketing, the following steps are appropriate:

Step 1

Carefully establish the objectives. The incentive may be triggering action to switch brands or buy a new product, or it may be reinforcing loyalty.

Step 2

Separate out the target markets and use private media as much as possible. This will avoid wastage. The example in Exhibit 10.3 highlights the advantages of using direct marketing.

Exhibit 10.3 The advantages of incentives using direct marketing: a 'Wine Direct' operation versus a retailer

Let us compare a wine retailer with our database driven 'Wine Direct' operation. We can take a typical promotion, say a free bottle of new Romanian wine on any purchase of a box of 12. In Tables 10.2 and 10.3, each column represents different target markets, while the two rows split those who are not motivated by the incentive from those who are. Look at the differences between the retailer's (Table 10.2) and Wine Direct's (Table 10.3) sales promotions.

Table 10.2 Retailer's sales promotion

	Possible new entrants into market	Loyal to competitor	Brand switcher	Loyal to company
Motivated by sales promotion	Activate?	No effect?	Activate	Waste
Not motivated	No effect	No effect	No effect	Waste

Table 10.3 Wine Direct's sales promotion

	Possible new entrants into market	Loyal to competitor	Brand switcher	Loyal to company
Motivated by sales promotion	Increase offer	Increase offer	Activate	Do not promote
Not motivated	No effect	No effect	No effect	Do not promote

Wine Direct uses sales promotion in a superior manner in the following ways:

- It adjusts the promotion to its own loyal customers, thus avoiding wastage.
- It increases the offer to audiences that are tougher to get to respond to incentives.

Step 3

Calculate the allowable marketing spend per sale (acquisition) or the lifetime value of customers (retention). (These calculations were covered earlier (see Chapter 3).) Then estimate from this how much you can afford to spend on the incentive.

Our starting principle is that the more valuable the incentive is, the more response it will pull, until a point is reached where the returns will diminish and the incentive will no longer be cost-effective. This point can only be accurately determined through testing, although perhaps research could help in the decision.

To calculate the optimum budget to spend on incentives, we can use 'what if?' analysis.

Let us take the example of a direct-mail programme to 10,000 prospects (marketing cost of £5,000). We want to test both a £5 and a £10 incentive. The costs of these incentives depend on response, as we only pay out to responders.

Suppose the £5 incentive achieves a 2 per cent response, while the £10 incentive achieves a 3 per cent response. The product gross margin is £30.

To see which incentive to use, set out a table as in Table 10.4.

In this instance, we should choose the £10 gift, as the returns outweigh the extra costs.

By 'plugging in' other incentive costs, the necessary number of responses to reach your profitability targets can be estimated and assessed as a possible test programme.

You can see from trying out a few of these calculations that the profitability of the exercise depends on the gross margin of the product sold, and the extent to which a more valuable incentive improves the response rate.

Be aware too that there is a school of thought that says the size of the incentive makes less difference than may be first imagined. The marketing department at a direct sell travel insurance retailer were split over just how important the incentive was in encouraging response. They tried a split run mailing, one half being offered a free prize draw to win £1,000, the other half were offered a free prize draw to win £25 in M&S vouchers. The bigger prize drew the bigger response, but careful analysis showed that it was so close as to be statistically insignificant. What is more important, the extra profit generated fell slightly short of covering the bigger prize offered.

Step 4

Choose the incentives carefully so that the brand franchise is built upon, and the positioning of the product is reflected in the promotional device. Check that you are rewarding desired behaviour rather than promiscuity.

There are a large number of different sales promotions, of which the following are suitable for direct marketers (Jobber, 2010, p. 588):

- Free samples
- Prize promotions
- Loyalty cards

Table 10.4 'What if?' analysis for incentives

Incentive	Percentage response	Incentive costs (£)	Mailer costs (£)	Total costs (£)	Sales revenue (£)	Profit (£)
Test 1: Gift of value £5	2	1,000*	5,000	6,000	6,000	0
Test 2: Gift of value £10	3	3,000	5,000	8,000	9,000	1,000

* 2% of 10,000 instances = 200, and 200 × £5 = £1,000.

- Free goods
- Competitions
- Coupons
- Premiums
- Price discounts/money off

Other ideas suggested include (Kotler and Armstrong, 2007):

- Frequency purchase schemes (now commonly known in the UK as 'loyalty schemes')
- Self-liquidating premiums
- Product warranties
- Third-party offers (affinity offers)
- Finance offers (0 per cent interest loans to help purchase, for example)

So as you can see, the range of promotional tools is large and varied. Sales promotions not used by direct marketers are the retail environment specialities, such as price off pack, extra pack free, bind-in offers, etc.

To help us to choose incentives to reward loyalty, O'Brien and Jones (1995) propose five attributes that a successful scheme should have. The incentive should:

- give cash value (at least 5 per cent of product value is recommended)
- offer convenience (incentive should be offered easily within the transaction, avoiding vouchers if possible)
- be relevant (link the incentive to the product or service)
- have aspirational value (incentive should reflect the brand)
- offer choice (points systems redeemed for a choice of rewards)

The digital age has made loyalty schemes easier to use all round. The likes of Tesco (Clubcard), Sainsbury's (part of the Nectar programme) and Boots (Advantage) issue points on a card that is scanned at point of purchase and can even be used for buying on-line. This is far more convenient than earlier coupon collecting, which inevitably meant lost coupons, the inconvenience of counting fiddly pieces of paper and writing off for whatever reward you had been saving to get.

A large number of credit cards offer reward schemes linked to the amount you spend on the card. There is no need to do anything else, just spend, and you are sent an update on your points (or in some cases cash rebates) with your monthly statement – again, much more convenient and less hassle for all concerned. As a result, people are more likely to sign up for such schemes and to use them than before, which can only be a good thing.

Exhibit 10.4 Incentives in direct marketing: Dove

Dove is well known as a beauty products brand with a range of soaps and similar products. In 2006, Dove started its famous 'Campaign for Real Beauty' in which the brand positioned itself as making a point against the ever increasing trend towards using 'size zero' models – ultra skinny models promoted by the fashion industry. Dove launched a powerful TV driven ad campaign featuring everyday women as models.

Dove wanted to do something using direct marketing to encourage more interactivity with its customers. So they launched an on-line campaign inviting people to join in by sending their photos to a Web based album. Agency OgilvyOne had the idea of surprising each of the participants by using an individual photo on the cover of their customer magazine: the magazine's title was *Dove & Me*.

See: **www.ogilvy.com**.

Step 5

Test different incentives against one another in small volumes to establish the most effective.

Step 6

Roll out.

Having examined incentives in detail we now need to consider both offers and incentives together as 'programmes to existing customers'.

10.3 Programmes to existing customers

Programmes to existing customers can be split into those for which the primary objective is to help retain customers, and those that are designed to maximise the profitability of existing customers through extra sales. Figure 10.2 shows how.

We will concentrate on these programmes. Tailored service programmes have been described earlier (Chapter 6), so we will look at dialogue, loyalty schemes, and cross- and up-selling.

10.3.1 Dialogue

Dialogue with customers has been made much easier by digital media. Interested consumers can find out more about their company, products, policies and so on through well designed websites. Direct marketing on-line is used to provide information, newsletters, digital product catalogues, and other vehicles that deliver help, news, information and ways of making the product more valuable to consumers. As well as creating value for existing customers, these Web and e-mail links can provide ways of keeping the relationship alive between purchases. A package holiday operator could keep its name in the minds of its customers, who may be a year from their next purchase.

Traditional direct media can also be used to open a communication channel. Persil distributed thousands of postcards door-to-door, with a help line number included. The number was little used but served as a reminder that Persil does care, positioning Unilever as more than a washing powder supplier.

Among the 'best in the business' here are the charity fundraisers. Given that donors seldom get to see the benefits of their money directly, charities know that communicating clearly what the money is used for can be vital to ensuring donor satisfaction. Some charities see the best solution as offering a 'menu of communications' – often on-line – to the regular donor. Donors choose from pdf files of magazines, reports, accounts or updates of particular projects of interest to them.

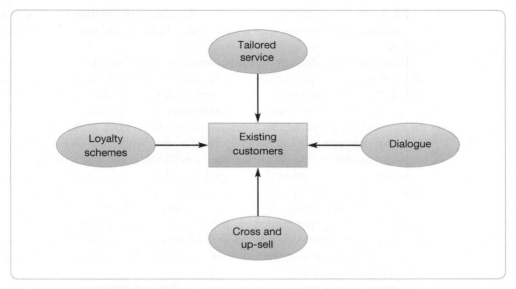

Figure 10.2 **Programmes to retain and maximise profitability of existing customers**

Driven by the need to make it easy for customers, 'carelines' have grown considerably in importance throughout Europe, while they have long been standard practice for US companies, from insurance to packaged supermarket goods.

Carelines are essentially reactive rather than proactive. Their objectives are to build reassurance and to provide accessibility, rather than being a major part of data driven marketing. They can, however, be important data gathering devices.

However, carelines are important because people who call carelines are (self-selected) high involvement purchasers of your products. There is a high chance that they are among your most valuable customers, and making sure they are happy is then top priority. Careline interactions can be included in the customer's record and future direct marketing adjusted accordingly. For example, if a bank's careline takes a call from a customer who is unhappy about existing loan arrangements, it makes sense not to mail them the next day with a mass mailed loan offer!

'Outbound calling to existing customers' can be used to enhance the value of the core product or service. The call from American Express to confirm safe arrival of a customer's card is welcomed and valued. American Express measures this activity in terms of customer retention, and has established a positive effect. Using the telephone to foster relationships and loyalty is more crucial in business-to-business marketing. A supplier of computer training services will keep in constant touch with its customers' personnel departments to ensure high levels of satisfaction. The importance of the telephone is discussed in detail later (Chapter 11).

But it does not stop there, and nor should it. When we go shopping on the high street or at an out of town shopping centre, we expect to be approached – or perhaps that should be accosted – by staff asking 'Can I help you at all?' Usually we just sort of mumble a reply on the lines of 'I'm alright thanks' and hope they will leave us alone and, if they do not, we find ourselves wishing we had gone on-line to look for what we wanted in peace.

Now, websites are increasingly employing 'call back' buttons, where you click, put your telephone number in a text box and within minutes – or even seconds – someone is calling you to discuss your requirements. Other sites use a pop-up dialogue box which offers you the option of a live on-line chat session with a trained sales assistant, or other appropriate person.

These dialogue boxes can be pinpointed to appear at a time in the customer journey where it would be appropriate to make contact. British Telecom currently uses software provided by solutions provider LivePerson to identify points at which users of its retail site are having difficulty in making a decision; and when the behavioural analysis shows that the customer requires help an invitation to chat to an agent is offered (Clawson, 2012). At this point the customer can either accept the offer by clicking on one button or reject it by clicking on another – the online equivalent of shuffling off, 'just looking'!

Another 21st century equivalent, perhaps, of the careline is the advent of allowing customers to post comments on your website. If carefully selected and edited, these can be a great testimonial for your site and your company but, if the posts are allowed to go directly on-line without any moderation or intervention from the site's owner, well, it really is a case of hoping for the best! When NatWest suffered a major systems failure during the installation of a software update, their website's customer comments were far from favourable for a few weeks afterwards!

Another area of particular importance in dialogue programmes are loyalty magazines, also known as 'customer magazines'.

Loyalty (or 'customer') magazines

'Customer' or loyalty magazines are a way of providing high quality, added value communications to existing customers, in an effort to create extra value and, hence, provide another reason to stay with that supplier. By 2007, loyalty magazines (contract publishing), were worth over £500 million as an industry, up from a modest £50 million in 1990. Loyalty magazines have gone from strength to strength throughout much of Europe and the USA. In the UK loyalty magazines now account for the biggest circulations, over and above the paid for magazine sector. This has to be one of the success stories of the loyalty industry – one cannot imagine this sort of sustained growth unless firms were at least reasonably happy with their measures.

Customer magazines enjoy wide use across international markets and products from credit cards to cars, clothing to cigarettes. The sector is dominated by retail – supermarkets in particular – and entertainment. But organisations as diverse as BMW, Barclays, Saab, Benetton, BT, News International and Oxfam all use magazines. Research by Tapp back in 1995 in the charity sector showed 65 per cent of the top 500 charities have launched magazines to their donor base. There is little doubt that, even in this on-line age, customers seem to welcome magazines. In fact, dedicated on-line companies now realise that they need an off-line presence as well: *Lastminute.com Magazine* was launched in 2006.

Magazines achieve loyalty related objectives by providing awareness of products and services, getting feedback from customers, helping to clean the database via customer calls, and prompting the provision of extra information to customers. Citroën's magazine, *Directions,* is an example. Citroën says that its customers are informed and entertained by the magazine, thereby feeling 'warmer' towards the company.

The key to success for these magazines is that they must be worthwhile in their own right. To be successful, they must be capable of competing with news-stand magazines; the acid test is whether the loyalty magazine is potentially capable of commanding a price in its own right. Sainsbury's retail magazine is bought in its stores for £1 but mailed free to high value existing customers. Customer magazines now have production values and quality to match glossy consumer magazines, with many staffed by ex-consumer magazine journalists

Loyalty magazines require high quality editorial with relevant, entertaining features. In some sectors, interesting aspects of the product itself can be a major focus for the magazine; for example, the UK roadside recovery organisation Automobile Association focuses on travel and auto articles. Other sectors will probably largely ignore their product. Barclaycard's magazine or a telecommunications magazine will go for 'lifestyle' features of popular appeal. For example, a magazine from Sun Alliance Financial Services, *Foresight*, had articles on a major TV star, how to sell your home in six weeks, tips on being safer on the roads, and the chance to win an all inclusive trip to the USA. Any mention of Sun Alliance's products was strictly 'soft sell', and occupied only a minor proportion of editorial.

Companies with tightly defined audiences find it easier to produce relevant loyalty magazines. Saab, with its high skew to AB males, can safely include articles on golf and rugby, knowing they will be well received. On the other hand, companies with loosely defined audiences may segment their magazines according to different needs. In 2007, TV multinational Sky launched two new magazines *Sky Movies* and *Sky Sports* to complement its long standing *Sky Magazine*. *Sky Magazine* has for some time been the largest circulation loyalty magazine in the UK, but recognises that a segmented approach will appeal more.

Clubs

Creating a membership scheme or club as part of the loyalty strategy was well established in direct marketing by classic direct marketers. They originally set up 'clubs' that had no fundamental basis other than to act as a type of contract, locking in customers to an offer. These devices are used more for acquisition and are discussed later. In this section we will discuss clubs that have been created to help engender loyalty.

In what instances will the creation of a membership club for our existing customers be a good idea? Think for a moment about leisure or social clubs you may belong to. You may have joined because of a high level of interest in an activity, or because you feel comfortable with the type of people who have already joined. You may also enjoy the status that club membership gives you, and even 'subconsciously' use membership to help define your position in society.

It is these reasons for joining that provide the clues to successful direct marketing clubs. Direct marketers should consider the tactic of creating a club to create customer value when the following applies:

Exhibit 10.5 Customer magazines: *Land Rover Onelife*

'If Land Rover were a person, he'd be an explorer, adventurer and an adrenalin junkie.'

Land Rover is a classic example of a brand for which loyalty magazines were made. There is plenty of customer interest, and plenty to write about. Land Rover understands that, although most of its customers drive about in places like Surbiton, in their heads they are crashing about off-road in somewhere like Peru. *Onelife* magazine invites customers to participate in Land Rover events and off-road adventures. Direct agency Craik-Jones helped Land Rover run a programme called 'A Country Affair', a series of one-day events in which customers were invited to enjoy a range of country pursuits as well as put the latest Range Rovers through their paces on and off the road. It also runs Discoverers Days – a programme of events geared to the more family/adventure orientated owners of Discovery

---

vehicles. Research with customers shows that the magazine achieves a high readership level and is welcomed by customers.

Across the sector the customer magazine industry is enjoying an increase in usage of its branded content across different channels including podcasts, on-line, radio and TV, and *Land Rover Onelife* is no exception. It was winner of Magazine of the Year at APA's Customer Publishing Awards 2006, Best Use of Photography and Best Use of Film at the 2009 APAs, Customer Magazine of the Year at the 2010 PPA Awards, and Best International Publication at the 2011 APA awards. The magazine is now translated into 14 languages and is adapted and delivered to 36 international markets worldwide, including the US, China, Japan and Europe, and the combined print-run is 450,000 copies. An iPad version of the magazine is also created for both the UK and US markets. *Onelife* is being shown on Land Rover's 24/7 TV Network, 'Go Beyond', as well as on-line at **www.landrover.com,** a truly multimedia approach to customer contact and engendering loyalty.

Sources: **www.landrover.com**; **www.apa.co.uk**, **http://redwoodgroup.net/land-rover-onelife-magazine**

1 **Customers have high involvement with the product.** Examples include Pedigree Petfoods' 'Sheba' Club, Buitoni's Pasta Lovers' Club and Walt Disney's Children's Club. Some cat owners are quite obsessive about their pets, devoting more love and attention to them than to members of their own family. This obsession extends very naturally into the cats' welfare, including their diet; which is where Sheba, positioned as top quality cat food, comes in. Membership of the Sheba Club entitles consumers to all manner of cat related offers, such as personalised pet plates, books on cats, events and so on. On informing Pedigree that their cat has died, members receive a 'mortality' mailing expressing how sorry Pedigree is that Tiddles has died and the hope that they will eventually buy another cat! Websites have added a great deal to the way these kinds of clubs are run. On-line is a cheaper and more interactive way to set up a club, and if people are interested they will access websites and join in activities on-line.

2 **Membership bestows an element of status.** Obvious examples here are clubs run for customers of BMW, the BA Executive Club for frequent flyers and the Hilton Hotels Executive Club. Club membership is restricted, and customers may discreetly enjoy the exclusivity bestowed by their status as club members. Club privileges are positioned accordingly.

3 **Customers would value the association with other members.** People who own unusual or niche products often feel a strong sense of association with one another. Harley Davidson motorbike riders see their pastime, and their bikes, as a part of their identity. They define their personality through this shared interest, and product purchases are, therefore, made very carefully. Such products are an obvious area for direct marketing run clubs.

10.3.2 Cross- and up-selling

Delighted customers not only make repeat purchases, but also become willing marketing partners and 'customer evangelists' who spread the word about their good experiences to others (Kotler and Armstrong, 2012, p. 37). This is something that has been known by direct marketers; 20 years earlier Professor Derek Holder, the late Managing Director of the Institute of Direct Marketing recognised that a firm's loyal customers are far more likely to buy its products than are new prospects (Holder, 1992). According to Holder, many sectors operate a cycle of contact programmes, shown in Figure 10.3.

The 'welcome' stage may resist any attempt at an overt sale, but experience has shown, in sectors such as mail order, that customers often buy again soon after their most recent purchase. Nevertheless, the primary objective of welcome mailers or calls should be service related.

If customers are satisfied with the product they first bought, they will be favourably inclined to purchase more of it, or to purchase an upgrade. Computer software consumers who enjoyed the basic product of a computer game are likely to be hot prospects for a higher priced upgrade. This is 'up-selling'.

As customers get used to you and learn more about your offerings, the logical next step is to cross-sell. Thus, a bank may interest a current account customer in a credit card or loan.

This has been going on for decades. Over 25 years ago, at Norwich Union Life Insurance 'cross-selling' was described as a 'strategic must' (Durand, 1987). Although much cross-selling in financial sectors is often poorly targeted, it is still one step better than prospect mailing of cold lists, because at least we are selling to our existing customers. One worry for the industry is that response rates have been dropping slowly for cross-selling as time has gone on: the ease of the Web in helping people proactively buy has lessened the effectiveness of semi-targeted guesswork – which is what cross- and up-selling effectively is.

That said, some sectors, such as subscriptions to publications, car breakdown services and car insurance, have definite 'renewal' cycles, and the critical moment arrives when a customer makes an active choice to stay, lapse or defect to competitors. Holder recommended a series of relevant communications before, during and after the renewal date (Holder, 1992). Thomas and Housden suggest breaking renewals down by category, giving an example of a magazine that may divide lapsing subscribers depending on whether they have an automatically renewing direct debit or not, the latter being sent a more in-depth set of communications over a longer run-up to the lapse date (Thomas and Housden, 2011).

Making the effort in increasing retention is a worthwhile exercise. Research (Weitz *et al.*, 2007, pp. 196–7) has shown that:

- when customer retention increases by 5 per cent a year, profits rise by as much as 25 per cent
- improving customer retention by just 2 per cent can decrease costs by up to 10 per cent

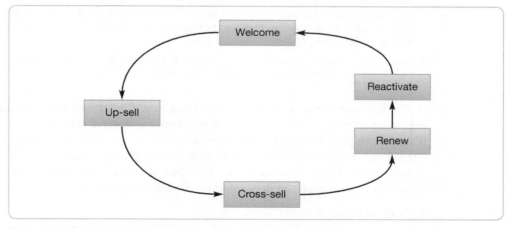

Figure 10.3 Contact cycle to increase revenue from loyal customers
Source: Holder, D. (1992).

At some point (this point is identified through testing) it becomes uneconomic to continue contacting people and they then become lapsed customers.

Exhibit 10.6 Cross-sell – Wells Fargo

Every financial services company tries to master 'cross-selling', offering pre-existing customers multiple products. Wells Fargo, which averages 5.9 products per customer in its retail banking business, does it better than anyone. The average household has roughly 16 products – mortgages, checking accounts, credit cards, various insurance policies and the like – across various financial institutions. Wells and its rivals compete fiercely to own as much of your wallet as possible.

'When I first became CEO, I got a call from another big bank CEO who said, "I'm coming through town. You guys are big in this cross-sell. I'll buy you lunch. Tell me how you do it," ' recalls Wells Chief, John Stumpf. 'I told him, "I can't eat that long and I can't eat that much because it would take hours – days – weeks to talk about it." ' Stumpf was being polite. He'd as soon reveal his methods as Coke would the ingredients of its syrup.

The more services you sell to individuals, the more profitable those customers are (even with discount bundles for multiple services) – and the harder it is for them to break away. 'We expect to sell at least one more product to every customer every year', intones the company handbook. Competing divisions within the bank have a healthy incentive to cooperate with one another. Brokers need to make nice with retail bankers, say, because those folks' clients are an easy target for mutual funds and retirement accounts.

On the institutional side the payoff is customers like Public Storage, a self-storage company with the $1.65 billion in sales, which has been banking with Wells Fargo since 1984, when it had $12 million in revenue. Today it uses the bank for primary lending, depository and treasury services, retirement plan administration and overnight investments; Wells also serves as a joint book runner and underwriter for Public's preferred-share issuances. In the last 12 months Wells has helped provide financing totalling $2.3 billion.

'When things are good everyone wants to be your banker and lend you money,' says Public Storage Chief Executive Ronald Havner Jr. 'It's when things are bad you find out if you have a bank or not.' Wells has stuck by him because a known customer is a lot less risky than a new one.

As the 37-page book, Vision& Values, signed by Stumpf and distributed to all the company's 264,000 employees, puts it: 'There are only three ways a company can grow. First, earn more business from your current customers. Second, attract customers from your competitors. Or third, buy another company. If you can't do the first, what makes you think you can earn more business from your competitors' customers or from customers you buy through acquisition?"

Sources: Adapted by the author from articles appearing in Forbes Magazine, 13 Feb 12 (Touryalai, 2012), (Schifrin & Touryalai, 2012). Also available online at **forbes.com** (accessed 30 June 2012).

The final stage may be to attempt to 'reactivate' former customers with reminders to renew membership. These people are still better prospects than those who have never bought from you. Rapp and Collins (1994) found that the majority of defection comes as a result of company indifference rather than an active switch. Other research by the Direct Marketing Association and the Future Foundation (cited by Thomas and Housden, 2008) shows that customers claim they defect for the following reasons:

- 72 per cent due to poor customer service
- 31 per cent give quality issues as their reason for stopping buying from a company
- 25 per cent say it is because of price

- 16 per cent for special offers
- 12 per cent for reasons of functionality
- 9 per cent for convenience
- 9 per cent because their needs have changed

This research also asked companies why they thought their customers left them. They gave a completely different weight to the above categories, with 48 per cent of companies thinking the main reason was due to price and 36 per cent believing the customers' needs had changed. Only 22 per cent identified customer service as a reason.

In any case, we can see clearly that renewal and reactivation tactics, therefore, have a sound theoretical foundation.

10.3.3 The use of loyalty schemes

There can scarcely be a soul left among us who has not encountered a loyalty scheme somewhere. Imagine a weekend trip to Paris. You take your car to the airport, picking up your petrol points on the way and using your credit card to pay, racking up credit card points towards your next car purchase. You park in the long-term car park, promoted by its points scheme, and go to the terminal. There you pick up your daily paper, the choice dictated by your involvement in its 'Fantasy Football' loyalty competition. You jump on the plane, redeeming your Arios collected through your other credit card over the past year. While in Paris you stay at the hotel that attracted you as a business person on its prestigious 'gold card' bonus scheme, while the car you rent has a similar deal. On the way home you stop off at the supermarket to replenish supplies, participating in your eighth loyalty scheme of the weekend!

In truth, there cannot be many people who are as obsessed with loyalty schemes as our Paris tourist. In fact, the danger of 'loyalty overload', causing customer confusion and apathy, has led to the plethora of points schemes launched in the mid 1990s drying up considerably. At the time of writing, in the UK the biggest loyalty schemes operating are Tesco Clubcard and Nectar. This last case is examined in detail at the end of this chapter.

Early research suggested that loyalty schemes were very popular with the public (although there have been variations between countries). However, analysts (Mitchell, 1997) have noted that consumers do not perceive loyalty schemes as a strong benefit and, hence, increasingly they do not bother to participate. As a personal example, I frequently shop in Sainsbury's and when I go to pay I give them my Nectar card (because I am being loyal to Sainsbury's), and then pay with my Tesco credit card where I receive Clubcard points (because I am being loyal to Tesco!).

When we speak of 'loyalty' we need to recognise that not everyone is loyal to an organisation for the same reasons, and not all loyalty is the same. The following types of loyalty have been identified (Baines et al., 2011); other authors will have their own version of this list:

- **Emotional loyalty.** This is a true form of loyalty and is driven by personal identification with real or perceived values and benefits.
- **Price loyalty.** This type of loyalty is driven by rational economic behaviour and the main motivations are cautious management of money or financial necessity.
- **Incentivised loyalty.** This refers to promiscuous buyers: those with no favourite brand who demonstrate through repeat experience the value of becoming loyal.
- **Monopoly loyalty.** This class of loyalty arises where a consumer has no purchase choice owing to a national monopoly. This, therefore, is not a true form of loyalty.

Some of these problems and ways round them were discussed in detail earlier (Chapter 6). Here we will confine ourselves to an understanding of the schemes themselves. Let us first define what these schemes are.

Loyalty schemes can be defined as:

'Systems which persuade customers to prefer one supplier to another through 'spending-related rewards' and related marketing activities.'

(Andy Wood, Head of European Marketing, NCH Marketing Services Ltd)

Loyalty schemes tend to be most useful in 'frequent purchase markets', and have been particularly prevalent in airlines, hotels and retail markets around the world. The core mechanism to all schemes is essentially quite simple: customers accrue 'points' or some other measured unit of value in return for spend with that company or brand. These points may be redeemable by the customer for something of value, be it money off a future purchase, gifts, cash back or privileged services.

Loyalty schemes are also commonly found in markets where the core product is a 'commodity' and companies have great difficulty differentiating themselves. Sectors such as telecommunications or car insurance are largely price led, and suppliers may attempt to keep their customers through 'loyalty pricing' schemes, in which customers who spend more obtain volume discounts. In car insurance, the accumulated 'no claims bonus' is an example of this.

Loyalty pricing is an example of the strategy of sharing value (Reichheld, 1996); or 'sharing the sweeties', as it has rather more picturesquely been described (Cram, 1994). As you trade more efficiently with long-term customers, you can afford to charge less. Cram, however, recommends offering better value rather than straight price discounts, because the latter are so easy to copy. Another problem with price discounts is that there is always someone with deeper pockets than you, and they do not have to be 'much' deeper, just deep enough to last one day longer than you can stay in business, as Exhibit 10.7 illustrates (again, rather more picturesquely than normal, perhaps!)

Exhibit 10.7 The cheetah in the long grass

While on safari and walking in the savanna plains, two tourists were stopped by their guide who urgently hushed them into silence. Following the guide's stare, they saw a cheetah staring at them from its hiding place in the long grass about 30 metres from them. One of the tourists froze, the other began to take a pair of trainers out of his backpack very quietly and put them on.

The guide turned to him and whispered: 'Are you mad? That's a cheetah, the fastest animal on dry land. It can run at up to 70 miles per hour! You'll never outrun it, even with the best trainers in the world!'

The tourist kept on changing and replied: 'I don't have to run faster than the cheetah, I only have to run faster than you two can, and not for very long.'

Let us remember the key issues discussed earlier (Chapter 6). These schemes do not engender loyalty by themselves; they must be 'part of' a retention strategy to work. By themselves, they are only sales promotions – incentives for a particular purchase. When used properly, these schemes become an integral part of the direct marketing system: they act as the vehicle through which customer transaction data is collected. Without them, no direct marketing as such would take place. With them, the company can understand who its most and least valuable customers are, the importance of which is highlighted all through this book. Finally, these schemes combine both loyalty and sales objectives, in that they are designed to encourage customers to spend more as well as staying with one supplier.

Loyalty schemes are implemented in various ways. The original method, 'proof of purchase', has been largely replaced by 'card based schemes'. These, in turn, have developed into 'co-branded partnership' marketing schemes. A recent variant has been the use of 'competitions' as a way to promote loyalty. However, some companies avoid this paraphernalia and employ loyalty pricing schemes with the data held within the company. We will now examine these different executions.

Exhibit 10.8 Supermarket wars: how Clubcard saves Tesco money

British retailer Tesco uses its loyalty card data intelligently in its on-going battle with supermarket giant Wal-Mart, owner of Asda. Asda will routinely discount on multiple products, in line with its low-cost, low-price approach. For Tesco to copy directly all price drops would be very costly. Instead, it adopts a much more precise, though equally aggressive, 'rifle shot' promotion. Tesco analyses individual customers' shopping carts to determine which are the 'killer' products that drive us into stores in the first place. If any of these are threatened, Tesco will match these prices, but again only with customers it has identified as more price sensitive. Ultimately, Tesco Clubcard is a key player in the big game of minimising the profit damage of aggressive price competition. Just another example of how 'loyalty cards' have only an indirect relationship with loyalty.

Proof of purchase based loyalty schemes

The traditional mechanism, proof of purchase, is still used, especially by packaged goods manufacturers who have no way of easily using cards. In the restaurant sector, Pizza Hut has used incentives and competitions to categorise its customers by frequency and scale of patronage in order to target heavy and medium users. Heavy users are sent vouchers that must be redeemed within four weeks and are encouraged to buy special value meals. Meanwhile, medium users have eight week vouchers, and so on.

In markets where margins are very tight, in particular packaged goods sectors, the rewards are often self-liquidating; that is, customers are asked to pay a small fee in addition to the vouchers to receive their reward. This fee covers the company cost of the gift. For example, a premium dog food company may offer personalised plates, leads, etc. in return for both proof of purchase and a small charge. These schemes can add value to relationships while also stimulating extra sales within it – achieving the twin objectives of retention and increased sales.

As ever, the Internet has taken the idea of proof of purchase schemes to another level. Sites such as Quidco have opened the offering of cash back to people who shop through their site. Although they do not sell anything themselves, they are effectively an introducer to other (often mainstream) retailers such as Tesco, eBay, Vodaphone and npower.

The idea of such cash back sites is relatively simple: you register and when you buy on-line you visit the same retailers as usual, but via a link on your chosen cash back site. When you make a purchase, the retailer pays a commission to your cashback site, who in turn gives you a cut of the money (Stevens, 2010). In effect, the loyalty in this case is price driven and to the cash back site, rather than to any particular retailer, but it is an example of how technology has taken an old idea and developed it in new ways.

Card based schemes

The use of loyalty cards was an extremely important development in the 1990s in most developed world markets. Loyalty cards originated with the 'Divi' from the Co-op supermarket, which dates back to the nineteenth century and started life as the dividend paid to members from profits (hence the name 'Divi'). Replacements included the once famous Green Shield trading stamps and coupons. Loyalty cards are now used in a number of sectors: retail (petrol, supermarkets, DIY, some high street sectors such as clothing and music), leisure (restaurants and pubs), business executive markets (airlines, car rental, hotels) and, more recently, business-to-business markets, for example the ICI bonus points scheme aimed at painters and decorators who buy Dulux paint products.

Exhibit 10.9 The Wacky Warehouse

Allied Domecq has spotted a big gap in the market in UK pubs: catering for families with young children. It has built a series of pubs, branded Big Steak, with adjoining Wacky Warehouse play areas for children. Customers are offered the chance to join a loyalty scheme by Wacky Warehouse staff, and fill out a questionnaire asking for birthdays, anniversary dates, etc. The scheme is administered by a Gold Card that records transactions. Customers get one point for every £1 spent and £5 reward vouchers for every 100 points. Quarterly statements are sent to customers keeping them up to date. In addition, 'exclusive' special offers are run, such as vouchers offering 15 flowers free with 15 purchased for an anniversary.

Allied Domecq has combined excellent niche marketing, carefully meeting the needs of families with young children, with a loyalty scheme designed to maximise existing behaviour traits. The company knows that parents of young children will often get into routines and will return time and again. The loyalty card encourages this.

Source: Allied Domecq consumer communications.

Magnetic stripe and smart cards

Loyalty schemes are run on either magnetic stripe or smart cards. Smart cards carry computer chips within them and have greater off-line functionality and data capacity than magnetic stripe cards. Customer data is held within the card, not on a database. This hands control over their own data from the company to the customer.

Magnetic stripe cards have been much cheaper (a few pence) than smart cards but these differences are disappearing, and smart cards are increasingly being introduced for debit and credit cards as well as loyalty cards. Magnetic stripe cards are more likely to be compatible with existing store 'electronic point of sale' (EPOS) technology, and a good database makes the need to hold the data on the card less apparent, but smart cards are essential for coalition cards such as Nectar.

Cards are ideal for the crucial role of tracking transaction data and building the customer record.

The economics of a card based loyalty scheme need to be carefully thought through, as it is not a cheap option. A company with a six figure customer base would expect to pay, probably, £5 to £10 million in set-up costs, and then perhaps 50p per customer per year in ongoing administrative charges. Finally, there are the costs of the reward itself. This investment will only pay back if the incremental customer retention revenue achieved from the scheme outweighs these costs.

In some sectors, such as telecommunications or utilities, transaction data is automatically collected internally and cards are not necessary for loyalty schemes to be run.

Cross-category promotion schemes (co-branded cards)

Most loyalty schemes are unique to one supplier in that the points earned are for purchases from that supplier, with rewards obtained within the scheme. However, cross-category promotion schemes have become popular. Here, the scheme involves a number of suppliers from different sectors. Consumers can earn points from purchases from all these suppliers, which are then redeemed for rewards in the normal way. The scheme may be set up and administered by an independent company, which makes money from selling points to suppliers at a higher rate than their pay out on redeemed points from consumers.

Exhibit 10.10 Airline frequent flyer programmes

Airlines have been described as 'a lousy business to be in'. Always operating with tight margins, the trauma of 9/11, a weakening of consumer confidence and tough competition from low cost carriers have combined to bring many airlines to their knees. Swiss Air and Belgian Airlines effectively closed down in 2002, Northwestern Airlines filed for bankruptcy, and even mighty American Airlines was taken to the brink.

However, since then there has been a recovery in global flying with growth in the numbers wanting to fly and the emergence of new and very large Asian markets. Part of the picture has been the re-launch of frequent flyer schemes. These began because traditional airlines have historically been starved of information about their customers as only about 15 per cent book direct. Loyalty schemes give them priceless transaction data on their most valuable customers: frequent business flyers.

Frequent flyer programmes are now a global phenomenon. The majority of the world's major carriers, from Air Portugal to Cathay Pacific, now have well-established schemes. But note the loyalty paradox yet again: increasingly people switch between 'loyalty' programmes! There are websites like **www.frequentFlier.com** that have newsletters, news of the best deals and a chat forum.

The biggest market is in the USA, part of over 50 airlines worldwide with around 250 million members in total around the world. The world's biggest scheme is run by American Airlines, called AAdvantage, with 26 million members worldwide including partner airline members. This scheme was launched as far back as 1981. Credit card programmes, such as the American Express Business ExtrAA corporate card, have developed partnerships with airlines, so that consumers can convert points to airline miles. The airlines have a number of partnerships with hotels and car rental firms that allow more attractive points gathering opportunities.

Sources: Charlton, P. (2004) 'Targeting – The Achilles' heel of frequent flyer programmes', **Thewisemarketer.com**. **FrequentFlier.com** Accessed 2008. *Potentials*, (2003) **36** (7), p. 7.

Examples of card consortia of various types have included:

- Tesco (UK retailer) Clubcard/NatWest Bank. Points are collected from Tesco retail store and redeemed for vouchers based on supermarket spend.
- Takashimaya (Japanese retailer)/Fujitsu, Visa, Development Bank of Singapore. This is a co-branded Visa credit card that also acts as a loyalty card. Points are redeemed for parking rights (a big deal in Japan!), delivery of purchases and gift offers.

Ideas such as Shell's Smartcard were seen as ground breaking when first launched. For instance, Mitchell (1997) described it as developing as a brand in its own right – with its own identity, image and values – driven primarily by direct marketing. It was hoped this would be an umbrella loyalty scheme involving ten-plus non-competing companies from different sectors including Hilton Hotels, Shell, and a number of retailers from wine to stationers. In fact, Shell encountered significant practical problems in making the scheme work, with players arguing over who was entitled to what. There were also problems over the branding being Shell driven. Subsequently, Shell replaced Smartcard with Pluspoints – a scheme with more modest outcomes than Smartcard.

The plans for cards such as this are to tie in a large number of companies across as many sectors as possible, in particular frequent purchase markets.

Such 'constellation brands' may be a big growth area of the future because of the added value that can be created for customers without adding costs to individual suppliers.

Future developments

With smartphones becoming ever more ubiquitous, it is surely only a matter of time before these become the mechanism for managing loyalty schemes. Tesco and others are currently offering apps that will let you carry your Clubcard on your phone, other third parties (Loyalty Card and the French fidme among them) are offering apps that will allow you to scan and store multiple cards and combine this with geo-locating to find the nearest branches of the stores to which you are loyal. Sainsbury's Nectar has an app that allows you to see your points balance, shop on-line and find local stores.

It is surely just a matter of time before all of these are brought together with app driven shopping and order placing, payment, tracking of orders and purchase driven loyalty rewards, all managed from our smartphones.

10.3.4 Creating a complete programme of contact

Taking our offers, discussed earlier, and incentives all together, we arrive at a complete programme of customer contact. The scheme in Figure 10.4 indicates what such a programme might look like.

10.4 Programmes of contact to attract new customers

Contact programmes to acquire customers have been used by direct marketers in traditional direct marketing sectors for a long time. Direct distribution companies such as mail order, publishing, book clubs, china collectibles and so on, have become masters of the art of using incentives to acquire customers at the lowest possible cost per sale.

Recalling Jones' (1996) comment that firms should 'acquire with product and retain with service', there is perhaps some truth that direct marketing within the acquisition situation is often better described as 'direct selling'. Within this context, the objective of incentives within an acquisition programme becomes clearer. It is to provide that final push: to trigger a response from a customer who is interested but needs that final stimulus to act on the impulse to buy.

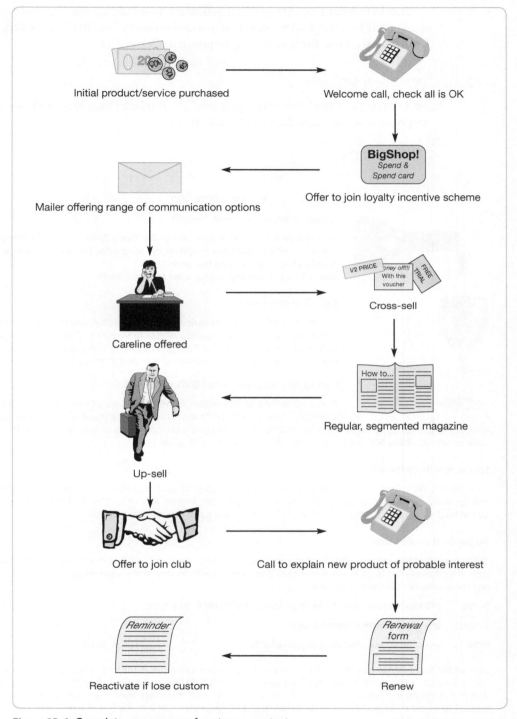

Figure 10.4 Complete programme of customer contact

Thanks to extensive testing, direct marketers have built up considerable cumulative wisdom on the best ways to trigger action in a cost-effective way. To illustrate this, let us examine a typical classic direct marketing acquisition offer in detail.

10.4.1 Whitten's Wine Club

As an example of the 'offer with conditions', let us take a closer look at the specimen direct-response advertisement shown in Figure 10.5.

Whitten's Wine Club

Quality wine, free delivery, free gift

As a special offer for new members of Whitten's Wine Club, we're offering FREE delivery, and a saving of over £50 off the shop price for this superb selection of quality wines from around the world!
That's 12 bottles of top quality wine for just £19.99.

Save over £50 now!

At Whitten's Wine Club, we believe that good quality wine shouldn't be an elitist hobby but should be made easily available to everyone. That's why with your first order you will receive detailed Tasting Notes along with more information about each bottle – a service designed to make wine buying as easy and pleasurable as possible.

Sign up now to receive a free DVD wine course!

If yours is in the first 500 responses we receive, we will send you – FREE OF CHARGE – this fantastic DVD wine course, giving you expert guidance and advice into selecting and tasting wines from around the world – but you must act quickly to qualify for this extra free gift because we only have 500 copies and when they're gone, they're gone!

Special monthly wine offers

As Whitten's Wine Club member, you'll receive an option to buy 12 bottles of quality wine each month for just £40, and for every third case you buy at this price, we'll let you take another for just £19.99. All we ask of you is that you buy at least six cases at the full club price of £39.99 at some point over the next two years.

No payment needed now!

Simply complete the payment details below, we'll send you your wine and won't take any money from you for ten days after delivery has been made. Better than that: **if you don't like any of the wine we send you – ever – you don't pay for it** – we can't be fairer than that!

POST: Whitten's Wine Club, 1 The High Street, ANYTOWN, AT1 1WC

E-MAIL   offer101@whittenswineclub.com

WEB   www.whittenswineclub.com/join-offer101   Expires 26 Feb 15

I would like to join Whitten's Wine Club. I am enclosing payment of just £39.99 for the Special Introductory Offer 101, for which I will receive 12 bottles of top quality wine, POST FREE, and agree to buy at least six cases of twelve bottles (for the normal club price of £39.99) in the next two years. For every third case I buy at this price, I will be entitled to a case of 12 bottles at the special price of £19.99. If this reply is in the first 500 received, I will get a free wine course on DVD.

Figure 10.5 Whitten's Wine Club

Name: _____   Address: _____

_____

Credit card details: _____   _____

Name on card _____   _____

Card number _____   _____

Expiry Date _____   Postcode _____

Signature: _____   **I am 18 or over (Order invalid without a signature)**

Offer closes 26 February 2013. All orders subject to acceptance. All offers subject to availability. One membership per household. Allow up to 10 days for delivery. Offer applies to UK, CI, Eire and BFPO only. P&P and insurance charges quoted are based on rates at time of going to press and may vary.

I understand that I can return the wine in this offer, unopened, within 10 days of receipt and I will not be charged and my membership will be cancelled. As a member I agree to buy at least six more cases of 12 bottles for just £39.99 in the next two years. This is my only commitment. I am not obliged to buy every month and, if I do not want to receive wine in any month, I will return the order form to you to indicate this.

Whitten's Wine Club is registered under the Data Protection Act (1998). From time to time we may pass your name and address to other companies who we believe offer products in which you may be interested. If you wish to avoid this, please tick here [ ]

Your 12-bottle introductory case will be delivered to you within 10 days

Remember the Whitten's Wine Club money back guarantee: if you are not completely satisfied for any reason, we will refund your money. If you don't like the wine, you don't pay!

Figure 10.5 (*continued*)

As you can see, there is some complexity to the customer offer. Let us take a closer look. The following analysis highlights how the design of the offer pays back for the company while also providing instant value for the customer.

The return on investment

The economics of the use of incentives will have been carefully calculated by the company. The figures in Table 10.5 illustrate the general principle 'but are not based on actual data'.

From Table 10.5 we can see that gross margin is, therefore, £65 on a turnover of £260.

The introductory case of 12 bottles of wine represents Whitten's Wine Club's front-end revenues and costs. As we can see, the company will lose a few pence on the initial sale,

Table 10.5 Typical return on investment figures

	Typical costs	Typical revenues
Introductory wine case offer	£20.00	£19.99
Six subsequent cases at £39.99	£120.00	£239.94
Gift (wine course DVD)@ £5 each	£5.00	
Media costs per customer (press, catalogues)	£50.00	
Total	£195.00	£260.00
Return =	**£65.00**	

because of the high value of its incentive to join the club. It is with the sale of the six subsequent purchases, the back-end revenues, that the payback is achieved.

The key to success is that the offer demands a future obligation from customers by contracting them into future purchases. This could be:

- customer agreement to automatic billing for a year's subscription
- club-style conditions, e.g. 'I agree to buy six more cases of wine at full price over the next two years'

This example is typical of classical direct marketers in offering multiple incentives. The direct marketers' assertion that these give multiple reasons to buy is borne out by testing. They also take care to use incentives (the wine course DVD) that are related to the core product.

Exhibit 10.11 Groupon – taking coupons to groups of people on-line

Groupon is a website that brings together sellers and buyers to the advantage of all concerned.

On behalf of their business clients, Groupon makes 1,000 offers every day to geographically targeted segments of their 142 million global subscribers in 45 countries. The offer may be something like a memory foam mattress at 67 per cent off the normal price or a large discount on beauty treatments from a local provider. What makes their approach different is that, unless a given number of people sign up for the deal (that number is predetermined by the seller), the deal does not become 'active' and nobody can have it; as soon as the prescribed number is reached the seller has to sell at the price stated to all who signed up. Sellers retain control in that they can stop the deal at any given point in time or when a certain number of people have signed up, so (assuming they have done their maths) they should not end up out of pocket.

The sellers gain extra customers (and Groupon even provides them with their details for future marketing activity), the customers get a bargain, and Groupon takes a cut of the sales revenue as their payment, so the seller does not even have to find any payment up front. It is a situation where everybody wins.

10.4.2 Techniques for eliciting direct response

One of the most knowledgeable writers on the subject of acquisition offers is Stone (1996), who outlined many of the most common techniques used. We can now examine the most important of these.

The opt-in/out mechanism

These were based on techniques honed within the mail-order sector, and are perhaps increasingly 'old fashioned' outside of classical direct marketing. But as much as anything, they illustrate a mentality of marketing professionals to push techniques to the limit in almost manipulating their customers. Let us describe the techniques – see what you think: are there any ethical issues here?

One variant on the 'contractual' design, illustrated by the example, is the opt-out. Here a higher initial response is sought by promising no 'lock-in', that is no obligation to buy in the future. The company then sends products at regular intervals to the customer; if they do 'not' want these, they must act by sending back the product. This technique is often used in publishing. If the customer wants to cancel the subscription, they must write to the publisher to do so.

The success of this technique is due to the direct marketer's understanding of customer inertia. There will be a middle ground of customers who perhaps would not have made the effort to buy the products but who also are not sufficiently motivated to cancel the subscription, being reasonably happy with the value they are receiving. These are the people who are captured by the opt-out mechanism.

Opt-out is frowned upon by many people who see it as deceptive and giving marketers a bad name. The alternative is to opt-in. Here customers have to act if they 'do' want the product.

The question of which is better has to be carefully addressed and tested. Stone reports that opt-in offers tend to give lower initial response, because the acquisition offer is likely to be less valuable to the customer. However, retention sales are likely to be higher, because more customers with a genuine interest in the product rather than the incentive will have been attracted.

Free samples

Used extensively by the packaged goods industries, free samples can be delivered by targeted door drops. This is direct marketing if some sort of response, perhaps further information, is sought. In this way the sample offer helps to build a prospect database.

Unit of sales

In order to shift more volume, a 'two for X pounds, saving Y' may be offered. However, compared to price off, this is likely to reduce the number of customers who will respond, which may be a disadvantage if you are looking to build up your database.

Credit options

Offering payment by credit cards increases response when compared to cash demands (Stone, 1996). The ability to accept credit card payment by phone was a major driver in the growth of direct marketing when it was introduced in the 1980s.

More recently, the advent of electronic payment systems such as PayPal have made on-line trading much easier as well as more secure and reliable for all concerned. Londoners know that it is possible to pay the daily Congestion Charge on their mobile phone bill, and many local authorities are adding this payment method to parking facilities, reducing the need for ticket machines/parking meters (which are costly to maintain and empty). Traders – both on- and off-line – have been taking advantage of using the revenue from premium rate phone numbers to pay for goods and services (such that it is necessary to make a five minute call at (say) £1.50 per minute to place your order; the call is billed to the user's phone and the revenue split between the phone company and the trader). This method is becoming less common now because of the poor image of such premium numbers, the inconvenience of a long call and the availability of other payment methods.

Free trial

Stone describes this as the 'bell-wether of mail order'. The key to this incentive is that it removes the barrier of immediate pain (having to pay!) while also providing reassurance that customers will not have to pay for a product they subsequently do not like. In any purchase made remotely, this is very attractive.

Exhibit 10.12 'Giving them a puppy to look after'

Fercell Engineering is a market leader in the UK dust extraction and air filtration market. They provide equipment to remove harmful substances such as dust from manufacturing processes, excess spray from paint booths and so on, as well as solvent recovery systems, ducting for factories and other specialist industrial equipment. Much of their product range is incorporated into the building's structure at the time of fitting, but some smaller machines sit under a work bench and remove harmful substances as materials are worked and, with these systems, it is possible to employ a marketing technique not available to the factory sized equipment.

When someone shows an interest in their Mini Range, Fercell gives them a free trial of the system for a month. Founder and Managing Director, Malcolm Fletcher says: 'It's like giving someone a puppy to look after for the weekend. At the end of their time with it, it's made a big impact on them and the way they work; they love it and they simply don't want to give it back. It's the easiest route to a sale that I can think of!'

The author wishes to thank Malcolm Fletcher of Fercell Engineering for this example.

In the digital age, it is even possible to give free samples immediately. Owners of Amazon's Kindle e-book reader will know that it is possible to download a free sample chapter of most books before you buy, so you can see if the book is as interesting as the write-up makes it sound. Certain music and film clubs (like **lovefilm.com**) let you download products immediately you have supplied your details to them, and some of them offer a 30-day no obligation free trial period.

The following incentives are 'related to customer knowledge'.

Member get member

'All things being equal, people will buy from a friend. All things being not quite so equal, people will still buy from a friend.'

(Mark McCormack, CEO, IMG, 1984)

'Member get member' schemes offer incentives to current customers in return for their recommendation of someone they believe will be interested in that company's products. It is based on a fundamental principle of (direct) marketing: the people most likely to buy from you are those most like the people who already do. And the people most like them are their friends.

Member get member is most likely to work if it is part of a strategy of maximising customer satisfaction and, hence, loyalty. This is because only very satisfied, happy customers will recommend a supplier to friends.

Bounce-backs

Not to be confused with the term describing an undeliverable e-mail, this refers to the notion that often the best time to sell to someone is when they have just bought from you, a phenomenon well known in the mail-order industry. The customer, therefore, receives a 'Thank you for purchasing . . . by the way have you seen our tremendous offer running on . . .?' message.

Gifts/premiums

'These six books are truly, truly great novels. They are absolutely right for Dewhurst customers.'

(Dewhurst Butchers' spokesperson, on the offer of free, unpublished Barbara Cartland novels when purchasing meat products)

Remember that customers who can be bought by a gift can be bought by someone else offering a better gift, so gifts should be used as a 'thank you' rather than as a 'please' (Thomas and Housden, 2011, p. 193).

Gifts should be something that meets the following criteria (Blythe, 2009, p. 599):

- It should not be too expensive for the promoter to supply.
- It should add extra value for the consumer.
- It should be relevant to the product being promoted.
- The offer should not look too good to be true because, if it is, the consumer may suspect there is a catch.

The overuse of gifts as incentives by financial services companies in the 1980s led to a number of problems for the sector. The first mistake was to use gifts as a primary differentiator between very similar offerings, promoting the gift to top spot in the advert. At the very least, this would have done little to build brand values in an already weakly branded market. Second, financial services companies all found through testing that consumer durables were their most effective premium. This led to a plethora of similar looking offers, hence lacking any distinctiveness. Our attraction for telephone clock radios soon waned. Once the lesson had been learned, direct marketers realised that their use of gifts is subject to changing trends and, as time moves on, more imagination is required to provide value and distinctiveness.

In sectors with high margins it is perhaps easier to be imaginative. Land Rover offered picnic baskets as an incentive to attend a sales day for its new Discovery marque. However, these were offered only to carefully chosen existing customers.

One senior practitioner commented that unusual items, loosely related to the product, are very successful. A book club selling a European history set could offer a limited edition print of a painting by a classic European artist. Buyers of the product are arguably likely to value such an incentive more than another clock radio.

Of course, there is always one example that completely bucks the trend. David H McConnell, founder of Avon Cosmetics, did not originally intend to create a beauty company. A travelling book salesman, he founded Avon in 1886 after realising his female customers were far more interested in the free perfume samples he offered than in his books (Avon Products Inc, 2012)! In this case I suppose the lesson is to find out what the customer wants, and then provide it.

Competitions/prize draws

The use of competitions and prize draws continues, but their popularity has waned somewhat with middle class responders who see them as marketing gimmicks. They have acquired a rather downmarket image, aimed at low income groups whose keenness for a bargain makes these schemes attractive. Against that, Peattie and Peattie's work back in 1993 pointed to trends such as size of prizes being offered (you may remember British Airways' 'World's greatest offer' featured £6 million worth of free flights) and, in the UK, the enormous success of the Lottery in establishing itself quickly as a national institution, but these are exceptions: incentives are still mostly tactical in nature.

Competitions have been a popular acquisition incentive in classic direct marketing sectors for decades, but are probably on the wane outside of sectors aimed at down-market audiences. *Reader's Digest* has been using competitions to attract custom since the 1950s and has refined its methods to a high level of sophistication. For example, the use of prize draws by the *Digest* is often related to deadlines: 'Your prize will be £1,000 more for every day you beat the deadline', but such headlines are misleading and response rates have deservedly dropped. Research in 1992 reported that the most popular prizes were cash, cars and holidays, in that order (McKibbin, 1992). In 2007, cash was still top of the pile (Reynolds, 2007) and there is little to suggest that will change in the near future.

Some industry practitioners have commented that competitions and free prize draws related to acquiring names may improve initial responses, but poor quality names have resulted. The *Reader's Digest* has found that using prize draws and competitions success-fully takes a great deal of experience. In most sectors, competitions are perhaps best used as secondary incentives, but many classic direct marketers have used competitions as an important part of their creative. Book club offers to prospects may have 'You may already have won . . .' messages emblazoned across the envelope, and practitioners have had great success with such approaches.

To many marketers, this sort of approach goes against their natural instincts. How can such approaches build brand values? Why ignore the core product and concentrate on the incentive? Such approaches have been tested and shown to obtain higher responses than others within these particular markets. In answering the critics, practitioners point out that white collar, AB marketers who find the approaches unattractive may not understand the motivations of people who lack their education and wealth.

Further insight into consumers' reactions to competitions came from a large study that developed the audience segmentation shown in Exhibit 10.13 (Peattie and Peattie, 1993).

Exhibit 10.13 Competitions: turning shopping into a treasure hunt

Six types of consumer were identified in relation to competitions (Peattie & Peattie, 1993):

1 **Non-competitors:** consider competitions a waste of time.

2 **Passive competitors:** enter a competition, which they qualified for as part of their normal purchases but would not switch in order to enter.

3 **Brand switchers:** switch brands from their normal purchase, within the same product category, in order to enter a competition.

4 **Product switchers:** buy a product they do not normally buy in order to enter a competition.

5 **Hoarders:** alter their buying behaviour between product and brand types, and will alter their timing of purchases to enter competitions or increase their chances of winning a competition.

6 **Dog fooders:** buy almost anything to enter a competition, regardless of core product's utility. Make excuses to buy these products. Known as hobbyist competitors. Buy any product with 'win' on the pack, including bags of Winalot – hence their name.

Direct marketers who have a high number of people from segments 4, 5 and 6 (see Exhibit 10.13) in their target audience will find competition-led approaches most lucrative.

Exhibit 10.14 Acquisition incentives: tricks of the trade

Time limits

Delay kills response. As an incentive to act immediately, you can set time limits for your offer: 'You must reply within ten days to take advantage of this unique offer.'

Quantity limits

This idea could be a 'Hurry while stocks last' message. In markets where there is an implied prestige in ownership of the product, the offer could include a deliberate quantity limit to act as an incentive in its own right. China collectibles is one such market: 'Only 500 of these beautiful hand-painted dolls have been made. You will need to act quickly.'

Guarantees

Guarantees should never be passed up in any direct distribution market (Stone, 1996). World-class mail-order exponents, such as L.L. Bean, a US outdoor clothing supplier, have made this into a competitive differentiator. It offers 'lifetime, no quibble, money-back guarantees' for all its lines. This represents tremendous value, in the form of peace of mind, to L.L. Bean's customers.

Summary

In this chapter we identified the difference between offers and incentives as being one of level – the incentive is part of the offer. We found that both offers and incentives are an important part of the message that customers receive from direct marketers.

The differences between the use of incentives in direct as opposed to general marketing were identified. In particular, incentives can be segmented and targeted using direct marketing, thereby avoiding wastage.

The use of activities such as magazines and loyalty schemes to help retain customers was explored. Loyalty schemes should not be relied upon without having carefully built into the business one of the routes to their success.

The well-established use of 'lock-in' offers to acquire new customers profitably was outlined, showing how initial losses are compensated by profitability over time. The success of premiums and competitions in improving response was also established.

QUESTIONS

1 What is the difference between sales promotion and direct marketing?

2 What are the major factors to consider before using incentives to tempt purchase of a product in a direct marketing context?

3 Explain the difference between opt-in and opt-out offers.

4 You are the marketing manager of a medium-sized chain of restaurants and are considering the use of a loyalty card to boost retention rates. However, there are a number of other leisure related loyalty cards already launched, none of which seems to stand out. State the factors that you, as the manager, must take into account before making a decision, and give recommendations on the approach that would have most chance of success.

5 What is the role of a loyalty magazine in the retention strategy of a car manufacturer? Justify the expenditure versus alternative uses of the money.

6 A 'wine direct' operation is considering the use of premiums to stimulate take-up of an offer. Recommend an appropriate choice, explaining your reasoning clearly.

References

Avon Products Inc (2012). *Experience Avon's History*. Available at: **http://www.avoncompany.com/aboutavon/history/index.html** [Accessed 01 July 2012].

Baines, P., Fill, C. and Kelly, P. (2011). *Marketing* 2nd edn, (ed.) Oxford University Press, Oxford.

Bolger, M. (2011). *Case Study: Barclaycard Freedom*. Available at: **http://www.themarketer.co.uk/articles/case-studies/case-study-barclaycard-freedom/** [Accessed 24 August 2012].

Boothby, K. (2002a). Campaign Planning and Management – converting strategy into action plans. In: R. Fairlie, ed. *The New IDM Practitioner's Guide*, pp. 1.3-8, The IDM, Teddington.

Clawson, T. (2012). *It's Good To Talk*. Available at: **http://www.themarketer.co.uk/trends/its-good-to-talk/?locale=en** [Accessed 28 June 2012].

Cram, T. (1994). *The Power of Relationship Marketing*, Pitman Publishing, London.

Dahlen, M., Lange, F. and Smith, T. (2012). *Marketing Communications – A Brand Narrative Approach*, John Wiley and Sons Ltd, Chichester.

Dibb, S., Simpkin, L., Pride, W. M. and Ferrel, O. C. (2012). *Marketing Concepts and Strategies*, 6th edn (ed.) Cengage Learning EMEA, Andover.

Durand, P. (1987). *Norwich Union: Development of Cross Selling in a Growing File*, EDMA Conference, Montreux.

Holder, D. (1992). 'Finders Keepers – The Basics of Customer Acquisition and Retention', in: B. Halsey, (ed.) *The Practitioner's Guide to Direct Marketing*, The Institute of Direct Marketing, Teddington.

Jobber, D. (2010). *Principles and Practice of Marketing*, 6th edn, McGraw Hill, Maidenhead.

Kotler, P. and Armstrong, G. (2007). *Marketing Management*, 12th edn (ed.) Prentice Hall, Upper Saddle River, NJ.

Kotler, P. and Armstrong, G. (2012). *Principles of Marketing*, 14th Global edn, Pearson Education, Harlow.

Marketing Magazine (2009). *Inaugural study claims brand owners spend £25.6 billion on BOGOFs and other sales promotions*. Available at: **http://www.marketingmagazine.co.uk/news/946464/** [Accessed 29 June 2012].

McDaniel, C., Lamb, C. W. and Hair Jr, J. F. (2013). *Introduction to Marketing*, International edn (ed.) South-Western, Cengage Learning, Canada.

McKibbin, S. (1992). 'The Importance of Incentives in Direct Marketing', in: B. Halsey (ed.) *The Interactive and Direct Marketing Guide*, The Institute of Direct Marketing, Teddington.

Mitchell, A. (1997). *Marketing Week*.

O'Brien, L. and Jones, C. (1995) "Do Rewards Really Create Loyalty". *Harvard Business Review*, May–June, pp. 75–82.

Ogilvy, D. (1985). *Ogilvy on Advertising,* Random House, New York.

Peattie, K. and Peattie, S. (1993). Sales Promotion, Playing to Win. *Journal of Marketing Management,* Volume 9, pp. 255–69.

Rapp, S. and Collins, T. (1987). *Maximarketing,* McGraw Hill, New York.

Reichheld, F. (1996). *The Loyalty Effect,* Harvard Business School Publishing, Boston, Mass.

Schifrin, M. and Touryalai, H. (2012). 'Wells Fargo: The Bank that Works' *Forbes,* 13 February.

Smith, P. (1993). *Marketing Communications – An Integrated Approach,* Kogan Page, London.

Stevens, J. (2010). 'Cashback sites: Do They Deserve Any Credit?' *The Observer (London),* 17 January.

Stone, B. (1996). *Successful Direct Marketing Methods,* 5th edn, (ed.) NTC Business Books, Chicago IL.

Thomas, B. and Housden, M. (2011). *Direct and Digital Marketing in Practice.* 2nd edn, (ed.) A & C Black Publishers Limited, London.

Touryalai, H. (2012). 'The Art of the Cross Sell' *Forbes,* 13 February.

Weitz, B., Castleberry, S. and Tanner, J. (2007). *Selling,* McGraw Hill, Burr Ridge, IL.

CASE STUDY

Bounty

The arrival of a new baby into a family is a life changing event, and just one of the many things a parent has to get used to is how much they will spend on the infant. In one year, a typical parent will spend £1,500 on their precious new arrival. Clearly, then, this is an important and sizeable market, with around 770,000 babies born in the UK alone every year.

Companies such as Unilever, Procter & Gamble, and Nestlé are keen to show mothers how their products can help with raising the child. They also know that, once a habit of behaviour is instilled with a particular product, there is a high likelihood that mothers will stick with that product. But how do they target mothers at the right time? This is the problem that Bounty set out to solve. Bounty acts as a conduit for the product manufacturers because of the direct contact it sets up with mothers.

The key to the data gathering lies with hospitals granting Bounty access to mothers-to-be and new mothers, in return for a fee. The process starts with pregnant women who are handed *Bounty's Pregnancy Guide,* a 150-page booklet on pregnancy, containing advertisements from the above companies. Hospitals receive 30 per cent of advertising revenues. The women are encouraged to fill in a form and hand it in to the local Mothercare retail store, where they are handed their first Bounty Pack, containing free samples of baby products. Data is collected and stored at this stage.

The second phase occurs when the baby is born. Bounty representatives travel through the ward collecting data and dispensing a second bag of freebies. Again the hospital makes a charge – about 50p per mother. A baby care guide and a voucher for a third free bag, collected from Boots, the retail chemist's, are also included. Both Mothercare and Boots distribute these bags of samples free, because they benefit from the extra store traffic generated. At Boots, more data is collected, including the baby's sex and date of birth.

The value of the data gathered by Bounty is in the accuracy of targeting that it offers to manufacturers. The resulting database of mothers can be rented and mailed by interested companies, offering vouchers or frequent-purchase incentives to encourage brand switching and loyalty. Mechanisms can be set up to ensure that data on the usage of vouchers is captured.

Case study (*continued*)

Analysis of Bounty case

Why should the likes of Unilever and Procter & Gamble pay £65,000 to place leaflets and up to £500,000 to place a sample in one of Bounty's bags? The answer is that the payback is better than would be obtained through traditional sales promotion methods. Let us look at a comparison of the use of baby product incentives through traditional and direct methods.

Traditional sales promotion methods

Here the samples would be in store or delivered through mass media, perhaps *Mother and Baby* magazine. Costs per thousand of distribution would be lower than using Bounty's sample bags. However, wastage would be much higher because two audiences you did not want to attract would take samples:

- Mothers already loyal to the firm's products
- Mothers loyal to deals rather than brands

Vouchers could be distributed on pack, through mass media, or by door-to-door methods. Again wastage would be high because the vouchers are less likely to get to new mothers at the crucial times that they make these habit-forming decisions, but will again be used by already loyal users and deal conscious switchers who will quickly switch away from your brand to the next incentive.

Direct marketing methods

The case study highlights the extra *costs* of using a highly targeted distribution system like Bounty's. The 'payback' comes from the immense power of direct marketing when used to its full potential:

- **Targeting**. Wastage is at an absolute minimum. All sample bags will be relevant to the recipients.
- **Timing**. The samples are given at exactly the right point when the consumer is making decisions about product use and brand choice.
- **Continuity**. By collecting voucher usage data, companies can understand who is using their vouchers and how much these customers are worth to them. Ongoing incentives can be targeted accurately, with the level of the incentive set so that both company and customer benefit.

Source: Based on Denny, N. (1995) 'Bounty bags', *Marketing Direct*, November.

CASE STUDY

Barclaycard Freedom

Barclaycard Freedom reaped the reward of new local business partners with its loyalty scheme launch

The Brief

Mention a loyalty scheme to customers and chances are their eyes will glaze over. Loyalty cards have become ten a penny, and time pressed customers tire of stuffing wallets with cards while mentally totting up the value of points and vouchers. Many loyalty cards remain unused or are dumped in the dustbin. The marketing team behind Barclaycard's new loyalty scheme, Barclaycard Freedom, knew it had to set its card apart from the glut of plastic weighing heavily in punters' purses, if the scheme was to gather customer data and attract new B2B partners.

'We wanted to appeal to a wider audience through a reward programme, and to develop a programme that would actually deliver for a broader range of customers,' says Barclaycard marketing director Sarah Alspach. The brief was straightforward: boost card usage among existing customers and attract business partners from the retail sector to the new scheme.

The strategy

As well as attracting new business partners, Alspach needed to find out why customers shunned existing loyalty schemes. 'We spoke to people who had a number of reward cards in their wallet but were not using them. We talked to them about their perceptions of existing programmes and discussed what wasn't working for them,' says Alspach. It quickly emerged that customers wanted reward schemes to be as straightforward and simple as possible.

'We tried to design a programme based on the idea of effortless rewards – which were easier to earn, easier to use and easier to redeem,' she says. The main advantage of the scheme was that Barclaycard customers could use their existing card instead of having to apply for and carry another card. In addition, the rewards were featured in pounds and pence rather than in points, to make it easier for the customer to see the value of what they had earned. This reward money could then be redeemed from other retailers in the scheme.

The execution

With a budget of £10m, Barclaycard kicked off the campaign by posting a welcome pack to every customer. This pack emphasised the participation of shops in customers' local areas, and included directions to the local retailers involved. 'One of the key differences of the programme is that we include local merchants. The scheme does not just feature major high street chains,' says Alspach.

The direct mail was followed by a television campaign and advertising in the national press. The TV ad, by agency Bartle Bogle Hegarty, used the classic blues track 'Green Onions' by Booker T & The MGs. Each time someone is shown using their Barclaycard in a transaction, the card reader plays notes from the song.

'You hear the music being created by the sound of the pin pad entry, so that forms a tune and creates a sense of an upbeat shopping experience,' says Alspach. 'The use of music underscored the simplicity of the new system for customers,' she says. 'We wanted to demonstrate how easy it is for people do their shopping when using Barclaycard Freedom.'

The campaign also had a digital element, namely a virtual game entitled High Street Beats, where consumers could create the 'Green Onions' track by hitting shopping items. A full version of the game became available through the red button on Sky and Virgin Media, with shorter versions for Facebook and YouTube.

But Barclaycard had to target B2B partners as well as existing customers. The marketing team engaged with smaller businesses in the local areas to encourage them to

Case study (*continued*)

participate. 'We emphasised the simplicity of the scheme; it can be operated through retailers' point-of-sale system, which means that it is much easier to execute in store. We also stressed the scale of the project, because obviously one of the things our business partners are interested in is their ability to reach a wider number of potential customers,' says Alspach.

Barclaycard Freedom also carried out a direct mail and telemarketing campaign to reach small and medium sized businesses with news of the scheme. For larger businesses, Alspach used a bigger sales force to target decision makers face to face.

The outcome

During the course of the campaign, the scheme attracted the participation of 20,000 retail outlets including LA Fitness, Yo! Sushi, Goldsmiths, Nationwide Autocentres, Gourmet Burger Kitchen, Flight Centre, Pizza Express and Shell.

A year after the campaign launched, 1.3 million of Barclaycard's 10 million customers were regularly using their card to accrue reward money in these outlets.

According to Alspach, the scheme partners have seen a rise in spend of 14 per cent since the launch. On average, Barclaycard customers take £4.56 off their card bill by using the loyalty scheme – double the amount recorded during the first month of the scheme. 'We expect this to increase as customers have the time to accrue more reward money. In April, customers redeemed over £0.5m and, as the number of customers increases, we expect the amount saved to continue to grow,' she says.

Barclaycard also wanted to extend customer awareness of the Freedom scheme. The target was set at 50 per cent awareness, but this reached 58 per cent by the end of the first month. Alspach also saw an 11 per cent rise in customer satisfaction levels with the scheme. But there is still work to do – less than half of her customer base (46 per cent) see Freedom as offering value for money.

Analysis

'We were happy with the way the campaign worked. We overachieved on our awareness level targets, so that aspect of the campaign worked well for us,' says Alspach. 'We see our card holders pulling their cards out of their wallets more frequently and generating more spend for our business partners.'

But she admits that the marketing efforts behind Barclaycard Freedom will steer away from a costly national advertisement campaign in future. While she has been given the green light to roll out a follow-up campaign for Freedom with a similar budget, the priority will be on emphasising benefits in customers' local areas. She says: 'The intention is not to do the same thing this year, but rather to focus our efforts on local engagement activities.'

She adds that B2B partners experienced more benefits from this approach. 'We worked with Shell and ran local campaigns for the company where it was opening retail outlets in new locations, and this had real success in driving business there.'

Alspach says that Barclaycard needs to place more focus on digital marketing. 'We have customers seeking out information through our mobile websites, and we have started putting out some of our offers through Facebook and Twitter. So we are testing the water, but it is something we need to better understand and exploit.'

Source: Bolger, M., (2011). Case Study: Barclaycard Freedom. Available at: **http://www.themarketer.co.uk/articles/ case-studies/case-study-barclaycard-freedom/** [Accessed 24 August 2012]

CASE STUDY

ARK Skincare

After a successful e-commerce launch in 2009, ARK Skincare decided to pursue a more aggressive marketing strategy for 2012. The on-line branding agency, Pomegranate, was approached to help plan and then implement the 12 month strategy.

After reviewing the past marketing performance and the current market situation, it was agreed that the strategy would focus on using the positive PR gained since launch to appeal to the factors that motivate women to adopt new skincare products.

Campaign strategy

The ARK Skincare marketing strategy uses multiple channels to gain maximum exposure and engagement across the brand's three core audience profiles:

- Age Prepare (teens to early 30s);
- Age Maintain (mid 30s to 50);
- Age Repair (50s and beyond).

For the most recent campaign the focus was on helping women prepare their skin for the summer months.

Website updates

Before the marketing programme began some fundamental updates were carried out on ARK's website, to create a more appealing user experience, to focus on promoting the facts that the ARK products are natural and that they address key skincare concerns. At the same time the design was refreshed to create a lighter more feminine interface and bring user testimonials to the fore.

E-mail marketing

The ARK brand has built up a loyal following, and also has a strong network of salons in London. The 'Prepare For Summer' campaign was designed to re-engage with the ARK audience and launch the new refreshed brand.

The initial e-mail campaign was sent to the ARK database. It contained information and tips on how to get ready for summer, as well as links to some of ARK's most popular products. The e-mail also included a promotional code incentive, and promoted the new Facebook presence where ARK experts would be on hand to give professional skincare advice. Finally, a link to a new free samples form on the website was provided after a review of conversion rates showed a dramatic increase when the customer had managed to try the product in advance. This free samples offer was also widely promoted across social media and voucher sites for a limited two week period.

Social media

To run alongside the campaign, and to be carried forward as a regular feature of the ARK brand, a regular programme of Facebook and Twitter activity was initiated.

For the summer campaign this included tips on looking after your skin during the summer months, user polls and a reintroduction of 'Acts of Random Kindness' (the ethos behind the brand). This is now promoted weekly and monthly, with free sample sets and prizes being awarded to ARK's top fans.

Case study (*continued*)

Campaign results

The first six months of 2012 have seen site traffic increase by 200 per cent on the same period of 2011, with sales and social media interactions on a similar trajectory.

Question

Explain the factors that have led to the success of ARK Skincare.

With thanks to Pomegranate for this case study.

CASE STUDY

Friend get Friend Campaign*

Agency name: Publicis Dialog   **Client name: Beam**

Category: Direct Marketing   **Country: UK**

Background

Trading conditions

- The UK single malt Scotch whisky market was expanding through new brands entering the market place.

- In the UK, LAPHROAIG® was enjoying growth through attracting new consumers to the brand; however, frequency of consumption was declining among existing consumers due to the new level of choice available to malt explorers.

- The total malt whisky market was around 600,000 nine litre cases in volume and worth over £178 million. However, it was in decline: –9.7 per cent by volume, –8.1 per cent by value year-on-year (Source: ACNielsen, December 2006).

- LAPHROAIG had around 59 per cent distribution on the ten-year-old 70cl in the Off trade (i.e. to be consumed off the premises where it was sold) (Source: ACNielsen Scantrack).

- Sales/share position: total brand was in growth +22 per cent by volume, +19 per cent by value year-on-year.

Competitor and brand position

- When entering the single malt market consumers initially drink less 'challenging' single malts, or the easier 'Glens' before trying LAPHROAIG due to its differentiated taste profile.

- Glenfiddich (12 year old) and Glenmorangie (10 year old) are the top two malts in both the On (i.e. to be consumed on the premises) and Off trade. It, therefore, became a priority to drive recruitment among the wider single malt drinking universe.

---

*The Friend get Friend campaign won the following: Bronze in the UK IMC European Awards for Best Direct Marketing Campaign; Gold in the UK ISP Awards, in the 'Alcohol' category; and Silver in the UK ISP Awards in the 'Direct Marketing' category.

Case study (*continued*)

- Friends of LAPHROAIG (FoL) is a growing on-line community and loyalty programme with over 300,000 members worldwide. Members receive news from the distillery, post questions for the master blender, take part in on-line auctions, gain access to limited editions and special bottlings as well as chat with other friends around the world.

Objectives

- Drive awareness of FoL and LAPHROAIG amongst 20,000 target consumers.
- Sample 4,000 new users with the ten-year-old expression.
- Encourage existing members to 'mentor' their friends and introduce them to LAPHROAIG.

Strategy

LAPHROAIG is an inherently down to earth brand and behaves as such.

Research indicated that the first time you try LAPHROAIG is a memorable one, often with a mentor. Being included within the LAPHROAIG circle demonstrates a rite of passage in your malt whisky journey.

The FoL website community provides the perfect on-line vehicle to drive awareness and trial by encouraging members to talk about LAPHROAIG.

LAPHROAIG's target audience are males 35+, with a higher education, discussion leaders with above average income. They appreciate good quality food and drink and are willing to pay for it. Interests include rugby, golf and the arts, and they enjoy entertaining people at home.

Their appreciation goes beyond taste; they are interested in learning more about whisky. They want to become experienced connoisseurs – intelligent and discerning in their choices.

Strategy – pack shots

To drive awareness and trial through the FoL community, a programme was created to encourage recommendation from existing FoLs through an enticing, premium mailer that included a LAPHROAIG ten-year-old 5cl miniature.

Case study (*continued*)

Source: Publicis Dialog.

An e-mail was sent to 25,000 UK Friends of LAPHROAIG inviting them to provide e-mail addresses of up to three friends who would appreciate an introduction to LAPHROAIG. (Recommenders were asked to provide permission to be contacted on behalf of their friends.)

New contacts were e-mailed for age verification, opt-in requirement and their postal details. Contacts were then mailed a personalised LAPHROAIG gift box, complete with the ten-year-old LAPHROAIG 5cl miniature and information about the product.

The leaflet enclosed was designed to reflect the square foot of Islay that friends receive when they join. The barcode on the miniature bottle allowed them to become a Friend of LAPHROAIG on-line.

Existing members were incentivised to provide their recommendations through a competition to win an exclusive trip for four to Islay, as VIP guests of the Master Distiller at the world famous (and notoriously difficult to attend) Islay Festival that took place in May 2007.

Additional information

To join FoL consumers enter their details and the bar code found on a bottle of LAPHROAIG on the website, **www.laphroaig.com**. In return, consumers receive a certificate stating they are entitled to a lifetime lease on their own personal square foot of Islay (where LAPHROAIG is produced). They can view their plot on-line, go and visit it and collect their annual rent from the Distillery – a dram of Laphroaig. They also receive regular news, offers and information from John Campbell, Distillery Manager.

With thanks to Publicis Dialog.

Chapter 11

Direct marketing media

Objectives

Once you have read this chapter you will:

- understand and be able to apply a step-by-step guide to media decision making for direct marketing
- understand the main features, strengths and weaknesses of direct mail and telemarketing

Introduction

Media decisions are very important to marketers because they are one of the biggest resource allocation decisions that we make. The question we need to answer is this: given the business situation we are in, what are the best media we should use to contact our customers or prospects?

In this chapter we will discuss in detail how to go about making these decisions. Naturally, they should be based on a good understanding of the media themselves. Therefore, the bulk of this chapter will concentrate on an analysis of the merits of each medium from a direct marketer's perspective.

How this chapter is structured

After introducing the broad range of media available to direct marketers, a decision making framework is offered to help direct marketers choose the right media. The rest of this chapter (and most of the following chapter (Chapter 12)) contains a detailed look at each medium, outlining the strengths and weaknesses of each. Finally, the use of media in contacting the same customer 'over time' – a contact programme – is discussed.

11.1 The range of media in direct marketing

Figure 11.1 summarises the main media choices open to direct marketers. The main ones for our purposes are discussed below, but all are dealt with in depth in practitioner guides.

The most important media for direct marketers were traditionally direct mail, the telephone and press, and these are still important choices. However, these are all under pressure from new media and from their unpopularity with the public. There is growing use of direct-response TV, door drops but, in particular – without doubt the most significant recent development for direct marketing – search, social media, e-mail, and other digital media.

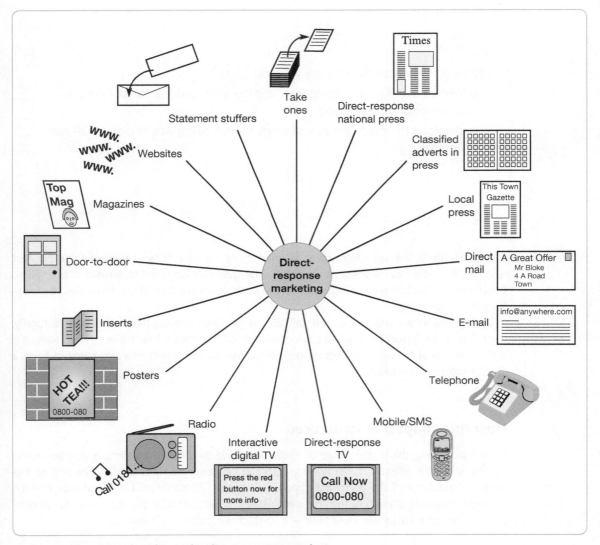

Figure 11.1 The range of media used in direct-response marketing

> ### Exhibit 11.1 Better the devil you know
>
> Some businesses have a tendency to stick, out of habit, to one or two media, and they drift out of the discipline of testing. On being challenged, this routine is defended with the argument that they have found the 'best' media. On being persuaded to test, they often find that this is not the case!
>
> The reality of business is that each situation – each campaign, each new product launch or price drop – has an element of uniqueness attached to it. The objectives of the campaign, the message that needs to be communicated, the response requirements, the handling of responses: all of these things may change slightly each time. In each case, media choices should be assessed anew.

In the next section we introduce the main factors to consider before choosing media. After this, we will take a detailed look at each medium in turn.

11.2 Factors affecting media choice

It is important to establish a way of objectively and consistently judging each medium. Direct marketing authors (Chaffey and Ellis-Chadwick, 2012; Thomas and Housden, 2011; Stone, 1996) have discussed each medium in terms of its strengths and weaknesses. Meanwhile, marketing communications texts (Smith and Taylor, 2004) have discussed a number of issues that are important in media choice.

These can be brought together into a framework that will help us be consistent in making media choices. This framework, dubbed AIMRITE, consists of the following:

Audience: Does the medium reach the desired target audience?

Impact: Does the medium have impact; that is, does it ensure the message has a chance of getting through the clutter?

Message: Does it help to ensure the message is clearly communicated? Does it add to the message?

Response: This does not refer to the percentage response but rather, does the media make responding easy?

Internal management: Does it enhance the efficient management of the campaign?

The end result: What are the costs and projected likely revenues? Taking all the above into account and looking at typical response rates for your medium, how likely are you to hit target for the campaign?

Before discussing this framework a little more, it is worth pointing out that, in direct marketing, we can usually be quite specific about what we require. Usually, the direct marketing communications objective is to get a response of some sort. Media choice often pragmatically boils down to 'that which will get the maximum desired response at minimal cost'.

Each of AIMRITE's components is now analysed in more detail.

11.2.1 Audience

Media choices are heavily influenced by the way the target audience is defined. If you need to target a 'lifestyle' grouping, say lovers of vintage cars, you are likely to go for websites that target this sector, car magazines or direct mail or e-mail to a lifestyle list. Narrow 'geographic' targeting lends itself to door drops or to targeted advertisements in social media. A pizza takeaway restaurant will use door drops to make offers to its local catchment area. An audience that knows its own mind, such as independent travellers, will want to control its own marketing – so uses search marketing and websites.

Target audiences that are tightly defined can be addressed by more precise media. The most well-known audience is usually a firm's existing customers, while at the other end of the scale we have suspects – a broad category of people fitting our target description, but with no known prior contact with the company. These would be approached with very different media.

To illustrate this, let us take the example of a firm selling theatre guides to Birmingham. If the best you can do with your audience definition is 'people in Birmingham' then you are more likely to use Birmingham radio or the *Birmingham Evening Mail* as your media. If, however, you define your audience as 'people who have been to the theatre in the past year in Birmingham', then you can target blogs that are concerned with the arts in Birmingham, or use direct mail or e-mail to a list of such people obtained from the theatres themselves. The latter course is likely to bring an efficiency gain, not because direct or e-mail are 'better' media than radio or press, but because in this particular situation the direct or e-mail audience is very well defined (and likely to be responsive to the offer).

The relationship between media choice and target audience in this example is summarised in Table 11.1. (Note that this target audience split was discussed fully earlier (Chapter 6).)

Note the way that, in Table 11.1, the size of the audience decreases as it becomes more highly defined. Media choice is likely to shift from broadcast to more highly targetable options.

Another 'audience' factor to consider is the inbuilt 'media responsiveness' of the target market. This has been true of direct mail though is less so now. Direct marketers knew that certain media were more 'responsive' than others. Media responsiveness is the 'natural predisposition of some people to prefer to do business through one particular medium'. Nowadays, many people are particularly tuned to the social media, e-mail or the phone. Direct marketers should take into account any information they have on the media responsiveness of their target audience.

Finally, it is worth noting that each medium will have 'black holes' of audiences that cannot be reached at all by that medium. Outbound telephone selling has become very

Table 11.1 Media choice according to target audience definition

Audience type	Example	Medium
Suspects	People in Birmingham	B space advertising, targeted website display or pay-per-click
Prospects	ABC1 people in well-off areas of Birmingham	Door drops to selected areas
Enquirers	Mainly existing theatre visitors	Direct/e-mail to list of Birmingham theatre customers
Customers	Users of the guide	Direct/e-mail to your own list

difficult in some countries, none more so than the UK, where well over half of households have signed up to the Telephone Preference Service, a system that bars companies calling them. Some people do not use fixed line telephones, others are not on any direct mail lists, a minority do not read any daily paper, according to Ofcom (2012) 24 per cent of British households do not have broadband access at home and 20 per cent of all households have no access to the Internet at home.

11.2.2 Impact

It is vital to make an initial impact on your audience. In a world where people have their senses constantly bombarded with messages of various types, they have to notice that you are there before you can begin to persuade them to respond. A big part of impact is the creative approach, discussed later (Chapter 13), but the medium also has a big role to play in getting your message through the clutter.

There are two dimensions to media impact. One is the extent to which the media can get the audience's undivided attention. Private media, such as direct or e-mail, are more likely to achieve this than broad scale media like press advertising. The second dimension is summed up by the phrase 'the medium is the message' (see Exhibit 11.2).

Exhibit 11.2 'The medium is the message'

We have all heard this expression, but what does it mean and to what extent is it relevant to direct marketers?

If you were to consider the magazine *Vogue*, you would probably agree that the magazine itself has a strong brand identity. It is easy to picture the type of person that reads it, the articles it carries and, of course, the advertisements it contains. Here the medium, in a sense, creates a halo effect around the adverts it carries. Just the fact that a company has advertised in *Vogue* carries a message to the reader. This message would be an implication of prestige, of the product being upmarket and aimed at an exclusive audience. This is what we mean by 'the medium is the message'.

There are other examples of the same principle. Channel 4 gives an image of young, trendy viewers, and advertisers sometimes take advantage of this ambience with products that fit this image. Virgin, for example, often uses Channel 4. The *Financial Times* has a businesslike, serious brand and adverts seen in the FT would benefit from this background.

11.2.3 Message

Once your prospect's attention has been obtained, the medium must then help you to get across the necessary information in a persuasive manner. Thus, TV has always been a compelling medium for inspiring an emotional response, because of its sound and vision qualities. Direct mail, on the other hand, is good for imparting large volumes of information about complex products such as, say, financial services. A website can combine both aspects of the two previous media with the potential for long copy but also the ability to link to video or other emotionally engaging collateral. Thus, to get the best match of medium and message, we should consider both 'volume' and 'type' of the information we want to impart.

11.2.4   Response

Here we are **not** considering size of response. This factor is concerned with how much effort is required by the consumer to respond to different media.

Certain media are much easier to respond to than others. Direct marketers who use poster adverts are expecting consumers to remember a phone number or a URL until they get home or until they can get to a phone, and then still be motivated to ring it. Not easy. A well-known saying among practitioners is 'time kills response', and if one imagines a car driver seeing a response advert on a poster, then another hour passing until he is home, it is not hard to see why posters are still a little used direct-response medium. The use of posters with QR codes printed on them or, in rarer instances, using Bluetooth technology makes it a more responsive medium.

The ideal response medium is one, then, which makes the act of clicking, ringing up or filling in a form on-line (the two primary methods of responding) as easy and quick as possible. Old style 'direct mail coupons' are seldom used now except in specialist mail-order sectors often targeting the older generation. People are more likely to respond from the comfort of their own home, at a time when there is nothing else going on to distract them, and when very little effort is required. The telephone, direct or e-mail, and the Internet, offer the most advantages here, while at the other extreme, posters and radio present many obstacles to success. The basic rule is to remove as many barriers to responses as possible.

11.2.5   Internal management

Mike De Domenici has just been made marketing manager for Prestige Motorcycles. He discovers that a lot of Prestige buyers do not actually ride their motorbikes very much at all. Instead, they like to add endless accessories to them and possess them as fashion extras. Mike decides to promote a new line of silver chrome exhaust pipes, and commissions an advert to go into *Men and Motorcycles* magazine. It is time to give them a ring to place the ad. He is stunned to find a lead time of four months before the ad can be placed. All his carefully laid plans hit the dust.

This story highlights the need to get those management issues carefully understood. Which are the best media when it comes to testing different creative approaches? Which have the shortest lead times? What media are relatively easy to manage if you do not have much experience? These are some of the issues that need to be considered.

11.2.6   The end result

We have now pulled together the issues to consider before making that final choice in favour of a particular medium. The initial considerations are an attempt to whittle down the media to those that will get the best end result. At this final stage, our focus is on those media which we believe will give us the 'highest possible response at lowest cost'.

Before committing our entire budget to one medium, we should test different choices. This is a key process within direct marketing and is outlined later (Chapter 14). However, here we are concerned with the step preceding this: which media do we put into the test process?

Experience has shown that we do need to go through the disciplined approach of AIMRITE to make the right decisions. This is because no one medium has stood out as clearly superior in fetching the highest response at lowest cost. In fact, it is a general rule that 'those media which elicit a higher response also tend to be the most expensive'. For example, although telephone responses are potentially the highest of all the media, the costs are also the highest.

We can call this effect the cost/response 'rule', which offers a rough guide:

> In general, the higher the response that a medium achieves from an audience, the more it costs to reach that audience.

Sometimes, in a particular sector, extensive testing reveals a medium that out performs all other media in that area. China collectibles tend to sell best using Sunday supplement press advertising, whereas charities use direct mail to recruit possible donors 'cold'. However, when totalling up all marketing activity, the average cost of getting one response has been roughly similar across all media.

Digital media have challenged this rough guide. You can see that e-mail has many similar characteristics to direct mail but at a fraction of the cost. Websites have low ongoing costs, and search engines help us find them cheaply. But e-mail (for new customer acquisition) has been wrecked by the spammers. However, it remains true that the average cost per acquisition remains broadly similar today to what it was in the early part of the 2000s.

So what is this 'average cost' of getting one response? Here we enter a very dangerous area, because response will always depend on the specific business situation: a well thought out offer, good timing, incentives and so on. There is, therefore, a huge variation around the mean response rate for a medium, even within one industry sector. A major player in the loans sector of financial services reckons on different campaigns delivering costs per response 'varying from £12 to over £600', with an 'average' of £250. A recent marketing Sherpa report shows that 64 per cent of companies are achieving qualified leads at $99 or less, which means that 36 per cent of companies are achieving leads at over $100 (Marketing Sherpa 2013). These 'real world' figures illustrate the dangers of generalisation by just quoting the average.

Nevertheless, it is important to press on and develop some practical 'rules of thumb', because these can be useful for media planning in the absence of more specific data. 'Official' figures are hard to come by for many media, but there are some we can use for direct mail. The Direct Mail Information Service (DMIS) surveys of companies using mail for acquisition have found average response rates of about 1 per cent. If the average cost per thousand mailers is typically about £500, and 1 per cent of 1,000 is ten responses, then we can see that it typically costs £500 to obtain ten responses, or £50 per response.

With the above warnings on large variations around the mean ringing in our ears, here is a rule of thumb that can be used for planning if no other data is available:

> **A rule of thumb for quick calculations is that it costs typically about £30 to £70 to obtain one response in an acquisition programme. However, there are often exceptions to this 'rule'!**

Typical costs and response rates for the different media are compared in Table 11.2.

Before we move on to the individual media in more detail, we just need to consider the different media performances when used with existing customers compared with new prospects.

11.2.7 Media for acquisition and retention

All media can potentially be used for acquisition, but the best media for contacting existing customers held on a database are the 'individually addressable media': e-mail, direct mail, the telephone, mobile media and websites.

Table 11.2 Comparison of media costs and typical relative response rates

Medium	Cost per thousand (£)	Responses to acquisition programmes (broad averages) (%)	Targeting
Direct mail	500–700	1–2	High to absolute
Telemarketing outbound	6000	10–20 (retention only)	High to absolute
Press	4–20	0.01–0.1	Low to medium
Magazines	10–50	0.02–0.5	Medium
Inserts	40–70	0.1–1.0	Low to medium
Household delivery (door-to-door)	40–250	0.1–2.0	Medium to high
Direct-response TV	7–15	0.01–0.05	Low
Direct-response radio	2	0.005	Low
Websites	Say £10 000 to set up	–	Passive
Search engine marketing	£0.5 per click	0.1–2 clickthrough rates	Medium to high
E-mail	5–20	Low–1	Medium to absolute

Sources: Authors for 2012 updates, originally based on the 1st edition of the IDM Media/*Educators' Guide* and IDM course content.

One reason for noting this early in the chapter is to point out that a different set of standards should apply when judging media used for contacting existing customers. Responses should be much higher, results better, and the control you, as a marketer, can exert with your own database is much better than when trying to contact new customers. This is something to be aware of when comparing media performance. If someone tells you that such and such got 15 per cent response using e-mail, the first question to ask is whether this was an existing set of customers or new prospects that were contacted.

11.3 Discussion of individual media

Each of the major media used in direct communications, shown in Figure 11.1 earlier, will now be discussed. For each medium, key qualities will be highlighted that are unique to the medium, along with a summary of relative strengths and weaknesses compared with other media.

Let us start with the biggest growth area: digital media.

11.4 The Internet

The Internet is set to grow hugely as a 'media cluster' – search, websites, and e-mail all working together. Strategically the Internet was covered in detail earlier (Chapters 8 and 9), but here we confine ourselves to the communications media issues. The Internet is stealing media spend from other media because customers and sellers like it so much. It is convenient, quick and the customer is in charge. Consumers largely control their Internet experience – the 'interruption' model of TV and press ads is easy to bypass with the rise of search and the decline of pop-ups and bypassability of banner ads.

We can use characteristics such as 'lean forward' versus 'lean back' (active or passive media) and information or entertainment driven when comparing the Internet to other media (see Figure 11.2).

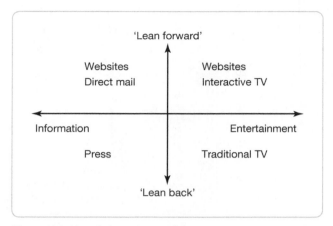

Figure 11.2 User interaction model

11.4.1 Characteristics of websites

Websites are complex media to consider. Websites themselves can act as both content of various types – entertainment, business, information – with adverts as part of this content, or as standalone commercial advertising in their own right. Both types, but the latter in particular, require ways of alerting the consumer to the existence of the site and of perhaps motivating access to the site. Hence 'pay-per–click', 'search engine optimisation' on-line display and classified adverts must all be seen as part of the chain of direct-marketing communications that leads the customer from search to purchase.

In some ways websites compete with the telephone, as an inbound medium in particular. The latest UK DMA Census (2012) shows that, as the Internet continues to spread through populations, their use of it for shopping is growing at a rapid rate; hence the recent announcements of the closure of major high street retail businesses (see Figure 11.3).

As hinted at, websites have one fundamental difference from all the other media, which is that 'it is customers, not advertisers, who initiate the process of contact'. Complete control over the messages they are exposed to, therefore, switches to the customer. This requires a completely new way of thinking by the advertiser.

Organisations, therefore, need to do one of a number of things:

- Register with the search engines (Google, Yahoo, Bing and Ask are the best known), to ensure that your pages are being indexed. Then use search engine optimisation techniques to improve the search table position of your firm (see Figure 11.4).

- Ensure that copy in your site is optimised to help the search engines find your site. Techniques include:

  - Keyword density. Ensure that the copy in your site contains the words that are being used by the people searching for products and services.
  - Optimising your website source code for the search engines. This means having a clear sitemap with efficient navigation within the site and inserting relevant keywords within the code, for example in title tags and in meta descriptions.
  - Developing links into the site. Google describes itself as a reputation engine and it wants to displays the most relevant search returns to its users. A link to your site is

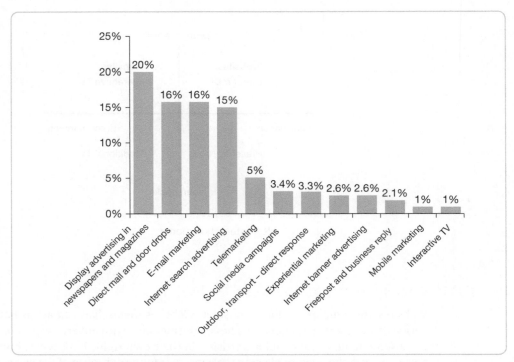

Figure 11.3 Proportion of direct marketing spend by medium 2012

Source: DMA/Future Foundation Research (2012).

seen as an endorsement. Therefore, using links to and from reputable affiliates or partners is important for SEO. You should not use techniques that are designed to deceive search engines, as you will be found out and delisted. This happened to BMW in the mid 2000s when an agency working on their behalf used a device designed to improve search rankings.

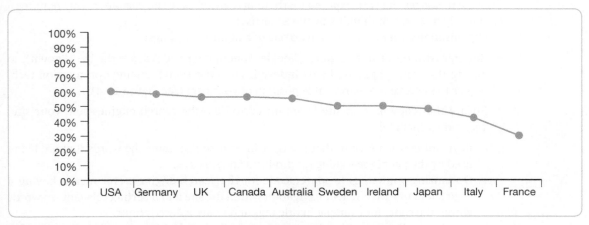

Figure 11.4 Percentage of which businesses use the Internet for marketing activity

Source: Adapted from DMA Census (2003). Reproduced by permission of the DMA (UK) Ltd.

- Carry out pay-per-click advertising. These are the ads that appear on the right hand side of the search engine return page (SERP) or in the shaded box at the top left of the Google SERP.

- Use affiliate sites to facilitate click-through from other sites to their site. This may be done by establishing 'affiliate networks' – maybe thousands of non-competing sites to help promote your website.

- Advertise on a key 'portal' site. For example, it may be increasingly vital for financial services companies to have a presence on **www.moneysupermarket.com**.

- Advertise your website off-line through conventional off-line media, or through other on-line channels, for example Twitter and Facebook.

There is a wealth of information on SEO on-line and for detail here we suggest using Google's Business Services; for example, their webmaster tools or the on-line starter guide (Google, 2013).

Different countries tend to have different rates at which businesses use the Internet. Within Europe, close neighbours can have markedly different take up for business use, with the Italians lagging somewhat compared to Germany and the UK. A useful guide to international take up of internet communications can be found on the Ofcom website (see Figure 11.5).

Search engines

These are vitally important tools and probably the most significant marketing development of the past 20 years. Google is perhaps set to be the most important organisation in marketing history.

From a media perspective search engines are so important because they are the key driver of traffic on to commercial websites. When we want to hunt down an offer for, say, car insurance, the first thing the majority of us now will do is punch 'car insurance' into Google or Yahoo! and examine what we find. The success of search engines is such that they are a major, everyday tool that has become part of people's lives. Advertisers have followed these trends and about 70 per cent of all on-line spend is now with search engines.

Being registered with a search engine is just the start. The organisation then needs to consider 'search engine optimisation' and search advertising known as 'pay-per-click'.

Search engine optimisation

Advertisers believe the truism that the higher up your firm is in the search engine rank for a keyword or phrase, the better your chances of being chosen by the searcher. Research suggests this is largely true, with the top three positions in SERPs accounting for around

	UK	Germany	France	Italy	USA
Internet universe millions	39.1	44.9	44.9	25.7	199.3
Fixed broadband connection %	70	69	62	49	76
Cellular broadband connections %	16	7	3	16	n/a
Internet access via mobile phone	38	30	31	37	33

Figure 11.5 Internet penetration by country 2010

Source: Ofcom 2012.

70–80 per cent of all clicks. However, research also suggests that consumers are willing to search for two or three pages (20–30 searches) before starting a new type of search or trying elsewhere. Search engine optimisation involves deploying a series of techniques to place your site as high up the natural listings of a search as possible. Search engines use algorithms to calculate how high up the search rankings a site should go.

The first step is to identify the keywords or phrases consumers will use. So, if you are easyJet, things like 'cheap flights' will be close to your heart. But they will also be interested in a host of others like 'cheap holidays', 'flights abroad', 'flights' and many others. The next step is the use of various website 'dark arts' to improve ranking. Chaffey and Ellis-Chadwick (2012) report:

- frequency of occurrence of body copy (so, easyJet might use the phrase 'cheap flights' a lot in its website)
- maximising the number of inbound links (the links to easyJet from other sites)
- maximising the occurrence of a keyword in the HTML code of the website title
- ensuring your meta tags include search keywords

Meta tags are less important than they used to be but are still important. They are part of the HTML file, hidden from users, but read by the search engine 'spiders' or 'bots'.

Pay-per-click advertising on search engines

The diagram below illustrates pay-per-click ads on a typical Google search.

Google allows text adverts only, with a clickable link, that is displayed when a user types in a certain search. Google makes it clear what are adverts and what is the 'natural' search (though do not forget this is manipulated by search engine optimisation). The advertiser only pays when the user clicks on the ad. Of course, a click does not mean a sale. Indeed, conversion to sale is a very important measure of success and may be pretty low – perhaps

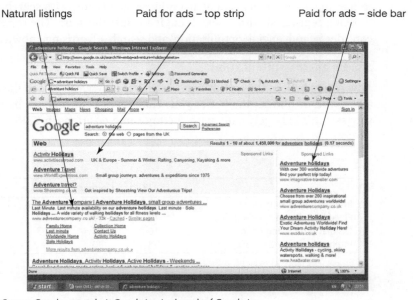

Source: Google screenshot. Google is a trademark of Google Inc.

just 1 or 2 per cent in some cases, maybe 20–30 per cent in others. The advertiser may pay, say, $0.50 per click, so if conversion to sale is 10 per cent, their cost per sale is $5. This would be good going! Conversion is usually lower than that. You also have to factor in competitors deliberately clicking on your adverts to raise your costs. (It is a dirty world out there.) Search engines will do some work in minimising this but typically about 8–10 per cent of clicks are fraudulent.

Pay-per-click prices are either decided by bidding or charged at a set rate. The highest bidder for say 'cheap flight' keywords takes top spot for the advertised links. For high value products the price-per-click can be much higher than the figures quoted above. Prices for valuable keywords like say 'best mortgage' might be $20 or more.

Exhibit 11.3 Get your best clothes on – it's time for the Google Dance

What is the Google Dance? It used to refer to the 3–5 day period when Google updated its search engine rankings. This used to lead to wild fluctuations but, since 2004, this has smoothed considerably as Google updates more often and with less dramatic effect.

Exhibit 11.4 Search engine optimisation (SEO) and pay-per-click advertising (PPC): tricks of the trade

1 PPC can be used to do 'tests' quickly on keywords, which can then be used in SEO.

2 PPC can also be used to 'test' two landing pages. You can use two approaches to try to understand which of the two approaches is more likely to convert customers. Or you can do the same page twice, but attach different keywords to each in an attempt to understand which keywords are more successful.

3 The more content (words) your web page has the easier it is for SEO. However, typically you should aim for a maximum of 250 words per page and certainly no more than 500 words per page. The objective of SEO is to try and get as much text indexed as possible.

4 You should consider the purpose of the Web page and write the page accordingly. What is the pages aim? Product introduction? Conversion to a sale? Search engine optimisation? Brand building? Once you have identified the purpose of the page and it has been built you can monitor its success. For example, if a page is designed to convert to sales you can track the individual to see if they get to the 'thanks for placing an order' page. Similarly, if a page is designed to push traffic towards picking up the phone to you, you can track them to the 'contact us' page.

5 With PPC, the keyword that you bid on and the phrase or words that customers search with are not necessarily the same thing. Therefore, it is best to use the broad match function in 'Google ad words', unless you are confident of the exact keywords used. For example, broad match: 'insurance', might yield 'car insurance', 'house insurance', etc. Use Google's keywords tool to help with this. **https://adwords.google.com/o/KeywordTool**

6 Business-to-business searches are likely to be shorter in length than personal searches done by an individual at home. At home you are more likely to browse as you will have more time.

7 Avoid overloading a page with keywords. This is keyword stuffing and Google will recognise this and delist your URL.

8 Type the name of your organisation into the search engine to see what pages it has picked up and indexed. You can try this for different keywords, as they may pick up different pages. You can use the Google search operator site url to check which pages Google is indexing.

9 Three word phrases are usually the optimum. People tend to use three words to search. One or two word searches are typically too general.

10 SEO is better if high quality sites link into your page rather than the other way around. Google 'pagerank', named after Larry Page, is their measure of website quality and it is believed to be more effective to link to pages with a higher pagerank. In 2012, the Google algorithm was updated and these were known as the Penguin and Panda updates. These changes aimed to shut down SEO tricks, including low value link building that previously helped improve the search return.

Affiliate networks

The highest profile example is that of Amazon, which has millions of affiliates: websites that provide a click-through facility to **Amazon.com** in return for a commission in the event of a purchase. Amazon has run affiliates since 1996 when apparently the founder of Amazon got chatting to someone who had a website and wanted to sell books about divorce on-line. The UK bookmaker William Hill pays £10–£20 for a new account generated through its affiliate partners. In general rather unsophisticated promotions have deployed poor targeting with the result that the affiliate sites have only the vaguest resemblance to the host site.

Banner ads

Banner adverts are paid-for adverts often placed across the top of the website – hence the term 'banner'. An interested prospect simply clicks on the banner to be whisked off to the advertiser's website where tempting offers await them. Banner ads may have nothing to do with the host website, and could simply be paid-for space hoping to catch interested people. Used in this way they are poorly targeted and will suffer low response rates.

Exhibit 11.5 Different types of banner adverts

Ad formats in this area are changing and the **IABUK.org** is a good source of information on formats. Alternatively, you can go direct to the media owner. Generally, formats are becoming 'richer' with animation and sound included or larger, for example mid page units and sky scrapers.

The top three formats are the medium rectangle, leaderboard and skyscraper. These, according to Google Doubleclick (2013), comprise nearly 80 per cent of all served impressions. Common formats include:

- Animated banner ads. Moving and changing images displayed in sequence to attract attention.
- Interstitial pop-ups. Many people find these irritating, including the author. Interstitials pop up in between pages that the user has asked for. They often have to be manually removed; very irritating but can be blocked by PC software.

- Overlays or superstitials, which pop up over the top of a website that has been opened, Again, they have to be removed by the user; equally irritating but can be blocked.
- Interactive banner ads. Becoming more popular, for example, an airline website ad prompting the user to enter a particular destination to find out the cheapest fare.

See Chaffey and Ellis-Chadwick (2012) and Rowan (2002) for more details.

Banner ads should follow the usual good commonsense rules of marketing communications, with good creative approaches, incentives, making sure the responses can be handled well and so on, but their big weakness is targeting. **www.DoubleClick.net** reports the latest situation (see Exhibit 11.6).

Exhibit 11.6 Banner advertising

After its poor early performances, banner advertising is changing. Formats are being used that intrude directly into the Web page (though it has to be said many people find these extremely irritating); also more banners now contain 'rich media', video and movement based, that is more eye catching. Flash animations and interstitials are also more common. Ads are becoming bigger, with half-page sizes used much more. One interesting trend is that the onset of rich media has meant a move away from just direct response ads towards a mixture of DM and brand building adverts being deployed. Nevertheless direct response remains crucial – the seductive nature of 'click-through' from the advert to the advertiser's Web page remains high. Click-through rates from rich media sites are estimated at 0.1 to 2 per cent of Web page readers, though purchase (conversion) rates will of course be much smaller again.

Measurement is improving, with some firms tracking surfer behaviour from click-through to purchase more accurately. Targeting too is improving with ads being served based on browsing behaviour (for example ads will be served based on which pages have been visited within a site or which websites have been visited) or at particular times of day, or days of week, or against registered profiles.

Source: Based on Google Doubleclick (Feb 2013).

The bottom line for banner ads is that click-through rates may average 0.1 per cent at best. Not surprisingly consumers who have arrived at a page looking for something are unlikely to click on an advert for something else. So, on average 1 in every 1,000 website views leads to a click-through. Of these click-throughs, perhaps 5 per cent will make a purchase. Let us say the original website charges the advertiser £10 per thousand impressions (1,000 people download the Web page). If 0.1 per cent click through, each click-through costs £10. But if only 5 per cent make a purchase, each purchase has cost the advertiser £200.

The deficiencies of banner advertising compared to affiliate marketing are clear enough: affiliates have a natural link to the seller website and click-through rates are higher; they also do business using a commission of sales model rather than charging an ad rate per impression, so the advertiser can check that their cost per sale is economic. Banner ads suffer from many of the problems of traditional 'push' advertising that you have off-line. Of course, good banner ads will be interesting and, if well placed, can be reasonably relevant to many of the site viewers. Contextual and behavioural targeting is still quite clunky but is improving the relevance of banner advertising.

In summary, a consumer has a variety of routes to get to the website, illustrated by Figure 11.6 showing us some possibilities for, say, **www.easyjet.com.**

Customer behaviour with websites

It is very important that marketers develop an understanding of customer behaviour in processing websites as a medium. Braithwaite *et al.* (2000) compared the Internet to TV, outdoor and print media. They found that consumers used websites in a goal-orientated mood, whereas people were more relaxed, seeking interest or emotional gratification with other media. We tend to process TV in an episodic, superficial way, but websites are consciously, cognitively processed – words are more important than pictures. Everything is done in an active manner with website consumption, whereas outdoor and TV media are consumed passively.

The AIMRITE analysis to follow looks at how these issues affect our choice of websites as a medium.

11.4.2 Websites as a medium

Key AIMRITE qualities

The most important issues when comparing the Internet with other media are:

- Websites are electronic – the speed of data gathering, effecting transactions is very fast
- Interactivity – websites are an important interactive tool, andit is important to remember that e-mail 'is not as quick, or as effective', as the telephone for use as a genuine one-to-one medium
- Unlike most media, the consumer can initiate the dialogue if they are Web browsing

We will now quickly look at each AIMRITE element one by one, beginning with audience

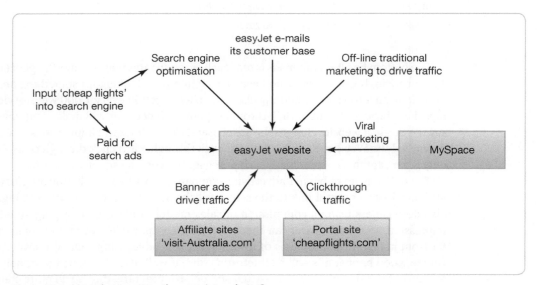

Figure 11.6 How do we get to the easyJet website?

Audience

The Internet has grown phenomenally over the last 20 years. Google, founded in 1998, has improved the functionality of the Web for most users and what in the mid 1990s was a niche medium, attracting primarily upmarket male audiences, has democratised, become gender neutral and has globalised to become a truly global network. There remains an important issue relating to digital exclusion; in the UK according to Ofcom (2013) 20 per cent of all households have no home access to the Internet and these patterns are replicated across the 'developed' world. They raise important issues for central and local governments who are increasingly pushing services on-line. In the UK the government is pushing to develop a high speed train network. However, this technology from the industrial revolution might be better replaced with high speed broadband access for all citizens. The Internet remains a young person's playground, although things are equalising even here as, for example, middle aged women are the fastest growing sector in the on-line gaming market.

Segmentation is an interesting item of study on-line. Because users are in control of their access to the medium, customers can segment sites, rather than the other way round.

Therefore, sites will all deploy 'handraising' techniques in which they make themselves as conspicuous as possible so that users can find them. Newsgroups, blogs and discussion boards are effective in offering a type of 'lifestyle segmentation', and these are of undoubted value to marketers. For example, **www.mumsnet.com** has become influential, not just in the area of marketing to mothers but also in raising issues in gender politics at national level.

The story is rapidly improving for existing customers of a site: firms will use tracking tags and cookies with permission, usernames and passwords to identify previous browsers, then create personalised on-line experiences and offers for identified customers – classic DM activity!

Impact

Peters (1998) points out a media attribute that she calls 'social presence'. This refers to the ability of the media to facilitate the communication's sociable, warm, personal and sensitive attributes. Channels that convey tone of voice, facial expressions and quick interactions will rank highly on the social presence scale. As you would expect, the telephone will rank highly here, while e-mail will rate poorly. The use of video and audio on websites helps convey warmth, and of course there are myriad ways in which users can interact with websites, clicking on hundreds of features to obtain different responses. At present most interaction is done using HTML and Java software, i.e. the program language in a sense acts as a barrier between the customer and a human representative of the firm. Nevertheless, the 'social presence' could still register from good creative approaches for both websites and e-mail.

Message

Websites are very powerful message carriers. They offer considerable, almost infinite multidimensional message opportunities. Full colour, illustrations or photographs, videos, plus as much information as companies wish to add, are all possible (for example computer firm Dell has thousands of pages of technical information). The use of hypertext makes consumer scanning of a lot of information painless and easy. Recent trends in Web design have improved the user interface considerably and now designers who have successfully worked on rendering sites in tablets and mobile devices are working to render up into large screen formats. It is rumoured that Apple will launch its own branded TV in 2013 and the use of Web enabled screens in cars also demands new skills of the Web design world.

Exhibit 11.7 Siri coming to a car near you

Legend has it that late Apple co-founder Steve Jobs once dreamt of an iCar. That dream will be one step closer to reality in early 2013 when General Motors introduces Apple's chatty voice assistant Siri into several of its car models.

The feature will be available to iPhone 4S and iPhone 5 owners, and Siri will be working through these cars' standard Chevrolet MyLink infotainment system.

To minimise distractions while driving, Siri will be available in 'Eyes Free' mode, meaning users will be able to interact with it without their iPhone's screen lighting up.

As far as features go, users will be able to make hands-free calls to contacts on their iPhone, play songs in their iTunes library, listen to, compose and send messages and add appointments to their calendar.

'Complex questions to Siri that require displaying a Web page will not work', GM says.

Other car manufacturers such as BMW and Honda have also announced Siri integration, but GM tries to differentiate itself by making the feature available in small cars first.

'It says a lot about our commitment to small-car customers that Chevrolet has announced that Siri Eyes Free capability will be available in the Spark and Sonic well before the luxury brands,' said Cristi Landy, Chevrolet marketing director for small cars.

Source: Mashable 2012. Copyrighted 2013. Mashable, Inc. 102589:813PF.

However, back with websites, consumer control is a big plus. Peters (1998) reports research by Carson, who found that the ability of customers to control 'the pace and presentation of their contacts' via websites was the biggest factor on willingness to use this media. As Peters points out, consumers can also control 'content' as well as contact, although it has to be said that this is not the case in the majority of commercial interactions. Controlling content means, for example, the use of customer bulletin boards, consumer home pages, or by supplying content that is used in the corporate website. It is interesting to note the difference in power of websites compared with direct mail on customer control of pace, presentation and content.

Exhibit 11.8 Some thoughts on Internet brand advertising vs direct marketing

At the Procter & Gamble summit conference in the summer of 1998, 'Why Isn't [Brand] Advertising on Websites Working?', Procter & Gamble invited competitors, consultants and Internet agencies to discuss the failure of Internet advertising. Experts pointed out that no one had coined a memorable slogan on websites. Even worse news: people ignore banner ads. The conclusion (which is pretty obvious if you understand media) was reported in multi-page stories in both the *New York Times* and the *Wall Street Journal*: websites are a direct marketing medium, not an advertising medium.

Advertising is a right-brain hemisphere communications discipline. It works best on television (a right-hemisphere medium), ideally by inculcating shards of impressions into the passive brains of half-alert couch potatoes. As soon as you call for behaviour, the spell is broken.

> Websites – like direct mail – are an interactive medium, by definition left-hemisphere. The advertising industry wants websites to be like television, but they can't be – the wrong part of the brain is involved. It takes time to sort all of this out: cf. the McLuhan quotation, 'Media are put out before they are thought out'.
>
> *Source*: Rosenfield, J.R. (1999) 'The Internet, **Amazon.com** and Book-of-the-Month Club: the old, the new, and the future view', *Direct Marketing*, June, 62 (12), pp. 44–8.

Response

Peters (1998) pointed out that there are two types of media – those that have a time lag between sending and receiving information, and those with no time lag. In fact, the only truly interactive medium is the telephone, which has no time lag. But this may be closely followed by websites that companies may use on a 'real-time' basis, responding to requests for information or confirming sales orders almost immediately. However, this is not the whole story. Once again, we must return to a key advantage of a website: 'it is always available to customers'. This means that customers can conveniently plan their responses to suit themselves.

Some companies operate response facilities on-line. Many websites make it possible for people to order on-line. By quoting a credit card number after choosing the order, customers complete the entire transaction without leaving their computer. The acceptance of on-line transactions and the ability to point and click to order a product, for example Amazon 1-Click, make websites 'the most powerful of all major media from the point of view of easy response'.

Exhibit 11.9 Everyone's a fruit and net case. . .

In June 1997, a 15-year-old boy in Dublin was surfing the net and came across a company offering home delivery of chocolate. A couple of minutes later he had ordered $2,000 worth of Dairy Milk, Toffee Crisp and Mars Bars. Payment was on-line, and when asked for credit card details he just punched in the first 16 numbers that came into his head.

Four days later three huge boxes of chocolate arrived outside his front door, and the boy began to tuck in. However, the owner of the credit card, who lived in Argentina, complained, and eventually the Dublin police paid the family an uncomfortable visit.

The chubby youngster's surfing days were over . . .

Internal management

Setting up a website can involve big learning curves for companies. Websites potentially cost very little but there are considerable hidden costs in learning how to set up and maintain them. However, direct marketers will be delighted that:

- testing should be very cheap, but not necessarily as easy as the telephone or direct mail in separating out target audiences
- lead times should be very short
- supplier control is high, as media ownership is not an issue at present

The role of data management, however, is a different matter. The ability to optimise the site around the user experience and to test multivariate formats within a site is a key part of the functionality of the website. To set up a site and leave it static is poor business and will influence search rankings and customer satisfaction. Once a website is established it should be worked on and improved and the use of 'Google website optmiser' and active use of tracking software, such as 'Google analytics', gives us the opportunity to improve site performance over time. These mean that time and budget must be allocated to site maintenance and development.

The end result

Entry costs for website marketing is low, and ongoing costs are extremely low. The potential for direct selling, database building and acting as a prime tool to do business is huge.

We might expect the following average figures:

- 2 US cents per impression to generate awareness (an impression may be a prospect accessing a Web page that has an advert for the supplier's site)
- 50 cents per click-through (those prospects who click through to the end site)
- $5 per lead on preference (i.e. some kind of lead where the prospect has shown an interest)
- $100 per sale

This last figure, though rather anecdotal, 'is nevertheless highly significant'. If we compare this cost per sale figure with those of other media using the 'cost per response' rule introduced early in this chapter, we see 'that yet again the average cost per response comes to somewhere around the £25–£75 area'. The developing economics of websites for direct sales is hugely important: if these average cost per sale figures remain steady, then websites will be very competitive alongside other major media, and better than many. But, in time, will websites dominate direct marketing? The consumer may have the last word: consumers like websites! Consumers are in charge: direct mail, inserts and outbound telephone just irritate.

Table 11.3 Summary of advantages and disadvantages of websites as a medium

Strengths	Weaknesses
Search engines make reaching your audience easier	but some sections of society are cut off
Content can be effectively communicated	
Very popular with customers	but still a lot of technical support needed

11.5   E-mail

11.5.1 Characteristics of e-mail

E-mail is huge. It has been estimated that 300 billion e-mails per day are sent globally. And although half the 300 billion are for male impotence cures, on an everyday basis e-mail has probably had a bigger impact, particularly on working life in westernised countries, than any other electronic development in the past 20 years.

E-mail has already emerged as a powerful business tool, with many firms using its flexibility and very low cost as an excellent way of keeping in touch with customers. However, there is a sharp divide between using e-mail to attract new customers versus keeping in

	Phone	E-mail	Chat/IM	SMS/Text	None	Social media
Male	67	52	22	8	7	3
Female	65	55	21	5	6	2
16–24	53	55	26	9	14	5
25–34	58	57	29	12	12	4
35–44	70	52	27	5	4	1
45–54	76	55	17	6	1	1
55–64	71	48	9	2		3
Total N=1009	66	53	22	7	6	3

Figure 11.7 Preferred method of communicating with customer services according to 'Internet Users in the UK, 2012'

Source: Sitel and TNS Omnibus 2012 Cited in **www.emarketer.com**.

touch with existing customers. On the retention side, e-mail has replaced direct mail as the favoured medium of retention marketing, as it is cheaper and easier to deploy than direct mail, and creates an instant dialogue channel with quick customer response. Both companies and customers like it. According to Ofcom (2013) face-to-face is the most used and preferred method for communication with businesses. Three in ten (28 per cent) UK adults say that they communicate with businesses such as banks or other services face-to-face on a weekly basis, followed by 24 per cent who e-mail, and around one fifth who call via a mobile or fixed line. Around one in ten (13 per cent) use postal services. Almost nine in ten (88 per cent) respondents indicate that they prefer to speak with a real person than an automated service. According to a Sitel TNS survey published on **www.emarketer.com**, e-mail comes second after the telephone in a list of customers' preferences for contact with companies (see Figure 11.7).

For acquisition marketing e-mail looked attractive on paper but e-mail 'spamming' has largely wrecked the entire industry.

Exhibit 11.10 E-mail: spamming and fraud kill the golden goose

Consent has long been vital with commercial e-mail. 'Spamming' is the use of technology to send the same e-mail to thousands or even millions of addresses on an e-mail list. Spamming is enabled by the very low costs of sending huge volumes of e-mail, and made possible by spider software that combs websites looking for e-mail addresses, which are automatically added to the list. Targeting is utterly non-existent of course and response rates extremely small but, when sending millions of e-mails, the cost per thousand is also minute.

It has been estimated that over 75 per cent of the world's e-mails are spam. Interestingly, 90 per cent of spam comes from only about 180 points of origin, mostly in the USA and Africa. Pornographic offers ('enlarge . . .'), financial scams ('I am transferring 20 million dollars and need you to hold it for me in your bank account . . .'), and the usual lotteries ('win a million!') seem to predominate.

Rowan (2002) and Ryanand Jones (2012) offer the following rules for prospective e-mailers:

- E-mail is always opt-in.
- Always offer unsubscribe buttons.
- Do not solicit on-line with chatlines that forbid commerce.
- You cannot sell e-mail addresses on to another company without permission.
- Subject lines must not be deceptive.
- Source of the e-mail must be traceable.
- Include a full postal address.
- If your customers or prospects think your email is spam, then it is.

Responsible companies are largely following these rules; but they cannot control the spammers. The result? Frustration and irritation will lead to a tendency to ignore or block out anything other than the personal, lowering response rates for the medium as a prospecting vehicle.

As if spamming was not enough, fraudulent e-mails have proliferated. The most prevalent are fraudsters posing as well known banks or financial companies. Their trick is to pose as your bank, tell you that your security records need updating, then click you through to a scam website posing as your bank's. If you then enter your details these are used to rob your account.

Needless to say these unpleasant developments have had a huge impact on the use of e-mail for customer acquisition.

11.5.2 Key AIMRITE qualities

Audience

E-mail has, in theory, a greater audience flexibility than any other media, with a range from one-to-one dialogue based communications to global mass advertising. In practice, these two extremes are used with spam at one end and good retention marketing from firms like Land Rover at the other.

However, there is little scope for detailed segmentation work outside of private data held by companies. External data firms like Experian are working hard on building credible e-mail lists, which they segment using other data held on that individual, but, in general, list-brokers have a hard job linking personal or business data to an e-mail address. This is leading to bulk e-mails to members of an interest group, say, being the norm (better than spam but still fairly hit and miss). Many e-mailers would not care over much about segmentation however: the cost of sending 50,000 e-mails is similar to sending 5 million – everything at present encourages mass advertising rather than more 'scientific' targeting.

One important development is the use of 'viral' referral e-mails. Here, a recipient is encouraged to pass on the offer to friends who may be interested. The secret here is the convenience and ease with which we can copy mails to our address books. In this way, rapid spread of relevant offers to similar people may be effected. This particularly works if the mail contains entertainment or humour, or if it contains useful business information. You will find much more information on viral campaigns earlier (Chapter 10).

Impact

A strength of commercial e-mails is that they are received by the recipient alongside their personal e-mails and, hence, are highly likely to be noticed. But this is more than countered by their current weakness, which is the suspicion with which they are now generally regarded: people are highly likely automatically to delete them without even opening, more so even than 'junk' mail through the post.

This is a pity because the characteristics of the medium have developed such that full colour, pictures and text, video attachments and, especially, clickable links make e-mail a potent force for conveying attractive messages. Of course it lacks the impact of TV or the tactile nature of direct mail. The varied interface also limits dramatic effect. For these reasons e-mail may not be used to build symbolic brand values; its strengths do, however, lend themselves to relationship building approaches, using its responsiveness to build dialogue.

Message

It is incredibly cheap to send extremely large volumes of information using e-mail. It is likely that the only constraining factor on message volume is the amount of information the consumer wishes to digest, rather than any media limitation. Chaffey and Ellis-Chadwick (2012) have compiled a commonsense list of creative recommendations for e-mailers. These include the need to grab attention in the header and early in the copy; hyperlink to websites for more information; be personalised; have a clear call-to-action, and so on. All of these ideas are based on principles that were developed for direct mail and are discussed in depth later (Chapter 14).

Response device

It is very easy to respond by e-mail: this is one of the secrets of its success. Only the telephone and perhaps point-and-click interactive TV could claim to be easier. As a response device e-mail shares with Web response the ability to offer 'delayed response' a few hours after receiving a message from a customer.

Internal management

Businesses need to plan for both outbound and inbound e-mail back from customers. The latter will be a minefield unless the firm has made provision to answer the queries reasonably promptly. One study done in 2002 found that only 30 per cent of e-mails were answered at all, let alone within a few hours or days. While firms preach service, they often do things to cut costs. E-mail lends itself very well to testing, with its data driven nature allowing the set-up of control cells to check and compare response rates.

The end result

The spammers and fraudsters have probably prevented e-mail marketing from achieving its potential. In theory, e-mail threatens to re-write the economic balance of marketing media – that most media deliver a similar cost per response. The potential advantages of e-mail, particularly as a retention media, are terrifying. Its cost per thousand reduces significantly with bulk, but a marketer going to his own list may expect to pay about £20–£30 per thousand sent. A 1–2 per cent response rate should not be unreasonable for an offer sent to an in-house list: this leads to a cost per response of only about £1, well under the best any other medium can usually manage. So, for retention marketing watch out for e-mail continuing to progress in importance. For acquisition marketing, the suspicion with which the prospect will view the campaign as possible fraud will severely limit its effectiveness.

The future probably lies with in-house lists and newsletter groups, with some well-directed acquisition offers using reputable list builders. That is, if the regulators and the consumers will allow.

Exhibit 11.11 The changing face of e-mail

E-mail is rapidly changing its rather basic interface. Anderson (2003) highlighted the case of RedV, an on-line company that sells privacy and security software. It has moved from simple HTML e-mails that click the recipient to its website, to e-mails that contain pictures. Following good direct marketing practice, it tested three. One displayed a picture of a man, one a picture of a woman, the third, the control, had no picture. RedV's target audience are mainly young men.

Guess which campaign did best? Some might not be surprised that most respondents clicked on the picture of the woman. The final twist, however, came in the conversion to sale figures: those who clicked through via the man's picture were more likely to buy. Yet again showing us the value of testing when trying to unravel how people actually do behave when responding to adverts.

Source: Based on an article by Heidi Anderson, **www.clickz.com** 17 April 2003.

Exhibit 11.12 The Battle of Hastings: using e-mail to overcome small budgets

How did Hastings Hotels generate a profit of £115,249, all from an expenditure of only £27,160?

The date was December 2006. The Hastings Hotels Group is an indigenous hotel brand in Northern Ireland, having grown out of, and survived, the years of the 'troubles'. By 2006 there was still a lot of work to be done to improve the image of Northern Ireland as a holiday destination. The Hastings Hotels Group had to compete in a slow-to-thrive tourism market. Hastings Hotels had optimised its website to enable it to receive on-line bookings.

It spent three years using a variety of methods to grow a customer database of over 8,000 people who were interested in receiving regular updates from the group. A campaign of e-mail marketing was recognised as the most cost-efficient and effective method to generate bookings.

Over a two-year period, Hastings Hotels sent 12 regular e-mails to its customer database. Each e-mail was a direct-response vehicle that communicated special bed and breakfast rates with a strong call to action to encourage the receiver to take up the offers by booking on-line.

Hastings Hotels also used a tactical pricing strategy to stimulate demand at times of projected low occupancy levels. The offers communicated in these e-mails would be better than at times of projected higher levels of occupancy.

Each e-mail was distributed to the Hastings customer database at the end of the month, when the receiver had more disposable income available to spend.

The key to converting these e-mails into actual sales was to make the message relevant and beneficial to the receiver. Different themes were chosen for the regular e-mails, which

Source: http://**www.hastingshotels.com.**

captured the mood of the receiver for the time of year and encouraged them to treat them-selves to a well-earned break. The focus of each e-shot was seasonal, with e-mails themed on St Valentine's, winter, spring, summer, autumn and Christmas breaks.

The following straplines used in the e-shots are some examples of how each e-mail's message tried to capture the mood of the receiver for the time of year:

- January 2006: Make this Valentine's Day special and escape to a world of luxury and romance.
- September 2006: Ward off the Winter Blues with some Red Hot Autumn Offers!
- November 2006: Treat Someone Special This Christmas . . . Or Treat Yourself!

The interactivity and insightfulness of each e-mail's call to action buttons (book now, refer a friend, gift vouchers, other offers and contact us) coupled with the relevant season-ality of each e-mail's message, aimed to present Hastings as an intuitive and user friendly brand, which was providing something of benefit to the receiver's life.

Each e-shot incurred costs for design in HTML and dispatch by a third party database manager:

design of e-shot in HTML, £480

dispatch by a third party database manager, £200

total cost per e-shot, £680

As Hastings sent 12 e-mails to their customer database in 2005 and 2006, the total implementation costs for e-mail marketing was £27,160.

By tracking room nights booked from the e-mails in 2005 and 2006 and the associated amount of revenue generated by these room nights, it was clear that e-mail marketing was a consistent income generator for Hastings Hotels, generating 2,464 room nights and £195,000 of revenue.

The revenue generated by each e-mail is based on the cost of a bed and breakfast rate and does not take into consideration any additional money spent by the visitor on evening meals and drinks during their stay.

Source: Hastings Hotels Group – Battle of Hastings 2005–06: how e-mail marketing overcame heightened competition to generated increased room occupancy and return on advertising investment for Hastings Hotels. Institute of Practitioners in Advertising, *IPA Effectiveness Awards, 2007,* pub. WARC Ltd.

Table 11.4 Summary of advantages and disadvantages of e-mail as a medium

Strengths	Weaknesses
E-mail very easy and convenient for both suppliers and customers	but little targeting capability at present
Cheap to set up and on a per thousand basis	but interface reduces dramatic impact
Very quick to organise, personalise and send, so an ideal one-to-one medium	but recipients drown in unwanted spam

11.6 Direct mail

11.6.1 Introduction

Direct mail is targeted distribution of 'personally addressed' mailing packages through the postal service.

Such is the historical importance of this medium, direct mail is often mistakenly seen as synonymous with direct marketing. However, in most countries it is no longer the pre-eminent direct marketing medium (in the UK, more marketing budget is spent on the telephone and new media have overtaken direct mail) and it is in decline, but direct mail remains important, even if its public perception with consumers is of 'junk mail'. Recently the authors have noticed a resurgence of interest in direct mail as a lead generation medium as recipients receive less direct mail so it has increased impact.

The difference in popularity of direct mail between consumers is mostly explained by examining the differences between acquisition and retention direct mail usage. Customers may welcome 'letters from the company' when receiving a mailer from a favoured supplier who knows their current situation and is writing to them with a relevant message. In contrast, 'junk mail' from companies mailing a prospect list arouses as much anger as ever. Across Europe in particular direct mail is under attack as being wasteful, environmentally damaging, contributing to recycling costs and generally irritating to consumers (. . . except when they respond). In the UK, politicians increasingly threaten to legislate to convert direct mail to an opt-in medium: in other words, direct mail to prospects will be barred unless that prospect has actively opted in to say they wish to receive mail. This will severely curtail the entire industry and is a great worry to its employees.

However, direct mail has long been the target of forecasts of decline by many in the industry. Given the ruthlessness of direct response – no hiding place for poor performance – you are advised to keep an eye on declining response rates, as much as political sabre rattling, as your guide to the future of direct mail. Average industry response rates are pretty much guesswork, but there does seem to have been a sense that they are declining a little – probably as people migrate to search Web e-mail ways to market. More evidence comes from the UK Direct Marketing Information System figures, which show that, while in 1985, 83 per cent of direct mail was opened, by 2007 that had reduced to below 60 per cent.

Exhibit 11.13 Rory Sutherland Direct Mail and Bloggers

How does mail work with blogging? Can an ad last 20 years? Rory Sutherland explores the unexpected strengths of a traditional medium.

1. Testing and measurement

New? Hasn't this always been the most trumpeted virtue of mail as a medium? Yes. The only problem was that a traditional obsession with response rates has long hobbled the mail medium with small-time metrics and an obsession with immediate transactional response. In a multi-channel age, where people don't necessarily respond to mail in easily trackable ways, this had become dangerous: mere coupon-counting can both fail to record many immediate responses while neglecting to record long-term effects at all.

But it needn't be that way. If you have a customer database or a loyalty programme you now can track long-term customer behaviour and value – one customer at a time. That means you now see the longer term pay-off of any addressable communication. The effects of this can be startling. In one test, loyalty card data showed us that the actual return on a mailing was eight times higher than previously thought. Why? Recipients to the mailing were buying the products without bothering to redeem the vouchers.

With mail you know who has received your message and – just as important – who hasn't. By and large, it's then easy to compare the behaviour of the two groups, giving the hard-pressed marketing man true accountability.But be careful not to use 20th-century measures to appraise 21st-century marketing. 'Not everything that counts can be counted; not everything that can be counted counts.'

Measurement is how you know your mail is working. But testing is how you discover what works, or what could work better. The freedom mail gives you to work with small, discreet test cells is liberating, as it gives you permission to be far braver.

2. Money and information

Every customer has two things of value: money and information. If they don't want to give you any of the first, ask for some of the second. When you use mail, market research is already included in the price.

3. The chance to transact – and to be personal

You can sell things from mail and catalogues with an efficiency not even on-line channels can match. But, just as important, you can use mail not to sell things. You can say thank you or sorry. You can say goodbye or welcome back. It's called a relationship. Maybe you even value your customers as human beings, not as wallets on legs. Wonders will never cease.

4. Timeliness

Perhaps your target audience isn't a 'who' at all. Maybe it's a 'when'. Maybe you have a target moment instead. Mail lets you target individual timelines, not just collective ones – birthdays as well as Christmas. People who have just bought a house. People whose insurance is up for renewal. People who are getting married – or divorcing.People also have a moment in the day – or week – which they reserve for 'dealing with stuff'. Paying bills, answering queries, organising their holidays. Miraculously your mail advertising reaches them at precisely this moment.

5. Personalisation

With digital print, it's perfectly possible to have as many creative variations in a mailing as there are people reading it. Microsoft recently wrote to people showing an aerial photograph of their business.

6. Flexible and creative messaging

Do you want a 30-second mailing or a 30-minute mailing? The space and time constraints of other media don't apply to mail. Need to show a range not a single product? Or need to talk about the intricacies of a financial product? No problem – you can be as detailed, precise, expansive, loquacious, articulate or circumlocutory as you want. Or as brief.

7. Attention-grabbing

High attention processing (HAP) means people pay attention to the post. Sure, they chuck some of it away – we don't deny it. But when they open it they look at it. Mail is unusual like that. You can't read your post while surfing the Web or driving a car. Even if just for a minute, you do gain someone's undivided attention.

8. Keepability, tangibility and texture

Most ads last 30 seconds. Send someone something they want to keep and you have an ad which lasts 20 years. In a virtual world it's nice to experience a little reality. Something you can touch, feel and even smell. And pass on to someone else.

9. It's cost-effective – whether cheap or expensive

The simple door drop is still the least expensive way to reach every household in the country. On the other hand, you can send an elaborate mail which looks a million dollars and costs a little less. Why? Well, it shows you care. And it gets talked about. One US agency routinely produces mailings costing $100 or more per head. The target audience? Bloggers. Mail one person nowadays and a million people may get to hear about it.

10. It translates intentions into action

On a final, serious, note, most charities in the UK depend on mail for their existence. That's not because other media can't do a great job persuading people to save the whale or the planet. It's because no medium can match mail for translating soft opinions into hard action.

Source: Market Reach 2013.

The answer – the message of this book – is good database marketing aligned to attractive offers.

The following discussion outlines the circumstances in which direct mail is a sensible option.

11.6.2 Key AIMRITE qualities

Audience

Anyone with an address can be reached by direct mail. In the UK, that means about 26 million households and businesses. There is a large industry revolving around the production and sale of lists, catering for target audience needs. If direct mail wants to be employed as a medium but the audience is not well defined, a company can use general lists, such as the opted in electoral roll, the Postcode Address File which has all the UK's addresses or, as a last resort, the telephone book or compiled lists.

Of course, the audience is best known when they are your own customers. In this instance, mail is often used because of its addressable qualities giving it a precise targeting ability.

When used in acquisition, direct mail requires a list of target prospects. These lists come in many forms, and are available to the marketer for a fee.

Lists

Lists are big business throughout Europe, Asia and the USA. In the UK, the key players in list broking include Dun & Bradstreet, Kompass, Call credit and Experian. But agencies are increasingly pulling in list broking so they have the whole offering in-house, allowing them to link list buying very closely with their data analysis team.

There are two broad types of lists in existence for both business and consumers: compiled lists and responsive lists.

Compiled lists

These are lists put together deliberately by a third party, such as the UK's ACORN geodemographic list, or a list available in the public domain, such as the telephone directory. The broad groups are:

- electoral registers (since 2001 the public have the opportunity to opt out of their Electoral Register details being used for commercial promotions, and, according to the Ministry of Justice in 2009, 40 per cent of individuals had opted out of the Electoral Register for marketing purposes and, in some areas, this was as high as 70 per cent (Minstry of Justice, 2009)
- geodemographic lists
- psychographic lists
- geo-lifestyle lists
- business lists from firms such as Blue Sheep or Dun & Bradstreet

The cream end of the market is lifestyle data, because it involves bigger volumes and a greater understanding of data selection. Geodemographics and lifestyle databases were covered earlier (Chapter 4).

Responsive lists

These are lists put together as a by-product of someone else's business, for example mail-order buyers of catalogues, subscribers to *The Economist* or store card holders. These are often the most responsive lists (hence the name), because they usually contain people who have responded to direct marketing programmes. Remembering the earlier point about 'mailing responsiveness', the importance of a predisposition to do business by mail should be noted here. In the same way as retail has shopaholics, many responders to mail order may actively enjoy shopping through the post. These people are more likely than average to respond to mailers on 'any' topic.

Recent changes to the list industry

The list industry is changing. List brokers are increasingly concerned that they are commodities that can only be differentiated on price. They are also increasingly being subsumed into

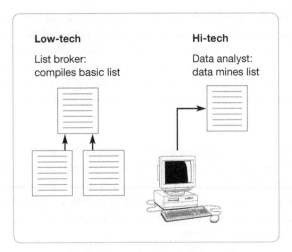

Figure 11.8 List brokers repositioning themselves

data agencies that can add value by helping clients analyse their data. Hence, list brokers are repositioning themselves as 'data analysts' more and more (see Figure 11.8).

What about over use of the lists? One development is that list brokers are adding in data about responders, and doing regression analysis that can predict list responses. This again increases the pressure to over mail 'responsive' people with poorly targeted offers: yes, some people prefer direct media, but this does not mean they will respond to any old offer!

To summarise, the issue for the direct marketer is to be on their guard and to know their stuff: the list broker is not media neutral or even list neutral – so the client must decide.

Impact

Direct mail is not regarded as a sexy media by the industry, but direct experts know that mail can still communicate very strongly. As something with the customer's address on it coming through the door in the morning, it can cut through competitors' clutter or noise, maybe more effectively in some ways than press, inserts or broadcast media. But, compared with, say, a much loved favourite magazine, the medium of direct mail will not generate the same 'halo effect' around the message.

Exhibit 11.14 What do consumers see as junk mail?

Research (Smith, 1996) found that in the public mind junk mail means anything they do not find interesting, in particular 'cold' mail making offers they do not find relevant. Nothing surprising there. More subtly, however, consumers do not describe mailers they find useful as either 'direct mail' or 'junk mail': they call these 'letters from the company'. Much research will, therefore, fail to pick up consumers' attitudes to the totality of direct mail because consumers and practitioners do not share the same language.

Message

If segmentation is important, a key strength of direct mail is its ability to use personalised letters to carry a different message to each recipient. Potentially millions of different messages could be sent, according to each prospect or customer's situation. A conference organiser could thank a businesswoman for attending a recent event, and, based on that customer's unique history of attendance, invite her to future events. Thus, direct mail can be an important element in turning a one-to-one strategy, as discussed earlier (see Chapter 6) into reality.

If your message is a long or complex one, another advantage of direct mail is its flexibility for carrying a lot of information. It can arguably carry more than any other medium. The only creative boundary is what fits through a letterbox and complies with Royal Mail guidelines on size if you want the lowest postage costs.

Direct marketing practitioners produce a massive range of direct mail, ranging from a simple one-page letter to packages containing 'gimmicks' that help get the message across.

Exhibit 11.15 Even cool bandz use direct marketing

Client:EMI
Agency: M&C Saatchi/Mark Sydney
Product: Gorillaz – *Plastic Beach* album
Campaign Title:Plastic Flowers
Media:Dimensional Direct
Country: Australia
Date:July 2010

Gorillaz is a virtual group, with real marketing objectives: to propel *Plastic Beach* to number one in the Australian charts, and go gold, within a month of release. And the glam showbiz budget? Just $3,000. That's more like a Direct Marketing one.

Actually, big bucks don't sell albums. Bloggers do. But they need a story, so one was told: *Plastic Beach* was recorded on a floating island of marine litter, somewhere in the South Pacific. A direct mailing to 20 top bloggers followed, each containing a unique souvenir plastic flower, and a letter from 'bandmember' Murdoc Niccals, personally decreeing the blogger to 'go and tell [your] bloggy minions'.

Fourteen top bloggers blogged as instructed by Murdoc's letter. Much social babble ensued. Most importantly, *Plastic Beach* reached number one in the Australian charts within a week of launch, with 35,675 CD, and 7,188 digital sales, going gold as hoped.

Source: Market Reach, 2013.

Further up the bulk scale, there are the loyalty magazines now favoured by many companies as a prime mechanism for keeping in contact with their existing customers. Boots has a high quality magazine aimed at ensuring its customers are reminded of the Boots brand values in between their car purchases. Redwood publishing specialises in this medium **(www.redwoodgroup.net)**.

People read less than they used to, and they watch more TV. Even with the rise of the Internet, TV viewing figures have increased. We can blame Simon Cowell, Bruce Forsyth and the credit crunch for the fact we are staying in and watching more TV. Mailings can contain anything from plastic flowers to chocolate, golf balls and DVDs. DVD production is very cheap. These trends mean more DVDs can be sent as part of direct mail – with the audience receiving the message in a totally different way. In spite of its expense (costs of a DVD mailer average about £1), these are quite widely used and may be a growth area albeit in a slightly declining medium.

Response

Direct mail sits alongside the telephone, e-mail and websites as the key media used for retaining existing customers. Direct mail in itself is not as convenient to respond to as the telephone, e-mail or websites but the mail marketer will usually point the buyer to respond via these media.

Internal management

Direct mail presents formidable management challenges to avoid making mistakes with the execution. The devil is in the detail. Consider the steps involved:

- Writing and communicating the brief
- Agreeing copy and artwork
- Printing and production
- Organising the customer data: briefing, selection, de-duplication, and so on
- Lasering of individual details
- Enclosing all the mail pieces and then finally mailing

Exhibit 11.16 Brand development through direct mail: Nick TV

In its launch of Nick TV, Nickleodeon wanted to do more than just make a splash, it wanted to use direct mail to help build the brand over time. So, mailers with a 'gel filled slime wallet' and 'pond scum floating frogs' doubling as a pencil case gave the ideas some playground currency. The mail shots were timed during the spring break holidays to maximise synergy with viewing time. A section of the mailer went to parents to ask for consent contact details of the children for longer term contact.

Customer acquisition through direct mail: Cadbury

Christmas time is important for well known chocolate firm Cadbury with its popular brands 'Roses' and 'Heroes'. An acquisition campaign sought to build traffic for their Cadbury Gifts Direct service – mailing presents of more expensive chocolate gifts. The acquisition ideas in the mailer included a Cadbury's Christmas countdown cut out calendar, and a Cadbury Christmas tree for the family to dress with Heroes and Roses. This was the most successful Cadbury mailer ever, with very high recall and, not anticipated, over 200 requests for more trees.

Building relationships through direct mail: Persil

'Your little ones could set a world record' so said the pack sent out by Persil to mums of pre-school kids. The 'create a big mummy' asked everyone to help build the world's largest picture mosaic. Over 15,000 pictures were submitted as a result of the campaign mailed to 11,000 playgroup leaders, supported by press and radio. All the children received a certificate from Guinness World Records.

Source: Case studies on Royal Mail website **www.royalmail.com** (accessed 2008).

As you can see, this is very complex and there are more hazards in its implementation than, say, in producing a press advert and placing it.

Typical 'lead times', from the marketing brief to the mailer hitting the customer's door-mat, are at least six weeks and sometimes longer, and this needs to be borne in mind when choosing the medium.

On the plus side, however, direct mail offers superb opportunities for 'testing' of all aspects of the campaign. This could range from which list to choose to the minutiae of different creative approaches. Direct mail is an excellent medium in which to test because of the control we can exert on all the campaign variables, especially audience: we know 'exactly' how many mailers are sent and who receives them. When compared with, say, press, the extra control of mail is readily apparent.

Lastly, there is the issue of 'privacy' from the competition. When Coca Cola launches a sales promotion offer in supermarkets, the effect is often deliberately masked by a counter-offer introduced within days by Pepsi. Ideally, a company would like to be able to conduct many of its marketing activities without letting the opposition know what is going on. Direct mail offers the chance to do just this because it is a private medium.

The end result

The best judge of the value of direct mail is the bank of accumulated knowledge obtained by direct marketing practitioners over the years, based on testing direct mail against other media and comparing actual customer behaviour, that is their responses. The accepted wisdom is that response rates for direct mail are typically 1–2 per cent for offers aimed at so-called 'cold lists' of prospects but, as was pointed out earlier, direct-response percentages are generalised at our peril: prospect lists can often give responses much higher or lower than this. But the signs are that responses are slowly declining as on-line media become more popular.

Exhibit 11.17 Getting results through direct mail: Great Ormond Street Children's Hospital

Great Ormond Street Children's Hospital knew that its existing donors responded best when they knew exactly what the function and role of the equipment provided by their donations was. One such was the mobile ultrasound diagnosis scanner. So, the agency idea was the headline: 'If you could see inside every envelope, would you open every one?' This was described as 'clever use of the media to make a point' by award judges who gave it gold in the DMA awards in 2005. The campaign response was 15 per cent with an average donation of over £18 for a cost per mailer of 55 pence: a return on investment of 500 per cent.

Source: Case studies on Royal Mail website **www.royalmail.com** (accessed 2008).

Table 11.5 summarises the strengths and weaknesses of direct mail.

Table 11.5 Strengths and weaknesses of direct mail

Strengths	Weaknesses
Highly targetable	but you need a suitable list or database
Responsive	but expensive
Payback can be outstanding	but internal management is committing
Creative medium	but regarded as downmarket
Good for detail	but can be intrusive

Exhibit 11.18 IBM Tivoli: the invisible IT expert

Tivoli is software from IBM that is designed to automatically and intelligently look after every aspect of a company's IT system. IBM simply wanted to make IT directors in three key industries aware of what Tivoli was and what it could do for them. Letting Tivoli handle your IT is basically like placing an IT expert at the very heart of your IT system. It is virtually the same as a real IT expert – except you never get to see them, they work around the clock, and they never take coffee breaks. In other words, an invisible man (see Figure 11.9). Agency Harrison Troughton Wunderman's off-the-shelf software solution plays on 'Action Man' style packaging and arrives in a typical IT component's anti-static bag. So far it has generated a 1.1 per cent response rate in the financial sector and 0.5 per cent and 0.2 per cent in the public and distribution sectors respectively. Just one sale would generate revenues of between $500,000 and upwards of $5 million.

11.6.3 The telephone in direct marketing

The telephone is a major force in our lives. The average British person now spends over 20 minutes a day on land or mobile phones, more than triple the rate 15 years ago. Mobile phones have completely changed the culture of communication, and land line use is

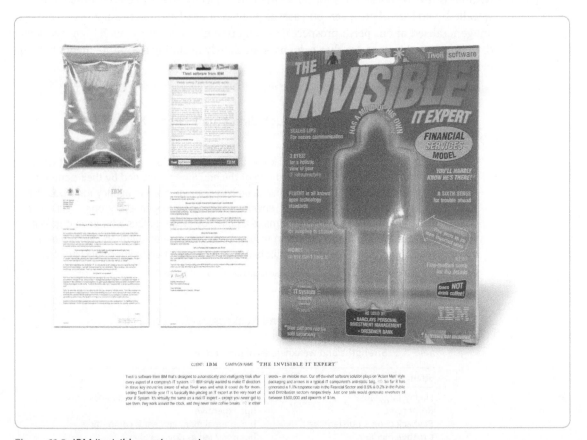

Figure 11.9 IBM 'invisible man' campaign

Source: Reproduced by kind permission of IBM United Kingdom Ltd and Harrison Troughton Wunderman.

relatively static – being used much more for Internet access in comparison. Mobile phone marketing is discussed later on.

The land line telephone in direct marketing is used in two ways. One is to make outbound calls to customers and prospects, known as outbound telemarketing, and the other is to use the telephone to take calls from customers, known as inbound telemarketing. But calling customers (outbound) is very unpopular, and has led to legislation with enormous opt-out rates amongst the population in the UK and across much of Europe and the USA. Customers calling (inbound) to companies is popular but expensive and firms struggle to cope with good service delivery.

Taking inbound and outbound use of the telephone together, total spend on this medium was estimated by the DMA at close to £7 billion in the UK in 2012 (DMA, 2013), making it the most important of all direct marketing media. Most of this spend was accounted for by the salaries of teleworkers, predominantly in call centres throughout the UK and of course in Europe and beyond too. The UK is the largest call centre sector in Europe, and our love affair with the telephone looks set to continue, though buying on-line competes hard as a channel and will increase.

11.6.4 Outbound telemarketing

Outbound telemarketing is the planned use of the telephone to make structured calls to the audience in a measurable and accountable way.

In theory at least, the telephone is the most powerful of all media in helping firms build relationships with customers. This would supplement its tactical use in helping make a sale. The link between the phone and relationship marketing is because of the key role of the telephone in providing 'service'.

Examples of the latter may include something as simple as saying 'thank you', which, although it is touted as a relationship marketing idea, was advocated by McCorkell, a leading direct marketer, back in 1989 when he said that 'the two most powerful words in advertising are not "new" and "free", they are "thank you"'.

Unfortunately, saying thank you has been the last thing on the minds of most outbound callers in the last decade. Aggressive cold calling, selling under the guise of service calls or 'research', and silent calling (using auto dialling that rings multiple homes at the same time, leaving only silence when some people pick up the phone) have all led to anger and dismay amongst the populace. An opt-out system called the telephone preference service now has over 60 per cent of all UK households signed up. Practitioners have made a collective mess of their use of this powerful medium.

Key AIMRITE qualities

Outbound telemarketing is probably the most powerful medium in terms of impact on the customer, the potential for response and the potential for getting it disastrously wrong.

Audience

As we have just noted, 16 million households have opted out of any outbound calling. Cold calling is a very poor business practice. The majority of telemarketing in this country consists of calls to a firm's existing customers, rather than new customers. Telemarketing is primarily used to increase the profitability of existing customers, either by encouraging them to spend more by up-selling or cross-selling, or by creating value for them in some way, thereby encouraging them to stay loyal to the firm.

Exhibit 11.19 Cold calling

You are sitting at home, settling down in front of *Coronation Street* with a bag of your favourite crisps and a cup of tea when suddenly the phone rings. Family or friends? No, it's a caller talking about PIPS saying it has your details and you are due compensation. Reactions to this would be varied, but experience shows that many people will react strongly against using the phone in this way. Unlike other media, the telephone generally forces a response answer from consumers, even if it is no. Not surprisingly, people resent having to say no and to explain why they are not interested, perhaps at a time when they would expect to be relaxing away from sales approaches.

Cold calling is the telephone selling of products to an untargeted list of people who have not been selected for any reason other than that they have a telephone. This is 'officially' not recommended by the industry bodies, the Institute of Direct and Digital Marketing and the Direct Marketing Association.

Impact

In terms of its ability to get messages through clutter, and in terms of the receivers' reaction to it as a medium, the telephone has the greatest impact of all media. It is very difficult to filter out telephone marketing in the way people filter out other marketing communications. Customers can screen calls using answering machines; otherwise people are forced to respond in some way (and generally to another human, not just to an advert). In this sense, the medium carries enormous impact, which means it is imperative it is used sensitively.

Exhibit 11.20 To phone or not to phone?

The Royal National Lifeboat Institution (RNLI) uses outbound telephone calls very rarely for any fundraising activity, even to its own donors. This is because the RNLI believes that its donors, who have rather traditional, conservative views, would not take kindly to being rung up by the charity.

On the other hand, both Shelter and Amnesty International, with a much younger profile of support, make active use of telefundraising, particularly for membership renewal. Both find they get much higher responses than for mail.

Message

Compared with media such as direct mail or inserts, the telephone can be used only for relatively straightforward messages. People can only take on board limited information aurally – try listening to a lecture without overheads, for example! The telephone is often used for 'announcement' or 'urgent' top-line messages that can then be backed up later, often with direct mail, to interested parties.

One technique worth highlighting is the need to have a 'reason to call'. Sudden calls out of the blue to someone about mortgages or to ask for a donation to a charity tend not to be well received unless they make sense to the recipient. So, for example, when BT made calls to its top-spending residential customers (often with bills well over £200 per quarter) the telemarketer might start by saying, 'We have noticed that your bills are very high and we were wondering if you might be interested in a scheme that could save you money?' A charity might call its supporters just after a major disaster to ask for emergency funds; charities have found that donors see this as a perfectly natural thing to do.

What does a telemarketing script look like? Exhibit 11.21 gives an example.

Response

Response, uniquely among media, is 100 per cent of people contacted. (There will be people who cannot be contacted because they refuse to answer, screen with an answering machine or are not in.) Politeness usually dictates that of those contacted some sort of response will be given, even if it is to decline the offer. Uniquely, therefore, negative responses are recorded and can be probed, gathering valuable research on the campaign.

The telephone is the easiest medium to respond to, as response comes naturally as part of the call. If the offer is rejected, the caller can either try to counter objections or at least note why the offer was not accepted.

Exhibit 11.21 Script for Red Cross Gulf War Appeal

The Red Cross launched an appeal three days after the Gulf War broke out on 15 January 1991. Its multi-media campaign consisted of direct mail to known supporters, a national press campaign and, finally, a telemessage backed up by outbound telemarketing to business leaders in major companies. The whole appeal was created and executed in a few days after the war broke out.

Outbound telemarketing script:

Good Morning/Afternoon Mr/Mrs/Ms . . .

My name is. . . and I'm calling on behalf of the British Red Cross. The reason for my call is that we recently sent you a telemessage asking for your help and support. Did you receive that?

Yes – That's great. Then you will be aware that . . .

No – I'm sorry about that. Let me tell you about it . . .

. . . The war in the Gulf is causing great suffering. As you know, prisoners of war have already been taken and thousands of refugees are fleeing from the war.

They need all the help we can give them. At home and abroad the Red Cross plays a vital role. We are determined to do all we can, but we urgently need funds, which is why we have launched an appeal for £56 million and why I'm asking for your support today.

Can we count on your support at this critical time?

No – May I ask why that is? (Discuss objections – see sheet)

Yes – Will your company be making a cash donation?

Cash donations can be made by . . .

Will you be dealing with this personally? (If no, get details) That's great.

Finally, thank you very much for your time and support.

Source: The British Red Cross. Reprinted with permission.

Internal management

There are many management issues to consider, and a detailed analysis is beyond the scope of this book. However, we will cover the key points that you need to factor into your media decision making, and which may prompt you into further exploration with specialist texts should you need to.

The first telemarketing decision is whether to attempt it in-house or use a bureau. Telemarketers need a lot of 'training' before they can be let loose on your precious customers, and they also need back-up systems to help them with the call. This back-up comes in the form of computer based scripts, which enable the caller to 'jump around' the basic 'script' depending on how the customer responds. Call centres tend to have teams of callers who are set demanding targets, with 'incentives' on reaching these, matching the way salespeople are given incentives. Putting together all this recruitment, training and scripting, and managing everything as the calls take place, is no mean feat, and for this reason a first time user of telemarketing is usually advised to use a specialist bureau. As time goes on, if your firm is a committed user of outbound calling, you may be tempted to bring the operation in-house, thereby avoiding paying a supplier.

Many companies, particularly those in the service industry, have well-established inbound telephone operations that take calls from customers about orders, repairs, complaints and so on. It is tempting to use these facilities to make outbound calls but not advised. This is because very different personalities are needed for the respective operations. Outbound callers tend to be more assertive, perhaps more outgoing and extrovert, whereas inbound operators are more sensitive to customers' problems, less driven by targets and goals and more reactive as people.

One of the biggest pluses for telemarketing is that it is a fabulous medium to carry out testing. To maximise the effectiveness of your campaign it is a good idea to test the major factors – the audience, the offer, the script, time of calling, to name but a few – before rolling out the final campaign. Telemarketing is undoubtedly the most manageable medium for testing, for two reasons. The first is the high response rates, which mean only a small number of customers need to be contacted to give a valid test. This means that many tests may be carried out and the results known within a short time, often within a day. The next day's tests can be formulated accordingly, learning from the previous day. The second factor is the control that managers have over the campaign elements. The audience, offer, time of call and script can all be tightly controlled.

We should also note that the telephone is not a good medium for contacting 'large volumes' of people, except in rare cases. This is partly because of the high cost per contact, and partly down to the relatively low number of contacts that an operative can make. Contacts by telephone are measured in 'decision maker contacts' (DMCs) per hour; a typical number may be about six contacts per hour, much lower than might have been supposed. Even with, say, 50 people making calls, a bureau would only expect to make about 2500 calls a day. This low number could be due to engaged lines, the person not being available or willing to take the call, and so on.

The end result

At its best, results with telemarketing can be astounding. Used appropriately, perhaps with a well thought out offer, well targeted at one's own customers, positive responses well in excess of other media can be achieved. One telecommunications company achieved 60 per cent take-up to an offer of telephone related services. Stone (1996) claimed that telephone generated leads are 'four to six' times more likely to close than mail generated leads.

In the Red Cross Gulf War Appeal highlighted in the exhibit earlier, the outbound calls to business directors were highly successful, generating a return of 9:1 on investment.

However, at a cost of about £6 per contact on average, high responses are needed just to break even. Even at 10 per cent response, a gross margin of £60 would then be needed on the sale in order to break even. This simple calculation shows why telemarketing is never likely to be used for single sales of low margin goods such as FMCG, which typically have gross margins per item of only a few pence. As a relationship building tool, however, customer lifetime values may well justify the telephone's use for some high value customers, even in FMCG markets.

Exhibit 11.22 Reassurance – the telephone

The telephone is an excellent medium when the recipient is likely to require careful explanation of the campaign's messages. This was the case with the International Fund for Animal Welfare's (IFAW) programme to improve average donations and switch donors from standing order to direct debit. The telephone enabled the charity to deal with queries in a reassuring way. Only existing donors were rung up, and because of their high level of trust in this excellent charity, the anticipation was that complaints of 'junk' telemarketing would be close to zero.

This proved to be the case, with 62 per cent of those called converting to direct debit, and 45 per cent agreeing to increase their gifts. These percentages illustrate the power of the telephone in eliciting response from existing customers. As a result IFAW decided to implement an annual calling programme to its 90,000 'Champions for Animals'.

Source: Based on DMA case study (1999) 'Best use of DM media – telemarketing', **www.dma.org.uk**.

Exhibit 11.23 Marjorie at the dealers here . . .

Simon Roncorroni, a leading marketing practitioner, tells the story of how he bought a Citroën from his local garage, and the day after he bought it he had a phone call:

'Everything all right? Marjorie at the dealers here . . .' 'While we are on, your next service is due in about six months or so. Shall we book you in now, so that you can plan around the date?'

'OK, that's all fixed up.'

Financial justification? The dealer's customer follow-up operation amounts to one woman working five hours a day (four hours making calls). She is paid cash, £25 a day. She is selling £1000 of incremental business every day.

Source: Roncorroni, S. (1992) 'Using the telephone for profit' in Halsey, B. (ed.) *Practitioners' Guide to Direct Marketing*, Institute of Direct Marketing, Teddington, UK.

Table 11.6 Summary of the strengths and weaknesses of outbound telemarketing

Strengths	Weaknesses
Highly specific in its targeting	but the most expensive medium
Very powerful in getting response	but poor practice has severely alienated consumers
Intimate	but needs close management
Immediate response	but message must be kept simple
Summary: the best relationship medium	

11.6.5 Inbound telemarketing

Inbound telemarketing is the use of paid or free telephone services to carry an invited response from other media.

The use of inbound telephone calling is now widespread in most developed countries, ranging from carelines on supermarket goods, and customer service centres to help with repairs, through to response handling for direct marketing campaigns. The Direct Marketing Association (DMA) reported UK spending on special lines (0800, 0845, etc.) as over £500 million in 2005 and this sector has become more sophisticated since then.

Inbound telephone service is highly valued by both consumers and business customers. As we have seen, recent surveys by Sitel and TNS rate the phone as the most preferred medium for customer contact (**Emarketer.com**, 2013). This primary importance of good interface for business customers was a key factor in the huge worldwide spend on CRM systems between 2005 and 2012.

Key AIMRITE qualities
Audience

Inbound telemarketing's audience is increasingly becoming universal. In 1970, almost no mail-order companies took orders by telephone. But in 2012, nearly all direct response was either through the telephone or through website/e-mail/mobile.

Impact

If (and it is a big if) the inbound service is good, people like this medium. Unlike outbound telephone promotion, which is viewed with heavy suspicion and hostility, inbound telephony sits alongside websites in handing control to consumers – this is very popular.

Message

The telephone is the most interactive of all media – the only one where a true dialogue with customers can be held. Messages can, therefore, be as flexible as the script and/or the training of the operative will allow.

Service companies can up- or cross-sell to consumers calling about something else. People ringing in to First Direct to ask about their bank balance would be informed about First Direct's new mortgage rates and asked if they wanted to switch.

The most far-sighted companies are using inbound calls to check on overall customer satisfaction, asking callers if they have anything that needs attention.

Response

Enabling easy response is, of course, exactly what inbound telemarketing is all about. In the western world, consumers are used to having their lives made easier and easier, and they want convenience and minimal effort expended when they buy goods.

The other big driver of quick response, which goes hand in hand with the telephone, is the credit card, which has also been a big contributor to the growth of direct marketing.

Internal management

Inbound telephone marketing management is not easy. As Rapp and Collins (1987) said, 'If you are going to do it, be sure you do it well or you may offend more people than you sell to.'

They recommend that managers try their lines out frequently themselves, and see how they get on.

The broad management issues are as follows:

1 **Predicting call volumes.** You can estimate forward trends from previous experience on the basis that 'the past is a good guide to the future'; or you can ask a consultant to estimate for you. Either way, this is critical to get right because, if you get it wrong, you will lose valuable leads, and you will annoy potential customers who have been kept waiting. If you cannot handle the volumes, you can use a bureau. This is particularly recommended with direct-response TV, which generates large volumes of calls in a very short time after the advert has been screened.

2 **Training.** The importance of front line staff to a business's image has been well documented. Some of the top exponents of this art, such as Direct Line or First Direct, use highly trained operators who can, if necessary, work away from a script. Such people do not, of course, come cheap, and it is marketing's job to decide whether the costs are worth the payback in terms of enhanced image, differentiation from competitors through superior service, and ultimately extra revenue as a result.

3 **Campaign management.** The marketer needs to write the operational brief, monitor the progress of training, set out the script, define the reports that are required and project manage the campaign as a whole, so that it happens on time, on budget and on brief. One key action is to make test calls throughout the process as a quality check.

The end result

Using a bureau, set-up costs for a major campaign might average £15,000 and then about £1 per call as typical inbound phone costs of a campaign. The marketer's role is to justify this cost in terms of the extra revenue it will bring in. This revenue will come through:

- responses that would not otherwise have come in because customers could not be bothered to send in a coupon;
- up- or cross-selling that was carried out while the customer was on the phone about something else;
- extra loyalty generated through the service element of the call; in other words, customers who would otherwise have gone elsewhere for future business will stay with you because they liked your service.

Table 11.7 summarises the strengths and weaknesses of inbound telephone marketing.

Table 11.7 Summary of strengths and weaknesses of inbound telephone marketing

Strengths	Weaknesses
Fast and convenient for customer	but can be expensive for the company and service delivery often poor
Most customers very comfortable on the telephone	but some sectors still reluctant
Flexible: use for service and sales simultaneously	but requires investment in staff training

11.7   Mobile marketing

A keen sports follower, you are watching the world athletic championships on the TV. Your mobile alerts you: there is a text message. It is from a well-known shoe company, inviting participation in a competition. Name the winner of the 100 metres from the last three Olympics. The first correct answer back wins two holidays to the Athens Olympics. Everyone gets the message at the same time so you are under time pressure. Come on. . . Maurice Green? Linford Christie? Donovan Whatsit. . . You respond, caught up in the small excitement of the game. It's fun, and easy to respond. You are asked by the company if you wish to receive marketing from them in the future. OK, providing it's interesting. Dull shoe promotions not required. You like them and you download their app, it gives access to personalised content about the sports and sports celebs you love.

The secret here is to interweave promotional material into the fabric of news, events, competitions and so on.

This is just one version of a growing phenomenon: using Mobile Marketing as a direct marketing medium.

According to the Mobile Marketing Association (2013):

'Mobile Marketing is a set of practices that enables organisations to communicate and engage with their audience in an interactive and relevant manner through any mobile device or network.'

These practices include simple calls over mobile, as well as SMS and application to person messaging, (these are 'texts or multimedia message sent from a network based mobile application, typically to a handset'(Mobile Marketing Association, 2013)). An example of this is when your mobile network tells you your bill is ready to view.

Mobile has grown from its original use as simply an alternative device for telemarketing, with the added feature of SMS messaging, to a medium that, through the use of smart phones and SIM enabled tablets and mobile data storage through cloud solutions, embraces all the features of Internet marketing. This comes with the additional benefit of location based marketing through the use of GPS. Gone are the days when we had to contact a building to talk to a person.

According to Ofcom, smartphone ownership in the UK reached 39 per cent in 2011, up from 26 per cent in 2009, and this is set to grow rapidly over the next three years (see Figure 11.10). An estimated 5 billion mobile handsets are in circulation worldwide.

In the near future the promise is of what Drayton Bird in a different context once called 'perfect marketing': real time one-to-one marketing. This works using the geographic positioning satellite facility that enables the network operator to pinpoint exactly where you are anywhere in the world. Location based services such as Foursquare allow McDonald's to send a promotional message to checked in prospects as they pass an outlet:: 'Hungry? Try our new McThai Surprise – 800 yards first left. . .' Time and place specific marketing is now possible using mobile devices. Speculating, one can see the growth of mobile marketing – but it must be personalised (so that we all receive only messages relevant to us), useful and entertaining. If marketing can deliver on this then we have the prospect of true one-to-one marketing. One-to-one media costs have dropped, but the management of one-to-one data and insight across channels, and co-ordination of this into personal marketing remains the issue.

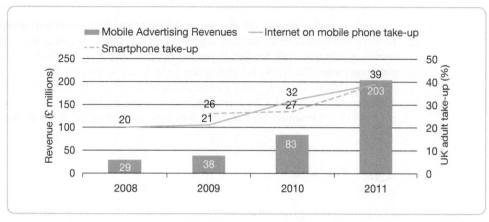

Figure 11.10 Smartphone ownership, mobile Internet and mobile advertising revenues in the UK 2008–2011

Source: Ofcom 2013, IAB/PWC.
Note: Take-up figures are from Q1 of the previous year.

Exhibit 11.24 Great mobile net bores of today

Ya the latest thing is the 'mobilemediary'. . . it's going to reconfigure the value chain you know. . . it will serve up your wife's wish list when you are in the mall shopping for a birthday present. . . let you download an app to help you trade stocks when the market is plunging and you are stuck on the train. . . theme park. . . lets you know it's your turn in five minutes for the ride. . . petrol – Mobil speedpass – a digital wand that you wave in front of an electronic reader at the gas pump. . . It's less about content and more about context – hence 'contextual marketing'. . .

These are just some of the issues for debate in what promises to be a fascinating future for SMS and mobile based marketing. 4G has been launched in the UK, offering better mobile user experience and the prospect of richer more compelling content to users. In effect, this means better quality video and photography and faster Internet access, all delivered through a single platform. The technology will continue to improve – who knows whether simple SMS text messaging, still a mainstay of this market, will survive another ten years?

SMS, and spend on mobile marketing generally, has grown significantly in 2012. The DMA put the level of spend at around £270 million (DMA, 2013). It is clear that marketing to consumers via our smartphones – whatever form this device takes – will continue to grow. Let us now use the AIMRITE framework to assess mobile as a medium for direct marketers.

Exhibit 11.25 How good is your teen texting?

Text messages cannot exceed 160 characters. To save space, text language has quickly evolved. Translate the following:

I cnt hr u. Im@ a RS concrt!
U no I lke u really. CU l8r
Thx 4 gr8 party. BCNU soon. Wan2 do dnr 2moro? Luv*:-)

> If you're having trouble, go to **www.mobileedge.co.uk/freesms/textexplained.htm** for easy-to-read translations. Text language is taken seriously by marketers wanting to communicate with the youth market. If you are MTV, then looking fuddy-duddy is not on. By the same token, the Prudential attempting to look cool is like your dad dancing at a wedding, or William Hague wearing a baseball cap at Notting Hill. According to Haig (2002), marketers for firms like the Ministry of Sound examine the language of text messages they get from their consumers carefully, and then they respond using the same language.

11.7.1 AIMRITE analysis

Audience

Mobile phones occupy an increasingly intimate place in our lives (see Figure 11.11). They may be a fashion statement, a lifeline or a crucial part of our daily social whirl. We look forward to messages from our friends, to important calls from work, sharing content or updating or checking our Twitter feeds and Facebook status. Into this fabric comes the marketer – and it is easy to miss the sensitivities and end up with a clunky, clumsy promotion that serves only to irritate. It is tempting to conclude that any use of this medium should probably be to existing customers only, but clever acquisition marketing is also possible, though rarer. In fact, most marketers use other media to attract 'handraisers', who respond using text or e-mail. Hence, in the first instance mobile is used as an inbound media for acquisition. It is then used as an outbound media only to those who have already responded.

Intimacy is one characteristic of mobile media, but fun and entertainment are also part of mobile marketing in particular, and it is this that marketers can turn to as a way of getting 'permission' to talk to new prospects. Whether it is Carlsberg sending m-coupons (i.e. coupons delivered via a mobile device) to responders of messages during the World Cup

UK internet and web-based content market	2007	2008	2009	2010	2011	2012
[1]PC/laptop take-up (%)	71	72	74	76	78	79
[1]Internet take-up (%)	64	67	73	75	77	80
[1]Total broadband take-up (%)	52	58	68	71	74	76
[1]Fixed broadband take-up (%)	n/a	n/a	68	71	67	72
[1]Mobile broadband take-up (%)	n/a	n/a	12	15	17	13
[1]Internet on mobile-phone take-up (%)	n/a	n/a	20	21	32	39
[1]Social networking online take-up (%)	n/a	20	30	40	46	52
[2]Internet advertising expenditure (£)	2.8bn	3.4bn	3.5bn	4.1bn	4.8bn	n/a
[2]Mobile advertising revenue (£)	n/a	29m	38m	83m	203m	n/a

Figure 11.11 UK Internet and Web based content market, 2007–2012 Bureau/PwC

[1]Ofcom consumer research, Q1 each year
[2]Internet Advertising Bureau/PwC
Source: Ofcom (2012).

qualifiers, or the Ministry of Sound inviting clubbers to respond to a number as they queue up, or advertising placed in the free download of the Angry Birds App, marketers can take advantage of the youthful nature of the medium. Indeed age is another consideration here. When SMS took off in 2001 the users were primarily teenagers attracted by the low cost – a few pence – of sending and receiving messages. Texting has since been adopted by older demographics, but amongst 55+ audiences there is still a distinct lowering of interest in this way of communicating.

Mobile media can be broadcast or narrowcast, with messages capable of being sent to millions of prospects, or a single customer. Hence, this medium has greater range than most of its rivals. In practice, the strengths of mobile lend themselves to narrower targeting, with relevant messages sent to individuals who have given permission to be texted. Mass campaigns would probably be largely dismissed as spam, and may irritate or anger the recipients.

In summary, if you are marketing to 18–30-year-olds about 'fun' products then Mobile is very powerful. On the other hand, if you are communicating with 45–55-year-olds about mortgages then it may be less likely to be of use, but by no means should be ruled out of court altogether.

Impact

Our discussion earlier highlighted how important the mobile phone is to its users. It is, therefore, hardly surprising that mobile messaging can rival the (land line) telephone as a medium of huge impact. SMS can rival the intrusive nature of telemarketing, and is much cheaper, though without the forcing power of having to respond to a person. SMS also gains impact through its possible usage as a database driven media to existing customers, hence improving the targeting of the media. Mobile also has a spontaneity and immediacy to it that land line telephony lacks. In visual or aesthetic terms SMS has to be one of the weakest media – the 'plain Jane' of media as Haig (2002) described it. Users are limited to 160 text characters, so building strong visual brand signals is not an option here. However, its low cost allows easy linkages into multi-media campaigns, particularly with press, TV, e-mail and websites. This flexibility can offset the low visual impact of SMS.

All this will change as we move to 4G technology, which will allow multi-media messaging service (MMS) to take over from SMS. MMS will allow the usual panoply of visual effects, graphics and so on, removing the need for text only discipline.

Message

The limited message capability clearly positions SMS as a medium that needs to be used as part of a multiple media delivery. Typically, SMS may be used to alert prospects to a sales promotion or event that is more fully explained elsewhere, often a website. Often directly responding will propel the customer into a series of back and forth communications with a firm, maybe allowing some kind of pseudo-dialogue to be established (but let us not overstate this: real dialogue is very rare – more commonly, consumers are nudged into pre-structured replies, typically using questionnaire style approaches).

Message content is much more likely to be related to encouraging response to an event or promotion than it is to brand building or direct selling, especially in the first instance. A two- or three-stage campaign will progressively pinpoint those in the market to buy, and will allow more direct sales approaches to be made.

However, the broader functionality of Internet enabled smartphones allows all the flexibility and functionality of the Internet to be harnessed in mobile communications.

The use of apps enhances this considerably. Apple's App Store and Android Market have been phenomenally successful. Apple App Store in February 2013 contains over 755,000 different apps, up from 200,000 in 2010, and today it is possible to generate a basic mobile app very cost effectively 'App kits' can be bought on-line for under £100.

Successful apps are easy to use and focus on a good user experience and a great interface. Apps with longevity are useful and relevant to the user group targeted. Sounds familiar, doesn't it?

Response device

SMS will rank ahead of TV, press, or even direct mail as a medium easy to respond to, but behind telemarketing or e-mail, which is quicker and easier to type into. Marketers can encourage easy response using questionnaire devices, such as asking a question needing only a Y or N response. Mobile media generally share the response characteristics of the Web.

Internal management

According to Haig (2002), 'most mobile marketers have learned that do it yourself SMS delivery is a recipe for expensive disaster'. He recommends marketers doing what they can in-house, then outsourcing more technical procedures.

Software is available that allows users to compose messages and then send them to prospects simultaneously. However, as always in direct marketing campaigns, handling responses is the toughest part of the operation. With large campaigns, these will come in by the thousand, requiring automated handling.

Outsourced services on offer will include the use of a text messaging server, multiple messaging support and response handling for incoming messages.

Text media campaigns can be created and sent within days of conception. As part of 'relationship' programmes, they can be integrated into daily activity within the marketing department. However, it is likely that a great deal of prior planning and trial and error will have to be experienced before this happy state of affairs is reached.

The end result

Mobile marketing generally shares the same metrics as the Internet but there are a few specific issues for 'mobile applications'. Clearly the number of downloads is important. For SMS messaging there are some industry standard rates.

Prices quoted recently (e.g. **www.websms.com**) place sending SMS messages at between 2 and 6 pence per message. Typically, sending to a large volume of prospects may cost about £25 per thousand messages. Smaller volume messages may rise in cost terms to about £60 per thousand. Response rates of 0.1 per cent would then yield a cost per response of £60. Publicly available case studies trumpet response rates much higher than this, but the reader is advised to interpret with care. That said, it may be that SMS, like e-mail, has the power to re-write the 'cost-per-response rule'. An average response of, say, 1 per cent, similar to direct mail, is hardly out of the question. This would bring cost per response down to less than £6, perhaps ten times cheaper than direct mail.

Overall, mobile marketing can produce rich data and this needs to be integrated into the data produced from other channels.

Summary

In this chapter we found that media choices in direct marketing depend on a number of factors and, therefore, should be made carefully. These factors can be applied systematically using the AIMRITE formula.

Direct marketers have a large number of media choices, of which some of the most important are websites, e-mail, direct mail, the telephone and mobile. On-line marketing has made life more difficult for direct mail and the telephone. The biggest development of recent times has been search engine marketing, which is now the dominant player in the on-line marketing mix. Banners and pop-ups have declined in importance but can still be effective. Website and e-mail costs per response are getting more and more competitive, although they often sit at similar levels to traditional media. Moving off-line, direct mail is still excellent at carrying large amounts of information, giving consumers a permanent record and presenting messages creatively. Even with the advent of Web and e-mail marketing, the telephone remains the best 'relationship building' medium, if it is used properly (sadly all too rare).

E-mail has the potential to be arguably the most powerful of all direct-response media. Some direct mail usage in particular is under threat in the long term from the easier and cheaper alternative of e-mail.

QUESTIONS

1 In what circumstances should you never use the telephone for contacting prospects? Give examples of companies or situations where this is the case.

2 Critically analyse the relative strengths and weaknesses of direct mail and e-mail.

3 A large regional car distributor with outlets in the Midlands is planning to introduce the telephone into its acquisition and retention programme. Draw up a proposal that explains:

the possible use of search engine marketing;
how the company might benefit from some form of telemarketing;
the ways in which the telephone maximises short- and long-term returns;
what major practical difficulties will be encountered and how to overcome them.

4 'Apart from some specialist applications, SMS will never be of much use for direct marketers.' Discuss the extent to which you agree with this statement.

5 A high street bank has set up a major calling centre in-house, capable of taking inbound and making outbound calls. Outline how such an asset could form part of a direct marketing approach to improve relationships with customers.

6 'Direct mail works best when integrated with other marketing media.' Evaluate this statement, outlining examples where it is and is not the case.

7 Bartlett's Office Services is a full range supplier of office equipment. Until now it has used trade press advertising and a salesforce to operate, but is now considering the use of websites to both generate and convert leads. Using the AIMRITE formula, evaluate the effectiveness of websites for this firm.

8 Imagine you are the director of a new theatre company, and you need to acquire new customers for the start of the season. Compare and contrast websites as a medium with direct mail and the telephone – what are their strengths and weaknesses using the AIMRITE formula?

References

Braithwaite, A., Wood, K. and Shilling, M. (2000) 'The medium is part of the message – the role of media in shaping the image of a brand', ARF, ESOMAR Conference, Rio, Brazil, 12–14 November.

Chaffey, D., Mayer, R., Johnston, K. and Ellis-Chadwick, F. (2006) *Internet Marketing Strategy, Implementation and Practice*, 3rd edn, Financial Times Prentice Hall, Harlow.

Chaffey, D. and Ellis-Chadwick, F. (2012) *Digital Marketing Strategy Implementation and Practice*, 5th edn, Pearson, Harlow.

DMA Census (2012) Direct Marketing Association, London.

DMA (2013) *Putting a Price on Direct Marketing* [on-line] Available at: **http://dma.org.uk/sites/ default/files/tookit_files/putting_a_price_on_direct_marketing_2012_0.pdf**. [Accessed January 2012].

Emarketer (2013) [on-line] **http://www.emarketer.com/Article/UK-Still-Prefers-Traditional- Customer-Service-Channels/1009424** [Accessed February 2013].

Google Search Engine Optimisation Starter Guide (2013) [on-line] Available at: **http://static.goog- leusercontent.com/external_content/untrusted_dlcp/www.google.com/en//webmasters/ docs/search-engine-optimization-starter-guide.pdf** [Accessed Feb 2013].

Google Doubleclick (2013) *What's Trending in Display for Publishers* [on-line] Available at: **http://static.googleusercontent.com/external_content/untrusted_dlcp/www.google. com/en//doubleclick/pdfs/display-business-trends-publisher-edition.pdf** [Accessed February 2013].

Haig, M. (2002) *Mobile Marketing – the Message Revolution,* Kogan Page, London.

Ryan, D. and Jones, C. (2012) *Understanding Digital Marketing,* 2nd edn, Kogan Page, London.

Market reach, 2013 [on-line] Available at: https://**www.marketreach.co.uk/why-mail/10-reasons- make-mail-your-medium** [Accessed February 2013].

Marketing Sherpa (2013). [on-line] **http://www.marketingsherpa.com/data/members/bench- mark-reports/11855_2012%20Lead%20Generation%20Benchmark%20Report%20-% 20EXCERPT%20-%20Launch%20Price%20Savings.pdf** [Accessed February 2013].

Mashable (2012) [on-line] Available at: **http://mashable.com/2012 ÷ 11 ÷ 27/siri-chevrolet/** [Accessed February 2013].

Ministry of Justice (2009) [on-line] *Electoral Registers Proposed Changes to the Edited Register,* Available at: **http://www.justice.gov.uk/downloads/consultations/electoral-reg-changes-ed-reg- consultation.pdf/** [Accessed February 2013].

Mobile Marketing Association (2013). [on-line] Available at: **http://www.mmaglobal.com/wiki/ mobile-marketing** [Accessed February 2013].

Ofcom (2012) Communications Market Review **www.ofcom.gov.uk** [Accessed February 2013].

Ofcom (2012) International Communications Market Review **http://stakeholders.ofcom.org.uk/ binaries/research/cmr/cmr12/icmr/ICMR-2012.pdf** [Accessed February 2013].

Peters, L. (1998) 'The new interactive media: 1 to 1, but who to whom', *Marketing Intelligence and Planning,* 16 (1), pp. 22–30.

Rapp, S. and Collins, T. (1987) *Maximarketing,* McGraw-Hill, USA.

Roncorroni, S. (1992) 'Using the telephone for profit' in Halsey, B. (ed.) *The Practitioners' Guide to Direct Marketing,* Institute of Direct Marketing, Teddington, UK.

Rosenfield, J. R. (1999) 'The Internet, **Amazon.com** and Book-of-the-Month Club: the old, the new, and the future view', *Direct Marketing,* 62 (12), pp. 44–8.

Rowan, W. (2002) *Digital Marketing,* Kogan Page, London.

Smith, I., Education Director, Institute of Direct Marketing (1996) *Personal communication,* Institute of Direct Marketing.

Smith, P. and Taylor, J. (2004) *Marketing Communications: An integrated approach,* 4th edn, Kogan Page, London.

Stone, B. (1996) *Successful Direct Marketing Methods,* 5th edn, NTC Business Books, Lincolnwood, Ill

Thomas B and Housden M (2011) *Direct and Digital Marketing Practice,* A & C Black, London.

CASE STUDY

Xerox wins gold – how to make direct mail interesting

The Xerox Work Centre Pro is a digital printer which needed to be launched across eight European markets. We needed to find an idea that was meaningful to all markets and able to cut through the language and culture differences. Our target was 60,834 IT managers in small to medium-sized companies. We knew they had

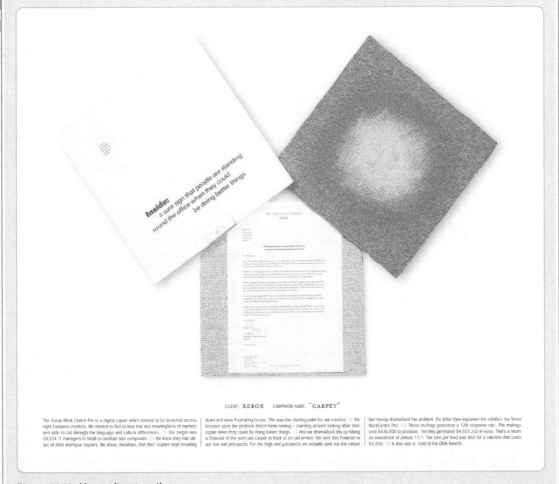

CLIENT: **XEROX**   CAMPAIGN NAME: "CARPET"

The Xerox Work Centre Pro is a digital copier which needed to be launched across eight European markets. We needed to find an idea that was meaningful to all markets and able to cut through the language and culture differences. Our target was 60,834 IT managers in small to medium size companies. We knew they had old, out of date analogue copiers. We knew, therefore, that their copiers kept breaking down and were frustrating to use. This was the starting point for our creative. We focused upon the problem they'd been having – standing around looking after their copier when they could be doing better things. And we dramatised this by taking a Polaroid of the worn-out carpet in front of an old printer. We sent this Polaroid to our low end prospects. For the high end prospects we actually sent out the carpet itself! Having dramatised the problem, the letter then explained the solution: the Xerox WorkCentre Pro. These mailings generated a 12% response rate. The mailings cost $436,000 to produce. Yet they generated $4,633,332 in sales. That's a return on investment of almost 11:1. The cost per lead was $60 for a machine that costs $4,400. It also won a Gold at the DMA Awards.

Figure 11.12 Xerox direct mail
Source: Reproduced by kind permission of Xerox (UK) Ltd and Harrison Troughton Wunderman.

old, out-of-date analogue copiers. We knew, therefore, that their copiers were near the end of their life and could be frustrating to use. This was the starting point for our creative. We focused upon the problem they'd been having – standing around looking after their copier when they could be doing better things.

And we dramatised this by taking a Polaroid of the worn-out carpet in front of an old printer. We sent this Polaroid to our low-end prospects. For the high-end prospects we actually sent out the carpet tile! Having dramatised the problem, the letter then explained the solution: the Xerox Work Centre Pro. These mailings generated a 12 per cent response rate.

The mailings cost $436,000 to produce. Yet they generated $4,633,332 in sales. That's a return on investment of almost 11:1. The cost per lead was $60 for a machine that costs $4,400. It also won a Gold at the DMA Awards.

Question

Making business direct mail work is extremely difficult. Executives receive so much that getting a response is ever harder. Give five reasons why the Xerox Work Centre Pro copier mailer worked so well.

Told by award winning agency Harrison Troughton Wunderman.

CASE STUDY

Dell

Legend has it that Michael Dell started out as a college student in the 1980s dismantling an early version IBM PC, putting it back together and realising that he could assemble and sell the thing for over $1,000 less than IBM. Thus was born a firm that became the world's biggest PC seller and one of the darlings of the Internet age. By 1998 Dell had become the first player to make selling over the Internet work. It claimed sales over the Internet of £3.7 million per day worldwide, even then an impressive figure. But as it moved into the late 2000s life had got a lot harder for one of the maverick kick-ass firms of the dot-com boom. What could Dell do to get away from the pack once again?

The story of Dell

Dell originally made its fortune by ignoring the traditional PC distribution model, avoiding middlemen and selling directly to corporate customers. Dell's extraordinary success with this approach caused the traditional computer makers, the likes of Compaq and Hewlett-Packard, to sit up and take notice. They had sold through retailers such as PC World, Currys and Dixons, which accounted for most of the sales to consumers and small business (the 'Small Office Home Office' (SOHO) sector). But as the market matured

and second-time buyers became the majority, buyers became more confident about purchasing computers. This meant they no longer needed the face-to-face reassurance of a retail channel: buying on-line or over the phone became a reality, especially for busy small businesses.

Branding was still important, however. Intel showed it was a vital weapon where customers trust suppliers to deliver a quality product in a high-ticket complex product sector. In the PC market increasingly, branding techniques – traditionally the forte of consumer marketing – are being used in preference to the product specification type of selling (often led by salespeople) previously favoured by business-to-business marketers in this sector. This enthusiasm for branding came as firms moved toward targeting their business consumers direct. For the resellers in the middle, the future seemed increasingly uncertain, as the big names wanted direct dialogue with their customers.

Coupled with branding, direct marketing is on the increase in the business-to-business sector as it recognises the success this element of the marketing mix has enjoyed in its neighbouring consumer field.

The move towards brand building/direct operations for business-to-business hardware firms meant a matching rise in media spending. Apple made one of the most significant branding pushes of the IT pack with its 'Think Different' brand building campaign. Alan Hely, Apple UK's marketing director, said the campaign helped to build 'the only lifestyle brand in the industry' and said the aim was to communicate 'what Apple stands for; it's not about the product'.

However, in its early days Dell eschewed the trend towards the 'corporate personality', instead focusing its efforts on the small and medium-sized enterprise sector, with '99.9 per cent of advertising in the UK directed at SMEs'. Its marketing strategy reinforced its direct-sell approach via very targeted direct mail, site visits by salespeople, telesales, sales promotion and direct-response advertising. It often ran 30 or 40 marketing programmes at any one time. One Dell executive said that: 'We are trying to use the products to carry the brand attributes. In the SME market, value for money is the key.'

Dell segments its customers into five sectors in the UK, according to size of company from corporate sales to the *Times* top 100 down to its consumer-only business. It tailors its marketing activities accordingly.

Dell's use of the Internet

Internet marketing now accounts for most of Dell's worldwide sales. With Dell the flow of information is upwards from the customer to the company, allowing something close to Pepper's ideal one-to-one scenario. First, the company made computers according to customer orders – it does not keep any stock. This allowed it to produce precisely what customers want, rather than nudging customers towards something that did not quite fit their needs. Secondly, the zero stock eliminated a whole series of costs, which fell out of the supply chain, allowing lower costs to be transferred to the customer and improving the company's competitiveness.

By 2005, Dell was the biggest PC seller in the world and nearly all these sales were on-line. Fortune named Dell 'America's most admired company'. Add in record revenue of $52.8 billion over the last four quarters, and the brand could not have looked in better shape. But by 2006 things had changed. Dell did something its owner had always scoffed at: it opened a retail store. What had happened? There were two market trends working against Dell. The first was the swing of products towards matching computing power with entertainment. High-end specs were

needed for game playing in a home environment. 'We're seeing more and more of our technology intersecting with home entertainment', says Ro Parra, a senior vice president of Dell's home and small business group. Secondly, while 80 per cent of Dell's sales were to businesses, that market had become a lot tougher. Businesses wanted standardised machines that are basically commodities, and prices had gone into free fall in the face of steep competition. So, domestic consumers were powering the industry's growth: by 2005, consumer sales were growing twice as quickly as businesses.

This coincided with a resurgence from the likes of Hewlett-Packard, which for years had suffered against Dell. But HP was not finished yet. By 2005 it had narrowed the gap in productivity and price and Dell had to get to grips with its new reality: its business model no longer gave it a competitive advantage over its nearest rivals.

'Michael broke the paradigm about how to run a computer business, but they haven't been so great at finding the next paradigm', says David Yoffie, a professor at Harvard Business School, in 2006. 'That's the big challenge for Dell, the company and for Michael.'

2006 was a tough year for Dell. Customer service studies showed that its once incomparable customer service standards had plummeted to 'just above average' and the company acknowledged the decline. Meanwhile, competitors such as Hewlett-Packard Co., Acer Co. and Chinese giant Lenovo (which bought out IBM's PC arm) threaten to dilute the brand in the US and abroad.

'Dell currently leads on the value attribute, but HP is seen as more creative and complete when it comes to solutions', said one commentator.

Dell's marketing strategy in 2008–09

Not surprisingly for a brand that exists mainly on-line, Dell does a lot of direct and Internet marketing. Twenty-five-year-old Dell continues to market its PCs and an array of products and services using the direct marketing model with which it built its reputation. 'Direct marketing has worked for us and continues to work for us,' said a marketing spokesman. 'The workhorse for us is our catalogue. We mail several different versions each month and touch the entire small and medium-sized business universe.'

Dell's agencies are expected to carry out high-volume direct mail campaigns, including door drops

Case study (*continued*)

and inserts, as well as on-line work. In the past most Dell campaigns have focused on price.

Dell has also done a lot more work recently on its brand image. It hired former National Football League marketing guru, Shawn Dennis, as VP-global branding to shake up its image.

Dell also markets via TV, e-mail, on-line and print, and ran a campaign using free-standing inserts (FSIs) and radio. The radio ads drove traffic to an easy-to-remember URL and the results were very promising.

The company is careful to measure media impacts. Marketing director Thompson and his team used regression modelling to determine the impact of TV spots on sales. He said television generates an 80 per cent lift to direct marketing. 'People might see the TV ad and dial the number on the back of the catalogue,' he said. 'In the past, we might have attributed it to the catalogue and missed the link from TV.' Thompson also discovered that on-line banner ads were actually cannibalising business, so Dell pulled back its investment there.

But Dell's on-line marketing is vital for its success on the Web. Try typing into Google keywords like 'PC', 'computers' or 'home computing'. The chances are Dell will be the first link in the paid-for ads section of Google search. Or, go to **www.Dell.com** and you will see straightaway how important on-line is to Dell. Another of its strategies is launching microsites showing how it is helping small business customers succeed. In March 2006 Dell introduced **www.dell.com** a microsite developed by T3, Austin, Texas. The site shows how Dell technology helped the 15-person World Triathlon Corp. put on the Ford Ironman World Championship. Small businesses are encouraged to share their success stories on the site. 'This site talks about how Dell is helping small businesses and is focused more on the human side than the transactional side.' Dell has also launched its own blogs and attempted to use viral marketing campaigns.

Questions

1 How did Dell put the customer in control of the buying process? How does the Internet help in this feature of Dell's business?

2 What can Dell do to regain eminence with its core B2B market? How can it move into the consumer market successfully?

3 Why don't consumers prefer on-line buying for entertainment based products? Why has Dell been forced into retail?

4 Compare and contrast Dell's direct approach with the brand-building approaches of HP and IBM.

5 How should Dell use Web search, e-mail, affiliate marketing and direct mail to best effect to support its inbound Web and telephone sales channels?

6 What are the key success factors for business-to-business direct marketing compared with consumer direct marketing?

References

Advertising Age's Business Marketing (Chicago) (1999) 'Past NM top 10 winners', 84 (8), p. 36.

Auer, J. (1999) 'Is going direct going cheaper?', *Computerworld,* 19 July.

Clancy, H. (1999) 'What does "direct" mean, anyway?', *Computer Reseller News,* Manhasset, 11 October.

Coates, T. (2006) 'Dell goes retail. . . and why that's a tough sell', *Time,* 31 July, 168 (5), pp. 56–7.

Krol, C. (2004) 'Dell sees continued success with DM', *B to B,* 25 October, 89 (12), p. 8.

Lee, L. (2006) 'It's Dell vs. the Dell way', *Business Week,* 3 June, (3974), pp. 61–2.

Littlewood, F. (1998) 'Direct connections', *Marketing,* 27 August, pp. 27–9.

Maddox, K. (2006) 'Marketers find Web effective way to reach small companies', *B to B,* 13 November, 91 (15), p. 30.

Marketing (2006) 'Dell reorganises direct business', August, p. 3.

Mitchell, A. (2000) 'In one-to-one marketing, which one comes first?', *Interactive Marketing,* pp. 354–68.

Slavens, R. (2005) 'Brands: DELL', *B to B,* 24 October, 90 (13), p. 23.

Trilling, D. (2006) 'Five ways companies can use the internet to target your wallet', *New Statesman,* 28 August, 135 (4807), p. 26.

Wasserman, T. (1999) 'IBM's magic moment', *Brandweek,* New York, 9 August.

CASE STUDY

Pimm turns gold

PIMM'S Summer Party

Challenge

The challenge was to position Pimm's as a national, everyday summer drinking brand, rather than a drink for 'Southern toffs' on special occasions.

Strategy

TMW's strategy was to create a 'participation platform' called 'Join the Pimm's Summer Party'. The idea was to use the 'Summer Party' as a pastiche political party to help people celebrate everything that is brilliantly eccentric about the British summer. The agency then identified those channels that we felt would be the most influential in helping to create a movement amongst the target audience and which could deliver rewards to all who participated and shared in it.

Solution

Like all political movements, TWM started with a party. They organised an event to launch the 'Summer Party' the night the clocks went forward. Through on-line rich media, social, press, radio, an experiential bus tour of all the major festivals, TV and outdoor digital advertising, TWM raised awareness of the movement and ultimately invited the nation to join the party on Facebook and claim free party prizes. They also created a 'Pimm's My Summer Party' Facebook app to host a competition offering Facebook fans the opportunity to win the ultimate Pimm's Summer Party. The broader Facebook community were encouraged to participate by voting for their favourite entry.

The brand partnered with Sainsbury's to offer people the chance to buy a bottle of Pimm's and redeem that against a Summer Party pack of much sought after branded jugs and bunting. A limited edition bottle was also created in just one month. Iin-store point of sale was developed including six sheets, security shrouds, barkers, in line plinths, gondola ends and merchandising units to engage customers and direct them to purchase in Sainsbury's.

Results

Over 50 per cent YoY increase in sales.
Almost 1,000,000 limited edition bottles sold.
35,000 Party Packs distributed.

Told by award winning agency TMW.

CASE STUDY

Heinz *At home*

In the summer of 1998, *Campaign* magazine announced that marketing executives at Heinz had withdrawn its direct marketing magazine in 1998 after deciding the Heinz brand communicated itself more readily through television and poster advertising. *Campaign* reported that Heinz believed its products

➡

would sell without the use of direct marketing and would revert to TV brand building.

Campaign, a magazine that champions brand building and advertising, suggested the following reason for the failure of the Heinz *At Home* project. Tylee (1998) reported:

> Want to know why Heinz is axing its customer magazine, *At Home*? Then try this simple test. Put your thumb across the Heinz logo on the front cover. Now imagine another name in its place. Sainsbury's, Asda or Safeway perhaps. Does the magazine look a neat fit with any of those brands? If your answer is yes, you are some way to understanding why Heinz *At Home* has bitten the dust.

Tylee suggested that, while the Heinz brand oozes warmth and homely values, the magazine had struggled to sustain them, being instead a mere bolt-on to the brand's distinctive multi-million pound TV advertising. Damningly, *Campaign* said that the move 'almost certainly ends Heinz's four-year flirtation with direct marketing'.

It had all started so well. . .

The announcement in May 1994 that Heinz was switching emphasis to an extensive direct marketing programme and dropping all product advertising in favour of 'umbrella' TV branding was much hyped at the time. It was probably the case that Heinz brought in direct marketing as an extra weapon in its armoury to match the growing power of the major retailers. Heinz had some experience of direct marketing from its US operation and a strong baby foods division that used direct marketing. A central plank of the initiative was Heinz *At Home* magazine, which was to be sent to customers responding to promotions: in-store campaigns, on-pack vouchers and so on. The aim was to gather customer data on an ongoing basis using the data gathered from vouchers redeemed in-store. This would help Heinz identify its most valuable customers, profile attractive prospects, target up-selling and cross-selling opportunities precisely, and improve loyalty to Heinz through the brand building values of *At Home* magazine.

Early results looked impressive. . .

Richards (1995) reported that of the 3.5 million households that were mailed the first magazine in September 1994:

- 68 per cent spontaneously recalled having received it;
- 40 per cent said they would keep it for future reference.

The number that actually took up the magazine's coupon offers or contacted its helpline was an impressive 1.5 million households. But did the activity actually result in increased sales? Heinz claims that in October 1994, a month after the first magazine went out, its soups' share increased 6.4 per cent on the month. Tomato ketchup was up 7.7 per cent and pasta meals rose by 4.9 per cent.

According to Booth (1998), by 1996 the agency had taken the scheme from a simple magazine to a highly targeted and segmented approach to customers. It whittled down the base to those customers who were genuinely responsive, and Heinz seemed happy with the return on investment the approach generated.

So why did Heinz withdraw the programme? *Campaign* offered its own analysis:

> You can see the point of a supermarket launching a magazine because it has so many products to talk to its customers about', an agency chief who has worked on Heinz business points out. 'But Heinz makes tinned foods. There's a limit to the amount of new information it can offer – and who is bloody interested anyway?

Some commentators felt that this was an example of the customer magazine being overused as a tool. However, as *Campaign* suggested, for the right advertiser with the right product, a customer magazine is a fantastic marketing tool. Some examples of successful magazines include the AA, British Airways' *High Life*, *Saab* magazine, and in-house magazines from Tesco and Sainsbury.

One possibility is that customers get too many and suffer from magazine overload. *Campaign* again:

> Broadly speaking, a middle-class family in the UK could find itself in receipt of titles for at least one car brand, a building society, a bank, Sky's listings magazine, a supermarket, a holiday company and so on. With that kind of volume it isn't long before receiving a customer magazine stops being a bonus and becomes a chore (or a bore).

Booth (1998) quotes another agency director: 'Putting a [postage] stamp on communications to sell a 30p can of beans does not make sense.' If one estimates the net margins on a Heinz product as about 3p per item, there is no doubt the economics of direct marketing need to be worked out carefully for FMCG. Adding to the difficulty would be the hard work that had to go into data gathering. Customer transactions could only be recorded by Heinz using redeemed vouchers. Ironically, the supermarkets probably knew more about Heinz customers than Heinz did.

Was the magazine good enough? Tylee (1998) was sceptical:

> If 'Beans on toast with a twist' and 'Have a pizza romance' (and let's shoot whoever came up with that pun) are the two best features they can come up with, then killing off the magazine was undoubtedly a humanitarian gesture.

Questions

1 Why did Heinz UK decide to pull out of its direct marketing approach?

2 What are the key features of FMCG markets that make it so difficult for database and direct marketing to thrive?

3 Produce a cost/benefit analysis for Heinz *At Home,* estimating the costs of the campaign from the material in the case study and the revenue benefits. Revenues were based on increased cross-selling of different goods. Assume typical margins were about 3–5p per product. Your calculation should also include revenues accrued from incremental loyalty gains: as a result of the programme, a certain percentage of customers chose Heinz rather than competitors.

4 Comment on the use of direct mail to promote fast-moving consumer goods. Outline the advantages and disadvantages versus its media competitors.

5 What do you think the major role of direct marketing is in FMCG markets?

References

Booth, E. (1998) 'Where next for FMCG loyalty?', *Marketing Direct,* July/August, p. 10.

Richards, A. (1995) 'Traditional twist to new campaign', *Marketing,* 29 June, p. 14.

Tylee, J. (1998) 'Heinz gets burnt in customer magazine market', *Campaign,* 5 June, p. 14.

Chapter 12

Acquisition media

Objectives

Once you have read this chapter you will:

- understand the main features of the various acquisition media
- understand their strengths and weaknesses

Introduction

This chapter concentrates on support media, or media often used for prospecting competitor customers or prospecting in new markets. We will look at press, magazines, inserts, door drops, radio and direct-response TV, as well as new or unusual media. Each of these will be assessed using the AIMRITE formula, covered earlier (Chapter 11).

The chapter ends with a look at how media should be put together over time to deliver a coherent message to customers.

12.1   National press

Direct-response press is space advertising in daily or Sunday papers and supplements, inviting a specific response.

The DMA definition of a direct-response press advert states that it must include 10 per cent of space being devoted to the response element. Hence, brand building adverts that merely contain a number or website are not counted as direct-response press. This has accounted for the declining figure attributed to direct-response press spend in recent years. However, there has to be serious doubt about the efficacy of such a definition – many press adverts may be direct response but will display Web addresses or phone numbers in relatively small fonts. The use of coupons is, not surprisingly, seriously declining. The '10 per cent of space' requirement accounts for the apparent decline in direct-response press between 1995 and 2005. The percentage of press adverts counted as direct response has declined from over 60 per cent to about 20 per cent.

Instead, perhaps it would be more sensible to consider what constitutes 'direct marketing' rather than what counts as a direct marketing advert. There are many definitions available, including:

- 'The techniques used to make a purchase from their home, office or other non-retail setting. These techniques include direct mail, catalogues and mail order, telemarketing and electronic retailing' (McDaniel *et al.*, 2013, p. 546).

- 'The planned recording, analysis and tracking of individual customers' responses and transactions for the purpose of developing and prolonging mutually profitable customer relationships' (The Institute of Direct Marketing, 2002, pp. 10.3–10.15).

- 'Direct connections with carefully targeted individual consumers to both obtain an immediate response and cultivate lasting customer relationships' (Kotler and Armstrong, 2012, p. 432).

These are perfectly serviceable definitions but (as is often the way with such things) they tend to be rather long winded and try to encompass everything in them. My preferred definition, the one I use is simply this:

Any marketing activity which solicits a direct response from the consumer or customer

At the time of writing there are more than 20 national daily and Sunday press titles in the UK and, according to BRAD, over 4,300 trade, technical and professional media that carry advertisements (BRAD, 2012). The national press can be very cost-effective for national advertisers. From a marketing point of view, the UK is exceptionally well served by national media, many European and Asian countries having a much more regional press.

Press advertising is extensively used by the big players in financial services, automobile, mail order and retail. The low 'cost per thousand' of national press makes it ideal for customer acquisition if the target audience is broadly defined. In addition, the broad scale nature of the press makes it ideal for 'double duty' brand building and response advertising.

Exhibit 12.1 Nerdy but nice – attracting application developers

Business press allows the advertiser to get straight to the point. In the case of an award winner from Lotus, intimacy was taken to new levels. The advert was written entirely in HTML code and was intended to raise awareness among application developers of a new aid, a constantly updated website (**www.lotus-dev.net**). Only the developers would get the point: if they typed the code into their Internet browser, a colour advert appeared describing **dev.net**. Clicking on the advert then took you straight into the website. Between May and August 1999, over 800 members enrolled.

Source: Based on DMA Case Study (1999), **www.dma.org.uk**.

12.1.1 Key AIMRITE qualities

Audience

If you are looking for high volumes of exposure then the national press could be your best choice. The *Sun* is bought by 3 million people and read by about 8 million. Your advertisement, therefore, could theoretically be seen by about 20 per cent of UK adults, with just one placement in one title.

> ### Exhibit 12.2 How newspapers are becoming multi-media platforms: Rebranding California State
>
> #### Objectives
>
> California Tourism wanted to encourage awareness of what the state has to offer, dispelling the view that all people visit for is the beaches and the sunshine.
>
> #### Solution
>
> *The Times*/*The Sunday Times*/Times Online developed 'Totally California' - a cross platform solution across in-paper and on-line to give readers the chance to learn all about the wider appeal of visiting California.
>
> Using themed advertorials and co-brands in paper, and an interactive map and timeline, readers had the chance to gain an insight into California, research areas of interest that they could visit, and view events that would be taking place during their stay.
>
> They were also given the chance to win one of four exclusive holidays tailor-made to suit each of the targeted audiences, from a skiing break to a tour of the wine country.
>
> #### Results
>
> The competition had 10,881 entries, and the Microsite achieved 102,417 page impressions with 58,008 unique users over three months.
>
> High recall levels across the campaign, 29 per cent recall having seen California co-brands, 32 per cent remembered California advertorials and 50 per cent found the advertorials interesting.
>
> After seeing the advertising, almost 1 in 3 were likely to consider California as a holiday destination and 23 per cent of a 45+ audience.
>
> *Source*: © News International Commercial, News Syndication, 2012.

Press is likely to be used in favour of other media in two situations. One is when the audience is quite broadly defined because it is not yet fully understood what type of people buy the product. For example, a new chain of hotels may enter an advert in the *Daily Mail* promoting weekend breaks. This is known as 'handraising', when the audience identifies itself from the mass. Once customers have been identified, a description is obtained by profiling – the weekend breakers here being perhaps 'older empty nesters from cities'.

Secondly, some product or service has a genuinely mass audience. Household items – kitchenware, for instance – may fit this category.

Impact

Compared with direct mail or the telephone, press adverts have low impact on the consumer, often being ignored altogether or glanced at, at best. As long as the advert is read by people who are in the market at that time, it does not matter that it is missed by the rest. However, most of us tend to read papers by scanning through to certain pages of editorial, often not looking at adverts at all. It is easy to see then why your message is more likely to be noticed in, say, direct mail than in the press.

The impact of the advert can be greatly enhanced by the medium surround – the editorial. A student bank account offer is more likely to be noticed opposite an article on 'What to do when entering university'.

The specific media brand also adds value to the advert. A full-page advert for a financial or business product placed in the *Financial Times* can convey a lot of credibility, just because of the medium.

However, the opposite is also true – the effectiveness for an advert for a bank, for example, could be killed stone dead if it is opposite an article decrying the size of bankers' bonuses, and there is seldom anything advertisers can do about such bad behaviour on the part of media owners.

Message

Press adverts consist of pictures and words presented within a fixed space. Colour can be used, particularly in supplements, but otherwise the creative constraints are substantial. Much less information can be communicated compared with inserts, door drops or direct mail, although press is still better than TV, radio or the telephone at imparting volumes of information.

Press is a public medium. This may help generate word of mouth, as you know that your friends have also had a chance to view the advert. Advertising in public confers some legitimacy on the advertiser: we associate press adverts with the company being at least pretty sizeable; also that, if it is willing to advertise in public, it is probably a legal operation.

Response

Websites are now the dominant response medium, rivalling the telephone. Coupons are becoming less frequently used.

Internal management

Press adverts can be created and space bought very quickly. If an opportunity is spotted, say to capitalise on an unexpected news event, then a press ad can be created and placed in the next day's edition of a national newspaper. A mortgage broker may want to get in quickly alongside an item on an interest rate drop. The press, therefore, has the potential to be one of the quickest of any media from brief to execution, perhaps just behind search marketing ad placements, e-mail or small website changes.

However, there are exceptions to this speed rule: special positions in newspapers, such as the back page of the tabloids (where there is usually only one advert, referred to as a 'back page solus spot') are generally booked up several months in advance. This is so popular because not only does its solitude make it stand out but, when held up (by train passengers, for instance), the advert is on show to the rest of the world (or carriage) to see.

Exhibit 12.3 Press variables to consider when testing

Size

A doubling in space size usually produces less than double the responses. Often direct marketers find the optimum size may be a quarter- or half-page advert.

Barker says that the relationship between an increase in the size of an advert and the response it pulls is approximately the square root of the increase in size (Barker, 2007, pp. 5.2–5.35). In other words, if you double the size of an advert you will gain approximately a 40 per cent increase in responses, not double the response, but the price will probably double.

Frequency

Responses drop off dramatically with repetition of the ad in the same press. Direct marketers could typically expect over 80 per cent of responses from the first two insertions, with rapidly diminishing returns thereafter. However, there is a case for running full-page ads with low frequency. Many direct marketers have found this is the best combination of the above two variables.

Although this will differ from product to product, company to company and industry to industry, personal experience suggests that adverts in a newspaper will generate the most responses the day after they appear, tailing off to virtually nothing within seven to ten days.

Colour

Colour will usually boost response, but will be slightly less cost-effective than black and white. However, colour works similarly to size, in that many direct marketers use colour but keep frequency low.

Barker suggests that the increase in response for a colour advert over a black and white equivalent is about 15 per cent (Barker, 2007, pp. 5.2–38). Companies test these variables to get their cost per response down, once the main media variable has been established.

Sun Alliance did just this with its new mortgage product launched in 1992. It used a series of colour adverts in quality and mid-market nationals targeting BC1s, and started its campaign in April. By the end of the summer it was using strip-shaped (like a ruler standing on end) ads only, but still using colour. The campaign generated 5,000 enquiries, well above target.

Sources: Halsey, B. (ed.) (1992) *The Practitioners' Guide to Direct Marketing*, Institute of Direct Marketing, Teddington, UK. Halsey, B. (ed) (2002) *The Interactive and Direct Marketing Guide*, Institute of Direct Marketing, Teddington, UK; (Barker, 2007).

Testing is more difficult to execute than it is with the private media: mail and telephone. Although the creative approach, the specific press title, offer and timing can all be tested, it is with rather less precision than direct mail or telephone. This is because the exact number and 'type' of audience exposed to each test cannot be completely controlled.

When testing, remember only to change and test one element at a time. If you change from black and white to colour and from half a page to a full page, how will you know which was responsible for the increase in responses you (hopefully!) enjoy?

The end result

It is very easy to just scan across an advert, recognise it as something that does not interest you at that time and not even register its presence. This explains why typical response rates for press adverts are very low in comparison to, say, direct mail, door drops or inserts. A press advert may only generate 0.01 to 0.05 per cent response to a typical advert. However, the media costs are low in terms of cost per thousand reached, often at well under £10 per thousand, and so the press is as competitive as the other media in terms of cost per response. The example calculation in the following box shows how to make quick calculations of cost per response.

Exhibit 12.4 Example calculation

A full-page advert in *The Sun* may cost £30,000. The circulation is 3 million.
Cost per *thousand reached* is then:

$$30,000/3,000 \ = \ £10 \text{ per thousand}$$

Let us say 0.03 per cent of the audience respond. What is the cost per response? First, calculate the number of responders:

No. of responders = 0.03 per cent of 3 million = 900 responders

As the advert cost £30,000, the cost per response is:

Cost per response = 30,000/900 = about £33 per response

The point is that, although responses are low, costs are also low when measured in cost per thousand reached. The cost per response is broadly comparable with other typical media performances.

The press, like the broadcast media discussed later, may have a 'dual objective' set for its use. As well as eliciting responses, the press can be used for general marketing goals of generating awareness or building brands. This can be dubbed the 'double duty effect'.

In summary, then, the national press is a valuable part of the direct marketer's media armoury. Returns are usually adequate, and the handraising abilities of press advertising make further definition of your target market possible. Occasionally, returns can be spectacular (see Exhibit 12.5 on the Labour Party).

Table 12.1 summarises the strengths and weaknesses of the national press.

Exhibit 12.5 Return on investment: the Labour Party

An old classic ad shows that if you can get the target audience, the medium and medium format, the offer and, crucially, the timing all just right, then press direct response can be spectacularly successful.

The UK's Labour Party bought 20cm by two-column slots on the *Guardian's* front page for the day after the announcement of the General Election call in 1992 by the Conservatives. The headline was 'Give £30 now for a Labour victory'.

The return on investment was an incredible 14:1 for this advert. **The Labour Party's most successful fundraising advertisement!**

12.2   Magazines

Magazines are used for acquisition via space advertising inviting a response.

It may be noted that, while magazine direct-response advertising has held fairly steady, so-called 'image and response' ads have grown while 'pure' direct-response ads (from, say, mail-order firms) have declined as a percentage of the whole.

Table 12.1 Strengths and weaknesses of the national press

Strengths	Weaknesses
Low cost per thousand	but low response
Fast production	but low creative options
Double duty effect (brand building and response)	but lack of secrecy

This is an interesting trend that is explained by three factors: first, the growth of direct marketing in sectors such as personal care and health; second, the movement within marketing communications towards 'brand response' marketing that mixes brand building with direct response; and, third, the increased use of the Internet as an advertising (and even a delivery) medium leading to a sea change in the way printed advertising works.

The increasing omnipresence of smartphones combined with the advent of QR (Quick Response) codes – also known as Snap Codes – in advertising has meant that printed adverts can be easily made into a digital-friendly environment, directing readers to a Web page for further details. This has the advantage of being quick, easy and not requiring a pen or any memory skills on the part of the reader. It also means that the response mechanism is available to the reader to follow up on in their own time, the advertiser has unlimited space and multi-media capabilities in giving further information and, let's face it, using the Internet to explore further information is a lot more enjoyable as an experience than ordering a brochure and waiting several days for it to arrive before you can flip through it.

Research by GfK MRI Starch Advertising research (cited by Kelly in Forbes) states that, between July and December 2010, 1.34 per cent of 61,000 adverts analysed contained a QR (Quick Response) code. In the following eight months, this had increased to 5 per cent of 72,000 adverts measured (Kelly, 2011). In terms of reader engagement, the study found that 5 per cent of readers of such adverts followed the QR code, though this was as high as 18 per cent in some cases of advertising for 'gadgets' and 'guy stuff'. This lag in the take up of the technology is only to be expected as readers travel along the learning curve to acceptance of the new technology as an everyday medium.

Magazine readership in the UK remains behind that of much of Europe but has grown a lot recently. Perhaps reflecting the fragmentation of society, the UK has become a nation of magazine readers to a much greater extent than ever before. There are now over 2,100 consumer titles and 4,300 trade and technical journals.

12.2.1 Key AIMRITE qualities

Audience

Whereas local press or door drops tend to target according to geography, magazines tend to separate consumers according to their 'interests'. If you need to segment your audience by lifestyle, therefore, magazines are a useful channel to consider.

What is more, we can seek out some pretty unusual audiences using magazines. Your local newsagent will have the standard women's magazines, *Woman's Own*, *Cosmopolitan* (although at least 25 per cent of *Cosmo's* readership are men!), and the men's section, for example *Computer Weekly*, which, according to popular myth, is read predominantly by anorak wearers; and then there are football and car magazines of all shapes and sizes. However, lest it be thought that we are all obsessed with relationships, fashion, sport, computers and cars, there are a host of incredibly varied titles lurking beyond these – everything from *Army Quarterly and Defence Journal* to *Audiophile with HiFi Answers,* and *Potholing Weekly* to *True Romances* are out there!

Impact

Magazines offer more impact on your audience than will newspapers. The saying 'the medium is the message' is perhaps more apt for magazines than for most media. There are a number of reasons for this. First, the magazine brand itself may be relevant to the product you are selling, and you may gain from association with the media brand values. Second, magazine production values are higher than those of newspapers, with higher quality paper and full colour, usually throughout; this helps to heighten the impact on the reader.

Third, people exhibit a different behaviour when reading magazines. They see a magazine as a pleasure, an indulgence, and will linger over the read in a way quite different from reading a daily paper. This, again, makes it more likely that adverts will be scanned.

Message

Have you ever picked up a motorbike magazine? If you are one of the majority who are not motorcycle riders, but have flicked through such a magazine, you might quickly be nonplussed by the language used within. What on earth is 'top end grunt'? Why are engines described as 'bomb proof'? (In case you are wondering, the former is engine power at high speeds, and the latter refers to reliability.)

The point is that magazine audiences are like 'clubs' in that they are talking to people with a shared interest. This shared interest leads to a sense of belonging to the group and, as a result, a sense of exclusivity is encountered by anyone not in 'the club'. In many instances, these products are the outward sign of 'membership' of the club. If Kawasaki were advertising its bikes in *Ride* magazine, it would use very different language (e.g. What torque does the bike have? How much brake horsepower?) to that used in an advert in the *Evening Standard*. As Dibb *et al.* put it, 'to communicate effectively, an advertiser must use words, symbols and illustrations that are meaningful, familiar and attractive to the people who constitute the advertising target: the target audience' (Dibb *et al.*, 2012).

Response

Because magazines are often kept by their readers, responses can come in months, and sometimes even years, after the advert was placed, often confusing the marketer who has moved on to another campaign!

This is especially the case with magazines that are not related to current affairs in any way, and which often get passed from one 'owner' to another. For instance, in some families the *Reader's Digest* finds itself a home as reading material in 'the smallest room in the house', and it is often borrowed by visitors to take home, where it resides in a similar place. From there it may be donated to the doctor's waiting room and/or the dentist, with other visits to homes between as people 'borrow' the highly portable magazine to finish reading the article they started in the waiting room. Several more laps may follow and, at any point, advertisers can gain infrequent but welcome responses.

Internal management

In common with the press, testing directly against a control is difficult, although this is partially overcome by A/B split run and cross-over testing, covered later (see Chapter 14).

One major disadvantage of magazines for direct response is the lead times typically required to place an advertisement. Three to four months is typical, and so significant forward planning is required and it largely makes the medium inappropriate for short-term tactical offers.

The end result

Cost per thousand is higher for magazines than for national newspapers, but the audience tends to be better defined, leading to higher response percentages and higher quality repeat purchasers. If you are after volume, then many titles can deliver large mass audiences too: women's magazines in particular having a readership of over 500,000 in many instances.

Table 12.2 **Strengths and weaknesses of magazines**

Strengths	Weaknesses
Segment audience by interest	but high cost per thousand
Medium's halo effect; colour adds to brand/message	but still has creative limitations of press
Superior targeting to newspapers	but longer lead times

Table 12.2 summarises the strengths and weaknesses of using magazines for direct response.

12.3 Direct response television

Direct response television (DRTV) is the use of commercials on local or national television to generate a direct response.

When we come to compare media, quite simply, TV is different. O'Guinn *et al.* say that television advertising is unique in that it gives the ability to send messages using both sound and vision, it has an almost 100 per cent household reach, and (although actual costs are high) it offers a low cost per contact because the audiences are so huge (O'Guinn *et al.*, 2009).

Consider how often you hear people say 'I saw a great press ad yesterday' or 'Have you seen this mailer? Look at that offer!' But we do talk about TV commercials. This word of mouth, this pizzazz, is a unique facet of TV adverts and, if it is important to the business problem you are considering, should be included in any decision about media.

In 1990, Drayton Bird recognised that DRTV worked better in the USA than in the UK because in America there was 24-hour television on a wide range of channels, whereas in Britain (at that time) there were four channels, two of which were commercial and none of which broadcast around the clock (Bird, 1990, p. 141). We have finally caught up with the States in this area, and DRTV is coming into its own here, too.

In an unscientific count of a selection of adverts broadcast on various UK digital channels in July 2012 (Whitten, 2012), it was noted that:

- 01 per cent only gave a phone number as a response method
- 40 per cent gave only a Web address for responders to contact
- 33 per cent gave at least two forms of contact method
- 26 per cent had no kind of response mechanism at all

Since 1990, in another sense, however, things have not happened as may have been predicted. 'Classic' DRTV advertising used a very particular style that was pioneered by book and record clubs, and mail-order firms. Long adverts concentrated on the call to action straightaway, with the telephone number to call permanently displayed, and detailed descriptions and demonstrations of the product. The chances are you will never have seen an ad like this but there are plenty of them about if you wish to look, on TV shopping channels. Go to, say, QVC channel and have a look. But in most mainstream TV adverts, direct response plays second place to brand-building content.

Nevertheless some trends run in favour of more direct response – even on mainstream channels. Factors compelling greater use of DRTV include the following:

- A survey carried out by Ofcom, the UK broadcast regulator, found that the Digital Switchover in the UK (where the analogue signal is being switched off) means that digital penetration had reached 97 per cent by December 2011. This is the highest in Europe and higher even than in the USA (87 per cent) (Garside, 2011).

- Freeview – the basic package in the UK after the Digital Switchover – means that households now have up to 50 channels (depending on signal area) as standard. In addition to the Freeview option, there are some 10.7 million subscribers to Sky's services in the UK (**www.cable.co.uk**, 2011) and 3.78 million Virgin Media cable subscribers (O'Reilly, 2011).

- These penetration levels have led to a fragmentation of television channels, meaning that direct marketers can more easily reach smaller, highly defined audiences.

- There has been a shift away from food or everyday purchase sectors towards an increase in advertising for high price items, such as cars or financial services, which traditionally use more direct-marketing techniques than low price ticket items.

- An increasing push to make image advertising more accountable. One way to achieve this is through the inclusion of a response element in the advert.

- There is now almost complete acceptance of website addresses and telephone numbers as channels for purchasing goods – more than 10 per cent of Britons had visited an auction site such as eBay by May 2012, compared to between 3.4 per cent and 6.7 per cent on the Continent (Garside, 2011).

12.3.1 Key AIMRITE qualities

Audience

One of the big attractions of TV for image advertisers has been the massive audience coverage that the medium offers. Although TV advertising is often expensive in terms of its production costs and prices for airtime, in terms of cost per thousand of audience reached it is very cheap. TV cost per thousand is typically £5–£12 per thousand, which compares very favourably with most other traditional media.

Although targeting is less well defined than for most other media, this is less of a problem than it used to be. If, say, you wanted to target 18- to 35-year-old 'AB' men who were interested in computers, you might have previously advertised in the breaks of a Formula One sports programme, but this audience would still have a lot of non-AB men who were not interested in computers. Now, there are specialist cable and satellite channels devoted to such target audiences, and even more speciality channels available on the Internet. It is also possible to advertise regionally or, in some cases, locally on certain TV channels now.

Even so, targeting on television can only be as good as the accuracy with which TV programme audiences are defined, and as viable as the number of people watching. Some of the smaller channels measure their audiences in the thousands, and that is at peak time. Rather like two overlapping circles, it is almost impossible to get a TV spot that exactly matches the intended audience requirements. It is this which led Lord Leverhulme, the founder of Unilever, to say, 'I know half of my advertising is wasted, but I don't know which half.' The cost per thousand of 'target' audience reached is, therefore, higher than the paid-for figure, which represents the cost per thousand of 'total' audience.

Exhibit 12.6 Moving DRTV forward – Cable & Wireless

Up against the might of BT, Cable & Wireless made a huge success of its move into DRTV for acquisition. Helped by a good offer of a 50p cap on weekend calls and free local calls, Cable spent less than £6 million in 1999 on the campaign, but achieved more than 600,000 responses. Response rates of 0.08 per cent were achieved, which for DRTV is considered excellent. Initially off-peak slots were used, which were further refined as the programme unfolded and analysis could be done on responders. Costs per response were reduced to about £5. This campaign proved to be one of the biggest acquisition campaigns in DRTV history, and has been an oft-quoted case study by those in the industry arguing for a shift in acquisition budgets towards more DRTV.

Source: Based on DMA case study (1999), **www.dma.org.uk**.

Exhibit 12.7 Using DRTV to increase sales – T-Mobile

Mobile is not a place for the shy and retiring and T-Mobile was setting some tough targets. The mobile giant had traditionally used other direct channels, such as inserts, national press and door drops to drive sales and market share in the contract market.

With targets heavily increasing, it was proposed that DRTV should be added, given its track record as an effective sales channel and also the mass-market profile of T-Mobile. After overcoming client concerns that the use of daytime TV would cheapen the brand, that the call centre might be overwhelmed and that the cost of TV meant it would not be cost-efficient, the first test was carried out.

The TV solution

T-Mobile's brand ad was edited to contain a more direct sales message. Key information to drive response (price, handset and offer) were overlaid on to existing creative, alongside a phone number and website address. Test activity was planned so that results could be captured via all channels. Initially multi-channel stations were selected based on their match with the existing T-Mobile customer base, using a range of times of the day (day-parts) and programme genres. This was then rolled out into regional terrestrial stations to increase volume.

Using different phone numbers for small groups of TV stations allowed the agency to analyse the most efficient day-parts and spots. The 30-second ad ran during the day to coincide with the call centre opening hours, with the bulk of the spots appearing on weekdays.

DRTV activity has gradually increased from an initial test of £50,000 per month through to the current £300,000 a month.

Results

Results measurement has shown DRTV to be a strong and efficient sales generation method for T-Mobile, pulling in customers via the phone numbers on the TV spots, retail, other phone numbers and also the T-Mobile website. Analysing all data, eliminating the impact of market conditions and the strength of the particular offer, shows DRTV to generate the highest number of responses (at the lowest cost per response) where it was part of an integrated campaign.

T-Mobile continues to invest in DRTV month after month, with more tests planned to find even cleverer ways of using the media in the future.

Source: Adapted from Thinkbox (2012).

Impact

Television is unique. It can arguably generate more impact than any other medium. If we consider the effect of popular campaigns such as Compare the Market's 'Compare the Meerkat' campaign or Cadbury's 'Gorilla' advert, what we have is adverts that permeate the public consciousness in a way that is unmatched by any other medium. There is also a sense, sometimes, that what is communicated on TV is somehow 'important' or 'true', a quality that media such as direct mail do not have. It also has both sound and vision, allowing it to make a more concerted effort on our senses. To summarise, the key impact values of TV are its 'ability to generate word of mouth, authority and credibility'.

In spite of these attributes, DRTV still has relatively low usage as a direct marketing medium. The reasons for this centre on the difficulties of generating action from customers. These difficulties are discussed in the Response section below.

Message

Television has powers of 'emotional persuasion' arguably unmatched by any other traditional medium. TV's ability to demonstrate USPs and to show the product in action make it a highly desirable medium to use for many products. On the negative side, however, it is impossible to leave any permanent reminder of how to respond.

DRTV comes in a number of formats. Commercials vary from pure direct sell (which was first used in the late 1940s in the USA with adverts that could be 30 minutes long, making them effectively the forerunners to today's specialist shopping channels on mainstream TV) through integrated brand and direct-response commercials, to primarily brand building commercials, with a website or, less often, a response number tagged on to the end.

Charities find that DRTV works better for those that have an emotional message to get across. Typically children's or international distress charities do very well.

Response

One reason that TV is not used more as a direct-response medium is because customers watch it in a passive state. TV is known as a 'lean back medium' whereas on-line media are 'lean forward'. 'Lean back' is that quality that one notices when entering a room full of TV watchers: everyone looks half asleep, staring without expression at the box in the corner. This relaxed state means we are not in the active mode necessary for making purchase decisions.

To maximise the chances of prodding us into action, a number of 'rules' have been identified as a result of extensive testing. The following sets of rules (Pearson, 2012) are from a paper by DRTV specialists The DRTV Centre, who are based in London. Many of them are similar to the recommendations made following tests carried out, particularly in the USA in the 1980s (Young, 1994), which suggests that, even though the technology and spread of channels may have changed, the overall approach is remaining constant.

General rules

- Be sure you are crystal clear about your objectives.
- Have a strong, clear, simple proposition.
- Consider using a specialist DRTV advertising agency.

- Feature an 0800 number, as memorable as you can buy.
- Say the phone number over and over in the commercial.
- Use titles to highlight your phone and text numbers and emphasise selling points.
- Test your commercial on low-cost small-audience channels.
- Consider using a call centre.
- 'Test, test, never rest'.

Scriptwriting

- The absolute top objective is to stimulate instant response.
- The proposition should be self-contained, clear and complete.
- Key selling messages must be reinforced with big, bold titles.
- Place strong emphasis on the words spoken in the soundtrack.
- Humour generally does not work.
- The phone number must be stressed and repeated.
- The more you tell the more you sell.

Booking TV Airtime for DRTV

- Big rating, peak time spots are normally to be avoided because they produce unmanageable numbers of phone calls.
- Double the number of small audience spots work better than half the number of large audience spots.
- Daytime spots are usually much more cost-effective than evening spots.
- Paradoxically, low interest programmes pull well.
- Small scale test markets can be reliable predictors of more expensive campaigns.
- Planning needs to take account of call centre capacity and working hours.

Call handling

- 50 per cent of the response to each individual TV spot will be received within 5 minutes.
- 80 per cent of the response will be received within 15 minutes.
- Between spots the phones will be just about dead, so it may be that call handling may be better managed by a specialist call centre.
- If all you need is to collect names and addresses an automated system may be sufficient.

Testing DRTV

- Try different lengths of commercial.
- Try different TV stations.
- Try different times of day.
- Try different days of the week.
- Try weekends instead of weekdays.
- Try different genres of programme.
- Try different creative approaches.

Exhibit 12.8 Home shopping channel

'Basically, in the DRTV world, we're appealing to a customer who is bored', said a commentator. 'DRTV exists in a space where people have downtime, and their brains are fried, and they're flipping channels looking for something to do.'

Imagine flicking through your TV channels one day and coming across one where a man and a woman are discussing the most intimate details of a new product – the Kitchen Wizard. Throughout the broadcast, the price and a telephone number for ordering are shown on the bottom of the screen. Twenty minutes later, the advert is still running, you are still captivated by the number of applications for the Kitchen Wizard, and wonder whether it would make a good present for your mum.

This is home shopping on the QVC (Quality, Value and Convenience) channel.

QVC, Inc., a wholly owned subsidiary of Liberty Media Corporation attributed to the Liberty Interactive Group (Nasdaq: LINTA), is one of the largest multimedia retailers in the world, with annual revenue of more than $7 billion. QVC provides its customers with thousands of the most innovative and contemporary beauty, fashion, jewellery and home products. Its programming is distributed to more than 166 million homes worldwide. The company's website, **QVC.com**, is ranked among the top general merchant Internet sites.

TV channel is interesting: home shopping is less like direct-response TV and more like an electronic catalogue; in other words, it is equivalent to mail order off the screen. There have been a number of spectacular failures of this technique in the USA and experience has suggested that to be successful, home shopping channels have to conform to quite specific rules.

QVC are also expert direct marketers, with a full transaction database, including channel preference data. Consumers tend to be aged 30–45, consist of slightly more females, and are skewed slightly downmarket. The product range is primarily jewellery, home products and collectibles.

Source: Quinton, B. (2006) 'As seen on the web', **www.directmag.com**.

Of course, there are always exceptions that prove the rule. One of the most spectacular successes in DRTV history was that of Tango, which ran adverts that had response numbers up for only three or four seconds. As part of a light-hearted campaign, consumers were invited to respond if they needed help in talking about their addiction to Apple Tango.

Internal management

Lead times are often long. One might expect at least 12 weeks from brief to execution, with production of the advert rather than media buying being the main time-consuming feature. Alternatively, using existing film and buying airtime at the last minute can cut down on both costs and time.

According to specialist DRTV agency, The DRTV Centre, 'low budget DRTV commercials can be made for less than £10,000; these would normally utilise animation, stills or library footage. Original DRTV filming costs from £15,000 dependent on the complexity of the DRTV script and the desired production values. More ambitious DRTV scripts may cost £30,000 or more' (The DRTV Centre, 2012a).

The other major headache is response management. Testing on a small scale should be done first to establish the likely scale of response. It is vital to get this right because the response can come in very quickly after the advert is screened. It is quite a sight to see an inbound centre, at first quiet, suddenly burst into frantic life seconds after an advert goes on air, with lights flashing showing the level of response, and people running around to cover any extra lines.

Responses must then be allocated to each station, region and individual spot in order to analyse return on investment. This can be achieved by either asking people where they saw the advert (the simple approach, prone to errors) or by having unique phone numbers on each channel or group of channels (the more complicated, expensive but foolproof approach).

The end result

DRTV is a major medium for us. The US experience has been replicated in Europe and now in Asia. There have been instances of great success in the UK with direct-response. Direct Line Insurance has built up a customer base of over 4 million UK customers who buy more than 5 million products each year. The little red phone attracts 97 per cent identification with Direct Line, and front of mind measures are now well ahead of rivals with spontaneous brand awareness at 70 per cent compared to 54 per cent for its nearest competitor. Mind you, this comes at a price. In the period 1990–2002, Direct Line spent £249 million on advertising – almost £21 million a year – and that is a lot in anyone's books!

TV is cheap in cost per thousand terms, but response rates are unlikely to match even the press, and typically could be about 0.01 per cent or less for a direct-sell campaign. However, this could still be profitable, depending on the gross margin of the good being sold and the lifetime value of the resulting customer.

One area of direct-sell DRTV that has seen significant growth is the use of DRTV by charities to raise funds. Charities find that DRTV works better for those campaigns that have an emotional message to get over. One such charity is the RSPCA (Royal Society for the Prevention of Cruelty to Animals) whose DRTV story is told in Exhibit 12.10.

'Double duty' direct response: building brands

Within DRTV, this is probably the biggest area of growth. Advertisers are increasingly looking to build brands as well as obtain responses. Here, the return on investment is in two parts: the direct revenues obtained from the immediate response, and the long-term revenues acquired from brand goodwill that the advert is helping to generate.

Exhibit 12.9 Example calculation for DRTV profitability

ITV's regions vary in size, but let us suppose we run a daytime commercial in the Central region, which comprises 7.3 million adults, selling a product with a gross margin (before marketing costs) of £100. The costs of advertising are £7,300.

Assume the daytime spot is watched by 4 per cent of adults.

Audience is then 4 per cent of 7.3 million = 292,000 viewers.

Assume an excellent response level of 0.05 per cent: $\dfrac{0.05}{100} \times 29,000 = 46.$

No. of responses is, therefore:

The cost per response is 7,300/146 = £50

Therefore, a final margin of 100 − 50 = £50 per sale, is made.

Exhibit 12.10 How the RSPCA used DRTV to boost donations during the recession

There is much comment in the media regarding a downturn in donations to charities. The Royal Society for the Prevention of Cruelty to Animals (RSPCA) found that by making a compelling case for public support this need not be so.

The RSPCA has been a stalwart user of television since 1997, using it as direct response television (DRTV) to recruit new donors and measure its effectiveness on a return on investment basis. Typically, DRTV is used to recruit regular donors who set up direct debits to give between £2 and £5 a month, and was performing well for the organisation until 2007. Response rates started to decline, dipping further as the credit crunch started to bite in 2008.

In summer 2008, Mike Colling & Company (MC&C), together with creative agency Whitewater, recommended a completely new approach.

Four key insights drove their thinking:

- Recognising that changes in legislation, together with the economic environment, allowed RSPCA to demonstrate an increased need for their services.
- Realising that asking for a single gift rather than a regular donation would be more appropriate for consumers in these straightened times.
- Testing the idea that encouraging donors to text rather than call or go on-line could dramatically increase response rates.
- Identifying that integrating the television activity with inserts, door drops, search, on-line display activity and a dedicated micro site would improve both volume of response and total campaign ROI. Crucially the message made more use of terrestrial TV and day parts outside the traditional DRTV schedule of Monday to Friday daytime TV.

Creative showed how the Animal Welfare Act enabled the RSPCA to take action earlier where animals were believed to be suffering. Images of animals being helped at RSPCA centres appeared over commentary revealing how the charity was now dealing with 15,000 more complaints each year. The charity dubbed the situation its 'biggest animal rescue'.

Results

A first test in September 2008 was an immediate and dramatic success. Response rates to the commercial nearly tripled compared with the previous campaign; response to integrated door drops and inserts rose by more than 25 per cent compared with control cells, and on-line response showed uplift of more than 75 per cent where integrated.

The total campaign return on investment rose by more than 40 per cent compared with the previous campaign.

The campaign rolled out in November 2008, and a special Christmas version was created starting on Boxing Day 2008.

Source: Adapted from a case study on **youtalkmarketing.com** (**youtalkmarketing.com**, 2009).

DRTV as support

Another role for DRTV is in its support of other media. Tests by a range of firms have shown that TV can significantly improve response. Weight Watchers supported its mailings to past members by TV, and these mailers in turn are co-ordinated with press advertising offering free membership to new members.

Table 12.3 **Strengths and weaknesses of direct-response TV**

Strengths	Weaknesses
Massive coverage at low cost per thousand	but low response rates
High powers of persuasion and credibility	but messages must be simple
Targeting improved with channel proliferation	but still dfficult to reach prime upmarket audiences cheaply
Unrivalled ability to build brands and obtain response simultaneously	

Table 12.3 summarises the strengths and weaknesses of direct-response television.

12.4 Interactive television

Launched in 1998 in the UK, interactive TV has arrived for the long term. Interactive TV is offered to consumers of digital TV services through satellite or cable. Viewers press a red button on their control for services that include direct shopping.

As mentioned earlier in this chapter, the digital switchover means that 97 per cent of households in the UK have access to digital television (and, therefore, some level of inter-activity) as of December 2011. In addition to the basic Freeview service, 14.5 million households – something just over half of the total – have services provided by Sky or Virgin Media.

Services such as voting for pop stars, or watching football matches using personally cho-sen camera angles, are now commonplace. Here, we are primarily interested in the poten-tial of these services for shopping. This may take place through direct advertising, where the viewer is taken through a series of steps that may lead to a product trial, or sale.

An Admap article in 2001 asked whether 'Direct marketing would knock the spots off TV advertising?' (Fox and Burrows, 2001). They proposed the possibility of a revolution that would change the whole face of DM communications (see Exhibit 12.11).

Exhibit 12.11 **How iTV could change direct marketing**

Traditional model	New model
TV ad awareness	iTV ad awareness
Direct mail pack – puts offer into the hands of the customer	iTV ad – delivers information to the customer
Call centre and website pick up those who you seek out and handle real-time interaction	iTV – website can handle real-time interaction

Source: (Fox and Burrows, 2001).

The theory was that we have a sea of eager consumers interacting with brands that take them through the initial advert via their remote to a new world of commerce. However, this has not really taken off. So far, every 'next big trigger' – such as penetration levels reaching large numbers, the convergence of computers and television and the conver-gence of telephones and television (and computers) – has failed to produce the increased surge in take up predicted. Maybe this is still an idea whose time is yet to come – only time will tell!

Figure 12.1 Mercedes-Benz encourages viewers to vote for the scenario they will see in the next ad break. This approach is seeking to tap into the growing phenomenon of 'second screening', whereby the majority of UK viewers now watch TV at the same time as looking at another device such as a smartphone. It is also hoped that this approach will increase Mercedes-Benz's appeal to younger audiences.

12.4.1 iTV in practice

One of the very interesting trends is the increasing link between predictive database marketing methods and iTV. Companies such as Mercedes are trialling self-selected adverts from a menu of options (see Figure 12.1).

Exhibit 12.12 How to avoid the big DRTV mistakes

According to Grossman (2006), 'Direct response TV advertising [means] marketers and advertisers are no longer being given carte blanche to create, on location, beautiful 30-second spots that are measured only by their ability to win awards in France'.

Procter & Gamble are advertising different products with the same TV spot, depending on a viewing database. Lifestyle data firms may be able to offer a kind of TV audience 'to order' to advertisers looking for a market definitely interested in, say, car insurance. Only those in the market would receive the ad.

Before we all get too carried away, it should be noted that early attempts to use iTV were fraught with problems. Woolworth's, a (now defunct) UK retailer, closed its t-commerce centre in 2002, announcing troubles with its payback on the project. Anecdotal reports from innovators at Procter & Gamble suggest that it is not easy to get success from iTV. That said, FMCG manufacturers such as Procter & Gamble are, it seems, having some success from their approaches to kids – games, puzzles and so on are enticing the children into participating. Products such as Fairy are experimenting with these approaches – it seems the mums are being educated by their young children into the interactive world of digital TV. It should also be noted that there are ethical issues here – as there always are in advertising to children. Ultimately legislation may be needed to catch up with these new possibilities, and the chance for exploitation of audiences.

Grossman (2006) has some advice. He says 'It is made to make the phones ring immediately. It should be modular, so that offers can be exchanged and the spot optimised based on response. It is not meant to subtly entertain and thus be memorable. There is nothing subtle about direct TV. It is made to drive behaviour, right there, at that very instant.'

He cites the use of Video on Demand (VOD), which 'allows marketers to "telescope" targeted advertising along with programming, custom-matched to the targets' consumer profiles and the downloaded content. The VOD spots can also be interactive, with opportunities to navigate from the advertisement to other branded content, creating a highly customised, interactive experience'.

Exhibit 12.13 Your 'home shopping' in 20 years' time: lean back or lean forward?

In many respects iTV is a direct competitor of Web based Internet marketing. The battle between TV and the personal computer to see which will be the dominant home media continues. Of course, this battle may become less coherent as time goes on and computers and TVs start to resemble one another more and more. Currently the Internet has unrivalled search capability; TV is the superior interface for entertainment. The idea of TV as a 'lean back' media and the net as a 'lean forward' media has merit. Perhaps they both have a place yet – but as part of the same machine? The technology will converge sooner rather than later.

(**www.itvt.com** is useful for more information on the future of iTV)

It must also be remembered that, while iTV is of interest to direct-response marketers, the case for such approaches in brand building terms is less clear. Brands are public things – shared ways in which we communicate to one another. Hence, the mass advertising model has worked well in creating a common language of brands. This is in danger, if advertising breaks up into micro-markets because of over precise targeting.

12.5 Inserts

Inserts are loose-leaf, bound-in or tipped-on (i.e. glued on to the page with a small dab of sticky) paper/card leaflets carried by many papers, supplements and magazines. These carry a coupon or telephone response number.

Inserts are those things that cascade out of your Sunday paper like autumn leaves when you shake it on arriving home from the newsagent. A frequent mistaken belief of newcomers to direct marketing is that inserts do not work because they just get thrown in the bin. However, the facts are somewhat different.

Inserts, along with perhaps door drops (unaddressed promotional material dropped through your letterbox) and 'take ones' (leaflets available in retailers), are one of those media that would scarcely get a mention from a general marketer, but which can form an important part of the direct marketer's armoury.

Inserts work because they draw attention to themselves before the reader has had a chance to be distracted by the editorial of the paper or magazine. At the very least, they will usually be glanced at before being discarded, which is more than often happens with press advertising. 'Bound-in' (to the spine of the publication) or 'tipped-on' (glued) inserts tend to have even more impact; standing out of the page with their physical presence, they are a natural draw to the curious eye.

Inserts cost about £50 per thousand, with about £25 per thousand due to the charges made by the carrying media, and another £25 per thousand attributed to cost of production. On-line printers, such as **www.vistaprint.co.uk**, are able to produce very small runs at a low total cost (though the price per item is higher due to lost economies of scale) such as 50-off 216 × 319mm flyers for £12.99, or 100-off either 139 × 107mm or 95 × 210mm flyers for just £16.24. For about double the price, you get around 1,500 items; good for even the smallest businesses to use as 'take-me' flyers and with invoices or quotes.

Spend on inserts has grown hugely over the last few years, with well over £1 billion spent in the UK in a typical year (DMA Census, 2005), making it the fourth largest medium in spend terms. This growth can be attributed in the UK market to the growth of appropriate carriers – weekend supplements, more magazine titles, growth in men's market, etc.

12.5.1 Key AIMRITE qualities

Audience

Most national dailies and Sunday newspapers will take inserts, most commonly in their magazine supplements. Most trade and technical journals will happily carry loose inserts. Most large magazine titles will also take inserts and, of course, the business press and magazines will too.

Audiences are, therefore, defined by readership of newspapers and magazines, discussed earlier in this chapter.

Impact

Inserts tend to have higher impact than press adverts, because of the way they attract attention to themselves. The downside is that many people are irritated by inserts, regarding them as 'junk'. Any research findings that proclaim unfavourable attitudes to inserts do need to be treated with care, however. There is almost universal claimed dislike of direct mail in the UK by the public, and yet their behaviour is different: people respond, and in sufficient numbers to make mail a successful medium. The same is true of inserts.

Exhibit 12.14 A direct marketing junkie in denial?

When I met my then new partner's mother for the first time, she asked what I did for a living. I told her I was the direct marketing manager for a well known company and, when she asked what that meant, I explained that it involved advertising on TV, radio, in magazines, newspapers. . . as well as sending out direct mailshots and using door drops. She stood there with a fixed grin on her face. 'I hate junk mail', she said. 'Nothing but clutter and rubbish; why on earth do companies send it?' I bided my time.

Over the course of the afternoon, she proudly showed us her garden. 'I got some great seeds through the door the other day. I planted them over there and then bought some more for that corner next time I was in the garden centre'. That's one, I thought.

Come the evening, she demonstrated the new cable TV system she had had installed to beat the cessation of the analogue signal in 2012: 'They're giving me the first six months at half price. It was on one of those awful flyers that fall out of magazines'. Two.

In the next three hours, she also showed us the new saucepans she had bought from a catalogue, as well as some slippers from another. Three and four.

> Given that response rates to such media vary but are rarely above 2 per cent, the fact that my partner's mother had responded to four items in a week meant that, if she totally ignored the next 196 items through her door, she is an average responder. Having demonstrated such a responsive attitude, the chances are that she won't ignore that many, or anything like it. When I pointed out that she is actually a direct marketer's dream, I was greeted with the fixed grin and the restated reassurance that she hates junk mail.
>
> We all do, but if it's sent to someone who is interested in the product offered at a time when they have the money and inclination to buy, it's not junk, it's well targeted marketing.

Message

The insert has much of the flexibility of direct mail and door drops, in that different colours, shapes and sizes can be used, and there is room for a lot of information to be included. Response devices and even envelopes are often included as items within the standard insert format. These advantages give the insert superiority over the press advert or broadcast medium in terms of the volume of information that can be carried.

One variation of inserts is the use of product samples, with offers attached requiring a response. Packaged goods companies make use of this facility.

Response

Responding to inserts is relatively easy. As a consumer, you are probably in the house when you read the insert, giving you a chance to respond. You can save the insert until you want to get around to responding; whereas a radio ad cannot be saved, though with Digital Radio (also known as DAB) the programme/adverts can be rewound if required. The only easier to respond media are the telephone (instant and verbal), websites and e-mail.

One feature of inserts is that they are sometimes kept by consumers for reference and can still pull responses months later.

Internal management

Inserts are quite good for testing. Happily, a printer can cope with as many inserts as you wish to use. An unlimited number of formats can be tested for a title, although Goodwin (1992) recommended testing only up to a maximum of six at a time, in order to control events. Some advice never goes out of date.

One reason inserts are popular with direct marketers is their physical flexibility for use in different settings. As long ago as 1990, inserts were described as 'the chameleon of the business, because they can be used in so many ways and can appear in so many guises' (Bird, 1990). This is still the case, as inserts often double up as brochures within mailers and are also used as take ones or door drops. Needless to say, this saves on costs of creation and production, and avoids wastage.

The end result

Inserts nearly always attract more response than press advertising, although this is counterbalanced by their higher cost per thousand. Insert costs are usually four to five times those of press ads (£50–£60 per thousand against £10 per thousand for off-the-page national press), but inserts are often more than five times more responsive (typically 0.1–0.5 per cent against 0.02–0.1 per cent for press). Stone (1996) reported that a printed ad with a bind-in card will outperform the same ad without a bind-in insert by up to 600 per cent.

Many organisations base their entire acquisition media strategy around inserts. The Institute of Direct Marketing, which ought to know, uses inserts as its major medium when recruiting new students for its diploma programme, and claims responses of over 1 per cent in relevant business media.

Exhibit 12.15 Trident (Metropolitan Police) – making a small budget go a long way

Creativity was right at the heart of this story of how the Met Police in London used a small budget to make a big impact in reducing gun crime.

In 1998, the Metropolitan Police set up a special initiative called 'Trident', to tackle gun crime in London's black community. There were a number of challenges, not the least of which was that the issues were not being debated, people were, not surprisingly, afraid to come forward, and that London's black community distrusted the police.

The use of inserts exhibited a brilliant piece of creativity to help raise the issues. Thousands of music magazines were left in black barbershops. Each magazine had been pierced by a hole, running right through the publication. On the final page, an insert explained to the bemused reader that gun crime tore through whole communities and encouraged witnesses to come forward.

These inserts were combined with posters, microsites, ambient media and cinema to encourage calls to 'Crimestoppers' and raise a debate within the audience.

The team also commissioned an anti-gun music track ('Badman'), from a top 'Grime' act, Roll Deep. To begin with, this was distributed without any Trident branding, to a select group of club DJs, music shops, TV and radio stations. It was also e-mailed to Roll Deep's 30,000 MySpace friends and made available as a download on Roll Deep's MySpace page and website. It was not until six weeks later that the team revealed Trident's involvement, via a four minute branded video released on their **www.stoptheguns.org** microsite

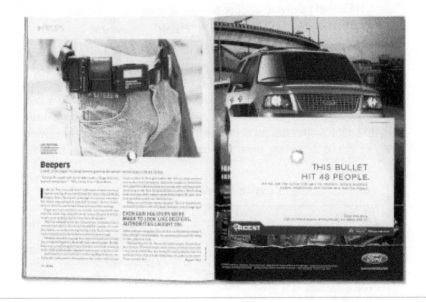

(including PSP and iPod formats), YouTube and **RWD.com**. After years of increases, gun crime in London fell significantly, to its lowest level since 2001 (see Figure 12.2).

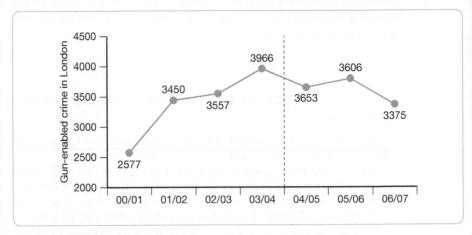

Figure 12.2 Falling gun crime
Source: Metropolitan Police Service. *Note:* all FY data runs April–March.

Source: Andy Nairn and Matt Buttrick (2007) 'Trident (Metropolitan Police) – making a small budget go a long way', Institute of Practitioners in Advertising, *Grand Prix& Gold, IPA Effectiveness Awards* (2007), pub. WARC Ltd.

Table 12.4 summarises the strengths and weaknesses of using inserts for direct response.

12.6   Household delivery/door-to-door distribution

Household delivery or door-to-door distribution is the targeted distribution of unaddressed leaflets or packages through the letterbox.

Door drops are 'unaddressed' leaflets or packages delivered through the letterbox. Like all direct mail, door drops are stealth marketing at its best. Not only do they offer a cost effective method of getting the printed creative you want to use (with no space restrictions) to the prospect, but it is also the case that your competitors will not know what areas you have targeted, why you have targeted them or how many door drops you have done. It is sometimes claimed that door drops offer most of direct mail's advantages but at a lower cost. With no postage to pay and no list to buy, the distribution cost can be as low as one-tenth that of mailers.

Table 12.4 **Strengths and weaknesses of inserts**

Strengths	Weaknesses
More impact than press	but often seen as 'junk'
More creative freedom than press	but production requirement means longer lead times than press
Overall: medium responsiveness at medium cost per thousand	

Nevertheless, door drops do have notable disadvantages compared with direct mail. Targeting door drops is clearly less accurate than for direct mail, being based on geodemographic (and/or lifestyle) profiles rather than individual addresses. It is this broader targeting that usually leads to lower responses than with mail. As a result, Bird (1989) recommended that only those companies that have products of fairly universal appeal should use door drops.

Door drops are distributed in the UK by specialist distribution companies such as NLM (National Letterbox Marketing), DBS Marketing and the Royal Mail's Household Delivery Service, as well as a host of other local and regional players.

Exhibit 12.16 How to target prospects with the best potential when you do not know their names

TNT Post is the UK's second largest postal delivery service, behind only the Royal Mail. They sort and transport business mail and packages to 26 million households, processing more than 22 per cent of all the mail that comes through the letterbox. One of their key services is that of door drops, delivering some 2.2 billion unaddressed items per year.

TNT uses Mosaic to work with their customers and improve targeting of door drop messages at a low cost. Says Mark Davis, Managing Director of TNT Post: 'In the current climate where marketing budgets are constrained clients need us to demonstrate a real return on investment. Mosaic has answered these needs and underpins the targeting innovations we have brought to market to answer our clients' requirements. Our clients have reported a 30 per cent improvement in response rates using Mosaic, helping to show how door dropping is still a highly effective distribution channel. Mosaic UK classification demonstrates true innovation.'

Source: Based on an Experian press release (Experian PLC, 2009) and TNT Post's website (TNT Post, 2012).

12.6.1 Key AIMRITE qualities

Audience

If your desired target audience can be accurately described geographically, then door drops may well be your best medium. You can also target on postcode sectors that average 3,000 households. However, you can also be more lateral in your approach: if you know your customers buy brand x, you can find more people like them using more sophisticated tools like the Target Group Index (TGI), which holds profiles of people who buy major brands (Royal Mail, 2012). Picking discrete addresses for the drop is not cost-effective and is, therefore, not offered as a service.

Door drops are used by firms for which locality is important: the local branches of services such as grocers, pizza delivery or local hairdressers spring to mind. However, big players also use door drops in certain circumstances, for example if distributing a sample of a fairly universal product. TalkTalk Telecom Group plc, one of the UK's largest broadband and voice customer providers, delivers some six million door drops every month (The Direct Marketing Association, 2011).

Cable TV and telephone companies used door drops extensively as a part of their marketing effort to sign up customers once a street had cable installed. The initial targeting for cable companies was based on profiling their existing customers according to geodemographic characteristics, and then using companies such as Experian to help them find similar streets.

If your audience is described best in purely lifestyle terms, for example 'young women who enjoy outdoor pursuits', then door-to-door targeting is likely to be less effective. You may be better off choosing magazines, or using direct mail on rented external lists from lifestyle database companies.

Impact

Again we have a medium that would get 'a panning' in research. One can almost hear indignant citizens recounting horror stories of ever increasing 'junk' coming though their doors morning, noon and night. Naturally, they will vehemently deny ever having responded or made any use whatsoever of such material. Yet the fact remains that, on average, far more people respond to door-to-door leaflets than will act on a TV commercial!

People tend to notice door drops, pick them up and look at them. The 'impact' value of a door drop is, therefore, high.

Exhibit 12.17 Knock and drop

This phrase refers to the practice of fieldworkers knocking on doors, asking a qualifying question about brand usage and dropping a product sample or coupon accordingly. Sometimes questionnaires are completed on product and brand usage for subsequent analysis.

These practices greatly decrease the wastage of door-drop targeting through broad geodemographic categories, but at a cost. The payoff may be worthwhile if the objective is to build a database, or if the product sample or coupon is of high value.

Message

Once again, the big advantage of this medium compared with general advertising media is its ability to carry large amounts of information. Although a lot of door drops are of standard C5 brochure style, practically anything goes, provided it can be posted through a letterbox. Door drops can even be used to deliver multi-media communications, such as CDs or DVDs, thus taking the medium into the digital age. Alternatively, flyers can incorporate QR codes or website addresses to achieve the same more cheaply.

Compared with TV, magazines or even direct mail, door drops do not imbue much natural authority. People do not say 'Well, that door drop I received today said so, so it must be true'. This may be one reason why traditional brand advertisers are often reluctant to use it as a technique.

However, door drop messages can be personal, even intimate. 'Singles clubs' tend to use door drops to recruit new members. Cards are dropped that ask people to fill in half a dozen simple questions such as 'Do you have lots of friends but no one very special?'. On returning the card, these people are then targeted directly using mail.

Door-to-door is an important medium for distributing free samples. FMCG sectors in particular make extensive use of door drop sampling. When Gillette was looking to increase market share of the disposable razors with the launch of a razor system, they devised a unique and innovative sampling technique. On Day One they door dropped a bag that encouraged disposable razor users to identify themselves and place the bag outside their door. On Day Two Gillette left a razor sample in the bag and posted it back through the door.

It was the most successful promotion in Gillette's history, with an incredible 40 per cent opt-in rate, incremental sales of £30 million over 3 years and a 23 per cent conversion rate (TNT Post, 2012).

Response

Response devices are typically integral to the door drop, and the issues match those recorded earlier for inserts.

Internal management

One of the criticisms of door-to-door distribution is its reputation for variable quality control. The industry does suffer from tales of skips being found with thousands of leaflets fluttering within instead of sitting on customers' coffee tables.

Exhibit 12.18 Environmentally friendly door drop is no longer a contradiction of terms

Based in the village of Ockley, at the edge of the Surrey Hills, farm shop 'Village Greens' is making a big contribution to the local environment. Everything they sell – from chicken and chocolate to ice-cream and cheese – is either grown on owners James and Catherine Dampier's own farm or sourced locally. 'Most of our range has been grown or reared within 30 miles of the shop, with 18 suppliers based within 10 miles,' says James.

Every year, Village Greens mounts a 20,000 volume door drop campaign to sustain interest and widen their customer base. The door drop is scheduled for May, June or July, the so-called 'golden months' when the farm crops come into season. 'We specifically want to let people know what's becoming available,' says James. But with such an obvious commitment to the environment, the Dampiers were faced with something of a dilemma: how to mount a door drop campaign without compromising their green principles. Enter Royal Mail's Sustainable® door-to-door service

The Sustainable Mail® service is aligned to PAS2020 environmental standard for direct marketers and provides guidance as to how to minimise the environmental impact of any campaign. The service employs effective targeting and data management to ensure the items are sent only to target audiences. Additionally, all paper and materials used will be recyclable and the mailing will carry a 'Recycle Now' logo and/or statement to encourage customers to recycle. The service can also prove cost effective thanks to, for example, the more efficient use of inks and paper.

'We're great fans of the scheme,' says James, whose principles of 'local, natural and ethical' are reflected by the Royal Mail Sustainable® door-to-door service. 'It really fits in with the ethos of the business . . . we wanted whatever form of advertising we employed to have minimal impact on the environment – not just because that's what we believe in, but also because that's what our customers expect. Any concerns that a mass leaflet distribution might sit a bit uneasily with our ethos have been dealt with by Sustainable® door to door.'

Source: Adapted by the author form a Royal Mail case study (Royal Mail, 2008).

Quality control, then, needs to be stringent, and industry suppliers will routinely use the practice of back checking to maintain quality standards. This is where a manager will follow on behind a door drop and check with a sample of each street that they actually received the drop. The manager will obtain signatures from the sample to that effect.

Apart from quality control, we need to consider testing. In fact, testing of door drops is quite easy. The target area can be split into geodemographically similar regions, and

Table 12.5 Strengths and weaknesses of door-to-door distribution

Strengths	Weaknesses
Lower cost per thousand than direct mail	but lower responses
Same creative versatility as direct mail	but not personalised
High impact compared with broadscale media	but lumped with 'junk mail'
Better targeting than inserts	but lacks double duty brand building

different executions of the drop tested. Alternatively, the same households can be tested at different times, allowing a suitable period to elapse between drops.

The end result

As a rule of thumb, door drops will cost from £40 to £250 per thousand, and may typically give about 0.1–1 per cent response, depending on product category, offer and so on, provided the campaign is well thought out.

12.7 Direct response radio

Direct response radio comprises adverts placed on commercial radio stations that invite a direct response.

Much as everything else nowadays, radio is going digital. After a shaky start, penetration of DAB radio has increased massively in the last eight years, from just 3.9 per cent in Quarter 1 of 2004 to the point where 42.6 per cent of UK adults (aged 15+) claimed to own a DAB set at home during the first half of 2012 (RAJAR, 2012).

Other than the switch to the digital platform, radio shares a few of TV's broadcast attributes. It can generate word-of-mouth debate, and pizzazz, although not often to the degree that TV is able to. Nevertheless, this should not be underestimated: radio commercials can offer publicity and credibility, and these need to be considered as part of the medium's set of attributes for direct-response work.

Radio is always likely to be a support medium rather than lead medium for any DR campaign, given the difficulty of retaining the details of response numbers.

In general, there is an upward trend in the use of radio by advertisers, because:

- It is cheap! You can reach a radio audience for about £2 per thousand, making it the cheapest of all the major traditional media.
- It has a higher ABC1 catchment than is typically thought. A lot of upmarket individuals listen to commercial radio on their way to and from work.
- Radio has been found to work very well with other media, increasing the response to media such as direct mail. The Radio Advertiser's Bureau (RAB) calls this the 'multiplier effect' (RAB, 2012a).
- The volume of commercial radio stations available has grown tremendously. At the time of writing, there are 326 UK stations (RAB, 2012b), including national coverage from Virgin, Classic FM, Talk Radio and Kiss FM. Regional stations, such as Capital in London and BRMB in Birmingham, have large audiences in their own right.

However, it is likely that there will always be a limited growth in direct response radio, because of the difficulties in responding, which are discussed in the Response section below.

Exhibit 12.19 Using SMS text messaging to make immediate short-term offers

The Hilton Hotel group has successfully used SMS messaging to increase guest numbers to its hotels and build customer loyalty.

The hotel sent out important marketing messages, such as on-site specials and promotions, directly to its members' mobile handsets. SMS allowed the hotel to get the messages out instantly and at the most appropriate time of day.

The use of SMS as a direct marketing tool resulted in a 10–25 per cent increase in offer redemptions sent out by the hotel and proved to be an integral part of its direct marketing and loyalty strategy.

Source: **www.EmailMobileMarketing.com** cited on **www.textsmsmarketing.com**, textsmsmarketing.com (2012).

12.7.1 Key AIMRITE qualities

Audience

A major characteristic of commercial radio audiences is that they are often young. Young people are typically notoriously difficult to reach through media: they are not on external lists, they do not read newspapers, they do not watch much TV. They do, however, listen to music channels on the radio, and are sympathetic to appropriately creative adverts aimed at them. Car manufacturers, financial services, charities and retail are all big users of direct-response radio, in order to attract the youthful audience.

Advertising in off-peak times has been recommended, on the grounds that anyone listening to radio at 2 a.m. has nothing else to do except reply to your offer! (Bird, 1990).

Local commercial radio has an audience defined primarily by geography. It, therefore, appeals, not surprisingly, to local businesses.

Impact

Generally, the impact of one radio advert is quite low, and is only made up for by repetition. Radio is often a background medium: one that people listen to while doing something else.

Message

Taking in information purely aurally is harder than taking it in visually, especially if we are doing something else, like driving, at the same time. Radio adverts should, therefore, be stimulating, to get our attention, and contain a simple, 'short' message that is easy to internalise.

Repeating adverts is universal in radio, the opposite of direct-response press or TV. Repetition is cheap, and it is essential in order to get the advert noticed. The best users of the medium will, however, vary their creative to give a number of different adverts. Using the same old advert in every slot, or for weeks/months at a time, turns it into wallpaper (at best), where people do not even notice it any more or it will very likely become irritating to listeners. Most stations will not let you buy spots in more than two consecutive slots to minimise irritation from repetition.

Response

If someone tells you a phone number, the chances are you will have difficulty remembering it an hour later. Radio is perishable. It cannot be torn out or read carefully at a more convenient time.

One tactic that works well with this medium is to use it as 'support' for other media, in particular websites. Raising awareness of an offer using radio, then ending with 'Look out for more details on the website' (using a very simple and easy to recall URL), makes the most of radio's strengths – the publicity factor of broadcast – and minimises its main weakness: response.

If you do need to go for direct sell, then freephone numbers that are easy to remember are a great asset. An excellent example was the ingenious Guardian Direct telephone number, based on its logo, an owl. The number is 0800 28 28 20, with an owl hooting 'too-whit too-whit too-woo' in tandem with the number! Such numbers are becoming increasingly hard to find.

Internal management

Lead times are very short with radio – a major advantage if you are in a hurry. An ad can be created, recorded and out on air within days if necessary, although wise counsel may prevail and more time be spent, in particular to get the creative right.

Buying radio ad time is time consuming. The 326 stations in the UK are owned by 30 different groups, and each will have different prices. It is best to use specialist buyers.

Testing is difficult (except for tests of different areas of the country, which are easy), as most commercial radio stations are geographically based and discrete from one another. Each station, therefore, attracts a unique audience, not matchable with other audiences in an accurate way. Time of day and day of the week are also worth testing. Peak radio listening is in the mornings, with troughs in the evenings. Weekends often attract higher percentage responses than weekdays, but from lower audiences.

The end result

Radio is excellent at getting large coverage for a business' message cheaply, and in a way that can generate word of mouth. Response rates using radio are very low compared with other media, but cost per response can be competitive. If you pay £2 per thousand of audience reach, a response of 0.001 per cent will mean you have obtained one response for £50, which is roughly on a par with typical performances of other media.

Table 12.6 summarises the strengths and weaknesses of direct-response radio.

Exhibit 12.20 Using radio to get inside the world of teenagers

The aim of the 'Frank Brain Crashers' campaign was to communicate the risks associated with cannabis use and bolster the resistance skills of the core 11–18 year old target audience. It augments the highly successful work achieved by a previous 'Frank' cannabis campaign and establishes that the risks of using cannabis are significant, alarming and potentially damaging to both your health and social status.

Radio stations are often felt to be part of people's peer group, and for these teenagers it was stations like Galaxy and Xfm, which have a youth orientated and somewhat subversive character. Messages on these stations tend to be seen as credible in both senses: believable and worthy of respect.

Table 12.6 Strengths and weaknesses of direct-response radio

Strengths	Weaknesses
Wide coverage cheaply obtained	but low response
Good public medium	but simple messages only
Good support medium	but needs creative to vary or risk annoyance

The campaign was a development of the core creative idea, which is that side-effects of drugs are like uninvited guests at a party. When people smoke cannabis, 'Giggles' come along but so do 'Panic Attacks', 'Paranoia' and the rest. Radio highlighted for discussion specific areas of risk, and the airtime was scheduled for moments when the target group would be most likely to be close to risky behaviour – not only evenings before they went out, but also very late night, early morning and 'chill-out' times at weekends. The Frank website and text number was signposted in the ads, so listeners knew where they could go to find out more or ask questions.

The radio ads were well integrated with the rest of the campaign, helping to achieve 81 per cent campaign recognition. Radio was particularly successful at driving word of mouth: 29 per cent of those who heard the radio campaign went on to discuss it with friends. The radio campaign was also effective at driving response. In periods where the radio ads ran, texts to FRANK increased by as much as 100 per cent. The campaign successfully communicated the risks of cannabis use, such that 75 per cent of respondents agreed that the advertising made them realise that cannabis is more risky than previously thought.

Source: (RAB, 2010).

12.8 New or unusual media

A number of other media are in use for direct-response marketing. These include some strange alternatives, such as underground tickets, Automatic Teller Machines (ATMs), the sides of cows in fields near motorways, the back of beer mats, balloons and so on. Just a few of the media are now discussed.

12.8.1 Electronic kiosks

Now becoming more common in the USA than in Europe, electronic kiosks were originally brought to prominence by Don Peppers as a fast way of delivering a one-to-one mass customisation strategy (Peppers and Rogers, 1993). Kiosks bring together the convenience of the Internet with the convenience of instant collection. Shoppers can use a kiosk in a large department store quickly and conveniently to purchase items without the bother of physically looking for them in the store.

The retailer can more closely control their inventory, while the consumer has the chance to browse through the entire product line whether or not the store carries the product. Some customers prefer to search electronically then buy face-to-face: in this sense kiosks are a mixture of 'bricks and clicks'.

Across the USA, kiosks can be found in local gyms, where members can order vitamins, nutritional supplements and other fitness related products, and at cinemas. In the UK, hotel chains such as Premier Inn use kiosks to speed up the process of checking in and out.

12.8.2 Using new on-line media for acquisition

A survey in *B-to-B Magazine* found that, when it comes to business-to-business marketing, blogs are considered the most effective social network for B2B prospecting, followed by LinkedIn, Facebook, Twitter and YouTube (Gillin & Schwartzman, 2011). Let us look at each of these media, briefly, in (almost!) that order.

Blogs

A blog (the word is a contraction of Web log) is simply a space in which the author can publish his/her views and opinions on a certain matter. In commercial terms a blog gives an organisation a presence on-line more quickly and cheaply than they could probably otherwise manage (it's possible to set up a blog in minutes at **blogger.com** or any of the other blog sites), which in turn gives a chance to connect with a wider audience than would otherwise be possible.

Blogs are a good way to hook new customers who have an interest in your company or the product/service you offer. As ever, it's a case of 'acquire with offer, retain with service', so use your blog to make appropriate and attractive offers to your prospects.

In a survey from Internet marketing firm Hubspot (**marketingvox.com**, 2010) 46 per cent of companies claim to have acquired new customers via a blog. This rises to 51 per cent when looking at business-to-customer (B2C) organisations. The same report says that 100 per cent of companies who post multiple times a day have gained customers, declining to just 13 per cent for companies who post less than monthly. Business blogs are most successful at customer acquisition when they have more than 24 articles posted (*ibid*) possibly because this critical mass is required for search engines to find the blogs in the first place.

The lesson here is that frequency pays!

Facebook

Facebook needs no introduction. With predictions of a billion users by August 2012 (Wasserman, 2012), it is the most popular social site on the planet at the time of writing.

There is a wealth of information on how to advertise on Facebook available on the site itself. Click on 'advertising' on your Facebook homepage to see it.

Creating an advert on Facebook is simply a matter of filling in forms, uploading links, photographs and so on, then clicking buttons when prompted. What makes it such a powerful prospecting tool is the ability to define the target audience you want to see your advert accurately. You can select by location, gender, age, education status, defined keywords, political views and many other discriminators. As you make your selections, Facebook very helpfully tells you how many people you will reach in this way (Holden, 2008). Your advertisement is then delivered to the sidebar of the Facebook pages of people whose profiles match that you selected.

Facebook lets you set a budget that will allow you effectively to reach your target audience, and checks your campaign performance often. Several options are available (Facebook, 2012):

- **CPC vs CPM:** Determine if you want to pay on a cost-per-click (CPC) or cost-per-impression (CPM) basis.
- **Daily Budget:** Set the maximum amount you want to pay each day. Once you hit your daily budget your ad will no longer show.
- **Bid Price:** Bid prices fluctuate often. Set a bid within or above the suggested range, and check your Ads Manager often to update it when the suggested range changes.

LinkedIn

LinkedIn could be described as Facebook for business professionals. With 161 million members (almost 10 million in the UK, 40 million in Europe), it lets users create a page about themselves and their professional background/career, and link to other people they know, taking professional networking into the digital age.

You can target your adverts by skill sets, geographic location, company or school name, age, gender and other differentiators. The site will automatically generate statistical analysis for you of who has clicked on your advert, and you can limit your financial commitment to predefined amounts starting at just US$10 per day (**www.linkedIn.com**, 2012).

Twitter

Twitter allows messages of up to 140 characters to be sent to anyone who chooses to receive them – known as 'following' a person or organisation. You can have 'Tweets' sent to your blog or Facebook account, and you can do this from a mobile phone so you do not even have to be sitting at your computer (Holden, 2008). The Tweets can also contain links to Web pages.

This makes Twitter ideal for attracting new customers, if you can give them a reason to follow you. Dell recorded $3 million in sales from Twitter, and California Tortilla, a chain of 39 casual Mexican restaurants in Rockville, Maryland, sends coupon passwords through Twitter, which customers must say at the checkout to redeem the offer (Solis, 2011, p. 53).

YouTube

YouTube is a website that allows users to post their own video (or, less commonly, audio) files and share them with the world, or only people to whom you give the URL pointing at your uploads. In effect, it is a TV channel for the masses.

Users can 'tag' descriptors of their videos to allow the site's search to find them. There is a tool that lets you see what search terms are popular at that particular time, which may be of help when deciding how to tag your upload.

In acquisition terms, simply think television without the big budget or delays! However, you do need to remember that a brand (or product, service, company, etc.) will be enhanced or tarnished by the quality of the promotions it uses and, if the files you upload are of poor quality, this will rub off on your overall image.

12.8.3 QR Codes – conveniently attracting customers to you

A QR (Quick Response) code, also known as a snap code, is a square barcode that can be read by smartphones equipped with the correct software and used to take the smart phone directly to a Web page or location. As such, they are not a medium but a signpost to a medium.

QR Codes can be placed on T-shirts, packaging, posters, catalogues, direct mail, business cards, print adverts – pretty well anything that is printed, in effect! We all carry mobile phones with us, and with smartphones becoming the way forward, QR codes take away the need to remember long Web addresses, which can only make your marketing more effective.

In practical terms, a QR code can increase website sales to promote new or slow moving products, increase subscribers to your blogs, direct people to your YouTube uploads – and from there you need to see the other sections and chapters in this book!

12.8.4 Sell during 'hold' on inbound telephone calls

According to Simon Roncorroni, a leading UK consultant, this is an undervalued opportunity in the UK. The experience of Rapp and Collins (1987) in the USA supports him. For example, they report that Polaroid once generated a 16–20 per cent response from its promotions on 'hold tapes'.

12.9   Combining media to maximise efficiency: the contact strategy

Direct marketers often need to combine media in a multi-contact programme that makes sense to customers over time, rather than expecting them to plough their way through a set of unrelated campaigns. Putting together a combination of media is often known as a 'contact strategy'.

Contact strategies can vary, depending on the situation, from single contact to many contacts over time. Examples are given in Figures 12.3 and 12.4.

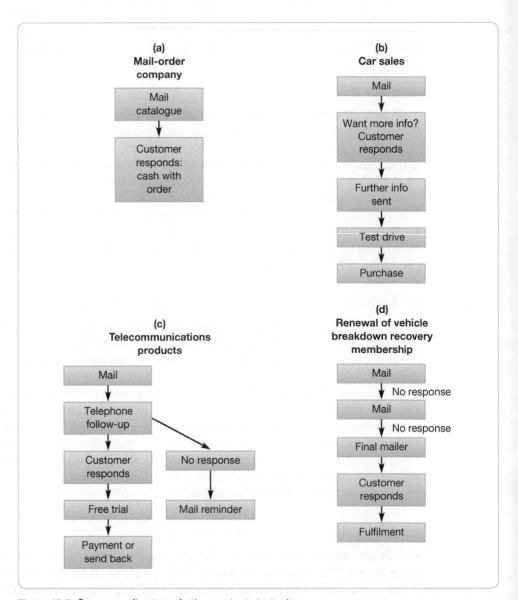

Figure 12.3 Consumer direct marketing contact strategies

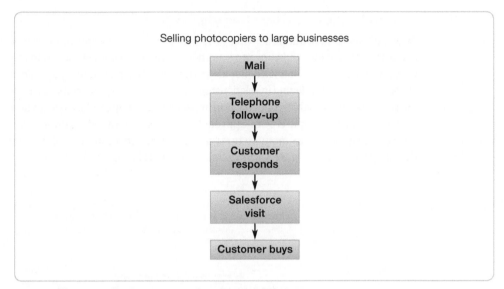

Figure 12.4 **Business-to-business contact strategies**

12.9.1 Guidelines for choosing a contact strategy

The *Educators' Guide to Direct Marketing* (Institute of Direct Marketing, 1996) outlines the following key areas to take into account:

1 **Expense of the product**. If the product is expensive, consumers are likely to need a multiple contact approach: they are less easily parted from their money! More communication is needed.

2 **Complexity of the product.** Particularly complex products may need communication to the consumer in stages to avoid overloading them with information. It may be that multiple decisions by the consumer need to be made; in this instance, they may need to be guided through slowly. Products such as personal pensions would fit this category.

3 **The need for reassurance.** Here, the remoteness of selling direct presents a problem. People need reassurance in lots of different ways: prior recommendation, well-known brands, and guarantees. Free trial offers may be the answer, adding another stage to the contact programme. Household goods, say stereo equipment, may fit here.

4 **Demonstrations.** The need for demonstrations would add to the number of required communications to the customer. If you are selling cars, for example, you will invite customers to test drive your vehicles, then perhaps follow up with more information and offers.

5 **Cost versus payback.** This should always be the final consideration. Total contact costs need to be calculated and assessed against gross margins obtained to ensure that the desired profit is made. There is a trade-off, of course: the more contacts you make, the more prospects you will convert to customers. So both costs and revenues will rise. The amount of contact needs to be fine tuned so that profits are maximised. This will usually come down to testing different approaches.

In addition to these five areas of consideration, there is the need to acknowledge the different contact strategy that a relationship approach would engender, compared with a traditional 'programme' approach.

Relationship approach versus campaign approach

As was discussed in detail earlier (Chapters 5 and 7), there is a strategic decision to be made: are you better off running marketing programmes in a discrete way, with separate programme objectives through the year? Or is it a better idea to manage customers rather than campaigns, and look at each customer's marketing in relationship terms? More and more companies are starting to use the latter approach, and this does have an impact on how they conduct a dialogue with customers.

It is useful to compare both approaches, using a detailed example. Figures 12.5 and 12.6 contrast how a car manufacturer might contact its customers, depending on whether they are 'campaign' (Figure 12.5) or 'relationship' (Figure 12.6) orientated.

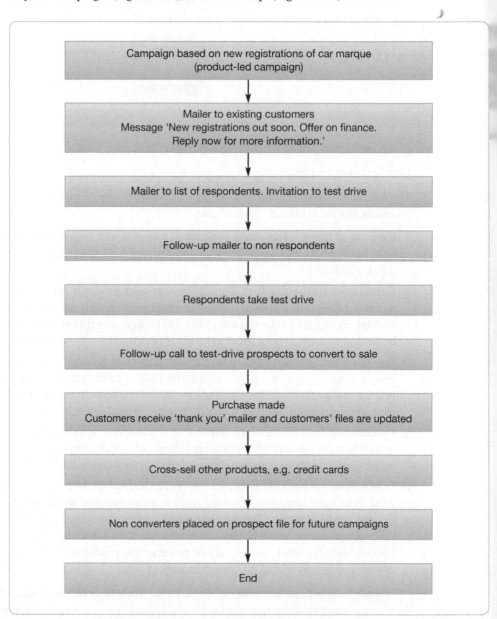

Figure 12.5 Contact strategy for a car manufacturer: the campaign approach

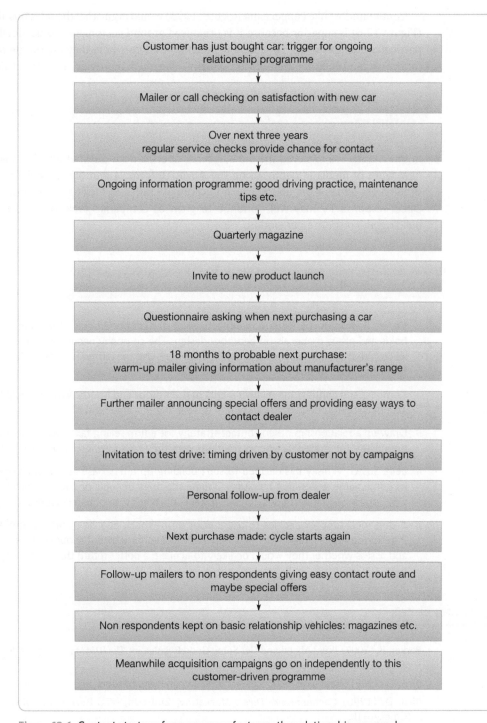

Figure 12.6 Contact strategy for a car manufacturer: the relationship approach

Commentators like Peppers and Rogers (1993) would argue that the relationship approach (Figure 12.6) is superior because it is organised around customers and acknowledges their particular circumstances. For example, it acknowledges where they are on the buying cycle for the car, and each communication is likely to be much more relevant as a result.

Summary

In this chapter we explored the press, inserts, door-to-door distribution, TV, radio and some new types of media in depth, using the AIMRITE formula introduced earlier (Chapter 11). While press remains popular, the split in channel options is fuelling a fast growth in DRTV. Direct-response TV may well continue to grow as companies look for double duty brand building and response generation.

QUESTIONS

1 Comfy Bedrooms is a leading manufacturer of designer bedrooms. It visits individual households and offers proposals on bedroom design. The company needs a continual feed of sales leads. What acquisition media should it consider? Use the AIMRITE formula to decide on the best candidates to test.

2 Compare and contrast the relative merits of door drops and inserts. Which would be the probable better bet for a pizza delivery firm advertising in a small town?

3 Draw up a relationship based contact strategy for a firm selling fax machine solutions to large businesses. Integrate your media solutions with the firm's salesforce activities.

4 Bell's Scotch Whisky has decided to start building up a database and intends using DRTV as its prime name generation medium. Outline the main benefits of DRTV to Bell's, and explain what practical considerations it needs to take in using TV to obtain responses.

5 A dog food supplier decides to use a door drop 'knock and drop' programme to distribute 2 million coupons nationwide. Explain what media alternatives it should have also considered, and assess whether they would be likely to achieve a better return than door drops.

References

Barker, B. (2007) Press Ahead and Get Some Good Results, in: *The IDM Marketing Guide*, The Institute of Direct Marketing, Teddington.

Bird, D. (1989) *Commonsense Direct Marketing*, Kogan Page, London.

Bird, D. (1990) *Commonsense Direct Marketing*, 2nd edn, NTC Business Books, Lincolnwood (Chicago) IL.

BRAD (2012) *Email from Tom McMullen*, BRAD, London.

Dibb, S., Simkin, L., Pride, W. and Ferrell, O. (2012) *Marketing Concepts and Strategies*, 6th edn, Cengage Learning EMEA, Andover.

DMA Census (2005) Direct Marketing Association, London.

Experian PLC (2009) *Mosaic UK 2009: Experian reveals the changing face of UK society,* Experian PLC, Nottingham.

Facebook (2012) *Facebook for Business – Promote your business with ads and sponsored stories.* Available at: **https://www.facebook.com/business/ads/en_GB** [Accessed 13 July 2012].

Fox, N. and Burrows, O. (2001) Direct Marketing Will Knock the Spots Off TV Advertising. *Admap,* March, pp. 31–36.

Garside, J. (2011) *UK is Europe's most digitally aware nation, Ofcom study finds.* Available at: **http://www.guardian.co.uk/media/2011/dec/14/uk-europe-top-digital-nation** [Accessed 04 July 2012].

Gillin, P. and Schwartzman, E. (2011) *Social marketing to the Business Customer,* John Wiley & Sons Inc., Hoboken, NJ.

Goodwin, J. (1992) *'Inserts: Press advertising with direct mail appeal',* in Halsey B (ed) *The Practitioner's Guide to Direct Marketing,* The Institute of Direct Marketing, Teddington.

Grossman, L. (2006) 'How to avoid the big DRTV mistaken', *Admap,* 468, January.

Holden, P. (2008) *Virtually Free Marketing,* A & C Black, London.

Institute of Direct Marketing (1996) *Educators' Guide to Direct Marketing,* Institute of Direct Marketing, Teddington.

Kelly, A. (2011) *How Many Readers Use Snap Codes in Magazine Ads?* Available at: **http://www.forbes.com/sites/annemariekelly/2011/11/14/how-many-readers-use-snap-codes-in-magazine-ads/** [Accessed 05 July 2012].

Kotler, P. and Armstrong, G. (2012) *Principles of Marketing,* 14th edn, Pearson Education Limited, Harlow.

LinkedIn.com (2012) *LinkedIn Ads – Frequently Asked Questions.* Available at: **http://help.linkedin.com/app/answers/detail/a_id/1015** [Accessed 13 July 2012].

marketingvox.com (2010) *Social media aids customer acquisition.* Available at: **http://www.marketingvox.com/social-media-aids-customer-acquisition-046777/?utm_campaign=rssfeed&utm_source=mv&utm_medium=textlink** [Accessed 13 July 2012].

McDaniel, C., Lamb, C. and Hair, J. (2013) *Introduction to Marketing,* 12th edn, South-Western: Cengage Learning.

News International Commercial (2012) *News International Case Studies.* Available at: **http://nicommercial.co.uk/timesmedia/case-studies/california-tourism** [Accessed 03 July 2012].

O'Guinn, T., Allen, C. and Semenik, R. (2009) *Advertising and Integrated Brand Promotion,* 5th edn, Mason OH: South-Western Cengage Learning.

O'Reilly, L. (2011) *Virgin Media marks 2010 as its 'best ever' year.* Available at: **http://www.marketingweek.co.uk/virgin-media-marks-2010-as-its-best-ever-year/3023598.article** [Accessed 04 July 2012].

Pearson, D. (2012) *DRTV – Absolutely Everything You Need to Know.* Available at: **http://www.drtvcentre.com/absolutely-everything-free** [Accessed 06 July 2012].

Peppers, D. and Rogers, M. (1993) *The One-to-one Future.* New York NY: Doubleday.

RAB (2010) *Frank: Using radio to get inside the world of teenagers.* Available at: **http://www.rab.co.uk/showContent.aspx?id=9128** [Accessed 12 July 2012].

RAB (2012a) *Radio effectiveness research – the major multiplier studies.* Available at: **http://rab.co.uk/why-use-radio/effectiveness-research/the-evidence-for-radio's-effectiveness** [Accessed 12 July 2012].

RAB (2012b) *Frequently Asked Questions.* Available at: **http://www.rab.co.uk/faqs#How per cent 20many per cent20Commercial per cent20stations per cent20are per cent20there per cent20in per cent20the per cent20UK per cent20at per cent20the per cent20moment?** [Accessed 12 July 2012].

RAJAR (2012) *RAJAR Data Release, Quarter 1 2012 – May 17 2012.* Available at: **http://www.rajar.co.uk/docs/2012_03/2012_Q1_DAB_Ownership.pdf** [Accessed 10 July 2012].

Rapp, S. and Collin, T. (1989) *Maximarketing,* McGraw Hill, New York.

Royal Mail (2008) *Sustainable Dream Comes to Fruition.* Available at: **http://www.royalmail.com/ sites/default/files/docs/pdf/final_ROY242_village_case.pdf** [Accessed 12 July 2012].

Royal Mail (2011) *Doordrop case studies – Putting Cravendale Milk on 270,000 new shopping lists.* Available at: **http://www.royalmail.com/what-5p-buys-case-studies** [Accessed 12 July 2012].

Royal Mail (2012) *Hit the right drop zone – how to target a door drop.* Available at: **http://www. royalmail.com/marketing-services/new-direct-mail/how-use-mailshots/target-door-drop** [Accessed 12 July 2012].

Solis, A. (2011) *Engage,* John Wiley & Sons Inc, Hoboken, NJ.

textsmsmarketing.com (2012) *SMS Text Marketing Case Studies.* Available at: **http://www.textsms- marketing.com/sms-text-marketing-case-studies.php** [Accessed 13 July 2012].

Stone, B. (1996) *Successful Direct Marketing Methods,* 5th edn, NTC Business Books, Chicago, Ill.

The Direct Marketing Association (2011) *Door drop case study: MCHI's campaign for TalkTalk.* Available at: **http://www.dma.org.uk/toolkit/door-drop-case-study-mchis-campaign-talktalk** [Accessed 12 July 2012].

The DRTV Centre (2012a) *How Much Does DRTV Advertising Cost?*Available at: **http://www.drtv- centre.com/drtv-cost-less-than-you-think-drtv-centre-specialist-drtv-advertising-agency- agencies** [Accessed 06 July 2012].

The Institute of Direct Marketing (2002) A Glossary of Direct Marketing Terms, In: R. Fairlie, ed. *The New IDM Practitioner's Guide,* The Institute of Direct Marketing, Teddington.

Thinkbox (2012) *T-Mobile dials sales using DRTV.* Available at: **http://www.thinkbox.tv/server/ show/ConCaseStudy.1570** [Accessed 06 July 2012].

TNT Post (2012) *About Us.* Available at: **http://www.tntpost.co.uk/ABOUTUS/AboutUs/ WhoWeAre.aspx** [Accessed 12 uly 2012].

TNT Post (2012) *Door Drop Media Case Studies.* Available at: **http://203.129.207.187/dnn6.0/ tntpost/ABOUTUS/AboutUs/casestudies/doordropmedia.aspx** [Accessed 12 July 2012].

Wasserman, T. (2012) *Facebook to hit 1 billion user mark in August.* Available at: **http://mashable. com/2012/01/12/facebook-1-billion-users/** [Accessed 13 July 2012].

Whitten, I. (2012) *Research carried out for this book.* London: s.n.

www.cable.co.uk (2011) *DTR predicts continued growth for satellite TV.* Available at: **http://www. cable.co.uk/news/dtr-predicts-continued-growth-for-satellite-tv-800619289/** [Accessed 04 July 2012].

Young, M. (1994) Direct Response Television. *Journal of Targeting, Measurement and Analysis,* 2(2), pp. 125–38.

youtalkmarketing.com (2009) *How the RSPCA used DRTV to boost donations during the recession.* Available at: **http://www.utalkmarketing.com/pages/article.aspx?articleid=14016&title= how_the_rspca_used_drtv_to_boost_donations_during_the_recession** [Accessed 06 July 2012].

CASE STUDY

Crocs Mobile Coupon campaign

When Crocs wanted to increase their sales they used analysis of known behavioural attributes to gain an understanding of their customers and decide on a strategy for contacting them. The resulting decision was to send digital – instead of traditional printed – coupons, to their target audience of consumers between the ages of 18 and 50.

'Crocs customers are on-the-go, very active individuals,' said Jay Custard, global on-line marketing director at Crocs Inc. 'Being able to connect with them in a meaningful way via their mobile device allows us to create a valuable shopping experience and to have a one-on-one dialogue with our customers'.

Posters were placed in 185 Crocs retail locations throughout the United States posing the question: 'What is a foot's bestest friend? Find out and save 15 per cent off today! It is as easy as one, two, three. . .'. The store number and a short code followed, with customers being invited to text CROCS and the Crocs store number to 63103. They would then receive a 15 per cent off coupon by immediate text reply to their mobile phone. The coupon was redeemed by showing it to the cashier at the checkout.

Store associates were trained and motivated to support the programme, spoke with customers about the mobile coupon, and encouraged them to stay opted-in to receive further communications and discounts from Crocs.

Crocs has discovered that mobile marketing is an extremely efficient and effective way to engage consumers, with engagement and enthusiasm both being described as 'off the charts'– 94,000 requests for coupons were received during the first month of the campaign.

'Mobile helps us reach our customers, regardless of their location, and provide them with valuable, useful information,' said Custard.

Going forward, Crocs plans to offer additional coupons and information via SMS to customers, as well as using the mechanism to drive traffic to retail locations and its website. Further, there are plans to use advanced mobile tactics such as sending targeted messaging to consumers based on anything from its previous shopping experience, purchase history, on-line activity and demographics.

Questions

1 Given that the posters were located in their stores, how could crocs be sure that they were not just giving money away to people who were going to buy from them anyway?

2 How could they track how many coupon redeemers were new customers and how many were returning buyers?

Source of case: Adapted from Butcher, D., (2010). Crocs rolls out nationwide mobile coupons campaign: case study. Available at: http://www.mobilecommercedaily.com/2010/05/17/crocs-gets-100k-texts-requesting-mobile-coupons-in-1-month-case-study [Accessed 24 August 2012].

CASE STUDY

Choosing media – Gillette

In the razor selling business, Gillette's most cut-throat competition is itself. Dominating the market with a reported 85 per cent of sales, Gillette builds on its success with constantly evolving product innovations and prestige-pumping campaigns to boost total category usage.

Armed with two new sets of product to promote – the Gillette Fusion Power 'Phenom' razor as well as the Gillette Series of toiletries for men – the company wanted to maximise awareness of the new shaver and the supporting merchandise, while simultaneously generating demand by challenging the stereotypically male reluctance to practise any kind of skincare routine.

The strategy

'Our target market, aspirational males between the ages of 18 and 35, is hard to reach in advertising terms,' says Nathan Homer, Gillette business director. 'The problem is exacerbated because we look to achieve retail level consumer engagement in shops such as Superdrug, which is a store environment that favours females.'

Gillette briefed the digital brand experience agency Iblink to help it realise its campaign. 'We have a history of shopper marketing activities with Superdrug and Iblink is the partner of choice for Superdrug when carrying out in-store activities. We'd also carried out successful events with Iblink previously, such as the Fusion Stealth razor amnesty marketing campaign,' says Homer.

Gillette decided that an introductory promotional discount combined with a competition, with entry via product purchase, would provide the right hook to reel in the attention of its male consumers.

Out-of-home media was selected as the primary channel of communication for the campaign, as it would target males proactively where they are known to congregate in large numbers, specifically when commuting to work in central London.

'Iblink helped us to bring our ideas to the next level, making sure we were following the shopper in his commuting day, with all available tools, such as digital outdoor media, Bluetooth messages and so on,' says Homer.

The execution

Digital six-sheet-poster sized advertising appeared in all London rail terminals from the last week of February for two weeks. The campaign ran in 10 railway stations on a total of 106 poster screens, broadcast when the railway stations were at their busiest. The digital creative, which used eye catching moving imagery, introduced the Gillette Series products and the 33 per cent price promotion, and invited entry to a competition.

Accompanied by the tagline 'Live like a Champion – Experience the Best' the competition offered winners a choice of 'aspirational' prizes, all with 'man appeal': a tailor made Savile Row suit, a supercar for the weekend, or a chauffeured speedboat trip to a show at the O2 arena.

'The winning opportunity was perceived to be high, with every participating Superdrug store having its own winner,' says Homer. 'Entry – via product purchase – could be made only in-store on a given day. To facilitate participation, GPS based messaging enabled consumers to text for the location of their nearest store.'

On the day of the competition, roaming street teams toured the vicinity of the 50 busiest Superdrug stores to catch the attention of consumers and drive more shoppers into outlets. Gillette embraced its target market's interest in gadgets, while covering all bases with additional traditional advertising. 'Armed with "bluecasting" pods housed in branded Gillette rucksacks, our street teams communicated the competition and price promotion by broadcasting Bluetooth advertising to mobiles, as well as distributing conventional leaflets,' says Homer.

The street teams were supported by in-store brand ambassadors who were instructed to engage shoppers and explain the benefits of Gillette's three-step grooming process, to mention the 33 per cent offer and to hand out competition entry leaflets.

On the following day the focus switched to support the Phenom razor. The above formula was repeated at store level, although this time the competition was replaced with the offer of a free skincare kit for purchasers of the Phenom razor, with the brand ambassadors briefed to talk up the features and benefits of the razor.

On top of this, a £146,000 Lamborghini Gallardo car was placed in the centre of London's Victoria station, both for the PR potential and as a focal point from which a dedicated field team directed shoppers into Superdrug's store on the station concourse. A 30-second in-store radio commercial also advertised the Gillette range and invited competition entries on the day.

The outcome

Network Rail statistics showed that 4,578,390 adults passed through the stations that broadcast the campaign, 2,418,628, (53 per cent) of whom were males. Meanwhile, 10,622 Bluetooth mobile messages were sent and 20,000 leaflets and 12,000 product samples were distributed.

Analysis by the company Continental Research found 8 out of 10 who recalled the campaign rated it positively overall; the campaign scored most positively among those exposed most often to the various communication activities; and the majority agreed it was 'better than most advertising for razors' (78 per cent), that it 'made Gillette seem cutting-edge' (67 per cent) and that they 'enjoyed seeing it' (59 per cent).

On the two in-store event days (the competition day and free skincare kit day) sales of Gillette Series products were three times greater in the 50 trial stores than in the non-supported Superdrug control stores, which also benefited from the 33 per cent off price promotion.

Similarly, sales of Gillette Fusion Power Phenom Razors were six times greater than in non-supported Superdrug control stores.

'Early rate-of-sale indicators across the two Superdrug trading periods of mid-February to mid-April indicate significant uplifts were maintained post-promotion, versus the non-supported control stores,' says Homer.

Analysis

'Overall we view the campaign as good evidence that we can use new tools versus traditional media to drive significant awareness and trial at the launch of new products,' says Homer.

'We think we could probably reduce the competition prize fund in favour of more field staff and promotional activity days, as there didn't seem to be a need for prizes in every store.'

Gillette is intent on staying a cut above. 'Our priority in campaigns is to continue to build on the trust and heritage we have with the men by bringing them better and better products.'

Case study (*continued*)

Questions

1 The brief describes Gillette's target market as 'aspirational males between the ages of 18 and 35'. Explain the concept of segmentation, targeting and positioning.
2 Critically discuss the communications strategy used by Gillette in the case study.
3 Discuss the role of branding in any company's marketing strategy.
4 Recommend and justify an alternative promotional campaign that Gillette could have used instead of the one they used.

Source of case study: Barda, T. (2009). Case Study: Gillette. Available at: **http://www.themarketer.co.uk/articles/case-studies/gillette/** [Accessed 21 August 2012].

Chapter 13

Creative practice and consumer behaviour in direct marketing

Objectives

By the end of this chapter you should understand:

- what constitutes creative practice
- how creative approaches rely on good understanding of consumers
- the origins and competing philosophies that have guided creative practice
- where the creative element fits into the wider direct marketing planning picture
- the strategic drivers of creative practice
- how to create a direct marketing advert

Introduction

'A lot of what passes for interruptive work is anything but interruptive. . . . . . 90% of marketing communications are self-indulgent, vague, dull, irrelevant wastes of the client's money, the prospect's time and the earth's resources.'

(Steve Harrison, 2009)

Steve Harrison makes his point strongly but it is strange that the creative department is one of the few areas of creative life that has to have the word 'creative' on its door. It is also true that everyone in business and beyond has a view on creative output and the magic dust that agency creatives sprinkle on the brands they work with.

In this chapter we try to lay down some drivers of effective creative work. We start by examining the background to direct marketing creative practice, and compare the various philosophies which guide different creative approaches. These are driven by differing views on how consumers behave. We then outline where creative fits in the planning process, and show how the different marketing functions influence the creative output.

The second section of the chapter outlines how to create a direct marketing advert, based primarily on the well-known AIDA model of consumer information processing.

13.1 Introducing creative practice

13.1.1 The popularity of creative study

Direct marketers tend to pay a great deal of attention to the art of creativity. There are a lot of books on the subject (some are mentioned at the end of this chapter), and training courses on creativity run by organisations such as the Institute of Direct and Digital Marketing are always popular. One reason for this fascination is the 'sexiness' of the subject – even hard-bitten business managers can be seduced by the glamour of thinking about their product in the bright lights of a Californian blockbuster advert. Advertising has been described (Martin, 1989) as 'the poetry' or 'the artistry' of marketing, although Ogilvy (1983) argued strongly that advertising has only one job: to sell. We will take a brief look at competing philosophies in the next section.

13.1.2 What is 'creative'?

Strangely, this question is not often addressed in texts. True to character, David Ogilvy (1983) comes up with a strong riposte to this question:

> 'I have to invent a Big Idea for an advertising campaign before Tuesday. Creativity strikes me as a highfalutin word for the work I have to do between now and Tuesday. The Benton and Bowles agency holds that if it doesn't sell, it isn't creative. Amen.'

So, 'creative' is a word that summarises how brands jazz up their messages in order to increase their attractiveness to potential consumers.

13.1.3 The importance of creative

Bird (2007) describes the creative contribution as the 'moment of truth' for direct-response communications. This refers to the moment when prospects or customers engage with the advert. In his view, therefore, the importance of the creative element lies in its visibility and tangibility for consumers.

However, Bird would have been the first to agree that, compared with other campaign elements – the targeting, the product, offer and incentive, and the timing – the creative element assumes 'lower' importance. This has been demonstrated many times in market tests, discussed later (see Chapter 14). However, isolating the effect of creative is not always easy. What is clear is that it doesn't matter how good your creative is, if the product is wrong and you are targeting the wrong audience at the wrong time with the wrong offer you are whistling in the wind. As Barack Obama famously said, 'You can put lipstick on a pig but it is still a pig'.

The primary purpose of good creative is, indeed, to sell. That said, one interesting twist on our appreciation of creative approaches is that they can help us to understand customers better. By analysing creative in relation to corresponding behaviour, we can use it as a form of research. The role of testing here cannot be underestimated. In the past it was very hard to isolate why certain creative campaigns outpulled others. The increased use of testing allows us to isolate variables and encourage creatives to think about how to drive physical response. This has to be nuanced by the impact of hard sell techniques on brand values. Have a look at **www.whichtestwon.com** and later in this book **(Chapter Fourteen)** for the power of this technique in refining creative execution.

13.2   Using creative as a form of research

Bill Bernbach, one of the giants of advertising history (the 'B' in DDB, the advertising agency), was asked what he thought would change in the future (Ogilvy, 1983). Referring to marketers' obsession with changing trends, he said:

> 'It's fashionable to talk about changing man. A communicator must be concerned about unchanging man – what compulsions drive him, what instincts dominate his every action, even though his language too often camouflages what really motivates him. For if you know these things about a man, you can touch him at the core of his being.'

Bill Bernbach stressed that understanding customers was critical to good advertising. In direct marketing this is just as true. However, because of the body of knowledge we have built up on direct marketing creative approaches, we have generated a 'feedback loop'. We can use creative tests as a driver to understand customers, as well as the other way round. In doing so, we are actually providing a key feedback loop to the beginning of the planning process – analysis – as well. In this chapter, therefore, a major role will be to gather together as much of this customer understanding as possible. This will enable us to be better informed about 'how and why' direct marketing works, not just 'what' works. Figure 13.1 summarises this feedback loop.

Before examining modern creative practice, it is useful to understand the historical influences and competing philosophies of creativity.

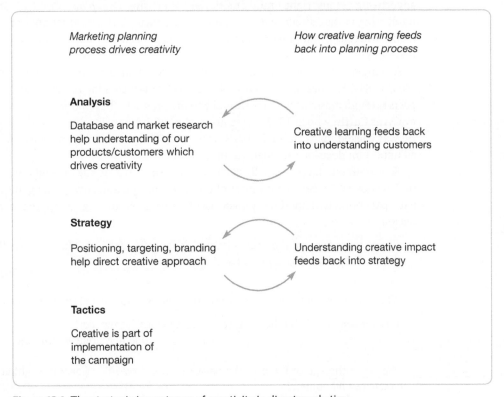

Figure 13.1 The strategic importance of creativity in direct marketing

13.2.1 The origins of creativity in advertising

'The purpose of advertising is to persuade.'

The advertising community

In this section we will look at different creative philosophies. In order to do this we must view the entirety of advertising, and so cast our net, briefly, a little wider than direct communications.

According to American commentators on advertising (Bovee *et al.*, 1995; Martin, 1989; Rapp and Collins, 1987), the readers of this book can be divided into two camps. If you are interested in a career as a 'creative' in an advertising agency, the chances are you are a 'right-brain' (intuitive, artistic) thinker. If, however, you see yourself in business, perhaps managing a marketing department, you will be a 'left-brain' (cognitive) dominated person. Left-brain people are logical, persuaded by words and argument, and take a step-by-step approach to solving problems. Most of this book is written using such an approach.

Right-brain people are different. If you are right-brain dominated, you use intuition rather than logic, may use emotion not reason, and are more interested in romance than rationality.

The reason for the above introduction is that this split of thinking lies at the heart of the creative debate, and to understand direct marketing creativity we need to understand how it fits into the wider context of this fascinating creative debate that has been rumbling on now for about 100 years. This argument can be summed up as 'left brain' logical advertising versus 'right brain' emotional advertising (Rapp and Collins, 1987). What is interesting is that direct marketing has been heavily influenced by one side of the argument, whereas brand advertising practice has chosen another route. So what are these two sides?

As long ago as 1904, John E. Kennedy described advertising as 'salesmanship in print' (Fox, 1984). He said that the best advertising 'contained a logical approach', leading prospects through reasons why they should buy the product. The opposing camp was epitomised by Cyrus Curtis, who in 1911 talked about the 'atmosphere in adverts' as the key ingredient. He was backed up by Dunn, in 1918, who said, 'The psychoanalysts have found that nearly all important decisions are made in the subconscious.'

This argument has essentially carried on the same way to the present day. Major figures such as Rosser Reeves, the inventor of the USP concept, and advertising giant David Ogilvy have passionately, sometimes provocatively, advocated the logical approach, appealing to reason:

'I have never admired the "belles lettres" school of advertising. I have always thought them absurd. They did not give the reader a single fact.'

(Ogilvy, 1964)

Whereas other, equally eminent practitioners have advocated the opposite approach:

'It is not what is said but how it is said that influences us the most.'

(Pierre Martineau, *Chicago Tribune*, 1957)

'We are in the age of the eye. We have less time to read . . . only the lightning strike of a picture can hit home.'

(Margot Sherman, President, McCann Erickson, 1959)

In summary, the left-brain enthusiasts would argue that advertising focuses on 'selling' by leading the prospect through a series of reasoned, logical arguments. Unique selling points are important to help persuade the customer. Words tend to be more powerful than visual images. Functional brands, such as Intel, are built up in these ways.

The right-brain advocates will claim that people make purchase decisions on emotional grounds, (although they will justify their purchases on logical grounds in research); but in fact people are ruled by their emotional subconscious, and it is this which advertising needs to play to. In this case, visual imagery is more important than words. Symbolic brands, for example Coca-Cola, are based on this premise.

Exhibit 13.1 Left brain versus right brain appeal

Let us say you enrol on a marketing course, 'Strategic digital and direct marketing: the future'. Your right-brain reasons for doing this might be the following:

- Impressing your friends
- Getting one up on your colleagues
- Fear of confronting a problem at work and looking for answers on the course
- Hope: you want to move on to better things in your career
- Getting excitement, brightening up a routine
- Looking good back at the office as you casually drop hints of your in-depth knowledge of marketing strategy

Whereas your left-brain reasons might be:

- It was the cheapest course of its type
- It was the most convenient to get to
- It minimised the disruption to daily work
- It had the best value
- It had the most knowledgeable speakers

What has made the argument even more entertaining has been the accusation from the champions of reason and logic that the 'intuition and romance' camp are more obsessed with winning awards than making sales.

So, was David Ogilvy right when he dismissed image and emotion led marketing communications in favour of a facts/benefits driven approach? Most classical direct marketing over the years was benefits based – 'here are the ten reasons you should buy this product', and so on. Ogilvy's stance is still valid for many sectors today – those that involve a step-by-step approach to buying, with a clear information search phase undertaken by consumers who buy on rational grounds. Pension plans spring to mind. But there is enormous evidence that we are rarely this robotic or logical in our purchasing. We feel strong emotions – the urge to show off, to treat ourselves after a hard week at work, to get 'one over' our friends, to feel better about ourselves through what we own. These are emotions. Brand advertisers have long understood the importance of emotions in our consumerism.

One manifestation of so-called emotion based buying may be impulse buying of perhaps quite expensive items without much thought or information search. Ever come home from shopping with an unexpected purchase? You should also consider low involvement repeat buying of standard or lower value items, in which the consumer uses their own experience to make an instant decision.

The Foote, Cone and Belding (FCB) Grid grid outlined later in this chapter helps us to resolve some of these issues. What is clear is that, for most decisions, thoughts and/or knowledge are moderated by emotion and if something 'feels' right then we react in a positive way. Conversely if it 'feels' wrong we turn away or ignore it.

This debate has profound importance for consumer behaviour models, such as the well-known awareness, interest, desire, action (AIDA) model. The AIDA model tends to hold up pretty well for more considered purchases but less well for impulse or repetitive purchases.

So, when designing creative to maximise sales, the suggestion is that you think through the type of buying process your consumer is likely to go through. And remember, in spite of academic claims to model all of this accurately, the 'science' behind human behaviour is fraught with uncertainty.

Turning to some specifics now, let us start with a look at the extent to which advertising needs to entertain.

Advertising: should it be entertainment as well as selling?

The following quotes summarise some of the arguments for and against the need for advertising to be entertaining:

'The people who know what they are doing are the direct marketing people. They know exactly what they've sold. And you don't. You don't have the faintest idea whether the advertising sells anything or not. And you don't really care. You just want to win an award at Cannes, or one of those rackets.'

(David Ogilvy in Martin, 1989)

'Our job is to kill the cleverness that makes us shine instead of the product.'

(Bill Bernbach, Managing Director of DDB)

'We sell; or else.'

(O&M advertising agency company motto)

Ad writers forget they are salesmen and try to be performers. Instead of sales, they seek applause.

(Claude Hopkins, 1923)

'Advertising began as an art, and too many people want it to remain that way: a never never land where they can say 'this is right because we feel it's right.'

(Reeves, 1961)

Martin (1989) advocated that advertisers should match entertainment with selling:

'Each message must indelibly lodge the brand in the viewer's memory and seed the mind with emotional reasons to buy, as well as providing entertainment.'

Broadbent (1997) said:

'There is no genuine clash between selling and "being creative". It is only that the criteria differ. Even when brand sales get the benefit of effective advertising, this can still be done entertainingly. We cannot intrude on the public without repaying them. We must not put at risk the media audiences. "Effective creativity" I can understand and admire. Unconnected creativity frightens me.'

So, where does direct marketing fit into the arguments, firstly for cognitive versus 'emotion based' advertising, and secondly for the need for entertainment?

13.2.2 The origins of direct marketing creative practice

Direct marketing creative practice has traditionally been dominated by the cognitive, left-brain approach. Direct marketing creative is to some extent still based on techniques developed by mail-order companies decades ago, which have always served that industry well. Rapp and Collins (1987) showed why direct marketing has historically been left-brain dominated:

1 Mail-order products had to have an element of 'uniqueness' about them to overcome the inertia of people at home; this led to a USP driven approach.

2 The items were often 'intangibles', or services, which were traditionally sold in a logical way.

3 Direct marketing products and services are still usually relatively 'highpriced items', and it was felt that items of such value cannot be sold solely through emotion. Reasoned arguments were, and still are, required if you want a consumer to buy a pension from you. John Watson, one of the great DM creatives, talks about consumers being motivated through fear and greed. He produced one of the great lines for financial services products 'cash if you die, cash if you don't'. This appeal to the whole brain, i.e. rationality and emotion, has actually outlasted the company that commissioned the line.

The culture within direct marketing remains largely driven by creative that presents logical propositions to customers (see for example the IDM's *Direct and Interactive* Guide, 2006) that advocate making rational arguments inspiring people to act.

In contrast, brand building creative has predominantly been right-brain led. If we consider products such as Marlboro cigarettes, Coca Cola or Levi Jeans, their advertising is pure emotional symbolism. The reasons for this are:

1 Brand building through imagery and association with attractive symbols is needed when you are advertising a product that is similar to others.

2 Brand building is similarly important for low involvement, low price ticket products, such as FMCG where consumers make impulsive, subconscious decisions.

3 Brand building has traditionally been used to sell tangible items such as food and clothes. But most of all because . . .

4 People like brands. Brands can help people create their identity, express who they are and what they represent. Brands can of course be status emblems. They can sometimes inspire strong emotions – think about brands like Harley Davidson.

5 Brand building remains a development area for direct marketing and on-line marketing. A good website can build or support a strong brand. Try **www.Guinness.com** to see how a good engaging website can use direct principles to support and develop a strong brand heritage.

Direct marketing's traditional stance on entertainment has been even more clear: there was no room for it in direct communications. The argument has been that even if it were required, there is simply no room for deflecting the prospect from the crux of the advert in order to obtain a response.

Recent developments in the direct marketing creative approach

Developments that started in the 1990s suggest that direct marketing needs to embrace a wider creative influence, taking more of a generalist perspective to add to the specific direct skills already present. Graeme McCorkell's (1994) long time observation that most of the best direct-response adverts he ever saw were produced by 'general' agency trained creatives, such as John Watson or Drayton Bird, and still holds true. One of the most successful recent agencies in the UK in terms of awards won was Harrison Troughton Wunderman (HTW), which specialised in 'brand response' marketing – a marriage of brand building and direct response. Steve Harrison, the eponymous creative director of HTW, describes a very simple but inspiring approach to the creative process, talking about a 'relevant abruption'. Relevance comes from understanding the customer in detail and abruption from demonstrating the product or brand in an engaging and interesting manner in a way that creates attention to the message being promoted.

Direct marketing has matured in sectors previously dominated by general marketing techniques. The car industry is a classic example of this. Cars are sold through a mixture of both symbolic branding, appealing to emotional benefits, and left-brain rational argument. It follows that there is an increasing need for direct-response creative approaches to help in brand building strategies as well as doing the job of driving sales directly. Indeed, when the authors hear that brand owners are 'losing control of their brands in the social media space' alarm bells start ringing. Brands represent significant value to the companies that own them and their promotion and protection, in whatever channel they are experienced, is at the heart of the marketing function. Poor creative execution can easily damage the value of the brand; and the hard sell messages that were once the mainstay of the traditional direct marketing community are now more subtly developed to produce the sales that all companies require, whilst reinforcing the long-term position of the brand. The launch of the Audi A1 is a great example of brand building Direct Marketing creative that protected the core Audi brand whilst delivering the successful launch of the new model.

OK, so can we summarise what kind of situations typically arise, requiring different creative solutions? Thinking about the above discussions, and thinking back to our earlier points about the different models used to explain behaviour, the Foote, Cone and Belding (FCB) Grid offers a neat theoretical framework. Their grid helps us pinpoint what kind of consumer behaviour we are dealing with, and what kind of creative response we need. The grid is shown in Figure 13.2.

Some have long argued that such differences between these four segments can be closed considerably. Over 20 years ago, Rapp and Collins (1987) proposed an holistic solution which, being practitioners, they called 'whole-brain advertising'. This approach advocates appealing to both 'thinking' and 'feeling'. Part of the communication would focus on symbolism, imagery and emotion, while the rest would home in on logic, reason and argument.

Exhibit 13.2 Whole-brain advertising

In the commercial break of the American Superbowl on New Year's Day, 1984, Apple Computers launched a one-minute advert introducing the Macintosh computer. Based on the George Orwell book *1984*, this was a piece of pure right-brain symbolism, costing more per second than a Hollywood movie. Apple then ran a 30-page ad in *Newsweek*, which

	Thinking	Feeling
High involvement	Learn-feel-do Home computing: Dell *Creative*: product demonstration, long copy, features, benefits	Feel-learn-do Fashion, make-up: Dior *Creative*: large space visuals, impact, symbolism, identity
Low involvement	Do-learn-feel Routine household items: Procter & Gamble *Creative*: reminders, quick, easy calls to action	Do-feel-learn Instant pleasure goods: Cadbury, Budweiser *Creative*: illustrate instant enjoyment, visuals, show emotion

Figure 13.2 The FCB grid – illustrating the product sector
Source: Based on the ideas of Vaughan (1980).

told prospects everything they needed to know about Macintosh computers: pure left-brain advertising.

Sales of Apple Macintosh computers rocketed.

Rapp and Collins did not argue for whole-brain advertising as a panacea for all problems. They reason that some products, say Dior fashion, should always need right-brain-only advertising, whereas others, say computer hardware accessories, should need left-brain only.)

Other leading practitioners from the traditional arm of DM offered a view more in line with classical direct creative practice. Nash (1995) argued that 'the direct marketing communications job is not to make an impression; it's to make a sale. Response and brand imagery are often two different beasts in an advert'. He advocated that writing a subtle headline in direct marketing means that the phones will not ring as often. The latest Guinness advertising campaign featuring the cloud contains surreal imagery, the line 'made from more . . .' is offered with no further explanation. (The idea is that Guinness and its customers are unique in this way.) Nash would argue that this approach would not win you any friends in direct marketing!

As direct marketing becomes a growing influence in sectors such as packaged goods for example, we have seen Procter & Gamble open a direct to consumer operation in the U.S., which has reinvented its creative approaches. The move into so-called whole-brain advertising is matched by a need to provide entertainment, engagement and relevance as part of the communication and, as we move into the social media space, the ability of consumers to amplify and pass on these messages through their social media networks becomes an important and valuable consideration. Martin's argument that brand advertising needs to entertain to stand out from the clutter should also stand up as an argument for direct marketing, if it wants to avoid 'junk' criticisms.

These debates will continue, but it is time to move on and examine how creative practice is derived from the elements of direct marketing strategy.

13.3 The strategic drivers of creative practice

'The stroke of creative inspiration is a rare phenomenon that comes only to those immersed in research, strategy, planning and tactics.'

(Nash, 1995)

Exhibit 13.3 Real-world planning

In principle, we should always set the broad direction before we set about our creative process. But what actually happens? In reality, planning is rarely linear, in the way described in textbooks. A creative 'big idea' may spring forth at any point in the planning process – and if it's powerful enough, may survive through to production.

Direct marketing writers have differed in what they see as the main drivers of creativity. For instance, Nash (1995) and Bird (2007) saw 'positioning' as the key strategic precursor of creative thinking. Stone (1996) cited 'the product, market, medium, and budget' as essential to creative strategy. In addition to these factors, modern users of direct marketing are stressing the importance of 'branding' as a strategic driver.

The creative effort should be looked upon as the 'last' piece in the planning and implementation jigsaw. If the creative brief is written before decisions have been made on the other planning elements, it lacks the guidance it needs to be successful. Norman Berry, the creative director of Ogilvy and Mather Direct, once said, 'Give me the freedom of a tight brief.' He would probably have applauded this planning principle.

Figure 13.3 outlines the specific links between the elements of strategy and the creative effort. It reveals that some of the drivers are strategic: the product, the market, positioning and branding. The remainder are tactical features: the campaign budget, media choice and the offer that will be made. Let us look at how these elements influence creative effort.

The product

An understanding of the product or service benefits is crucial to good creative practice. What is it that customers want the product to do for them? How does the product fit into their lives? The key is spending time researching the product. Ogilvy was famous for this; he once spent three weeks reading nothing but product manuals on the Rolls Royce, before creating a classic advertisement.

The customer/prospect

An intimate knowledge of your customers can greatly help in producing convincing creative material. Once you have got under the skin of your customers, you can reach out to them, knowing what to say and how to say it so that they respond to you.

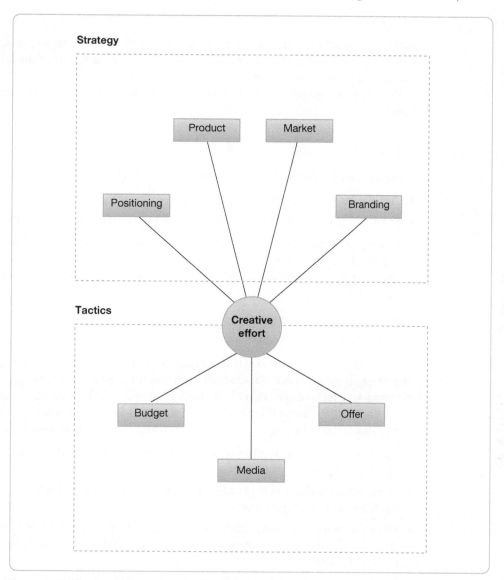

Strategy

Product

Market

Positioning

Branding

Tactics

Creative effort

Budget

Offer

Media

Figure 13.3 Planning influences on the creative effort

The budget

The biggest element of the budget is usually for media spend, but creative considerations are clearly also important. Including a glossy photo of the product on expensive material will raise the 'cost per thousand' considerably. Can this be justified?

The media

The media choice has an enormous bearing on the creative, and it is essential that media choices are made before the serious creative process begins. One only has to imagine the creative necessities of, say, on-line display ads or direct-response TV, compared with those of e-mail, to realise how vital it is to marry creative output with the needs of the medium.

The offer

Although arguably less critical than the choice of medium, the incentive decision is nevertheless an important part of the creative brief. The incentive is part of the message of the advert, and can also set the tone.

We will now expand on two areas that merit further attention, namely positioning and branding.

13.3.1 Positioning

We saw earlier (Chapter 6) that positioning is two things:

1 The dimensions chosen by the marketer to describe the product

2 Where the product fits in the consumer's mind compared with its competitors

As we observed earlier, it is the consumer who decides the hierarchy of competing products within that dimension.

The creative approach should reflect the positioning stance taken, and in particular try to emphasise:

1 the most flattering dimensions of the product

2 the most appealing dimensions to the consumer

Bird (2007) describes successful companies as having a clear positioning from which they rarely, if ever, deviate. For example, Audi has the positioning of 'being at the forefront of automotive technology'. This has a direct relationship with its creative line: 'Vorsprung Durch Technique'. This positioning has been sustained for over 30 years.

Bird draws the following lessons from his experiences in creating positions:

1 Your positioning should reflect the reality of your product or service. 'The best car service in town.' Who says?

2 Vague boasting about being the best in your category, with no back up, does not work, e.g. 'The ideal TV rental for you.'

3 Make sure your positioning dimension is relevant. 'Our car has the safest bodywork in its class.' No use if you are in the sports car category, whose buyers love speed and excitement, not safety.

4 Positioning may be relevant, but insufficient by itself. A successful example of this is Tango soft drinks. 'Have you been Tango'd?' is a 'wacky' positioning which works well, but the product has other support positionings – good value for money, refreshing taste and so on – which are vital for its success.

Exhibit 13.4 Typical positioning dimensions used in direct marketing

- 'New!' versus 'A tradition for centuries';
- 'Tough. Built to last' versus 'Easy to carry';
- 'A very personal service' versus 'You won't know we are here';

- 'This offer is only available to a limited few' versus 'The new product that will be all the rage';
- 'This service is with you in hours' versus 'A high-quality service will be tailor made to your situation'.

Price is, of course, a common positioning dimension to take:

- 'Everyday low pricing' versus 'The very best in quality'.

Nash (1995) developed what he termed 'horizontal positioning' as a way of generating a platform for creative effort.

Horizontal positioning

Nash suggests taking the point in the consumer's buying process that they have reached and establishing that as the basis for the creative approach. Taking the example of a mobile phone:

1 **Create a need.** 'Hey you! You need to communicate on the move.'
2 **Fulfil a need.** 'The new lightweight personal mobile for the stylish woman.'
3 **Sell competitively.** 'We offer the lightest mobile phone on the market . . . lowest price or your money back.'
4 **Overcome inertia.** 'Suppose you broke down today . . . send off now! You don't have a moment to lose.'

Steve Harrison (2009) puts it very simply: 'think about the problems that your prospect might be experiencing and then show how the brand helps to solve these problems'. Much successful advertising follows the problem/solution model. Ogilvy (1964) said that great advertising sells the problem and the solution. The work done many years ago on Listerine presents this effectively. The word 'halitosis' was invented by Listerine's adverting agency as bad breath was a social problem but 'halitosis' sounded like a medical condition.

13.3.2 Branding

Direct marketers have not always seen branding as an important part of their strategy. For example, *Reader's Digest* did not have a powerful corporate brand, yet it was regarded as one of the world's most successful direct marketers from the mail-order era. More recently, a number of direct marketing sectors have emerged to which branding is very important. These include retail, packaged goods and automobiles. Brands such as Next, British Airways, Tesco and Land Rover have used direct and interactive marketing to enhance and support their brands.

According to de Chernatony and McDonald (2010), these marketers can choose between symbolic (emotional, covert reasoning) and functional (rational, overt reasoning) brands. The creative approach must then support the chosen strategy. This is because the creative approach is important in giving brand 'clues' to prospects that are then interpreted from

Figure 13.4 Direct-response press advert illustrating typical business-to-business functional brand

Source: Reproduced by kind permission of Marketscan Ltd.

brand images in the consumer's mind. Thus, an exclusive brand such as American Express is unlikely to be supported by adjectives such as 'smashing', 'super' and 'unbeatable'.

All aspects of creativity – copy, illustrations, layout and production values – must support the brand strategy.

Copy

Copy is particularly important in supporting 'functional' brand values.

The 'Directors at Large' direct-response press advert in Figure 13.4 illustrates a typical business-to-business functional brand. Benefits are outlined in a logical way, with no recourse to brand symbolism.

Copy can also be used to communicate symbolic brand values. The typical American Express direct mailer conveys prestige and status to recipients, in a sense inviting them to become one of a 'chosen few'.

Illustrations

Illustrations are particularly important in supporting 'symbolic' brands.

The RSPCA has used powerful illustrations to communicate its brand in its direct-response advertising. The RSPCA, a charity over 175 years old, has recently moved decisively to change its previously rather 'comfortable' brand into one that is much more aggressive. Its direct marketing has reflected this, with direct-response adverts and mailings (see Figure 13.5) making strong brand statements reflecting the charity's stance over animal issues.

Layout/production

These elements are just as important. An example that highlights the difference between a classical direct-response approach and a more overt branding approach is that of Compaq, outlined in the case study Exhibit 13.5.

In the following section, we take a more detailed look at how to create a direct marketing advert. We will investigate the collective experience of direct marketing and see what does and does not work.

Exhibit 13.5 Compaq – a case study

Compaq is the world's biggest personal computer manufacturer. This position has been achieved through two distribution networks: one is through IT solution experts who sell to large corporations; and the other is through wholesalers such as PC World.

Figure 13.5 Examples from a fundraising appeal pack using a powerful image
Source: Reproduced by kind permission of the RSPCA.

However, the new consumer and small business growth had led to the need for a different channel – direct selling. This had already been done, successfully, by companies such as Dell, Gateway and Viglen, with classical direct marketing adverts off the page selling on rational benefits. For Compaq, however, branding was a key part of its added value, and for its direct operation it was important to reflect this in the creative approach.

The two adverts shown reflect the classic direct 'straight sell',Time Computers (Figure 13.6) and the branded sell, Compaq (Figure 13.7). Here, Compaq must break some of the 'rules' of direct marketing in order to accommodate its brand aims in the creative approach.

13.4 Creative execution

'I see the canvas and I begin!'

(Willem de Kooning, Artist)

13.4.1 The development of direct marketing creative 'rules'

Direct marketing's precision and control when testing allows even small changes in creative to be 'accurately' related to 'behaviour changes' by consumers. (This is something that brand marketers cannot do. For all the effort that goes into researching advertising effectiveness, practitioners are all too often reduced to making educated guesses about what effect their adverts have had. Not so with direct-response advertising.)

As a result, much of the myth and aura behind creative ideas has been steadily dissected by the direct marketing fraternity, and pulled together into a set of creative 'rules' that, if followed, even by a relative novice, allow the possibility of considerable success.

Figure 13.6 Classic direct 'straight sell' ad

Source: Reproduced by kind permission of Time Group Limited.

i want

A TOP CLASS PC ON MY DESK AS SOON AS POSSIBLE. THAT'S IN *days* NOT *weeks*. I HAVEN'T GOT TIME TO WORRY ABOUT INSTALLATION. I NEED SOMEONE TO TAKE CARE OF ALL THAT FOR ME. NATURALLY, I WANT TO ORDER IT OVER THE PHONE AND IT'S GOT TO HAVE THE LATEST SOFTWARE. I ALSO WANT A FULL ON-SITE WARRANTY BACKED-UP WITH TECHNICAL SUPPORT FROM PEOPLE WHO REALLY KNOW (AND CARE ABOUT) WHAT THEY'RE DOING. BUT I DON'T EXPECT TO PAY A PENNY TO GET

it up and running

THE NEW COMPAQ PRESARIO 2212
(HOME & OFFICE).
THE COMPLETE PC PACKAGE.

- 180 MHz PROCESSOR
- 16 MB TOTAL SYSTEM MEMORY
- 1.6 GB HARD DISK
- 8 x CD ROM DRIVE
- 14" MONITOR
- 3.5" FLOPPY DISK
- 33.6/14.4 DATA/FAX MODEM, UPGRADEABLE TO 56K*
- KEYBOARD, MOUSE, INTEGRATED SPEAKERS
- MICROSOFT® OFFICE 97 SMALL BUSINESS EDITION PRELOADED: EXCEL 97, WORD 97, SMALL BUSINESS FINANCIAL MANAGER 97, OUTLOOK™ 97, PUBLISHER 97, AUTOROUTE EXPRESS™ GREAT BRITAIN, INTERNET EXPLORER 3.0
- MULTIMEDIA BUNDLE INCLUDING ENCARTA® 97 WORLD ATLAS

- **FREE** DELIVERY TO YOUR HOME OR OFFICE WITHIN 3 WORKING DAYS**.
- **FREE** INSTALLATION (UNPACKED, SET UP AND CHECKED BY AN AUTHORISED TECHNICIAN).
- **FREE** YEAR'S ON-SITE WARRANTY.
- **FREE** ONE YEAR CUSTOMER SERVICE AND SUPPORT†.

ONLY £899+VAT
(£1,056 INC VAT**).**

OR FROM **ONLY £32.90** (INC VAT)
(15.9% FIXED APR) PER MONTH††.
TO PLACE YOUR ORDER
CALL US **DIRECT** ON:

0800 611 722

LINES OPEN 8AM – 8.30PM MONDAY TO FRIDAY.
9AM – 5.30PM SATURDAY AND SUNDAY. PLEASE QUOTE CQ5803.

COMPAQ DELIVERS MORE

COMPAQ.

Figure 13.7 Branded sell ad

Source: Courtesy HP UK.

Martin Troughton and his team were presenting to the Foreign and Colonial board. By chance the board also contained the chairwoman of the World Gold Council. The WGC exists to ensure the price of gold remains buoyant by lobbying governments. She explained to Martin that WGC had a problem. Gordon Brown, then UK Chancellor, wanted to shift the reserves from gold to currency (Dollars, Euros and Yen). Could they change his mind?

↓

So she gave the agency £100,000 with a brief to make things 'uncomfortable' for the Chancellor and raise awareness of the sell-off. They decided to use direct response press adverts but needed a strong idea.

↓

The creatives sat down and kicked around ideas. Gold itself . . . it's very heavy, it looks distinctive. Very unlike paper money. The team wanted to generate anger: why swap gold for mere paper? This thinking led to the headline:

↓

'If you can tell the difference between Gold and Paper tell us'

↓

The call to respond generated 70,000 protestors. MPs were written to, a petition was delivered to Downing Street. One week before the sell off the WGC came back to Martin: do us a poster outside the Houses of Parliament please. The team checked: no poster allowed! What could they do?

↓

There was a river . . . Someone suggested a barge flowing past Parliament. The barge reminded the team of scrap metal . . . that's it! We'll do a 'Gordon Brown scrap metal sell off' stunt! Production bought a load of junk metal for £600, hired a barge, painted the scrap using gold spray and gold wrapping paper. They hired a PR firm to tip off the press. This is what happened:

CLIENT: WORLD GOLD COUNCIL   CAMPAIGN NAME: "SCRAP METAL BARGE"

The World Gold Council approached us to organise opposition to Chancellor Gordon Brown's plans to sell off half the UK's gold reserves. ⇨ At the time, public awareness was minimal. So we created an old scrap metal barge and piled it high with gold painted scrap – cars, fridges, bikes etc. Then we erected the 96 sheet poster you see in the photograph. At noon (when the first sale began) we moored it outside the House of Commons. ⇨ The barge appeared on the Channel 4 news that evening. It also featured on the hour, every hour on Sky News throughout the day. The following day it appeared in national and international papers. ⇨ In combination with a small budget press campaign it generated over 70,000 responses and an estimated £800,000 worth of publicity. All for just £7,000.

Figure 13.8 World Gold Council – scrap-metal barge

Source: Courtesy ITN Source (left); Harrison Troughton Wunderman (top, middle); Sky News (bottom middle); Financial Times (right).

Exhibit 13.6 Creative 'rules' versus originality

Rules

Many people ask, 'How can creative practice be set by 'rules' of what to do? Surely creativity, by definition, cannot be rule bound?' Here's what David Ogilvy had to say in his brilliant book, *Ogilvy on Advertising* (1983):

> I am sometimes attacked for imposing rules. Nothing could be further from the truth. I hate rules. All I do is report on how consumers react to creative. I may say to a copywriter, 'Research shows that commercials with celebrities are below average in persuading people to use a product. Are you sure you want to use a celebrity?'

In other words, Ogilvy believed in 'guidelines' – rules that can be broken, provided there is a good reason to do so.

Originality

Respected advertisers like Bird and Ogilvy have warned against the cult of originality. Bird in particular warned against 'irrelevant originality', which wins awards and sells nothing. There are many great adverts that owe nothing to originality.

Ogilvy started his career by copying. Later he moved on to original work. He saw no problem in admitting this in his book (Ogilvy, 1983). Ogilvy often quoted Mozart, who said: 'I have never made the slightest effort to compose anything original.'

The agency HTW worked on a brief for the World Gold Council. Figure 13.8 shows what happened.

There are almost as many formulas for helping you to dream up a new idea as there are direct marketing writers. Most of them seem to agree on the main issue, however, although Ogilvy (1983) probably put it most forcefully. He and the others were quick to extinguish the romantic notion that brilliant ideas will effortlessly fall into a creative's mind as if by an act of God. Their view is summed up by the old adage:

'Genius is 99 per cent perspiration, 1 per cent inspiration.'

(Thomas Edison)

The 'perspiration' in advertising is the hard work of researching the product and the market exhaustively. World class creatives see the client's creative brief as only the first step in acquiring knowledge on the marketing problem.

Bird (2007) proposed a three-step process for producing creative ideas (see Exhibit 13.7).

Exhibit 13.7 Where ideas come from

Drayton Bird offers the following advice in his book, *Commonsense Direct Marketing*:

1 **Master your subject.** Become thoroughly familiar with your product/service and customers. Find out the truth about your marketing situation. 'Your imagination will never dream up anything to beat the truth.'
2 **The inner game.** Once the ideas are in, let your subconscious take over. 'Don't try to force ideas and they will pop out, probably while you are doing something else.'

> **3 Use sounding boards.** When you have an idea, expose it to your colleagues, however painful this might be. The chances are they will see things you can't, maybe because you have got too close to the problem.
>
> Bird's final piece of advice on this subject is salutary: 'Lead an interesting life! Don't be dull!'

On a similar note, Nash (1995) offered three secrets of advertising. They are 'research, research and research'. He explained that meaty copy – lots of anecdotes and examples, intimate details about the service or product that are more convincing than bland claims – is good copy. He then suggested that, after the hard work of research, you should do the following: think, 'dump' (that is, get everything in your head down on to paper), write up and, finally, 'make it sing!' Don't say a book is entertaining: give an example of the humour. Don't talk of the need for strategy: give a strategy.

Harrison (2009) describes a five stage process:

1 Gather as much information as possible.

2 Chew it over to get your first ideas out of your system.

3 Stop thinking about the subject and let your subconscious go to work.

4 Be ready for the ideas to flow at any time.

5 Shape and develop the ideas for practical usefulness.

The process of creating an advert is greatly helped by the use of one of the available frameworks. One useful framework is the 'AIDA model', which we will follow in detail a little later. First we can cover 'practitioner frameworks' and the 'consumer buying process'.

13.4.2 Practitioner frameworks

There are plenty of alternative frameworks offering a structure for creating a direct-response advert. These have been mainly conjured up by practitioners and, although they may not have any particular academic basis, they are based on a lifetime's practice of advert creation and testing. It is, therefore, well worthwhile repeating two such frameworks here, outlined in the following exhibits. They are Nash's Five Ss, and Stone's seven-step formula for copywriting.

Exhibit 13.8 Where does great creative come from?

An interview with Frazer Howard

'We don't produce ideas in a vacuum: great creative starts with the client'. So says Frazer Howard, Creative Director of EHS Brann, a large DM and interactive agency based near Bristol in England. What is the start of the process? 'I always say that great creative is like panning for gold' says Frazer. 'The McCann Erickson definition of advertising is "truth well told". Clients and agency can work together to find these little bits of truth. Look at the recent American Airlines campaign (late 2007). A tiny bit of data from the client powered

---

an entire multi-million dollar campaign. At a client presentation, someone at the agency noticed that AA flew more New Yorkers than any other airline. The idea that New Yorkers were more demanding than most consumers grew into the campaign that if AA can keep New Yorkers happy, it will probably keep you happy as well . . . .'

'Beware the kitchen door syndrome,' says Frazer. What's that? 'Ask someone – "Do you know what colour your kitchen door is? Yes of course. What is it then? Err . . . ." The point is that people don't notice stuff that is under their nose day in day out. Clients know loads of things about their business that becomes wallpaper, invisible to them. But these are often the nuggets, the "gold" creatives are looking for. Clients are very immersed. The agency job may be to take them out of that immersion for a moment and take a step back. One of our clients is Volvo. In the old days the Volvo dealers would think "show them the metal" would be enough to sell the car, but life has got more competitive.' How did you help turn that round? 'Well, the market perception is that other marques have caught up on the safety front. But Volvo still leads the way, so we wanted to re-establish that. We watched videos of their safety tests and they even tested on dummies of pregnant women. Talk about going the extra mile. So, the idea became "To Volvo the unborn child is already a passenger". We used this on our acquisition work. Direct mail included items like "mum to be on board" safety rear stickers. These ended up for sale on eBay at £2.50 each! For the dads we had "imagine having the best pushchair in the playground", humorous and ironic but struck a chord. We needed to aim at mothers and fathers together because there's some good research suggesting that men do most of the searching about but women often make the final decision on cars.'

'So – good research is worth its weight in gold. Ideas don't come in a vacuum. Back to our work with Volvo once again. Volvo have a good foothold in the fleet (business) market. To compete with the bigger players Volvo have developed a high quality service offering day-to-day management of the fleet on behalf the client. The fleet managers are very busy and need help – their lives are often hassled in solving day-to-day problems. They work in a busy office environment. Now, the point is that business-to-business direct marketing is often consumed in such an office environment where stuff is picked over and kicked about the office. So the team devised a mailing campaign with the idea "How can Volvo make your everyday life that little bit easier? What if you had a magical key on your computer keyboard to make your hassles disappear." The team devised fun stickers to place on colleagues keyboards in the office. So, stickers like "Undo last night", "Order massage", "CTRL temper", "Create evil twin" and so on were created. The idea was a fun way to dramatise Volvo's extra help, but based on the knowledge that having a bit of fun in the office is very important.'

Some of the work Frazer is most proud of came with the charity 'Practical Action'.

Practical action

Practical Action works to alleviate poverty around the world. Its slogan is 'technology challenging poverty'. At the start of 2007, agency EHS Brann organised a day listening to a few of the project workers, based in Peru and Kenya, who had got together. One of them, Lucy, worked in Kenya. She began 'I've spent the last six months in Kitale which as you know is famous for its flying toilets and we . . .'. 'Hang on, what was that about flying toilets?' This little exchange led to an extremely successful campaign. The extremely poor sanitation conditions in Kitale had led the locals to devise a way to cope, which was to 'go' in a plastic bag and then throw it out of the window – flying toilets. The agency devised a fundraising campaign with an envelope 'flying toilet enclosed'. Inside the envelope a plastic bag was included as a way of dramatising the problem.

Someone at the agency also suggested that 'flying toilet' had shades of a Monty Python sketch about it. It was known that Terry Jones of Monty Python fame was a strong supporter of charities. He was approached and became the signatory on the campaign – this worked well with the key audience of 50–55-year-old men for whom Monty Python were heroes.

The moral of the story is that there is no substitute for talking to the people who are at the front line. EHS Brann worked hard with Practical Action to get the best insights. Creative Director Frazer Howard went to Kenya, while the MD, Alison, took time out to go to Zimbabwe. There she met a grandmother looking after her grandchildren with 25 people living in tiny houses. Each morning she counted her charges to make sure one had not been kidnapped. This led to the idea of an envelope with the counting rhyme '1,2,3,4,5 once I caught a fish alive' . . . etc. adapted for the fundraising idea.

Some exhibits of work done for Practical Action by EHS Brann include the following:

Exhibit 13.9 Stone's seven-step formula for good copywriting

1 Promise your biggest benefit in your headline.
2 In the copy, immediately enlarge on your most important benefit.
3 Tell readers specifically what they are going to get.

4 Back up your statements with proof and endorsements.

5 Tell readers what they might lose if they don't act.

6 Rephrase your prominent benefits in your closing offer.

7 Incite action. Now.

Exhibit 13.10 Nash's five Ss for a direct marketing advertisement

1 Give a headline or picture that people notice.

2 **Show 'em.** Use visual images to communicate powerfully.

3 **Seduce 'em.** Appeal to higher psychological needs than just the basic product needs: emotion, self-image, changing the world.

4 **Satisfy 'em.** Show how the product fulfils their needs.

5 **Sell 'em.** Ask for the order.

13.4.3 The consumer buying process

From an academic standpoint, what we need is a theoretical framework that allows us to understand what the job of a direct-response advert is. Consumer behaviour models were divided by Foxall and Goldsmith (1994) into 'high-involvement' purchases and 'low-involvement' purchases. Remember the FCB grid we discussed earlier (Vaughan, 1980)? This showed high- and low-involvement examples of different creative practice. In direct marketing, we have been more concerned with high-involvement models because we tend to deal with higher price ticket purchases (cars, mortgages) in which the consumer goes through a significant decision-making process. However, the scope of direct marketing has expanded into 'low involvement sectors' such as food marketing, where the decision to buy may be impulsive or routine.

So, we need guides – models – that explain how consumers respond to marketing activities. AIDA has been mentioned earlier (awareness-interest-desire-action) model. This model has been used since the 1930s, and remains in active use today. It is useful in mimicking the process that consumers go through when buying high-involvement products that require a logical, thinking approach to their purchase. But as we alluded to earlier, the AIDA model has been criticised by some theorists as assuming too rational a consumer. As we saw earlier, consumers make decisions on emotional grounds as well as rational grounds. So, we need an expanded 'choice of models' to take us forward. Let us go back to the FCB grid. Figure 13.9 illustrates the product sector (rational emotional/high–low involvement) and this author's view of the best guidance models in each instance.

In a moment we will take a detailed walk through how direct marketers might use the AIDA model, as this helps us understand many of the 'tricks of the trade' in creative practice. Before we do, let us take note of the other FCB grid boxes.

Routine purchases – low involvement, thinking segment

For low involvement, routine purchases like washing powder, baby nappies (diapers) or cereal, Ehrenberg proposed that consumers absorb advertising to become aware of a brand,

	Thinking	Feeling
High involvement	Learn-feel-do Home computing: Dell Model to use: Awareness ➤ interest ➤ desire ➤ action	Feel-learn-do Fashion, make-up: Dior Model to use: (based on Rossiter-Percy model) Motive + emotional sequence ➤ action
Low involvement	Do-learn-feel Routine household items: Procter & Gamble Model to use: Awareness ➤ trial ➤ retrial	Do-feel-learn Instant pleasure goods: Cadbury, Budweiser Model to use: (based on Rossiter-Percy model) Action + motive + emotional sequence are concurrent

Figure 13.9 The FCB grid

Source: The author, based on the FCB grid (Vaughan, 1980).

then will perhaps try it for themselves and, if satisfied, rebuy with little thought. Here, the role of a direct marketing creative will be to reinforce existing behaviours with appropriate benefit led messages. Reminders will be the key here.

Instant pleasure goods – low involvement, feeling segment

You have had a hard day. You stop off at the garage to fill up. Waiting to pay, you spot that swirling purple colour of the Cadbury Fruit and Nut chocolate bar. Your decision is instant – one of those please. You deserve it – a little treat. This is the kind of decision making that goes on with most of us, often a few times each day. Direct marketing cannot predict these moments, but it can serve to help lodge attractive emotional messages with us, or to give us tangible reminders with neat creative devices like quizzes or involvement devices. The Rossiter–Percy model suggests identifying the key motive – for an instant chocolate treat it could be basic sensory gratification – then linking this motive to an emotional sequence:

Motive	Emotional sequence
sensory gratification	unstimulated ➤ sensory excitement

and this guides the creative treatment.

High involvement, feeling segment

Here we might be talking about our 'going out' clothes, a sports motorbike or a luxury holiday. The high margins on goods like these mean a lot of marketing spend is possible. Direct marketing creative can support the brand values with, for instance, expensive, high-quality paper for a mailer, or high-ticket photography for a website. The lead taken by emotions means that again the Rossiter–Percy model may be useful here: but more attention, more effort, and more emotion is deployed because of the high-involvement, high-importance sectors. So, in buying a sports motorbike:

Motive	Emotional sequence
attention seeking	disappointment ➤ pride

The remaining box is the 'high involvement, thinking' segment. Let us investigate how the well-known AIDA model helps direct marketers plan their creative.

13.4.4 The awareness, interest, desire, action (AIDA) model

(Direct) marketers have used the well-known AIDA model as perhaps the simplest way of helping explain how (direct-response) adverts work (Smith, 1993). First constructed in 1928, the Awareness, Interest, Desire and Action model is still popular as a way of explaining how we notice, internalise and respond to advertising. It is particularly important to help explain direct-response advertising, because direct response is primarily about getting the prospect from awareness through to action (response) 'all within the one advert'.

Taking each of the headings in turn, the following section describes the key elements of creative that take the prospect from awareness to action. It is important to understand the limitations of this approach before we proceed, however.

In line with Foxall and Goldsmith's comments on consumer decision-making processes, the AIDA framework is probably most realistic when applied to high-involvement products such as financial services, holidays or cars. It may be less relevant to impulse purchases.

Most of the following guidelines refer to the written media: mail, press, inserts and door drops. Many of the principles outlined are also relevant to the broadscale media and the telephone, but guidelines will vary. For more information, you are referred to one of the specialist creative texts suggested in the reference section.

Awareness

The moment of truth is nearly at hand. Your mailer lands on the mat. Your full-page press ad lies there on page 7, between the feature on cooking and the TV guide. Your insert falls out onto the hallway floor. The first crucial question is: will it get the audience's attention? To some extent this depends on the medium, the offer and so on, but the chances of you succeeding also lie with the quality of your creative.

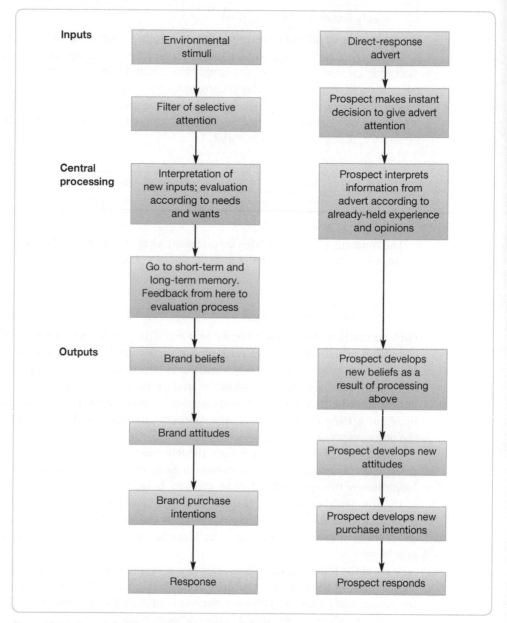

Figure 13.10 A model of consumer decision making
Source: Adapted from Foxall and Goldsmith (1994). Reprinted with permission.

Exhibit 13.11 Getting attention: tricks of the trade

- In e-mail the subject line is key. A good subject will improve open rates dramatically.
- In direct mail, outer envelope messages get attention by playing on curiosity: 'You start telling a story, then just when it gets interesting you . . . (please see inside).' According to Bird, envelope messages work because they encourage those who are interested to get into the envelope right away. It puts off uninterested people, which does not matter.

- In print and display advertising, 'eye camera' tests have shown the eye settles around the middle of the page. Ogilvy advises that you put the headline under the picture, not above it. This will lift response.
- In direct mail, attention getting devices are sometimes used. Tricks like plastic cards with the consumer's name on can increase response by as much as 70 per cent, according to Bird. He reported a very successful mailer in which a plastic frog that hopped out with a message: 'Hop it! Act now!' was used to get the attention of businesspeople.

The job can be likened to a person in a crowd trying to attract someone's attention some way away. This may explain why the two key tools used to attract attention in all written direct marketing media are the 'headline' and the 'picture'. Research done by using cameras to follow readers' eye movements has shown that the eye is attracted to an advert by these two main elements.

Headlines

When writing a direct-response press advert, what is the role of the headline? Given that the average broadsheet paper has 350 headlines, the primary job of the headline is to stop the reader from moving on. A similar role for headlines can also be envisaged in other media: direct mail, door drops or inserts.

If you concentrate your headline around the self-interest of your reader, maybe promise some news, or arouse their curiosity with something unexpected, you will be on the right lines. Additonally, think about the following:

1 **Maximise your chances of hitting the right audience.** Bob Stone underscored the pragmatism of direct response with his principle that out of 100 potential readers or viewers of the advert, only a very few are prime prospects to buy. Therefore, although it is tempting to write a highly creative headline that may catch the eye of many readers, it is better to make sure that you definitely catch the prime prospects by laying out clearly what it is you have to sell.

2 **Promise a benefit.** Stone revealed more details of typical benefits, emotional and rational, which may appeal to the self-interest of readers. He outlined two kinds of benefits. First, the obvious type related to the product; for example, Stephen Hawking's book, *A Brief History of Time,* is a quick way to satisfy one's curiosity about how the universe is formed. Second, we should consider a deeper benefit, related to possible emotional reasons for purchase; for example, Hawking's book will enable the buyer to sound well educated in front of their friends.

The following examples are based on Stone's ideas. Suppose we are selling a recruitment agency service. We could concentrate on the following benefits:

1 **Health.** 'Is your current job making you ill?'
2 **Money.** 'You're undervalued at work, right? Up your salary by £10K . . .'
3 **Security.** 'These days it's hard to feel safe, but 80 per cent of our clients feel more secure in the post we found them.'
4 **Pride.** 'Do you yearn for the job that will make your friends look at you with envy?'
5 **Enjoyment.** 'You spend half your life there. So for God's sake enjoy it. Get a new job with . . .'

6 **Excitement.** 'Remember the last time you woke up with that thrill of wondering what the day at work will bring. You can't? Maybe we can help . . .'

Finally, Ogilvy offers the following advice for writing winning headlines:

1 **Offer helpful information**. 'How to win friends and influence people.'

2 **Specify your audience in the headline or picture**. 'Do you live in a detached house?'

3 **Be specific.** Not 'Save money with us' but 'Save £12.50 every time you buy a pair of shoes'. It's more credible.

Exhibit 13.12 Soundbite headlines

'I want to be tough on crime; tough on the causes of crime.'

Why do soundbites work? Why use little jokes or plays on words as a headline or strapline? Because soundbites or straplines are retained in our short-term memory very easily and are associated there with other chunks of information in the mind, forming weakly held beliefs about a brand. When it comes to purchase we then recall these feelings and they can have a big say in the product choice.

In direct-response adverts leading straight to purchase, it may not be necessary to use soundbites, since we are trying to convince the prospect to act straightaway.

Illustrations

In the past, direct marketers have used visuals much less than have brand advertisers. As Stone points out, however, nowadays this may be a mistake in many markets. He found that the 'rules of the game' for direct mail changed considerably in the 1990s, as direct marketing communication's role in the marketing mix expanded. He identified two key changes:

1 **Copy has become shorter and better.** The 'TV generation' is less inclined to stay with a company if it does not get its message across very quickly.

2 **More visuals are being used.** There are three benefits to advertisers of using illustrations:

1 Brand advertisers have known for a long time that 'pictures can communicate more quickly and possibly more forcefully than copy'. Direct marketers in recent years have increased their use of pictures quite considerably.

2 Illustrations are crucial as attention getters within a direct-response advert because, compared to copy, 'visuals are easy to look at and take in'. Taking websites as an example, research has found that many readers will look at the picture on a site but not move on to copy.

3 A number of writers (Nash, 1995; Bird, 2007; and Jones, 1992) have emphasised the importance of visuals in 'communicating the positioning' of the product or service. This is explained in Exhibit 13.13.

Exhibit 13.13 Semiotics: the hidden science of signs

A product can be quickly repositioned, moving it upmarket or downmarket, without changing any of the words, by the use of simple visual signs.

Typefaces are important. Ogilvy used a classic serif typeface in his advert for Rolls Royce to convey elegance and a sense of history.

Production values, such as the thickness of paper and the use of models or actors in photos, will all make a huge difference. It is easy to see that using Jeremy Paxman *Newsnight* presenter, rather than, for example, a game show host, will move the position of a brand upmarket.

All these apparently minor changes are very important because people want to buy products that reflect their self-image, and the picture gives hugely powerful clues to people about whether the product is 'for them'.

Naturally, words can also be used powerfully to change a product's position. If we change 'Now's your chance to win!' to 'By an act of serendipity, an opportunity befalls you', we have altered the whole feel of the advert.

Exhibit 13.14 outlines a number of art directors' 'tricks of the trade'.

Interest

Most people who glance at an advert in the press or a banner ad on-line do not go on to read the body copy. The average readership of body copy in magazines is about 5 per cent. In daily newspapers it is even lower at about 1 per cent. With direct or e-mail, prospects may glance at the top line then discard.

However, this does not matter as long as the highest possible number of good prospects have noticed the advert. Unlike brand advertisers, direct marketers do not need to appeal to a mass audience, just those who are considering purchasing in their product sector.

Exhibit 13.14 Tricks of the trade: art direction

The lessons from classical mail order should not be lost. Experts like Nash (1995) recommended choosing models who are a little thinner, wealthier, younger or wiser looking than the target audience. People want to see themselves represented by what they want to be, not the reality of what they actually are. If you are marketing to retired people, use models who are 55–65, not over 65.

Cycles seem to exist in advertising art direction and copy. Look at the e-mailers you get from a particular sector, or look at TV adverts. It is clear that a lot of copycatting goes on!

Ogilvy (1983) offered the following guidelines for print advertising, which still seem to be relevant today:

- Pictures that arouse curiosity are the most powerful. Ogilvy described this as 'story appeal'. Faces and eyes in particular attract attention. A lot of children's charities use children's 'big eyes' in attracting attention.
- People want to see people with whom they can identify and to whom they can aspire. If you put a man in the picture, women may ignore it, and *vice versa*.
- Of all illustrative forms, cartoons will attract the most attention; but direct-response marketers have found that photographs pull the biggest response.

At the 'interest' stage, the prospects are looking at your advert with their curiosity aroused. They are looking for something of interest. The next requirement of the advert is to foster that interest by building on the primary benefit you presented in the headline or picture.

What has to be borne in mind here is that the reader/viewer is always looking for a reason to stop reading and move on to something else. It is an effort to read; your prospect will constantly evaluate whether it is worth it. The job of the copy is to keep them reading through to the end by making it very difficult not to read on.

There are a number of ways of creating and keeping the reader's interest:

Artwork/layout

1 Whether in a mailer, press or on a website, the principles are the same. Lead the reader naturally from the headline/picture to the copy, building up interest.

2 Dropped capitals make entering the copy easier on the eye.

3 Use a short first paragraph. It is less intimidating.

Copy

1 Help the reader into your advert with bullets, arrowheads or asterisks.

2 Break up the copy on a website with interactive features such as clickable links or videos.

3 Highlight key phrases with italics or bold type.

4 According to Bird, busy layouts outpull neat ones. They seem to add interest.

5 Write short sentences and short paragraphs. Use simple words.

6 Ogilvy advises copywriters to stay away from bragging with unsubstantiated 'our product is the best' copy. In his view, such claims are very unconvincing.

7 Give people reasons to buy; cut off their reasons not to buy. Lead them through the argument so that by the end they have no choice but to buy.

8 Expand on the product benefits. The more you can present the better.

Exhibit 13.15 Appealing to the audience's needs

Here are just some benefits that can be highlighted: independence, importance, fame, wealth, popularity, sex and romance, love and affection, not being lonely, excitement, variety, happiness, helping others, making progress, security, having a change, fitting in, gaining respect, pride in performance, feeling good through looking good, enjoyment of humour, feeling smarter, getting 'one over', being energetic, aesthetic pleasures such as food or art.

---

9 Present your message as news. Presenting something as news appeals to our sense of curiosity. We also have a desire to keep up to date. News feeds both these elements of psychology.

10 Tell a story. Charities often use this technique to highlight the human interest in what they are doing. Amnesty International has won a number of awards with its powerful, shocking and compelling copy detailing atrocities throughout the world (see Figure 13.11). This brands Amnesty as a serious organisation confronting these issues head-on.

11 Personalise your copy. At a fairly trivial level, personalisation works because we like seeing our own name. However, personalisation can be taken well beyond just merging the name and address of the individual into a standard letter. True personalisation means tailoring the message to include details unique to that individual. This would reflect a 'one-to-one strategy', as outlined previously (Chapter 6).

Figure 13.11 Amnesty advert using hard-hitting copy

Source: Reproduced by kind permission of Amnesty International.

> ### Exhibit 13.16 Practitioners' views on long versus short copy
>
> 'Good copy takes you by the hand and leads you gently from where you are to where the advertiser wants you to be.'
>
> (Schwab, 1985)
>
> Ogilvy (1983) always maintained that long copy worked better in direct-response press ads. Nash (1995), however, took the view that short copy is better. He quoted Victor Schwab: 'Tell me quick and tell me true, or else my love, to hell with you.' Nash asserted that the old style '49 reasons why you should buy this product' approaches no longer work. He is probably right in most cases given the extent of copycatting of product features by competitors.
>
> Bird (2007), a believer in long copy, felt that persuasion rarely came through brevity.
>
> Stone (1996) asserted that modern times demand shorter copy because the amount that people read has lessened.
>
> McCorkell (1994) took the commonsense view that, if marketers can still edit their copy without detracting from the power of the sales message, then it is too long!

Involvement devices

Involvement devices include scratch-off cards, clickable links, on-line games, toys, quizzes, stickers, half-completed elements which the reader completes, and 'highlight' devices like coins or bits of product.

Involvement devices are commonly associated with traditional direct marketing sectors such as book clubs, subscriptions, collectibles, weight watchers and so on. These 'direct marketing led' companies have ruthlessly tested the use of involvement devices in their campaigns, and the results speak for themselves. Involvement devices in these markets raise response. As Drayton Bird puts it, 'Why are they used? Because they work!'

The idea of involvement – inviting the prospect to actively do something – has reached new popularity with website marketing. Websites are ideal for interactivity.

However, there is a lot of resistance to the use of involvement devices among sectors like financial services companies, car companies and so on. This resistance is largely down to perceptions among marketers that such devices will damage their brands because of a perceived downmarket image. Traditional direct marketers argue that this premise is unproven.

So should mainstream market sectors make more use of involvement devices than they do at present? *Prima facie*, these devices do not fit very well with a serious brand/product category. However, there are increasing examples of strongly branded companies using involvement devices successfully, as Tango showed with its 'helpline' for consumers. This 'fun' approach worked very well; after one ad, Tango generated over 300,000 calls to this 'helpline'! Guinness has taken on such ideas with an excellent website full of ideas on how to engage people.

Finally, let us note that these devices, including toys, quizzes and stickers, are commonly used in business-to-business mailers, often aimed at 'senior' managers . . . with great success!

Practitioners have claimed a variety of psychological drivers underpinning the success of involvement devices. Some examples are:

1 **Scratch-off cards, executive toys.** 'Within every person there is a child, and that child likes to play' (Nash, 1995).

2 **Quizzes.** Practitioners claim that these work because we love the chance to test or show off our knowledge, even to ourselves.

3 **Completion.** It is felt that some people have a compulsive desire to obtain order. Picture yourself in front of a jigsaw, nearly complete with one piece lying close by waiting to be placed. How many could resist completing the jigsaw? There is a great deal of pleasure, aesthetic satisfaction, in completion.

4 **Making choices.** Many people enjoy making choices, especially when they feel they are getting a bargain. This is the basis for the 'Which three books do you want for a pound?' type of offer.

Desire/conviction

At the interest stage, the prospect is still hedging their bets. The frame of mind is one of appraisal, which tends to be made on a logical, calculating basis.

Desire is different. Here, your prospect has started to have some 'emotional feeling' for the product or service. They start to 'imagine' what it is like to own or experience what you are selling; they picture this happening. With desire, emotion takes over from logic and the powerful motivations leading towards a sale are in place.

The point of good creative is that it triggers and then fosters these emotional feelings. Emotional benefits are linked with the product: looking good, arousing envy in your friends, being successful, having control and so on.

The flip side of accentuating positive benefits is the reassurance required that the buying decision will be a good one. Here, 'conviction' is the required emotion for your prospect. You must convince them that they have nothing to fear, that you are trustworthy, that your product will be what you say it is in the advert. Above all, you must convince them that they are getting value for money.

Desire and conviction are built using the following techniques:

Testimonials

Ogilvy quoted James Webb Young, one of the best copywriters in history: 'Everybody in advertising has the same problem: to be believed.' Social media can amplify this basic principle.

Description

Bird extolled the use of words in such a way as to arouse desire: 'thick cream on scrumptious puddings'. This is also true of the incentive: 'Imagine winning a holiday in the Caribbean. Feel the tension release as the warm sand trickles between your toes, you hear the clink of the ice in your drink and the sea gently slides its way up the shore.' Alternatively show the experience on your YouTube channel or allow your customers to share their experiences via review sites and social media.

Tone

Bird advised making sure that the tone is appropriate; do not overstate by using 'fantastic, tremendous, superb' and so on *ad nauseum*.

Illustrations/pictures/videos

To trigger emotional feelings, pictures or video are often very powerful. Here the role of the art director is key. The art director helps to identify pictorial ways of communicating themes related to emotions, fantasy and self image. People want to be able to associate the product with themselves.

A lot of emotional messages have much more credibility with people if they are communicated visually rather than in the written word. For example, a picture of the use of perfume making a model feel younger and sexier would be completely natural. However, imagine a headline explaining that you can feel sexier with perfume. This would be ridiculous.

An important part of arousing desire is ensuring the product fits in with the self-image of the buyer. The most powerful way of doing this is through pictures. Off- and on-line retailers know that the choice of models in their catalogues or on their sites is critical to sales; consumers want to identify with the models. Take a look at **warbyparker.com.** This is one of many websites giving prospective customers the chance to see how the product looks on them before they buy.

Building credibility and trust

Well-known powerful brands such as British Airways should not have any trouble obtaining trust from prospects. A small on-line retail operation asking for cash with order is in a very different situation. It may use:

- testimonials from peers who have endorsed the product
- reviews on review sites and in social media
- famous personalities who have bought the product to endorse it
- the fact that it has advertised publicly, 'As advertised on TV', in its merchandising

Action

There are two creative strands to generating action. One is to emphasise the need to act straight away; the other is to minimise the effort required.

Encouraging immediacy

You have the reader's attention. You stimulated their interest through well worked copy and layout. You triggered their desire with pictures showing the emotional benefits of your product. You must now seize the moment! You must inspire action. Many authors (e.g. Nash, 1995) report an old saying in direct marketing: 'Delay kills response.' If your prospect puts down the advert, or the checkout page takes too long to load, or you give the prospect the chance to log off the website and maybe to look at it another time, the chances are the sale is lost. Direct and Internet marketers use various creative techniques that maximise the sense that time is short:

- Creative exhortations to be urgent, strongly allied to an offer that rewards urgency (for example, 'Limited edition product', or 'Free gift if you reply in ten days')
- Creative approaches that emphasise the urgent need for the product ('Act now to avoid paying/discomfort/loss later' approaches may be appropriate for products such as antifreeze, roof coating or children's school clothes)
- Simply telling the consumer what you want them to do in clear terms (Nash describes this as 'command terminology'; e.g. 'Send it now', 'Act straightaway' and so on)
- A sense of immediacy (this is most easily done on-line where firms like **lastminute.com** will trade on the idea that you can catch a bargain by being in the market at the right time).

Minimising effort: making it easy to respond

Direct and website marketers are past masters at making it easy for customers to respond. Consumers increasingly look for more convenient ways of living their lives; this is one of the main reasons for the growth of direct marketing. Given that buying is a function of reward divided by effort, marketers should minimise the effort involved in purchase. Thirty years ago, buyer and seller would have exchanged polite, courteous and well-written letters acknowledging the sale. No longer!

Direct marketers make it easy for consumers to respond using websites, telephone and credit cards. These have had a massive influence in driving the growth of direct marketing. Most mail-order companies now offer Web and telephone alternatives for ordering, and the trend towards the use of the telephone increases. Stating in the advert that credit cards are accepted, and using the credit card logos, Visa, Access, and so on, will raise response. Credit cards are extremely popular, and the brand names will enhance credibility. Paypal, Worldpay and other payment systems also help this on-line. Freephone numbers are worth prominent display; they enhance credibility and are popular. Forte Hotels once used 0800 40 40 40 in its direct-response TV adverts. Amazon 1-Click is a good example of how this can work on-line.

13.4.5 Putting it all together: layout

Nash (1995) outlined what he called the Five Cs of layout. These apply to both on-line and off-line creative work:

1 **Concentration.** A small-space ad with one large element in it will get more attention than a large-space ad with no large element in it. For example, a small press ad with a bold headline 'How to be happier' will be more eye-catching than a large article next to it without a headline.

2 **Cohesion.** Each element of the execution – the headline, picture, caption, body copy and coupon – should lead to each other rather than to the outside of the ad. In on-line work this applies equally to elements with, for example, a Web page and the way that the navigation of a site is designed.

3 **Convention.** As children we are taught that certain shapes have certain meanings; for example, a pencil is always recognised by its shape. These conventions are locked in our minds very strongly and, if a picture goes against these conventions, we get confused. Devices such as reversed-out copy, white on black, will lower response because we are not used to reading this way. Similarly, certain typefaces have greater credibility. For example, times new roman appears authoritative and handwritten signatures look more credible, and this is why in certain instances they work to drive response. Contrary to popular belief, handwritten-style signatures are not used because they fool readers into believing they have had a letter personally signed by the chairperson. They are used because that is what convention demands.

4 **Contrast.** The first law of layout is 'to be noticed'. Your ad must stand out from its environment. However, a balance needs to be struck between getting noticed and swamping the sales message. The best way to get noticed is through some creative way of enhancing the benefits of your product. A truth told in an interesting way is perhaps one definition of advertising. One radio advertisement, sponsored by the government, used long periods of 'silence', punctuated by a voice explaining how much the advert cost per second, to dramatise how money was wasted through heat loss in buildings! This ad worked because of the contrast it created with adverts played before and after. Getting noticed is one thing, however, being relevant is yet another.

5 **Convection.** Flow, or convect, the reader from one element to the other, from the headline to the coupon. Ogilvy, a master of print advertising, recommended the following ways of keeping the reader moving through the advert:
   - Use columns of 35 to 45 characters.
   - Use drop capitals to start your body copy.

- Captions are widely read – use them.
- Subheadings that break up the body copy are a good idea.
- Direct the reader to the coupon at every opportunity – (Nash recommends that when writing an advert you should start with the coupon).

In the on-line world this applies equally. Browsers are usually scanning text on websites, looking for relevant content and relevant links. So make it easy on them. The rules for engagement and readability have been evolving since print was invented. Largely the rules for copy and design off-line are replicated in the on-line world. Have a look at Jakob Nielsen's website **www.useit.com** for more on this, it will surprise and challenge you. Or read Steve Krug's book, *Don't Make Me Think*.

Exhibit 13.17 The secrets of typeface

Nash, Stone, Bird and Ogilvy have all emphasised the importance of typeface in direct-response adverts. The following guidelines are offered:

- Sans serif is associated with modernity, but . . . sans serif is difficult to read for long passages of text. Serifs, the little 'feet' at the edge of the letter characters, keep the eye moving horizontally along the line of type.
- Times Roman is associated with books and papers and so suggests reliability, authority and credibility.
- *Typeface at an angle gives an impression of speed.*
- **A bold typeface conveys loudness.**
- Gothic implies traditional.
- CAPITALS ARE MORE DIFFICULT TO READ. This is because they have no ascenders or descenders to help reading and tend to be read letter by letter.
- Small type on coupons inspires distrust.
- Reversed-out type is tiring on the eye in any great volume.
- Type set at funny angles, over pictures, or in large columns across the page is very difficult to read. Do not do this.

Summary

In this chapter we found that there is a strong basis in classic creative direct response from the 'left-brain' school of advertising. There are signs that this is changing to include some brand building techniques, as the two objectives of branding and response merge in certain sectors.

Direct marketers have been able to test different creative approaches, and the cumulative wisdom from these tests has led to a number of 'rules' or guidance for maximising response. By following the AIDA model of consumer behaviour, the novice direct marketer gives him or herself the best chance of success.

QUESTIONS

1 You are shown a website and asked to identify it as either a brand-building advert, a direct-response ad, or a mixture of the two. What clues would you use from the advert itself to help you identify its objectives?

2 Picking any Sunday colour supplement, go through the magazine and identify the objectives, target audience and creative principles of the direct-response adverts contained within.

3 Define positioning and branding, and explain why they are so important in creative considerations.

4 Outline what creative principles an international distress charity should take into account before e-mailing prospective donors.

5 In what instances, if any, is it acceptable to break the direct marketing 'rules' of collective wisdom gathered in this chapter?

6 You have been asked to put together a creative execution of a direct-response ad for Stilton blue cheese, a relatively expensive cheese sometimes eaten on special occasions. Explain how you would approach the problem and what creative factors you would take into account.

References

Bird, D. (2007) *Commonsense Direct and Digital Marketing,* Kogan Page, London.

Bovee, C., Thill, J., Dovell, G. and Wood, M. (1995) *Advertising Excellence,* McGraw-Hill, New York.

Broadbent, S. (1997) 'Accountability – the flaming sword', *Admap,* June.

de Chernatony, L. and McDonald, M. (2010) *Creating Powerful Brands,* 4th Ed. Butterworth-Heinemann, Oxford.

Fox, S. (1984) *The Mirror Makers,* Morrow and Co., New York.

Foxall, G. and Goldsmith, R. (1994) *Consumer Psychology for Marketing,* Routledge, London.

Harrison, S. (2009) *How to do Better Creative Work*, Pearson, Harlow.

IDM, (2006) The IDM Marketing Guide: Best Practice in Direct, Data and Digital Marketing, 3rd Ed. The IDM, London.

Jones, C. (1992) 'A visual language – the role of art direction in print', in Haldey, B. (ed) *The Practitioner's Guide to Direct Marketing*, Institute of Direct Marketing, Teddington, Richmond-upon-Thames.

Martin, D. (1989) *Romancing the Brand: The power of advertising and how to use it,* Amacom, New York.

McCorkell, G. (1994) *The Best of Graeme McCorkell,* DRM, London.

Nash, E. (1995) *Direct Marketing: Strategy, planning, execution,* McGraw-Hill, New York.

Ogilvy, D. (1964) *Confessions of an Advertising Man,* Longman, Harlow.

Ogilvy, D. (1983) *Ogilvy on Advertising,* Crown, New York.

Rapp, S. and Collins, T. (1987) *Maximarketing,* McGraw-Hill, New York.

Reeves, R. (1961) *Reality in Advertising,* Knopf, New York.

Schwab, V. (1985) *How to Write a Good Advertisement: A short course in copywriting,* Wiltshire Book Co., Chatsworth, CA.

Smith, P. (1993) *Marketing Communications: An integrated approach,* Kogan Page, London.

Stone, B. (1996) *Successful Direct Marketing Methods,* NTC Business Books, Chicago, Ill.

Vaughan, R. (1980) 'How advertising works: a planning model', *Journal of Advertising Research,* 20 (5), pp. 27–33.

CASE STUDY

England and Wales Cricket Board Limited

The brief

While the attendences of international one-day and test-match fixtures was as high as ever, the ordinary county cricket scene in England was not well supported. The profile of cricket followers was older than that of its much bigger rival, soccer. The brief from England

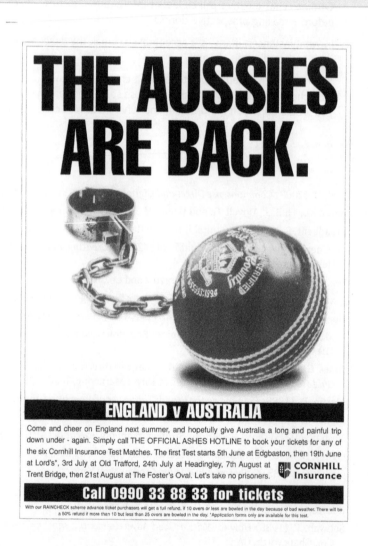

Figure 13.12 Advert using humour to appeal to broader age range

Source: England and Wales Cricket Board Limited and Bates Direct.

and Wales Cricket Board Limited was for the direct-response advertising to help whip up some appeal across a broader age range, while still fulfilling its primary role of pulling in response for tickets.

The solution

The agency, Bates Communications, decided to take an irreverent, humorous approach to the forthcoming test series between Australia and England. The picture and copy (in Figure 13.12) refer to the fact that some of the original white settlers in Australia were convicted British criminals carrying out penal service. The campaign attracted good publicity, with the *Daily Mirror* describing it as a 'provocative' campaign, and also attracting quotes from Australian cricketers.

Questions

1 From the brief, and referring to the classical direct marketing 'rules' in the chapter, critically analyse the off-the-page advert. In what ways does it differ from a classical direct-response advert?

2 Given the brief, produce your own version of the advert.

CASE STUDY

Friends of the Earth

Friends of the Earth is one of the highest profile charities in the UK. Barely a week passes without its name appearing in connection with its key campaigns including 'industry and pollution', 'biodiversity and habitat', and 'biotechnology'. In 2000, the hottest issue was probably the tests on GM modified foodstuffs, something that did not appear popular with much of the general public. 'We are here to transform society, and have a track record going back 30 years,' said Steven Montgomery, development manager. Founded in 1971, FoE strives to offer a 'better future' through campaigning, research and education.

As ever, fundraising is important. The direct marketing team looks after more than 100,000 supporters, and has its own mailing house in Luton. The fundraising mix is typical of sophisticated charities: members get a quarterly magazine, *Earthmatters,* and regular mailings containing appeals to fund specific campaigns. The typical FoE supporter is aged 35–55, well educated, geographically biased to London and the South East. Some 55 per cent of them are female. This profile is similar to the typical charity giver, with the exception of age: FoE supporters are younger than other donors. Not surprisingly, ideology is very important to FoE donors. They are committed enough about a better world to support their ideals through hard cash.

Montgomery and his team were particularly concerned to develop what they called 'major donors'. They trawled the database and came up with more than 800 names who had given more than £250 per year. The decision was made to contact these people in an effort to increase the average donation by a considerable amount. Issue specific appeals would be the focus, with the first three being toxic pollution, food and climate change.

Case study (*continued*)

Future plans for major donors included invitations to special meetings and evenings to see behind the scenes, and find out where their money was going.

Before that, however, plans were being laid for the all important direct-mail campaigns to the 800 key supporters. A powerful creative approach was needed. Montgomery had good resources available to him. What should he do?

Source: Based on information in Booth, E. (1999) 'Back to the planet', *Marketing Direct*, October, pp. 39–40.

Extract from 'Mailing do's and don't's'

- Don't forget to keep your mailing simple and single minded if you want a good response.
- Don't forget who your customers really are and what they want from you.
- Avoid the three Gs in copy: grovelling, grammar-ridden, gobbledegook.
- In other words, get straight to the point, don't feel the need to stick to formal grammar, and avoid jargon.
- Think about the medium – direct mail is tactile.

Source: *Marketing Direct* (1999) November, p. 42.

Questions

Outline the key messages of the Friends of the Earth campaigns. Make creative recommendations for the copy tone of voice, artwork and layout. Your creative solution should consider key messages, audience, the outcomes desired, brand values of FoE and any other considerations you think are important.

CASE STUDY

Lynx Attract

Background

For the first time ever, Lynx were launching a female variant – Lynx Attract for Her. The TV advert for the new product launch demonstrated the power of the Lynx Effect by showing the chaos that would ensue when men and women wearing Lynx came into contact with each other.

In order to bring this to life on-line TMW needed to continue this train of thought. However, a series of supporting videos wouldn't cut it – the agency wanted the target market to feel like the chaos was ubiquitous, a pandemic spreading up and down the country. They needed to show the chaos happening everywhere, in a tangible way.

This was tackled with a multiphase approach. Starting with a rumour stage, TMW drove the rumour mill, seeding out little bits of content to get people talking. At launch, they staged a real life occurrence of the chaos for the nation's press to see. Finally, they sought to report on the chaos caused by the new product launch, taking a breaking news-style approach to make it all the more compelling.

Creative execution

TWW already had penetrating TV ads but, to create intrigue and demand for the female product before launch, they targeted bloggers and key influencers to leak information about Lynx Attract - setting the rumour mill in motion. The agency also sold a black market can of Lynx Attract on eBay.

Facebook fans were then offered 100 exclusive cans of the fragrance before it hit the shops.

The product launch saw an outbreak of chaos at a real life launch event in Superdrug with model Abbey Clancy – who spurred an in-store flash snog by spraying the two fragrances.

Chaos sightings were recorded on-line via Chaos Watch, a hub for tracking the epidemic – which pulled in tweets, photos, videos and more.

Another flash snog was staged on a public bus and produced a series of short guerilla films to show the epidemic spreading. Tapping into real world trends, they found ways to link the product message to timely events. For example, a news story about a woman falling in love with the statue of liberty trended on Twitter. The cause? Lynx Attract.

The final phase of the campaign saw chaos infiltrate every touch point. Aligned with the TVC, their social spaces assumed a newsreader tone urging fans to 'stay safe' and avoid using Lynx Attract in an attempt to reign in worldwide attraction chaos.

Chaos survival tests and tips were created and posted on Facebook to help fans 'deal' with chaos. Adaptations of culturally popular content also did particularly well.

Results generated from this approach

The black market eBay can was sold for £23, while the cans on Facebook disappeared in less than three hours, showing that they had built a real demand for the product amongst their fans and target audience. They also saw interest from the blogging community who reviewed the product, which helped increase awareness.

In-store launches with Abbey Clancy at ASDA and Superdrug generated an unprecedented amount of PR coverage. In addition, the brand/product reached over 5.3 million people on Twitter and received over 9,000 on-line mentions – all of which helped drive product awareness and trial.

Lynx Attract For Her became the second fastest selling SKU (stock-keeping unit) at Superdrug and captured 24 per cent of the female body spray market.

Lynx Attract For Him became the third best selling product at Superdrug and was ranked as the brand's second highest selling product overall.

The product launch positively affected Facebook growth increasing their fan base by 157,000 fans (22 per cent uplift) and gaining 46,000 new likes and 15,000 comments.

This ubiquity, defined phases, and approach to content generation and distribution would give us an engaging platform that would endure for the length of the campaign. It would give opportunities to be reactive – commenting on the chaos in the real world and attributing it to Lynx as well as staging their own chaos to create experiential and on-line engagement. It was also a fantastic way to encourage fans to submit their own chaos sightings and become part of the campaign themselves.

Chapter 14

Testing, budgeting and research in direct marketing

Objectives

Once you have read this chapter you should:

- be able to set up a direct marketing test programme and interpret its results
- be able to structure a direct marketing budget and use it to aid decision making
- appreciate how research and direct marketing can work together

Introduction

There are three distinct techniques that direct marketers use to control their activities. They are setting a budget that includes target responses, testing to maximise return on spend, and market research to understand the qualitative impact of campaigns. The actual measurement of the campaigns themselves is based on direct response, not surprisingly, and these results, fed into the budget, give a precise, accurate measure of success or otherwise. There is no hiding place for direct marketers!

This chapter will show why direct marketing measurement exhibits clear superiority over general marketing's equivalent. The problem in general marketing is the lack of precision in relating spend to revenue. On increasing its advertising, a packaged goods supplier notices its sales rise. But how does it know the improvement was down to advertising? At the same time as the adverts were being shown, perhaps other competitors put their prices up; maybe footfall through the retail outlets rose, or its salespeople completed some breakthrough contracts to increase distribution.

The key to direct marketing's control lies with its ability to connect any spend precisely to corresponding revenues. We link money out to money back in. We can focus on an identified group of customers on their database, and track exactly how much is spent on them over the year, and how much revenue they generate for the company. Return on marketing investment is easily and accurately calculated, as we will see.

How this chapter is structured

This chapter covers three topics. The first is testing; we will look at what testing is, what we should test, and how to do so. The second section brings testing and budgeting together, showing how to set overall marketing budgets and then how to set out a series of tests for programme budgeting. Finally, we take a look at how market research can help with direct marketing analysis and campaign planning.

14.1 Testing

'By his actions shall you know him.'   (Matthew 7.16)

Testing is more than just an operational detail in direct marketing. It is a crucial advantage that direct marketing has in comparison with general marketing. A key aspect of business and marketing strategies is assessing and understanding the risks inherent in any particular chosen route. All other things being equal, the strategist should choose the least risky option. The point about direct marketing is that it is strategically a low risk option to take. This is because the unrivalled testability of its direct communications means that the success or failure of its campaigns is predictable, allowing returns to be maximised. Building and maintaining a customer database requires a large investment (Kotler *et al.*, 2009, p. 183).

In this section, we cover the operational details of testing. The structure will be:

- what testing is: a definition
- why we test
- justifying testing financially
- what variables to test
- how to design a test programme
- the effect of sample size on the accuracy of the roll-out predictions

14.1.1 What is testing?

Testing is the marketers' word for what scientists call experiments. The method has been used for as long as science has been practised, which says something about its validity.

The mechanics of a basic test are extremely simple. A test of a campaign is run concurrently against a control campaign. The test will have all elements kept the same as those of the control, apart from the element under investigation. For example, let us say a bank is offering a new credit card to its customers and wants to test different offers.

The 'control' elements could be:

- random sample of bank's database
- *Offer:* new credit card with no annual fee in first year
- *Timing:* May
- *Creative:* simple mailer with no brochure, reply envelope and response device

While the 'test' elements are:

- *Audience:* as above
- *Offer:* new credit card with annual fee at £12
- *Timing:* as above
- *Creative:* as above

As you can see, the golden rule is to vary only one element at a time. This way any differences in percentage response can be attributed to the element being varied: in the above case, the annual fee waiver.

Exhibit 14.1 How to get testing spectacularly wrong

A financial services organisation (who has asked not to be named!) decided it was time to change the creative treatment used on their radio advertisement. There was not anything 'wrong' with the old one, *per se,* it had just been hanging around a while and was getting a bit too familiar to work as well as it once had.

Things were going well for the company, both in terms of overall business and in terms of radio advertising effectiveness, so they decided to push the boat out and make a serious investment in their radio budget – after all, they knew it worked well, so what could go wrong?

Fed up of the old script, they decided to change it completely, coming up with brand-new creative. Previously they had used unknown voiceover artists, but this time they decided to invest £20,000 in paying for a household name actor (who, research showed, would be thought of as a trustworthy ambassador) to work with them. Finally, they decided to expand the number of stations they broadcast on, as well as the frequency with which their adverts were aired throughout the day. Then they sat back and waited . . . as the responses took a dive.

That in itself was a big enough problem, but the situation was only made worse by the fact that they did not know what had gone wrong – was it the new creative, the well-known voiceover, the new stations or the increased frequency of airing? There was no way to tell.

Several fraught meetings later, it was decided to start unpicking the layers of the problem one by one. They could not get out of their pre-spent airing commitments, so the first step was to change the celebrity voiceover for an unknown voice. They tried that and response improved back to where it had been – but it should have been higher as a result of the extra airtime, so they changed the script next. That too helped matters, and the process of rectifying 'schoolboy error number one' (as the marketing manager calls it) was well underway.

Subsequent posthumous research showed that, although the household name was indeed thought of as a safe and reliable personality, he was not associated with financial services so listeners thought 'he's been paid to say this', whereas with the unknown voiceover they thought 'he sounds knowledgeable'.

The lesson here is to test one thing at a time, so you can see what makes a positive difference, what makes no difference and what damages your product or service.

We are now ready for a formal definition of testing.

Definition

Testing is the small-scale measurement of the performance of individual campaign elements in order to maximise returns on rolled-out full marketing campaigns.

Let us expand a little on this definition.

Small scale

Typically a full, roll-out campaign may involve expenditure of hundreds of thousands of pounds in order to reach many thousands of potential customers. A direct marketing test, usually carried out before the full roll-out, typically consists of a mailer to 5,000 customers costing, say, £10,000, including all fixed costs.

Measurement

The most important performance measure is the response to the campaign, measured as a percentage. The other critically important performance measure that is used, directly related to response, is profitability. More secondary objectives would include awareness, percentage of mailers read, change in attitudes to the product and so on.

However, a key strategic performance measure for direct marketers is customer retention.

Maximising returns on roll-out

The idea with testing is to make the individual elements of the campaign as effective as possible so that when large expenditure is committed to the roll-out returns are maximised.

Individual marketing elements

What should we test? This is discussed later, after we have understood all the benefits of testing.

14.1.2 The benefits of testing for direct marketers

We have already covered the primary reason for testing: that is to minimise financial risk. As well as this, there are other secondary reasons for testing. They are:

- Protecting existing customers from unsuccessful campaigns. By using only small samples with each test you can treat the bulk of your customers to a proven offer.
- Stimulating creativity. There is a fascination for the creative team in designing a new treatment to beat the current control and testing provides healthy internal competition.
- Helping us to understand customers better. Testing can work alongside research in helping to understand customer behaviour. Testing provides a real environment in which to validate claimed behaviour in research. The two do not always tally!

Doing without testing

Some marketers believe they can put together the 'optimum' campaign based solely on intuition and experience, and without the need for prior market testing. This has been proven time and again to be a fallacy. The combined collective experience of the direct marketing industry has been that testing is the only sure, systematic way of maximising campaign profitability.

However, let us call the practitioners' bluff and try to beat the testing 'system'. Take a look at the six creative approaches in Figures 14.1–14.3 (a) and (b) for car insurance. Using your skill and judgement, try to pick the two that gained the greatest response.

(a)

Grab a bumper 20% off motor insurance.

Call The Insurance Service and you could look forward to cheaper motor insurance and a host of benefits.

- Friendly, efficient staff
- Free loan car
- Easy ways to pay
- 24hr windscreen replacement
- £50,000 of free legal expenses insurance in the first year

Full details supplied with your quotation

FREE £20 M&S VOUCHER
when you take out your first policy with us.

0800 989898

CALL FREE AND QUOTE REF:-W01

Mon to Fri 8am - 8.30pm Sat 9am - 4pm

For your benefit we record or listen to telephone calls to ensure high levels of customer service are maintained.

The Insurance Service
a member of the
🜲 **Royal Insurance**
group of companies
The Insurance Service plc. Registered in England & Wales no. 2145778. All offers are subject to change. Offer only available in mainland Britain.

(b)

Figure 14.1 Direct-response ads for the insurance service
Source: Reproduced by kind permission of Royal and Sun Alliance.

If you chose Figure 14.2 as the 'winning' adverts, well done – you get the star prize! In descending response order, the adverts were ranked as follows:

Figure 14.2 (b)

Figure 14.2 (a)

Figure 14.1 (b)

Figure 14.3 (b)

(a)

BUYING CAR INSURANCE

CUTTING YOUR PREMIUMS DOESN'T HAVE TO MEAN CUTTING YOUR COVER

When car insurance is due for renewal, nobody wants to pay more than they really have to. Royal & Sun Alliance – one of the UK's leading direct insurers recognise this, so they have developed a superbly priced package for drivers with good records.

They treat each customer individually, taking into account their driving history, and rewarding them with savings and discounts. It's little wonder their customers make an average saving of £50 when they join – just by making one free phone call!

Royal & Sun Alliance also recognise that lower priced car insurance is of no use without adequate cover which is why their policy includes immediate authorisation of repairs at their network of Quality Assured Recommended Repairers, a free courtesy car whilst yours is being repaired and 24 hour windscreen repair and replacement.

Not only that but customers get a discount of £25 when they insure a second car and up to 30% off Green Flag National Breakdown cover.

With savings like this, can you afford not to give them a call?

'Money saved, a courteous service...and a courtesy car!'

Maurice Pack-Davison called Royal & Sun Alliance and saved over £100. "What's more, the service was efficient and friendly - especially after someone ran into the back of me. Within 24 hours Royal & Sun Alliance had arranged for my car to go to one of their Quality Assured Recommended Repairers and gave me a courtesy car. One week later my car was back as good as new!

ROYAL & SUNALLIANCE

£20 M&S VOUCHER FREE
WHEN YOU TAKE OUT A MOTOR POLICY

0800 300220

CALL NOW & QUOTE MLA 938

Lines are open Mon–Fri, 8am to 9pm, Sat 9am to 5pm

For your benefit we may record or listen to telephone calls. Offer only applies to Mainland Britain. If you would prefer not to receive information on other group services, please make us aware when you call. Checks may be made with a licensed credit referencing agency for risk rating purposes. Offer subject to normal underwriting criteria.

(b)

Cut your motor premiums without cutting cover

Most of us recognise that buying motor cover direct can provide substantial savings, but it pays to look really closely at what you actually get for your money.

Using The Insurance Service as an example, some people have saved as much as £100 on their premiums, yet also received additional features like free legal cover up to £50,000 in their first year and a discount of up to 30% with Green Flag National Breakdown.

But what would happen if someone ran in to you?

The Insurance Service's Claims Action Line operate one of the fastest, friendliest services around. If you have an accident their Recommended Prime Repairers can be given instant permission to begin work on your car and you could have the use of a free courtesy car while yours is being repaired.

Can you afford not to give them a call?

"I got £100 worth of savings and complete peace of mind"

Susan Harding, a housewife from Whitchurch, Shropshire drives an E reg Rover. She was surprised at the savings The Insurance Service offered. "I was delighted to find that including the Green Flag National Breakdown discount, I saved nearly £100. Plus, if I'm on holiday in the UK and I have an accident, they'll recommend a quality garage and supply me with a courtesy car whilst mine is being repaired."

Call now for a free motor insurance quote

0800 98 98 98   Quote ref: MIR 919

Monday to Friday 8am - 8.30pm   Saturday 9am - 4.30pm

FREE £20 M&S VOUCHER WHEN YOU TAKE OUT YOUR FIRST POLICY

The Insurance Service
a member of the Royal & SunAlliance Group

For your benefit we record or listen to telephone calls. If you would prefer not to receive information on other Group services, please make us aware when you call. Checks may be made with a licensed credit referencing agency for risk rating purposes.

Figure 14.2 Direct-response ads for the insurance service
Source: Reproduced by kind permission of Royal and Sun Alliance.

Figure 14.3 (a)

Figure 14.1 (a)

Although you may have been successful this time, you would probably agree that it is extremely difficult to pick the winners consistently for a number of programmes over time. This is why we test.

However, testing costs money and also takes up a lot of time and management effort. The question of how much to test and how much to leave to management judgement is still a difficult one to answer. Some clarity can be obtained by taking a look at the following financial justification.

(a)

(b)

Figure 14.3 Direct-response ads for the insurance service

Source: Reproduced by kind permission of Royal and Sun Alliance.

Exhibit 14.2

A garden tools manufacturer wanted to test whether using male or female models in his catalogue would affect response. To his surprise, response jumped some 20 per cent when female models were illustrated with the implements, even though many of them were heavy and difficult to handle. He was unable to explain why. This is an example of testing showing what happens, and that such results are often hard to predict. Here the role of research would be to explain why it happened.

Source: Halsey (1992).

14.1.3 Justifying testing financially

The mathematics of testing can be illustrated using the following example.

A children's toy manufacturer has a number of possible products it could lead with as a special offer in its next catalogue, aimed at upmarket young families. Its total database is 600,000 households. It decides to test each product idea before rolling out. Each test is to 5,000 customers. The tests are:

Test A: board games	Test C: computer games
Test B: outdoor garden toys	Test D: children's books.

1 Costs are:

$$\text{Fixed costs per campaign} = \text{£}2,000$$
$$\text{Variable costs per catalogue} = \text{£}1,000 \text{ per thousand}$$
$$\text{Total marketing costs per test} = \text{£}7,000$$

2 The response rates obtained from the tests were as follows:

Test A: 7 per cent

Test B: 8 per cent

Test C: 5 per cent

Test D: 4 per cent

The gross margin on each purchase averages £20 for all the products.

3 Financial returns per test were as shown in Table 14.1.

4 The manufacturer rolls out with the outdoor garden toys (Test B) as the special offer.

Roll out

$$\text{No. mailed} = 600,000 - \text{tests} = 580,000$$
$$\text{No. of responses} = 46,400$$
$$\text{Total margin} = \text{£}928,000$$
$$\text{Total marketing costs} = \text{£}582,000$$
$$\text{Net return on roll-out} = \text{£}346,000$$
$$\text{Overall return on test plus roll-out} = \text{£}342,000$$

5 What would be the alternative if the test had not taken place? This depends of course on which product had been chosen for the roll-out:

Clearly, unless the company is lucky enough to guess right with its campaign elements, the tests were worth doing even though they lost a small amount of money, because the alternative may have been a loss of a much larger magnitude.

Table 14.1 Financial returns per test

	Test A	Test B	Test C	Test D
No. mailed	5,000	5,000	5,000	5,000
No. of responses	350	400	250	200
Test gross margin	£7,000	£8,000	£5,000	£4,000
Costs of marketing	£7,000	£7,000	£7,000	£7,000
Net margin	0	£1,000	(£2,000)	(£3,000)
Overall net tests margin = (£4,000)				

Table 14.2 Products chosen for roll-out

	Product A	Product B	Product C	Product D
No. mailed	600,000	600,000	600,000	600,000
No. of responses	42,000	48,000	30,000	24,000
Gross margin	£840,000	£960,000	£600,000	£480,000
Total marketing costs	£602,000	£602,000	£602,000	£602,000
Net return	£238,000	£358,000	−£2,000	−£122,000

With on-line marketing, measuring results is made that much more difficult because on-line advertising may be sold on a CPM, CPT or CPC basis – the first thing we need to do is understand these terms and then know how to convert from one to the other so that we can compare like with like.

CPT stands for 'cost per thousand', CPM is cost per mille and means the same thing – the two may be used interchangeably. CPT/CPM are usually applied to the likes of banner adverts on a website where you are charged the CPT price for every thousand times the advert appears on someone's computer screen. The total number of times your advert will appear can be calculated as follows:

$$\text{Total impressions} = (\text{Total cost or budget})* (1,000/\text{CPT})$$

Alternatively, you can work out how much you will pay for a given number of advert appearances, thus:

$$\text{Total cost} = (\text{Total impressions}* \text{CPT})/1,000$$

CPC stands for Cost Per Click. Google Adwords works on this basis; it does not matter how many times the advert is displayed on computer screens, you only pay if someone clicks on that advert and is taken to your website. Cost per click is, then, the total cost of your campaign (i.e. your budget) divided by the number of times someone clicks through to your site. Alternatively, the total campaign cost of your campaign will be the number of click-throughs you get multiplied by the CPC.

The problem is that you need to be able to compare a campaign based on CPC with another based on CPT, so how do you do that? Fortunately, Batra has come up with a pair of useful formulae to do just that (Batra, 2012).

CPC to CPM conversion

Below is a formula that you can use to calculate a CPM equivalent of a CPC model:

$$\text{CPM} = (\text{CPC}*\text{clicks}*1,000)/\text{Total impressions}$$

Let us take an example of a campaign that costs £4 per click and generates 100 clicks, resulting in a total spend of £400. Let us say it took 50,000 impressions to generate those 100 clicks.

Table 14.3 Calculating campaign metrics

		Formula
CPC	£4	Known value
Clicks	100	Know values
Total cost	£400	CPC*Clicks
Impressions	50,000	Impressions* CPM/1000
Cost per 1000 impressions	8	Total cost/(Total Impressions/1000)
CPM	£8	Cost per 1000 impressions

The CPM value you get when you convert CPC into CPM is also known as eCPM (effective CPM).

Having converted the measurements to the same units, the next essential measure is the ratio between clicks and sales. For instance, if you know that it takes 105 click-throughs from a given site to generate one sale, you can work out the cost per sale (as well as how much you need to budget for that site to meet the targets you have for it).

From that point, the approach to measuring tests beyond CPC/CPM and into financial justification is the same as outlined in the direct mail example above.

Social media

Social media is all too often seen as being somehow special, where measurement should be limited to the number of followers, likes or views a site has. This is all very nice to know, but what we really need to know is the same as with every other medium: what's the return on investment (ROI)?

Unfortunately, there is not a simple way of measuring this, except for the e-marketing equivalent of putting a code on a flyer and asking people to quote that when they contact you. With e-marketing it's both easier and more sophisticated in that you can have dedicated landing pages as destinations embedded into hyperlinks on Facebook or Twitter (for example), but not everyone will use those links.

In his book *'Social Media ROI – Managing and Measuring Social Media Efforts in Your Organisation'*, Blanchard suggests a complex set of eight steps to do what the book title suggests (Blanchard, 2011, pp. 227–237). Unfortunately, even this relies on human examination of various charts in the search for trends.

In reality, it could be argued that this makes social media similar to public relations in that it is difficult to measure accurately its effectiveness with any real accuracy. With the greatest of respect to our colleagues in PR, from a DM point of view, this is a real weakness.

Having established the need to test, we are now ready to tackle what variables we should be concentrating on. What exactly should direct marketers be testing?

14.1.4 Test variables: what we need to test

We can test just about anything. However, it is important to test only those variables that matter.

'Test the Big Things.'

(Stone and Jacobs, 2001)

What are the most important elements to test? In the 1980s, a very large test was put together by Stewart Pearson, a senior practitioner in the UK. Pearson wanted to understand which elements of direct marketing had the biggest impact on response. He put together an enormous matrix of 57 variables, all within one broad product/market area. He varied the media, the offer (the price, incentives, etc.), the timing and the creative treatments.

His results, shown in Table 14.4, were a critical lesson for direct marketers.

What does Table 14.4 tell us? First, it says that the target audience is the most important thing to get right, for any given product. As we saw in the strategy section earlier, the product market investment decision is the most important strategic decision a marketer makes, so this result here is perhaps not surprising.

Table 14.4 Varying elements to test impact

Element	Percentage impact – extent to which the best test outperforms the worst test
Media/audience	600 per cent (i.e. the best medium gave a response six times higher than the worst medium, with other elements held constant)
Offer	200 per cent
Timing	100 per cent
Creative	33 per cent

Source: Pearson (2008).

Everything else is less important, with the creative element (often the most tested) being the least important. This does not mean creative differences are not worth exploring; a third gain in percentage response can still be critical. But it is necessary to get the importance of the creative element in perspective, compared to other elements of the direct marketing mix.

Exhibit 14.3 The relative importance of getting the audience right above all else

A simple example that often clarifies the relative importance of targeting over all else is that of a company selling Viagra, the drug to cure impotence, via direct mail.

If they were to create the most beautiful creative, printed on glossy paper in full colour and offer 50 per cent off the normal price with a simple reply mechanism. . . and send it to a list of eight-year-old girls, they'd get no response worth talking about, and a lot of bad publicity.

On the other hand, they could probably handwrite a message on toilet paper – with no money off and not worry about the simplicity of the response mechanism – and get a response, if they sent it to men who were known to be impotent and their partners.

Of course, Viagra sales via direct mail are illegal in most countries and lists of impotent men are not easy to find, but this mythical example does illustrate the point clearly!

Pearson's results will not hold exactly true for every situation; they are only guidelines. However, they do lead us to a more profound conclusion. As a marketer, what you say and who you say it to is more important than how you say it. This is particularly important because, in marketing, we often seem to concentrate on the latter at the expense of the former.

14.1.5 Testing with different media

There is a lot of detail behind the design of a complex test programme, which is outside the scope of this book. The reader is referred to the excellent *IDM Marketing Guide* (The IDM, 2007) for more information. What we will do here is to touch on the different ways that testing is carried out in different media.

Direct mail

As outlined previously, just about any element of direct mail is easy to test, because the marketer controls every aspect of the campaign, including the exact time that the mailer is released.

Telemarketing

Telemarketing is extremely easy to test, and this is a powerful part of the telemarketer's armoury. Indeed, testing in telemarketing is easier than in direct mail. At the start of an evening's calls, the operatives can be asked to promote a particular product. Because response is instantaneous and high, it may only take 100 calls before a good indication is obtained of the success of that offer. On the same evening, a new offer can be tried and its results compared. Script changes are also commonly tested.

Press and inserts

Inserts and press space are both testable, although not as easily as the above media.

Split-run testing (only applies to inserts)

In a split-run test, advertisers will have between two and, maybe, six or eight different inserts to be put into a given newspaper or magazine. Each insert will differ in one way only from the 'control' (i.e. the best performing insert to date). This could be in terms of price, incentive, headline, body copy, pictures and so on. The inserts are supplied to the publisher not as separate piles of flyers, but so that they are all together as Insert 1, Insert 2, Insert 3, Insert 4, Insert 5, Insert 6 and so on. The publisher then places each insert in turn into the publication as it comes off the press, which gives a random split because nobody can tell who will buy each individual magazine. This lets the advertiser test which of several variables works best.

A/B splits

Each magazine or paper is split so that a certain number will include Advert (or Insert) A, a certain number will have Advert (or Insert) B and so on. As above, one of the treatments will be the best performing version to date, others are trying to beat that 'control' item in terms of response.

Cross-over testing

This is best described through an example, shown in Table 14.5.

In Table 14.5, the first issue of Press 1 is compared with the second issue of Press 2, and *vice versa,* and then a comparison is also made between creative approaches. In this way, a comparison is possible between the creative and also the press title. The flaw is that not all other variables are held constant: a second issue has had to be used. There is, however, no better way.

Other media

Testing on DRTV is possible, though not easy to achieve without disturbing external variables, rather like press testing described earlier.

Table 14.5 **Cross-over testing**

	Press 1		Press 2	
	Creative	Response	Creative	Response
First issue	A	400	B	200
Second issue	B	250	A	300

New electronic media such as the Internet provide excellent possibilities for testing offers, creative formats and so on, and these are dealt with elsewhere in this book.

We have seen how test results are used to 'predict' what would happen in a roll-out. However, to what extent can we be sure that on rolling out we would obtain the same result as the test? Because we only used a sample to test, there is a degree of 'uncertainty' in the prediction that we need to take account of. The following section shows how.

14.1.6 Calculating uncertainty in roll-out predictions

The level of uncertainty in our test results depends primarily on the sample size of the test. The smaller the test, the more uncertain we are of its applicability to the entire database. Having said that, direct marketers want to use as small a test sample size as possible, because testing costs money. What is the minimum test size we can use?

The answer depends on how certain we want to be that the test results represent the whole customer base. The relationship between certainty and sample size can be obtained from a few simple statistics.

The following worked example explains what direct marketers need to do to calculate test sample sizes.

Let us say we test an offer of a free wine appreciation course DVD on joining a wine club. We obtain a response of 2.5 per cent. Our break-even for roll-out is 2.3 per cent. Can we confidently roll out, being certain the roll-out will achieve a response of 2.5 per cent?

If we were to run the same test to another 5,000 people within the same target market, would we get exactly the same result? What would your instincts tell you? The answer is that it is possible we would get the same result, but we would not be surprised if the results were slightly different, say 2.4 per cent. If we were to run the test eight times to different samples of the same group, one might envisage the following results:

Test 1:	2.5%	Test 5:	2.7%
Test 2:	2.4%	Test 6:	2.3%
Test 3:	2.6%	Test 7:	2.6%
Test 4:	2.5%	Test 8:	2.8%

We have obtained a variation in test results, with an average of 2.55 per cent. We can say that, of our test results so far, the likelihood is that the full roll-out will lie between 2.3 per cent and 2.8 per cent. This bracket within which the roll-out result would be likely to fall can be estimated using statistics. The lower and upper figures (2.3, 2.8) are called the limits of error. The 'limits of error' give us a range within which we would expect the roll-out result to lie.

There is one more expression of our uncertainty we need to include. This arises from the fact that, although we believe that the true roll-out response lies within the limits of error calculated, we cannot be 100 per cent certain that it lies therein. There is a small possibility that the rest of the customer base would give a result outside this range. Statistics allow us to calculate how confident we can be that our result will lie within our limits of error. We use 'confidence levels' to express this part of our uncertainty. By far the most often used level is the 95 per cent confidence level. So, in our example, we could say that 95 times out of 100, our roll-out figure should lie between 2.3 per cent and 2.8 per cent. The other 5 per cent of the time it may lie outside that range, purely by chance.

To summarise, we want to express our level of uncertainty: it is possible that the roll-out result will be different from the test result. There are two aspects to expressing this uncertainty: limits of error and confidence levels. We will complete the picture now by showing how to relate these measures to the test sample size.

Relating sample size to uncertainty

Provided we fix our level of confidence (nearly always set at 95 per cent), the level of uncertainty in a sample result depends on two things. They are:

- The sample size
- The response percentage

However, uncertainty is particularly sensitive to sample size, and so it is this which the direct marketer needs to concentrate on to control the predictability of the test. Note that the size of the 'roll-out population', perhaps surprisingly, is not a factor in uncertainty.

Suppose we tested a sample of 5,000 people. The response obtained is 2.5 per cent. What are the limits of error associated with this result?

The formula for calculation is:

$$\text{Limits of error, } L = k\sqrt{\frac{R(100 - R)}{n}}$$

where:

k = constant depending on confidence level chosen (k = 1.96 for 95% confidence levels)
R = response percentage obtained for the test
n = sample test

For our example,

$$L = 1.96 \times \sqrt{\frac{2.5(100 - 2.5)}{5,000}}$$

$$L = 0.43$$

It is always best to write out in full what this result actually means to us. We can be 95 per cent confident that the roll-out will be 2.5 +/- 0.43 per cent. Put another way, we are 95 per cent confident that the roll-out response will be between 2.07 per cent and 2.93 per cent.

How is this useful to us? Bearing in mind that the break-even was 2.3 per cent, we can see that this test result leaves us in a quandary. It is possible that the full roll-out will yield a response as low as 2.07 per cent, placing us in a loss-making situation. The answer is to test again with a bigger sample size, thereby obtaining a prediction with a smaller limit of error.

14.2 Budgeting for direct marketing programmes

In this section, we approach budgeting at two levels. The first is the high level planning budget that may be set for the year's activities – a strategic budgeting exercise. The second is the individual programme budget, created to manage a discrete activity.

14.2.1 Setting total marketing budgets

Setting the overall budget is a fairly simple process, utilising the concepts of lifetime value and allowable marketing spend that we introduced earlier (Chapter 3). Ideally the key input that dictates the budget is an accurate target/objective-setting process.

Figure 14.4 shows how the overall yearly budget may be calculated.

Having constructed the total marketing budget, our next task is to divide this into individual programme budgets as efficiently as possible. To do this we use the following seven-step process.

The seven-step process to constructing a programme budget

Let us say our first programme has a target of acquiring 2,000 new customers buying computer accessories. From the lifetime value calculations, the allowable marketing spend has been set at £50 per customer. Our programme budget is, therefore, £100,000 for the programme (2,000 × £50).

The gross margin of each sale is £20. This is less than the targeted spend of £50, but the assumption here is that these customers are highly profitable later on in their 'lifetime' with the company. (In fact this mirrors many actual direct marketing situations.)

The seven-step process enables you to:

- draw up a test budget to meet the targets set
- calculate 'target' response rates
- undertake 'what if?' analyses with different tests
- calculate the percentage of the programme budget to be spent on testing

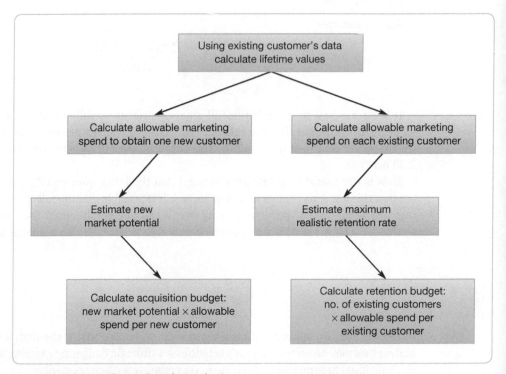

Figure 14.4 Setting the total marketing budget

Table 14.6 Typical test cell sizes for media

Medium	Test cell size
Direct mail	5,000 customers
Telephone	1,000 customers
Inserts	50,000 customers
Press or magazine advertisement	say 200,000
DRTV/radio	say 500,000

- input the actual test results and calculate the best options for roll-out;
- plan the final roll-out and predicted return.

Step 1: Decide what you want to test

Our first step is to draw up a list of tests depending on our need for more knowledge. Let us say we wanted to test media types. A typical list of media types (we will not go as far as actual titles here) for our example might be as follows:

- Direct mail to existing customers
- Direct mail to prospects
- On-line advertising
- Social media
- Telephone marketing to existing customers
- Computer magazines
- Direct-response television during computer programmes
- Direct-response radio

Step 2: Calculate your total test budget

This depends on how much testing you wish to do before moving on to the campaign roll-out. If you are following a well-understood direct marketing campaign, you may be carrying out one or two tests only to look for small improvements. If, however, you are trying something totally new, you have a significant learning curve. In this instance, the test budget can often be as much as 30 per cent of the total budget.

To estimate total costs for our test we need to decide its size in terms of audience, and then multiply this by the cost per thousand for each medium. Table 14.6 lists typical test cell sizes for different media.

Using the test sizes in Table 14.6 we can calculate the costs of testing, as shown in Table 14.7.

Table 14.7 Calculation of the total costs of testing

Medium	Cost/000 (£)	Size of audience	Total cost (£)
Direct mail to existing customers	400	5,000	2,000
Direct mail using lifestyle lists	500	5,000	2,500
Direct mail using mail-order lists	500	5,000	2,500
Telephone marketing to existing customers	6,000	1,000	6,000
Computer magazines advertisement	50	200,000	10,000
DRTV during computer programs	10	500,000	5,000
DR radio	5	500,000	2,500
Total costs			**£30,500**

Table 14.8 Calculation of number of responses required to hit target

Medium	Total cost (£)	No. of customers needed to hit target
Direct mail to existing customers	2,000	40
Direct mail using lifestyle lists	2,500	50
Direct mail using mail-order lists	2,500	50
Telephone marketing to existing customers	6,000	120
Computer magazines advertisement	10,000	200
DRTV during computer programs	5,000	100
DR radio	2,500	50

Therefore, we are spending 30.5 per cent of our total budget on testing.

Step 3: Calculate the number of responses required to achieve target

Our target is to spend less than £50 per customer. If we divide the total costs (from Table 14.7) for each medium by £50 we obtain our target recruitment per medium, as shown in Table 14.8.

Step 4: Calculate estimated target response rates

$$\text{Target response rate} = \frac{\text{No. of customers needed to hit target}}{\text{Total size of audience}} \times 100\%$$

We can, therefore, work out the target response rate for each medium, as shown in Table 14.9.

Step 5: Decide which tests to implement

Assess the response rates in Table 14.9 in terms of previous experience. Decide which tests actually to run with. In the case of the media tests in the example, we would use the AIMRITE formula outlined previously (Chapter 11) to evaluate the validity of our test choices. Are there any other media that should be tested in place of our choices?

Let us say we decide that the list of media in Table 14.9 is our final test choice.

Step 6: Identify test winners

When the actual test results come in, calculate the return on investment. This is done by multiplying the actual number of responses by £20 (margin per sale), which gives the total

Table 14.9 Calculation of estimated target response rates

Medium	Size of audience	No. of customers needed to hit target	Target response rate (%)
Direct mail to existing customers	5,000	40	0.8
Direct mail using lifestyle lists	5,000	50	1.0
Direct mail using mail-order lists	5,000	50	1.0
Telephone marketing to existing customers	1,000	120	12.0
Computer magazines advertisement	200,000	200	0.1
DRTV during computer programs	500,000	100	0.02
DR radio	500,000	50	0.01

Table 14.10 Calculation of net profit margin

Medium	Total media cost (£)	Actual response rate (%)	Actual no. of customers	Total gross margin (£)	Net profit margin (£)
Direct mail to existing customers	2,000	3.5	175	3,500	1,500
Direct mail using lifestyle lists	2,500	2.0	100	2,000	(500)
Direct mail using mail-order lists	2,500	1.5	75	1,500	(1,000)
Telephone marketing to existing customers	6,000	25	250	5,000	(1,000)
Computer magazines advertisement	10,000	0.20	400	8,000	(2,000)
DRTV during computer programs	5,000	0.06	300	6,000	1,000
DR radio	2,500	0.025	125	2,500	0
Total	£30,500			£28,500	(£2,000)

margin. The net profit is then total gross margin minus total marketing (in this case media) costs. Table 14.10 shows these calculations.

Marketers often feel guilty about making a loss in tests. This is wholly unnecessary because you are not £2,000 down on the deal, you are £2,000 better educated. You now know exactly what works and what doesn't. Had someone come to you before the test and said 'for just £2,000 I can tell you – absolutely and without mistake – which media will work and which won't' you would have given them the money without hesitation.

Step 7: Roll out the test winners to the full audience

Our final step is to roll out to the full audience using the best media. We start with the test medium showing the best 'percentage return on marketing investment', calculated by dividing net profit by marketing costs (expressed as a percentage). When that medium is used up, move down to the second best, and so on, until our budget is exhausted.

In the example, we have £100,000 minus our test budget of £30,500 = £69,500 to apply to the roll out. The best medium is direct mail to existing customers (with a 75 per cent return on marketing investment); the only other profitable medium is DRTV (with a 20 per cent return). Therefore, the roll-out in this example might look like Table 14.11.

The budget left after this roll out is £31,500 (£69,500 − £38,000). This dictates the roll-out to the other remaining test success: DRTV (see Table 14.12).

Thus, from Tables 14.11 and 14.12, the gross margin from roll-outs using these two media is £104,300 (£66,500 + £37,800). Deduct from this the costs of the tests from Table 14.10 and we arrive at an overall gross profit of £102,300.

Table 14.11 Calculation of total gross margin for roll-out of best medium

Winning medium	Maximum quantity	Maximum quantity minus test quantity (actual roll-out)	Roll-out costs (£)	Percentage response (%)	Total gross margin* (£)
Direct mail to existing customers	100,000	95,000	38,000	3.5	66,500

Total gross margin = actual roll-out quantity percentage response margin per sale (£20).

513

Table 14.12 Calculation of roll-out using remaining medium

Medium	Budget left (£)	Roll-out quantity*	Percentage response	Total gross margin (£)
DRTV during computer programs	31,500	3.15m	0.06	37,800

* Here, the roll-out quantity is dictated by the budget remaining.

By inputting the 'actuals' into these calculations, valuable clarity can be gained for the next round of budgeting decisions. This is why direct marketing can exhibit such tight control over its returns on marketing investment.

14.3 Market research in direct marketing

There has been something of a traditional rivalry between direct marketing and market research, with each claiming they know the true facts about customers and the market in general. In truth, the two disciplines should go hand in hand.

Market research has a number of roles in direct marketing that mirror its traditional strengths in general marketing. The core advantage that market research has over testing more succinctly is that, although testing can tell us 'what' consumers' behaviour is and how much they will respond or stay with us, only market research can tell us 'why' they do so. It is vitally important to answer the 'why' question in order to analyse accurately and develop effective strategies for the future.

On the other side of the coin, the codes of practice of most market research bodies around the world prohibit the use of research data for sales purposes (a practice known as 'Sugging' – Selling Under the Guise of Research), whereas direct marketing data has usually been gathered through that very route in the first place.

We need to focus on two main areas of work that can be assisted by market research. The first of these is database analysis, and the second is campaign planning and development.

14.3.1 Database analysis

We saw earlier (Chapter 3) how the database can be used to analyse our markets. Market research and the database can be used very effectively in tandem, drawing from the complementary skills of each technique.

In general marketing, a large part of the market research budget is used in descriptive research. Descriptive research takes a snapshot picture of the marketplace, providing marketers with data on customer profiles, product preferences and underlying attitudes that may underpin their purchases. Most of this research is quantitative, and is concerned with measurement: the number of customers who fit a certain profile, and so on.

These analyses are familiar territory to direct marketers, but we use a database rather than descriptive market research as our analytical tool. The database offers the advantage of looking at populations rather than samples, and behavioural data (what customers actually purchased) rather than claimed behaviour from research surveys.

Another advantage is the vast numbers that can be used for quantitative analysis. Techniques such as cluster and factor analysis, correspondence techniques and so on, are far more effective with large volumes of data. Databases offer tens or hundreds of thousands of customers: market research typically makes do with samples of a few hundred.

However, market research can provide tailor made causal studies that look specifically to understand what the dependent factors are for customer purchase. This can be better than the database equivalent, which is applying techniques such as regression analysis to data that 'may not have been collected for that specific analytical purpose'. Customer databases contain data from a variety of sources, which is there primarily to help in understanding individual customers' value to the company and their needs from that company. We may know that someone plays golf and is wealthy; we may have other lifestyle data about him, but none of this may be related to his psychological drive to buy other golf products, even if regression analysis suggests a correlation. This is where carefully done causal market research can provide an advantage.

Perhaps the greatest value market research can add to direct marketers is in the use of 'qualitative' research in an 'exploratory' role to increase understanding of marketing situations. Imagine a scenario where a company is faced with a sudden, unexpected increase in customer defections. It is obviously necessary to understand quickly what is going on. Exploratory market research using qualitative techniques, such as in-depth interviews and focus groups, is an excellent way of increasing our understanding of what drives customers in our market. Although experienced direct marketers of, say, china collectibles (porcelain dolls, decorative plates and so on) know what makes their customers tick, how does a new entrant operate? What is it that drives someone to spend hundreds of pounds every year collecting china dolls? Answers to questions such as this are best obtained through carefully executed in-depth interviews, group discussions and other qualitative techniques.

To summarise, when analysing markets in order to develop strategies, direct marketers traditionally use databases to replace a lot of measurement work that quantitative research performs in general marketing. Probably the most valuable role for market research in direct marketing is in the use of qualitative research to increase our understanding of our marketing situation.

14.3.2 Campaign planning and development

Let us take the example of a new product launch through direct marketing. A six-step model that illustrates the role of market research is shown in Figure 14.5 (Mouncey, 2007, pp. 2.1–29).

Each step in Figure 14.5 can be summed up as follows:

Step 1. Use the database to select samples for market research to test the initial product concepts.

Step 2. Use postal quantitative research to forecast demand, obtaining a low-cost measure of intended take-up. This early forecast enables test product and pricing issues to be solved before test costs are incurred. Postal research replicates the direct-response technique of the direct marketing exercise itself.

Step 3. Use knowledge from database analysis and qualitative research to develop communications material.

Step 4. Move to test; lists/media and product offers are vital to test at this stage.

Step 5. Roll out.

Step 6. Use the database to carry out response analysis, and back up with qualitative and/or quantitative research to understand consumer attitudes to the campaign.

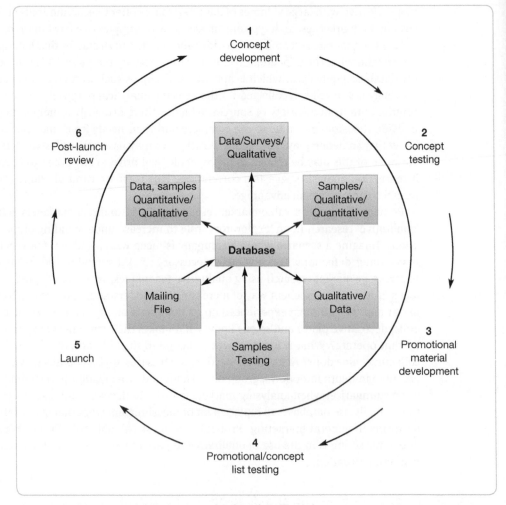

Figure 14.5 Six-step model illustrating role of market research
Source: After Mouncey, P. (2002). Reproduced with permission.

Summary

In this chapter the use of testing in direct marketing was attributed to the close control direct marketers can exert over the various campaign elements. By varying only one factor at a time, marketers can learn a great deal about how to maximise response, while keeping risks of big losses to a minimum. The accepted wisdom is that the audience and the product offering have the biggest impact on response, while the creative element has the least.

Because direct marketers can directly relate costs to revenues, highly accurate cost/revenue budgets can be produced. These can be integrated with testing using the process given, and a full top-level and individual programme budget can be drawn up to be used for 'what if?' analysis.

QUESTIONS

1 Why is testing so important to managers, and why is direct marketing better suited to testing than conventional marketing?

2 John Brown Supplies sells office equipment to small and medium-sized businesses in its locality. Each sale averages a gross margin of £30, and next year's budget is £100,000. Use the seven-step process of budgeting outlined in the chapter to draw up a 'break-even' test budget, drawing on cost assumptions covered earlier (Chapters 9 and 10) if necessary.

3 Most mail-order operations make very little use of market research as a tool to help them, preferring to rely on testing instead. If you were addressing them as a market researcher, what benefits of market research could you point out to them?

4 City Products is a mobile phone retailer in London. It wants to test an offer to its own database using direct mail, and has calculated its break-even response rate to be 3.0 per cent. Previous results indicate that this test result should be about 3.5 per cent. Given that it wants to ensure any roll-out is in profit, what size sample should the company use for the test?

5 Merchants Financial Services has a customer base of 500,000 existing customers. In September, the marketing manager will mail the complete file but wants to test two new formats, two new creative approaches and two new incentives against the existing control mailer. The cell size in each case will be 10 000. Devise a matrix that makes optimum use of the minimum number of customers for the tests.

6 A university wants to recruit students for the next academic year, and wants to use press advertising for the first time to achieve this. The marketing manager decides to test two creative approaches in an A/B split of the *Guardian* education section. She does not see the need for any other tests. What comments would you make about her testing priorities?

References

Batra, A. (2012). *Cost of Advertising: CPM, CPC and eCPM Demystified.* Available at: **http://webanaly-sis.blogspot.co.uk/2012 ÷ 01/cost-of-advertising-cpm-ecpm-and-cpc.html#ax-z20ylUtrSR** [Accessed 18 July 2012].

Blanchard, O. (2011). *Social Media – Managing and Measuring Social Media Efforts in Your Organisation,* Pearson Education Inc., Boston MA.

Halsey, B. (1992). *The Practitioner's Guide to Direct Marketing,* The Institute of Direct Marketing, Teddington.

Kotler *et al.* (2009). *Marketing Management,* Pearson Education Limited, Harlow.

Mouncey, P. (2007). *Understanding Consumers: The Essential Role Played by Market Research* in: *The IDM Marketing Guide,* The Institute of Direct Marketing, Teddington.

Pearson, S. (2008). *Personal Communication.s.l.:s.n.*

Stone, B. and Jacobs, R. (2001). *Successful Direct Marketing Methods,* 7th edn, McGraw-Hill, New York.

The IDM (2007). *The IDM Marketing Guide,* The Institute of Direct Marketing, Teddington.

CASE STUDY

The Royal National Lifeboat Institution

Setting the scene

'It's almost unbelievable isn't it? Over 75 per cent of our income comes from people who have never set foot in a boat in their lives.'

This comment by one of the fundraising team really summed up a worry for the fundraising department of the Royal National Lifeboat Institution (RNLI). Its traditional donor base (recruited and supported by direct marketing methods) often lived many miles from the sea. With their help, the RNLI had grown to be one of the five biggest charities in the UK, able to offer a complete sea rescue service for Britain and Ireland's 5,000 miles of coastline. However, this comfortable picture hid looming threats to income: the age of the RNLI's core supporter base indicated a decline in volume, threatening the long-term financial base of the charity itself. What were the fundraising team to do about it?

The Royal National Lifeboat Institution

In 1824, The National Institution for the Preservation of Life from Shipwreck was founded by Sir William Hillary as a voluntarily supported organisation. The folklore of the charity includes the famous story from this time of Grace Darling, a young girl who, on her own, rescued a foundering ship in stormy weather. In 1854 the organisation was renamed the Royal National Lifeboat Institution, which remains unchanged to this day.

The RNLI is a registered charity whose mission is simple, but powerfully expressed: 'to save lives at sea'. It has a legal responsibility to the governments of the UK and Ireland to provide a statutory 24-hour emergency service, to cover search and rescue requirements up to 50 miles out from the coast in all conditions.

Things have changed a lot for the RNLI since those early days. In 1995, RNLI lifeboats were launched 7,382 times, with a staggering 52 launches every day, on average, during August. Over the past ten years, calls on lifeboats have increased by nearly 50 per cent. This is due mainly to the numbers of people using the water vastly increasing. There has been an increase in the number of 'beach rescues', and also rescues to pleasure craft, commercial power and sail, as well as surfers and swimmers. On average, every day, a lifeboat is launched 16 times in the UK and 4 lives are saved each day.

This rescue service costs a great deal of money. The RNLI now uses the most modern rescue equipment, including 11 different types of lifeboat, ranging from the 50-foot-long Severn class of boat with a crew of six, capable of 25 knots, to the 16-foot D-class inflatable boat, which operates with a crew of three. Each D-class now costs over £11,000 to buy and more to run each year. This modern fleet is required to ensure that the RNLI's future commitment to reach any point 50 miles off the coast within two-and-a-half hours is met.

With over 400 lifeboats operating in 219 lifeboat stations, the RNLI costs £70 million to run annually, or £194,000 per day. Its fundraising budget is about £7 million p.a. Running costs are used for:

- operational costs
- a new lifeboat building programme
- training crews (vital)
- back-up and administration (less than 4 per cent of revenue)

RNLI funds are raised entirely through voluntary contributions, unlike some charities which get state support as well.

The RNLI's supporters

The RNLI has a quarter of a million members and donors, and about 40,000 volunteers who raise money through community fundraising activities. Only about 70,000 of the members are seagoers – about a quarter of the membership base. The RNLI's income currently comes primarily from 'middle Britain' supporters with traditional values.

Middle Britain supporters: a profile

Middle Britain supporters donate because they admire the bravery and self-sacrifice of the RNLI's volunteer crews, who risk their lives to save the lives of others. These donors typically hold 'conservative', traditional values of honour and chivalry, and are attracted to the qualities of bravery and calmness under pressure that are attributed to the RNLI crews. An example of the material that has worked well with this audience is shown in Figure 14.6.

Over two-thirds of the database are over 65 years old, and 75 per cent are male. They may typically read the *Daily Telegraph* and have some prior connection with the navy, civil service or similar organisation with traditional values.

However, this membership is facing slow decline. There are a number of reasons for this. The 'middle Britain' and wartime generation – the core demography

Figure 14.6 Classic insert used to recruit traditional support

Source: Reproduced by kind permission of the Royal National Lifeboat Institution.

of the members – is in decline. Another problem is that the RNLI is increasingly in direct competition with other charities for donors' income.

Most of the RNLI's income is from legacies: in 1992 about 70 per cent of its funds came from those who left something to the RNLI in their will. This figure has now declined to 60 per cent and may continue to fall. The reason for this appears to be the increasing costs of long-term elderly care, which is depleting retired people's life-savings at an alarming rate. The Henley Centre's research in this area suggests that legacy income to charities may continue to decline for the next 15 years. However, legacies are still tremendously important to the RNLI. Sixty per cent of its income comes from only about 2,000 people who leave money in their wills.

Of the five million people who use the sea, only a tiny percentage support the charity that could save their lives. Only about 2.5 per cent (50,000) of the 2 million boat owners regularly support the RNLI.

There has also been little growth in the number of younger supporters – a worrying trend with such an old base of donors. The problem here is that the RNLI has a low level of saliency among younger people. The values of the RNLI had their strongest resonance among a society with traditional values. There was also a relationship between the RNLI and Britain as a symbol of civilisation, via the Empire, around the world. With the decline of British influence, young people do not identify with this sense of national pride and the RNLI has suffered; it is no longer something younger people feel 'proud of'.

The RNLI's appeal to donors has been the courage and bravery of the crews. These volunteers go out in any weather, at any time of the day or night, and stay out until the job is done. The RNLI's core message to donors was, 'They'll face 30-foot waves, blizzards, force 9 gales and sub-zero temperatures. All we ask of you is £ . . .'

The problem for the RNLI's fundraisers now was to retain their traditional values in fundraising while changing their approach so as to appeal to seagoers. A meeting within the RNLI had yielded some early thoughts about how to achieve this. They felt that seagoers would still relate to the image of the lifeboat helmsman, but would have a more pragmatic view of him and what he and his crew does. The question was: what values should the helmsman project?

Charity fundraising generally

Charity fundraising is very different to commercial marketing. When someone gives to a charity, they are receiving something back, but establishing exactly what is often not easy. For 'inner-directed' people, it may be a satisfaction that they have helped make the world a better place, that by supporting the charity they have done something concrete to uphold their own beliefs and values.

'Outer-directed' people may get satisfaction in expressing their giving as part of their personality. They will associate with the brand values of the charity by giving, and will want to show others that this association says something about them. Thus by giving to, say, Greenpeace, they are identifying with Greenpeace's values of defiance, youthfulness, non-violence and so on.

Others may give for other reasons. Some will give because they get a direct benefit from the charitable service, or they know someone who has benefited.

Although some charities have a big retail presence, the importance of repeat donations from a relatively small number of big givers means that direct marketing is a critical part of the charity fundraising mix. The large charities all have databases of many hundreds of thousands of donors, some of whom give thousands of pounds a year in support. Recruitment is achieved through a variety of methods, of which direct mail has traditionally been the key medium. However, intense competition has led to an overuse of 'cold' direct mail, now regarded by many recipients as 'junk'.

Many charities swap lists in an effort to recruit more donors, although the RNLI has refused to do this. The RNLI will also limit the use of the telephone to its donor base, whose age and values make them highly sensitive to privacy issues and less comfortable with the phone than young people.

Most recruitment is done at a loss: the Charity Aid Foundation's figures found that the average return on investment for acquisition activities is about 0.7:1. Break-even on acquisition is considered good. The money is made from repeat donations, perhaps through automatic schemes like direct debit. In contrast to their public image, charities are now very professional outfits, and maximising returns through statistical modelling of their donor base or using relationship-building techniques to build closer links are very important activities.

Some charities have found that offering tangible benefits works well for them. The Royal Society for the Protection of Birds offers a range of 'products' (which may include information, access to sites, certificates, car stickers and so on) that donors or members can opt for in return for guaranteed donations of various sizes. Others set up special clubs or membership schemes for committed givers, in which they may be invited to special events, to receive privileged information, or to see the results of their donations. Action Aid's 'Sponsor a Child' campaign is a long-running example of this.

More recently, growth in donations has come through partnership projects with corporate partners. These could take the form of allowing access by the corporate partner to the donor file for marketing initiatives, or a PR-style connection in which the corporate partner gains from association with the charity. In return, the charity may get help with its own donor recruitment, or direct donations may be made by the partner.

A paper by Saxton (1996) on charity fundraising strategies outlined the primary choices taken by the larger charities. He detailed the following five choices:

1 **Donation-led strategy.** The most commonly used strategy (often inappropriately), the core elements are the need for a large number of new recruits, a heavy frequency of subsequent appeals and high supporter attrition rate. Average lifetime values are low. This approach depends on a constant supply of motivating new stories or topics to provide new stimulus to donate.

2 **The intimacy strategy.** A limited number of new supporters is recruited, but each is carefully nurtured to maximise lifetime value. Communications are carefully put together in such a way as to create a feeling of closeness. This strategy is often suited to major donor departments of large charities.

3 **Audience-led strategy.** A specific audience is taken and a close and lasting relationship is sought, often through membership. The group can be based on attitude and lifestyle. More donations and better relationships are then sought through offers that are carefully put together to take account of the sensibilities of the group. In many ways, the RNLI's approach to its traditional base fits into this strategy.

4 **Product-led strategy.** Here the donor is offered a clear product, such as membership. The Royal Society for the Protection of Birds organises its fundraising clearly around its membership scheme, which offers assorted benefits.

5 **Multi-product strategy.** This is a mix of donation-led and product-led strategies. An array of catalogues, appeals, newsletters and different opt-in membership schemes are communicated to the donor.

Offshore

To counteract the slow but radical changes in its membership profile, a firm policy decision was made to recruit and retain more 'seagoing' members. This was to be achieved through the launch of 'Offshore', a new grade of membership especially for sea users. This scheme was to offer a variety of marine-related benefits.

The team at the RNLI wanted to get over a feeling of belonging: that for seagoers, the RNLI is 'their' charity. There could also, with some justification, be grounds for marketing 'Offshore' as a thing of duty, or personal responsibility. If anyone should support the RNLI, seagoers should; it is they and they alone who benefit. Why should they rely on the support of others without giving themselves? However, the team knew that attempts to instil feelings of guilt could backfire. Good fundraising was all about arousing such strong feelings of empathy with the cause that instant action was the result. However, such feelings had to be built around values and beliefs if they were to remain beyond a one-off donation.

One possibility was to promote 'Offshore' as the sea equivalent of car breakdown insurance. Whether or not this was a good idea for a charity had yet to be discussed.

Seagoers: a profile

The segment of seagoers defined within the charity as top priority were those who use the sea for pleasure purposes. These were mainly owners of pleasure craft – weekend sailors, and so on – but also users of other craft such as windsurfers and surfers. Sailing is not a cheap sport, and so the profile of seagoers is accordingly quite upmarket. It is also rather younger than the RNLI's core support.

Seagoers' attitude to the RNLI was rather different to that of traditional supporters. Clearly, the RNLI is more relevant to them: they viewed it as a background presence, always there, and the ultimate safety line, but did not have high everyday awareness of it. They respected the RNLI's abilities – for example, seamanship, knowledge of sea safety and their experience of rescues were all acknowledged, but remained very much in the background of sailors' lives. 'Yachties' in particular were difficult to approach. They were notoriously independent, free-spirited people who disliked being pressured into anything. They were extremely proud of their seamanship, and some saw the RNLI as being only for 'incompetent' inexperienced sailors, although this was not the case.

RNLI research showed that seagoers were always interested in the latest sea safety information, and had a need for all kinds of sea-related products, from sailing accessories and clothing to boat fashion goods.

Official surveys found that seagoers:

- were younger than traditional supporters (66 per cent were under 44)

- were affluent (63 per cent had a combined income of £25,000 or above)

- comprised more women than traditional supporters (32 per cent of seagoers were women)

The surveys also suggested that seagoers were likely to be style-conscious, aspirational, self-interested and less altruistic than traditional supporters. They are more aware of marketing techniques, and so would assess approaches rationally rather than emotionally.

Programme issues

An initial analysis document drawn up by the fundraising team revealed the following issues to consider:

- There was a need to get past the 'taken for granted, always there' state that all rescue services suffer from.

- There was a need to remind seagoers that the sea is an unpredictable place.

- A new proposition, repositioned brand values, and a different tone of voice was needed in order to account for the differences between seagoers and middle Britain donors. However, it was important to remember that any material produced for 'Offshore' may be seen by traditional supporters, and they should not feel alienated or 'short changed' by this alternative scheme.

- At the same time, current brand values needed to be upheld for middle Britain support, but adjusted in tone for seagoers' support, while maintaining a credible overall image. This was a considerable challenge, but could not be ignored by the fundraisers.

- The team stressed the need to keep recruitment costs as low as possible. It needed to find ways to spread the message and attract supporters at an average of less than £50 per new supporter.

- 'Offshore' was to be offered to prospects at £40 per annum, i.e. probably making an 'initial' loss on the first year's income. However, surveys found that seagoers had suggested a fee of only about £23, on average, for such a package. There was, therefore, a strong need to offer a package that is perceived as good value for money, but which also puts the correct value on the RNLI's service.

- The RNLI had given a presentation to some potential business partners. The RNLI was looking for help in promoting the scheme and, in return, it would ensure the assisting company would benefit by association with RNLI's powerful brand values.

- The fundraising team was investigating the possibility of using volunteers to help with the recruitment of 'Offshore' members, but as yet had not developed detailed plans.

- Various lists of seagoers were available, ranging from subscribers to sailing-related magazines, to the possibility of sponsored questions on lifestyle databases (estimated quote was £1,500 per question, plus £100 per thousand names obtained).

- Seagoers read a wide variety of publications ranging from *Motor Boats Monthly* to *Yachting Life*.

- The RNLI maintained a strong presence each year at the London International Boat Show, and also ran an RNLI day each year in which fundraising opportunities were maximised. The RNLI was due to celebrate its 175th anniversary in 1999, another major fundraising opportunity.

The task

The RNLI team had a number of planning and implementation issues still to resolve:

1 Formalising objectives and strategies. The key target was to recruit 50,000 Offshore members within three years.

2 The launch of Offshore such that 60 per cent of sea-goers were aware of the scheme within six months of launch.

3 A set of programmes to recruit and retain Offshore members, such that each member was recruited at an average of less than £50 each, and gave a return of at least £40 per annum for at least five years.

Questions

With the help of Appendices 1–3, provide a detailed action plan for the launch and delivery of Offshore, giving details of marketing programmes that will deliver the required targets. Your plan should include:

1 A description of what programmes will be delivered to whom and when, with justification. In particular:

- Target audiences
- Product/price offers
- Incentives
- Media
- Tests
- Required target response rates

2 Decisions on other marketing mix elements and an explanation of how they integrate with direct marketing.

Appendix 1
Membership rates and grades

Name	Aimed at	Rate
Stormforce	Junior members	£3
Shoreline	Traditional supporter	£15 (in line with World Wildlife Fund, National Trust) £40
Offshore	Seagoers	£40
Governors	Major donors	£50–£100
Life governors	Major donors	£1000 one-off payment

Appendix 2
Headings from previous RNLI creative briefs to its direct marketing agency, Burnett Associates

A GUIDE FOR TONE AND APPROACH

TARGET AUDIENCE

TONE

AIMS

PROPOSITION

Appendix 3
List of questions in survey of yacht club members to be carried out within three months of the brief

General

How long have you been sailing?
How often do you sail?
For what purposes do you sail:

- Work
- Cruising
- Racing
- Other?

Which publications do you read regularly (if any):

- *Motor Boats Monthly*
- *Practical Boat Owner*

- *RYA News*
- *The Lifeboat*
- *Yachting Monthly*
- *Yachting World*
- *Yachts and Yachting?*

    Have you heard of the RNLI?
    Do you support the RNLI?
    If so, how?

Other charities

Do you regularly support other charities?
In what way?

About yourself

Gender

Age

Occupation

Income

Marital status

Reference

Saxton, J. (1996) 'Five direct marketing strategies for nonprofit organisations', *Journal of Nonprofit and Voluntary Sector Marketing*, **1** (4).

Chapter 15

Legal impacts on direct, database and digital marketing

Please note

The information provided in this chapter is not comprehensive and does not constitute legal advice. If you require legal advice on these issues you need to consult a solicitor.

Objectives

By the end of this chapter you will understand:

- the organisational obligations under the Data Protection Act (1998)
- what rights individuals have under the same Act
- the difference between opt-in and opt-out
- the new requirements relating to the use of cookies
- the direction in which data protection is likely to move in the next few years

Introduction

There are many rules, regulations and legislations affecting the way in which we can and cannot market our products to our customers and prospects. We will be focusing on the following of these:

- The Data Protection Act (1998)
- The difference between opt-in and opt-out
- The regulations relating to the use of cookies on computers
- The future of data protection in Europe

You should be aware that these are not the only regulations you need to follow. We are not even going to start looking at the various codes of conduct issued by the many different professional bodies related to marketing. These can be found instead on the individual bodies' websites.

How this chapter is structured

This chapter begins with a look at the Data Protection Act (1998) and how it affects both businesses and the individuals about whom data is held. The next section looks at the debate and best practice relating to opt-in and opt-out when it comes to marketing, and then we move on to the new regulations relating to the use of cookies on electronic devices. Finally, we will consider some of the plans for the future of data protection in Europe.

15.1   The Data Protection Act (1998)

15.1.1   Background to The Data Protection Act (1998)

Most people are surprised to learn that, in the United Kingdom, there is no legally enshrined right relating specifically to the privacy of an individual. Consider the cases of the following high profile people who were all the victims of invasion of privacy, usually by the press and other mass media:

- Ryan Giggs, who was 'outed' as having an extra-marital affair (BBC News, 2012a)
- Former Prime Minister Gordon Brown, whose son's medical condition was revealed in the *Sun* newspaper without consent of the family (Sabbagh *et al.*, 2012)
- The family of Millie Dowler, the murdered 12-year-old whose phone-hacking (after her abduction) by the *News of the World* led to Rupert Murdoch delivering a personal apology to her family (Taylor, 2011)
- Diana, Princess of Wales

The Data Protection Act (1998), which will be referred to as 'The Act' for the rest of this chapter, was a response to a European-wide requirement for data protection to be in place in all member states (The European Data Protection Directive 95 – 46/EC). It replaced the Data Protection Act (1984) – but we won't confuse matters by going into that Act! It should be noted, however, that The Act is just that – an Act of Parliament, which means it is a legal obligation in the UK. It is not an option to adhere to it or not!

It is a popular misconception that The Act gives us a right to privacy – it does not, it is merely concerned with the ways in which data is processed – and we will come to quite what is meant by 'processed' later in the chapter. Furthermore, The Act is only concerned with 'Personal Data. . . which relate to a living individual who can be identified from those data' (Carey, 1998, pp. 89–90) or from those data in conjunction with other data that may be reasonably available. It is also concerned with expressions of opinion, worth noting when we get on to the Principles of The Act.

15.1.2 The role of the Information Commissioner

The Information Commissioner's Office (ICO) 'is the UK's independent authority set up to uphold information rights in the public interest, promoting openness by public bodies and data privacy for individuals' (The Information Commissioner's Office, 2012a). We will come on to penalties for breaches of The Act in due course, but the ICO is on record as saying that it would like custodial sentences for serious breaches of The Act (The Information Commissioner's Office, 2012b), (The Information Commissioner's Office, 2011), and this has been supported by Members of Parliament (BBC News, 2011).

The ICO covers The Act and also the Freedom of Information Act (FOI) in England and Wales. Scotland has its own FOI Commissioner, but Data Protection is covered by the UK Commissioner. The role of the Information Commissioner itself is that of a Crown Servant, i. e. it is independent and reports to Parliament rather than any single minister or MP, which removes party political appointments.

The Information Commissioner's Office is responsible for covering the following (The Information Commissioner's Office, 2012c):

- Upholding information rights – promoting understanding of the various Acts, etc.
- Taking action against people and organisations that breach those Acts
- Maintaining a register of data controllers, which can be searched on-line at **ico.gov.uk**
- Working with data processors in audits, advisory visits and self assessments
- Handling complaints from people who feel they have been wronged
- Monitoring compliance
- International duties – generally working with the ICO equivalents overseas and promoting best practice

15.1.3 Some definitions

Term	Definition	Explanation
Data	'Information which a) is being processed by means of equipment operating automatically in response to instructions given for that purpose, b) is recorded with the intention it should be processed by means of such equipment, c) is recorded as part of a relevant filing system or with the intention that it should form part of a relevant filing system, or d) does not fall within. . . a), b), or c) but forms an accessible record as defined by Section 68 [of The Act]' (Carey, 1998, p. 89)	Information held in such a way that a computer can be used to manipulate it, or held in a paper based system that is organised so anyone can find a requested file with minimal instruction on how to do so. Also, certain information held by local authorities (as defined in Section 68 of The Act).
Relevant Filing System	'Any set of information relating to in-dividuals to the extent that, although the information is not processed by [a computer] the set is structured . . . in such a way that specific informa-tion relating to an individual is readily accessible' (Carey, 1998, p. 90)	Any paper-based filing system where anyone can find the file with minimal instruction on how to do so.

Term	Definition	Explanation
Personal Data	'Data which relate to a living individual who can be identified a) from those data, b) from those data and other information which is in the possession of, or likely to come into the possession of, the data controller' (Carey, 1998, pp. 89-90)	Data relating to living people, but only if you can tell who that person is from those data or from those data with things you already know or will probably find out eventually.
Processing	'Obtaining, recording or holding information or data, or carrying out any operation or set of operations on the information or data, including: a) organisation, adaption or alteration of the information or data, b) retrieval, consultation or use of the information or data, c) disclosure of the information or data by transmission, dissemination or otherwise making available d) alignment, combination, blocking, erasure or destruction of the information or data' (Carey, 1998, p. 90)	If you can do it with, or to, data, it is processing. It is worth noting that this includes merely looking at it on a screen and also deleting it.
Data Subject	'An individual who is the subject of personal data'	No translation needed.
Data Controller	'A person [or organisation] who determines the purposes for which and the manner in which any personal data are, or are to be, processed'	The body in charge of the database or relevant filing system.
Data Processor	'Any person (other than an employee of the data controller) who processes the data on behalf of the data controller'	An example may be a contractor or temp worker, perhaps.

15.1.4 Notification under The Act

The Information Commissioner's Office maintains a public register of Data Controllers. Each register entry includes the name and address of the Data Controller and details about the types of personal information they process. Individuals can check the register to find out what processing of personal information is being done by a particular data controller – see **http://www.ico.gov.uk/ESDWebPages/search.asp**. Notification is the process by which a Data Controller's details are added to the register.

Notification is a statutory requirement and every organisation that processes personal information must notify the ICO, unless they are exempt. (The ICO's website (**www.ico.gov.uk**) has a useful tool to determine whether you need to notify or not. Search the site for 'do I need to notify?') Failure to notify when needed is a criminal offence. The main purpose of the public register is transparency and openness. The register includes the name and address of Data Controllers and a description of the kind of processing they do (The Information Commissioner's Office, 2012d).

A notification fee of £500 applies to Data Controllers with either turnover over £25.9 million and 250 or more members of staff OR if they are a public authority with 250 or more members of staff. The fee for all other non-exempt data controllers is £35 per annum. Registered charities and small occupational pension schemes do not come into the higher tier, regardless of size and turnover.

15.1.5 The eight principles of The Act

The central tenet of The Act is the eight 'Principles'. These are listed below (The Information Commissioner's Office, 2012g) and then discussed in more detail.

1 Personal data shall be processed fairly and lawfully and, in particular, shall not be processed unless:

   a. at least one of the conditions in Schedule 2 is met, and

   b. in the case of sensitive personal data, at least one of the conditions in Schedule 3 is also met.

2 Personal data shall be obtained only for one or more specified and lawful purposes, and shall not be further processed in any manner incompatible with that purpose or those purposes.

3 Personal data shall be adequate, relevant and not excessive in relation to the purpose or purposes for which they are processed.

4 Personal data shall be accurate and, where necessary, kept up to date.

5 Personal data processed for any purpose or purposes shall not be kept for longer than is necessary for that purpose or those purposes.

6 Personal data shall be processed in accordance with the rights of data subjects under this Act.

7 Appropriate technical and organisational measures shall be taken against unauthorised or unlawful processing of personal data and against accidental loss or destruction of, or damage to, personal data.

8 Personal data shall not be transferred to a country or territory outside the European Economic Area unless that country or territory ensures an adequate level of protection for the rights and freedoms of data subjects in relation to the processing of personal data.

Principle 1 – Fair and lawful

The Act says that Personal data shall be processed fairly and lawfully. There is an assumption that data will have been obtained fairly where it has been obtained from someone who is authorised or obliged to supply it (Carey, 1998, p. 25).

Lawful processing is a much more complicated matter. The Act says that data shall not be lawfully processed unless:

a. at least one of the conditions in Schedule 2 is met, and

b. in the case of sensitive personal data, at least one of the conditions in Schedule 3 is also met.

   (Carey, 1998, p. 21)

   We will come on to what Schedule 2 and 3 conditions are in due course.

   In practice, the first data protection principle means that you must:

- have legitimate grounds for collecting and using the personal data

- not use the data in ways that have unjustified adverse effects on the individuals concerned

- be transparent about how you intend to use the data, and give individuals appropriate privacy notices when collecting their personal data

- handle people's personal data only in ways they would reasonably expect; make sure you do not do anything unlawful with the data

(The Information Commissioner's Office, 2012f)

At the start of this section, mention was made of Schedule 2 and Schedule 3 conditions for processing. Schedule 2 refers to the conditions for processing data and Schedule 3 refers to the conditions for processing sensitive data.

Schedule 2 – conditions for processing data

In short, one of the following must be present for processing to be held to be lawful (The Office of the Information Commissioner, 2012e):

- Consent of the data subject
- Contractual necessity
- Non-contractual legal obligations of the data controller
- Vital interests of the data subject
- Functions of a public nature
- The processing is in the 'legitimate interests' of the data controller

When it comes to conditions for lawful processing, consent of the data subject is king.

Consent is not defined in the Data Protection Act. However, the European Data Protection Directive (to which The Act gives effect) defines an individual's consent as: ' . . . any freely given specific and informed indication of his wishes by which the data subject signifies his agreement to personal data relating to him being processed' (The Information Commissioner's Office, 2012g). Note that this says consent must be indicated. It is not enough to send (for example) a letter to someone and say that you will assume they are happy with your data processing arrangements if you do not hear from them in the next two weeks. Note also that Data Subjects may choose to withdraw their consent for processing at any time.

Contractual necessity refers to cases where processing is necessary either in relation to a contract that the individual has entered into or because the individual has asked for something to be done so they can enter into a contract (The Information Commissioner's Office, 2012g). For instance, credit card companies will not give anyone a credit card without undertaking credit reference checks on the applicant first and they would be within their rights to do so under the 'contractual necessity' test of legitimate processing. Of course, the data subject is within their rights to say they do not want such processing to take place, in which case the credit card company is equally within their rights to refuse you a card!

Non-contractual legal obligations of the data controller – for instance, although contracts of employment do not generally mention anything to do with the amount of tax the employee will pay, employers legally are required to pass on earnings and other data to the tax authorities, whether the employee gives their consent or not. This has nothing to do with the contract, but it is a legal obligation on the employer/data controller.

In certain conditions, it may be in the 'vital interests' of the data subject to disclose their data. For example, one of your employees has been diagnosed as having a heart condition and informs you in your role as Human Resources Manager. He tells you that he does not want this to become general knowledge because he does not want his peers to give him special treatment, so you make a note of this on his file and say nothing to anyone. One day, the employee collapses at his desk and an ambulance is called. At that point, it would be in the vital interests of the employee for you to disclose his heart condition to the medics at the scene so that they can render the best and most appropriate treatment to him. One hopes you would do so discreetly and away from work colleagues, rather than broadcasting it over the company radio system!

Functions of a public nature are when processing is necessary for administering justice, or for exercising statutory, governmental or other public functions (The Information Commissioner's Office, 2012g). This is generally held to cover the public sector more than the private sector, and will include things such as disclosures required for taxation or the prevention of crime, for instance.

The 'legitimate interests' condition is The Act's recognition that it may fall short of including all the reasons why a data controller may wish to process data and provides a way in which other processing may be permitted, providing certain conditions are met.

The following explanation and examples are from the Information Commissioner's website (The Information Commissioner's Office, 2012g).

The first requirement is that you must need to process the information for the purposes of your legitimate interests or for those of a third party to whom you disclose it.

Example 15.1	A finance company is unable to locate a customer who has stopped making payments under a hire purchase agreement. The customer has moved house without notifying the finance company of his new address. The finance company engages a debt collection agency to find the customer and seek repayment of the debt. It discloses the customer's personal data to the agency for this purpose. Although the customer has not consented to this disclosure, it is made for the purposes of the finance company's legitimate interests – i.e. to recover the debt.

The second requirement, once the first has been established, is that these interests must be balanced against the interests of the individual(s) concerned. The 'legitimate interests' condition will not be met if the processing is unwarranted because of its prejudicial effect on the rights and freedoms, or legitimate interests, of the individual. Your legitimate interests do not need to be in harmony with those of the individual for the condition to be met. However, where there is a serious mismatch between competing interests, the individual's legitimate interests will come first.

Example 15.2	In the above example, it is clear that the interests of the customer are likely to differ from those of the finance company (it may suit the customer quite well to evade paying his outstanding debt). However, passing his personal data to a debt collection agency in these circumstances could not be called 'unwarranted'.

Finally, the processing of information under the legitimate interests condition must be fair and lawful and must comply with all the data protection principles.

Example 15.3

Continuing the above example, the finance company must ensure that the personal data it passes to the debt collection agency is accurate (for example, in the known details of the customer's identity); that it is up to date (for example, in the amount outstanding and the customer's last known address); and that it is not excessive – the agency should only get as much personal data as is relevant or necessary for the purpose of finding the customer and recovering the debt.

Schedule 3 – conditions for processing sensitive data

When it comes to processing 'sensitive data', as well as satisfying one of the Schedule 2 conditions above, it is necessary to satisfy one of the conditions in Schedule 3 of The Act. We will come to what these are in a moment, but first we need to understand exactly what constitutes 'sensitive data'.

Sensitive data is defined in Section 2 of The Act. This may be summarised (Carey, 1998, p. 28) as follows:

- The racial or ethnic origin of the data subject
- His political opinions
- His religious beliefs or other beliefs of a similar nature
- Whether he is a member of a trade union
- His physical or mental health or condition
- His sexual life
- The commission or alleged commission by him of any offence
- Any proceedings for any offence committed or alleged to have been committed by him, the disposal of such proceedings or the sentence of any court in such proceedings

The conditions which make processing lawful under this schedule are:

1 The data subject has given his explicit consent.

2 The processing is necessary to allow the exercising of any legal right or obligation imposed on the data controller, for example various employment laws.

3 Processing is necessary to protect the vital interests of the data subject, as in Schedule 2 (above).

4 Processing is carried out as part of the legitimate activities of a not-for profit body organisation. By definition, any database of members of a church or trade union will contain sensitive data; it is in the legitimate interests of such data controllers to hold and process such data.

5 The personal data has been made deliberately public by the data subject.

6 The processing is necessary in relation to legal rights, for example obtaining legal advice or defending the data subject in legal proceedings.

7 Processing is necessary for the administration of justice; processing by the police and courts, for example.

8 The processing is necessary for medical purposes. Think about your family doctor, the NHS (in the UK) or hospitals, for instance.

9 Processing is necessary to trace equal opportunity policies and practices. Think about job application forms that ask you to tick the right box to indicate your ethnic background and nationality.

10 Any other condition made by the Secretary of State. This is another 'catch all' to allow The Act to be modified as time passes and new situations arise.

(Carey, 1998, pp. 28–30)

Principle 2 – data can only be used for the specified and lawful purposes notified

This comes back to notification again. As part of the notification process, data controllers are required to tell the ICO the reasons for which they will be using the data held. To use data for any purpose that is not listed in that notification is a breach of The Act.

Example
15.4

If your company sells travel insurance and has decided to make a natural expansion into selling holidays it would seem logical to use the data you have collected about your travel insurance customers to use in selling your new holidays product. Unfortunately this would not be permissible under The Act unless you first contact all the data subjects concerned to ask them for permission to use their data for the new purpose of selling holidays.

Principle 3 – data held must be adequate, relevant not excessive

There are no interpretation provisions for this principle in The Act (Carey, 1998, p. 33). However, the ICO's website tells us that we should identify the minimum amount of personal data required to adequately fulfil the purpose for which it is being held and hold only that data. This practice is known as 'data minimisation' (The Information Commission's Office, 2012h).

Principle 4 – data must be accurate and kept up to date

To comply with these provisions you should:

● take reasonable steps to ensure the accuracy of any personal data you obtain
● ensure that the source of any personal data is clear
● carefully consider any challenges to the accuracy of information
● consider whether it is necessary to update the information

(The Information Commissioner's Office, 2012i)

There is a degree of common sense applied to this, in as much as you would be expected to keep address details relating to a regular customer up to date but you would not be expected to check that the man who bought from you once, ten years ago, still lives at the same address.

You will not be in breach of The Act if you obtain data from a third party (rather than directly from the data subject) as long as you have accurately recorded the data provided, you have taken 'reasonable steps' to ensure its accuracy and (if the data subject has challenged the accuracy of such data) this is clear to those accessing it.

Principle 5 – data must be retained no longer than necessary

How long is necessary is a question of some debate. For some data controllers it may be necessary to hold data only for the fulfilment of one transaction, for others (financial services, for example) it may be necessary to hold the data for a period specified by the industry's watchdog, and in some cases this may be a large number of years or even indefinitely.

At the end of the period determined as being reasonable, data may be permanently deleted or archived. In the latter case, data is held off-line, which reduces access to it and the possibility of misuse or mistake, but the data is still held and as such is subject to The Act (The Information Commissioner's Office, 2012j).

Many companies are reluctant to delete data because they wish to use it for sales and marketing analysis and to identify trends in sales. Bearing in mind that The Act is concerned only with data relating to living persons who can be identified from those data, a simple way to achieve the desired goal while not breaching The Act is to anonymise any such data by removing anything that would allow the identification of the data subject.

Principle 6 – data subject rights

Data subjects have the following rights:

- A right of access to a copy of the information comprised in their personal data
- A right to object to processing that is likely to cause or is causing damage or distress
- A right to prevent processing for direct marketing
- A right to object to decisions being taken by automated means
- A right in certain circumstances to have inaccurate personal data rectified, blocked, erased or destroyed
- A right to claim compensation for damages caused by a breach of the Act

Let us take a look at these rights one at a time.

Access to personal data

The process when a data subject asks to see their data is known as a 'subject access request'. Data subjects have the right to be:

- told whether any personal data is being processed
- given a description of the personal data, the reasons it is being processed and whether it will be given to any other organisations or people
- given a copy of the information comprising the data
- given details of the source of the data (where this is available)

For a subject access request to be valid, it should be made in writing. You should also note the following points when considering validity (The Information Commissioner's Office, 2012k):

- The request should be received in writing (e-mail or fax is acceptable) but it may, depending on the circumstances, be reasonable to respond to verbal requests (as long as you are satisfied about the person's identity), and it is good practice at least to explain to the individual how to make a valid request, rather than ignoring them.
- If a disabled person finds it impossible or unreasonably difficult to make a subject access request in writing, you may have to make a reasonable adjustment for them under the Disability Discrimination Act 1995.
- If a request does not mention The Act specifically, or even say that it is a subject access request, it is nevertheless valid and should be treated as such if it is clear that the individual is asking for their own personal data.

535

- A request is valid even if the individual has not sent it directly to the person who normally deals with such requests – so it is important to ensure that you and your colleagues can recognise a subject access request and treat it appropriately.

Responses to subject access requests must be provided in a manner that is capable of being understood by the average person. In other words you cannot provide a list of coded data fields that would not mean anything to anyone outside your organisation (The Information Commissioner's Office, 2012k).

Organisations receiving a subject access request may charge a fee for dealing with it, and you need not comply with the request until you have received the fee. The maximum fee you can charge is £10, though there are different fee structures for organisations that hold health or education records (where the maximum fee is £50, depending on the circumstances). If a subject access request is not accompanied by the fee, you cannot ignore it; rather you should contact the data subject promptly and tell them what they need to pay and how (The Information Commissioner's Office, 2012k).

Subject access requests may be made by, or on behalf of, a third party under certain situations. Solicitors may make such requests on behalf of clients, or adult children may act on behalf of their elderly parents, for example. If you are not certain that the data subject fully understands the nature and extent of the data that will be provided to the third party in such a situation, you can choose to send it directly to the data subject (The Information Commissioner's Office, 2012k).

When it comes to subject access requests from (or relating to) children, even if a child is too young to understand the implications of subject access rights, data about them is still their personal data and does not belong, for example, to a parent or guardian. So it is the child who has a right of access to the information held about them, even though in the case of young children these rights are likely to be exercised by those with parental responsibility for them (The Information Commissioner's Office, 2012k).

Before responding to a subject access request for information held about a child, you should consider whether the child is mature enough to understand their rights. If you are confident that the child can understand their rights, then you should respond to the child rather than a parent. What matters is that the child is able to understand (in broad terms) what it means to make a subject access request and how to interpret the information they receive as a result of doing so (The Information Commissioner's Office, 2012k).

When considering borderline cases, you should take into account, among other things:

- The child's level of maturity and their ability to make decisions like this (The Information Commissioner's Office, 2012k)
- The nature of the personal data
- Any court orders relating to parental access or responsibility that may apply
- Any duty of confidence owed to the child or young person
- Any consequences of allowing those with parental responsibility access to the child's or young person's information (particularly important if there have been allegations of abuse or ill treatment)
- Any detriment to the child or young person, if individuals with parental responsibility cannot access this information
- Any views the child or young person has on whether their parents should have access to information about them

At this point, it is well worth mentioning that expressions of opinion are included in the data that needs to be provided in response to a subject access request. If a customer record includes statements meant to be helpful to your colleagues when dealing with the customer – such as 'Mr Monday is an obnoxious egotist who takes pleasure in being an awkward pedant' (or worse!) – you should remember that Mr Monday has the right to see that data. As a result, it is always a good idea to write as if the data subject is going to read your comments!

Prevent processing likely to cause damage or distress

A much misunderstood part of The Act is that it is often thought to give data subjects the right to stop processing of their data, full stop. This is not the case. The Act allows individuals to object to processing only if it causes 'unwarranted and substantial damage or distress'. As a result, it may be that you have to stop processing in certain circumstances and, equally, it may be that you will find yourself explaining to data subjects why you do not have to stop (The Information Commissioner's Office, 2012l).

A data subject who wants to object to their data being processed needs to object in writing, stating why your processing is causing them damage or distress and what they want you to do to stop this happening. This is known as an 'objection to processing' or a 'Section 10 notice', and can only relate to their own personal data being processed in a way that is causing unwarranted damage or distress. The data subject has no right to protest if they have consented to the data being processed in the first place, or if you are processing due to some legal requirement or for the data subjects 'vital interests' (The Information Commissioner's Office, 2012l), all of which have been covered earlier in this chapter.

Perhaps somewhat unhelpfully, The Act does not define what is meant by 'unwarranted damage or distress', though the ICO does say that 'substantial damage would be financial loss or physical harm; and substantial distress would be a level of upset, or emotional or mental pain, that goes beyond annoyance or irritation, strong dislike, or a feeling that the processing is morally abhorrent' (The Information Commissioner's Office, 2012l).

If you fail to respond to an objection, the data subject may decide to take the matter to court where, if the decision is that the objection is justified, you will be ordered to comply (The Information Commissioner's Office, 2012l).

Prevent direct marketing

This is perhaps the most relevant right for our purposes. Data subjects have the right to opt out of receiving direct marketing material by simply telling you of their wish. Once informed of this, you must comply. You are not required to respond to such a request, merely to comply 'within a reasonable period', which the ICO defines as being 28 days (for electronic communications) to two months (for letters) (The Information Commissioner's Office, 2012m).

Although it is normal for data subjects to ask you to remove their details from your database, best practice (approved by the ICO) is to add their name to a suppression file instead (The Information Commissioner's Office, 2012m). This is because, if you delete their name completely, there is nothing to stop you from subsequently buying their name again on an externally purchased list, whereas if you match all such lists against your suppression file the chances of that happening are much reduced.

See also the sections on the various Preference Services covered earlier (Chapter 2).

Automated decision taking

Much comedy has been made of the jobsworth whose response to customer requests for help or information is the simple reply 'the computer says no'. Such an approach is contrary to The Act, which says:

- An individual can give written notice requiring you not to take any automated decisions using their personal data.
- Even if they have not given notice, an individual should be informed when such a decision has been taken.
- An individual can ask you to reconsider a decision taken by automated means.

(The Information Commissioner's Office, 2012n)

This provision only becomes an issue when two conditions are met: firstly, the decision must have been made using personal data processed purely by automated means and, secondly, that decision has to have a significant effect on the data subject (The Information Commissioner's Office, 2012n).

Many personal loan companies provide a service where you can apply on-line and receive an immediate decision based on the answers you give to the questions asked. There is no human intervention in such cases, and the decision could have a major impact on the applicant's financial livelihood. As such it would be covered under The Act.

Correcting inaccurate personal data

The fourth principle requires that data must be accurate. If a data subject tells you that your record of his data is inaccurate, you are obliged to correct it in any and all places where it is held.

Compensation

If you have breached The Act, it may be that a data subject is entitled to compensation.

The right to compensation can be enforced only through the courts. There are no guidelines about the level of compensation that may be awarded. It is either for the data controller and data subject to come to an agreement or for the courts to decide for them if they cannot.

In all cases, it is better to simply comply with the Act and avoid such unpleasantness altogether.

Principle 7 – data security

The Act says that 'Appropriate technical and organisational measures shall be taken against unauthorised or unlawful processing of personal data and against accidental loss or destruction of, or damage to, personal data'. What is appropriate to one organisation (say the Ministry of Defence) may be wholly inappropriate to another (say a company of three plumbers and an administrator).

This means that organisations need to look at their own circumstances and determine what is appropriate to their situation. They should also be clear about who in the organisation is responsible for information security, provide suitable training to staff and be ready to respond to any breaches swiftly and effectively (The Information Commissioner's Office, 2012o).

You are required to ensure that data can be accessed only by those who need to do so, that such people act within the scope of their authority and that, if any personal data is lost, altered or destroyed, it can be recovered in order to prevent damage or distress to the data subjects concerned (The Information Commissioner's Office, 2012o).

In most cases, the application of passwords to restrict access to data is considered to be a sensible precaution, and the availability of back-ups is never going to go astray. Who among us has not suffered some form of data loss due to failing to save a document or accidentally deleting the most recent version of a file instead of the old version?!

Training staff to understand the importance of data protection and their duties under The Act is also a sensible approach (The Information Commissioner's Office, 2012o).

Physical security – such as keeping data servers behind locked doors, perhaps disallowing the use of USB sticks and the sending of large e-mail attachments, encrypting files that are taken off site and so on – should be considered (The Information Commissioner's Office, 2012o).

If data processors are employed (see definitions at the start of this chapter) then contracts should be drawn up detailing who is responsible for what, minimum security levels expected, methods of delivery of such security and processes for the transfer of data between data controller and data processor (The Information Commissioner's Office, 2012o).

Should you be the victim of a security breach, whether deliberate (e.g. through theft) or accidental (equipment failure, perhaps) then the ICO's office suggests four important elements in a breach management plan (The Information Commissioner's Office, 2012o):

1 Containment and recovery, including, where necessary, procedures for damage limitation.

2 Assessing the risks. In particular, you should assess the potential adverse consequences for individuals; how serious or substantial these are; and how likely they are to happen.

3 Notification of breaches. You should be clear about who needs to be notified and why. You should, for example, consider notifying the individuals concerned; the ICO; other regulatory bodies; other third parties such as the police and the banks; or the media.

4 Evaluation and response. It is important that you investigate the causes of the breach and also evaluate the effectiveness of your response to it. If necessary, you should then update your policies and procedures accordingly.

Principle 8 – overseas transfers

'Personal data shall not be transferred to a country or territory outside the European Economic Area (EEA) unless that country or territory ensures an adequate level of protection for the rights and freedoms of data subjects in relation to the processing of personal data' (The Information Commissioner's Office, 2012p).

There are no restrictions in transferring data between the countries in the EEA. Presently these are:

Austria	Greece	Netherlands
Belgium	Hungary	Norway
Bulgaria	Iceland	Poland
Cyprus	Ireland	Portugal
Czech Republic	Italy	Romania
Denmark	Latvia	Slovakia
Estonia	Liechtenstein	Slovenia
Finland	Lithuania	Spain
France	Luxembourg	Sweden
Germany	Malta	

Other countries are considered as having an adequate level of protection and, as such, transfers to these countries are acceptable under The Act:

Andorra	Faroe Islands	Israel
Argentina	Guernsey	Jersey
Canada	Isle of Man	Switzerland

If you wish to transfer data to a country that is outside the safe countries list you can still do so by using contracts to draw up acceptable levels of data protection (The Information Commissioner's Office, 2012p).

The Act differentiates between transfer (when data is sent to a country) and transit (when data passes through a country without being processed). It is only the former that is of interest to The Act. Companies that send paper records to India, for example, to be put onto computer are transferring data. Putting personal data on a website is also transferring the data, even if that website is hosted in the UK, because if anyone outside the EEA looks at the data they have processed it (The Information Commissioner's Office, 2012p).

It is a surprise to many that the United States of America (US) is not included in the European Commission list. However, the US has introduced a 'Safe Harbor' scheme, which applies to individual organisations rather than the country as a whole. If a company is a member of this scheme, it is considered to be adequately protected in terms of The Act. When a US company signs up to the Safe Harbor arrangement, they agree to follow seven principles of information handling and be held responsible for keeping to those principles by the Federal Trade Commission or other oversight schemes. Certain types of companies cannot sign up to Safe Harbor (The Information Commissioner's Office, 2012p). You can view a list of the companies signed up to the Safe Harbor arrangement on the US Department of Commerce website: **www.export.gov/safeharbor/**.

Furthermore, in July 2007, the EU and the US signed an agreement to regulate and make legal the transfer of passenger name record information (PNR) from EU airlines to the US Department of Homeland Security (DHS). This agreement is regarded as providing adequate protection for the personal data in question (The Information Commissioner's Office, 2012p).

In all of the above cases, there is a wealth of additional help and direction to be found at the excellent website run by the Information Commissioner's Office: www. ico.gov.uk.

15.2 Opt-in versus opt-out

Opt-in versus opt-out is the topic of much debate (and some confusion) in the direct marketing industry.

- Opt-in is where it is assumed an individual does not want to receive marketing material from your organisation unless they positively say they do.
- Opt-out is where it is assumed the individual is happy to receive marketing material from your organisation unless they positively say they do not.

The benefits of opt-out over opt-in are clear. If the assumption is that people want to receive literature from you, then there is a bigger pond in which to fish for prospects. However, the less obvious other side of this argument is that by only marketing to those who have said they want to hear from you, you are not so much fishing in a big pond (to carry on the metaphor on), but fishing where the fish are by sending your materials to people who have said they want them. As well as better targeting, this will mean shorter production runs and save money.

Consent by definition requires some sort of positive action on behalf of the recipient (Pinsent Masons, 2008). As a result, by itself, failing to register an objection will be unlikely to constitute valid consent. However, in context, failing to indicate objection may be part of the mechanism whereby a person indicates consent. For example, if you provide a clear and prominent message, the fact that a suitably prominent opt-out box has not been ticked may help establish that consent has been given (The Information Commissioner's Office, 2012q). On the other hand, the same page of the ICO's website also tells us that 'The fact that someone has had an opportunity to object which they have not taken only means that they have not objected. It does not mean that they have consented' (The Information Commissioner's Office, 2012q). Perhaps now you can see the reason for confusion in this matter!

To help control the increased use of e-mail for direct marketing and, in part, to deal with the risk of spam, in 2002 the EU issued a directive on privacy and electronic communications. This was brought into force in the UK by the Privacy and Electronic Communications (EC Directive) Regulations 2003. These are often referred to as PECR (pronounced 'pecker'), but will be abbreviated to 'The Regulations' for this book. The Regulations apply to all organisations that send out marketing by telephone, fax, automated calling system, e-mail, SMS, MMS or using any other form of electronic communication (Pinsent Masons, 2008). It is worth noting at this point that the rules on e-mails apply to individual subscribers (**james.monday@hotmail.com**) but not to e-mails sent to organisations (**james.monday@companyname.com**), though in the latter case you must identify yourself and provide an address (The Information Commissioner's Office, 2012r).

The Regulations provide that organisations cannot send unsolicited marketing communications by e-mail to individual subscribers unless the recipient has given his prior consent (Pinsent Masons, 2008). However, there is an exception to this rule. Known as the 'soft opt-in' it applies if the following conditions are met (The Information Commissioner's Office, 2012r):

- Where you have obtained a person's details in the course of a sale or negotiations for a sale of a product or service
- Where the messages are only marketing similar products or services
- Where the person is given a simple opportunity to refuse marketing when their details are collected and, if they do not opt out at this point, are given a simple way to do so in future messages

Recommended best practice

The approach known as 'double opt-in' is perhaps the gold standard when it comes to best practice in the arena of electronic marketing communications. This is where a subscriber indicates that they are interested in receiving marketing material from you (so they have opted-in once) and, in response to this, you send them an e-mail asking them to confirm they have made this request. That e-mail tells the subscriber that, in order to receive the marketing material they have requested, they need to click on a link in the e-mail (they opt-in for a second time). This prevents malicious signing in to receive marketing literature by third parties, whose sole objective may be to cause inconvenience to the ultimate recipient of the promotions by filling their inbox with e-mails they have not requested.

The final word on this should probably go to the ICO, which recommends that marketing campaigns are always permission-based and that it is explained clearly what a person's details will be used for. A simple way for recipients to opt out of marketing messages should be provided, and there should be a system in place for dealing with complaints (The Information Commissioner's Office, 2012r).

15.3 The use of cookies

A cookie is a small file, typically of letters and numbers, downloaded on to a device when the user accesses certain websites. Cookies are then sent back to the originating website on each subsequent visit. Cookies are useful because they allow a website to recognise a user's device (The Information Comissioner's Office, 2012s). Not all websites use cookies. Those that do, use them for a variety of different purposes, including (but not exclusively):

- Protection. Banks use cookies for security to protect customers from fraudulent activity. Without cookies, customers would not be able to access on-line banking so easily.

- Functionality. Cookies can be used to help speed the process of form filling on websites by using previously stored data to auto-populate fields.

- Improved user experience. Organisations may use systems such as Google Analytics to count and track how visitors come to their site and, once there, how they navigate their way around the site. This helps the organisations improve their sites and make the user experience more friendly and efficient.

- For marketing purposes. Cookies help organisations keep track of how effective their marketing campaigns are and Flash cookies count the number of times Flash files are played, thus indicating popularity and impacting on the website's design.

- Other cookies may originate with services that appear on an organisation's Web pages. These may include the likes of Facebook or Twitter, where users are encouraged to 'like' the host organisation's website.

As this book is being written, The Regulations have just been updated by The Privacy and Electronic Communications (EC Directive) (Amendment) Regulations 2011 (for the sake of ease and differentiation from The (original) Regulations, this will be referred to as 'The Amendment'). The Amendment came into force on 26 May 2012 with the major changes relating to the use of cookies on computers, the need for public electronic communications service providers to report personal data breaches, and the powers the Information Commissioner has to enforce these regulations. We will concentrate on just the first of these.

The law states that websites can store cookies on your machine if they are essential to the operation of the site but that for all other cookies the website's owner needs your permission to do so (Pinsent Masons, 2012a). An example of a cookie that is essential to the operation of the website may be, for example, the use of cookies to remember the contents of a user's shopping cart as the user moves through several pages on a website (Pinsent Masons, 2012b).

In practical terms, The Amendment requires that users are given this option on their first visit to your site. Cookies or similar devices must not be used unless the subscriber or user of the relevant terminal equipment:

a. is provided with clear and comprehensive information about the purposes of the storage of, or access to, that information; and

b. has given his or her consent.

(The Information Commissioner's Office, 2012t)

The Regulations are not prescriptive about the sort of information that should be provided, but the text should be sufficiently full and intelligible to allow individuals clearly to understand the potential consequences of allowing storage and access to the information collected by the device should they wish to do so (The Information Commissioner's Office, 2012t).

There has been much debate around the nature of the consent to be given, and whether this should be implied or express. Express consent involves the user making a positive decision to allow your cookies. A simple method of doing this would be through the use of pop-ups (where users are told why the website wants to place a cookie on their device and are required to give their consent positively to this).

How to gain implied consent is much less clear, but the ICO tells us that those who seek to rely on it should not see it as an easy way out or use the term as a euphemism for 'doing nothing' (The Information Commissioner's Office, 2012t). The implied consent route seems to be following one of two paths at this stage: relying on the settings in the user's browser and adding pop-ups (with a different type of message to the express approach) to your site. The former is not generally considered technically robust enough because not all browser settings (or users) are sophisticated enough to rely on this as the sole method of gaining permission while the latter, at this stage, seems to be winning favour.

Marketing Week ran a story – 'Implicit consent, best practice on cookies' –stating that organisations adopting an implicit approach to complying with The Amendments are seeing 99.7 per cent acceptance of their cookies, compared to just 57.2 per cent on explicit consent. The difference is that users were faced with pop-ups telling them either that the site would like to use cookies and asking for permission to place them on the user's machine (explicit permission) or pop-ups saying that the site would like to use cookies and then allowing users the option to disable them (implicit permission) (O'Reilly, 2012).

The Amendment is new and it is not clear how things will eventually develop, or how the ICO will feel about the above interpretation of implied consent. Only time will tell, as is the case with all new legislation!

15.4 The future of data protection legislation

In a document entitled 'Why do we need an EU data protection reform?', the official website of the European Union (The European Union, 2012) suggests the following developments in data protection legislation are on their way. There are some very sensible ideas in here that will improve data protection to the benefit of all concerned . . . and some rather odd ones, which may be somewhat difficult to implement. The proposals are presented without further comment!

- A 'right to be forgotten' would help people better manage data protection risks on-line. When they no longer want their data to be processed and there are no legitimate grounds for retaining it, the data will be deleted.

- Whenever consent is required for data processing, it would have to be given explicitly, rather than be assumed.

- There would be easier access to one's own data and the right of data portability, i.e. easier transfer of personal data from one service provider to another.

- Companies and organisations would have to notify serious data breaches without undue delay, where feasible within 24 hours.

- There would be a single set of rules on data protection, valid across the EU.

- Companies would only have to deal with a single national data protection authority – in the EU country where they have their main establishment.

- Individuals would have the right to refer all cases to their home national data protection authority, even when their personal data is processed outside their home country.

- EU rules would apply to companies not established in the EU, if they offer goods or services in the EU or monitor the on-line behaviour of citizens.

- There would be increased responsibility and accountability for those processing personal data.

- Unnecessary administrative burdens, such as notification requirements for companies processing personal data, would be removed.

- National data protection authorities would be strengthened so they can better enforce the EU rules at home.

References

BBC News (2011) *MPs call for tougher personal data abuse laws.* Available at: **http://www.bbc.co.uk/news/uk-politics-15465349** [Accessed 12 June 2012].

BBC News (2012a) *Ryan Giggs can be legally named as 'affair' footballer.* Available at: **http://www.bbc.co.uk/news/uk-17114875** [Accessed 12 June 2012].

Carey, P. (1998) *Blackstone's Guide to The Data Protection Act 1998.* One ed, Blackstone Press Limited, London.

O'Reilly, L. (2012) *Implicit consent best practice on cookies.* Available at: **http://www.marketingweek.co.uk/4002151.article?cmpid=MWE09&cmptype=newsletter&ern=7DDDF374E648E38A4621A18D2773CCDE&email=true** [Accessed 18 June 2012].

Pinsent Masons (2012a) *Use of cookies on* **Pinsent Masons.com** *and other Pinsent Masons websites.* Available at: **http://www.pinsentmasons.com/en/legal-notices/how-pinsent-masons-uses-cookies-on-its-sites/** [Accessed 18 June 2012].

Pinsent Masons (2008) *Email Marketing – When to use opt-in and when to use opt-out.* Available at: **http://www.out-law.com/page-5657** [Accessed 18 June 2012].

Pinsent Masons (2012b) *Cookie Law.* Available at: **http://www.aboutcookies.org/Default.aspx?page=3** [Accessed 18 June 2012].

Sabbagh, D., O'Carroll, L. and Carrell, S. (2012) *Gordon Brown launches fierce attack on Rupert Murdoch at Leveson inquiry.* Available at: **http://www.guardian.co.uk/media/2012/jun/11/gordon-brown-attacks-rupert-murdoch-leveson** [Accessed 12 June 2012].

Taylor, M. (2011) *Rupert Murdoch apology to Milly Dowler family was sincere, says lawyer.* Available at: http://www.guardian.co.uk/media/2011/jul/15/rupert-murdoch-apology-milly-dowler [Accessed 12 June 2012].

The European Union (2012) *Why do we need EU Data Protection Reform?* Available at: http://ec.europa.eu/justice/data-protection/document/review2012/factsheets/1_en.pdf [Accessed 18 June 2012].

The Information Commissioner's Office (2012s) *Guidance on the rules on use of cookies and similar technologies.* Available at: http://www.ico.gov.uk/for_organisations/privacy_and_electronic_communications/the_guide/~/media/documents/library/Privacy_and_electronic/Practical_application/cookies_guidance_v3.ashx [Accessed 18 June 2012].

The Information Commissioner's Office (2011) *Cashier spied on sex attack victim's bank records.* Available at: http://www.ico.gov.uk/news/latest_news/2011/cashier-spied-on-sex-attack-victims-bank-records-13092011.aspx [Accessed 12 June 2012].

The Information Commissioner's Office (2012a) *Home page.* Available at: www.ico.gov.uk [Accessed 12 April 2012].

The Information Commissioner's Office (2012b) *Private detectives jailed for blagging: ICO Statement.* Available at: http://www.ico.gov.uk/news/latest_news/2012/statement-private-detectives-jailed-for-blagging-27022012.aspx [Accessed 12 June 2012].

The Information Commissioner's Office (2012c) *What we cover.* Available at: http://www.ico.gov.uk/what_we_cover.aspx [Accessed 12 June 2012].

The Information Commissioner's Office, 2012d. *Register of Data Controllers.* Available at: http://www.ico.gov.uk/what_we_cover/register_of_data_controllers.aspx [Accessed 12 June 2012].

The Office of the Information Commissioner (2012e) *The conditions for processing.* Available at: http://www.ico.gov.uk/for_organisations/data_protection/the_guide/conditions_for_processing.aspx [Accessed 18 June 2012].

The Information Commissioner's Office (2012f) *Processing personal data fairly and lawfully (Principle 1).* Available at: http://www.ico.gov.uk/for_organisations/data_protection/the_guide/principle_1.aspx [Accessed 18 June 2012].

The Information Commissioner's Office (2012g) *Data Protection Principles.* Available at: http://www.ico.gov.uk/for_organisations/data_protection/the_guide/the_principles.aspx [Accessed 14 June 2012].

The Information Commission's Office (2012h) *The amount of personal data you may hold (Principle 3).* Available at: http://www.ico.gov.uk/for_organisations/data_protection/the_guide/information_standards/principle_3.aspx [Accessed 18 June 2012].

The Information Commissioner's Office (2012i) *Keeping personal data accurate and up to date (Principle 4).* Available at: http://www.ico.gov.uk/for_organisations/data_protection/the_guide/information_standards/principle_4.aspx [Accessed 18 June 2012].

The Information Commissioner's Office (2012j) *Retailing Personal Data (Principle 5).* Available at: http://www.ico.gov.uk/for_organisations/data_protection/the_guide/information_standards/principle_5.aspx [Accessed 18 June 2012].

The Information Commissioner's Office (2012k) *Access to Personal Data.* Available at: http://www.ico.gov.uk/for_organisations/data_protection/the_guide/principle_6/access_to_personal_data.aspx [Accessed 18 June 2012].

The Information Commissioner's Office (2012l) *Preventing processing likely to cause damage or distress.* Available at: http://www.ico.gov.uk/for_organisations/data_protection/the_guide/principle_6/damage_or_distress.aspx [Accessed 18 June 2012].

The Information Commissioner's Office (2012m) *Preventing Direct Marketing.* Available at: http://www.ico.gov.uk/for_organisations/data_protection/the_guide/principle_6/preventing_direct_marketing.aspx [Accessed 18 June 2012].

The Information Commissioner's Office (2012n) *Automated Decision Taking*. Available at: **http:// www.ico.gov.uk/for_organisations/data_protection/the_guide/principle_6/automated_ decision_taking.aspx** [Accessed 18 June 2012].

The Information Commissioner's Office (2012o) *Information Security (Principle 7)*. Available at: **http://www.ico.gov.uk/for_organisations/data_protection/the_guide/principle_7.aspx** [Accessed 18 June 2012].

The Information Commissioner's Office (2012p) *Sending personal data outside the European Economic Area (Principle 8)*. Available at: **http://www.ico.gov.uk/for_organisations/data_protection/ the_guide/principle_8.aspx** [Accessed 18 June 2012].

The Information Commissioner's Office (2012q) *What do opt-in and opt-out mean?* Available at: **http://www.ico.gov.uk/for_organisations/privacy_and_electronic_communications/opt_in_ out.aspx** [Accessed 18 June 2012].

The Information Commissioner's Office (2012r) *Marketing*. Available at: **http://www.ico.gov.uk/ for_organisations/sector_guides/marketing.aspx** [Accessed 18 June 2012].

The Information Commissioner's Office (2012t) *Cookies*. Available at: **http://www.ico.gov.uk/for_ organisations/privacy_and_electronic_communications/the_guide/cookies.aspx** [Accessed 18 June 2012].

Index